ISBN 978-1-5282-3716-1
PIBN 10913577

1 MONTH OF
FREE
READING

at

www.ForgottenBooks.com

By purchasing this book you are eligible for one month membership to ForgottenBooks.com, giving you unlimited access to our entire collection of over 1,000,000 titles via our web site and mobile apps.

To claim your free month visit:

www.forgottenbooks.com/free913577

PROCEEDINGS OF THE NATIONAL
TAX ASSOCIATION

PROCEEDING

OF THE

TWENTIETH ANNUAL CONFERENCE

ON TAXATION

UNDER THE AUSPICES OF THE

National Tax Association

HELD AT TORONTO, CANADA
OCTOBER 10–14, 1927

EDITED BY

W. G. QUERY, Secretary

ASSISTED BY

A. E. HOLCOMB, Treasurer

265553
17. 3. 32.

COLUMBIA, S. C.
NATIONAL TAX ASSOCIATION
1928

NATIONAL TAX ASSOCIATION

OFFICERS

1927-1928

President

HARLEY L. LUTZ

Professor of Economics, Leland Stanford Jr. University,
Palo Alto, California

Vice President

MARK GRAVES

Member State Tax Commission, New York

Secretary

W. G. QUERY

Chairman S. C. Tax Commission, Columbia, S. C.

Treasurer

ALFRED E. HOLCOMB

Assistant Secretary, American Telephone and Telegraph Co.,
195 Broadway, New York, N. Y.

Executive Committee

(In addition to above officers)

PAST PRESIDENTS

EDWIN R. A. SELIGMAN, Columbia University
CHARLES J. BULLOCK, Harvard University
ZENAS W. BLISS, Board of Tax Commissioners of R. I.
THOMAS S. ADAMS, Yale University
WILLIAM BAILEY, Nephi, Utah
THOMAS W. PAGE, Washington, D. C.
GEORGE VAUGHAN, Little Rock, Ark.
JOSEPH S. MATTHEWS, Concord, N. H.

ELECTED MEMBERS

Term expiring 1928

JOHN J. MERRILL

Member, State Tax Commission of New York

CLARENCE SMITH

Member, Public Service Commission of Kansas

T. M. MILLING

Counsel, Standard Oil Co. of La.

Term expiring 1929

FRANKLIN S. EDMONDS

Chairman, Pennsylvania Tax Commission

C. M. BROWN

Utah Copper Co.

E. T. MILLER

Professor of Economics, University of Texas

Term expiring 1930

HENRY F. LONG

Commissioner of Corporations and Taxation of Massachusetts

· PHILIP ZOERCHER

Member, State Board of Tax Commissioners of Indiana

S. H. CHASE

Chairman, State Tax Commission of Washington

Honorary Members

J. T. WHITE

Controller of Revenue, Province of Ontario

E. BRASSARD

Legal Adviser, Succession Duty, Province of Quebec

CONTENTS

(vii)

CONSTITUTION OF THE NATIONAL TAX ASSOCIATION

As Amended at the Seventh Annual Meeting, October 25, 1913, and at the Ninth Annual Meeting, August 13, 1915

ARTICLE I

Name and Objects

Section 1. The name of this association shall be "National Tax Association."

Sec. 2. Its objects shall be to formulate and announce, through the deliberately expressed opinion of an annual conference, the best informed economic thought and ripest administrative experience available for the correct guidance of public opinion, legislative and administrative action on all questions pertaining to taxation, and to interstate comity in taxation.

ARTICLE II

Membership

Section 1. Any person in sympathy with the objects of the association shall be eligible to membership. All memberships shall be continuing and the dues therefor shall be paid annually unless the membership is discontinued by reason of death, resignation or non-payment of dues.

Sec. 2. The annual membership dues shall be five dollars, and shall be payable in advance, on the date of application for membership, and annually thereafter. Any member who shall fail to pay his dues within one year from the date when payable shall be dropped from membership on account of such non-payment.

Sec. 3. All members not in arrears for annual dues shall be entitled to receive, without charge, one copy of the proceedings of the annual conference for the current year, and one copy of such reports, bulletins, pamphlets, and documents as may be issued by the association from time to time for general circulation.

ARTICLE III

ANNUAL CONFERENCE

SECTION 1.   An annual national conference on taxation shall be held under the auspices of this association during the month of September in each year, or at such time and place as its executive committee may determine. The details of each conference shall be arranged by the executive committee in cooperation with such special and standing committees as may be created by this association at its annual meetings for such purposes.

SEC. 2.   The administrative personnel of each annual conference shall be composed of three delegates appointed by the governor of each State, and public officials holding legislative or administrative positions charged with the duty of investigating, legislating upon, or administering tax laws.

SEC. 3.   The educational personnel of each annual conference shall be composed of persons identified with universities and colleges that maintain a special course in public finance, or at which that subject receives special attention in a general course of economics; members of the profession of certified public accountants; and public men, editors, writers and speakers who hold no educational or official position but who have developed a special interest in the subject of taxation.

SEC. 4.   The voting power in each conference upon any question involving an official expression of the opinion of the conference shall be vested in delegates appointed by governors of states; universities and colleges, or institutions for higher education, and state associations of certified public accountants, each of whom shall have one vote.

SEC. 5.   Voting by proxy shall not be allowed.

SEC. 6.   No member of this association shall have the right to vote in any annual conference by virtue of such membership.

SEC. 7.   The last session of each annual conference, or so much of it as may be necessary, shall be devoted to the consideration of the report of the conference committee on resolutions and conclusions. The report of this committee, as adopted by the conference, shall be its official expression of opinion, and it shall not be held to have endorsed any other expression of opinion by whomsoever made. The voting power of the conference upon an official expression of its opinion, is limited with the purpose of safeguarding the conference from the possibility of having its expression of opinion influenced by any class interest; or consideration for those who devote their time to the work or management of this association; or favor for those who contribute money for its support. The annual conference will be the means used by the association for carrying into practical effect its purpose to secure an expression of opinion that will formulate and announce the best informed economic thought and ripest administrative experience available for the correct guidance of public opinion, legislative and administrative action on all questions pertaining to taxation, and to interstate comity in taxation.

SEC. 8. *Organization of the Conference.* — The temporary and permanent chairman; secretary and official stenographer; address of welcome and response to the same; meeting place, accommodations for delegates, and all necessary preliminary details for each conference, and also the program of papers and discussions, shall be arranged for the conference by the executive committee of this association. All other details of the organization and work of the conference shall be arranged by the delegates present in such manner as they may from time to time decide.

ARTICLE IV

ANNUAL AND SPECIAL MEETINGS OF THE ASSOCIATION

SECTION 1. The annual meeting of the association shall be held in connection with the annual conference and at such time as the executive committee may determine. Sixty days' notice shall be given to all members of the time and place at which such annual meeting is to be held.

SEC. 2. Special meetings of this association may be held at any time and place, when called by its executive committee. At least thirty days' notice shall be given to all members of each special meeting, which notice shall specify the purpose for which the meeting is called, and no business shall be transacted at such meeting other than that specified in the call.

SEC. 3. A majority of all members present at any annual or special meeting of this association shall constitute a quorum for the transaction of business, but such quorum shall at no time be less than fifteen, and whenever the attendance of members and delegates exceeds one hundred, twenty-five shall constitute a quorum.

ARTICLE V

OFFICERS AND EXECUTIVE COMMITTEE

SECTION 1. The affairs of this association shall be administered by a president, a vice-president, a secretary, a treasurer and an executive committee consisting of the president, vice-president, secretary, treasurer and nine additional members to be elected by the association at its annual meetings and to hold office until their successors are duly elected. In the discretion of the association the same person may serve both as secretary and treasurer. The ex-presidents at their option may become *ex-officio* members of the executive committee, and two honorary members of the executive committee may be elected annually representing the Dominion of Canada.

SEC. 2. Officers shall be elected for terms of one year and shall be eligible for re-election. Three active members of the executive committee shall be elected each year for terms of three years each, except that at the first election following the adoption of this amendment three such members shall be elected for terms of three years, three for terms of two years and three for terms of one year each. After the election in 1915 no such member of the executive committee shall be re-elected to succeed himself thereon.

SEC. 3. A vacancy in any office or in the membership of the executive committee or of any standing committee may be filled by the executive committee for the unexpired term.

ARTICLE VI

DUTIES OF OFFICERS AND COMMITTEES

SECTION 1. The officers of this association shall perform the customary duties of their respective offices, and such other duties as may be assigned to or required of them from time to time by its executive committee, or by the association.

SEC. 2. When compensation is paid to any officer of this association, the amount thereof shall be fixed by the executive committee, and payment shall be made only as authorized by that committee.

SEC. 3. The Executive Committee shall have power to appoint additional officers, heads of departments and agents, from time to time, prescribe their duties, fix their term of office, and their compensations, and also to appoint standing or special committees and prescribe their powers and duties. All committees appointed by the executive committee shall report to that committee.

SEC. 4. The Executive Committee and all standing committees created by this association shall perform such general and special duties as may be assigned to them by the association.

SEC. 5. Such standing and special committees may be created from time to time by this association as may be deemed necessary for the efficient promotion of the work being undertaken. All committees appointed by the association shall report to the association.

ARTICLE VII

FINANCIAL MANAGEMENT

SECTION 1. This Association, its Executive Committee, or any of its officers, agents, or employees shall have no power to contract a debt, or liability of any kind, for which the association or its members collectively or individually can be held responsible, in excess of the amount of its funds available for the payment of the same.

SEC. 2. The fiscal year of the association shall begin with the first day of the month of July and end with the last day of the month of June in each year.

SEC. 3. The accounts of the Association for each fiscal year shall be closed on the 30th day of June in each year. They shall be audited by a chartered or certified public accountant, who shall certify to the correctness of the financial reports submitted to the association at its annual meeting.

ARTICLE VIII

GENERAL OFFICES AND LIBRARY

SECTION 1. The offices and library of this association shall be established and maintained at such place or places as may be determined by its executive committee.

SEC. 2. This Association shall accumulate and properly index, as rapidly as its funds will permit, a reference and circulating library which shall contain one or more copies of every useful leaflet, pamphlet, address, document, and book on the subject of taxation. As far as is possible with the funds available for the purpose, this library shall be kept continuously written up to date and indexed so as to enable its custodian to supply on application correct and full reference to all authorities on any phase of the subject of taxation, the decisions of courts, the statistical results of taxation laws and of changes made in such laws from time to time.

SEC. 3. The services of this library shall be without charge to all members of this association and to all legislative, executive, and judicial officers of states and of their political subdivisions, and to every person desiring to study, discuss or speak upon any feature of the subject of taxation.

ARTICLE IX

PROCEEDINGS AND PUBLICATION

SECTION 1. At each annual meeting the association shall elect, or authorize its president to appoint, a standing publication committee, under whose supervision a full report of the proceedings of the annual conference last held shall be edited and published. This committee shall also edit and supervise the publication of all reports, pamphlets, and literature in other forms issued by this association.

SEC. 2. The Executive Committee shall authorize the terms of sale or of distribution of all publications issued by this association.

(Ayes and Noes)

CHAIRMAN MATTHEWS: It seems to be a unanimous vote.

(Motion carried)

CHAIRMAN MATTHEWS: We have a communication from the Prime Minister of the Province of Ontario which I will ask the secretary to read.

SECRETARY HOLCOMB: Mr. Chairman, I have a letter from Hon. T. W. Ferguson, as follows:

> Toronto, October 5, 1937

EAR SIR:

I regret that my absence in the West next week will deprive me of the privilege of attending the meeting of your Association which is being held in the City

The information that has come to me with regard to the work of your Organization has convinced me that it is achieving tangible results that are of substantial value.

I am writing this note to express my regret at my inability to be in attendance and, as the Prime Minister of the Province, to extend a welcome to the members of your Association. I sincerely hope that your stay in the Province may be enjoyable and that the work you have in mind may be carried out successfully.

> Yours sincerely

> T W. FERGUSON

Tis letter is addressed to Joseph S. Matthews, President of the National Tax Association, Associate Justice of the New Hampshire Superior Court, Concord, New Hampshire.

I have a letter addressed to Hon. Joseph S. Matthews, President of the National Tax Association, as follows:

> TORONTO, 6TH October, 1937.

DEAR SIR:

It is with great regret that I find I will be absent from Ontario during the Conference on taxation.

I am deeply interested in all questions relating to taxation and revenue and was planning on attending all the sessions of the Conference, but circumstances over which I had no

will   essful meeting and that all the
ng t   be will enjoy their visit to the

wi   oronto on Friday next for
eting   of the Conference.

H,
Toronto.

J. T. WHITE (Ontario) : I wish to anno ce that the Prime Minister of the province has requested Mr. R(rt Faulkner, President of the University of Toronto, to deliver ¿ ew words of welcome on behalf of the Province of Ontario. Sir Robert is here.

SIR ROBERT FAULKNER (Ontario) : Mr President, Ladies and Gentlemen: You have heard the Prime Minister's letter read, in which he expressed his regrets that he is uıble to be with you this evening. Those regrets, I am sure, are sinre, and Mr. Ferguson is at present in Winnipeg engaged in a ve important conference that is being held there; and of course he mself, if he had been here, would have been able to give you soe definite information with regard to the financing of this provinc that would have been extremely interesting to you as coming firshand from him. But, of course, all I can do is, at his request, te you what he has told you by letter, that you are very welcomaagain in the city of Toronto and in this province, and that the rovince, as you have also heard from the letter of the Treasureris hoping that it will profit greatly by your deliberations here.

I remember very well when this associatic met here some nineteen years ago. You met at that time up inhe Parliament Building, as I remember. That is where you hel most of your meetings. I remember very well some of the geılemen who took part in those meetings, and I remember how interting they were.

At that time the University was representı, and again now the University is represented. We have one or ıo delegates, I think, who are to take part in your proceedings.

A society that is entirely a voluntary assoction, meeting for the definite purpose of discussing the underlyingprinciples that ought to be applied to public taxation and taxation í various sorts, must have a great deal of vitality if it can keep ıng, as your society has kept going all these years, and to be ableɔ come, as you have come, in such large numbers here today to hoı your meetings.

I suppose one reason that you have such a ral continuity is that the vitality of taxation seems not to grow lı. As far as I can judge, it does not seem to have necessarily ıy definite maturity beyond which it does not pass.

I know very well that the expenditures of u versities have gone up by leaps and bounds, and I know that our wn has very much kept in line with what has been going on in tı United States and in other countries of the world, and I find it ıe of my duties to try and justify increased expenditures. Thu Government, while they are very generous to us, sometimes wondı where our expenditures are to stop; and when Mayor Foster anıhe comptrollers of Toronto get to work at taxation, then the citiıns sometimes say, " Where are you going to stop?" I have enıʒh sympathy with

ARTICLE X

By-Laws

SECTION 1. The Executive Committee is authorized to formulate, adopt, and from time to time amend, such by-laws as it may deem necessary for the good government of the affairs of this associaion, and of the official conduct of its officers and committees.

ARTICLE XI

AMENDMENTS

SECTION 1. This Constitution may be amended at any annual or special meeting of this association by a two-thirds vote of all members present, PROVIDED, the full text of the amendment shall have been submitted to the membership by the executive committee or by the member or members proposing the same, at least thirty days before the date of the meeting at which such proposed amendment is acted upon.

FIRST SESSION

Joseph S. Matthews, President of the National Tax Association, presiding.

President Matthews: The convention will come to order. I will say before we start, for the benefit of any who may not have attended the conferences of the National Tax Association heretofore, that the National Tax Association is a permanent organization whose officers are elected by its members. The National Tax Association arranges for the conferences, selects the place, fixes the date, arranges the details, and prepares a program; but the conference itself is composed, as you will note, those of you who have a program, of delegates appointed by the governors of the several states and provinces, of teachers from the universities, those who are in actual service, and members of state associations of public accountants.

The conference conducts its proceedings in its own way, except that it must be in compliance with the constitution of the National Tax Association; and the first business, therefore, is to organize the conference.

Mr. Carl S. Lamb: Mr. Chairman, observing the time-honored custom of this association in nominating the president of the National Tax Association as permanent chairman, it gives me great pleasure to nominate Joseph S. Matthews of New Hampshire.

Mr. Philip Zoercher (Indiana): Second that motion.

Mr. Lamb: To save you embarrassment, all those in favor say aye.

(Ayes and Noes)

Mr. Lamb: Carried.

Chairman Matthews: I wish to express my appreciation for the honor. I shall endeavor to serve you to the best of my ability. The next in order is the election of a secretary.

Mr. Virgil H. Gibbs (Ohio): Mr. President, also following a long custom, I wish to present the name of Alfred E. Holcomb as secretary of the conference.

Chairman Matthews: The name of Alfred E. Holcomb is presented in nomination for secretary of the conference.

(Ayes and Noes)

CHAIRMAN MATTHEWS: It seems to be a unanimous vote.

(Motion carried)

CHAIRMAN MATTHEWS: We have a communication from the Prime Minister of the Province of Ontario, which I will ask the secretary to read.

SECRETARY HOLCOMB: Mr. Chairman, I have a letter from Hon. T. W. Ferguson, as follows:

TORONTO, OCT. 5, 1927.

DEAR SIR:

I regret that my absence in the West next week will deprive me of the privilege of attending the convention of your Association which is being held in the City.

The information that has come to me with regard to the work of your Organization has convinced me that it is achieving tangible results that are of substantial value.

I am writing this note to express my regret at my inability to be in attendance and, as the Prime Minister of the Province, to extend a welcome to the members of your Association. I sincerely hope that your stay in the Province may be enjoyable and that the work you have in mind may be carried out successfully.

Yours sincerely,

T. W. FERGUSON.

This letter is addressed to Joseph S. Matthews, President of the National Tax Association, Associate Justice of the New Hampshire Superior Court, Concord, New Hampshire.

I have a letter addressed to Hon. Joseph S. Matthews, President of the National Tax Association, as follows:

TORONTO, 6TH OCTOBER, 1927.

DEAR SIR:

It is with great regret that I find I will be absent from Ontario during the Conference on taxation.

I am deeply interested in all questions relating to taxation and revenue and was planning on attending all the sessions of the Conference, but circumstances over which I had no control will make this impossible.

I hope you will have a successful meeting and that all the parties attending the Conference will enjoy their visit to the City.

If possible I will return to Toronto on Friday next for the purpose of meeting the delegates of the Conference.

Sincerely yours,

J. D. MONTIETH,
Treasurer of Toronto.

J. T. WHITE (Ontario) : I wish to announce that the Prime Minister of the province has requested Mr. Robert Faulkner, President of the University of Toronto, to deliver a few words of welcome on behalf of the Province of Ontario. Sir Robert is here.

SIR ROBERT FAULKNER (Ontario) : Mr. President, Ladies and Gentlemen: You have heard the Prime Minister's letter read, in which he expressed his regrets that he is unable to be with you this evening. Those regrets, I am sure, are sincere, and Mr. Ferguson is at present in Winnipeg engaged in a very important conference that is being held there; and of course he himself, if he had been here, would have been able to give you some definite information with regard to the financing of this province that would have been extremely interesting to you as coming first-hand from him. But, of course, all I can do is, at his request, tell you what he has told you by letter, that you are very welcome again in the city of Toronto and in this province, and that the province, as you have also heard from the letter of the Treasurer, is hoping that it will profit greatly by your deliberations here.

I remember very well when this association met here some nineteen years ago. You met at that time up in the Parliament Building, as I remember. That is where you held most of your meetings. I remember very well some of the gentlemen who took part in those meetings, and I remember how interesting they were.

At that time the University was represented, and again now the University is represented. We have one or two delegates, I think, who are to take part in your proceedings.

A society that is entirely a voluntary association, meeting for the definite purpose of discussing the underlying principles that ought to be applied to public taxation and taxation of various sorts, must have a great deal of vitality if it can keep going, as your society has kept going all these years, and to be able to come, as you have come, in such large numbers here today to hold your meetings.

I suppose one reason that you have such a vital continuity is that the vitality of taxation seems not to grow less. As far as I can judge, it does not seem to have necessarily any definite maturity beyond which it does not pass.

I know very well that the expenditures of universities have gone up by leaps and bounds, and I know that our own has very much kept in line with what has been going on in the United States and in other countries of the world, and I find it one of my duties to try and justify increased expenditures. The Government, while they are very generous to us, sometimes wonders where our expenditures are to stop; and when Mayor Foster and the comptrollers of Toronto get to work at taxation, then the citizens sometimes say, " Where are you going to stop ?" I have enough sympathy with them, in my own line, to know that we must not be too hard on the subject of taxation.

If we were able to put ourselves back twenty years to where we were when this last meeting was held here, I think it might be found that the wealth of the country has gone ahead very rapidly and that we are not much more crushed today than we were then. However, I am speaking as a layman in that, and all that I know is that my own taxation is just about all that I want. If you can do anything to lighten my load I certainly would be glad to join your association, Mr. Chairman; and I think probably you would get a very large membership if you could only promise returns, as they do in life insurance companies. You know, profits is all we want. Just give profits to those who join the tax association, and you will have an enormous membership.

However, I am sure that your scientific investigation of taxation, the basis of taxation, the methods of taxation, your scientific investigation of the principles of taxation, the adjustments and everything of that kind, is a pursuit of enormous advantage to the average citizen.

In the University, of course, as in every great university, a very large part of the work that is done in the department of political economy does deal with such matters as these, and I presume that, as in other departments of human knowledge, there is a growing exactitude that some definite result come from investigation; and there ought to be every reason to expect that, just as in public health.

The knowledge of the laws of health have had an enormous influence upon longevity of the people, and on the general well-being of the people. So, the understanding of what underlies the financial structure of society and the necessary upkeep of society, the understanding of these things, must result in the long run in an application of principles which will make a healthier society. We shall learn better what thrift is, and how the applications of public money shall be developed in the best way possible. We do need to understand more and more in our country how to spend in the right way. That concerns everybody (applause). I am sure that is one of the great necessities of today. Money in the last generation has been made so rapidly that many people have acquired it who have not understood always how to use it in the proper way. And, I am very sure that the proper use of wealth, the proper expenditure of money, the way in which money should be spent, and the right attitude in the spending of it—to learn those lessons is one of the duties as well as one of the necessities of the people of this wealthy continent. Money is coming in to us in enormous quantities. We have a very, very rich country, both north of the line and you have south of the line, but we do need to know how to control what we are getting, and how to use it for the best advantage of the body politic, as well as for the individual; and if a group of people like you, Mr. Chairman, and your associates are able even in a small realm, in a small sphere, to spread abroad a more intelligent understanding of the right methods of expenditure and of also getting from the people, in the right way, what should be spent, you will undoubtedly be doing something for the good of the people as a whole and akin to what is done in other lines by scientific investigation.

However I have gone to much greater length as a mere layman than I should. Allow me again to say that I have the privilege and the honor of extending to you in behalf of the Premier of the Province a warm welcome tonight, and allow me again to express the hope that your meeting this time will be at least fully as satisfactory to you and this community as was that of twenty years ago. (Applause)

CHAIRMAN MATTHEWS: Is it true, Sir Robert, that you welcomed the convention nineteen years ago?

SIR ROBERT FAULKNER: I spoke at the time. Just how much responsibility I had at that time I do not remember.

CHAIRMAN MATTHEWS: I think that especially to those of us who have been connected with the association since those early days, it is a pleasure that Sir Robert should be the one to welcome us here the second time.

J. T. WHITE (Toronto): I wish to announce that His Worship, Thomas Foster, the Mayor of the City of Toronto, is in the room, and I think he would like to extend a few words of welcome on behalf of the city.

THOMAS FOSTER (Mayor of Toronto): Mr. Chairman, Ladies and Gentlemen: I appreciate this very distinguished honor I have of welcoming so very many distinguished ladies and gentlemen here tonight attending this convention. You are visiting the queen city of the west, the capital of the Province of Ontario, which I think is one of the finest provinces in the Dominion and one of the finest cities in the Dominion. Why should we not think that, those of us who represent this great city?

We have a population of about 650,000, and another 100,000 or 150,000 in the suburbs, which indicates the very rapid growth of the City of Toronto.

I might indicate a few things which go to show that the people of Toronto have great confidence in their city. Our waterworks and supply is owned by the corporation. We have invested in that some $19,000,000. We are duplicating that on account of being up to the peak, finding the growth of the population warrants increasing the supply. We have under way the expenditure of some $15,000,000 to meet the future growth of our city, which we think is very necessary. Our transportation, our railway system, which you will observe in passing through our city, is also owned by the city, but operated by a commission; and we have invested in that some $45,000,000. Our electric light system, which you see in all streets and hotels throughout the city, is also owned by public ownership, operated by two commissions, a provincial commission and a city commission. We have invested in that some two or three hundred million dollars, and I think we have the cheapest heat, light and power of any system of any other country in the world; at least it is said that is the case. Our streets are well lighted. We have some 40,000 or 50,000 lights throughout our streets. Our buildings are well illuminated, and that being owned by the public means a great deal to the people. There are no dividends to pay, no watered stock, but it is operated at cost, for the benefit of the masses.

Our survey of the city water front is costing the city and the railways and the Government some $30,000,000. The reason for that is, it has been very dangerous to go to the water front, and we have to build a viaduct there to eliminate the danger, and we have developed that from reclaimed marsh lands to the extent of 1100 or 1200 acres. That investment has cost us $25,000,000. The work is not yet completed. It will take almost another ten years to complete it.

We shall have dockage enough, I think, when the work is completed, to accommodate all the ocean liners, if they come up this far, and I think it is looked upon favorably here, as in the United States, that the St. Lawrence should be deepened and that boat transportation should come to the upper lakes, to all the principal terminals, which would mean a great deal to the western provinces. When that is completed and that transportation takes place we shall have accommodations.

As you know, there is now being spent some $150,000,000 or $200,000,000 for deepening the waterways between here and Duluth and Chicago and the western cities. That is all right between here and the north and western cities, but we must deepen the St. Lawrence to make it so the larger vessels can come through and go to the western cities. That, I think, will be in the near future. Our Government is hesitating a little, but your Government is very favorable, and I think we shall fall in line very soon, perhaps after the next election, and you may be better situated after your next election also (laughter). It is surprising what effect those elections have on the community in the way of progress. It delays for a time, but after the election is over we catch up again; and I suppose that will be our experience in the next year or two.

Also, in connection with our city, our north part is growing very rapidly, and to meet the demands of that growth we are spending in the north part of the city—and no doubt you will have the opportunity tomorrow or the next day to go through that part of the city— some $11,000,000 for a sewerage system to meet the demands of the growth of that part of the city.

We just closed our exhibition, at which we had many thousands from the United States. We had an attendance there of almost 2,000,000 people, which we think is the largest and best annual exhibition in the world.

We have, following that, in November, the latter part of November, the Royal Winter Show, something similar to what you have in Chicago, which is carried on yearly as a very successful and very interesting attraction. If any of you gentlemen have a little time about that period, it will be worth your while to visit that Royal Winter Fair. We have an exhibit, I think, there of some of the finest bred stock in the world, with products of every description; and, as you know, in some of our provinces we have some very fine producing fruit districts. It is worth while to visit that Royal Winter Fair. To meet the demands of that we have to put up a new stock building this year which is costing us from ten to twelve hundred thousand dollars, to give the necessary accommodations to that fine quality of stock.

We have also in connection with our city about 2000 acres of parks, and we have about 60 to 80 supervised playgrounds. We have a child population of about 105,000, and we find it worth while to spend hundreds of thousands of dollars to interest the children, under control, and teach them various games and interesting amusements, whereby physically and mentally they become better youths as they grow up. That means a great deal to the city, and a great deal to the children, being under supervision and safely guarded. I think Toronto is about the only city that to that extent spends hundreds of thousands of dollars for the benefit of the coming generation, and I think it is money well spent.

In connection also with our city, as Sir Robert did not indicate to you, we have some six or seven thousand students who are here from all parts of the world. We feel very proud of our university and the wonderful work that it is doing from year to year and has carried on for a hundred years. Last week the university celebrated its one-hundredth anniversary, and we had representatives here from all parts and from the principal cities in the world. I suppose there must have been some two or three thousand people here representing education from all parts. It was very interesting for the city of Toronto to have the honor of having so many distinguished educators from all parts of the world. If you have time it is worth your while to visit our university and our parks in connection with the university, and our Provincial House, and also the grounds surrounding that. We have some very beautiful parks and houses throughout the city, and no doubt you will have some time after you get through with your strenuous labors to have a little pleasure and see something of the city.

I hope that after your convention you will find it possible to remain a day or so over, so that you may visit and get an idea of the attractions in our city and also visit our large departmental stores. I am sure the ladies will be more than interested in visiting that part of the city. We think we have one or two of the largest departmental stores in the world; in fact, it is said that that is so; and it would be, I am sure, very interesting to visit some of those attractions, as well as other beautiful stores throughout the city.

We always appreciate Americans coming over to our city. We know the vast amount of money they have on the other side—so much that they hardly know how to invest it or get rid of it. When you come to Canada and come to Toronto you will find an opportunity here to dispose of some of that surplus gold in connection with our city in some of the wonderful bargains and attractions in the highest class of goods that you can see in any country.

I am sure you gentlemen who have undertaken to solve the problem of taxation or to do something towards improving it will make it easier.

Sir Robert spoke of the city levy, and how sometimes it is difficult to carry on, on account of taxation. I have always been striving to keep it down as much as possible, notwithstanding that I am not able to solve the problem of meeting the demands that are made upon the treasury of the municipality; but I suppose it also applies to the Province and to every community. It is a problem that requires a great deal of thought, and one that is hard to solve. It is very easy to make a levy, but it is very unpleasant, especially when you are a candidate. To me it seems that at election time, all the candidates are economists, but after the election it is surprising how they change in their principles of spending money.

Last year, on account of the great demands upon our city, because of large expenditures, some of which I have indicated, a great deal of money had to be raised. Our rate is higher this year than it has been for some time, on account of that great demand. Our assessment is fairly high also. If our assessment was low it would not be so bad to have a little higher tax rate, but to have a high assessment and high tax rate is pretty hard on the community and the taxpayer.

Now, if you can show us how to get away with a heavy assessment and a heavy tax rate, I am sure the community will bless you forever. When you send out your tax bills, that is the time they begin to think what their representatives have been doing for them.

Not only that: It is one thing to send out your bills and set a date when you expect they will respond and pay. Some are not able to do that; many are able. Then when the blue paper comes around, of course we get our blessings, which sometimes are not so very pleasant to receive.

However, these are things which take place in connection with all municipalities. If there is some way whereby through some community process or organization we could better that condition—I cannot solve it—that is what we are hoping for.

You gentlemen who are here and who have been following this up from year to year for many years no doubt have many ideas as to how better conditions can be brought about in taxation and the method of collecting. Some think you ought to collect in one installment, some think the better way is to divide it into installments. We have three, and I think that is an improvement on the immediate full demand; especially with the working people. As you know, the winter season is hard. The working man has to have some time in the spring to catch up, to make a payment. If you demand the whole of the payment it would be almost impossible, but if he has only to pay one-third of it, and another payment in the summer, and another later, it helps considerably.

If there is any other method that could overcome some of those difficulties and make it more easy for the taxpayer, that is something, perhaps, you will be able to solve. It is a very big problem, especially when you are dealing, many of you, with millions and millions of dollars. From every standpoint it means a great deal to work it out. I hope you will be able to solve the problem. I hope that your meeting will be very beneficial, and that those of you who have attended here will be anxious to attend the next convention.

There are many reasons why you should get the benefits of assembling in conventions similar to this. First, there is the acquaintance, the making of friendships. When you go back to your community you tell of the things that have taken place, which makes it interesting to those who are not able to attend as delegates. When the representatives go back to the communities and bring to them accounts of what has taken place during the convention, it makes it very interesting, and it makes those people anxious to become delegates and attend the next convention. In that way it is very interesting; in that way you feel the benefit of the knowledge that you have derived; you are anxious again for another year to pass around the thoughts that have passed through your mind which you think will be beneficial to this assembly in your congress again; and that makes it continuously interesting from year to year.

I hope after your convention is over that you will be sufficiently impressed to feel that it was worthwhile coming to the City of Toronto. I am sure we are delighted to know that we have not only representatives from throughout Canada, but that from every state in the Union there are so many distinguished representatives in this gathering.

It will mean a great deal to Canada if you are well impressed when you go back to your various communities and put a good word in for Canada. We presume that you are getting quite congested in the United States; your population has been growing very rapidly. You have about 110 or 120 million. In Canada we have less than 10 million. We have an immense country here, undeveloped, and immense wealth here to be developed. Those of you who want to become millionaires quickly, and you are a little bit crowded in the United States, come over to Canada. I am sure we will treat you well, and there are great opportunities here to make money rapidly.

We have within three or four hundred miles of Toronto, as no doubt you have read from time to time, some of the greatest mineral deposits that there are in the world—gold, silver, iron, steel, pulp wood, and fisheries, almost everything you can think of—that are yet undeveloped. It has been discovered that our lands are rich in minerals of every description. I am sure notwithstanding that we have thousands of Americans in the city of Toronto and throughout Canada, there is room for hundreds of thousands more; and I extend to you an invitation when you want more freedom in the way of open country, to come to Canada. I am sure you will be well received, with an open hand, and have a great opportunity that you have not got in the United States.

It is a great pleasure for me to welcome the delegates to the city and extend to you the freedom of the city. If I had been representing the Government I might perhaps have even done more than that. The Provincial Government controls some things that the Mayor of the city of Toronto does not, and if you had the Premier here he might have extended that control to some of those who would enjoy that opportunity, and perhaps make life a little more lively and interesting for your period here.

In extending the freedom of the city to you, that means that you are pretty free to come and go. In this city we have policemen that are very particular in some ways, but if you look pleasant at them they are not so bad, but if you get into an argument with them when you are traveling around, or should anything occur, just report yourself to me and everything will be all right.

Sir, I hope that you will be so well satisfied with this convention that it won't be eighteen or nineteen years before you come back. We want to see you back again in another two or three years. I am sure this is a great pleasure that we have this opportunity of having your convention here this year. Come any time. Come by airplane if you think the motor is too slow. I am sure we shall be delighted to have you come here during our Exhibition. I think we must have had two or three hundred thousand Americans come over to our Exhibition, who enjoyed our highways. Our highways are in splendid condition, the scenery is good; fishing is excellent, and the accommodations are good. I am sure you will be delighted to avail yourselves of that opportunity, and we shall be delighted to meet you. I am sorry I am going to leave, but I hope we shall meet and that you will be back again. (Applause)

CHAIRMAN MATTHEWS: We have among the delegates to this convention a gentleman who is a leading authority on public finance. He has been a member of this association for a long time and has come a long way to be present. I am going to ask him to say something in response to the addresses of welcome. Professor Plehn of the University of California.

CARL C. PLEHN (California): Mr. Chairman, Sir Robert, Your Worship the Mayor: Your kindly words of welcome have touched our hearts and surely strengthened the high purposes for which we have assembled.

The National Tax Association was at one time called the International Tax Association, and the purpose of that name was to include the Dominion of Canada with the states of the United States. We were forced to drop that name—the International—because we were afraid that the nations of Europe would come crowding into our assemblies and that by sheer numbers it would be embarrassing. But the association still includes Canada. It must always include Canada for two very good and sufficient reasons.

In the first place, the fundamental economic conditions of these two closely neighboring countries are the same, or very much the same. Our traditions in regard to social and political life are very much the same, and so far as the problems of taxation are concerned, the sources of our law regarding taxation, and the customs, more than the mere statutory law, upon which taxation rests in both countries, come from the same source.

Our ideas of fundamental justice and equity in taxation are the same and have the same source. We of the United States need your experience and your wisdom, and I think I may safely say without undue conceit that you may find in our experiments and our ventures and trials some lessons that may be equally useful to you.

For those reasons the National Tax Association will always be, so far as Canada is concerned, an international association, with a boundary line that I crossed the other night without knowing it, except that as I crossed it I had a curious dream which, if you will bear with me, I should like to recount briefly.

I dreamed that the train drew up and stopped, and as I looked out, there was a long picket fence, extending as far as the eye could reach in both directions. There was a gate over the railway track, and as we stopped there the fireman jumped down, ran ahead and opened the gate. The train pulled slowly through and stopped again, and he closed the gate and got up.

I dreamed that as I looked at that fence, as we came up to it on the United States side, it was painted red, white and blue, and when I got over and looked around at it on the other side, looking back, it was painted red, white and blue.

After I woke up I recalled the old, old story of the two knights who fought over the shield, one asserting that it was gold, and the other that it was silver, the fact being that it was different on one side from the other, and each had his different point of view in approaching it.

If there is anything in my dream at all, it is that there is no ground for quarrel over that boundary fence that seemed to be there, if the colors are the same on both sides; and they are bright colors, too, indicative, perhaps, of the joy of meeting there; but, of course, it is only an imaginary line. One cannot tell much by observation as to when and where he crosses it.

The conferences of the National Tax Association have been, and it is our endeavor to keep them, non-partisan and non-political, and the curious device by which we keep them that way is that the resolutions or other decisions reached in the conferences are binding in no way upon anybody. At first that might seem a source of weakness, but it is, per contra, a source of strength; for it means that whatever is said or is done or is resolved must stand on its own inherent wisdom and common sense. And it is because we have by threshing out these questions in the mutual interchange of ideas succeeded now and again in finding a piece of wisdom or in expressing some common sense. The statutes of our states are full of items—full of plans that have originated in these conferences. Of course, now and again designing men—faddists have come and endeavored to obtain authoritative support for their views or plans from the association, and they have not altogether succeeded. And I am afraid, Sir Robert, you will not succeed in getting your taxes reduced.

This is not a tax-saving association. This association is composed mostly of administrators. Somebody has said, and I think there is a great deal of truth in it, that good taxation is nine-tenths administration and one-tenth law. If you can have honest and fearless administration, you can give your administrator a patched-up law or a paragraph, and the results will be satisfactory; but you may write volumes of law and if you have poor administration the results are not a bit improved by the length of the statute.

I have, therefore, merely to conclude that we are grateful for your welcome and we are sure we shall find it an inspiration.

CHAIRMAN MATTHEWS: We have also with us this evening the Hon. Henry Hapai, treasurer of the Territory of Hawaii, who will say a few words to us.

HENRY C. HAPAI (Treasurer of the Territory of Hawaii, Hawaiian Islands): Mr. Chairman, Sir Robert, Ladies and Gentlemen: The Territory of Hawaii realizes the importance of the matters to be taken up at this conference and appreciates the honor of having our representative here at this convention.

We have a population of 333,000, twenty-one hundred miles from San Francisco. Sometimes Hawaii is termed the crossroads of the Pacific. The Treasurer of the Territory is blessed with the duties of assessing and levying the tax and collecting it. I have done my best. I have not got into trouble yet. We have our tax problems to solve as well as any other country. I greet you all from Hawaii with the word Aloha (applause).

SECRETARY HOLCOMB: Mr. Chairman, it is in order, I think, to suggest the rules of procedure for the conference. The rules that I am about to read are those that have been heretofore used, with slight change, and are such as have been approved by the National Tax Association through its executive committee. It is necessary that these rules be read, because we should like to have the speakers bear in mind the limitations, to the end that the proceedings will go off in due order.

RULES OF PROCEDURE

Constitution of the National Tax Association

The provisions of the constitution of the National Tax Association shall govern the conduct of this conference generally, and these rules of procedure shall be considered supplemental to and subject to interpretation by such provisions.

PROGRAM AND DISCUSSION

The program as printed and distributed is adopted and shall be followed, with such modifications as may be required, by reason of absence, vacancies or other causes.

The usual rules of parliamentary procedure shall control.

Each speaker shall be limited to twenty minutes for the presentation of a formal paper. He shall be warned two minutes before the expiration of such period. The time of such speaker may be extended by unanimous consent of those present.

In general discussion each speaker shall be limited to seven minutes, and such time shall not be extended. No person shall speak more than once during the same period of discussion until others desiring to speak have been given opportunity to do so.

The voting power in this conference, upon any question involving an official expression of the opinion of the conference shall be vested in delegates in attendance at the time the ballot is taken, appointed by the governor or other appropriate executive officer of the states and territories of the United States, the District of Columbia and the Canadian provinces, not exceeding three votes for any one state, territory, district or province; persons actively identified with and duly appointed delegates by universities and colleges or institutions for higher education, not exceeding one vote for each such institution; and members of state associations of certified public accountants, duly appointed delegates by such associations, not exceeding one vote for each such association. No person shall have more than one vote, by reason of appointment from more than one source.

Voting by proxy shall not be allowed. The voting shall be by ayes and nays, unless a roll call can be demanded by at least three delegates from three different states. On all questions other than those involving an official expression of the opinion of the conference, the voting shall be by vote of all in attendance. The receipt of reports made to this conference by committees of the National Tax Association shall not be considered as expressing the opinion of the conference on the subjects treated.

COMMITTEES

The following committees shall be appointed:

(a) A committee of three on credentials, to be appointed by the chairman, who shall designate the chairman of such committee.

(b) A committee on resolutions, composed of a chairman, to be appointed by the chairman of the conference, and one person from each state, territory, district or province, selected from among the delegates; but in case of the non-attendance of any such, any person from such location may be appointed. The chairman of this committee shall appoint its secretary and arrange for its organization.

RESOLUTIONS

All resolutions involving an expression of opinion of the conference shall be read to the conference before submission to the committee and shall be immediately referred, without debate.

Mr. Chairman, I move the adoption of these rules.

(Motion seconded)

DELEGATE: Mr. Secretary, do the rules regarding voting there permit the treasurer from Hawaii to vote? As I understood the reading, they do not.

SECRETARY HOLCOMB: Yes, territories are included.

DELEGATE: Territories of the United States.

CHAIRMAN MATTHEWS: It is moved and seconded, I believe, that the rules as read by the Secretary be adopted; are you ready for the question?

(Call for the question)

(Ayes and Noes)

CHAIRMAN MATTHEWS: Unanimous vote.

CHAIRMAN MATTHEWS: I will appoint as chairman of the committee on credentials, Mr. Charles J. Tobin of New York. The other members of the committee will be announced later.

The Chair will also announce the name of the chairman of the resolutions committee at the earliest opportunity. The delegates from the several states are requested to meet and select your representative on the resolutions committee at the very earliest opportunity, and hand the names in to either the secretary or to Mr. Tobin. It is exceedingly important that the names should be handed in at the earliest possible moment, and the chairman will be appointed some time tomorrow.

CHARLES J. TOBIN (New York): As president of the National Tax Association, I move you that you designate the ex-presidents of the association and appoint three other members of the association as a nominating committee, to nominate officers of the Association.

(Motion duly seconded)

CHAIRMAN MATTHEWS: This motion is made in behalf of the National Tax Association?

CHARLES J. TOBIN: Yes.

CHAIRMAN MATTHEWS: The motion, as I understand it, is that the Chair appoint a nominating committee to consist of the past presidents of the association present at this convention and three others. Are you ready for the question?

(Call for the question)

(Ayes and Noes)

CHAIRMAN MATTHEWS: Unanimous vote.

CHAIRMAN MATTHEWS: Are there any announcements?

SECRETARY HOLCOMB: Mr. President, before making a very important announcement that I hope you will all wait for, I want to make two or three incidental announcements.

(Incidental announcements)

SECRETARY HOLCOMB: One of the most important objects of this conference is the consideration of the federal income tax, a subject that is occupying the attention of the Government of the United States and of a great number of bodies throughout the United States.

Among others, the National Tax Association has appointed a committee of some of the very best talent in the States on that subject. I mention this because the report itself will be a 100-page printed document.

Now, those of you who are interested particularly in the subject of the federal income tax are requested to secure a copy of this report as early tomorrow morning as you can, and read it over, with the idea of at least noting the separate recommendations that are made and printed in black-faced type. It will be helpful, because the discussion comes on in the afternoon, and there is hardly time to run over such a document, yet it is highly important that those who are competent and feel interested in that subject should at least go through the report to that extent.

DELEGATE: Do we get the report tonight or tomorrow morning?

SECRETARY HOLCOMB: Tomorrow morning. George Holmes will be here tomorrow morning on the morning train with 500 copies. You will find it a highly interesting document. This is the report (exhibiting). It has 104 pages.

There are certain other documents that have been handed in that will probably be interesting to some of the members. Here is a pamphlet on the sales tax. Those of you who are interested in the sales tax will find a few copies of that in the hands of the Minnesota Tax Commission.

Here is a report on the question of public expenditures. It is entitled "Sanctified Squander." It is prepared by one of our members from Cleveland, Ohio, and he has some copies for your use.

Now I come to the really important announcement. I see here in our midst a man who can, I think, give us a delightful treat. Those of you who were at the Bretton Woods conference probably will remember that delightful evening we had when Judge Hough of Indiana was kind enough to give us recitations from James Whitcomb Riley. Ever since that time I have wanted it repeated, and I have finally taken to myself the privilege of asking Judge Hough if he will not entertain us again this evening.

WILLIAM A. HOUGH (Indiana): Mr. President and Ladies and Gentlemen: I expect to take you away from the consideration of facts and figures and taxation, and ask you to take a little flight with me into the realms of fancy and sentiment. It is pretty hard for an association of this character to get away from facts and figures and from the old well-known statement that figures won't lie. The fact about it is they cannot the way women dress nowadays.

I want to give you a few sketches and readings from James Whitcomb Riley and picture to you through his verse the Hoosier characters that he has made famous almost throughout the world.

This is a very appropriate time to talk about Riley. His birthday was celebrated in Indiana last week. He was born on the 7th day of October in 1849. His father was a country lawyer in the little town of Greenfield.

James Whitcomb Riley grew to manhood among the farmers who planned the little town, and the rather rough characters with whom he was associated led him to delve beneath the surface and to picture to the world the emotions of the human heart which were common to these men and which are common to all.

The great secret of James Whitcomb Riley's popularity grew out of the fact that when he wrote his poetry he pictured in every stanza of it a little piece of the human heart; and no man and no woman can read his poems but what he or she will find reflected in them something of his own feelings and his own emotions.

The power seemed to be intuitive with him. He was able to portray to his great audience all the feelings that a husband might have for a wife, in the little domestic happenings of the household, when she was away from home and he was looking for her return; in the great tragedies, and even when she lay dead he seemed to know intuitively just exactly how the husband would feel, and yet he never had a wife.

He seemed to know exactly how a father or mother would feel towards a little child—love mingled with hope and a desire that the child will grow up to be a happy and useful citizen—and yet he never had a child. He had this remarkable ability of portraying the emotions. It came from his intuitive love of human nature and of men and women.

And he had another faculty, which was the ability to picture in just a few lines the characteristics of a person, so that the reader would feel that he had known that person and would know throughout the whole life of the person the sort of character that had been back of it. As an illustration of that, I want to read one of his poems for you, which was one of Mr. Riley's favorites—" Out to Old Aunt Mary's."

I was going down to French Lick a short time ago, and when I was on the train I picked up a St. Louis newspaper, and I saw that the original of Old Aunt Mary had died out in Missouri some place. I made note of it, because that is the eighth one of those originals that I have seen announced in the paper as the original of Old Aunt Mary.

The truth about it is there was no particular woman who was the original. The character that he portrays is built up of the composite characteristics of many good women whom he had known in his life. The poem was written and sent as a letter to his brother, John Riley, who lived in Albuquerque, New Mexico, at that time, and was not published until many, many years after it had been written.

(Reciting " Out to Old Aunt Mary's.")

I don't think any man or woman can go back home without feeling some of the emotion that Mr. Riley felt when he wrote the beautiful verses that make up that poem, which is a picture of a woman, just in a few lines. Every man or woman who reads that poem feels that he or she knows just the sort of woman that Old Aunt Mary was. When a neighbor was sick she was there to help care for those who were ill; if a little child was ill or was hurt, you know what Old Aunt Mary would do; and the picture is drawn in just these few lines; and I think it was one of the most wonderful of all the poems that Mr. Riley wrote.

Mr. Riley had very little schooling. He went to school practically not at all after he was fourteen years of age. He loafed a good deal up and down the banks of the Brandywine, and in the shops and drug stores and the places where boys and men congregate. The old country store was a favorite place of his to visit on Saturdays when it would be half full of farmers; and in the markets and the shops they would tell stories to each other and exchange the news of the neighborhood.

In the study of those characters he became familiar with all the characters in the world, because beneath the skin there is that same love for our children, the same love for our fellowman, and it is found all over the world. That is what made people love Riley.

One of the favorite places he visited was Old Man Kreiter's paint shop. He loafed around Kreiter's paint shop a good deal, and old Mr. Kreiter who painted signs would line out the letters and Riley and some of the boys would fill in the other parts with the paint brushes, and after a while, Riley became a sort of a sign painter himself and painted a great many signs in Greenfield; and finally Riley and George Carr and John Skinner formed a partnership for the purpose of painting signs all over Hancock County, on the barns and fences and wherever they might secure permission to place a sign. Riley did most of the outlining, and Skinner filled in the letters, after they had been properly outlined, and George Carr furnished an old horse and wagon, which was his contribution to the partnership. They drove all over the country, advertised their wares and advertising merchandise which was sold in Greenfield at that time.

One hot afternoon in August during the war, while Riley's father was away, these three boys went out through the country, and as they were returning home about 6 o'clock in the evening they passed the home of a strictly religious old farmer who lived three miles east of Greenfield on the National Road. This old farmer belonged to a class of people who have almost entirely disappeared; not that all religious people are gone, but they are manifesting their religion in a different sort of way, mostly abusing everybody who does not happen to believe in their views of life.

This old farmer had painted on his barn in great wide four-foot letters "Praise Ye the Lord," and over the door of his home he had painted clear across the house, "Salvation Unto the Lord," and on his barn-yard gate he had painted the words, "What shall I do to be saved?"

Carr says, "Stop the horse. Here is a good place for a sign." He got out and painted beneath the words "What shall I do to be saved?" "Take Carter's Little Liver Pills."

They had a good laugh, and talked about the consternation of the old farmer when he would come out and discover what had been done to his sign. On the way home Mr. Riley said, "Old man Kreiter may not be willing to pay for that sign when he sees it out there," but they hoped he would. They went in the next morning and collected 50 cents from old man Kreiter for the sign that had been placed on old man Thornton's barn-yard gate.

About two weeks after that they were coming back from a trip to Charlotteville, Indiana, and as they were coming down the National Road, Riley said, "Let's stop at old man Thornton's and see what he did to that sign; I expect he painted it all out."

When they got to Thornton's house they discovered the old man had a pretty keen sense of humor himself, for beneath the words "Take Carter's Little Liver Pills" the old farmer had painted another religious motto, and he had on the next board below, "And then prepare to meet thy God." .

I will have to hurry along, because it is getting late, but this sign-painting led up to what Mr. Riley always regarded as one of the most delightful experiences in his life.

About this time an old traveling quack doctor, named Dr. McKrillis, who lived about three miles out in the country from Muncie, came to Greenfield in a large wagon, built up something after the style of a service wagon, with one of the sides let down and fastened back with chains to the wheels on the other side, making a sort of a platform. On this platform the old doctor carried a couple of young men who gave a musical entertainment, played on the banjo and guitar, and who gave clog dances and did a little singing, and after the doctor had collected a good crowd around he got up and expatiated on the wonderful qualities of the medicines which he carried around with him, and sold what he could in the crowd, and continued this sort of thing for about a week, after which he would move on to another place and leave his medicines on sale in the drug store. He was just a quack doctor, who manufactured his medicines out in his barn. I almost got into trouble at Muncie once by calling him a quack doctor. After my evening's entertainment was over, three or four people showed up in the audience who were related to the old doctor and though perhaps I ought not to have called him a quack doctor, and I never do that in the United States any more. I know that is all right here, just like a lot of other things are all right here that are not all right in the United States.

The young man Riley was perfectly fascinated with the entertainment, and when Dr. McKrillis was ready to leave the town he tackled him for a job. The old man said he had two boys and that was all he could afford to carry. Riley said he could play the violin, guitar, banjo, and was a pretty good clog-dancer, and he said, " Doctor, I can draw very well, too; if you get me a blackboard and let me draw pictures," he says, " I can help entertain the crowd and sell your medicines." The doctor said he could not afford to carry the young man to give the entertainment, but he said he could send him around the country to paint signs to advertise his medicines all the time. Riley said that was his regular business, and he persuaded the doctor to take him along; so Riley joined Dr. McKrillis' caravan of musicians and medicine venders, and he traveled two years with old Dr. McKrillis all over central and northern Indiana; and Riley recited as he drew pictures on the blackboard of how a man looked before taking the doctor's remedies and how he looked after taking a couple of bottles. It has always been claimed that he was the first man that used the " Before and After " method of advertising. It probably was not original with him, but originated back in the days of Rome.

While he was traveling with the doctor and reciting, he used nothing of his own writing. At that time he had a number of clippings that he had made from newspapers, and he recited poetry and short stories; things of that kind. One rainy day at Newcastle, Indiana, when the doctor and the boys were all together, Riley told the doctor the story of his former life over in Hancock County, and the doctor said, " Riley, if you just write that up in the form of a story it will make a good recitation." Said Riley, " Do you think it would?" The doctor said, " Yes, I am sure it would."

So Riley began to write up this story. He wrote it out in prose form first, and then he concluded that he would change it into the Hoosier dialect. It was always Riley's favorite dialect poem, and he had a great many he loved, but this particular one was his favorite. It was not written to be published; it was written to be used as a reading; and Riley worked on it while he passed from Newcastle up to Anderson and to Muncie and to Wabash, and finally in Warsaw, Indiana, one Saturday night, with the gasoline torches blazing on each side of the highly decorated wagon, Riley recited for the first time in public the poem that I am about to read for you now.

It is a picture of a Hoosier character, a pretty sharp, shrewd sort of a man with not a great deal of education, but one who had, through his business ability, made quite a success in life.

(Reciting: " I am one of these curious kind of chaps," etc.)

I see it is pretty nearly ten o'clock. I wish I might recite a dozen of Riley's poems and tell you a great many of the very interesting things I have learned from him, of his youth; but while I feel it is late I will give you one more recitation and then we will call it a day and let the tired people go to bed, and let those who have not secured any rooms yet go back to work on the hotel clerk.

In 1912 the Bobbs-Merrill Company in Indianapolis sent for Howard Chandler Christy to come to Indianapolis to illustrate " That Old Sweetheart of Mine," for the purpose of putting it out in book form; nothing else but the one poem. Mr. Christy came to Indianapolis and spent some little time there, familiarizing himself with the poem, talked with Mr. Riley about it a great deal, and submitted a number of sketches he prepared, to Mr. Riley and Mr. Wills of the Bobbs-Merrill Company. After he had been there for some little time he suggested that the poem ought to be a little longer in order to make it good. The fact about it was he had drawn more pictures than there were stanzas, and he wanted Mr. Riley to write some additional stanzas in order to make a little larger book. Mr. Riley was not in favor of it, but they prevailed upon him, and he finally did write a number of additional stanzas to the poem. He never liked the additional stanzas very well, although the book was a very great success. Mr. Riley got in royalties out of that one poem in one year's time $25,000, which is more than most people get out of a poem, particularly for " That Old Sweetheart of Mine." They sometimes do ring them if the sweetheart happens to be of the masculine persuasion, for even more than that.

Mr. Riley once told me he never looked at the remodeled poem but what it reminded him of a very beautiful woman with six large warts on her face. For that reason, when I read the poem I always leave the additional stanzas off.

I think it is really a very beautiful poem, illustrating, as I said when I began to talk this evening, Mr. Riley's wonderful power of placing himself in the character he was portraying in his poem.

(Reciting: " That Old Sweetheart of Mine.")

(Applause)

CHAIRMAN MATTHEWS: It is suggested that all of the delegates who have not yet registered should register as soon as convenient. Tomorrow's session is at 9: 30 A. M., and the meeting will now adjourn.

(Adjournment)

SECOND SESSION

CHAIRMAN MATTHEWS: If the members of the convention will take seats we will open the morning session.

The first item on the program this morning is a review of 1927 tax legislation, upon which subject you will be addressed by Miss Beulah Bailey, of the staff of the New York State Tax Commission. Miss Bailey.

MISS BEULAH BAILEY (New York): Mr. President, Ladies and Gentlemen: I once heard an after-dinner speaker say that the applause at the beginning of a speech is faith, during the speech hope, and at the end charity. I think that this year, with forty-four states in regular session and one state in extraordinary session, all of the applause is charity.

The trend of taxation is, of course, upward. In February I read an article in a paper, entitled " Canada again reduces her taxes." There is a 10 per cent reduction in the Canadian income tax, and a 20 per cent reduction in the sales tax. Possibly we all know why Canada can reduce her taxes, and possibly if we could we should go back to the states and do likewise.

I have tried to find out how much revenue the Province of Ontario took in from their last business venture, but they are keeping it a secret.

This year there were two tax commissions formed, one in Arkansas and one in Michigan. In Arkansas the tax commission was not a new departure, because they had one in 1923. Under the 1927 law a commission was created for thirty-two years, with three tax commissioners, each serving a term of eight years. In Michigan the tax department was abolished, and a commission created, with three commissioners, the ultimate term being six years. Of course, the first appointment was for two years.

The states of Connecticut, Pennsylvania and Texas this year passed blanket laws which in certain cases will validate acts which otherwise would not be valid, for certain omissions and irregularities. It might be beneficial if all states could pass such laws which cover up slips in red tape and procedure. This is especially true in the case of tax titles. There are very few people who like to buy in property at tax sales, on account of the impossibility of getting clear title. Arizona, Idaho, North Carolina, Utah and Minnesota tried to help this situation this year by legislation.

In the first four states they provided for foreclosure actions to clean up titles, and in Minnesota the law states that after five years all titles will be absolutely clear.

Arkansas and Montana this year changed their assessment of real estate from an annual assessment to biennial.

A 1927 law in Carolina provides for a much better assessment of their real property.

The most radical change in the assessment field has been Illinois. Formerly assessments there were at 50 per cent of the true value. This year it was increased to 100 per cent. The bankers of Illinois feel that this is going to react very unfavorably towards the taxing of the banks.

I think now the approximate assessment of property in Illinois is about 43 per cent instead of the 50 per cent as called for, and in Cook County about 35 per cent. Of course, under the new law the banks will be taxed on 100 per cent of book value, but it will be some time before property is raised to 100 per cent assessment, on account of the personal equation of the assessor, therefore some of the bankers feel that an income tax on the banks would be much fairer than the property tax.

Due to this increase in the assessed value, the rates in Illinois have been decreased in quite a few cases. Of course you know Illinois is still a devotee of the general property tax, classification being unconstitutional.

At a special August election an amendment providing for classification of property for the purpose of taxation was rejected by the people. A similar amendment will be voted upon in November by the people in North Carolina and Washington.

Connecticut this year made quite a few changes in her exemption laws, but these changes were primarily in administration and to clarify the 1925 act.

Of course you all know Connecticut made a very extensive study of their exemption problems, and this problem of exemption is yearly increasing in all of our states, on account of the great mass of tax-exempt securities, and because of authorization for harbor development, aviation fields, and so forth.

In our own state the joint committee on taxation and retrenchment, under the leadership of Senator Mastick, made a very good report on our exemption problem. The report is based on statistics and is unbiased. I know Senator Mastick is on the program to tell you about exemptions, but I was just afraid he would not tell you how good his report is. It would be serviceable to all states.

In Massachusetts they are trying by legislation to force the bachelor girls into matrimony, that is, if these girls have the proverbial

New England thrift. They formerly had a law giving $1000 exemption from local taxes to all unmarried women. This year that law was repealed.

New Hampshire allows the towns and cities by vote to exempt certain industries for a period of five years, and after four years by another vote they may exempt them for five more years, making a maximum of ten years.

Rhode Island and Maryland also granted similar exemptions. There are some people who doubt the wisdom of these exemptions.

There has been quite a little difficulty during the past year in the taxation of banks. This is especially true in Minnesota. The Supreme Court in the case of State of Minnesota vs. First National Bank of St. Paul, handed down a decision that the stock of national banks was taxed at a greater rate than that of moneyed capital coming in competition therewith, and therefore was discriminatory. However, the banks of Minnesota do not feel that this is the time to change the taxation of intangibles. To better enable them to persuade their shareholders that this tax should be paid, the state passed a law that no public money of the state or of any governmental division shall be deposited in any bank that is delinquent in its taxes. I don't know enough about law to know whether that is coercion or collusion.

In North Dakota the banks and trust companies are depositing about 50 per cent of their annual net earnings in a surplus fund. This is to continue until the surplus fund equals the capital stock. This fund is to be exempt from taxation. I see that no more banks in North Dakota are going to close their doors. In taxes they are not quite so foresighted, but they do not believe in hitting a man when he is down. No insolvent bank shall pay a tax, but after liquidation the bank taxes shall be paid before any of the shareholders get any of the money.

Kansas has been a little more specific in her millage tax of five mills on the dollar on intangibles—formerly 2½ mills—as to just what it applies. Kansas has also passed an alternative tax of one-tenth of one per cent on the face value of secured debts.

In Nebraska they have amended their tax on intangibles so that in accordance with the interpretation of Section 5219 of the federal law, the taxation of the national banks will equal that of moneyed capital in competition therewith.

Oklahoma classifies her intangibles and levies a tax of one-fifth of one per cent, again money coming in competition being exempted. The receipts from this tax go to the county, one-half to the general fund and one-half to the school fund.

In New York State there is no stock transfer tax levied on the . stock of domestic corporations, where the agreement of sale and the actual transfer of the stock takes place outside of the state. Of course, this becomes a matter of record, however, on the books of the corporation.

For some time now we have had only twelve states with an income tax, and, try as they will, it seems to be impossible to make that a baker's dozen.

Again, Oregon in the June election, defeated an amendment for income tax. Indiana, not at all daunted by the defeat of a similar amendment last year, this year passed a resolution for another amendment to come before the people. I think in many ways they are getting very courageous in Indiana; in fact, they will soon have a new government there.

South Carolina made some amendments in her income tax of last year, dealing with penalties and deductions and exemptions.

In North Carolina the income tax rate on corporations was increased from 4 per cent to 4½ per cent.

Wisconsin and Missouri made rather extensive changes in their income tax laws, the changes in Missouri being in the form of the law rather than in the substance. Formerly in Wisconsin the tax was on the current income; now it is on the average net income. The Tax Commission and the income assessors are to figure out this income, by averaging the current reported income with the net income and net losses of the two preceding years, of course special rulings being made for the first year.

They also introduced a rather new departure in Wisconsin in regard to exemptions. For instance, the exemption to a single person is $8, to the head of a family $17.50, to a dependent $3.

In Delaware you can now pay your income taxes on the installment plan, as it were. They are payable four times a year.

There has been much excitement in inheritance tax circles this year, due to the fact that New York State, one of the prime movers in reciprocity, has quite upset the foundation structure of it. Our Court of Appeals handed down a decision that our flat-rate tax— and I cannot call it the Matthews plan, because Mr. Matthews thinks that we kind of wandered and strayed away on that. They claim it is unconstitutional.

In the same law with this flat-rate tax on non-residents are our reciprocal provisions. The New York State Tax Commission has sent out notices to the effect that the reciprocal death tax exemption in New York State is inoperative until further notice. This year reciprocal provisions were made by California, Georgia, Illinois, Maine, Maryland, New Hampshire, Ohio and Oregon, Maine's becoming effective July 1, 1928.

With states that have reciprocity and those that do not tax intangibles, we now have twenty-one states and the District of Columbia which are safe to die in. Of course, we dare include New York, because in New York we still have hopes.

Georgia also adopted the Matthews flat-rate plan at the August session, the rate being 2 per cent of the value.

The 80 per cent credit was taken up by California, North Carolina, Ohio, Pennsylvania and Vermont. North Carolina states that the law will continue, even if the federal law is repealed, but at 80 per cent of the present rate.

North Dakota repealed the inheritance tax law and substituted an estate tax law. I do not think that they quite picked up the 80 per cent federal credit.

The inheritance tax rates have increased, especially in the higher brackets in New York and in Oklahoma.

Indiana, Nevada, North Dakota, Vermont and Wyoming memorialized Congress for the repeal of the federal estate tax.

Now, coming to the most popular of all taxes, the gasoline tax, two new states this year levied a gasoline tax, New Jersey and Illinois. The rate in each state is two cents a gallon. In Illinois the receipts go half to the state and half to the county, based on registration. In New Jersey the tax is not only on the gasoline used in motor vehicles, but also gasoline used in motor boats. Therefore, $90,000 of the receipts go to inland waterways, and the rest to the highways.

There was a man in our office last week making a study of the gasoline tax problem for the Municipal Research Bureau of New York City, and he said that it was his opinion that the Illinois law was the model gasoline tax law. But the people of Illinois are trying to get out an injunction, claiming it unconstitutional. The lower court upheld the state. The case was appealed, and is coming before the Supreme Court at this October term.

Fifteen states during the past year increased the gasoline tax. Now we have four states with a 5-cent tax, one state with a 4½-cent tax, nine with a 4-cent tax, three with a 3½-cent tax, fourteen with a 3-cent tax, and sixteen with a 2-cent tax. The day of the 1-cent tax has passed.

According to published statements, there was last year taken in from gasoline taxes in the United States 187½ million dollars. Two backward states, New York and Massachusetts, are still discussing the gasoline tax. Last year a bill passed both houses in Massachusetts, but was vetoed by the Governor. In New York State there were nine bills up, but none managed to weather the legislative storm.

Tennessee has taken over the control of the gasoline industry. To pay for this a special tax has been levied of $10 on every wholesaler of gasoline, and $1 on every pump.

Georgia has changed her registration from horsepower to weight.

Quite a few laws have been passed in regard to the taxing of motor common carriers. Nevada passed a specific license which is not additional to the other tax; and Wyoming passed an additional one.

In New Jersey an excise tax was levied of ¾ of a cent a mile traveled by motor vehicles in interstate business.

New Jersey also repealed her general property tax on motor vehicles.

Texas, feeling pity for her electric railroads, since the development of the motor business, has repealed her franchise tax, which was levied on the gross receipts of her electric railroads.

In New York State the additional franchise tax on electric surface cars, subways and elevated, has been decreased from 1 per cent of gross receipts and 3 per cent of the declared dividends in excess of 4 per cent, to five-tenths of one per cent of the gross receipts.

Maine also takes pity on her railroads. Where she formerly taxed them on the basis of the gross receipts per mile, she now taxes them on the gross receipts per mile compared with net receipts. The people of Maine have circulated a referendum petition in regard to this tax and also in regard to the increase in the gasoline tax. Both of these petitions are now in the hands of the Governor of Maine, awaiting further investigation.

In Connecticut, motor vehicles operated by street railroads are taxed in the same way as other operations of the street railroads.

Wisconsin and Minnesota enacted a yield tax of 10 per cent of the stumpage value of the forests, and one pays 10 cents an acre to the county, and the state also pays 10 cents an acre to the county for the classified land, that being the value of the land only, excluding the value of trees.

In Michigan the rate was increased to 10 cents an acre, instead of 5; and the tax on pine lands was increased from 5 to 10 cents, now being equal to that on their hard-wood lands.

In Minnesota the tax on the land itself is 8 cents on every dollar of assessment value.

I have not said a word about the changes in the corporation taxes, but in New York State the corporation tax can only be considered by those to the manner born, as it were.

I have here the digest of tax legislation for 1927, and if any of you are interested you can here find the facts or face the facts or do anything else with the facts that our program tells us to do.

I will say, though, that Pennsylvania has codified her taxes on corporations and has reduced the rate from ⅓ to ⅕ per cent.

In Alabama many additional taxes have been levied on public utilities, these taxes going to a special fund for education. A 15 per cent tax on the wholesale price of tobacco goes to the same fund.

Kansas levied a tax of 2 cents on every package of 20 cigarettes, and 1 cent on a package of 50 cigarette papers.

I think that in Wyoming they are trying to make a bid for the next Tunney-Dempsey prize fight, because they have created a boxing commission and are going to charge a tax of 5 per cent of the gate receipts on all boxing matches.

These are only the high lights of 1927 legislation.

There has been only about one-third as many laws passed this year as there was at the biennial session two years ago. However, I think there will be a great increase during the next two years, as ten states have created, or recreated special investigating commissions. Dr. Snavely in his paper will tell you about those.

Before closing I wish to thank the tax commissioners of the various states for their cooperation in making material available for this digest of legislation. Most of it has to be done before the session laws are in print.

Of the 45 states there were only two states I did not hear from, and that was due mostly to a misunderstanding.

REVIEW OF TAX LEGISLATION FOR 1927

BEULAH BAILEY

Librarian, New York State Tax Commission

During 1927, forty-four states were in regular session and one state, Virginia, in extraordinary session. The three states not in session were Kentucky, Louisiana and Mississippi.

CONSTITUTIONAL AMENDMENTS

Idaho

An amendment providing that all taxes shall be collected by the officer or officers designated by law is to be voted upon November, 1927.

Minnesota

In November, 1928 the people will vote upon the crediting of two-thirds of the proceeds of the gasoline tax to the trunk highway fund and one-third to the state road and bridge fund. At the present time the entire amount is credited to the trunk highway fund.

North Carolina

An amendment permitting the classification of intangible personalty for the purposes of taxation will be voted upon in November, 1928.

North Dakota

An amendment to be voted upon in 1928 will give the State Board of Equalization power to assess the property of electric light, heat and power companies and the property of all other companies which are used directly or indirectly in the carrying of persons, property or messages.

Oregon

At a special June election, Oregon rejected an income tax amendment and an amendment limiting the amount of the state tax.

Texas

Texas rejected an amendment providing for the classification of property in a special August election. In November, 1928, Texas will vote on an amendment authorizing the legislature to exempt from taxation any property owned by a church, strictly religious society or educational association.

Washington

Washington will vote upon the right to classify property, November, 1928.

SPECIAL TAX INVESTIGATING COMMISSIONS

Arkansas

A special Honorary Commission consisting of seven residents of the state is appointed by the governor for the purpose of investigating the subject of taxation and business and corporation laws. $6,300 is appropriated for the use of the commission. It is to report by October 1, 1928.

California

$75,000 is appropriated to be used at the direction of the governor for the purpose of a special tax investigation commission. The commission, numbers undesignated, is to be appointed by the governor and is to report in January, 1929.

Illinois

A joint Legislative Revenue Committee, consisting of nine members, four from the legislature and five appointees of the governor, representing varied industries, is appointed to study the laws and methods of assessing property, and to investigate the methods of taxation in Illinois. $25,000 is appropriated for this purpose.

A Revenue Investigation Commission of seven members, four from the legislature and three appointees of the governor is also appointed. $15,000 is appropriated for this commission.

Maryland

The governor may at any time appoint five people who shall constitute the Maryland Tax Revision Commission. They will serve without pay and the expenses of the commission so appointed shall be defrayed out of state funds.

Massachusetts

Massachusetts provides for a special commission to revise the laws of the commonwealth relative to taxation. The commission is to consist of one senator, three representatives and three appointees of the governor. It shall make a report not later than December 31, 1927, but it hardly seems probable that such an extensive study can be consummated in that length of time. $10,000 is appropriated for the work. The commission is also authorized and directed to consider an excise tax on the use of the public ways by motor vehicles. This refers to motor vehicles that escape taxation by avoidance of ownership on the first day of April.

Minnesota

A special commission consisting of six members, three from the senate and three from the house, is created. The commission is to make a study of the tax laws of the state, with particular reference to those relating to the taxation of intangible personalty. $7,500 is appropriated for this purpose.

New Hampshire

The governor is authorized to appoint a recess commission of nine members to study the subject of tax revision. The commission is to report at the next meeting of the legislature. The governor is also to appoint a commission of three members to study the re-organization of state government.

North Carolina

A commission known as the " Tax Commission," consisting of five members appointed by the governor is created for the purpose of making a comparative study of taxation.

Texas

A Tax Survey Committee of fifteen persons is created in Texas. Three members shall be from the senate, four from the house, and the remainder appointees of the governor. One of the latter to be a person who has made a special study of government and taxation. $25,000 is appropriated for this purpose.

STATE TAX ADMINISTRATION

Arkansas

A Tax Commission comprised of three members created in Arkansas in 1909, abolished in 1923, and its duties transferred to the Arkansas Railroad Commisson, and now in 1927 the law of 1923 has been repealed and a new Tax Commission has been created for a period of thirty-two years. The three commissioners are appointed by the governor for a term of eight years. The commission is charged with the assessment and equalization of general property and public utilities; the collection of the taxes and the supervision over the localities.

Michigan

The State Tax Department was abolished and the State Tax Commission created. The commission is to consist of three members appointed by the governor. The term of appointment is six years.

New Mexico

The powers of the Tax Commission have been increased. The number of days for which an associate tax commissioner may receive pay are increased from 150 to 180. The commission is given power to fix the actual value of livestock and grazing lands instead of the minimum value. The commission is given jurisdiction over the collection of all delinquent taxes and an office of special tax attorney is created and for each county the office of delinquent tax collector. Ten per cent of all delinquent taxes collected is to go into a fund known as the tax commission fund, to be used in paying the cost of collection.

Oregon

The Tax Commission has been given the power to direct and to order any county board of equalization to raise or lower the valuation of any taxable property and to add such property to the assessment list.

South Dakota

Either the Director of Taxation or the assistant director shall be a lawyer. This person shall have general charge and supervision of the administration of inheritance tax matters.

Tennessee

A division of motors and motor fuels has been established in the Department of Finance and Taxation, which division shall have charge of the regulation of the gasoline industry.

Virginia

The administration of the inheritance and the transfer tax will upon March 1, 1928, be transferred from the Auditor of Public Accounts to the Department of Taxation.

LOCAL TAX ADMINISTRATION

Connecticut

The fees of the tax collectors upon a levy and sale have been doubled.

The treasurer and tax collector of
shall be bonded. The size of the bor
officials and the form approved by the

The state tax commissioner may, upc
the books of the treasurer and tax (
average annual receipts from taxatior
ceding shall not exceed fifty thousand

Connecticut passes a most inclusive
which would have been legally valid,
ities and omissions.

Illinois

The maximum compensation of as
per day to $7.00.

Pennsylvan

All tax liens or municipal claims
of an error in the name of the registei
inadequate description are by a 1927 a

All ad valorem tax levies made b}
forceable because of the failure of tł
levies by ordinance are by a 1927 law

ASSESSMEI

Arkansas

Arkansas passed an act regulating
personal property in counties whose ʃ
is less than 75,000. Real property iɩ
odd-numbered years. Personal prope
A Board of Equalization is created in

Illinois

Property shall be assessed at its fɩ
its full value.

Minnesot.

The assessors are instructed by law
of land, to take special note of its loc
and streets.

The property of transient merchan
at the rate of levy for the curent yea
diately.

Montana

All real estate and improvements,
assessed by the state board of equaliz
future biennially, starting with 1927 ɩ

According to th Montana law, a tax due upon personal property is a prior lien up all such property and is also a lien upon the real property of owner. Under a 1927 amendment, if a mortgagor does not p his personal property tax, or his real property tax, the mortgage may request that the personal property and the real property of mortgagor be separately assessed. If so done the personal prop y taxes ceases to be a lien upon the mortgaged real property.

New York

The Tax Comn sion must approve of every assessment of state-owned lands bv tł assessing officers of a village, before the village taxes may be levi thereon.

North Carolina

In a 1927 law ·tter provision is made for local assessments. The qualification i the county supervisor who is appointed by the County Board of ommissioners are enumerated. The supervisor appoints three as ants or assessors. The compensation is not less than three nor m e than eight dollars a day. The county supervisor meets with · board of county commissioners when they sit as a board of equ zation and review. Any taxpayer has the right of appeal from county commissioners to the State Board of Assessments.

XEMPTIONS FROM TAXATION

Connecticut

As a result of findings of the special tax exemption commission appointed in)23, and reporting in 1925, a law codifying the recommendations as passed in 1925. Section 1 of this law was repealed in 1927 d a new section substituted. The changes made by the 1927 statu ıre chiefly in administration and for the purpose of clarifying the)25 act.

Some specific ınges in the exemptions are as follows:

The 1927 law akes use of the word " charitable " rather than " benevolent " a ı preceding Connecticut tax-exemption statutes, thus conforming ith the statutes of other states.

The 1927 law xempts property not owned by a Connecticut municipality, prc ded such property is exclusively used by the public in lieu of ..blic property and provided a nominal charge not in excess of $25 nually is made by the owner.

The 1927 law xempts up to $1,000, property belonging to an individual who s'ved in the army, navy, marine corps, or revenue marine service c the United States during the Philippine Insurrection or China elief Expedition and who received an honorable discharge theref `n·

3

The treasurer and tax collector of each town, city or borough shall be bonded. The size of the bond is to be fixed by the local officials and the form approved by the tax commission.

The state tax commissioner may, upon request, cause to be audited the books of the treasurer and tax collector of any town whose average annual receipts from taxation during the three years preceding shall not exceed fifty thousand dollars.

Connecticut passes a most inclusive act validating acts and deeds which would have been legally valid, except for certain irregularities and omissions.

Illinois

The maximum compensation of assessors is raised from $5.00 per day to $7.00.

Pennsylvania

All tax liens or municipal claims which are defective, because of an error in the name of the registered owner, or by reason of an inadequate description are by a 1927 act declared valid.

Texas

All ad valorem tax levies made by cities and towns but unenforceable because of the failure of the city or town to make such levies by ordinance are by a 1927 law made valid.

ASSESSMENT

Arkansas

Arkansas passed an act regulating the assessment of real and personal property in counties whose population exceeds 60,000 and is less than 75,000. Real property is to be assessed biennially in odd-numbered years. Personal property shall be assessed annually. A Board of Equalization is created in each county of this class.

Illinois

Property shall be assessed at its full value, instead of one-half its full value.

Minnesota

The assessors are instructed by law, when determining the value of land, to take special note of its location, with reference to roads and streets.

The property of transient merchants shall be assessed and taxed at the rate of levy for the curent year. Such taxes are due immediately.

Montana

All real estate and improvements, other than such as has to be assessed by the state board of equalization, shall be assessed in the future biennially, starting with 1927 rather than annually.

According to the Montana law, a tax due upon personal property is a prior lien upon all such property and is also a lien upon the real property of the owner. Under a 1927 amendment, if a mortgagor does not pay his personal property tax, or his real property tax, the mortgagee may request that the personal property and the real property of the mortgagor be separately assessed. If so done the personal property taxes ceases to be a lien upon the mortgaged real property.

New York

The Tax Commission must approve of every assessment of state-owned lands by the assessing officers of a village, before the village taxes may be levied thereon.

North Carolina

In a 1927 law better provision is made for local assessments. The qualifications of the county supervisor who is appointed by the County Board of Commissioners are enumerated. The supervisor appoints three assistants or assessors. The compensation is not less than three nor more than eight dollars a day. The county supervisor meets with the board of county commissioners when they sit as a board of equalization and review. Any taxpayer has the right of appeal from the county commissioners to the State Board of Assessments.

Exemptions from Taxation

Connecticut

As a result of the findings of the special tax exemption commission appointed in 1923, and reporting in 1925, a law codifying the recommendations was passed in 1925. Section 1 of this law was repealed in 1927 and a new section substituted. The changes made by the 1927 statute are chiefly in administration and for the purpose of clarifying the 1925 act.

Some specific changes in the exemptions are as follows:

The 1927 law makes use of the word " charitable " rather than " benevolent " as in preceding Connecticut tax-exemption statutes, thus conforming with the statutes of other states.

The 1927 law exempts property not owned by a Connecticut municipality, provided such property is exclusively used by the public in lieu of public property and provided a nominal charge not in excess of $25 annually is made by the owner.

The 1927 law exempts up to $1,000, property belonging to an individual who served in the army, navy, marine corps, or revenue marine service of the United States during the Philippine Insurrection or China Relief Expedition and who received an honorable discharge therefrom.

Except in one particular, the 1927 law exempts from local taxation and from the state four-mill chose-in-action tax, all cash on hand and money on deposit. Under the 1925 law such property, savngs deposits in the state excepted, was exempt only up to $500.

Idaho

The property belonging to veterans of the Spanish-American War, and the Philippine Insurrection has been added to the exempt list.

Iowa

Under a 1927 law the dependent widowed mother of a soldier, sailor or marine is allowed the exemptions if said soldier, sailor or marine has not benefited by such exemptions.

Maryland

The veterans of the Spanish-American War have been granted the same exemptions as the veterans of the Civil War and the World War.

The real and personal property owned by Chambers of Commerce or boards of trade and used solely by them is exempt from taxation.

For the purpose of encouraging industries certain industries are exempt in certain counties.

Massachusetts

Formerly unmarried women as well as widows, old people and certain minors were allowed, for local taxation, an exemption of $1,000. A 1927 act denies this right to unmarried women.

Nevada

Fraternities of the University of Nevada are allowed $7,500 exemption on each chapter house.

New Hampshire

Any town or city, by a two-thirds vote, may give a five-year abatement of taxes to any manufacturing concern, upon such terms and conditions as may be mutually agreed upon. After four years they may vote again, extending the time another five years, but not exceeding in all ten years.

New Jersey

Bonds or obligations issued by any public utility company of any state are exempt from taxation while owned by any savings bank or institution for savings of New Jersey.

New Mexico

$200 exemption from taxation of property belonging to the head of a family applied to personal property only; now it applies to general property.

New York

The real property of bar associations has been added to the exempt list.

North Carolina

The property of patriotic and historical associations is added to the exempt list.

Rhode Island

A special act authorizes the town of Warren to exempt from taxation manufacturing property which has been or shall have been idle for two years or more. The exemption shall be for a period of ten years from the date of the renewal of the operation of such property.

Rhode Island adds to its list of exemptions ·real and personal property, to the extent of $100,000, belonging to or held in trust for the benefit of incorporated organizations of veterans of any war in which the United States has participated, if actually used for such association or if the net income from the property is used for charity.

The veterans of the Spanish-American War and the World War are given the same exemption privileges as those of the Civil War.

South Carolina

South Carolina passed laws ratifying two constitutional amendments adopted in 1926, for the purpose of exempting in certain counties, all cotton and textile enterprises valued above $100,000 from all county taxes except for school purposes, for five years from the time of their establishment.

BANKS

Connecticut

Connecticut permits as a deduction from the taxes assessed against the savings department of banks and trust companies, the tax paid on real estate held as an asset of said department.

Minnesota

Under 5219 U. S. Rev. St. shares of national banks cannot be taxed at a greater rate than moneyed capital employed in competition with such banks. The Supreme Court of the United States held, in State of Minnesota v. First National Bank of St. Paul (47 Sup. Ct. Rep. 468), that the Minnesota state tax on national bank shares was greater than the tax on moneys and·credits, and hence discriminatory. As a result of this decision the national banks are not legally bound to pay the present state tax. However, the officers of the banks feel that for the time being, the taxation of bank shares and money and credits should remain as they are. In order to more forcibly persuade the holders of shares of stock in the various banks that the present bank tax should be paid, a 1927 act states that no public money belonging to the state or to any governmental subdivision shall be kept in any national bank that has not paid its tax after July 15, 1927, nor deposited in any after July 1, 1927. The newly created commission to study tax laws is to make a special study of this situation.

New York

An amendment was made to the law imposing the income tax on the net income upon banks providing that the tax of four and one-half per cent shall be for the calendar year in which it becomes due; except that with respect to corporations of classes previously subject to franchise taxes, this tax being in lieu of that tax, will be for the year that such franchise tax was formerly imposed.

North Dakota

For the purpose of strengthening the banking associations of the state, a law was enacted providing that every banking association and trust company shall annually or semi-annually convert into a surplus fund at least fifty per cent of its net earnings. This shall be done until the surplus equals one hundred per cent of the capital stock. This surplus is exempt from all taxation.

Texas

No franchise tax shall be assessed on an insolvent bank. However, if after liquidation there are any funds left, past due franchise taxes shall be paid before such funds are distributed to stockholders.

Wisconsin

Wisconsin levies an income tax on the income of state banks, national banks and trust companies. This tax is in lieu of all taxes upon the capital, surplus, property and assets of such banks, except that no real property owned by such bank or trust company shall be exempt from taxation. The rate is from 2% to 6%.

Wyoming

Formerly the surplus and undivided profits of loan or investment companies, banks and banking associations was assessed and taxed to the shareholder. Under a law enacted in 1927 the surplus and undivided profits of banks and banking associations are no longer thus taxed.

BONDS

North Dakota

The Tax Commission of North Dakota drafted and the legislature enacted with a few minor changes a uniform bond bill, governing borrowing by means of bond issues by counties, cities, villages, townships, school districts, park districts and all governmental subdivisions. The new bill makes the bond procedure uniform as to all taxes of taxing districts and places additional safeguards around sinking and interest funds.

In any county where the crops have been a total or partial failure on account of natural causes, bonds, certificates of indebtedness or warrants shall be issued to procure seed grain and feed for needy inhabitants.

Texas

Any county in the state, upon a vote of two-thirds majority, may issue bonds in an amount not to exceed one-fourth of the assessed valuation of real property in the county, for aiding navigation. This debt is in addition to all other bonded debts.

COLLECTION OF TAXES

Arizona

In an effort to remedy the delinquent tax situation all court actions of the county treasurers against tax delinquents are to be prosecuted as actions for the foreclosure of mortgages.

Idaho

Idaho provides for the foreclosure of tax liens by the county when it has taken a tax deed for delinquent taxes, and can't sell the land. The foreclosure shall be conducted the same as a foreclosure of a mortgage.

The taxes upon not over $1,000 of assessed personal property as written upon the real property assessment roll is a prior lien on the real property, but if the assessed personal property exceeds $1,000 in value, the lien of the taxes on the amount over $1,000 is subordinate to any recorded mortgage or recorded lien.

Iowa

Taxes due upon personal property are a lien upon real property owned by the person for ten years. Formerly the time was not limited.

Minnesota

Under a 1927 act the taxes assessed upon personal property are a lien upon such property. If lands are sold for non-payment of taxes, after five years absolute title is vested in the purchaser or in the state if they were not sold.

North Carolina

Any holder of a certificate of sale resulting from buying lands at a tax sale, has the right of foreclosure of said certificate of sale by civil action.

Oregon

The interest rate on unpaid taxes has been increased from five-sixths of one per cent per month to one per cent. When taxes are declared delinquent there is an additional penalty of two per cent per month, formerly three per cent.

Pennsylvania

Pennsylvania becomes a little more lenient in the matter of delinquent taxes, permitting the filing of tax liens and the return of property for non-payment without the necessity of levying on and selling the personal goods and chattels of the delinquent.

Utah

If any county claims a lien on real estate for delinquent general taxes which have not been paid for four years, said county may foreclose such lien by action in the district court.

CORPORATIONS

Alabama

In addition to all other license and privilege taxes, corporations must procure an annual permit. The fees for said permit range from $5 to $100 on foreign corporations, being based on the amount of capital employed in the state, and from $10 to $100 on domestic corporations, based on the amount of capital stock.

The annual franchise tax on domestic and foreign corporations has been increased from $1 to $2 on every $1000 of capital stock issued or capital employed in the state. Formerly one-tenth of this tax was returned to the counties, now one-fifth.

California

A foreign corporation when filing the certified copy of its articles of incorporation, or of its charter, or of any act creating it, with the secretary of state, shall pay a fee of $100. The fee for educational, charitable, religious, scientific, or foreign non-profit corporations is $5. A fine of $500 is imposed upon all foreign corporations failing to file such papers, or pay such fee.

The rate of tax on the franchises of all corporations other than public utilities, insurance companies, banks, savings and loan societies and trust companies, is raised from one and two-tenths per cent to one and eight-tenths per cent.

Maryland

If business corporations have issued no capital stock, which is the basis of the franchise tax, they shall pay an annual franchise tax of $10.

Formerly in determining gross receipts of certain corporations, income from any investment of capital or surplus was not included. In the case of the investment of money received or deposited, only the difference btween the receipts of such deposited money and the interest paid on such deposits was included in gross receipts. Under a 1927 law the only corporations to which all this applies are trust companies and title insurance companies.

For county, city and municipal purposes a tax of one per cent of the assessed valuation is levied upon the shares of stock of every commercial banking, finance, mortgage and other moneyed or financial corporation except state or national banks, and insurance casualty, surety, guaranty or fidelity companies. This tax is in addition to the state tax but in lieu of all other local taxes.

Massachusetts

The right of appeal is extended to sixty days in place of thirty days from notice of tax.

By a 1927 act, in assessing business corporations, instead of having to take the value as of April 1st, the taxing day in Massachusetts, the value can be taken as of the day returned to the Federal Government for taxation purposes. This law becomes effective January 1, 1928. At present the inventories given as of April 1st, are really the inventories of December 31st, adjusted by estimate or otherwise to April 1st. In estimating the value of all capital stock, the surplus and undivided profits shall be included.

New Hampshire

New Hampshire provides for the annual tax if the authorized capital stock of a corporation is reduced. The annual tax is one-fourth the original incorporation fee plus one-fourth of additional payments for increases in its authorized capital stock. If the stock is reduced the annual tax is one-fourth the amount required for the original fee of a corporation capitalized at the amount as reduced.

North Carolina

The franchise or license tax on telegraph companies has been reduced from $7.50 per mile for each pole mile of line to $5.

Ohio

The fee charged against corporations, domestic and foreign, is decreased from one-half of one per cent to one-eighth of one per cent of the value of the issued and outstanding shares of stock. After 1928 it will be one-tenth of one per cent.

The franchise fee of foreign corporations has been changed from one-tenth of one per cent of its authorized capital stock employed in the state to a graduated rate based on shares. The minimum fee is $25. The same rate holds for the increase of capital stock.

Pennsylvania

A 1927 act exempts domestic corporations owning all of the shares of stock, except necessary qualifying shares, of a subsidiary, from paying a tax on so much of the value of such stock as represents tangible property without the Commonwealth. In a decision of the Pennsylvania Supreme Court in 1926 it was held that shares of stock of a foreign corporation are intangible property, and their value may be included in determining the amount on which the capital stock tax is to be assessed against a domestic corporate owner.

There were six distinct corporation bonus bill laws in the Pennsylvania statute. An act of 1927 codifies these laws and repeals four of them specifically and all other acts inconsistent with it. The 1927 law reduces the bonus tax from one-third of one per cent to one-fifth of one per cent.

FORESTRY TAX

Michigan

The tax on classified pine lands has been increased from 5 cents an acre to 10 cents, corresponding now with the tax on hard-wood lands. The state also pays ten cents per acre, formerly five. Both of these sums go to the county, 25 per cent to the general fund and 75 per cent to the townships. Twenty-five per cent of the latter goes to the contingent fund and the remainder to the school district.

Minnesota

In accord with the constitutional amendment of 1926, Minnesota passed an act establishing auxiliary forests. Such lands are to be taxed at eight cents on each dollar of the assessed value of the land exclusive of the timber. In Minnesota the assessed value is one-third of the true value. In addition to this tax there is one of three cents an acre for forest-fire protection. The yield tax payable when the timber is cut is ten per cent of the true and full value of the timber.

Wisconsin

Wisconsin has levied a yield tax of ten per cent of the value of the stumpage cut on her forest crop land. Growing timber is exempt until cut, while from the land itself counties receive a total yield tax of twenty cents per acre, ten cents from the owned and ten cents from the state. This advancement by the state of money to local taxing districts that might otherwise be impoverished is a new feature of the law. The state will theoretically get this money back from the yield tax.

GASOLINE TAX

Arkansas

The gasoline tax is raised from four to five cents per gallon. The ten-cent per gallon tax on motor oil is repealed.

California

California increased the tax from two cents to three cents per gallon.

Delaware

Delaware increased the gasoline tax from two cents per gallon to three cents per gallon.

Georgia

Georgia increased the gasoline tax from three and one-half cents to four cents.

Idaho

Idaho has raised the gasoline tax from three cents per gallon to four.

Illinois

Illinois levies a two-cent tax, effective August 1, 1927, on gasoline used for motor purposes. The money is for the road fund, fifty per cent for the state and fifty per cent for the counties, based upon the amount of motor vehicle license fees collected in each county.

Iowa

The gasoline tax has been increased from two cents per gallon to three cents.

Maine

The tax on gasoline has been increased from three cents to four. Under the Maine law all gasoline is taxed, but a refund is made on every gallon used for purposes other than to operate motor vehicles on the highway. The amount of this refund is increased from two cents to three.

Maryland

Two separate acts have increased the gasoline tax from two cents per gallon to fóur cents per gallon. The receipts from an additional one and one-half cents goes to the Lateral Road Gasoline Tax Fund, while the receipts from the additional one-half cent is to be used for the elimination of grade crossings.

Michigan

Michigan increased the gasoline tax from two cents to three cents a gallon.

New Hampshire

The gasoline tax has been increased from two cents per gallon to three cents.

New Jersey

New Jersey levies a tax of two cents a gallon on gasoline used in motor vehicles and motor boats. $90,000 of the receipts from this tax is to go to the Department of Commerce and Navigation, for the inland waterways and the remainder to the highways, after first deducting the cost of collecting the tax. The annual license fee for selling gasoline is $2.

New Mexico

The tax on gasoline has been increased from three cents per gallon to five cents. The receipts from the tax go to the state road fund. The Highway Commission is authorized to anticipate the proceeds, by the issuance and sale of state highway debentures, not exceeding in the aggregate $1,250,000. The collection of the tax has been put under the jurisdiction of the state comptroller.

Oklahoma

Various counties of the state are to use the proceeds from the gasoline tax, in so far as may be necessary, in the payment of the interest on, and the principal of, bonds issued by the respective counties for the construction of hard-surfaced roads.

Pennsylvania

The permanent gasoline tax is increased from one cent a gallon to two cents, and the temporary tax of one cent is continued until June 30, 1929, making a total tax of three cents. Formerly fifty per cent of the permanent tax went to the county, now only twenty-five per cent of the permanent tax goes to the county, the rest of the permanent and all of the emergency going to the state for highway purposes.

Rhode Island

The tax on gasoline is raised from one cent per gallon to two cents. The proceeds will all go to the roads and, due to the increase in receipts, that portion of the state tax on cities and towns formerly applied to highway purposes, is to be diverted to the general purposes of the state.

South Dakota

South Dakota increased the gasoline tax from three to four cents per gallon.

Tennessee

A division of motors and motor fuels has been established in the Department of Finance and Taxation, which division shall have charge of the regulating of the gasoline industry. To defray the expenses of this, an additional license is levied on wholesalers and retailers. The license on the former is $10 per annum and on the latter $1 per annum, for each retail service station or curb pump.

Texas

The gasoline tax is increased from one cent a gallon to three cents until September 1, 1928, when it shall be two cents.

Vermont

Vermont increases the tax on gasoline from two cents to three a gallon.

West Virginia

West Virginia increases the gasoline tax from three and one-half cents to four cents per gallon.

Wyoming

The tax on gasoline has been increased from two and one-half cents per gallon to three cents.

INCOME TAX

Delaware

Many minor changes have been made in the administration provisions of the income tax. Some of the more material ones are as follows:

Every person, firm, corporation or division of government making payments to another person of $1,000 or more must report the same to the tax department.

The income tax may now be paid in four equal installments instead of the one payment at the time of filing the returns. The filing fee of $3 has been removed.

The credit allowed to certain corporations on their income tax returns for state taxes paid during the year, other than for a certificate of incorporation or of increase in capital stock, has been withdrawn.

Indiana

A resolution for an amendment to the constitution providing for an income tax was passed by the General Assembly.

Missouri

Missouri repealed eight sections of its former tax law, and substituted new sections which are about the same in substance but not in form. There are, however, a few changes and additions. All persons or corporations making payments to another person of $1,000 or more in any taxable year shall make a return of such information to the state auditor.

Income received under the workmen's compensation act, or through the war risk insurance act, or by any law for the benefit or relief of injured or disabled members of the military or naval forces of the U. S. shall be exempt.

Necessary traveling expenses in the pursuit of business are deductible from gross income.

Under the 1927 act, in computing the net income of a resident of the state all sums paid in the taxable year by said resident, as taxes assessed and levied by any other state, as income tax on property of non-residents, shall not be deducted from the amount of the income tax.

Under the 1917 act, income embraced in a personal return was credited with the amount received as dividends upon stock, or from the net earnings of any corporation taxable upon its net income. Under the 1927 act, the income is credited only with such proportion of the amount received from the same source as such corporation's income taxed in the state during the preceding taxable year bears to its total net income for the same period.

The law was tightened up in regard to the income from the undivided profits of corporations, trying to close up a few avenues of escape from taxation, made possible by holding companies accumulating profits, etc. After investigation the state auditor may determine whether in his opinion such accumulations are unreasonable for the purpose of the business.

Under the repealed act stock dividends were specifically designated as income and were taxable. In the 1927 act "dividends" include the share to which the taxpayer would be entitled, of the gains and profits of corporations, if divided or distributed, whether divided or distributed or not, stock dividends not being specifically designated as income.

New York

Any official or employee of the tax department is forbidden by law to produce or disclose the contents of any income tax report, except in an action brought on behalf of the tax commission.

In computing net income a taxpayer who regularly sells property on the installment plan may return as income that proportion of the installment payments actually received in a taxable year which the total profit realized when the payment is completed bears to the total contract price.

North Carolina

The rate of the income tax on corporations has been increased from four per cent to four and one-half. The time for appeal to the Commissioner of Revenue for a revision of the assessment has been increased from one year to three years.

Oregon

An act providing for a tax on income was submitted to the people at a special election in June. It was rejected. A similar bill was rejected in 1926. Oregon's former income tax was repealed by referendum in 1924.

South Carolina

South Carolina adds four new sections dealing with deductions, exemptions, depreciations and penalties, to its income tax law of 1926.

Charitable contributions not exceeding fifteen per cent of the taxpayer's net income are deductible.

Reasonable deductions are allowed for depreciation and obsolescence of property used in trade or business.

The exemption of $2,500 to husband and wife making separate returns may be taken by either or divided between them.

Wisconsin

The Wisconsin income tax law was extensively amended but the rates themselves were not changed. Formerly the tax was on all income, now it is on all average net incomes. The Tax Commission or the assessor of incomes determines this net average income by averaging the current net income reported, with the net incomes or net losses of the two previous years. Stock dividends are no longer considered as taxable income.

Wisconsin has made rather a novel departure from the methods of taking exemptions. Instead of a certain amount being taken from the measure of the tax, it is taken from the amount of tax. The personal exemptions are for an individual $8, head of family $17.50, and for a dependent $3.

In crediting overpayment of income and surtaxes against taxes to be subsequently collected, six per cent interest is allowed from certain specified dates.

INHERITANCE TAX

Arizona

Arizona memorializes Congress to repeal the federal estate tax.

California

California provides for reciprocity in imposing inheritance taxes on the intangible personal property of non-residents. This act is effective July 29, 1927.

California also enacts a law in order to obtain for the state the benefit of the credit of eighty per cent allowed under the federal estates tax.

The amount of fees allowed by law to the treasurer of each county in addition to his salary, has been increased.

Colorado

Colorado by law obtains the eighty per cent credit allowed under the federal estate act.

Georgia

Georgia enacted the Matthews flat-rate plan for the taxation of the property of non-resident decedents. The tax is two per cent of actual value. Coupled with this act is the reciprocal provision for the taxation of the intangible personalty of non-residents.

A 1927 amendment to the inheritance tax law provides for the filing of an amended return showing any changes made in the federal estate tax, and providing for payment direct to the Comptroller General instead of the local tax collector.

Delaware

Delaware passes an estate tax in order to take advantage of the eighty per cent federal credit.

Illinois

Illinois provides that intangible personal property of non-residents shall not be taxable, if the decedent was a resident of a state that exempts non-residents from such a tax.

Indiana

Indiana went on record in a concurrent resolution memorializing Congress to abolish the federal estate tax.

Maine

Maine will have reciprocity in the taxation of intangible personalty of non-resident decedents after July 1, 1928.

Maryland

Maryland provides for reciprocity in the taxation of the intangible personalty of non-resident decedents. Maryland went on record as being opposed to the federal estate tax.

Massachusetts

Massachusetts had reciprocity in regard to the taxation of all intangible personalty of non-resident decedents except stock in any national bank in the state, or in any corporation organized under the laws of the state. A 1927 act eliminates these exceptions and now Massachusetts has complete reciprocity in so far as complete reciprocity is possible. This is effective as of December 1, 1926.

Massachusetts makes permanent, for so long as the federal estate tax is in force, the estate tax levied in the commonwealth in 1926.

Minnesota

Adopted children have been classed with lineal issue in the levying of the inheritance tax. Cemeteries have been added to the corporations, gifts to which are exempt from the inheritance tax.

Missouri

Missouri amends its inheritance tax in order to pick up the eighty per cent federal credit.

Montana

Montana places additional taxes on estates over $1,000,000, in order to take advantage of the eighty per cent federal credit.

Nevada

Nevada memorializes Congress to repeal the federal estate tax.

New Hampshire

New Hampshire passed a law providing for reciprocity in the taxation of intangible personalty of non-residents. The law goes into effect March 9, 1927.

New Jersey

The inheritance tax rates have been increased in New Jersey, especially in the higher brackets. Father and mother of the decedent have been taken from the collateral-heir group and placed in the direct heirs. Formerly the rates for direct heirs ranged from one per cent on any amount from $5,000 to $50,000 to three per cent on any amount in excess of $250,000. Under the 1927 act the rates for direct heirs ranges from one per cent on any amount up to $50,000, to sixteen per cent on any amount in excess of $3,700,000. The rate for collateral heirs under the old law was five per cent on everything. Under the 1927 act it ranges from five per cent on any amount up to $300,000, to sixteen per cent on any amount in excess of $2,200,000. Under the former law all property not falling in either class was taxed at eight per cent. The present tax for such property ranges from eight per cent on any amount up to $900,000, to sixteen per cent on any amount in excess of $1,700,000.

There has also been a little change in the deductions allowed. Transfer taxes paid to or payable to other states or territories or the District of Columbia or foreign governments on any property the transfer of which is taxable according to the New Jersey law, is deductible. However, the federal estate tax is not allowed as a deduction.

New York

The Court of Appeals of New York State handed down a decision July 20, 1927, declaring the flat-rate plan of inheritance tax upon non-resident decedents, as written into the New York statutes, unconstitutional, under the provision of the Constitution of the United States whereby "the citizens of each state are entitled to the privileges of citizens in the several states." This same law also contains the New York State reciprocal provisions, in regard to the taxation of the intangible personalty of non-resident decedents. The New York State Tax Commission sent out notice under date of July 25th stating that the reciprocal death-tax exemptions are to be considered inoperative until further notice.

North Carolina

In addition to the inheritance tax North Carolina imposes an estate tax which provides for the 80 per cent credit allowed by the Federal Government. If the Federal Government should repeal the federal estate tax, then instead of the present state estate tax, a tax equal to 80 per cent of the present federal estate tax shall be levied.

The penalty for the non-payment of death taxes within two years after the testator's death has been reduced from ten per cent to five per cent.

North Dakota

North Dakota memorializes Congress for the repeal of the federal estate tax.

The inheritance tax law of North Dakota was repealed and an estate tax was substituted. The rates are one per cent up to $25,000; one and one-half per cent on the amount from $25,000 to $50,000; two per cent on the amount from $50,000 to $100,000; two and one-half per cent on the amount from $100,000 to $200,000 and then increasing one-half per cent for every $200,000 up to $1,000,000. The rate on the amount from $1,000,000 to $1,500,000 is six per cent, and seven per cent on all over $1,500,000. North Dakota in its rates does not take full advantage of the 80 per cent federal credit.

The exemptions are $20,000 to husband and wife, and $3,000 to lineal ancestor or descendant, unless the latter is a minor and then $5,000. All proceeds from life insurance policies are exempt. Debts, taxes, administrative expenses etc. are deductions.

Ohio

Ohio provides for reciprocity after June 30, 1927. Ohio also levies an additional inheritance tax, in order to pick up the 80 per cent federal credit.

Oklahoma

Oklahoma amends its inheritance tax by fixing the rate of tax on amounts over $100,000. The former law taxed all amounts in excess of that sum at four per cent. The amendment carries rates graduating from 4.8 per cent to sixteen per cent on amounts from $700,000 to $10,000,000.

Oregon

Oregon passes a law granting reciprocity May 27, 1927 in regard to the death tax on the intangible personalty of non-residents.

Pennsylvania

An additional tax, making the whole tax equal to the 80 per cent federal credits on estates of decedents was enacted.

The Auditor General instead of the Register of Wills is to appoint investigators, and appraisers on decedents' estates.

Vermont

Vermont memorializes Congress in regard to the repeal of the federal estate tax.

Vermont enacts a law obtaining for the state the benefit of the credit of 80 per cent allowed under the federal estate act.

Wyoming

Wyoming passed a joint resolution memorializing Congress to repeal the federal estate tax.

INSURANCE COMPANIES

Alabama

In addition to the insurance tax on the amount of business done, there is levied an annual filing fee of $200, to be paid into the state treasury. Insurance agents are charged an annual fee of $4.

4

North Carolina

The franchise or license tax on insurance rate-making associations is $350.

Pennsylvania

The tax on marine insurance companies is changed from one on gross premiums to one on underwriting profits. The tax is five per cent on the " underwriting profit." The law states how that underwriting profit is to be determined.

Texas

Hitherto there has been no law in Texas regulating how the property of fire-insurance companies and casualty companies should be assessed. A 1927 law says that the real property shall be valued the same as other real property in the state is valued. The personal property shall be valued as is other personal property but from the total valuation of the latter shall be deducted the reserve and from the remainder the assessed value of real property, and the final remainder shall be the taxable personal property of such companies, to be assessed as other property.

Wyoming

A tax of five per cent per annum is levied upon the gross premiums on insurance placed with companies not admitted to do business in the state.

INTANGIBLES, MONEY, CREDITS

Connecticut

In Connecticut only the amount of a mortgage which is in excess of the assessed value of the real property is taxable. The 1927 law states that if a note, bond or mortgage provides that the borrower shall pay all taxes assessed thereon, such excess tax shall be assessed against the owner of the real estate instead of against the lender.

Kansas

The millage tax on money and credits is raised from 2.5 mills on a dollar to 5 mills. The 1927 law states more definitely to what specific money and credits this millage tax applies. This is done in an effort to meet the difficulty which has been encountered regarding the taxation of national banks.

An alternative stamp tax of one-tenth of one per cent per year is levied upon the face value of secured·debts. If the taxpayer wishes to have the secured debt registered, there is an additional tax of one-tenth of one per cent of the face value. Either the millage tax or the stamp tax is in lieu of all further taxation, except the inheritance tax or an income tax, if Kansas should levy one. The stamp tax is administered by the state treasurer. Half of the proceeds from the stamp tax goes to the state and half to the counties according to their assessed valuation. The registration money goes to the general fund of the county.

Nebraska

Nebraska amended the intangible tax law in order to comply with Section 5219 of the revised federal statutes. All moneyed capital coming in competition with the national banks shall be taxed at the same rate as bank stock is taxed. Of the receipts from intangibles, one-sixth shall go to the state general fund, one-sixth to county general fund, one-third to the general fund of the city or village, and one-third to the school district. If the property assessed is not located in a city or village, two-thirds of the tax will go to the school district.

New York

The stock transfer tax has been removed on shares or certificates of stock or rights to stock or certificates of deposit of any domestic association, company or corporation, when the sale, the agreement to sell, the memorandum of sale and the delivery are all made outside of the state. However, a record of such transaction has to be kept on the books of the company.

Oklahoma

Intangibles have been taken from the general property class, and a special tax of one-fifth of one per cent is levied upon them. This tax does not apply to moneyed capital coming into competition with national banks, nor to certificates of stock or evidence of deposit issued by building and loan associations and held by depositors and certificate-holders, but does apply to the undistributed cash of such associations. The receipts from the tax go to the county in which the same was paid, one-half going to the general fund and one-half to the school fund.

Oregon

If the income tax act had become law, all stocks, except shares of stock in banks on other moneyed capital employed in competition with the business of national banks, bonds, notes and all moneys or debt due would have been removed from the general property tax, as the dividends, interest on other income from these would have been taxed under the income tax.

Vermont

A 1927 act has added perpetual or redeemable leases and the shares of stock of a corporation or joint stock company or business trust, except shares of stock in national banks, trust companies and savings banks and trust companies organized under the laws of Vermont, to the class of personal property to be taxed at the rate of forty cents on a dollar of one per cent of its appraised valuation.

In assessing stockholders for shares of stock in corporations there shall be deducted the value of the real and personal property and machinery taxed to such corporation in Vermont. Under the repealed section the value of the personal property taxed outside the state was also deducted.

MISCELLANEOUS LICENSES AND TAXES

Alabama

A tax of two cents a gallon is levied on all lubricating oils; this, however, does not include "kerosene oil," "fuel oil" or "crude oil."

Connecticut

Connecticut repealed its registration tax of ten dollars on each hundred feet of motion-picture film and substituted a tax upon places of amusement based upon seating capacity. The tax is as follows: $40 per week for seating capacity of 1500 or more; $25 for 1000 to 1500; $20 for 750 to 1000; $15 for 500 to 750; $10 for less than 500 and $5 for less than 500 where exhibitions are given not more than twice per week.

Georgia

Georgia levies a tax on kerosene of one cent a gallon. This is on the distributor. The revenue goes to the school fund.

Montana

A license tax of forty cents per head on horses, mules and cattle and ten cents per head on sheep is imposed on all live stock coming into the state to graze for any length of time whatsoever. The money is divided equally between the general fund of the school district in which the stock is grazing and the general fund of the county. This tax does not apply to any livestock on which the regular annual tax is levied.

New Mexico

The law levying an annual road tax of $3, or in lieu thereof, two days' work on the roads, has been repealed.

Oklahoma

Property used in the manufacture of lint cotton is taken from general property and classified. A statement of the business must be filed quarterly with the county assessor. The tax is one-tenth of one per cent of the gross value of the manufactured product and is payable quarterly to the county treasurer. This tax is in lieu of all others, except the ad valorem tax on the ground on which the buildings are located. Half of the receipts from this special tax go to the school district in which the mills are located, one-thirtieth to the state, five-thirtieths to the county, seven-thirtieths to the township and two-thirtieths to the sinking funds of the county school district and city or township on which the mill is located.

South Carolina

South Carolina re-enacted, with certain changes, previous revenue legislation in regard to documentary taxes, consolidating several acts into one.

Texas

People operating "endless chains" are required to be licensed, and pay an occupation tax of $25 per annum.

Wyoming

Water rights and reservoir rights acquired under or through permits issued by the state engineer, and having their origin within the state shall be assessed and taxed as real property.

An office known as the "State Boxing Commissioner of Wyoming" has been created. A tax of five per cent of the gross receipts from admission fees to boxing or sparring matches or exhibitions is levied on every club, corporation or association holding such a match.

MOTOR VEHICLES

Alabama

There are two sets of registration fees in Alabama for motor trucks. The fees on trucks using motor fuel, on which the excise tax has been paid, range from $15 on trucks less than one ton to $1000 on trucks of seven tons or over. The fees on trucks using motor fuel on which the excise tax has not been paid range from $265 to $1500.

Arkansas

An excise tax of two per cent of the gross receipts is levied on carriers of persons, property and freight. This shall be collected quarterly by the Commissioner of Insurance and Revenues. The money goes to the highways.

California

California added three new sections to the Political Code, to carry into effect the provisions of Section 15 of Article 13 of the constitution, as adopted by the people in 1926, in relation to an excise tax on motor vehicles used for transporting passengers and property.

The tangible property of these transportation companies is to be assessed by the local assessor and segregated on the assessment roll. The state will equalize such assessment and pay from moneys received from the excise tax to the localities, any taxes levied against said property to pay the principal and interest of any bonded indebtedness created and outstanding by any local government. This property shall also be included if a tax is levied for state purposes on all the property in the state.

A law passed in 1920 states that no transportation company shall hereafter begin to operate motor busses without first obtaining a certificate of public convenience and necessity from the railroad commission. A 1927 act charges a fee of $50 for such certificate.

Connecticut

Motor busses operated in connection with a street railway corporation or subsidiary to one, shall be taxed in the same manner as the street railway corporation is taxed upon its other operations.

Georgia

An amendment to the motor vehicle law changes the basis of registration fees from the horse-power of the vehicle to weight. The rate for pleasure cars is 50 cents per one hundred pounds, with a minimum of $11.25. Truck fees range from $15 to $1,125. The rate for trailers is $1 per one hundred pounds with pneumatic tires, $1.50, solid tires, and $2 metallic tires. A motor-cycle fee is $5, with an additional $3 for a side car.

Maryland

No automobile can be licensed unless all other taxes on said automobiles have been paid. Formerly this restriction applied to the City of Baltimore only.

Minnesota

A 1927 act requires public-service corporations paying gross earnings taxes to pay motor vehicle taxes on motor cars or trucks using the public highways. Prior to the enactment of this law the court held that such corporations were not subject to the motor vehicle tax, the gross earnings tax being construed as in lieu of all other taxes.

The registration fees on trucks, other than those used as common carriers and the transportation of farm products has been reduced from five per cent of the base valued to 3.4 per cent.

Missouri

Missouri levies an additional fee on common carriers. The rates range from $40 for omnibusses carrying seven passengers or· less to $230 for ones carrying twenty-four or more. These rates are for omnibusses operating over fixed routes. The fees for irregular routes are one-half the above, and for interstate routes, where less than ten miles is in Missouri, one-third of the above rates.

Nevada

A special but not an additional license under the supervision of the public service commission is levied on all common carriers. The rates are $25 for each passenger car plus $5 for each passenger-seating capacity. For trucks it is $25 flat, plus $1 for each 100 pounds of rated carrying capacity. Trailers are $15, plus the $1 for each 100 pounds. A combination passenger and freight is $25 flat, plus $5 for each passenger-seating capacity, computed on ten inches and 125 pounds to the passenger. The weight of the passengers is deducted from the total pounds of carrying capacity and the rate for the remainder is the same as for trucks, $1 for each 100 pounds. The money goes to the counties for roads.

New Jersey

The general property tax on motor vehicles is removed.

An excise tax of three-quarters of one cent for each one-half mile of operation over New Jersey roads is levied on common carriers engaged in interstate traffic. The tax is payable monthly at the same time a sworn statement is filed, to the commissioner of motor vehicles.

North Carolina

The operator's license fee on common carriers has been increased from one dollar to five dollars. They require a special permit.

North Dakota

A department of motor vehicle registration has been created in North Dakota. Formerly the supervision of motor vehicles was under the Board of Railroad Commissioners.

Trailers are required to be registered. The additional tax on commercial passenger transportation vehicles has been reduced from $10 per passenger-carrying capacity to $5. Automobile dealers must pay a flat-rate fee of $12 for each set of dealer's auto tags and $5 for each set of motor-cycle tags issued to them. Government-owned automobile shall pay only $1, the actual cost of the tags.

Oregon

The law enacted in 1925 in regard to a license tax on motor vehicles, when used as common carriers for transporting persons and property for hire, was submitted to the voters in 1926 and was carried.

Any person, firm or corporation engaged in buying or selling motor vehicles must be licensed and bonded. The license fee is $5 a year and the amount of the bond is $1,000.

Vermont

Snowmobiles are taxed at one-third the annual fee applicable to motor vehicles of like weight.

Wyoming

Formerly there has been no tax on common carriers, other than that applicable to all other motor vehicles. Under a 1927 act an additional tax is added. Common carriers are put under the supervision of the Public Service Commission, and the commission shall collect an annual license fee. The license fees range from $10 to $25 per vehicle, based on horsepower and seating capacity. This money goes ultimately to the highway fund.

POLL TAX

Connecticut

The 1927 law imposes a penalty of one dollar upon any person failing to pay his or her personal tax within sixty days after the same becomes due, thus making the amount due three dollars.

PUBLIC UTILITIES

Alabama

Additional taxes are imposed upon certain classes of public utilities. The money derived from these additional taxes is for education. These additional taxes are: two and one-half per cent of the gross receipts of railroads, telephone and telegraph companies and express companies. The additional tax on hydro-electric power companies is two-fifths of a mill upon each kilowatt hour of power sold during the preceding calendar year.

The flat-rate privilege tax on sleeping-car companies (except railroads operating their own sleeping cars and diners) is increased from $8,000 a year to $20,000. This tax also goes to education.

Formerly there was a license tax of 2 mills on the gross receipts of electric public utilities. This tax has been increased to 4 mills until December 31, 1931, when it will again be 2 mills.

New York

There has been a change in the measure and in the rate of the additional franchise tax on elevated, subway and electric surface railroads. Formerly the tax was one per cent of gross earnings and three per cent on declared dividends, in excess of four per cent upon paid-up capital. Under a 1927 amendment the only tax is five-tenths of one per cent of the gross earnings in the state.

Ohio

The excise tax on sleeping car, freight line and equipment companies is increased from one and twenty one-hundredths per cent to one and thirty-five one-hundredths per cent of the value of the capital invested in the state.

The excise tax on the intrastate business of electric light, gas, telephone, waterworks, etc. companies is increased from one and twenty one-hundredths per cent of the gross receipts from such business to one and thirty-five one-hundredths per cent.

Pennsylvania

Taxi-cab companies are exempt from the special public utility tax of 8 mills on $1 of gross receipts.

South Dakota

The tax on the gross earnings of express companies is increased from five cents to six.

Texas

The occupation tax based upon the gross receipts of street railways is repealed. They have now only to pay the franchise tax.

Vermont

The tax rate on telegraph lines is increased from 65 cents per mile of poles and one wire to $1, and from 56 cents per mile for each additional wire to 75 cents. This is an optional tax, the other one being four and one-fourth per cent of the gross earnings earned in the state.

RAILROADS

Maine

Under the former law gross transportation receipts were divided by the number of miles of railroad, to ascertain the average gross receipts per mile. The rate of tax was graduated according to the per mile receipts. The 1927 law bases the rate on a comparison of the gross receipts with the net. When the net receipts do not exceed ten per cent of the gross, the tax is three and one-half per cent of the gross; four per cent of the gross, when the net exceeds the gross by ten to fifteen per cent; four and one-half per cent, when the net exceeds by fifteen to twenty per cent; five per cent, when it exceeds by twenty to twenty-five per cent, and five and one-half when it exceeds by twenty-five per cent. Special provisions are made for short lines and narrow-gauge railroads.

Maryland

A tax of two per cent on the gross earnings of freight-line companies was repealed. In the attempted enforcement of this tax it was found that the state lost more revenue by reason of exemption than would be received if the tax were imposed.

On account of the effect on the franchise tax due to the additional issuance of stock, the electric railroad companies of Maryland have created additional indebtedness, rather than issue preferred stock when they had to acquire more funds for extension and improvement of their facilities. A 1927 act, in order to encourage the issuance of preferred stock, provides that said stock shall not be an added tax burden.

Nebraska

Nebraska enacted a law prescribing a new method for assessing railroad companies. The Board of Equalization and Assessment shall prepare a complete transcript of its proceedings as to the basis of the assessment and how the same was arrived at. Either the attorney general, acting for the state, or the railroad has a right to appeal from such assessment. The supreme court of Nebraska is given jurisdiction over the matter. No injunction can be granted restraining the levy of taxes under the assessment made by the Board of Equalization.

RATES AND LEVIES

Arkansas

The maximum school tax rate for a school district is raised from 5 mills on a dollar to 18.

Delaware

The state tax on real property is reduced from 25 cents per $100 to 15 cents.

Illinois

The maximum tax rate to raise money for specific purposes such as forest preserves, care of the blind, firemen's pensions, mothers' pensions, etc. has been lowered. This is probably not because less money is needed, but because the assessments on property are raised from 50 per cent of its value to 100 per cent.

Nebraska

The road district assessment was formerly limited to two mills on a dollar, now it is three.

An additional levy of one and one-half mills on the dollar is made for a redemption fund, for the purpose of reimbursing the general fund of the state.

New Jersey

New Jersey continues until December 31, 1928 its tax of one-half mill on each dollar of real and personal property in the various municipalities, the proceeds being for the benefit of the state institution construction fund.

Ohio

The various sections of the Ohio code regulating the rate of tax to be levied by governmental divisions has been repealed and new sections enacted. The limitation of a special levy without a vote of the people is raised from ten mills to fifteen.

Oregon

The amount of any continuing millage tax levied by a governmental division upon the assessed valuation is limited to the amount of the levy for the preceding year plus six per cent.

SEVERANCE TAX

Alabama

The rate of tax on mines has been increased from two cents a ton on coal to two and one-half cents, and from three cents a ton on iron ore to four and one-half cents. A tax is also levied on the output of mines, other than coal or iron, quarries and sand gravel pits, or slag pits, equal to three per cent of the net value of the output at the mine or quarry or pit. The money from these taxes goes to education.

Arkansas .

Arkansas has increased the severance tax imposed in 1923 on minerals, by one-tenth of one per cent of the gross market value. And by one mill on each ton of coal and manganese ore mined.

Montana

Petroleum has been added to the list of mine deposits taxable. Also all royalty and royalty interest in the mineral production of a mine are to be taxed on the same basis as the net proceeds of mines under the general property tax.

Nevada

The assessing of mines and the computing of the net proceeds is, by a 1927 act, put under the jurisdiction of the Nevada Tax Commission. It was formerly under the jurisdiction of the county.

TOBACCO TAX

Alabama

Alabama levies a tax equal to fifteen per cent of the wholesale price of all cigars, cigarettes or cheroots sold within the state. The tax is under the jurisdiction of the Tax Commission and the money goes to education, the fund to be known as the Alabama special educational trust fund.

Kansas

Kansas levies upon all cigarettes and cigarette papers a stamp tax of two cents on each twenty cigarettes or fractional part thereof and of one cent on each fifty cigarette papers or fractional part thereof.   The annual license fee for selling cigarettes at retail is $150 in cities of the first and second class and $50 in all other places.   The fee is $300 for selling them on railway trains or electric cars.   The receipts from the license fees go to the county and from the cigarette tax to the state.   The tax is administered by the state treasurer.

Tennessee

The tobacco tax act, which was originally enacted in 1921, re-enacted in 1923 and 1925, was again re-enacted in 1927, with a few minor changes as to the specific application of the receipts, all however being applicable to education.

CHAIRMAN MATTHEWS: I would say that a gentleman called my attention this morning to the fact that no mention had been made of our appreciation of the presence of the ladies.   I told him that on the part of the Chairman that was not an oversight at all; that I thought the appropriate time for us to express our appreciation of the presence of the ladies was this morning at the convention, after listening to Miss Bailey's address.

(Minor announcements by Secretary Holcomb)

CHAIRMAN MATTHEWS: The convention is now open for any suggestions that any member wishes to offer on the subject which Miss Bailey has discussed.

JOHN H. LEENHOUTS (Wisconsin): I should like to add to the resume of tax legislation, that Wisconsin took a very important step in placing her banks on the income tax basis.

CHAIRMAN MATTHEWS: Has any other member of the convention anything to say?

(No response)

CHAIRMAN MATTHEWS: I should remind the delegations that it is important that they should meet and select their member of the resolutions committee and hand the name in to the secretary as early as possible.

The next item on the program is a paper upon " Suggestions in Aid of State Tax Researches and Investigations," by Professor T. R. Snavely of the University of Virginia.

PROFESSOR T. R. SNAVELY (Virginia): Mr. Chairman, Ladies and Gentlemen: I know that you have all been wondering why the program committee made the mistake of placing such a dry subject as research in taxation at the very beginning of these meetings.

I am reminded of the advice which an old political campaigner gave to a youthful politician. He said, ."Begin your speech by flattering the audience, end it with a grand oratorical climax, and put in the middle any kind of inconsequential material that may be necessary to fill up the space." Under such an arrangement as that I think the paper on tax research probably should come somewhere near the mid-section of these meetings.

I have prepared a paper on this subject which I am not going to read at length this morning, but it will be printed in full in the proceedngs.

I want to summarize my paper by setting forth at the beginning the object that I have attempted to realize.

In state tax investigations it seems to me that at this time there are some four things that we might give special attention to. I may enumerate those as follows:

First, continuity in tax investigations. They must continue for a period of several years, under some systematic and uniform plan; secondly, tax investigations if they are to be effective must be broad in scope. At the present time the tax system reaches clear through our economic organization, and no incidental study will do the job sufficiently. In the third place, there is needed a clearer interpretation of tax reports than we have been accustomed to having. A mere statistical report, without some interpretation and exposition is not effective for the layman. In the fourth place, some competent body should be provided, in my judgment, by the National Tax Association, to act as a clearing house of information, to aid in promoting tax research work.

SUGGESTIONS IN AID OF STATE TAX RESEARCH AND INVESTIGATIONS

TIPTON R. SNAVELY

University of Virginia

There may be some question perhaps as to the wisdom of the program committee in assigning for discussion, at the beginning of these conferences, such a dry and dismal topic as research in taxation. I hope, however, that it will not have the disastrous psychological effect of reducing the attendance at future meetings. I am reminded of the advice given by an old-time political campaigner to a youthful politician. He said: " Begin your speech by flattering the audience, end it with a grand oratorical climax and place in the middle whatever inconsequential material may be necessary to fill in the space." Under an arrangement of this sort, the discus-

sion of research would no doubt have landed somewhere near the
mid-section of these meetings.

The increasing emphasis which is being laid upon scientific inquiry in the fields of taxation and finance is a fact of which the
members of the National Tax Association are altogether familiar.
The members of this body here in attendance, and others who are
not present, have steadily pointed the way toward juster tax systems
and the more equitable distribution of tax burdens. As pioneers in
whatever movements for tax reform have come into being, you have
recognized the value and importance of careful investigation, have
often felt the insufficiency of data at your disposal and have stressed
the need for more complete and accurate information. For me to
undertake a discussion of the subject with you, therefore, is, I fear,
very much like placing myself in the position of one " carrying
coals to Newcastle."

The importance of research in taxation and other social fields lies
in the shifting conditions of the forces involved. If we stop for a
moment to consider the swift changes in our economic organization—changes which appear to come faster and reach farther with
the dawn of each new day—the need for a consideration of tax
research not only at this conference but at each annual meeting of
this Association becomes apparent. If the processes of industry
would become static for a time, or even approach a condition of
stability, then we might catch up with the problems of taxation and
solve them in a reasonably satisfactory manner. As it is, we seem
to be chasing the elusive rainbow. at one moment believing it
within easy reach but at the next moment finding it farther away,
being all the while really in the midst of it. We do solve problems
of taxation, at least partially, but not before conditions have
changed and new problems have arisen. We often hear it re-
marked that the only thing about which we can have positive assurance nowadays is change itself.

It is not my purpose here to undertake a resume of current investigations and reports in the field of state taxation. If there were
sufficient time for it, such a summary might be highly profitable.
Suffice it to say, that the amount of work being done is undoubtedly
larger than at any time in the past. On the whole, it is more extensive in scope and is characterized by greater precision and
accuracy than at any previous time. Not only are contributions of
great importance being made by the regular and specially appointed
state tax commissions, but also private organizations and individuals are contributing much in the form of monographs and articles
on particular problems.

The last decade has brought a renewed emphasis upon research   ·
because the changes have been swifter and more far-reaching than
usual. This is true not only in the field of taxation but also in

nearly all other branches of economics. In the course of industry itself more attention is being given to such factors as the business cycle, the foreign exchanges, tariffs, over-production, and similar problems. Within the year notable works have appeared both in Great Britain and the United States on the causes and effects of the business cycle. A fact of much significance is the expenditure of time and money which large industrial corporations are devoting to research in all its forms as a means toward the improvement of their organization, product or services.

Recently a number of British business men have traveled throughout the United States, with a view to studying the causes of the great industrial advancement and progress of this nation. Numerous factors have been held responsible, but that which Mr. Ramsay Muir, noted economist and historian, places first is research and university teaching. He says: "Among the causes of American prosperity—the first place must be given to the immense facilities which are provided for research in every subject bearing upon industry, the strong practical belief of the leaders in all the more progressive industries that every problem can be solved by scientific methods of inquiry, and the readiness of the heads of great concerns to take infinite pains and incur vast outlay, in order to carry out the improvements suggested by these inquiries." Speaking further, he says: "American industry has, over the greater part of its range, accepted the methods of science, and pinned its faith to research and inquiry, in a degree not equalled in any other country. And this of itself is enough to account for American prosperity, and to insure its continuance." [1]

Research as thus described means, when applied to state and local taxation, that the various tangled problems in this field are capable of being explained by patient and methodical inquiry. Furthermore, it presupposes that an analysis of statistical data, a study of forces in operation as to their causes and effects, the results of given tax policies, etc., will form a basis for more intelligent legislation and administration. On this general point there is scarcely room for disagreement.

Almost every writer in the field of public finance since the close of the World War has laid great stress on the need for more comprehensive investigation. Let me quote briefly from three authors of books which have recently appeared. "Facts in the field of public finance," says Professor Hugh Dalton in his work on Public Finance, "are moving so rapidly at the present time, that realistic studies are soon out of date, and the form in which practical problems present themselves is constantly changing." [2] Professor

[1] *America the Golden,* by Ramsay Muir, pp. 27 *et seq.*

[2] *Public Finance,* by Hugh Dalton, p. 5.

Shirras in his notable volume, the *Science of Public Finance,* emphasizes the great need for accurate statistical studies. " Modern financial administration," he says, " depends greatly upon full and accurate statistics;" and again he asserts that the science of public finance " could not do without statistics as, for example, in budgets or in estimating the distribution of taxation among the various classes in a state." [3]   Finally, in a recent comparative study of the income tax in Great Britain and the United States, Mr. H. B. Spaulding declares, that the " need of enormous amounts of revenue has resulted in an intensive study of tax schemes on the part of many nations to place their revenue laws on a sound basis." [4]

Without further general statement, let me come at once to the main aspects of this subject.   In my judgment the National Tax Association can assume aggressive leadership in no more important function than that of fostering continuous, experimental research in state taxation.   The sort of research which will yield a maximum return is that which is carefully planned to reveal the facts necessary for the answer of vital questions.   Obviously, its usefulness is enhanced in proportion to the duration of the period in which it is carried on.   It cannot be too strongly urged that the sort of work required is a continuous process, lasting for a five- ten- fifteen- or twenty-year period, or even longer.   The chief benefit of a momentary study, however carefully done, seldom lies in the completeness of its own subject-matter, but more in its comparative value.   Each temporary report covering, for example, a given fiscal year, contains a body of factual material which presents a flashlight picture of the tax system for that period.   In that sense it is complete, but in a broader and more important connection it forms one unit in the continuous development of a state's tax system over a long period.   Economic facts are always co-related with other facts, either at the same moment or at varying times.   One annual report or special study of our tax system forms a single peak of an entire mountain range.   To get a perspective of the range, we are compelled to view it from a distance.

Suppose we illustrate the need for continuous research by means of a specific problem.   A given state, let us say, wishes to investigate the distribution of the tax burden as it falls on the various contributing classes.   This is a question of long standing, but it has been given much prominence in recent years, because of the increase in aggregate tax burdens.   It has become more important also because of the rapid shifting about which has occurred among income-receiving groups.   The equilibrium of economic conditions

[3] *The Science of Public Finance,* by G. Findley Shirras, p. 7.

[4] *The Income Tax in Great Britain and the United States,* by Harrison B. Spaulding, preface.

has been greatly disturbed.   Our problem, then, is a big one and ramifies clear through the tax system.   It touches the whole foundation of the economic structure.   Every part of it has the characteristic of being related to all other parts, making it impossible to split it into small compartments, or for each part to be regarded as a separate entity.

There are a number of approaches to this question of tax distribution.   We may, for example, attempt to place all groups on a property-valuation basis and make a comparison of assessments and rates.   Or again, we may take the net income as our guide and seek to determine the ratio of state and local taxes paid to the net income derived.   The approach through net income is more definite —more scientific—although some combination of the two methods may be found quite desirable.   At any rate, it is imperative, if we wish to arrive at the real measure of taxpaying ability, that we reduce all groups to some sort of common denominator.   The question obviously cannot be answered by loose generalizations.   We make no progress whatever until we obtain the facts.   We want to see a complete picture of the system—that is, see it in its relative aspects.

It is just at this stage of our proposed investigation of the tax burden, or similar question, that we run into difficulty.   No one is better aware of the scarcity of pertinent facts, or of their adequate presentation, than are the members of the various state tax commissions.   And yet we are compelled to have the facts impartially gathered and set out.   The final result we get depends, of course, upon something more than a mere collection of statistics or their quantitative measurement.   Great care must be exercised in the qualitative use of the data secured.   Good judgment, skill and commonsense are always at a premium in dealing with a mass of figures.   There have been tax reports, in the preparation of which it is to be feared little concern was given to orderly arrangement, while others have fallen short because they were unaccompanied by a forceful analysis of their contents.   In my own opinion, if an annual statistical report is worth publishing it is also worth a few pages of interpretation, such as might be attached to the profit and loss statement or balance sheet of a business firm.   The layman is fortunate when he finds a statistical report that has been elucidated by some one who is a genius at vivid exposition.

In studying relative tax burdens from a standpoint either of property valuation or net income, we are likely to find that in practically every state wide gaps exist in the statistical material needed. A large majority of states do not impose an income tax, thus making it difficult to arrive at the net income for many classes of taxpayers.   This is true for any given year and applies with even greater force over a series of years.   There are some groups of

industry in which there is still a marked deficiency of facts concerning net income and perhaps will continue to be. One of these
is the farm group. Farming continues as one of the outstanding
problems since the post-war depression; but in no state, even for
farm operations or farm land, do we have for a single year conclusive studies of income. We do not have precise figures to prove or
disprove the general belief that the farmer is bearing an excessive
tax load.

Our task is complex enough if we undertake a comparative study
of tax burdens for one year, but it grows more involved when extended over a ten or twenty-year period. Tax statutes are frequently changed; administrative policies are altered; there is a
varying personnel in tax departments. If the data for one year is
incomplete, or if it is not presented uniformly with that of previous
years, the sequence is broken. Yet, is it not vital that we be able
to visualize the structure of our tax system as an evolutionary process? The well-managed business corporation looks carefully to
the statistical analyses of its monthly and yearly trends. Each department is carefully studied, as related to other divisions and to
the business as a whole. The statistical material is prepared in
such a manner that it may be effectively scrutinized in the form of
charts and diagrams. Our state tax departments' have grown into
large business organizations in which business methods must be
employed. Their annual reports are of great importance and should
be prepared with a view to their future as well as to their present use.

Now there is still another factor in state investigations not to be
overlooked, and that is the desirability of comparing the tax systems
of the different states one with another. An investigation begun in
one state leads directly to an inquiry of the results and experiences
in other states. Suppose once more that we are interested in the
tax burden on farm lands; that a careful study has been made with
respect to all other taxes and that this has been done for a number
of years. It is reassuring to know whether more or less similar
conditions have obtained in other states. Our individual study is
likely to be incomplete at certain points because of the many forms
of corporate enterprise doing an interstate business. On railroads
and public utilities, for example, the tax burdens in one state bear
a definite ratio to the burdens imposed by all states in which operations are carried on. It is obvious that many advantages would
result if greater uniformity were effected in the reports of state tax
commissions.

It is gratifying to observe that quite a number of states are at
present undertaking a critical analysis of their tax systems. Special
commissions have been appointed in twenty or more states since the
year 1922. The states included are as follows:

Arkansas 1927
California 1927
Georgia 1923
Illinois 1927
Iowa 1927
Maine 1923, 1924
Maryland 1922, 1927
Massachusetts 1924, 1927
Minnesota 1927
New Hampshire 1927
New Jersey 1924, 1925, 1926
New York 1922, 1923, 1924, 1925, 1926, 1927
North Carolina 1927
Ohio 1926
Oklahoma 1923, 1924, 1927
Oregon 1925
Pennsylvania 1922, 1925
Texas 1927
Virginia 1924, 1926
West Virginia 1925

Special commissions for the year 1927 have been appointed in the following states: Arkansas, California, Illinois, Iowa, Maryland, Massachusetts, Minnesota, New Hampshire, New York, North Carolina, Oklahoma and Texas.

It is impossible to generalize about the work of the special commissions because of the varying conditions under which they are appointed. Many of their reports deserve high rank and have been used widely as pioneer efforts, by other states. All too frequently, however, their accomplishments have been restricted in scope either by statute or constitutional limitation; the information at hand has been too meagre and the time allotted for the investigation has been too short. I wish to emphasize more than anything else, however, that the work of special commissions will not be adequate and cannot have permanent value unless it be made continuous.

On this point a statement made by Professor H. L. Lutz at the annual conference of this Association in 1922 may well be quoted. "We are driven back to the conclusion," he said, "that if an investigation of this sort in any state is worth while, it must be done carefully and frequently by trained investigators, who are able to go into the problem involved and compile material upon which a sound step forward may be taken. . . . . Unless you are willing to provide a special tax-investigating commission or committee with funds and with ability to draw upon those who may contribute in a degree sufficiently ample to get results, there is no use undertaking it." [5]

Certain states, and it would be instructive to know how many,

[5] Proceedings National Tax Association, 1922, p. 67.

are making the sort of study of their tax systems that I have had in mind in the foregoing discussion. They are compiling the facts necessary to give a complete picture of expenditures, of governmental functions as divided between the states and localities, of the distribution of tax burdens, exemptions, uniformity of assessments, new sources of revenue and tax administration. They are doing this through special commissions working in cooperation with the permanent state tax departments. They are collecting and presenting tax facts in such a way that they will be comparable from year to year, so that our accumulating tax experience will be of more help in formulating tax policies than it has been in the past. They are publishing the facts for the instruction of legislative officials and citizens.

In this connection I want to speak of the original work of New York State through the reports of the Special Joint Committee on Taxation and Retrenchment and the Annual Reports of the State Tax Department. The committee has been a continuing one, and its reports, which have appeared at frequent intervals since 1920, have dealt with the tax system of New York in a scientific and exhaustive manner. The committee has had the assistance of trained investigators in the preparation of its reports. It has been able to rely on the State Tax Department for the facts used in its investigations. The annual reports of this department have been standardized for a number of years. They have made possible the constructive work of the special committee.

As was noted above, the State of Massachusetts has appointed a special commission to consider the problems in that state. The basic material for the commission is being prepared by the State Tax Commissioner. I have received from the Commissioner, Hon. Henry F. Long, an account of the statistical facts which he has in preparation. His statement is so completely in accord with the ideas which I wish to present that I am taking the liberty to quote it at length. It reads as follows:

"I have tabulated all of the figures available here in this office which, for practical purposes, is a complete picture of the situation in Massachusetts, the tables showing, first, the trend of taxation as to total taxes needed to run governments—our municipalities, our counties, and our State. Then I have shown where this money has gone to (that is, what activities of government in the cities and towns, the counties and the State have absorbed the money for increases). And thirdly, I have shown the sources from which this money has been obtained.

"In addition to this, I have of course made detailed statistical tables showing for the cities and towns, for the counties, and the State, the demands upon government—where the money has gone, over the comparatively last few years, not exceeding in any case one table in which I show a swing of seventeen years.

"I am in addition to that showing the classes of property that are standing the burden, in addition to showing the classes of property that are tax-exempt.

"I am using the word 'property' here in its broadest sense, including tangible as well as intangible, and what might be called in legal phraseology 'commodity' and what-not. The word 'property,' however, is to cover everything that can be possibly imagined.

"These tables which are being formulated, I suspect, with two or three changes, might very well apply to every single state in the Union. It would seem to me that the National Tax Association, as a central body, might very well take an investigation of this kind and mingle it with an investigation of a similar nature in other states, with statistical tables, and send it broadcast throughout the land. One difficulty, however, I foresee, and that is that very few states in the Union can really get the complete picture of what the tax burden is upon the picture. We here in Massachusetts can do it because of the records that we have here in this office, and the reports that we require. Many of the states have taxing units that never work through a central control body, and I have my doubts as to whether or not more than half a dozen of the states in the Union know, with any degree of accuracy, what their people are really paying in the shape of taxation.

"The central agency that you have in mind is an excellent idea, but it has got to be a disinterested central agency, and not one that is likely to color the statistics available for their own particular purposes. One or two associations spring readily to your mind as being financially capable of distributing this information but which are so situated from a practical point of view that they would soon work the information into propaganda for their own ends.

"In the matter of disseminated information, also, there would have to be a classification of states. That is, the farming states would be more or less comparable, the industrial states would be more or less comparable and the states of large wealth as represented by intangibles would be more or less comparable. Then, there would be divisions under this, but it would be a tremendous task to get it at all in understandable shape. We must encourage industry by favoring it in some way or another.

"When the National Tax Association becomes incorporated, it may be possible from time to time to publish information obtained by some active person in the Association, who has nothing else to do but to tabulate and arrange in proper order not only these special taxation reports, but also the regular reports annually made that contain much of value also."

In a statement which I have recently received from Hon. William H. Blodgett, Tax Commissioner of Connecticut, he concludes that, "Arms-length discussions and generalities in regard to matters of the kind avail but very little. There is the necessity of marshalling the details of facts to show the application of the law, its abuses, if any, and its correct use. Except as the details are in hand and facts positively known, discussions are purely academic, and statutes passed on academic conclusions altogether too frequently bewilder the tax administrator, lead to litigation, and disgust the taxpayer."

A valuable report was made last year by the Joint Legislative Committee on Economy and Taxation in the State of Ohio. The committee began the study of the tax burden in that state and strongly urged the general assembly to provide for its completion. "From this study," said the committee, "it was hoped that a generally true and unbiased picture could be had of the tax burden and how it bears upon different classes of industry and business. The committee is fully aware that any changes in the tax laws should preferably be based upon an accurate appraisal of existing conditions rather than upon so-called general knowledge. Therefore, this study was undertaken. It is believed that this is the first time so comprehensive a study of this sort has been undertaken in Ohio." [6]

If time permitted, I might refer to investigations that are being conducted in other states. From what has been said, it appears that the interest being manifested in state taxation, as shown by the number of research studies now in progress, is steadily increasing.

I wish in the concluding paragraphs of this discussion to make some observations in aid of research work. In the first place, there is an outstanding need for more uniformity and standardization of the regular and special reports of state tax departments. This need applies to the reports of each particular state, as well as to the almost total lack of standardization as between the different states. The advantages of some measure of uniformity are so well understood that they need not be repeated here. I am fully aware that no absolutely rigid form of report could be agreed upon. Assuming that the legislative statutes in each state would permit of that, other obstacles would be found to exist. Appropriations are very inadequate in many states and the tax departments are overburdened with administrative duties. Nevertheless, without much additional cost or effort, the material now being inserted in official reports could be so prepared and arranged that it would be more effectively used for comparative purposes.

The National Tax Association has already adopted a plan of standardization. In response to suggestions from various sources a committee was appointed to present an outline of a feasible plan

---

[6] *Report of the Ohio Joint Legislative Committee on Economy and Taxation,* 1926, p. 260.

·and it prepared a very able report which met the approval of the association. The committee consisted of tax experts, men who have had much experience in research work, and their recommendations were based on personal experience. Hon. Mark Graves, chairman of the committee, presented the report in part as follows:

> ·" Statistics are only valuable to the extent that they may be compared with something. In New York we have been publishing one kind of a tax report for many years. That has a certain value, because each year's report may be compared with those for preceding years. But our report would be of infinitely greater value to us if we could compare it with the tax reports of some of the other states; or better still, with the tax reports of all the other states. That is what lends value to statistics: the fact that they may be used for comparative purposes." [7]

The fact that the committee spent considerable effort in drafting its report in 1923 is sufficient indication of its hope that its labors would not be in vain. The question may well be asked now whether the outline for state tax reports recommended by the committee has been used by state tax departments. The National Tax Association through some official channel might consider the wisdom of taking more active steps to advance this work.

A second suggestion which comes to mind is that by some process there should be made continuously available to research workers and public officials, knowledge of the "most significant achievements" accomplished in taxation in this and other countries. Aside from state officials, there are many organizations and individuals that are interested in tax problems. Our universities, for example, are conducting surveys and studies through their respective faculties and graduate students. The monographs which are thus prepared are occasionally published, but in many instances they are given no attention by the public. The result is that there is much duplication of effort which might partially at least be avoided. Taxpayers' associations, chambers of commerce, trade organizations, banking groups, investment houses, and numerous other bodies initiate movements from time to time to investigate tax problems. They are nearly all working independently and we know that there is much lost motion and wasted energy.·

The National Industrial Conference Board has just published a study of the "Cost of Government in the United States, 1925-1926," in which it is stated that, "over a hundred taxpayers' associations were organized since 1920, but less than one-third of them are functioning at present. Active associations of state-wide scope in

[7] *Proceedings National Tax Association*, 1923, p. 420.

1927 were to be found in twenty-two states—eleven Western states, ten Eastern states, and one of the South Atlantic states." [8]

Is it not generally true that the bulletins and monographs which these various organizations issue remain inaccessible to other organizations? The consequence is that there is much bewilderment on the part of those who are just beginning tax studies. When a committee is appointed to investigate tax matters it is obliged to write these other bodies, including all state tax departments, for publications. The National Tax Association has done much to alleviate this situation, but I believe it might profitably do more. There should be a central clearing-house from which complete information could be distributed. It would have a library of tax works and publications, and should keep abreast of all new developments in every state. The New York State Tax Commission has collected through its special library what is perhaps the most complete assortment of tax material in this country and it is in a favorable position to render substantial assistance in the formation of a research department or clearing-house in the field of taxation.

Recently the National Municipal League and the Governmental Research Conference have established jointly a central bureau called the "Municipal Administration Service." The Director has expressed in a personal letter to me, in which he explains the purposes of the bureau, willingness to cooperate with the National Tax Association in any central information bureau that it might provide. He also suggests the possibility of combining the facilities of the two organizations in a larger and more useful agency. A somewhat similar movement was announced on October 1st by the United States Bureau of Education, in the form of a "clearing-house on current research work in education." The purpose of this new project, as announced, is to aid "universities and colleges in the elimination of wasted effort and duplication in the study of educational problems."

Finally, a third suggestion which seems appropriate relates especially to one phase of the work of the central research bureau. Assuming that such an agency were created, it should make an analysis of various reports and of the methods employed in the preparation of reports from state tax commissioners, special commissions, and private organizations. This analysis would be in the nature of an extended bibliography and of a paragraph report of matters listed in the bibliography. It would not include so much a recital of pertinent passages as a listing of the matters treated. There might then follow in a few paragraphs an abstract of the articles in the nature of a true digest. In this connection I should

---

[8] National Industrial Conference Board, *Cost of Government in the U. S.,* 1925-1926, Ch. VIII.

like to mention the notable contribution of Professor and Mrs. Roy G. Blakey in the new " Digest and Index " which they have prepared for the National Tax Association. No more important service has been rendered the association than this Digest.

In addition to making analyses of tax reports and articles, a central bureau should have the task of keeping abreast of legal changes and practices. Not only should data as to tax laws be kept up to date but also something upon a larger scale should be attempted by means of charts or reports, which would give a synopsis of the laws and tax rates for each state. Possibly the most convenient form would be that of a loose-leaf binder service. All of us have experienced the difficulties involved in trying to comprehend the tax systems of forty-eight states by an examination of the tax codes. We need for every state charts which are more extensive but similar in form, to those contained in the " Annual Reports " of the New York State Tax Commission.

The realization of these objects would not entail heavy financial outlays, nor require an elaborate staff of investigators. If sufficient funds became available, however, I should favor a somewhat broader undertaking through the central bureau of research. It should engage in statistical investigations on its own initiative, thereby making analyses and comparisons of the data contained in state tax reports. Through a rearrangement of figures under different categories, and by processes of refinement, it would endeavor to make the results comparable. The National Tax Association holds a position of unquestioned leadership in the general forward movement toward equitable taxation. Can we not in a practical way gradually extend the program of " mutual education," to the end that tax laws may be made " simpler, saner, more just and more effective " ?

Let me now summarize briefly the essential conclusions which I have endeavored to present, as follows:

1. Research in taxation must be made continuous. It must be carried forward over a period of years, so that a clear picture of the growth of the tax system may be obtained. From one single investigation we are able to get only a fleeting glimpse of a state tax system at a particular time. Such a study is insufficient for a comprehensive understanding of the system. Continuous investigation is necessary for comparative purposes.

2. Breadth of scope is essential in tax studies. Economic facts are always related to other facts. Hence, it is impossible to study any isolated part of a state tax system without reference to the whole.

3. Statistical reports bearing upon state taxation should always be accompanied by a clear statement of interpretation. The statis-

tical figures from only the skeleton of a report, unless properly explained and interpreted, are not effective. There should be a forceful exposition of the salient conclusions to be drawn from a given report.

4. There is the greatest need for uniformity and standardization of state tax reports; first, within each individual state, and secondly, as between the respective states. The National Tax Association has already accepted a report on a plan of uniformity.

5. A central clearing-house should be established for the distribution of information and literature. It would maintain a library of tax works and publications, and would keep abreast of all new developments in every state. Such a bureau should also prepare analyses of tax reports and should engage in statistical investigations on its own initiative.

In conclusion, let me add one word of caution, by saying that I hold no illusions in regard to the limitations of research in taxation. It is not possible, and perhaps never will be possible, to use wholly exact methods or to obtain absolute facts in an ultimate sense. Even if we could completely resolve all problems for a single day, new problems would immediately appear and we should need to resume our task. In our changing economic organization, the real hope lies in a closer approximation to the facts. For the time being, the challenge to those who are interested in state taxation is to seek to ascertain the facts and to present them in understandable form.

CHAIRMAN MATTHEWS: The subject of the last paper is one of much interest Is there anybody who cares to enter into the further discussion of this paper at this time?

R. WAYNE NEWTON (Michigan): Mr. Chairman, I am especially interested in the paper which was just read because for some years I have spent my time in research on the subject of taxation, first in the Department of Agriculture, and now for Michigan State College. Perhaps every commission in the United States has at one time or another received letters from one or the other officers with whom I have worked, asking questions; and I am sure that many of those questions have appeared foolish to the people who received them. The reason for that has been that it has been absolutely necessary for them to go into the most minute detail in order to get a reply that we can understand, from various states. Many words have entirely different meaning in different states.

In the State of Michigan the word " equalization " refers particularly to equalization between districts, and does not consider individuals. As a result, the best we can do by correspondence and by reading the letter is to prepare information concerning which we are not ourselves absolutely sure of.

I feel confident that such a central organization as Professor Snavely has mentioned would be not only of great service to research organizations, but would relieve you administrators of a whole lot of detail which must get very tiresome when we send you these letters.

CHAIRMAN MATTHEWS: Any further remarks?

OSCAR LESER (Maryland): Mr. Snavely said that one of the states that had appointed special tax commissioners was Maryland. I want to correct that. The commission has not been appointed. An act has been passed to authorize the appointment of such commission, but it is put in such form that unless a proper amount of money is forthcoming to do that work adequately, that act will remain indefinitely, until the time arrives when some money is provided for that purpose.

We had the experience three years ago of authorizing a commission to revise the laws, which it needed badly, and the commission went off at a tangent on the question of the state income tax; did not revise the laws at all.

I want to throw out the practical suggestion, that you need money, money, money.

GEORGE VAUGHAN (Arkansas): This subject is of great interest to me because I happen to be on one of those commissions that Professor Snavely has spoken of. I think it would be interesting at this time, if we have the time, to have some brief discussion from members of this meeting who happen to be on commissions of that sort. I believe there are about ten that are supposed to be operating new commissions; and while I am not going to take much time, I think it is not improper for me to begin, since my state alphabetically is in first place of that class of commissions.

I am reminded, however, of a very unfortunate situation that arose once in a circumstance between myself and a good life-long friend who was at that time attorney general of Arkansas, and this friend of mine was one of those unfortunate good fellows who was always hale and well-met but always broke. He had borrowed from Tom, Dick and Harry, and appeared to be not very much worried about his debts. Among others of his friends who had accommodated him at times was myself. One morning he came down with a smile on his face. He says, " George, I had a happy dream last night; I found out how I am going to pay up my debts, and it is the easiest thing in the world; it is going to relieve me; I will be relieved of that great burden." I said, " What is it?" He said, " I just decided to pay off my creditors alphabetically."

We in Arkansas should like to be first in a good many things besides the alphabet. You will notice in these various charts that

Arkansas is down at the bottom, which means that Arkansas has the smallest per-capita debt. We are not proud of that proposition at all, because I think that is one of the ways of accomplishing things which we as citizens strive for. But as to this commission I speak of, it is unique in one respect. I do not think there is a commission that has exactly the same functions as ours. This is a commission on business laws and taxation. The two subjects are combined. The commission consists of seven members, and at least four are outstanding business men, perhaps two of them with national reputation as being representative of "big business," so that the dual function of that commission is to work out any corrections to our laws and to recommend for correction any particular laws which seem unfavorable to business.

Of course the other proposition is to study the taxation system and to recommend methods of improving the taxation system.

Arkansas is the one state in the Union that has never had such a study commission before. Many of the other states have. Perhaps every state in the Union has had one, two, five or six. California, I think, had three or four. We are limited in our funds: Although there was an appropriation made, it is small.

For example in Arkansas only $6300 was appropriated for that work, as compared with California's $75,000. Now, I know that those of us who are charged with the work on these very important commissions would be glad to get expressions of a practical character with regard to procedure in this work. For myself, I have formed no definite idea as to program. Our committee has just been organized, but the outline of the scope and duties of such a commission, as given by Professor Snavely, has opened a field in my imagination for the work, and I think a great deal of good will come from that paper and from the discussion which I hope will be heartily participated in.

CHAIRMAN MATTHEWS: Anything further?

PROFESSOR JOHN E. BRINDLEY (Iowa): The thought occurs to me, in listening to the very able paper of Professor Snavely, that about ten or twelve states, of which Iowa is one, are making a special investigation now of this tax question, and quite a number of other states have cooperated with the Federal Government in research studies at one time or another.

I was wondering if it would be possible for that group somehow during this conference to get together. I should very much like to meet them.

In Iowa we haven't a special commission. They appropriated some money to our college, and I am anxious to get all the advice and counsel and information I possibly can from people working in other states. I am wondering if it is practical to do that. I should like to meet them some time during the conference.

CHAIRMAN MATTHEWS: I think I may say, Professor Brindley, that at all the conferences of the tax association as much information has been gleaned between the sessions, in the discussion of subjects between individuals in the corridors, perhaps, as has been obtained on the floor of the convention. Is there anything further?

PROFESSOR WILLIAM J. SHULTZ (New York) : This is rather a side issue from Professor Snavely's paper, but I think it is pertinent.

The Bureau of Internal Revenue at Washington has a wealth of material on taxes paid by individuals to the state and local governments, and on taxes paid by corporations to their state and local governments. All those have to be reported as deductions from income for the federal income tax.

Now, I do not think there can be disapproval of the administration's policy of economy as outlined, but I think one unfortunate aspect of that policy has been the rather strenuous cutting down of the appropriations to the bureau, which has resulted in cutting down the bureau's work in digesting that material that comes in to them through the reports of individuals and of corporations. I think that the National Tax Association could well go on record as making a plea, if it should be put that way, for a full appropriation to the federal bureau of internal revenue, so that it can carry on the very able work of digesting this material.

There are a number of states that through the records of their income taxes or of their corporation taxes of various kinds, get a great deal of material from taxpayers that would be of immense value for research purposes, though not of any immediate administrative value.

Now, the New York commission has done a wonderful work during the last five or six years in digesting and publishing in its report the materials that have come to it, and if other states could follow this lead they would provide for students of taxation an absolutely invaluable body of comparative material, a body which is not available now in any digested form, and which it is impossible for any one except the commissions themselves to work out.

RAY RILEY (California) : I am interested in the remarks of the gentleman from Iowa. Some members of the California Tax Commission are here in attendance, and I wonder if it is possible for the gentlemen of the new commissions to meet over in the corner for just a moment after this meeting and see if we cannot get together on a little program later.

We are starting work out there. We should be very happy to go along with the rest of the new commissions who have had a like undertaking. Would that be agreeable to you—just half a moment over here in the corner, any who are here from the new tax commissions, after this meeting?

T. R. SNAVELY (Virginia) : I want to say just one further word by supplementing what has been said by Professor Brindley and also Dr. Shultz.

In the first place, it seems to me an excellent idea for the various representatives here from the special tax commissions to get together and discuss a plan for work in the various states. I am sure that it will not only serve as a means by which they can become acquainted, but it will bring forth many fruitful ideas in regard to keeping in touch with the various phases of the work further on, and also of the general procedure in the work.

In the second place, all of us are acquainted with the general movement toward economy in governmental expenditures and in the various departmental expenditures of government. I am wholly in sympathy with any substantial and sane movement for economy, but it seems to me that sometimes perhaps appropriations have been cut off for making public reports, in some departments, especially in that of taxation and finance. That is unwise. If the reports are too brief it will be impossible to get the material that is necessary for an understanding of state taxation, and it seems to me a word of caution is necessary in regard to this general movement to reduce the publications of the various governmental departments, especially in taxation and finance.

GEORGE VAUGHAN (Arkansas) : Mr. Snavely, I suggest that you ask those present who are on such commissions to show hands, so that we get an idea of about how many there are here.

(Showing of hands)

SIMEON LELAND (Kentucky) : From what has been said in reference to the standards that are necessary for state reports and the need for information contained therein, members of commissions sometimes get the idea that it is impossible to bring their reports up to the standard, say, of the New York report, due to the lack of money, due to the lack of staff or what-not, but it seems to me there are a few other suggestions that might be made in line with what Professor Snavely suggested, which could be done without additional cost either for publication or for staff.

In the first place, in the analysis he suggests for the reports, it seems to me a great many historical comparisons are desirable. The early reports of many of the tax commissions are not only out of print but are unavailable. The statistics, therefore, with reference to some of the taxes, revenues, assessments, and the like, can only be obtained by the laborious process of personal letters or personal interviews, which commissions do not like and which investigators do not like to resort to.   If, then, the tax commissions could occasionally publish statistical summaries of an historical character concerning the material in previous reports, it seems to me that would be decidedly valuable.   A number of the commissions have not thought the reports of sufficient value to even summarize the statistical material or even to publish the totals of the columns of figures contained in their reports.   A number of the states have not thought enough of their reports to change from one year to the next, yea, even for a period of five years.   The analysis which they purpose to give is a discussion of the tax laws in those states.   It seems to me if you publish reports so frequently that you cannot make an analysis of that report, it would be much better to have a biennial publication with a slight amount of analysis than annual reports with only a few statistics and no analysis whatever.

Then, in the second place, it seems to me that the federal census publications of financial statistics of states and financial statistics of cities are not of much use to us.   The statistics, while valuable, are ofttimes not comparable with preceding issues, and it seems much valuable information is improperly classified or altogether omitted.

If the National Tax Association as a body, or its members individually, would take some interest in these publications, it seems to me that in the course of a few years they could be much more serviceable and much more valuable for our purposes.

FRANKLIN S. EDMONDS (Pennsylvania) : In connection with the very interesting suggestion of Professor Snavely, I should like to say a word about the experience of the Pennsylvania Tax Commission which has just gone out of business on May 31, 1927.   We had three or four years in which to do our work.   We had two appropriations, of $15,000 and $25,000—$40,000 altogether.   The larger portion of our appropriation was spent in the expense of public hearings, stenographic and clerical work; but there was one piece of major work which we did, costing $6,000, which I think will be of some value to the state.

We were very anxious to ascertain whether the various lines of business were taxed, either on their capital or their net income, at the same ratio.   In other words, was the burden of taxation equally great upon businesses of the same kind?

We classified 15,000 business corporations into twenty-one classes. In one was bituminous coal, anthracite coal, oil companies, railroad companies, transportation companies, other utilities, and so forth, making twenty-one classes altogether.

We collected from their corporation reports these facts: First, what was their capital in Pennsylvania; second, what was their net income for the year 1925; third, what did they pay in federal taxes for 1925; and, fourth, what did they pay in state and local taxes for 1925?

Then we made the ratios, and we found with very great interest that for the year 1925 certain lines of business in the State of Pennsylvania paid in taxes as high as 41 per cent of their net income. That was the highest ratio and was on anthracite coal.

The second highest ratio, I think, was 35 per cent on bituminous coal. There are other lines of business, in which including federal and state and local taxes, they paid as low as 10 per cent. That, I think, would apply to the newspapers and also certain other industrial lines, and is probably due to the fact that in Pennsylvania capital which is engaged in manufacturing does not pay our capital stock tax.

It was, however, a very interesting series of facts that showed, after a study of 15,000 corporation returns, that there was as wide a spread as from 10 to 41 per cent on net income in the relative tax burden borne by various businesses. To obtain that result cost $6,000 in the way of statistical study. We think the money was well expended, and that this table, which is published as a supplement to our report of 1927, will have quite a decided bearing upon future legislation in the state.

ARTHUR S. DUDLEY (Wisconsin) : This discussion has brought to my mind something I recall in reading the works of O. Henry. He says that statistics is the lowest form of information that exists.

Gentlemen, without the comment below your figures, I think all of us will agree that the figures are practically meaningless. I do not think it requires further argument to bring out the fact that we must have some comment upon the figures to make them of any service.

JOHN E. BRINDLEY (Iowa) : In addition to the special tax commissions, I should like also to ask that any present from the dozen or more states carrying on investigations now in connection with the federal government, meet also in this corner.

OSCAR LESER (Maryland) : I wonder if Mr. Edmonds can tell how much of the anthracite coal taxes are paid by the rest of us outside of Pennsylvania.

FRANKLIN S. EDMONDS : Very little, judging the way our exports are falling off.

CHAIRMAN MATTHEWS : I believe the secretary has one or two announcements to make before we go on with the next paper.

SECRETARY HOLCOMB : I am a little bit worried about these various calls to meet in certain corners of this room, because we have an important engagement outside at 12:30. Our photographer is fuming and fretting about the exodus from the hotel. It has not been announced heretofore, but we always like to have that photograph, so it is necessary that we meet at 12: 30 at the Leader Lane entrance to the hotel.

Now, this little card which I have in my hand, is a card which it is quite necessary should be returned before one o'clock. The committee on arrangements would like to know how many can be counted upon at these various social functions. There is a drive at 2: 30 on Wednesday, for instance. It is stated as 3: 30 on the card, but it is 2: 30; and the tea in the Crystal Room at 4: 30 on Wednesday; then there is a drive on Friday at 2: 30, and a banquet on Friday at 7: 00 P. M.

Now, you realize that it is quite important for those who have to arrange for these things to know in advance how many to count on, and they ask that these cards be immediately passed around.

Be sure your names appear on the railroad certificates. I notice that a lot of them have not the name, and I am hopeless without the name.

CHAIRMAN MATTHEWS: The next subject is " Sources of Public Revenue Supplemental to Taxes," and will be discussed by Professor Jens P. Jensen of the University of Kansas.

JENS P. JENSEN (Kansas) : Mr. Chairman, Delegates and others: I suppose that a man is entitled to his own opinion, however erratic and fantastic it may be. I am feeling just now as if my opinion, my idea in starting out on this analysis may be fantastic. If it does not provoke any very violent or vigorous protest, if people ignore it, I suppose the thing is harmless, and that is something to be said for it. I thought that anybody who is paying taxes might be willing to consider some ways in which supplemental revenues might be obtained; so it is my purpose not to settle but merely raise that question, whether or not revenue from other sources than taxes may not be obtained.

As a simple procedure, I took the Bureau of Census statistics, financial statistics of states and of cities and some other classifications, and took these revenues that could not be classified as taxes, and tried to analyze very briefly, and as simply as I could, the possibilities they might possess for additional revenue.

Now, those revenues that we can classify as taxes for the Federal Government and for all the state and local governments I think amount to about 80 per cent of the total. What I am concerned with is the remaining 20 per cent. The question is whether that can be increased to 40 per cent, or even a smaller percentage, and if it could, whether it will be worth while. Some of them I shall make short shrift of, because I do not think they need be studied very carefully. I think on the face of them we can tell that they cannot give us any relief.

(Reading paper)

6

PUBLIC REVENUE SOURCES SUPPLEMENTAL
TO TAXES

JENS P. JENSEN

University of Kansas

It is the purpose not to settle but merely to raise the question whether it is possible and desirable to supplement the public revenue raised from taxes, to a greater extent than is now done, by revenue from other sources. If these other sources can be made to yield more revenue, without involving new or aggravating present objections, taxes can be *pro tanto* reduced. Certainly, today, with rapidly mounting public expenditures and consequent complaints of excessive taxes, there are good reasons for seeking relief in any legitimate manner.

I. The Importance of Taxes

Taxes are today, and have long been the principal form of public revenue; in fact they are in many political units almost the only source. But that was not always so. The prince of feudal days relied upon taxes as a last resort only. Today the situation is almost entirely reversed. The maker of a modern public budget, knowing the total amount that must be raised for the fiscal period, deducts a fairly measurable but decidedly minor amount, derived from miscellaneous sources, and produced largely incidental to the public services. The balance, usually by far the largest part, and sometimes practically all, must be apportioned among the taxpayers according to some basis or other, or according to a combination of bases.

For the fiscal year 1926 the total federal revenue receipts, exclusive of postal revenues,[1] amounted to about $3,963,000,000. The receipts properly classified as taxes amounted to about $3,417,000, 000, or about 86% of the total. If we include the postal revenues, the percentage is of course somewhat less—in the neighborhood of 75%. The receipts include such items as payment on the principal of the debts of foreign governments, and of debts owed to the treasury by railroads and other enterprises, incurred during the World War. Such receipts represent conversion of assets, rather than revenue receipts, and should not properly be included among the receipts for the year. There are other items, such as receipts from the sale of surplus property, collection of back taxes in more than the average amounts, that are not properly creditable to the year in question. In fact, an accurate analysis of the net revenue receipts of the Federal Government for any year does not exist,

---

[1] Data from *Fifth Report of the Director of the Budget.*

apparently. But it seems that we are fairly warranted in saying that, one year with another, taxes constitute not less than 80% of the total federal revenue.

In the state budgets taxes figure only slightly less prominently. In 1915 taxes amounted to 79.8% of the total revenue receipts of the 48 states.[2] In 1925 that figure had shrunk to 74.6%. However, this shrinkage is misleading. It is accounted for chiefly by the rapid increase in receipts by the states from the federal treasury, in the form of subventions and grants-in-aid, chiefly for highways and education. Such receipts are not, in a sense, revenue to the states at all. In any event, they were taken from the general fund of the treasury, which was supplemented by taxes. Taxes are perhaps equally as important to the state treasuries as to the federal treasury.

It is worth noting, in passing, that there has been a change in the type of taxes accruing to the state treasuries. In 1915 the general property tax yielded 40.6% of all state revenues; in 1925 only 24.1%. This decrease was offset by a corresponding increase of from 20.3% to 34.3% in the so-called "business and non-business license taxes." The increase comes chiefly from taxes on motor fuels and registration of motor vehicles. The shift in emphasis has some bearing upon my subject. These new taxes are based largely on the benefit and cost-of-service principles, while the declining general property tax must be justified more upon the principle of ability to pay. The increased reliance upon this type of taxes we may accept as an outgrowth of a search for new sources, to ease the burden of taxes based upon property. Such new sources, other than taxes, or such increased amounts from such sources already in use, must, like the business and non-business license taxes, be justified largely upon the cost-of-service and benefit principles.

For the cities the case is about the same. Taking the 146 cities of 30,000 population for which the Census Bureau has continuous data, taxes amounted in 1903 to 73.4%; in 1915 to 70.2%; and in 1925 to 71.2%.[3] That figure will hold for the smaller cities as well. That the cities appear to make relatively less use of taxes than the states is explained in part by the fact that the cities derive about 10% of their total revenue receipts from various public service enterprises that are generally operated on a cost-of-service basis, while the states derive but negligible amounts from that source. The cities also make greater use of special assessments than the states. The cities, after eliminating the returns from the public service enterprises, derive not far less than 80% of their total revenue from taxes.

[2] Data from *Financial Statistics of States.*
[3] From *Financial Statistics of Cities.*

It is certain that the counties and other local political units make even greater relative use of taxes than the larger units of the cities, the states, and the nation. Many of them, in fact, have scarcely any other sources. We are certainly warranted in saying that, taking all our governmental units together, one year with another, they depend for their revenue upon taxes to the extent of over 80% of the total. And there has been no striking change in that ratio during recent decades. It is the remaining 20% that requires our attention. I shall employ the classification developed by the Bureau of the Census; and I shall have to rely chiefly upon data furnished by the Bureau.

II. Earnings of Public Service Enterprises

The largest single group of gross revenue receipts, other than taxes, consists of the earnings of public service enterprises. On the part of the Federal Government the largest item is that of the postal service. If the ambitions of our Postmaster General materialize, the postal revenues will soon amount to $1,000,000,000. And if the diminishing national debt, coupled with continued economy, can reduce the national budget or at least keep it from mounting appreciably, the postal revenues will soon amount to 25% of our total national revenues. The state governments receive but trivial amounts from this source, and the same thing is true for the local governments, except the cities. The latter, however, have succeeded better with public enterprises, if their revenue receipts are acceptable as a criterion. Between 1903 and 1925 this form of revenue increased in the 146 cities, for which the Census Bureau has continuous data, from $2.42 to $6.19 per capita. But expressed as a percentage of the total revenues the figures fell from 11.5% to 10%. The cities vary widely in the extent to which they have municipalized their service enterprises. For example, in 1925, of the 247 cities having populations of 30,000 or above, 9 reported no receipts at all, 22 reported receipts exceeding $10 per capita, and one, Pasadena, California, reported receipts of $44.43 per capita.

Can the revenues from our public service enterprises be increased so as to lighten the tax burden? Unfortunately no conclusive answer can be given. The total gross revenue could of course be increased if the public service enterprises were more extensively municipalized or nationalized. But to do so would not of itself lead to lower taxes, and might have the opposite effect. For it is probable that, taken as a whole, public service enterprises do not fully pay their way. And it is to be presumed that if additional service enterprises were to be municipalized or nationalized, they would be less efficient than those already publicly operated. Doubtless those least well adapted for public operation would tend to be reserved longest for private operation.

There seems to be no valid reason why the patrons of public services should be generally favored with less-than-cost rates, with a resulting obligation upon the taxpayers to make up the deficit, any more than they should be made to pay rates so high as to yield, above total cost, a surplus to relieve the taxpayers. Public opinion would probably not favor the idea of a fiscal monopoly. It doubtless favors rates based on cost. But what is actually included in costs? It is regrettable that public accounting fails to give us any adequate data as to the relation between revenue and total costs of public service enterprises. They are seldom credited with the value of the services rendered to the general departments. On the other hand, they are not infrequently charged with interest on all the capital employed; indeed the value of the capital employed is rarely known even approximately. And it is very rare, if it ever occurs, that a public service enterprise is charged with the taxes it would have to pay if it were a private corporation, and of which the public treasuries are deprived through municipalization or nationalization. With accounting so inadequate, for our purpose, it cannot have any significance that the operating revenues may exceed the operating costs. There are very good reasons for believing that the public service enterprises do not fully meet, from their operating revenues, all the costs, especially those of interest and taxes. If they were generally made to meet all the costs that must be met by a private corporation rendering the same services, it is possible that concealed deficits that now often occur, would tend to disappear, with some attendant relief to the taxpayers.

III. Fees or Administrative Charges

The next largest source of non-tax revenue is composed of what the Census Bureau calls "Earnings of the General Departments." And here is probably the source from which the most substantial relief to the distressed taxpayer can come. These fees or administrative charges are varied in character, since they are collected in varying amounts by practically every general service organization of practically every part of our government. The wide variations in the receipts among the same type or degree of governmental unit suggest possibilities of augmented revenues.

For the Federal Government, fees are probably relatively less significant than for the states and their local divisions. The consular and passport fees amount to about $10,000,000 annually, and render the State Department nearly self-supporting. Certain fees of the customs service, of the public land registers and receivers and others bring the total of federal fees to probably less than $25,000,000. Considered as a percentage of total federal revenue in excess [4] of $4,000,000,000, this is considerably less than 1%. It

[4] See e. g. *First Report of the Director of the Budget,* 1923.

does not seem probable that federal fees will increase so as to form a very important part of the total revenue.

The 48 states in 1925 received nearly $119,000,000 from general department earnings, or about $1.05 per capita, and 8% of their total receipts. The extent to which the 48 states, taken together, and to which certain selected states that received more than 10% of their total revenues from fees, made their different departments self-supporting, may be seen from the accompanying table.

EXTENT OF SELF-SUPPORT IN SELECTED STATES OF GENERAL DEPARTMENTS (PERCENTAGE WHICH EARNINGS WERE OF COST PAYMENTS), 1925.

	All departments.	General government.	Protection to persons and property.	Conservation of health.	Highways.	Charities, hospitals and corrections.	Education.	Recreation.	Miscellaneous.
Maine.................	15	2	20	9	40	13	8	..	9
Vermont	12	10	21	6	15	16	2	..	2
Minnesota	16	3	32	53	1	28	8	7	1
Iowa.................	19	13	38	26	1	55	23	12	4
Missouri	24	6	40	38	1	40	11	37	..
North Dakota	14	3	30	34	1	44	7	6	2
South Dakota	16	6	41	32	2	41	10	27	3
Kansas	22	4	72	24	143	18	23	..	5
Maryland	25	54	40	12	6	37	22	..	1
Alabama	31	16	90	7	12	95	15	..	1
Colorado	15	7	48	17	1	11	24	48	18
New Mexico	23	14	25	21	17	3	18	..	250
California...........	10	11	17	10	..	22	9	36	1
All States.........	11.5	10	33	16	29	11	9	11	1

NOTE: Based upon data from *Financial Statistics of States*, 1925.

Some of these figures are decidedly misleading. For example, the State of Kansas collected through its "highway department" 143% of its cost payments for highways. That appears to be a case of making highways sources of considerable income. But the total amount collected was less than $34,000; and the amount spent was less than $24,000—both amounts inconsequential. The explanation is that the state constitution forbids the state to engage directly in any internal improvement. It can therefore spend very little directly, and whatever is collected from miscellaneous sources looms large, relative to the negligible expenditures. No doubt there are other "freak" variations; and some of the variations can be explained away on other bases. But enough of variation remains to suggest that some states might derive additional revenue from fees. The 247 cities of 30,000 population or more received in 1925 nearly $67,000,000, or about $1.64 per capita and 2.7% of their total revenue from general department earnings. But 17 cities received more than $3.50 per capita; and Highland Park, Michigan, and Pasadena, California, received, respectively, $5.09 and $5.65 per capita. The extent to which the several departments were self-supporting in all the 247 cities and in those cities that received more than 8% of their total revenue from this source, may be seen in the table following.

EXTENT OF SELF-SUPPORT IN SELECTED CITIES OF GENERAL DEPARTMENTS (PERCENTAGE WHICH EARNINGS WERE OF COST PAYMENTS), 1925.

Cities.	All departments.	General government.	Protection to persons and property.	Conservation of health.	Sanitation and promotion of health.	Highways.	Education.	Charities, hospitals and corrections.	Recreation.	Miscellaneous.
Detroit	8	7	6	4	2	11	4	24	36	6
Cincinnati	8	10	5	3	1	4	12	1	3	..
Denver	8	26	11	2	..	13	2	10	14	3
Worcester	9	10	1	15	18	10	3	29	10	15
Sacramento	8	..	4	14	52	16	1	5	10	5
Highland Park	11	..	2	18	3	6	3	63	..	48
Berkeley	9	2	3	2	89	41	1	..	10	..
Brockton	10	5	..	13	78	28	2	20	67	..
Jackson, Mich.	14	25	2	62	26	4	2	51	31	..
Pasadena	10	16	3	5	7	57	2	3	10	10
Augusta, Ga.	13	..	2	..	2	9	1	64	..	2
Galveston	15	4	4	..	4	..	..	81	3	..
Columbus, Ga.	19	..	..	42	51	2	17	63	1	..
Fitchburg	8	5	1	12	2	2	20	45	4	13
Lynchburg	10	9	1	4	6	12	8	54	17	..
All cities having population over 30,000	4	9	3	6	5	5	2	11	13	4

NOTE: Based upon data from *Financial Statistics of Cities,* 1925.

It may be argued that the general departments are not organized for fiscal purposes. They are not revenue-producing, but service-giving organizations. That is true in the same sense that it is true that a meat-packing plant exists not to produce fertilizer or tooth-brushes. But every well-managed industry exploits its by-products, so long as their sale will yield more than the extra cost of their production. So also should the finance minister use every minor source of revenue whose tapping will cause less sacrifice than the same amount of taxes would cause.

It is obvious that not for every type of service rendered by the government can a fee be charged. Some of them, such as that of the legislature, furnish no occasion for such a fee, and contain no basis for determining the size of the fees. Generally speaking, there can be no charge unless the fee-payer can be identified with tolerable readiness, as being either the recipient of benefit from some definite service or a member of a class whose behavior necessitates the service. Any state or municpal government will furnish examples of organizations whose work is of an overhead, or general character. I have culled from the first Report of the Director of the Budget for the State of Kansas (1927), a number of officers and a number of boards. The selection of officers include the governor and the justices of the courts and others. The boards include, among others, the Board of Regents, the Livestock Sanitary Commission, the Board of Health, and the State Historical Society. The appropriations for this group totaled a little over $1,000,000. Not one cent in fees or charges was collected for the services of this group. And there were certain other organizations, such as the Attorney General's Office and the Public Service Commission, whose "earnings" were small. With variations for individual officers or boards, the situation is the same in all states and cities. It is not practical to charge, on a *quid pro quo* basis, for general governmental services. From this source taxpayers can hope for no appreciable relief.

But after all, the general governmental cost is only a minor part of the total governmental cost. Taking all our governmental divisions as a whole, it may be said that the general government requires considerably less than 10% of the total revenue. And it is probable that the cost of general government will be relatively less in the future than it is now. Nearly all of the new functions of the government are special rather than general. For many of the services, though not for all of them, some charge may reasonably be made. In individual instances this charge will probably not be large, but in many cases it may reasonably cover the entire cost. In some cases it may develop into a tax, when the cost of the service is more than covered. The best example in recent decades of such a development from a fee to a tax is found in our motor-vehicle registration charges, which are now everywhere properly regarded as taxes. In such cases fees represent merely the transitionary stage in the development of taxes.

I have taken, again from the state budget of Kansas although any other state might serve as well, seventeen boards of the type for whose services heavy charges may be made. The list includes the Athletic Board, the Grain Inspection Department, and the Hotel Commission. These boards collected during the fiscal year 1926 $581,000 in fees, and spent $417,000, or about 70%, leaving $164;000 for the general' fund. In the case of an increasing number of these boards, the legislature has in recent sessions required that 10% of the collections be deposited to the credit of the general fund, appropriating the balance for the use of the organization. This is one way of accomplishing two different objects: First to determine statistically the amount of the collections, with a view to fixing the proper rates; second, to require these special services to bear not only the direct cost of the agency performing the services but also all or a part of the overhead cost in which they involve the general government. On theoretical as well as on practical grounds such a procedure is justifiable.

In between the extremes, on the one hand, the services that are so general that no charge can be made for them, and on the other, those services that can bear their full cost, fall the bulk of governmental services. The cost of the services is partly met, in varying degrees, from the charges exacted. There is evidence to show that legislatures and budget-makers are considering the possibility of making the special governmental services as nearly self-supporting as possible.

Many of our governmental organizations are found upon analysis to render services of a composite character, some of which may safely be required to bear their total cost, while others can bear only a part of it or none at all. Consider, for example, the institutions of higher learning of the State of Kansas. The appropriations for these institutions for 1925 amounted to $6,488,000, of which they spent $5,834,000 or 89%. The fees collected, together with minor amounts of other kinds, amounted to $2,126,000, or about 36% of the cost.

If we analyze the services of, say, a state university, which we may take as typical of a higher educational institution, into its elements we see that for purposes of determining fees to be charged, the services are heterogeneous. And that generalization will hold for nearly all governmental organizations. For example, the University of Kansas, besides its general instructional service, for which a general fee is charged, maintains a cafeteria, dormitories, student health service, student extra-curricular activities, and the like. While probably no one would argue that this type of services provide a proper occasion for the levying of a tax, there is no serious objection to charges for them that will cover their cost. While such services help to swell the total cost of an educational institution, it is not regarded as proper that they should swell also that part of the cost that must be met from taxation.

But not only are such supplementary services more and more met from fees imposed; the fees for the general instructional services have almost everywhere doubled during the past decade. At its 1927 session the legislature of Kansas refused to increase the appropriations for the state educational institutions for the biennium, over the appropriations for the previous biennium. If more revenue were required, it was suggested that the fees might be increased. Accordingly the Board of Regents authorized an increase. Because of this increase and because of another increase, made two years earlier for similar reasons, the general tuition fees have been more than doubled. An inspection of the fee schedules of similar institutions discloses the fact that Kansas is following, rather tardily, a movement that is quite general.

In the tendency to increase the general tuition fees we may discern a principle of much wider application in determining the proper size of fees. Our earliest universities and colleges were endowed institutions, and the first state institutions joined in the practice of giving practically free tuition, or at least of charging nominal fees. This liberal policy served admirably to encourage attendance. We can understand that at that time such encouragement was in the public interest. But today such indiscriminate encouragement is not needed and has, besides, certain drawbacks. Among the hundreds of thousands that matriculate each year at our institutions of higher learning are many who do not have the requisite mentality to benefit from the facilities offered, and also many who for other reasons could more advantageously occupy themselves in some other way. In proportion as it is no longer in the public interest to increase the attendance indiscriminately, may the fees be safely increased, and made to cover a larger part of the cost.

The principle involved is of course that the charging of fees must be subsidiary to the public policy. But public policy, with reference to a given service, may change; and it is not likely to change with reference to all public services to the same extent and in the same direction at the same time. Nothing but constant vigilance and repeated study will develop an acceptable and justifiable schedule of fees.

It is obvious that the so-called " earnings of the general departments " can never equal their cost, at least not all of them considered as a whole. Fees cannot be charged except upon some fairly definite occasion, such as the issue of a marriage license or the inspection of a sample of grain. They cannot be charged unless the fee-payer can be readily identified as having some relation to the specific occasion, either by way of benefiting from the service or giving rise to the necessity for performing it. And finally, they should not be charged when or in such amounts that they will interfere with accepted public policies. The foregoing restrictions require that many public services be rendered free or at less than cost. On the other hand, without doubt, there are many possibilities for additional fees, or for increased fees. Though their payment may cause some sacrifice, it will often be less than the sacrifice involved in taxes to which their non-payment gives rise. It should no longer be possible to ignore the fact that non-payment of justifiable fees involves more than equivalent sacrifice through the exaction of resulting taxes.

IV. HIGHWAY PRIVILEGES, RENT AND INTEREST

The Census Bureau has grouped together a somewhat miscellaneous list of items under the caption "highway privileges, rents and interest." The wide variations in the receipts from this group of sources suggest the possibility of increases in many places. The average receipt per capita in the 48 states for 1925 was only 60 cents, but North Dakota received $4.09 per capita or 15.4% of her total revenue; Wyoming $4.36 per capita and 11.2% of total revenue; and South Dakota $6.12 per capita and 26.1% of total revenue.

Among the cities the variations are even wider. The average per-capita receipts for the year 1925 of the 247 cities of over 30,000 population was $2.91; but for many individual cities the receipts were much larger; and in one case, Long Beach, California, it was $18.56. The larger cities show larger receipts than the smaller. Thus for the cities of 500,000 or more the average was $4.74 per capita, while for the smaller, those between 30,000 and 50,000, the figure was only 88 cents. But the group of receipts is too heterogeneous. We must analyze a bit more.

The first sub-group is that of receipts from highway privileges. And the Census Bureau further subdivides into major and minor highway privileges. The receipts for major privileges consist chiefly of amounts received from private public-service enterprise, such as street railways and telephone companies, in exchange for the use of public property, such as streets and alleys, when exacted in accordance with the terms of the franchise. In 1925 the 247 cities of over 30,000 population received $23,423,000 for all highway privileges. But the 12 cities with populations exceeding 500,000 received $16,244,000; and Chicago alone received $7,280,000. With the large receipts of Chicago contrast the negligible receipts of Cleveland, of only $1,681. Of course the difference between the larger receipts of Chicago and the smaller receipts of Cleveland and other cities is explained partly by the large consideration exacted by Chicago for the use of her streets for rapid transit purposes, while other cities either have been less exacting for their street privileges or operate their service enterprises themselves.

The question of the character and magnitude of public utility franchise payments has always been and still is a vexed and vexing, as well as a never-settled one. It would certainly be rash to raise it here for detailed analysis. A settlement can never be avoided, and it can never be anything but a compromise. The value of the use of the public streets for traffic purposes can never have any meaning in terms of a definite amount of money. The best that can be done is to understand that, with effective public rate regulation, the franchise payments and the tax payments must vary inversely with each other; and to arrive at a workable compromise in the light of that understanding.

The receipts for minor highway privileges are much less voluminous at present; but the variations in the receipts suggest that they may be the source of greater net increases in public revenue than the major highway privileges. The minor privileges consist of privileges of maintaining private services, drains and vaults under the streets, fruit and other stands, and other property on the sidewalk, and of extending awnings, bay and show windows, and other structures and conveniences, including signs, beyond the building line.[5] These minor privileges differ in one important respect from the major privileges: the benefit goes to particular persons, in the main. It must be possible, in most cases, to arrive at a workable valuation of each particular type of privilege. Any reasonable charge collected will be almost clear gain to the public treasury. And if the use of some of these privileges is checked by the imposition of a charge, such checking will often be a cause of rejoicing.

It will probably be objected that the charges will often be small, and that the dignity of the public exchequer will be injured by its attention to such trivial matters. I do not think that objection is valid. On the contrary, I think that adequate financial consideration for such privileges, arrived at in the open, will injure the dignity of the exchequer less than the political considerations that will almost necessarily be involved if no charge is made.

The second item of this group, namely rents from public property, might have been much more important than it is had we not disposed of our public domain so completely, and often so recklessly of the public interest. The vast territory, once public property, with its varied natural resources, is in private hands, almost completely. In retrospect, it is easy to see that the disposition was accompanied with too little regard for the rights of posterity. One exonerating circumstance there was. It was, as far as agricultural land is concerned, in the public interest to speed the exploitation. That was less true of minerals and waterpower, and probably in case of oil, coal, and timber, seldom true. But today that remnant of the public

---

[5] *Financial Statistics of Cities.*

domain not yet alienated need not be disposed of to facilitate exploitation. The conservation of the public interest should now be—should long ago have been—jealously guarded.

Not only have we disposed with reckless liberality of the bulk of the public domain, but that part which was converted into cash has been spent for current purposes. And when we have made some attempt to conserve the patrimony of the state, in the form of permanent funds, we have seldom had the strength of character to refrain from raiding the fund on the first occasion of financial stress. Witness the public school lands in most of the states. Sold often for far less than they were worth—and the proceeds spent for current purposes. In only three or four states does there remain intact any considerable share of the original funds.

A great part of the receipts from public property is still of that sort, and the proceeds are still being spent for current purposes. Each year the Federal Government realizes something over $10,000,000 from the sales of public lands and from oil leases on federal lands, mostly from the latter. The amounts from rentals proper, that is, such receipts as do not involve the alienation of land or the removal of irreplaceable assets, is very small. From the rentals of public buildings and grounds the federal treasury realized possibly a little over $1,000,000 last year.

From rents of investment properties the states in 1925 realized $11,000,000, and the 247 cities $21,400,000, but nearly $16,000,000 was received by New York, Chicago, and Boston. It would not be desirable for the state or any part of it to acquire property for profits or rents, as a landlord. But the most profitable use of such public property as is held is a reasonable expectation.

It is not impossible that diligence may yet uncover valuable sources of revenue from such remainders of the public domain, as yet remain unalienated. Thus in 1925 oil was discovered in a certain river bed that was the property of Kansas. For one lease a $130,000 bonus, plus the regular 8% royalty, was obtained. The total receipts of the state amounted for the fiscal year 1925 to $184,000, of which $181,000 was credited to general revenue and spent for current purposes. There also accrues to the state royalties for pumping sand from the rivers for building purposes. Not large sums, but worth collecting. In the three-year period 1923-25 the City of Long Beach, California, collected nearly $3,500,000 from properties owned, mostly from oil rights.

To be sure, the chances that a city will become rich from the royalties on the oil rights of such properties as it possesses are rather remote. And the probability of that event for a state is not immediately impending, though for the Federal Government more of a chance exists to gain from mineral rights. And such rights as exist may prove to be valuable and should be conserved, if not for current, then for future use.

Many resources now perhaps quite or nearly without value may, with the growth of population, prove to be very valuable. At the present time New York State is considerably agitated as to the best method of conserving for the public such values as reside in the waterpower of the state. It is not improbable that other assets, now abundant, relatively speaking, may some day be scarce. A British engineer once raised the question as to whether some day there might not be an actual shortage of water, as population increases and the municipal requirements for water grow. In a new section such a contingency is quite remote. But already New York City is faced with a prospective shortage from her Catskill water supply, and it is certainly true that increased supplies will have to be obtained at increased costs. Other cities are in this position. While the conservation of natural sources of water supply is not likely to be made a source of revenue for the city and thereby lessen taxes, it may lessen taxes of the future quite as effectively by reducing the costs of the future supply.

The last item of the group, that of interest, is important. In 1925 the 247 cities received nearly $74,000,000 and the 48 states nearly $56,000,000. Of the federal treasury the receipts are larger, owing chiefly to interest receipts on the foreign debts and other domestic emergency investments.

Not all interest receipts are of the same significance. A considerable amount (nearly $45,000,000 in case of the 247 cities, and nearly $14,000,000 for the 48 states) of the interest received represent interest on sinking-fund investments. Large interest receipts of this kind mean a large public debt, and large reliance upon sinking funds for its liquidation. It might be preferable to employ the method of serial bonds to liquidate the debt. There is no net revenue from interest receipts derived from investments, the money paid for which could have been used to pay the public debt.

Another variety of interest is that received for account of public trust funds. The 48 states in 1925 reported over $28,000,000, and the 247 cities over $8,000,000. If the interest is for the account of, for example, the permanent school fund, the revenue is real enough, but such is not always the case.

It is from the two remaining types of interest, namely on investments and on current deposits, that it is probably possible to secure additional revenue, and at the same time probably improve the honesty and efficiency of the government. From this source, the 247 largest cities in 1925 realized about $17,000,000, and the states about $14,000,000. The federal Treasury does not exploit its interest resources as fully as would be possible. In the past, objectives other than revenue have been served. For example, deposits have often been made to "move the crops," and sometimes to further political purposes, although probably in this respect the federal

Treasury cannot hold a candle to the treasuries of the cities and the states. The franchise tax paid by the federal reeserve banks, out of their more or less arbitrarily defined excess earnings, are in one sense interest receipts.

The facts are not fully enough available to show the average rate of interest received by states and cities. At the close of the fiscal year 1925 the 48 states were reported to have cash on hand amounting to about $525,000,000, and to have collected interest on current deposits to the amount of $12,000,000, or nearly 2.5%. If the amount of cash on hand were representative of the average amount of deposits during the year that would be a very good showing, but obviously the average amount of cash on hand is much larger. At the close of the fiscal year the deposits and cash on hand are usually at a low ebb for good reasons of budget administration. It is the wide variation in the receipts from current deposits that lead me to suspect that in many states a more economically and politically sound method of custody of the public funds could yield increased revenues. States that are substantially similar show very wide variations, in the amount of interest. Thus in 1925 North Carolina received $357,000 interest on current deposits, and South Carolina only $4,420. While the amounts of cash on hand of North Carolina was larger, they were far from being as much larger as the difference in interest received. The cities are probably worse offenders than the states, and so far as the evidence goes, the smaller cities are in general worse offenders than the larger, which perhaps was to be expected.

I recall that Professor Merriam of Chicago once in his classes made a remark to the following effect: If you are looking for any single presumptive index of efficiency and honesty of a city administration, consider its custody of public balances. I believe he was right. It is not an infallible index. But if the balance of cash is not properly regulated, guarded, and used to yield such revenue as it may, that in itself is wrong; and something else is also likely to be wrong.

To be sure, such a test must be used with discretion. In the first place, it is not a mark of efficiency to have a large balance at all. It would be well if the tax payments and other revenues could be adjusted to come in such a steady stream that they could at once be paid out to meet the public bills. But in practical affairs this is not possible, and of such balance as it is necessary to carry, two things I think are required.

First, that it shall yield as much interest as is consistent with safety and availability. Presumably that can best be done by something like a tripartite division, investing that part which will be on hand for a relatively long time in marketable securities, placing a part of the remainder on inactive deposit, and the balance upon checking accounts at such rates as approved banks are willing to pay upon a competitive basis. More than the banks can afford to pay cannot be gotten, and less should not be accepted.

Second, there should be nothing, in the way of favoring deposits, which the fiscal officers can use for their own benefit. It is not necessary here to rehearse the scandals of Pennsylvania, Ohio and Illinois, and lesser scandals elsewhere, growing out of the circumstance that improper and wasteful arrangements pertain as to the custody of the balances in the public treasury.

V. MISCELLANEOUS SOURCES

There are other minor sources, some of which might be augmented, but none of them can be expected to yield great increases. Nevertheless it is worth trying.

Occasionally a public-spirited person makes a gift to the public treasury, either of money or other property, perhaps more often the latter. But the amount is small and uncertain, and is, besides, incidental. The finance minister cannot actively solicit voluntary contributions, as is possible for the financial secretaries of endowed institutions. Voluntary gifts, though there seems to be no good reason for discouraging them, cannot be expected to give much relief to the distressed taxpayer, unless in some way gifts to the public become more popular and fashionable than they are at present.

Occasionally also some money or other property escheats to the public treasury, because it is found to be without an owner. But such revenue is not only small, irregular, and uncertain; it is also beyond the control of the exchequer. The government cannot, by taking thought, increase its revenue from escheats, unless it reverts to the practices of the robber-baron days and confiscates the wealth of those who have, when it will be a crime to be rich. Nevertheless, whether the revenues from escheats can be augmented much or little, such wealth as comes to the treasury in this manner should be claimed with speed and certainty.

The Census Bureau also records small amounts of revenue from commercial forfeits, paid by persons or firms who fail to live up to the terms of their contracts with the governments. But such receipts are small and irregular, and should not be hoped for. They can not or should not be such as to yield net revenue to the treasury. For the vast majority of governmental contracts are acceptably fulfilled; and to fix the penalties in excess of the loss sustained by non-fulfilment will necessarily make contractors less willing to bid, and thereby tend to increase the bids. There can be no relief to taxpayers from such practice.

Only one more source remains to be suggested; and that one seems to me to offer limited possibilities, in some governmental divisions at least, for increased net revenue. The Census Bureau reports that for the fiscal year 1925 the 247 cities of over 30,000 population collected fines amounting to $17,136,000; and the 48 states collected $6,819,000 from that source. The variations in amounts between political units of the same degree and the same magnitude suggests that this source of revenue might safely be increased. For example, the state of Ohio collected $1,156,000, while the adjoining state of Michigan collected only $3,827, and Missouri none at all. The City of Los Angeles collected during the same year $1,307,000, while San Francisco collected only $69,000.

No one in his right mind would advocate that the administration of justice and the enforcement of the laws should be prostituted. by being turned into revenue-producing enterprises. The bad old days of Henry II of England, so well described by Adam Smith, when " the judicial authority of such a sovereign . . . far from being a cause of expense, was for a long time a source of revenue to him," fortunately are no more. Not that the power to impose fines is today free from abuse. Many a motorist has found himself caught in a speed trap and been made to contribute ungraciously to the coffers of some village or, what is much worse, in the form of fees to the prequisites of some village constable or justice of the peace. But fines are today imposed for penological rather than fiscal purposes. It is only one of the forms of penalties which the sovereign government may impose, in its attempt to suppress violation of law.

Nevertheless, the violation of law is a pastime that throws a considerable financial burden upon the shoulders of the taxpayer directly, besides being costly to society, indirectly, in many ways. It is very probable that in many cases a pecuniary penalty will have as satisfactory penological results as any other form of penalty. If the finance minister were also the administrator of justice, and had to choose definitely between saddling the cost upon the taxpayers or making the violator bear the cost, it is probable that the revenue from fines would show a marked increase. Some types of law enforcement may be better adapted to be " self-supporting " than others. Perhaps it is not with universal popular approval that Dr. Doran, in charge of prohibition law enforcement, recently announced that in the future fines would be more severe and numerous, in order to make the service self-supporting financially, thereby removing popular objection that the Volstead Act is a piece of legislation too expensive to enforce.

In conclusion, let me say that I have no intention to initiate or even support a movement to abolish all taxes and to make all governmental services self-supporting, but driving hard every one of the miscellaneous sources I have reviewed. I am not suffering from the illusion that such a condition is possible or even desirable. All that is contended for is that all of the suggested sources deserve further study in every governmental division. And the only prediction ventured is that such study, if its results are acted upon, will bring relief to the taxpayer in many states and cities. Of one thing I am sure: The taxpayer will welcome whatever relief can be had.

CHAIRMAN MATTHEWS: I want to call your attention to the fact that there are two of these cards: This small one is for the men, and the large one for the ladies. Make no mistake in using the right card.

Is there any discussion on the subject of Professor Jensen's paper?

(No discussion)

CHAIRMAN MATTHEWS: If not, I will remind you once more that the photographer will be ready to receive you at 12:30.

MARK GRAVES (New York): The New York delegation will meet in this corner immediately following adjournment.

CHAIRMAN MATTHEWS: If there are no further announcements, the meeting is adjourned.

(Adjournment)

THIRD SESSION

CHAIRMAN MATTHEWS: Before proceeding with the program of the afternoon, I will announce as the other two members of the credentials committee Mr. E. P. Tobie of Rhode Island and Mr. Simeon E. Leland of Kentucky.

The afternoon session wll be in charge of Mr. Thornton Alexander of Massachusetts. Mr. Alexander, will you please take the chair?

(Thornton Alexander of Massachusetts, presiding)

CHAIRMAN ALEXANDER: Gentlemen, this ought to be one of the most interesting sessions of the conference, if I can be prevented from spoiling the interest of it, for the reason that prior to the Volstead Act there were select but comparatively few people who were interested in the federal income tax act, but for some reason or another, since the passage of the Volstead Act the great indoor American amusement seems to have been to pass income tax laws, some eight or nine in the last thirteen years, I believe, and immediately having passed an income tax law, the next part of the game was to try to poke holes in the income tax laws and drive a team of oxen through the holes; and then the next thing was to pass another law to stop up the holes. So that, after a period of time, we find ourselves in 1926 with a new income tax law which appears to be—I judge from the comments I have heard from those who know something about, which I do not claim to—more intricate and more complex than anything that has gone before. Now the variation in this great indoor United States amusement of creating laws is to create an income tax law to simplify the previous structure of laws which has gone ahead. Every organization of a serious nature, whether business or purely intellectual, or what-not, has gone to work to create a committee to aid in the simplification of some new future income tax law; and every one of these organizations is hoping that its particular committee, with its particular recommendations, will be honored by having those recommendations adopted in the next law.

The National Tax Association has very properly appointed a committee upon the simplification of the income tax law, and that committee has today reported to you in the form of a printed report, with which I suppose each one of you is armed for this afternoon's

(99)

session. If you do not happen to be armed with one of these, I presume you can get it at the desk outside the door.

It is needless to say that this report of this committee is presented to you for discussion, and also, I am requested to say, for criticism, as well as discussion. The members of the committee who were charged with the duty of drafting this report are not going to be at all hurt if you discuss and criticize the report very freely. In fact, they welcome all suggestions, comments and criticisms with respect to it. If, however, your association at this conference adopts this report, or adopts it with amendments or supplements of any sort, it is needless to say that the report is going to carry very, very great weight when the next income tax act is finally drafted, for the reason that the National Tax Association is not only a nation-wide association, but it is also international in its scope, and any report which is accepted by this conference must necessarily, from the character of the association and the personnel, the ladies and gentlemen who compose it, carry weight, but also on account of the weight and standing of the members of the committee itself.

You all know the chairman of that committee, and no words of encomium which I might say could raise him any higher in your estimation than he is at the present time, by virtue of his previous activities and experiences. He is one of the leading, and perhaps the leading income tax scholar and legal practitioner in the income tax world, Mr. George E. Holmes.

As to the other members of the committee, their qualifications are set forth very modestly on page 3 of this report.

The members of this committee, it may be stated, are, with the exception of the chairman, men who have been privileged to observe the operation of the present income tax system within as well as without the Bureau of Internal Revenue, since the enactment of the Revenue Act of 1917.

Mr. Robert N. Miller, one of the members of the committee, was solicitor of the Internal Revenue; Mr. Hugh Satterlee was draughtsman of the prototype of the present income tax regulations; Mr. Albert E. James was a member of the Board of Tax Appeals; Mr. Henry Bond was a member of the Advisory Tax Committee appointed by Hon. Daniel C. Roper in 1918; Mr. F. Morse Hubbard was secretary of that committee, and Mr. Donald Arthur was assistant to the advisory tax committee. Those gentlemen helped to organize the stupendous work concerning the Bureau of Internal Revenue.

I am not going to attempt to summarize this report, except very, very briefly. The report is, as you see, somewhat voluminous, containing 104 pages, and very frankly I have had opportunity to do little more than glance hastily through it.

I may call your attention to a few points therein, very broadly.

The keynote of the report is found on pages 1 and 2. You may see that the whole report is built upon the theory that the present income structure ought to be entirely demolished, and must be if any new law is to be really successful in the way that we wish to see it successful—must be entirely rebuilt. It requires an entire revision, and the gentlemen suggest that in rebuilding it there should be an avoidance of all pleas of special opportunity and big interests.

These gentlemen do not expect that this income tax law is to be demolished and rebuilt at this coming session of Congress. They, in fact, say that there ought not be any hasty action by Congress, but that the present joint congressional committee's life ought to be extended for a period of at least one year, if not longer, in order that they may give the most careful consideration to the sort of an act which this committee thinks ought to be enacted.

They say in concluding their report:

"We have been deeply impressed with the very general opinion that the need for a thorough revision of the statute and improvement of administration is urgent and pressing; that a partial revision looking to improvement of the present structure is inadequate to meet the needs of the situation and should not be substituted for a thorough renovation of our income tax system; and that the existence of the Joint Congressioual Committee should be extended for as long a period as may be necessary to fully consider the manifold aspects of the subject in order that a new system of income taxation, simpler in its terms, sounder in its concept, and more flexible in its operation, may spring from the experience of the past."

That is quite a radical recommendation. Nevertheless, we all know, I suppose, that that is really the thing which ought to be done with our income tax system, if it is possible to do it. And then they go on to say that on account of the chameleon-like character—those words are my own—of our past acts, the fact that hardly do we have one act, before we put another act on top of it, it would at least be desirable that this new and more perfect act, or revision of the old act, should remain for a time—at least a period of years—unaltered, in order that not only the public but the employees of the Internal Revenue Bureau may become familiar with the new act.

From my experience at Washington and in my own office I think that it might be a very desirable thing, to have the act exist long enough so that we can become familiar with it.

Another thing they say, is that the administration of the law itself and the interpretation of the law should present no uncertainty

[...] from the point of view of the
1. Quest in Washington and
[...] the income tax admin-
[...] this committee does not
[...] certain conditions
[...] at work [...] to de-
[...] income tax act from Wash-
[...] until such time as the em-
[...] the [...] of administering
[...] until such time as they
[...] until time as they shall be
[...] believe than decentraliza-
[...] administration under local
[...] favoritism, in prejudice, and
[...] of the act with local politics.
[...] the long run that such de-
[...] carefully, cautiously, and
[...] [...]ure of office, have been
[...] have a nation [...] int
[...] such a [...],
[...] on [...] y

[...] ill
[...]
[...]
[...]cern
[...]hey
[...]s, b

[...]ntiv

The committee stresses and discusses th necessity of the stability
of the rate of tax, for instance. We all know—those of us who
have had any dealings with the Government with respect to income
taxes—that on account of the different res existing in one year,
as compared with the higher or lower rat in another year, it is a
chess game between the Government an the taxpayer; the Government makes a move to get a certain aount of tax into a year
in which there is a higher rate, and the kpayer makes a move to
get it into a year in which there is a loer rate; and they move
back and forth, until somebody finally ccides the thing, and it
takes a long period of years.

This committee thinks that by having sble rates this chess-game
proposition, while it will of course constatly go on to some extent,
will be more or less minimized. They so recommend a single
normal tax rate or single graduated scale f rates, if that is necessary, to take the place of the present rmal tax and sur-taxes.
They go on to discuss the double taxation f corporations in a particularly lucid and sane manner. They feel that the individual
stockholder ought to be held responsible or the tax on corporate
profits, taxing the corporation, for instant merely on the retained
profits.

The committee recommends that the prent provisions of certain
sections, such as those of Section 220—th ax on the undistributed
income of corporations—is perfectly usele in its present form, the
penalty of 50 per cent being too great. They characterize that
rathe   squely, as attempting to cra nuts with sledge ham-
me   y that this tax on the undistibuted income of a cor-
             d be reasonable, in order to e effective. The treat-
             nds, they claim, could be ve much simplified.
             attempt to go into any of ese questions in detail.
             to the determination of ga and loss, they make a
             ommendation, for instance, t Section 202—sustained
             obsolescence, amortization, letion to be subtracted
             of the property in determi g gain or loss—should
             usly allowed depreciation or bsolescence. The term
             eciation or obsolescence rept into the 1926 act
             deal of disturbance to e minds of our friends
             o a good many othe eople who have to deal
             r loss on sales o exchanges, they urge a
             nguage and subsnce of sections 203 and
             ave to deal w those subjects. They
             the exemptio n earned income.
             of the suggtions which they make.
             le for me discuss all the recom-
             report.

whatsoever. Anybody who has ever had any dealings with the income tax act appreciates the uncertainty not only of the law but of the interpretation and the administration of the law; the flood of rulings and office memoranda and solicitors' opinions, and general counsels' opinions, and opinions of one sort and another, which are published and perhaps filed; and in addition to that, the secret rulings with which the taxpayer is confronted, without ever being able to see those secret rulings.

All that they believe should be done away with, and the act, together with the more or less simple regulations as they are issued by the Government in book or pamphlet form or otherwise, should be the basis on which the Government, as well as the taxpayer stands, getting rid of the intricacy and multiplicity and complexity of all these other rulings and memoranda.

Another very startling proposition, from the point of view of the taxpayer who has been obliged to go down to Washington and complain about the great centralization of the income tax administration at Washington, is the fact that this committee does not recommend immediate decentralization, unless certain conditions are complied with. They say that if you go to work hastily to decentralize the administration of the income tax act from Washington—to put it under local agencies, until such time as the employees of the Government charged with the duty of administering the act are put under civil service, and until such time as they receive adequate salaries, and until such time as they shall be assured of adequate tenure of office—they believe that decentralization and placing the income tax act administration under local bodies would result in carelessness, in favoritism, in prejudice, and in flavoring the whole administration of the act with local politics. But they do say that it is desirable in the long run that such decentralization should take place, slowly, carefully, cautiously, and after a body of men have had sufficient tenure of office, have been trained at Washington, so that they may have a national viewpoint and not purely a local one; when they have such a body of men, they think that decentralization might be carried on in a reasonably satisfactory manner.

Pages 15 to 42 of this report, if you have it before you, you will notice contain 19 recommendations, the recommendations being set forth in heavy black type, the discussion and explanation of the recommendations being in the lighter and smaller type.

Those 19 recommendations are chiefly concerned with the form and administration of the income tax law. They relate to the entire cycle of the taxpayer's duties and obligations, from the point of view of the administration of the law.

The balance of the report is mainly substantive, and treats of such matters as rates of the tax.

The committee stresses and discusses the necessity of the stability of the rate of tax, for instance. We all know—those of us who have had any dealings with the Government with respect to income taxes—that on account of the different rates existing in one year, as compared with the higher or lower rates in another year, it is a chess game between the Government and the taxpayer; the Government makes a move to get a certain amount of tax into a year in which there is a higher rate, and the taxpayer makes a move to get it into a year in which there is a lower rate; and they move back and forth, until somebody finally decides the thing, and it takes a long period of years.

This committee thinks that by having stable rates this chess-game proposition, while it will of course constantly go on to some extent, will be more or less minimized. They also recommend a single normal tax rate or single graduated scale of rates, if that is necessary, to take the place of the present normal tax and sur-taxes. They go on to discuss the double taxation of corporations in a particularly lucid and sane manner. They feel that the individual stockholder ought to be held responsible for the tax on corporate profits, taxing the corporation, for instance, merely on the retained profits.

The committee recommends that the present provisions of certain sections, such as those of Section 220—the tax on the undistributed income of corporations—is perfectly useless in its present form, the penalty of 50 per cent being too great. They characterize that rather picturesquely, as attempting to crack nuts with sledge hammers. They say that this tax on the undistributed income of a corporation should be reasonable, in order to be effective. The treatment of dividends, they claim, could be very much simplified.

I will not attempt to go into any of these questions in detail. With respect to the determination of gain and loss, they make a particular recommendation, for instance, that Section 202—sustained depreciation, obsolescence, amortization, depletion to be subtracted from the cost of the property in determining gain or loss—should be the previously allowed depreciation or obsolescence. The term "allowable depreciation or obsolescence" crept into the 1926 act and caused a good deal of disturbance to the minds of our friends and, I must confess, to a good many other people who have to deal with that sort of thing.

With respect to gain or loss on sales or exchanges, they urge a complete reform in the language and substance of sections 203 and 204 of the statute, which have to deal with those subjects. They urge a complete abolition of the exemption on earned income.

I am only picking out a few of the suggestions which they make. It would be perfectly impossible for me to discuss all the recommendations contained in the able report.

Mr. Holmes, will you address the conference?

GEORGE E. HOLMES (New York) : Mr. Chairman; The chairman
of the meeting has stated in such a splendid and succinct manner
the chief points of our report that I do not feel it necessary for any
member of the committee to enlarge upon that explanation.

The committee unfortunately, but necessarily, was hampered by
lack of time to give this very large and important subject the consideration that is necessary and desirable. It was impressed with
the importance of quite a radical and drastic revision of the law,
instead of attempting to patch the law by amendments, leaving the
old basic structure intact.

We have gone along for thirteen or fourteen years, or perhaps
longer, if we consider the 1909 corporation excise tax as a part of
our income tax system, patching and adding to and taking from
our statutes, tying one revision after another into the preceding
revision, until the statute today fairly puzzles even those who spend
all their time studying its provisions.

I have heard men who have spent all their lives in studying questions of income tax—and I know it is my own experience—say that
they cannot rely on their recollection as to any provision of the law.
They do not remember whether a particular provision is in the
1924 act or the 1921 act or the 1918 act or the 1917 act or the 1916
act or the 1913 act, or perhaps even the 1909 act.

Such a jumble of statutes prevents any attempt at building a simplified system of income tax. We feel, therefore, that the present
series of laws ought to be allowed to stand, perhaps with some
amendments, to govern the collection of revenue up to the time a
new law is passed; but then we ought to take a very clear step, and
forget all about the present patchwork proposition of an income tax
system.· That is our most important conclusion.

We have attempted in our nineteen recommendations to indicate
some of the things that might be done to simplify the income tax
law. We think periods of limitation against the Government and
for the Government ought to be measured broadly by years instead
of by days.

Take, for instance, the period of limitation that runs against the
Government, which is now a certain period of time, depending
upon the day on which the return was filed. The commissioner
may, and in some instances has, failed to keep sufficiently in mind
the particular day on which the return was filed, and has permitted
the case of a taxpayer to slide under the bar of the statute of limitations and into oblivion, merely through forgetfulness.

We feel that the statute of limitations, instead of running up to a
particular day, three or four years after the return was filed, ought
to run broadly to the end of the calendar year in which any return

was filed. And similarly, all other periods of time within which things must be done ought to be measured broadly by calendar years. For example, claims for refund should be filed before the end of a calendar year following one, two or three years, as the case may be, after the year in which the return was filed.

We have endless trouble with our periods of limitation, and we also have endless trouble with our calculation of interest. Calculation of interest on taxes due or calculation of interest on refunds to be paid the taxpayer is almost impossible under the present laws. Interest runs, as we recite in our report, from some seven or eight different points of time to some seven or eight different points of time. We suggest a statutory provision which will permit the assessment of interest from the day the tax was originally due until the day it is paid, or approximately from and to those dates. We suggest that for that purpose, the tax should be due in quarterly installments, at the beginning of the months of March, June, September and December, instead of the 15th of the month, and that the interest rate should be one-half of one per cent from the due date of the tax to the end of the month in which that tax is finally paid. That gives a simple definite calculation of interest by months, without resorting to interest tables or going through all the figuring that is necessary, to arrive at the precise amount of interest due, according to the number of days which have run.

The committee feels, after a study of the subject, and out of the experience of its members, that for the purpose of simplifying administration, questions of fraud on the revenue ought to be removed entirely from the task of collecting taxes; that the tax collecting branch of the Government ought not to be concerned with the intent of the taxpayer or the question of whether or not there was fraud in making or failing to make a return, and be charged only with the duty of referring to the Department of Justice cases where there is evidence of fraud under the statute, after which the prosecution of the case for fraud on the revenue should be entirely within the province of the Department of Justice.

But we do feel that the most important thing the taxpayer is called upon to do is to report fully and frankly to the commissioner all of those transactions and all of those items on which a tax might possibly be assessed; so we suggest that the taxpayer should assess himself, to the extent that he admits a tax liability; but where he has transactions about which he may have been advised or with respect to which he may have reached his own judgment as to tax liability, and has decided that he is not taxable, he should, nevertheless, place on his return a brief description of those transactions, so that the commissioner may have notice of them and be at liberty to examine with respect to them if he so elects, within a period of three years. If the commissioner does not act within a period of three years, it will be conclusively presumed that the taxpayer's construction of those facts is correct, and that there was no tax assessable with respect thereto.

We have also touched on the subject of jeopardy assessments. We regard the present provision of the law as granting far too great power to the commissioner, without the right of review. A jeopardy assessment should not be made, merely because of the running of time against the Government, as has been done in the past. I understand that the Treasury Department is not so prone to do it at present as it has been, but the principal activity of the department under the statute which permits jeopardy assessment has been to threaten taxpayers with jeopardy assessment unless they file waivers and thereby extend the period of limitation within which the commissioner may act. We think the jeopardy assessment should only be made in cases where it is clear that the taxpayer has done, or contemplates doing, some act which will endanger the revenue; and even in those cases, an abuse of the discretion lodged in the commissioner should be subject to review by the courts.

Another provision which we refer to in the report is that relating to transferees. At the present time, under the Revenue Act of 1924, the commissioner may proceed to collect the tax from the transferee of a corporation or an estate or any separate entity subject to tax. Where the transferor has not paid the tax, the transferee, when he receives the property of that transferor or a portion of that property, may be proceeded against in a summary way, and the tax collected from him. It is uncertain whether the entire tax may be collected from a single transferee, regardless of the amount of assets he has received, but it is the practice of the Treasury Department to assert the entire tax liability against each transferee. The existing provision may be construed by the courts to limit the commissioner to collecting up to only the amount of the assets received. This committee regards even that as going too far, and thinks the amount of tax that the commissioner should be allowed to collect from a transferee should be only that proportion of the tax which equals the proportion of the assets he has received.

We furthermore recommend the insertion in the statute of a provision requiring a corporation, trust or other separate entity subject to taxation, to file a notice of a proposed distribution, at least six months before that distribution takes place, and if it awaits the expiration of that period of six months, the distribution should then take place without any liability upon the transferees. Present Section 280 of the statute does not, in our opinion, have any proper function in a permanent revenue system.

After making our nineteen recommendations the report proceeds to a discussion of a number of substantive provisions.

We feel that the tax on corporations and the relation between a

THE FEDERAL INCOME TAX 107

corporation and stockholders, for the purpose of income tax, is sadly in need of revision. We suggest as a method for bringing this about, the taxability of the stockholder for normal and sur-tax on dividends, and the exemption of the corporation from tax on that amount of its annual net income which is distributed by way of dividends, leaving a tax to be imposed on the corporation in respect of its undistributed income at a rate which roughly approximates the interest likely to be lost over a period of years by the delayed payment of the tax by the stockholder, and leaving that surplus to be taxed to the stockholder at normal and sur-tax rates whenever it is distributed, and even in process of liquidation.

We also believe that we have gotten far enough away from March 1, 1913 to consider the advisability of falling back on the old rule announced by the Supreme Court in the case of Lynch vs. Hornsby, namely; that a dividend paid in ordinary course by a corporation shall be regarded as income to the stockholder, regardless of whether it is from earnings or profits accumulated prior to March 1, 1913, or from value accrued prior to that date. The ordinary dividend ought to be regarded as ordinary income to the stockholder.

Our present system of calculating the taxability or non-taxability of dividends, as set forth in Section 202, is awkward, difficult, complicated and unscientific.

The committee touches on the question of reorganizations, but it admits that it has no solution that appeals to its members. Some of the members of the committee have advocated going back to the rule of the 1918 act and taxing reorganizations or persons participating in reorganizations as though they had sold the stock and received in exchange cash, or the equivalent of cash, in the case of property having a market value.

The committee is in agreement only on one thing; that where stock is received for stock in a reorganization, there should be no tax upon the participating stockholder. Beyond that, where property other than stock is received, serious consideration should be given to the taxable status of the recipient.

I will not take up the time of this meeting to discuss the various items enumerated on pages 80 to 83 of the report, relating to the calculation of net income. We think the calculation of net income is entirely too complicated, too artificial; that the statute should provide for the reporting of the taxpayer's net income, as nearly as possible conforming to the net income found in commercial practice and usages, and that having found that net income, such exemptions or special deductions should be applied as Congress may decide to authorize.

The definition of gross income in the statute, particularly the definition of what is not gross income, is as obscure and complicated, as complex, artificial and incorrect, as any statement could possibly be.

I will not take up any more of the time of this meeting to expound my views or reasons for this report, as I understand the purpose is to throw the meeting open to discussion by any members who wish to raise any questions.

SIMPLIFICATION OF THE INCOME TAX

Report of Committee of the National Tax Association
George E. Holmes, Chairman

Acknowledgment

The Committee has been assisted in the preparation of the following report by suggestions from a large number of contributing members from many sections of the country. To them we acknowledge our thanks. We regret that space forbids acknowledgment to each by name.

Preface

The undersigned Committee on Simplification of the Income Tax has approached its task with full appreciation of the difficulties of the work and the impossibility of presenting any program which would meet with the full approbation of that great body of citizens who are interested in paying—or not paying—income tax. It is not unaware of the cross purposes that motivate every discussion of income tax legislation; the selfish interests of taxpayers and groups of taxpayers that preclude academic discussion of theories or rigid adherence to principles. It has endeavored in this report to present its judgment of what should be included—or omitted—in a genuine revision of our income tax system. This committee knows full well that in many of its criticisms of the present system it may seem unduly harsh and in many of its suggestions too venturesome to be followed by the Congress. New ideas are startling to most people and appalling to the conservative. The National Tax Association, however, presents a forum for discussion of new ideas, and to that forum we present our views on the shortcomings of the present system of income tax and our suggestion for improvement.

The most important consideration, occurring to the minds of the members of this committee is the genuine need of demolishing the entire present structure of our income tax system, in order to build anew, along simpler and sounder lines, a structure more adaptable to present and future conditions. We recognize the difficulties under which our revenue laws have developed; the necessity which confronted Congress of imposing our war taxes on every item of receipt that came within the category of income, and at the same time preventing the heavy exactions of war-time revenue from bearing down disastrously in exceptional circumstances. But this committee thinks we have now reached a point where many refinements can be abandoned for the sake of certainty and simplicity. Absolute equality of the tax burden can never be obtained. In a genuine revision of the law, with a view to certainty of the tax and simplicity in administration it becomes necessary to avoid, as far as possible, the pleadings of taxpayers or groups of taxpayers to modify the law in certain respects to suit their special interests. It does not advocate a sudden change and would deplore hasty action by Congress on so important a matter. The new law should be thoughtfully considered and criticized before it is enacted, and for this purpose we advocate the extension of the life of the Joint Congressional Committee for at least another year and perhaps longer, in order to give it ample time to consider a new statute. When that new statute is finally enacted its effective date should be placed at some date in the future, to enable the country to become acquainted with the new law in advance of its operation. Above all, the practice of retroactive tax imposition by Congress should be forever abandoned. Remedial legislation of a retroactive character may be necessary at times but such legislation should extend relief to all taxpayers similarly situated and not be by way of amendment of a general statute, as in the latter case it may operate with gross inequality.

The members of this committee, it may be stated, are, with exception of the chairman, men who have been privileged to observe the operation of the present income tax system within as well as without the Bureau of Internal Revenue since the enactment of the Revenue Act of 1917, Mr. Miller as Solicitor of Internal Revenue, Mr. Satterlee as draftsman of the prototype of the present regulations, Mr. James as member of the Board of Tax Appeals, Mr. Bond as a member, Mr. Hubbard as secretary and Mr. Arthur as assistant to the Advisory Tax Committee appointed by Hon. Daniel C. Roper in 1918, to organize the stupendous work confronting the Bureau of Internal Revenue at that time.

This committee realizes fully the difficulties encountered by the Bureau of Internal Revenue in administering the income tax laws, and the sources of those difficulties. It has the highest regard for the sincere efforts and the accomplishments of the personnel in coping with conditions brought about by our war-time tax legislation. Before 1918 the bureau knew practically nothing of the intricacies of an income tax. The low rates of the Revenue Acts of 1913 and 1916 did not produce any baffling problems or require any complicated procedure. No important precedents were established; no comprehensive system of auditing formulated. Until 1918 the administration of the income tax laws was a relatively simple affair.

Then, almost overnight, it became necessary to establish the largest tax-gathering organization the world has ever seen. And it had to be done in the midst of the bewilderment of war. The problem was to find men—thousands of them—and to train them in work which required a high degree of care and discernment. Routine had to be established; legal, accounting and practical problems arising under entirely new principles of taxation had to be studied and solved. The statute was experimental, unprecedented, obscure and defective. On this base a practical system of administration had to be built in haste, to stem the avalanche of tax returns, and to impound the torrential stream of revenue that was overwhelming and swamping the bureau. The mighty efforts and the endurance of the men who brought order out of this state of chaos deserve to be recorded as an important chapter in the history of the war. Preeminent among these men are Dr. Thomas S. Adams, former president of this association, and Mr. J. E. Sterrett.

If ever the power to destroy by confiscatory taxation was delegated to administrative officials it was in the Revenue Acts of 1917 and 1918. On the whole, that power was sanely exercised. But under the conditions of stress and turmoil arising from the abnormally high rates were many of the precedents established that now serve to confuse and confound any attempt at co-ordination into a system of income taxation. The violent changes in rates between 1916 and 1917, and between 1917 and 1918; the application of those rates by statute to theoretical profits, as well as actual income, and the harsh rule that the taxpayer must first pay over the tax before he could question its legality, created conditions which made the orderly and logical development of a harmonious system of income taxation impossible.

Moved by a spirit of helpfulness to the taxpayers, the Bureau of Internal Revenue in 1919 began to publish, in addition to its general regulations, hundreds of specific rulings, office decisions, office memoranda and tentative conclusions as to the construction of the law or its application to specific facts. All of the rulings could not have the deliberate consideration of a single authority in the bureau; inconsistent rulings were bound to appear. Many rulings were influenced by the exigencies of a particular case and were not seasoned enough, when published, to operate as general precedents. No inconsiderable number of rulings were found on second thought to be incorrect and had to be revoked, modified or distinguished, when applied to other cases. Finally, a very large number of rulings were never published, for one reason or another, but were distributed privately among employees of the bureau. The importance of these "secret rulings" has probably been over-emphasized, especially by those who possessed them and thereby sought to swell their own importance, but failure to publish them, when the general policy of the bureau was so lavish in the publication of rulings, provoked widespread dissatisfaction and criticism.

It has been stated that the publication of these rulings was necessary to post the large number of employees of the Bureau, both at
Washington and in the field, in the intricacies of the tax, and was
helpful to taxpayers, in aiding them in an understanding of the law.
Both purposes, however, could have been accomplished by the dis-
semination of briefer and more guarded statements supplementing
the general regulations. The rulings recited the facts of a particular case, and gave in detail the reasons for reaching certain administrative conclusions—with all the ratiocination of court opinions.
In the publication of those facts and this reasoning lay the seed for
endless discussion and argument. A court decision is the product
of two opposing forces. An administrative ruling is largely *ex parte*
and lacks the independent viewpoint. It is not within the province
of an administrative office to lay down a body of judical opinion,
without the benefit of argument pro and con which is given to the
impartial judge in court. Under normal conditions, administrative
officials are concerned primarily with the protection of the revenue,
but our imperfect statutes and intemperate rates, forced the bureau
during the war years into a quasi-judicial position and compelled it
to weigh and balance the effect of the tax on individuals and on
businesses.

It should be borne in mind that the great mass of actual decisions
in income tax cases cannot be made by the legal department of the
bureau. The rank and file which makes those decisions is composed of laymen; that is, men without legal training. It was these
men who were posted by the rulings, opinions and memoranda referred to. But it is obvious that ability to understand a legal
opinion is based on a knowledge of legal principles. And certainly
the proper application of a legal precedent requires an understanding of legal principles. Rules couched in plain, simple and forceful
language would have carried more authority to the rank and file
than the judicial language of the rulings. Many representatives of
the taxpayers were also laymen, and they would have been better
guided by simpler and shorter statements than those which the
rulings contained. Where inconsistent or conflicting rulings covered a point, the taxpayer's representative would present the ruling
most favorable to his cause. It might not be the sounder ruling, but
if the government representative was not alert he might accept it,
without further search, as sufficient authority to settle the case.
But what more frequently happened was that the government representative discovered other rulings more favorable to the Government, and then would ensue ponderous argument between layman
and layman or between layman and lawyer, on the precise meaning
of the law and of the rulings, followed perhaps by extensive briefs
in writing explaining, distinguishing and drawing analogies, followed again by further hearings. All this discussion naturally chal-

lenged more and more fine distinctions, more and more plausible arguments, until by the time one or the other of the parties appealed to the legal division of the bureau the case fairly bristled with points and had become twice as complicated as it was in the beginning and was tending further and further away from consideration of the language of the statute. The specific rulings supplied so generously by the bureau produced, in representatives of Government and taxpayer alike, tendencies

    (a) toward extreme regard for technicalities,
    (b) toward a minute scrutiny of the law, for curious, narrow, hidden meanings.
    (c) towards sophistry in the minds of the acute,
    (d) towards quibbling on the part of the disputatious,

and served as plausible excuses for error of judgment.

Human beings are subject to moods. Any human institution reflects the moods of the individuals composing it. At the beginning of the high war-rates of taxation the bureau was in a helpful mood, realizing the plight in which taxpayers found themselves. Panic-stricken taxpayers besieged the bureau for guidance and aid in problems tragic in their aspects to individuals and whole industries, and the bureau responded, so far as the law would permit. But if the mood of the bureau changes and it grows indifferent to the essential importance of settling cases, we have sufficient provocation in our obscure and complicated statutes and in our multitudinous and casuistic rulings to swamp the Board of Tax Appeals and to keep the courts ringing with tax arguments for a generation to come. There lies a real danger. Up to the present time the bureau's administration of the income tax has been perhaps as reasonable, on the whole, as the statutes warranted. Administrative defects are the outgrowth of a system of settling cases that started inevitably from the combination of obscurity, complexity, faulty conception and immoderation of the revenue acts.

There is no question that great uncertainty is encountered in the ascertainment of tax liability under our present system of administration. Protracted hearings, arguments and appeals are the order of the day. This is due in some measure to the excess profits tax, that war-time excrescence on our tax system, which, happily, has been repealed. Invested capital, amortization of war facilities, special assessment and affiliation are vanishing causes of much perplexity. But we still have with us, and always will have, complication, uncertainty and delay in the settlement of income tax, unless more radical revision is made in the statute than any since the Act of 1913.

After thirteen years of experience, with thousands of administrative rulings and hundreds of court decisions, our income tax system still fails to point out any clear path along which taxpayers may tread with certainty. Each revision of the law has added new complications; almost every decision of the courts raises new questions; litigation is rife and the highest court of appeal is found to protest by implication and expression the litigiousness of parties in tax cases. Our courts decide many cases without laying down general principles—the technicality of the statutes prevents it. Decisions are difficult to reconcile and of doubtful value as precedents. Tens of thousands of individuals are unsettled and uncertain of their tax liability for periods of four, five or six years in the past. We have periods of limitation, albeit obscure, prescribed by statute, within which assessment should be made, but the principal effect has been to burden the mails with countless waivers or to subject the taxpayer to summary assessments before the merits of his case have been adjudged.

Why should we have uncertainty and perplexity, after thirteen years of experience with income taxation? The root of the trouble lies in the complexity of the statute, and that complexity is in large part caused by the striving of Congress to make the calculation of net income a matter of fine mathematical computation. In such complicated provisions as Sections 203 and 204 lie the seed of endless controversy. The amount of tax collected from that source (reorganizations and mergers) must be relatively very little in the aggregate, possibly a small fraction of one per cent of the total tax. Yet we have a very substantial body of rulings and a number of important—though utterly confusing—decisions on the subject. The amount of argument, time and vexation which these provisions have cost Government and taxpayer is immeasurable. The minute enumeration of conditions affecting the calculation of profits arising from transactions based on reorganizations—Sections 203 and 204 are full of " ifs ", parentheses and cross references— is an invitation to acute intellects to search for hidden meanings and unenumerated conditions which might serve as loopholes to avoid taxation. In fact, the legislative history of these and the corresponding provisions of preceding laws proves that to be the case. We have had before us for many years the spectacle of agile taxpayers pursued by eager tax-collectors in a maze of statutory provisions, the old outlets of which are assiduously closed by Congress as fast as discovered and new ones inadvertently opened in the process. That these provisions will prove an endless vexation to the courts seems inevitable.

The present complicated provisions regarding interest and periods of limitation are still obscure and capable of much clarification and improvement. Improvement in the form of the return is very necessary. Its complexity appalls the average taxpayer and makes the annual reporting of net income a nightmare. Such improvement,

8

however, must be preceded by simplification of the law. The form of the statute fairly cries aloud for simplification. It is in kaleidoscopic confusion. Over two hundred and fifty cross references serve to retard the reading and understanding of the law; special provisions are intermingled with general provisions and repeated with tiresome frequency; the statute is unduly elaborated with exceptions and distinctions; it contains too much minutia that should be left to administration in the first instance and to elaboration by judicial decision where necessary.

The attempt at meticulous definition in the statute hampers the development of a practical system. When courts must discard general principles and sound judicial sense, to hang on the meaning of statutory language, we have a serious hindrance to progress by other than statutory enactment. Improvement wholly through statutory enactment is not satisfactory and never can be. Legislative bodies are too large and political stresses too many.

Frequent changes in statutory language are an abomination. We are now laboring under no less than seven statutes, no two of which are more than remotely alike. Decisions, rulings, opinions and precedents have uncertain value, where the language has been changed. Yet changes in language go on with every revision and entirely new meanings are derived from them—often meanings not clearly foreseen by Congress. Of tremendous importance is a clear, stable and comprehensible statement of general principles. Knowledge of the law is an extremely important and valuable national asset, requiring in the aggregate, millions of hours of time to acquire. That knowledge has largely been destroyed and rendered useless every time Congress has tinkered with the language of the statute. The habit of making each revision refer back to prior acts adds complexity. The next revision should be written on a clean slate and with a sharp pencil. And it should be done in advance of the year to which it will apply. Retroactive tax laws are vicious, even though unconstitutional.

It is obviously no simple thing to simplify the statute, but it is equally obviously a most desirable thing. The actual workmanship should be that of a group of skillful men, with adequate time at their disposal. It should be done with due deliberation and far from the turmoil of the political arena. Once a clear statement of general principles is enacted, it should remain unchanged in verbiage. Five or even ten years may be necessary for a clear comprehension of a statute to sink into the intelligence of a great mass of taxpayers. Once that comprehension is acquired, the burden on the Bureau of Internal Revenue, on the Board of Tax Appeals and on the courts will be vastly less than it is today. But no clear comprehension will ever be grasped by taxpayers unless frequent changing of the statute ceases.

Let us have a statute of general rules as a foundation, on which the courts can build a just and equitable system. Let us have reasonable rates tempered to the taxpayer's real ability to pay. Let such an income tax stand at unvarying rates, except in cases of national crises. Take the income tax out of politics. Let temporary deficiencies in revenue be made up from other sources. Keep the income tax steady, as a reliable backbone of national revenue, at rates that the country will accept as not too burdensome. Then concentrated on keeping alert a tax conscience. Fostered by court pronouncements and supported by the public press, it would soon be backed by intelligent public opinion. The income tax would then tend away from what it now is—a game of wits, of clever manipulation of profits, of artificial forms and technical avoidance, a game in which the sophisticated win and the unsophisticated suffer.

RECOMMENDATIONS

The first recommendation of this committee relates to the form of the Income Tax statute. The Revenue Act of 1926 covers one hundred and ten pages of closely printed small type. Viewed from the standpoint of the average income-tax payer, who is concerned only with his obligations to pay income tax, it contains a mass of irrelevant matter. Fifteen pages are given over to a statement of the estate tax, three and one-half pages to a statement of the tax on cigars and tobacco, two pages to the tax on admissions and dues. one and one-half pages to excise taxes, four pages to special taxes, four pages to stamp taxes and two pages to the tax on distilled liquors—a total of thirty-two pages, almost one-third of the act, treating of matters in which he has no interest whatever as an income-tax payer, and in which an inconsiderable minority of readers have any interest. The statement of those minor taxes in the same act with the income tax is obviously a wasteful repetition. Thousands of copies of the income tax are printed by the Government and by private agencies for distribution. These copies are thumbed over millions of times. Simple principles of efficiency dictate that they should not be encumbered with the thirty-two pages of practically no interest. The committee, therefore, makes the following as its first recommendation.

FIRST RECOMMENDATION

The income tax should be contained in a separate act, dealing solely with the one subject.

Having removed the offending pages covered by our first recommendation, we again examine the Revenue Act of 1926, from the viewpoint of a reader intent on discovering his obligations as an income-tax payer. His interest would ordinarily be in somewhat the following order:

1. What is the rate of tax?
2. On what must he pay the tax?
3. What are his exemptions?
4. When must his return be filed, and where?
5. What statements must it contain?
6. How and when must he pay his tax?

He opens his copy of the Act and is immediately confronted by a number of general definitions, of no immediate interest to himself, following by general provisions relating to " Distribution by Corporations," " Determination of Amount of Gain or Loss," " Recognition of Gain or Loss from Sales or Exchanges," " Basis for Determining Gain or Loss, Depletion and Depreciation," " Inventories," " Net Losses," " Fiscal Years," " Capital Gains and Losses " and " Earned Income "—all esoteric subjects that he can have no interest in, until he has gotten far into the complex subject of income tax. Not until he reaches the twentieth page does he find the answer to his first question (and the question probably most frequently asked about the income tax), namely, what is the rate of tax? He then fiuds it necessary to search to page 32, before he finds a statement of the exemption to which he is entitled as a single or married man or head of a family.

If he happens to be employed part time in a foreign country he has to search further for the exemption granted him on that ground, and ultimately finds it tucked away under a most misleading title among a large number of items defining what is not gross income. The definition of gross income in Section 213 (b) is, by the way, about as artificial and obscure a place to hide exemptions as could be found. The great majority of items found therein defined as *not* gross income are items of gross income in every sense of the word and should be truthfully labeled as " income exempt from tax."

Our hypothetical taxpayer then proceeds to Section 223, to ascertain whether or not he is required to make a return; to Section 227, to find out when and where the return should be filed. He turns to Sections 212, 213, 214, 215, 221, 262, 263, 1125, 1208, 1209, 1210, 1211 and 1212, to find out what his return must contain or may contain, to protect his interests.

Then he returns to Section 270 to ascertain when the tax must be (or may be) paid, but only by inference can he then assume to whom the tax should be paid. If he prosecutes his search he will find in Section 1118 a statement which may fairly definitely lead him to the conclusion that taxes should be paid to the Collector of Internal Revenue, presumably in the district in which his return is filed.

The foregoing description of the travail of an inquiring taxpayer serves to illustrate the need for improvement in the form and arrangement of the statute. Our hypothetical taxpayer, in order to satisfy himself as to his simple duties and ordinary rights under the statute, has wandered from one end to another of its one hundred and ten pages. He has encountered every provision; he has found administrative provisions in which he has no interest; long and involved statements of his right to appeal (in Section 274 and again in Section 900, *et seq.*) ; he has glanced at endless statements of the duties of partnerships, fiduciaries, corporations, withholding agents, China Trade Act Corporations, etc., etc., and has encountered a number of confusing cross references to sections in which he has no interest. The committee therefore makes its second recommendation as follows:

SECOND RECOMMENDATION

In the next revision of the statute care should be taken to state, at the beginning, the entire cycle of the ordinary taxpayer's duties and obligations, segregating special provisions, including those containing definitions at the end, having in view the desirability of making those provisions of interest to the ordinary taxpayer most accessible. Administrative provisions should be segregated in a separate part of the act. All provisions relating to the Board of Tax Appeals and to appeals to that board should be incorporated in a single statement at the end of the act or preferably printed as a separate act or embodied in the judicial code.

Having proceeded to a point where the revenue act has been shorn of extrinsic provisions, and limited to income tax provisions, and those provisions have been so arranged that those most frequently consulted can be found segregated in the forward and most accessible portion of the statute, we examine the act again, from the viewpoint of the ordinary and most numerous class of taxpayers. It appears upon this examination that the language of the statute is unduly encumbered by cross references, tending to confuse the reader and distract his attention from the subject he is pursuing. A more logical arrangement will greatly reduce the need for cross references.

We believe the language of the act can be and should be simplified, by introducing first a statement of the principles governing the typical or average taxpayer who has no interest in such exceptional matters of infrequent interest as, for example, the China Trade Act of 1922, or the benefits of Section 262.

The purpose of the statute is obviously, by means of cross references, to save words and to lead the reader to all the qualifications and exceptions to a particular statement. The difficulty of the reader lies in the necessity of following blind cross references, whether or not of interest to him, and thus confusing his train of thought. We believe all qualifications and exceptions should either be stated in the text or, wherever possible, be gathered together under the head of the exceptional subject. Foot-notes carrying cross references would be much less confusing, and this work could be well left to annotators.

The nomenclature of the act can be improved in such instances as, for example, the confusing designations of " Credits allowed individuals " and " Credit for taxes allowed individuals."

Again, there is a tiresome repetition in the statute of the clause " under regulations of the Commissioner with the approval of the Secretary." The ordinary reader is not interested to know whether or not regulations under a particular provision of the Act must be approved by the Secretary. He is interested in comprehending the gist of the provision and is disturbed by every interpolation he en- counters. Section 1101 in fact now renders the frequent repetition of this clause unnecessary.

The necessity of using generally three references to cite the statute, e. g., " Sec. 213 (b) (7) " is a complication. We recom- mend a simpler method of enumeration in a new law—a consecutive use of section numbers instead of letters denoting subdivisions, and the use of figures without parentheses to designate paragraphs.

In addition to these criticisms of the form of the statute we be- lieve no small part of the language is archaic and stilted or unduly repetitious. The expressions we have in mind are sometimes car- ried over from earlier acts, with the idea that there is something sacrosanct in language that has been used for a long time. As an example we refer to the language of Section 213, defining " gross income " as being " gains, profits and income derived from * * * interest, rent, dividends, securities * * *." " Dividends " is the name of the income derived from stock. Income is not derived from dividends. " Interest " is the name of income derived from securities. " By way of interest " would be a correct expression, but there is no sense in the expression " income derived from in- terest and securities."

We agree with the general proposition that language which has taken on a definite meaning through court decisions or long usage should not be lightly disturbed, but we contend that many expres- sions in the present statute have not taken on accepted meanings and can be improved and made more readily understandable, and that the next revision should include a complete review of the lan- guage used throughout the statute. For example, the present statute defines gross income. We believe it would be more within the ready comprehension of the taxpayer to omit the definition of gross income and substitute in its place a definition derived from an abbreviation of the language in the Act of 1916, in somewhat the following language: " Subject only to such exemptions and deductions as are hereinafter allowed, the net income of a taxable person shall include his gains, profits and income from whatever source derived."

Our next recommendation, therefore, is as follows:

THIRD RECOMMENDATION

The language of the statute should be thoroughly revised, with a view to eliminating, so far as possible, cross references, repetitions of stereotyped expressions, parenthetical in their nature, and awkward, cumbersome and obscure words or phrases.

FOURTH RECOMMENDATION

Every person required by law to file a return should do so on or before March 1 (or on or before the first day of the third month following his fiscal year).

The return may be tentative, merely stating the taxpayer's estimate of his net income, in which event a final return shall be filed within twelve months after the taxable year.

Amended returns may also be filed within twelve months after the taxable year.

The last return filed within twelve months after the taxable year shall take the place of all preceding returns and shall be the basis of the taxpayer's self-assessment.

We suggest the filing of the return on or before the first day of March for the sake of simplifying interest calculations, as more fully set forth in our seventh recommendation.[1]

We advocate the simplification of the form of return—particularly those for small taxpayers. It should not be necessary for the small taxpayer to make his return under oath, which often entails time and expense. A false return signed by a taxpayer may carry

[1] The Committee is divided in opinion on the advisability of demanding returns on smaller incomes than at present required. It is recognized that the present requirement that a return need not be filed if the gross income is less than $5000, unless the net income is $1500 for a single person or $3500 for a married person, leaves a great spread for deductions (especially in the case of single persons) with respect to which the government has no check. A single person is left to his own discretion to decide on the propriety of deductions which might reduce his gross income of almost $5000 to a net income of $1500. There are perhaps many thousands of persons under no obligation to file returns on gross income who would be found taxable if a return were required. The minimum gross income with respect to which a return should be required might well be reduced to $4000 in the case of married persons and $2000 in the case of single persons in the opinion of some of the members of this Committee. Other members are of the opinion that the additional administrative work would offset the advantage to the revenue by way of additional tax. All are agreed that some method of occasional general check-up on all adults in each collection district would be desirable.

the same penalty as one sworn to. The signatures of two witnesses would ordinarily be sufficient to attest the signing by the taxpayer.

Tentative returns should be recognized by the statute. Such returns should be very simple, and purport to be no more than a *bona fide* estimate of net income. Thereafter the taxpayer should have ample time to prepare his final return. The tentative return is sufficient to start the machinery of revenue collection. The final report is necessary only for the purpose of the commissioner in checking the accuracy of the taxpayer's self-assessment. We see no reason why final returns should not flow in steadily over the entire period of twelve months following the taxable year. That would assuredly help the situation in which many business men now find themselves of having to rush the completion of the income tax return, at a time when other taxpayers are doing the same thing and accounting assistance is at a premium. To spread the filing period for final returns over the entire year would do much to stabilize accounting work and would permit of more careful preparation of returns. The revenue would not suffer, if a tentative return has been filed and a tax paid thereon, so long as interest runs on any deficiency.

Since the taxpayer assesses himself under our system, he should be allowed a reasonable period in which to correct his assessment. We propose that he should have the year following the taxable year in which to do this. The last return filed during that year should be his "return" for all purposes and should take the place of all prior returns. It would follow from this that he would not be penalized for omitting from his first return any item of income, so long as it was reported on an amended return before the year is over. The truth or falsity of his "return" would be predicated on the last return so filed.

Furthermore, if an error was made by which he returns more net income than he finds he should, the law ought not to require him to pay tax upon his larger and incorrect statement, as it now does, but he should be permitted to adjust his second, third or fourth installments, so far as possible, to total the exact amount he considers due from himself. At present he is not permitted to do this and instances are known where taxpayers have been compelled to pay substantial sums, when no tax was due, and cases where duplicate assessments made by assessors could not be offset against subsequent installments of the tax. At present the only recourse of the taxpayer is by way of claim for refund—often a tedious procedure. To the extent that the taxpayer should not be required in the first instance to pay more tax than he admits is due from him, we recommend a restoration of the right to file claims for abatement with respect to any installment of tax after the first.

FIFTH RECOMMENDATION

One-fourth of the amount of tax finally found to be due from the taxpayer shall be deemed to have been payable on March 1, June 1, September 1 and December 1, respectively, of the year following the taxable year (or the first day of the third, sixth, ninth and twelfth months following fiscal years).

We see no reason for departing from the present practice of paying the tax in four installments. A reduction of, say, 3% of the entire tax might be offered, if the payment is made in full on or before March 1. This might serve to induce many small taxpayers to make a single payment, and thereby reduce the clerical work of sending out notices and keeping account of such sums. The general tendency now is toward making payment in four installments, even where the tax is small.

SIXTH RECOMMENDATION

In the case of any underpayment of the tax, interest shall be added at the rate of one-half of one per cent for each calendar month or fraction thereof from the date the tax was payable to the date it is paid.

The necessity of simplifying the calculation of interest prompts this recommendation. At present the provisions imposing interest on underpayments are set forth in no less than fourteen paragraphs of the law in Sections 270, 274, 276, 279 and 283. The rate is variously stated at " 6 percentum per annum " and " 1 percentum per month." The words " 6 percentum per annum " are in practice considered synonymous with " one-half of one per cent per month." The interest runs " from the date when such payment should have been made * * * until the expiration of the period of the extension," " from the date prescribed for the payment of the tax (or, if the tax is paid in installments, from the date prescribed for the payment of the first installment) to the date the deficiency is assessed or, in the case of a waiver * * * to the thirtieth day after the filing of such waiver, or the date the deficiency is assessed whichever is the earlier," " for the period of the extension," " from the date of the enactment of this act to the date such tax is assessed," " from the date of the enactment of this act up to the date of notice and demand from the collector * * *," " from the date of the jeopardy notice and demand to the date of notice and demand under this subdivision," " from the date prescribed for its payment until it is paid," " from the date of the expiration of the period of the extension until it is paid," " from the date of such demand until it is paid," " from the time fixed by the period of the extension until it is paid."

We suggest a single statement that interest shall run from the date the tax was payable until it is paid. This would be the basic period in all cases. A double rate of interest is now prescribed in some cases, e. g., as a penalty for not paying the full amount self-assessed on the return and in cases of extension of time to pay the tax. Our opinion is that penalties should not be imposed as interest and that the extension of time to pay the tax should not be the occasion for charging more than a reasonable rate for the forbearance exercised by the Government. We advocate that the term " interest ", as used in the statute, should signify only that one thing and should not be used to designate a penalty, and that the interest rate should in all cases be the same.

Instead of stating the rate at 6% per annum, we suggest " ½ of 1% for each calendar month or fraction thereof " during which the tax remains unpaid. While this may perchance result in a payment of slightly over 6% per annum, the simplicity of the calculation would justify the change. Furthermore, any inequality between this rate and 6%. per annum would disappear if the collector was required to give a 30-day notice of the tax due instead of a 10-day notice, as at present. The taxpayer would then have the option of either paying the tax within the calendar month of the notice, or paying in the following month, with the addition of ½ of 1%.

Our suggestion is that the interest shall begin to run on the first day of March, June, September and December, respectively, with respect to one-fourth of the additional tax in all cases; that the interest to be added shall be ½ of 1% for each calendar month or fraction of a calendar month, until payment is made. The calculation can be quickly made, requires no interest table or lengthy computation involving days. The amount due could be calculated by the ordinary government clerk and verified by the average taxpayer with ease and certainty.

The corresponding provision relating to interest due the taxpayer on refunds would be equally simple, as shown below in a subsequent recommendation.

SEVENTH RECOMMENDATION

The penalty for failure voluntarily to pay the full amount of tax shown by a taxpayer to be due on his return should be equal to the interest on the underpayment.

In cases where the taxpayer reports a sum to be due but fails to pay any installment in full on or before it is payable, he should be required to pay the regular rate of interest on the underpayment. Such cases would most frequently arise where his first installment is estimated to be less than that shown on his final return. But in cases where he carelessly or deliberately fails to pay such deficiency as soon as it is discovered or delays payment of an installment, and the collector is required to take the initiative, the taxpayer should be penalized by the addition to his bill of an amount equal to the interest found to be due. This in effect doubles the interest on such underpayments, but the additional amounts should be designated as a penalty and not as interest. The present rule is also that all remaining installments immediately become due, and we see no reason to change that rule.

EIGHTH RECOMMENDATION

The penalty for failure to file a return should be divided into two parts, a specific penalty and an ad-valorem penalty. It should increase with the lapse of time after delinquency.

We regard the filing of a return as the most important act to be done by the taxpayer. It initiates the routine of collecting the revenue. The precise time in which the return is filed is of secondary importance. Therefore, if the return is not filed on time a small penalty should be asserted, but if not filed within an adequate period of grace after the due date, a very heavy penalty is properly due. We suggest a specific penalty of $10 plus an *ad valorem* penalty of 5% of the tax if the return is not filed on or before the due date and in its place a penalty of $25 plus 100% of the tax if no return is filed within 12 months after the taxable year. On the other hand, the commissioner should have power to remit such part of the 100% penalty as he may deem proper, in cases where the failure to file a return was due to inability of the taxpayer. If only a tentative return is required on or before the due date and the penalty for failure to file a return is low in the first instance, the present provision permitting collectors to grant extensions of time for filing returns could be omitted from the law. The filing of a tentative return estimating even no tax liability on behalf of a taxpayer would stay the penalty for failure to file a return and subject the taxpayer only to interest on the underpayment of installments shown to be due from his final return. In other words, the tentative return would take the place of the present request for an extension.

A tentative return would place the maker on the collector's list. It may or may not show his true tax liability. The final return or its amendments would purport to show the true tax liability. The statute of limitations should, therefore, not run on tentative returns. To start that statute running a detailed statement in the form of a final return filed at some time within the year following the taxable year should be necessary. The penalty for filing a tentative return and failing to file a final return would be twofold in its nature:

(a) The statute of limitations would not apply to the taxpayer, and (b) Any additional tax found to be due from the taxpayer filing only a tentative return would be doubled, as more fully shown in our next recommendation.

NINTH RECOMMENDATION

The penalty for omitting reference in the returns to any item of taxable income should be 100% of the amount of tax found to be due by adding such item to the taxpayer's other income.[2]

We consider this to be a very important provision. It contemplates that the taxpayer who frankly makes a full report of the facts in his case, including transactions regarding which there may be doubt as to their taxability, should be protected in every way. But the taxpayer who omits from his return transactions about which there may be any question of tax liability is not fairly putting the commissioner on notice, and the statute should not run in his favor. Furthermore, the charge of fraud should be practically impossible to make against one who has submitted the facts of all transactions about which there can be any question of tax liability. He should be permitted to draw any conclusion he sees fit from the facts, but he should not be excused, except at his own peril, from revealing those facts to the commissioner. It is the practice of cautious taxpayers now to attach riders to their returns stating the facts of transactions which they themselves believe not taxable, but with respect to which other conclusions of fact or law can possibly be drawn. We suggest this be made compulsory, as we believe it most essential to proper and speedy administration, that the taxpayer be frank in his disclosure to the commissioner and that concealing transactions which may be on the border line between tax and no tax, until he is forced to disclose them (often in the hope that they may not be discovered) is reprehensible.

Certainly the statute should not run with respect to matters not disclosed on the return, whether or not there was concealment with intent to defraud the revenue.

We advocate a penalty of 100% of the tax found to be due on items to which no reference is made in the return, but no penalty if the item is reported or referred to in the taxpayer's return. This we think should be stated on the return where the taxpayer is bound to see it when he signs. The deterrent effect of a penalty is strengthened, when it is called to his attention at the opportune time and is weakened if hidden away where it is not likely to be noticed.

As incident to the foregoing, we suggest that a space should be

[2] Some members think the penalty should not exceed 25%.

inserted in the return for the enumeration of transactions about which there is doubt of taxability.

It may be mentioned further at this point that tentative returns should be accepted, if signed by an agent of the taxpayer, but the law should provide that final returns must be signed by the tax-payer, unless he is physically or mentally unable to do so. Even though a return is prepared for him by another, the taxpayer him-self should sign it. Since he will have the greater part of a year in which to do so, present reasons of temporary absence, sickness, *et cetera,* will not be valid.

We suggest a penalty of 100% of the amount of tax found to be due with respect to any omitted item, the amount of such tax to be found by adding the omitted item to the taxpayer's other income. The present penalty for a fraudulent return is 50% of the amount of the deficiency found by the commissioner. This penalty operates in a very uncertain manner. For example, if the commissioner discovers that a taxpayer has fraudulently omitted a receipt of net income of $1,000 from his return but has also overlooked his right to claim deductions which properly reduce his tax by $1,000, there is no deficiency and consequently no penalty can be imposed. On the other hand, if the taxpayer has fraudulently omitted $1,000 and also has in good faith claimed deductions which are disallowed to an extent which increases his tax by $1,000, the penalty is imposed on $2,000, which is the amount of his deficiency. Our suggestion is that in both cases the penalty should be imposed on $1,000.

Furthermore, fraudulent intent is a difficult thing to prove. The administrative officers should not be required to concern themselves with the problem. The tax and penalty should be collected on the ground of failure to report the omitted item. If evidence of fraud is found to taint any return of a taxpayer the only duty of the ad-ministrative officers should be to properly notify the Department of Justice and to render such assistance to that department as may be required. Prosecution for fraud on the revenue should be entirely dissociated from the collection of the revenue. The collection of the tax, interest and penalties should be predicated upon facts readily capable of ascertainment.

TENTH RECOMMENDATION

The period in which the commissioner must act in revising a tax-payer's self-assessment should be three years from the end of the year in which the final return is filed, with respect to all items re-ported on the return.

As stated above, the statute of limitations should not run on ten-tative returns and should not run with respect to any items of in-come not reported by the taxpayer. With respect to all items reported by the taxpayer the commissioner should be required to send the taxpayer a final assessment letter before the end of the third year following the year in which his final return was filed. We suggest for the sake of certainty that this period of limitation end with a calendar year. Taxpayers having fiscal years would, under this provision. extend for one year the period in which the commissioner can act, by delaying the filing of their final returns until the calendar year following that in which their fiscal year ends. But if the return is filed promptly in the same calendar year as that in which the fiscal year ends, the statute of limitations would expire on the same day as in the case of those filing on the basis of the calendar year.

The advantage, it seems to us. lies in having a readily ascertainable date on which the statute expires. with respect to a general group of taxpayers. At present the statute requires assessment to be made within "three years after the return was filed." This necessitates a close watch being kept on the exact date on which a return was filed. Any uncertainty as to that date may endanger the collection of revenue. We recommend a definite date, namely December 31, to apply to all returns filed in a calendar year.

Instead of requiring the assessment to be made within that period, we suggest that the act to be done by the commissioner shall be the mailing of the final assessment letter. This is an act participated in by the taxpayer, while the act which must now be performed within the statutory period is an act done in secret, within the Bureau of Internal Revenue. It is not always easy to ascertain when an assessment is placed on the list. Last-minute entries on the assessment list always create uncertainty. We think the act of the commissioner to be done within the statutory period should be to challenge the taxpayer's self-assessment. All acts after that. namely appeal. assessment and collection should be subject to periods of limitation running from the date of the assessment letter.

In any case where the commissioner finds the taxpayer has overpaid the tax, refund or credit should be made without the necessity of filing a claim.

ELEVENTH RECOMMENDATION

The assessment should be made within six months after the date of the assessment letter and the tax should be collected or distraint or other proceedings for collection commenced within one year from such date, unless appeal is taken by the taxpayer or extension of time to pay the tax is granted by the commissioner.

We feel that the present period of six years after assessment in which to collect by distraint or by a proceeding in court is too long. It tends to encourage laxity in collection of the tax. Once the assessment has been made, prompt action should be required to protect the revenue. One of four things should happen within a year after the final assessment letter has been sent out: (1) Appeal should be taken by the taxpayer, or (2) The tax should be paid, or (3) Steps should be taken to enforce collection, or (4) A definite agreement should be reached with the commissioner for the extension of time of payment.

TWELFTH RECOMMENDATION

The time for filing a petition with the Board of Tax Appeals should be extended to ninety days after the assessment letter.

The present period is sixty days. It is believed that a longer period will result in better preparation of the petition and less occasion for amending petitions.

THIRTEENTH RECOMMENDATION

Jeopardy assessments should be authorized only in cases where the taxpayer's financial position or his act, or contemplated act, endangers the collection of the revenue. In all cases of jeopardy assessment the taxpayer shall be notified immediately, of the reasons for such assessment and the basis of the assessment. Action should lie in the District Courts of the United States to cancel or reduce such assessment, where an abuse of discretion appears.

Jeopardy assessments, we believe, should be limited to cases where the taxpayer has done or contemplates doing some act which will jeopardize the tax. The mere running of the statute should not be an excuse for assessments founded on surmise and often proved to be erroneous or excessive. The jeopardy provision has been used as a club to compel the taxpayer to waive the statute and that state of affairs should not find a permanent place in our income tax system. The arbitrary imposition of large assessments — and the amount of tax in jeopardy assessments is always found by resolving all doubtful points of liability in favor of the Government—and the consequent distress and financial loss to the taxpayer, who must either pay at once or put up a bond for the amount of the tax, are things contrary to good conscience, when the assessment is brought about by no fault of the taxpayer, but on the contrary by the negligence or inability of the Government, to keep pace with its work. The taxpayer should be notified immediately of the basis of the tax and the reason for the summary assessment. Since our suggestions include the proposition that the statute shall not run on matters not disclosed in the return, but only on matters disclosed in a return, whether reported as a part of the income statement or by rider or schedule attached, it does not appear to us proper that failure of the Government to act in due time upon the notice so given it, should be an excuse for compelling the taxpayer to extend further time for the settlement of his case.

The jeopardy assessment is so drastic an action that some power of immediate review should be vested in the courts. Jeopardy assessments are initiated in Washington and it is conceivable that misapprehension may exist either (a) as to the probable amount of tax due from the taxpayer or (b) his ability and willingness to pay. The taxpayer should have the protection of the courts against any possible abuse of this great power to assess taxes without first giving him his " day in court." The commissioner's action should be subject to review.

FOURTEENTH RECOMMENDATION

Taxpayers should be permitted to file claims in abatement in cases where the tentative or final return overstates the tax and a corrected return is filed before all installments have been paid.

At present a taxpayer has no relief, except by way of refund, in cases where he has made his self-assessment too high in the first instance and discovers the error after paying the first installment of the tax. He, therefore, finds himself in the position of paying into the Treasury, money which he knows is not owing to the Government. If a duplicate assessment is made by the collector, both assessments must now be paid and recourse had to a claim for refund. The use of claims for abatement would enable the taxpayer to avoid paying such palpably erroneous assessments. Such claims are now prohibited by the statute. We recommend the restoration of their use, in cases of mistakes in assessments, where the full amount of the tax has not been paid.

FIFTEENTH RECOMMENDATION

The right to file claims for refund should expire (a) at the close of the third calendar year following the one in which the return was filed or (b) at the close of the calendar year following the one in which final payment of tax was made and (c) in cases where the decision of a federal court of last resort materially affects the calculation of the tax for a prior year, the right to file a claim for refund should exist from the date of such decision to the end of the calendar year following the one in which the decision was rendered.

This recommendation is made to simplify the calculation of the period of limitation with respect to refunds. It follows the broad line of periods measured by the close of a calendar year, rather than by specific dates. We also suggest in this recommendation the introduction of a new period during which claims for refund may be filed, namely, from the date of a decision of a court of last resort to the end of the following calendar year. It is customary at present, when a case of general importance is pending, to file claims for refund based on the construction of the law urged by the taxpayer in such case. If the case is not decided within two years after such refund claims were filed, a great many new actions are commenced in the courts solely for the purpose of protecting the right to recovery until the test case is decided. Since there is a way for the sophisticated taxpayer to prolong his right to recovery until test cases have been decided, our suggestion is that the complicated procedure for so prolonging rights to recovery be abolished and the right to recovery be extended for a reasonable time to all taxpayers affected by the decision on the test case.

SIXTEENTH RECOMMENDATION

If the commissioner rejects a claim for refund or fails to act on it for a period of six months after it is filed, the taxpayer's right to commence action thereon should expire at the end of the calendar year following the one in which the claim for refund was filed.

This deals with the time in which the taxpayer must act, in case the commissioner fails to act on his claim for refund or rejects it. Here as in other instances, where periods of time are measured, we believe it advisable to specify a general date, measured broadly by the calendar year, rather than one which requires computation from a specific day. We believe such period will be easier to remember and to bear in mind. It may give one taxpayer more time than another, depending upon the accident of filing his claim early or later in a calendar year, but we do not see that this is a material objection. The offsetting advantage of knowing that his right ends with a calendar year is desirable as a simplification. It is infinitely easier to remember the year in which a thing was done than the day on which it was done.

The periods of time indicated in the last two recommendations would give a taxpayer at least four years after his taxable year, and at most five years, to file his claim for refund; and approximately two years more in which to sue thereon. Experience would show whether this length of time is sufficient. If not, the time to sue could be extended another year.

SEVENTEENTH RECOMMENDATION

All refunds, or overassessments credited against taxes due for other years, should bear interest from the date the tax was due to the beginning of the month in which the refund is paid or the overassessment credited.

Refunds now bear interest, but there is no clear delimitation of the period, and very often the taxpayer is made to lose a considerable amount of interest by lapse of time between the date the refund

9

is allowed and the date it is actually paid. We propose the same principle here as in the case of interest on deficiencies in payment of tax, except, however, that interest shall be paid from the original due date of the tax to the first day of the month in which the refund is paid, instead of the last day, as in the case of underpayment. This will tend greatly to simplify the calculation of interest. For the converse provisions, see our sixth recommendation.

EIGHTEENTH RECOMMENDATION

The filing of a claim for refund should open the return for the same year, for additional assessment.

Where the claim for refund affects the tax liability of the taxpayer for other years, the increase in tax liability should be offset against the refund allowed.

When an additional tax found to be due in one year affects the tax liability for other years, the additional tax should be offset by the consequent reduction of tax liability in other years.

The filing of a claim for refund should open the taxpayer's return for that year for all purposes, so that the commissioner may consider the tax for the year as a whole, in acting upon the refund. Many cases are necessarily settled by a species of compromise, that is, the commissioner will concede a doubtful point in favor of the taxpayer and decide another against him. If the taxpayer accepts the favorable part of a settlement and later on files a claim for refund on the points decided against him, the commissioner should not be handicapped by being unable to consider the case as a whole. If a taxpayer desires to press a claim for refund, he ought to be willing to have that claim settled with respect to his real tax liability. It is believed that if the commissioner is given this power it will have a salutary effect on the taxpayer and restrain him from claiming refunds unless he feels secure in the conviction that his case is not vulnerable on other points. Likewise, if a claim for refund is justly allowable for one year but an increase in tax follows logically in another year, only the net amount due the taxpayer should be paid. Similarly in the case of additional tax, such adjustments should be made, regardless of any statute of limitations.

NINETEENTH RECOMMENDATION

In case of the distribution of the assets of a corporation to a successor corporation or to its stockholders, and in the case of distribution of the corpus of estates and trusts, the commissioner shall be notified by registered mail of the proposed distribution and shall immediately examine into the liability for income tax of such corporation, estate or trust. After such examination has been made and the additional tax, if any be found to be due, has been paid, and in any event, after six months from the giving of such notice, the distributees may receive their respective shares of the assets distributed, without any liability for income tax. If distribution is made without giving such notice or within six months thereafter, unless in the meantime an examination has been completed by the commissioner and no tax found to be due, the distributees shall remain liable for the taxes due but unpaid by the corporation, estate or trust, each for that proportion of tax equal to the proportion of assets he received, and no more.

Section 280 must be regarded as an expedient to remedy a situation arising in the past. It is generally condemned and should not be a part of a new revenue system. Instead of waiting until a taxpayer has parted with his assets, action should be taken while the assets are still in his possession. Our suggestion is that before a distribution is made which will result in substantially all the assets of a corporation, trust, estate, or other taxable entity being distributed to stockholders or beneficial owners, the commissioner should be served with notice of the proposed distribution and should proceed diligently to settle the question of tax liability, in order that the recipients may receive their respective shares of the assets without danger of a liability for taxes of the preceding holder of title. If the commissioner neglects for six months to assert any additional tax liability against the transferor, the case should be closed against him as to the transferees and the liability, if any, should be solely that of the transferor. Only in cases where the transferor or transferees fail to give him notice of the proposed distribution, should the tax liability descend on the transferees, and then only in proportion to the amount of assets received.

RATES OF TAX

We have not considered the propriety of any particular rates of tax, and do not regard a discussion of rates within the scope of our report. We are convinced, however, that a most essential factor in the simplification of the law is stability of rates. Changes in the rates should be made as infrequently as possible and then with as slight an adjustment as conditions permit. It necessarily follows that reductions in rate should be made with utmost caution and only to the extent that may be regarded as somewhat permanent. We strongly urge that temporary needs for revenue be met by temporary taxes on other objects than income, leaving the income rates unvarying, except in the case of national crises. Much of the difficulty of administration in the past ten years has been due to violent fluctuation in rates. When rates in one year are two, three or four times as high as in adjoining years, the time element be_ comes of paramount importance. Inventory, installment sales, depreciation, depletion, and practically every difficult subject of dispute between taxpayer and Government loses importance, if the rate next year or the year after is the same as today. It is the desire of the taxpayer to have gains fall in years of low rates and deductions in years of high rates, pitted against a contrary incentive on the part of the Government, that has produced a very large part of our tax disputes. Unvarying rates would do much to ameliorate this condition; a single flat rate of tax would do the rest. Since, however, we are committed in our income tax policy to graduated rates, the lower the maximum rate may be, the nearer we approach simplicity, so far as the time element of taxable transactions is concerned. A graduated tax based on an average of three or five years' income of the taxpayer would also tend to reduce the importance of the time when income was received or deduction accrued. If high rates of surtax are imposed, the principle of the three or five years' average increases in importance. The lower the maximum surtaxes, the less it is important to smooth out the peaks of extraordinary receipts in the net income curve of the taxpayer.

The present rates of normal and surtax require simplification. We have now a graduated normal tax as well as a graduated surtax. The normal tax should be at a flat rate, and the first gradation should be the beginning of a surtax. The present complication arises from a desire to give the taxpayer of very small income a concession in his tax, at the same time giving other taxpayers the benefit of deduction of the "credits" against normal tax at a higher rate. We suggest at this point a search for a solution which will permit a simpler statement of rates, possibly a combination of normal and surtax rates in a single graduated scale. One reason for retaining the normal tax as a separate schedule is the exemption of dividends from normal tax. We believe a simpler and more equitable plan would be to tax dividends as ordinary income is taxed, that is for both normal and surtax. Our reasons are given below.

DOUBLE TAXATION OF CORPORATE INCOME

Net income of corporations is now taxed at the rate of 13½% to the corporation. It is exempt from normal tax. But the normal tax is only 1½%, 3% or 5%. The stockholder of small means pays indirectly 13½% to save 1½%. The differential is 12% against him. The intermediate rate payer has a differential of 10½% against him, while the most able taxpayers have a differential of only 8½% against them. Here is a beautiful example of a tax on the theory of ability to pay gone wrong.

Corporations may be regarded in one of two lights for purpose of income tax, either (a) separate entities, to be taxed as such, or

(b) mere conduits through which income passes to natural persons. Congress has now chosen neither position, although in the earlier income tax acts it chose the latter and for convenience collected the normal tax (which was then at a flat rate) from the corporation, giving the stockholder an equal reduction in his tax on dividends. Now it cannot be said that any of the tax is assessed on corporations, as a means of collection at the source, without implying that more is collected from some stockholders than from others.

We advocate, for the sake of avoiding double taxation on incomes derived through dividends, as compared with incomes derived from other sources, a return to the idea that a corporation is merely a conduit through which income passes and that the only recipient who should be taxed is the natural person as stockholder, who enjoys the income earned by the corporation.

Our argument against taxing corporations as such is that it results in an unfair discrimination (though not illegal) against corporations, as compared with partnerships and sole traders. Answer will probably be made that the partners and the sole traders are taxed at normal and surtax rates on the entire net income of the year, while the corporation is taxed only at a flat rate, and the stockholders only at surtax rates on that portion of the year's earnings paid out as dividends. This answer is not convincing, as ultimately all the net income of a corporation is likely to be paid out in current dividends or by liquidation in dissolution, unless it is lost in the business. In those cases where earnings are successfully accumulated over a long period of time, the consequent increase in value in the corporate assets is reflected in the value of the stock, and the stockholder who sells his stock pays indirectly a tax on the undistributed surplus. It is only in the case of stockholders who die and whose stock is passed on by devise or bequest, that a loss in revenue may occur—and then only by reason of the exemption granted by law to the heirs. The desideratum in a tax law is an equitable distribution of the tax burden and in the case of income tax, in accordance with ability to pay. Our present system of taxing corporations does not accomplish this end. To treat the corporation as a mere conduit of income, in the manner which we propose for consideration, will come nearer accomplishing the desired end.

If the corporation is treated as a mere conduit of income, the ideal manner of taxing the stockholders would be on their share of the earnings for the year, whether distributed or not. Aside from any legal or constitutional consideration, this is not feasible. For one thing, unless distribution were actually made, the minority taxpayer might not, except at great inconvenience, be able to pay his tax upon income which he has no power to presently enjoy.

One method might be to place a reasonable tax on the corporation on that portion of the income which it does not actually distribute. It is impossible to make this amount even roughly approximate the revenue which would be collected, if complete distribution were made, as the conditions vary in each and every corporation. It should therefore rather be considered as a premium tax paid by the corporation for its stockholders, in exchange for retaining the earnings in the business and thereby postponing the normal and surtax until a future day. For that purpose a tax of 10% on that amount of its net income which exceeds the dividends paid out in any year would be a reasonable tax.

Argument has been made that this form of tax is uneconomic, because it creates an incentive to pay out dividends instead of plowing the profits back into the business. One answer might be the question, Why should the Government permit corporations to accumulate partly tax-paid surplus to plow back into the business, where it insists on the full tax on surpluses of partnerships and individuals, even though they are plowed back into the business? The argument of an individual that he should receive an exemption from tax on that part of his year's earnings which goes back into his business would receive short shrift.

We emphasize again that the rate of tax on the undistributed earnings should be reasonable, bearing in mind that when those earnings are later distributed, they will bear the full normal and surtax. The tax on undistributed earnings must be looked on in the light of a premium paid for the privilege of deferring distribution and should be reasonable as viewed in that light.

Section 220

We are unanimously of the opinion that the present provision of the revenue act purporting to tax the undistributed income of corporations is a useless member of our income tax system. The record shows that it has not been effective to accomplish the purpose intended. Cracking nuts with sledge hammers has never been noted for success, and that is apparently what Congress intended to do, when it provided a penalty of 50% of the entire *net income* of a corporation for an offense which is *malum prohibitum* and not *malum per se,* one which is extremely difficult of proof, namely; the accumulation of profits beyond the reasonable needs of the business, for the purpose of preventing the imposition of the surtax on the stockholders. Let us pause for a moment to consider the many conditions which must exist before this tax can be imposed.

1. Intent to evade the surtax must be proved. Does this mean the intent of the corporation? or of its officers? or of its board of directors? of its principal stockholders who control the board of directors? or of all its stockholders? Unless it can be shown to be the intent of all the stockholders, the imposition of the penalty-tax

must necessarily be a visitation of punishment on the innocent as well as the guilty—a principal abhorrent to justice and foreign to our law. The difficulty of proving a fraudulent intent (which is the intent implied in the statute) of a group comprising minority stockholders who had no authority to dictate the policy of the corporation, and perhaps no knowledge of its affairs, is obvious, and any attempt to discover and prove such intent is futile and vain. Therefore, the provision must be limited in its application to corporations having only a very few stockholders, and the moment consideration is directed to a corporation having more than one stockholder the difficulty increases in geometrical proportion.

2. Having proved the intent or purpose for which the corporation was organized or is conducted to be the avoidance of surtaxes, it becomes necessary to prove that the corporation's gains and profits are actually accumulated in excess of the reasonable needs of the business. The word " reasonable " is a term extremely difficult to define. It requires particular inquiry into each set of facts and the exercise of fine judgment, based on experience and intimate knowledge of the business and affairs of the corporation whose acts are the subject of inquiry. Only in the most rare cases can conclusion be reached with any definiteness at all, regarding the reasonable needs of the business of a corporation. Corporations are formed primarily to grow and expand. It is unwise and uneconomic to prohibit that growth, and to subvert a most important factor in our economic system to the ends of a graduated surtax on individuals. If proof of the reasonable needs of a business is adduced before a court, it will naturally give great weight to the opinion of the managers or directors; their testimony would be practically conclusive, in the absence of a showing of bad faith. To pit administration officers against such difficulties is unwise if not absurd.

3. A penalty which amounts to 50% of the entire net income of a corporation, including dividends, which are not ordinarily taxed, and interest on United States obligations which have been solemnly declared in the acts under which they are issued to be subject only to certain definite taxes, is so drastic as to alienate the sympathy of administrative officers and courts, if not actually to be in violation of the constitutional provision against unwarrantable fines and seizures.

An example will serve to expose the unreasonable harshness of this provision.

A holding corporation with a single stockholder (whose surtax is in the maximum bracket) has an income of $100,000. It pays out $75,000 and is held to have retained $25,000 beyond the reasonable needs of its business. The total tax paid by the corporation and its stockholder would be

Corporation tax $15,606
Surtax 15,000
Sec. 220 50,000

Total................................. $80,606

The amount of revenue lost to the Government by the corporation failing to pay out all its income is $5,000—the penalty is $50,000. The figures speak for themselves.

It is no answer to say that the statute presents an alternative by which the stockholder could have included (*at the time of filing his return*) a fictitious amount equal to the undistributed income. For one thing, a stockholder often does not have any knowledge of the amount of net income of the corporation at the time of filing his return, as individual returns are filed in many cases before the corporation accounts are finally made up. Furthermore, the stockholder may have acted in perfect good faith in believing at the time of filing his return that the undistributed income of the corporation was necessary for its business, only to have his judgment overruled by the administrative officers, upon a later examination of the corporation return at which time they may be vastly influenced by subsequent events. It is no cause of wonder to this committee that the administrative officers have proceeded with utmost caution and reserve in attempting to administer this section.

The suggestion has been advanced that Congress intended the statute to be so drastic as to strike terror in the hearts of stockholders contemplating this form of tax avoidance. In short, that the provision is a bogey—a scarecrow. If so, it has long ago ceased to serve any useful purpose. It has been found out. Nothing is more undignified and contemptible than a scarecrow which has outlived its usefulness, and to this category we consign Section 220.

We recognize that it is highly desirable that profits of corporations, not necessary for the proper and reasonable current and prospective purposes of the business, should find their way into the hands of the stockholders, in order to be taxed along with other profits. We deplore the condition which now exists, whereby profits can be shunted from the class of current income subject to surtax rates into the class of capital gains, by the distribution of corporate surpluses in dissolution of the corporation. We have no doubt this avenue of escape is frequently used. We also do not question the fact that the accumulation of surplus by a great many industrial corporations may be somewhat in excess of the reasonable needs of the business, difficult as that is to prove. We believe a gentle but steady pressure should be placed on all corporations to make the fullest reasonable distribution to stockholders. That pressure will be exerted by adopting into the statute the plan of taxing corporations above described. If no tax is imposed on the corporation with respect to the net income paid out to the stockholders and a tax of 10% on that retained, every directors' meeting for the declaration of dividends will take into consideration, as a business proposition whether or not it is worth while to pay .10% for the privilege of retaining the earnings in the business, and unless a genuine reason exists for so doing, the incentive to save the tax will be added to the other incentives which actuate directors in paying dividends to stockholders. In short, the best qualified persons to judge of the reasonable needs of the business will have a steady pressure brought to bear on them to pare the surplus down to actual needs and reasonable requirements.

The present Section 220 has had no effect on the active industrial corporation. The proposed plan will.

The investment and holding company is often a personal or family affair, with few stockholders. If all the stockholders are wealthy and therefore pay surtaxes, in the maximum brackets, they may welcome the imposition of a 10% tax on the entire corporate earnings, rather than a 20% tax on dividends and permit the corporation to continue to accumulate its earnings until the stockholders die and their interests are passed on to heirs. But the heirs will be in no better position as respects the dividends and sooner or later, by division of the stock among descendants, the surplus will be drawn on and the consequent taxes paid. The result is merely a postponement of the tax on dividends—a privilege paid for by the tax on undistributed income. Assuming the income tax to be a permanent part of our federal revenue system, the delay in the payment of the tax is not an evil. The 10% on the undistributed income is equal to 50% of the tax on the dividend, assuming that tax to be 20%. The proposed tax on undistributed income therefore is tantamount to the collection in advance of 50% of the amount of tax to be paid at some future date. Even if the income is not distributed for fifteen years, a fair rate of interest will have been received on the postponed tax.

Another objection has been weighed by the committee. It has been stated that while the plan of taxing undistributed profits may operate fairly in general, it will militate against that class of corporation, frequently having large incomes, which, by reason of some exigency of the business, does not earn enough per share to warrant paying a dividend. Certain public utility corporations are said to fall into this class, by reason of limited income, due to fixed rates on the one hand and constant necessity for increasing equipment on the other. The mere fact that such incomes are large in amount, does not seem to us relevant. Whether income is $10,000 or $5,000,000, the rate remains the same, and it is no greater hardship on the larger corporations to pay $500,000 than it is for the former to pay $1,000. In either case it is ten per cent and only ten per cent.

The other argument, namely that income is fixed and need for extensions urgent, is in fact an argument that any corporation might advance. We can see no special need for sympathy here any more than in the case of the individual who protests against a tax on his income because he re-invests it in his business. It may or may not be an economic fallacy not to exempt saved income from tax, but we are committed to the principle of taxing income, whether saved or not, and the point is that a desire or a need to save income should not be recognized as an argument against a tax on undistributed income of corporations, any more than it would be recognized as an argument to exempt an individual on his saved income.

Our closing statement on this point is that the tax on undistributed income should be reasonable in amount: otherwise it will defeat its purpose and if too high, be an instrument of oppression arousing the just resentment of a substantial group of taxpayers.

DIVIDENDS—IN GENERAL

Section 201 can and should be very greatly simplified. There is a growing conviction on the part of many thoughtful students of taxation that we are now far enough away from March 1, 1913, to warrant us in returning to the simple rule in *Lynch* v. *Hornby*, 247 U. S. 339, in which case the United States Supreme Court declared, under the language of the Revenue Act of 1913, that a dividend paid *in ordinary course* by a corporation was subject to tax, regardless of when the earnings of the corporation had been accumulated. Later a rule was inserted in the statute that dividends from earnings or profits accumulated prior to March 1, 1913, could be distributed free from tax to the stockholders. This rule was later enlarged to embrace also "increase in value of property accrued before March 1, 1913." Such exemption was entirely justified in the years of high tax rates, but on return to normal post-war conditions and the consequent lowering of rates, a great step toward simplicity lies in the uniform taxation of dividends as current income, regardless of the original source thereof.

For one thing, such simple rule would obviate the awkward and complex rule as to order of distribution of corporate income. The rule now is that profits accumulated after February 28, 1913, must first be distributed before tax-free surplus, representing earnings, profits or increase in value prior to that date can be passed on to stockholders. This artificial rule ignores a well-settled rule of law that a surplus cannot be earmarked but that every dollar paid out as a dividend partakes of the character of the entire surplus and is in fact a slice of all earnings for all years. The rule in Section 201 presupposes that whatever surplus or value existed on March 1, 1913, continues in existence until distributed, regardless of losses since that date, at least so far as such losses can be offset by later earnings. It was an expedient rule in its day, but is not a simple or logical rule worthy of position in a revised law.

One complication of the rule referred to above is that tax-free distribution "shall be applied against and reduce the basis of the stock provided in Sec. 204." This is taken to mean that tax-free distributions are considered as returns of capital to the stockholders. That is a recent modification of the rule. At one time it was not considered so, but was regarded as tax-free income. The rule provokes complications in the computation of gain or loss from the sale of stock, under the statutory rule in Section 204(b). The rule is easily overlooked or forgotten by the taxpayer in calculating gain or loss, for, strange to say, in a statute replete with cross references, there is no reference to this rule either in Section 202 containing the rules for determining the amount of gain or loss, or in Section 204(b) describing the basis for determining gain or loss. One consequence is added administration difficulty in verifying the accuracy of the taxpayer's calculation.

A rule that all dividends paid in ordinary course should be subject to tax would simplify the calculation of annual income and of profit on the sale of stock.

The committee strongly urges, however, that the present rule exempting from tax dividends from earnings, profits or value accrued prior to March 1, 1913, should not be changed, without giving corporations a reasonable period in which to distribute such tax-free dividends to their stockholders. The rule having been in effect for a number of years is undoubtedly relied on by corporations having surpluses of the character specified and who contemplate tax-free distributions. Such corporations should have a reasonable opportunity to make their distribution before any new rule goes into effect. This observation applies particularly to "personal service corporations" referred to in Section 201(e).

DIVIDENDS IN LIQUIDATION

Pursuant to the plan hereinabove described of taxing corporations on the undistributed income, we suggest that dividends in liquidation be subject to normal and surtax, to the extent that the liquidating dividend represents a distribution of earned surplus. The present rule operates to subject liquidating dividends to the capital gains tax. It opens up an easy avenue for shunting profits from the higher rates of surtax to the lower rates of capital gains tax, by merely permitting the earnings to accumulate until liquidation takes place. An attempt is made in the statute to prevent this result, in Section 201(g), but that provision calls for the exercise of discretion and presents many administrative difficulties. A simple rule that all dividends shall be deemed to be from surplus, until the surplus is exhausted, would go far toward completing the simplification of Section 201, and would prove effective in preventing the escape of normal and surtaxes, through the channel of capital gains.

Any revision of Section 201 should omit subdivision (f) ."a stock dividend shall not be subject to tax." The language is not clear, for one thing, as it does not define the phrase "stock dividend" to include preferred stock, debenture stock or other special stock which may be paid to common stockholders, and purports merely to repeat a well-known rule of law laid down by the Supreme Court.

DETERMINATION OF AMOUNT OF GAIN OR LOSS.

The particular recommendation of this committee with respect to the substance of Section 202 is that the sustained depreciation, obsolescence, amortization and depletion, which must be subtracted from the cost of property, or other basis, should be that which has been actually allowed instead of that which has "been allowable." In using the word "allowable" Congress has strayed into the field of speculation and surmise, theory and conjecture. It is a necessary evil that administration officers and taxpayers must wrangle over the proper allowances for depletion, amortization, obsolescence, depreciation and similar deductions, in the computation of annual income. (A steady reasonable rate of tax will minimize the importance of fine calculations of depreciation, et cetera, with respect to annual income.) To calculate the actual profit of a seller of property, by reference to what an administrative officer thinks the annual loss by way of depreciation, et cetera, should have been in theory, is to invite dispute and litigation. The average revenue agent is so intent on making a showing of assessment of additional tax that he is incapable of exercising calm judgment on so delicate a problem. Only in exceptional cases does an adjustment of this character find acceptance from the taxpayer without appeal to Washington. At best such annual losses are mere estimates. In calculating annual income some correction of this estimate is possible as the taxpayer goes along, but in a final calculation on a sale, such current correction is impossible. The rule which obtained in the Revenue Act of 1924 is more equitable, namely: to reduce the cost by the depreciation, et cetera, "previously allowed." By this rule the taxpayer does not escape taxation, his adjustment can be precisely determined by reference to his books or tax returns, and there can be no dispute between taxpayer and administration over the result.

The purpose of Congress in adopting the word "allowable" in the 1926 Act was apparently to cover cases where the seller's basis is cost paid prior to March 1, 1913, and no depreciation was "allowed" prior to that date, because there was no income tax.

The fear expressed by the Committee on Ways and Means in its report was that "the taxpayer may receive too large a basis for determining gain or loss" if only allowed depreciation is taken into consideration. Our answer to this defense of the present statutory provision is: (1) There was a corporation excise tax in effect between 1909 and 1913, and to that large and important class of taxpayers the remarks of the committee would apply with considerably less force and the rate in the years immediately following 1912 was so low as to be comparable with no tax at all. Varying rates of tax make the annual depreciation allowance of varying value to the taxpayer, and if there is any merit in insisting on a theoretical deduction for years in which no income tax existed, it should be equally meritorious to make adjustments on the ground that in years of very low rates of tax, or of very high rates of tax, the allowance should be adjusted on the basis of the tax benefit derived by the taxpayer. For example, a taxpayer may have saved 80c. on the dollar by his deduction in 1918, 1c. on the dollar in 1913. In either event he now pays, say, 12½c. on the allowance formerly given him. It is impossible to make a fine compensating adjustment in his basis under such circumstances. Why, then, should he introduce deductions for years in which the rate was 0%, that is, no tax was levied? (3) The cases to which the Committee on Ways and Means referred are relatively few, and will become rarer with every passing year. The loss in revenue cannot be so great by returning to the 1924 rule as to justify the iniquities of the 1926 rule. It is such provisions as this that we have in mind when we say in our preface that complexity in the law is in large part caused by the striving of Congress to make the calculation of net income a matter of fine mathematical computation. Here we have a provison intended to cover a few rare cases, but which in its language permits the Bureau of Internal Revenue to rule (Reg. 69, Art. 1561) that the depreciation which must be deducted from cost on a sale is that which has been "allowable", whether or not such deduction were claimed or allowed. Under that regulation an administration officer may hold that notwithstanding the taxpayer claimed 10% depreciation and the government allowed him only 5% as an annual deduction, 10% is nevertheless the rate by which his cost must be reduced, in order to compute a taxable profit in the sale. A taxpayer may be conservative in his claim for annual depreciation allowance and find himself penalized by larger "allowable" deductions when he comes to sell, or, conversely, he may have been extravagant in his claims for annual allowances and be in a position to insist on lower "allowable" depreciation on sale. The right kind of taxpayer is in jeopardy by this provision—the wrong kind may profit. In the foregoing discussion we do not mean to imply that the administration officers have unjustly acted in any cases under this section. We merely cite the Act and the regulation to illustrate what can happen under the language of the present law.

Many instances can be given to illustrate the baneful working of this provision. For example, the case of a taxpayer who has not had income from his property against which he could charge depreciation. If he has actually had a loss in past years when he had no income to offset that loss for income tax, why should his loss be conjured up, when he sells the property, to haunt him again and subject him to tax. Let us assume the case of a woman who owns a house for two years, which she has been unable to rent. She has no income. At the end of two years she sells for precisely the cost of the property to her. What practical justification is there for taxing her on 6% of her cost, by requiring two annual deductions of 3% for "allowable" depreciation, when she has actually suffered a loss of interest on her money for that period. Such a theoretical calculation of net income would justify her in asking for a deduction of 12%, representing the loss of interest on her money during the two years.

The illustration of the purchaser of a patent is illuminating. It may take five years of development before he derives any income from it. Yet if he sells he must deduct 5/17 of the value from his cost and pay a profit thereon. Instances of this kind can be multiplied indefinitely.

If there is need for protecting the revenue at this point we believe it should be done by other language than that used in the law. If the loss in revenue is not relatively large, we believe that for the sake of simplicity and certainty the deduction for depreciation et cetera sustained, should be only with respect to that actually allowed the taxpayer and from which he has definitely already received a tax advantage.

Gain or Loss on Sales and Exchanges

Section 203 is one of the most complicated and difficult sections of the statute. We do not attempt within the scope of this report to suggest the plan of a complete revision. Any such proposition is tied up with too many fundamental considerations. We urge its complete reform in language and in substance and set forth below a statement of some of the criticisms we have considered in this respect.

A. All provisions relating to reorganizations, now spread in Sections 203 and 204 should be consolidated in one group of paragraphs. We believe the general plan of stating in the same place the circumstances under which a transaction or a closely related group of transactions, e. g., reorganizations, is taxable, together with the method of measuring the tax, is preferable to stating in one place the circumstances under which a tax may or may not accrue in a great many transactions and stating in another place the method of measuring the tax on those transactions which are taxable. The ordinary reader is not interested in a description such as that contained in Section 203. He is likely to be interested in only one of the several subjects and would find it more convenient to read consecutive paragraphs than to refer forward and back through Sections 203 and 204 as he is now compelled to do.

As to substantive matter in these sections, we believe, with respect to reorganizations, that a simpler statement could be evolved by defining non-taxable transactions and leaving taxable transactions to be defined by practice and by judicial decisions. A simple exchange of stock for stock in a reorganization can clearly be exempt from tax. Beyond that (and the present statute goes beyond that, as will be noted later) questions arise which require consideration, with the circumstance of each particular case in view. No general satisfactory rule can be formulated. Reorganizations will tend, wherever possible, to take the form which is expressly stated to be exempt, if such provision exists in the statute, and where novel features are involved, we believe the general principles enunciated in court decisions will furnish a sufficient guide for administration, always assuming the tax rate is to be moderate and steady, so as to relieve the administrative officers so far as possible from laying undue stress on the time element in the receipt of income.

The present law provides for the exemption from tax in cases where stock *or securities* are received in exchange for property. We are of the opinion that where bonds of a new corporation are received in exchange for stock of an old corporation, the taxpayer has changed his status in whole or in part to that of creditor and the propriety of his paying a tax might justly be raised for consideration. The present law exempts such transaction.

Cash or property, other than stock of the new or resultant company might *prima facie* be presumed to be taxable income, unless the stockholder can show that he should be allowed a deduction for the value of his proportion of interest surrendered as a result of the reorganization, but as a rule of this character cannot be more than indicated in a statute, its development must be a matter of growth through judicial decision, if it is to fit the variety of circumstances to which it will be applied.

We admit that the problem is difficult of solution and we can only make tentative suggestions for purpose of discussion.

BASIS FOR DETERMINING GAIN OR LOSS

Section 204 is another difficult and highly complex provision, rendered so by the desire of Congress to prevent avoidance of tax on capital gains through the making of gifts *inter vivos,* transfers in trust and the incorporation of companies.

It is complicated by long and involved statements of the extent to which sales of property received in tax-free exchanges or by tax-free reorganizations shall subject the seller to tax. In fact substantially two-thirds of the first subdivision of this section is given over to dealing with these exceptional cases.

The simplification of the substance of this section, therefore, depends upon simplification in the treatment of gifts, trusts, incorporations and reorganizations or in the abolition of tax on capital gains.

This committee is not prepared to advocate the abolition of the tax on capital gains. In principle an income tax should be confined to current income and should not embrace capital gains, but the practical difficulties lie in distinguishing between true capital gains and current income. And until our income tax system is more highly developed, the possibilities of evading taxation by masquerading current income in the guise of capital gains will be too numerous to warrant a complete abolition of tax on capital gains. A tax on capital gains reduces the incentive to such evasion. We are therefore in favor of a tax, but believe it should be at a flat rate, in reasonable ratio to the surtax rates. Sales and exchanges of property should not be discouraged, nor should the taxpayer who by intent nor necessity reduces his capital to cash be unduly penalized. We are inclined to the opinion, therefore, that the rate of tax on sales of property held for over two years should not be more than one-half the maximum surtax rate, and a lower rate, approximating one-quarter of the surtax maximum might properly be prescribed on sale of property held over five years.

Having committed ourselves to a tax on capital gains, we approach the problem of simplifying Section 204.

As to Gifts. A restoration of the rule in effect before the Revenue Act of 1921, namely: that the donee shall take the value of the property at the date of the gift as his "cost", would be a far step toward simplification. The objection to this is that it opens up an avenue to tax evasion. Owners of property having an unrealized increment would be invited by such a rule to make gifts of the property to persons near to them in order to avoid a tax. This incentive, however, would be lessened by reasonable rates of tax on capital gains, if the donor would be privileged to apply the capital gains rate to his profit, while the donee would be taxed at normal and surtax rates unless the gift were made over two years before the sale, as gifts so far in advance of realization can hardly be said to have been made for purpose of avoiding tax.

Coupled with the foregoing we make another suggestion affecting gifts. Gifts made for the purpose of avoiding tax under the rule here advocated, would naturally be made to some one close to the donor; that is, some one to whom he is inclined by ties of close relationship. In the case of wife, child, grandchild, parent, brother or sister, nephew or niece, friend, the likelihood of any being donee of a gift made for the purpose of avoiding tax is in the order stated. The likelihood of the wife being donee, under such circumstances is probably several times as great as that of the child; that of the child several times as great as that of the parent, that of the parent several times as great as that of the brother or sister, and so on. That is to say, a donor who makes a gift for the purpose of avoiding the tax is most likely to choose the person closest to him as donee, in the belief that although he has parted with legal title he nevertheless retains a genuine benefit, by reason of the close community of interest between himself and the donee. If then, a rule is prescribed by which either (a) the incomes of husband and wife and minor children are added together for purpose of assessing the surtax,[3] or (b) the husband and wife are given the privilege of dividing the family income between them (as in community property states), for purpose of assessing the tax, the incentive toward making gifts to avoid tax will be vastly reduced, and we might safely return to the older and simpler rule of allowing the donee to take as his cost the value of the property at the time of its receipt.

Few statutory rules, we may add in closing at this point, can be more indefinite and difficult of administration than the one in Section 204, which requires a donee to ascertain the basis of the donor or the last preceding owner in order to compute his own profit. The duty of the commissioner, if the donor is unable to ascertain the required basis, amounts to a direction to disregard the express rule laid down in Section 204(b), namely: that the basis shall be cost or value on March 1, 1913, *whichever is greater.* This provision has invited litigation and its constitutionality is now under judicial scrutiny.

As to Trusts. The class of trusts specified in Section 204 (a) (3) fall into the same category as gifts, the subject discussed in the preceding paragraphs.

As to Corporations. The present rule is that a corporation must take the basis of the preceding owner or owners of the properties

---

[3] Some members of the committee are opposed to compulsory filing of joint returns by husband and wife.

10

it acquires upon organization in exchange for its stock. This rule works a manifest hardship against stockholders who purchase stock in the corporation for cash. The situation is difficult to visualize from abstract statements, but the following illustration will bring out the point:

A has a business whose assets have trebled in value during his ownership. He incorporates his business for its present value, $1,000,000. He pays no income tax on incorporation. The corporation is limited to $333,333 cost basis for purpose of sale, depreciation, etc. A sells his stock for $1,000,000. His tax is on a profit of $666,000. The new owners have invested $1,000,000, but the corporation is still limited to $333,333—the basis of A. The assets of the corporation are sold and the corporation pays a tax on a fictitious profit of $666,000, being compelled to adhere to A's basis. But why should it adhere to A's basis when A has paid a tax between that and $1,000,000? The result is double taxation, and that is true none the less if the assets are not sold but used in the business, because the depreciation rate is applied to A's basis. It is true in a corresponding degree as soon as A sells a single share. The rule is justifiable only so long as A remains the sole stockholder. This is an instance of where the law is so intent on preventing A from gaining any tax advantage by incorporating that it disregards the rights of all who may become investors with him.

The allowance to the corporation of the actual value of the property at the time of acquisition, as basis for sale, depreciation, etc., is not an exemption from tax to that extent but merely a postponement of the incidence of the tax until the liquidation of the corporation takes place. The rule that the basis of the preceding owner of the property shall be used by the corporation is a denial of the separate entity of the corporation. The general rule in accounting is that a corporation shall take the value of the property it acquires for stock into its capital account, and that rule was long recognized for income tax until changed by statute with retroactive effect. We advocate the restoration of the former—and general—rule, notwithstanding the transferor of property in exchange for stock may under certain conditions be excused from tax until the stock is sold. That rule is eminently proper as a protection against heavy taxes on a transaction which is more in the nature of a change in the form of the taxpayer's assets than a realization of their value in cash or its equivalent.

The importance of the present rule, against which we protest will be minimized by the adoption of low, steady rates of tax, and would almost disappear if the plan of taxing corporations and dividends herein proposed were adopted. Whether or not that plan is adopted, we believe that for the sake of simplicity and reasonableness the present rule as to basis for corporations should be abolished and the corporation should be allowed to take the value of the property it acquires for purpose of sale, depreciation and all other allowances normally based on cost.

As to Exchanges. We are in entire accord with the rule that where property is exchanged for other property without being taxed under the law, the cost-basis of the property received should be that of the property surrendered.

As to Reorganizations. These special provisions can be greatly simplified by simplifying the basic statutory provisions relating to tax on reorganizations. We do not attempt to suggest a new form here, as it depends upon what is done with the basic provisions. We call attention, however, to the fact that the effect of the parenthetical expression "(other than stock or securities in a corporation a party to a reorganization)" should be carefully considered in any revision of the law. As now used it affords a method of lawfully avoiding, by means of reorganization, the rule that the basis for purpose of sale cannot be increased by a tax-free exchange.

NET LOSSES

Section 206 prescribes the rule under which a net loss in one year may be used to offset in a succeeding year or years. It attempts to serve a purpose somewhat similar to that accomplished in statutes of other countries which average the income over a period of years. That is, it recognizes the insufficiency of a twelve-month period in which finally to determine the taxpayer's ability to pay income tax. It does not go so far as other statutes, which recognize that the relative ability of taxpayers to pay is better measured by the amount of net income received over periods of three or five years than over a period of one year. The best measure of a taxpayer's ability to pay tax is his average net income over his entire life. Any period shorter than that results in an approximation—and the shorter the period the farther that approximation is likely to be from the absolute truth. Some of the inequalities of our system result from the adoption of the single year as an accounting period, and many of its problems arise from that cause.

The adoption of a rule of assessing the tax on the average of three or five years' income would do away with the necessity of Section 206, and would more completely accomplish the remedial or corrective purpose behind that section. If such averaging of income is not introduced into our system of taxation, Section 206 should be enlarged in its operation to include the net loss of any · taxpayer whether from business or not. Taxpayers not in business are excluded from the operation of this statute. Thus one who suffers a loss of income and has allowable deductions in excess of his receipts is not afforded any relief. There appears to this com-

mittee no reason why a net loss under such circumstances should not be recognized as fully as one sustained in business, if losses of one year are justifiable deduction from income of another year.

The calculation of net loss is unduly complicated. Consideration should be given to the simple proposition of allowing a net loss, if such loss is indicated on the return, that is found by taking all the deductions which the law allows in computing net income under ordinary circumstances. We couple this suggestion with the suggestion that the definition of net income be revised to eliminate, among other things, the deduction for contributions. Contributions by individuals are not deductions from gross income to arrive at net income. They are dispositions of net income, and Congress should allow them to be deducted under the head of exemptions, in which category they properly fall.

The suggestion of the committee is that such items as dividends (in the case of corporations) and tax-free interest should not be added to the taxpayer's income, for the purpose of reducing his net loss, when they are contemplated by the law as exempt income. There seems to be no consistent reason why a taxpayer should be deprived of his or its benefit of these exemptions, merely because his outgo exceeds his income in one year, when the law expressly grants them to him if he is in the more fortunate position of having his income exceed his outgo. The adjustments required by Section 206 evince a reluctant spirit in dealing with unfortunate taxpayers; a failure to fully meet the need which called the section into existence.

We are further of the opinion that these paragraphs of Section 206—(c) (2) and (d)—may well be omitted, for the sake of simplicity, leaving net losses to be applied against subsequent annual net income. Cases where adjustments would be made against subsequent capital gains are likely to be few and the effect on the revenue relatively slight. The complication of the statute is increased by the interpolation of provisions covering exceptional cases, and where such exceptional cases are likely to be rare or the effect produced on the revenue by including them in the general provisions is likely to be relatively slight, the importance of keeping the statute simple and general in its terms should overbalance the desire to exact the maximum revenue in every exceptional case. This is a sacrifice that must be made for the sake of simplicity whenever justified on practical grounds.

The limitation of two years in the application of net loss to subsequent income should be removed. A net loss, if deductible at all, should be deductible in toto regardless of the time required to absorb it by subsequent income.

Subdivision (e) of Section 206 is a temporary provision. Such provisions, which are intended to have effect for a temporary period only, should be segregated in one part of the act, from which they can easily be eliminated without disturbing the general structure when their usefulness has ceased.

Subdivision (f) can be eliminated in our opinion. This point is dealt with more fully below under the heading of " Fiscal Years." Our point is that with a rate that varies slightly, if at all, from year to year, the net loss occurring in a fiscal year might well take the status of a taxable year falling in the calendar year in which it ends.

FISCAL YEARS

We believe that Section 207 can be simplified by providing that in case the taxpayer elects to make a return for a period of twelve months beginning in one calendar year and ending in the following calendar year, the rate of tax, and all other statutory provision, in force in the calendar year in which such period ends, shall be applied to the net income and its calculation.

This is on the assumption that rates will not fluctuate violently from year to year. In case any exceptional statutory provision is enacted or any violent change in rates takes place, the taxpayer may always be protected by a special temporary provision, but such provision as that of Section 207 (a) should not be a part of the general law. Subdivision (b) can be supplanted by a simple statement that a partner shall be taxed on his share of partnership income according to the law in force in the calendar year in which the partnership fiscal year ends. Paragraph (c) is a temporary provision which should in no event find a place in the body of the act, but should be segregated at the end with all other temporary provisions.

CAPITAL GAINS AND LOSSES

As heretofore stated, this committee is in favor of imposing a tax on capital gains (see p. 64).

Where a capital net loss is so great that 12½% (or such other rate as may be adopted) exceeds the ordinary annual income of the year, the excess of such percentage should be applicable to the following year. Capital losses are often large and do seriously affect the taxpayer's ability to pay. If they should be so great as to exceed his net income for two or three years, remedial provisions of the law should take cognizance of his position.

As heretofore stated (see p. 65), we suggest consideration of one rate on capital gains where the property has been held for two years and a lower rate where it has been held over five years.

EARNED INCOME

We advocate the total abolition of this provision. The exemption extended to earned income is so niggardly as to be of no real advantage to the taxpayer. The method of calculation is so complicated that almost universal objection is voiced to it. The assumption that the first $5,000 is earned income (desirable as it is from the standpoint of administration) amounts to a general reduction of tax that might as well be accomplished by adjustment of the normal and surtax rates.

While we find no reason for continuing the present earned income credit, we are strongly of the opinion that earned income is grossly discriminated against in our present law. There is no "cushion" to ease the burden of the tax on the individual who earns his income as there is in depreciation, depletion, obsolescence and other devices for the protection of capital. The present surtax rates bear with relatively heavy weight on incomes within the range of substantial earnings. Congress has seen fit to absolve millions of small taxpayers from any tax and has reduced the surtaxes on very large incomes from 65% to 20%, but no substantial reduction has been made in the rates applicable to incomes between $20,000 and $75,000. The rate in the Revenue Act of 1926 is actually lower than the rates in the Act of 1916 on very small incomes. In 1916 a married taxpayer with two children paid $120—in 1926 he pays $111, subject to a reduction for earned income, or a net tax of $83.25. So far as the small taxpayer is concerned the return to normal pre-war tax is complete without the advantage of the earned income credit. So far as the very large taxpayer is concerned, his reduction has been ample, in the surtax reduction to approximately one-third of the 1918 rates on incomes exceeding $100,000, the present rates being approximately twice as high as those of 1916. In the great middle brackets the reduction has been to approximately one-half of the 1918 rates which are now approximately six times as high as those of 1916.

The result, obviously, is that the great mass of incomes between $20,000 and $75,000 are bearing the chief burden of post-war taxes. In this great class are the earners who might justly receive some consideration.

The taxpayer who earns an income between $20,000 and $75,000 per annum is likely to be in receipt of a fluctuating income, large in one year and smaller in another. Authors, artists, inventors, professional and technical men fall in the class who enjoy occasional large receipts, as the result of long endeavor. To tax them on a parity with recipients of income which flows steadily and in equal amounts from year to year is discrimination. For example, assume an inventor has worked for twenty years without an income and then realizes $500,000 on his invention. That would be equivalent to an average annual income of $25,000 for the period. His surtax alone would be $91,600. .The capitalist enjoying a steady income of $25,000 a year would pay only $10,200 in surtaxes over a period of twenty years. Here is an exaggerated case of the discrimination against earned income. The discrimination exists in a lesser degree in the great majority of cases.

Income has been likened to the fruit of the tree of capital. In the case of the earner it is the fruit of his toil and the margin above his expenses is in fact his capital. Income from capital can bear taxes at progressive rates, the capital remains intact and the owner is at most deprived of the use of a part of his wealth. The earner is attempting to grow his tree of capital and a heavy progressive tax is in effect cutting down the growth of his tree. A doctor's skill, a lawyer's intellect, an author's inspiration or a business executive's energy are not fixed and indestructible, capable of producing annual income forever. Yet the income they produce is taxed on a parity with that of capital. Capital is permitted to replenish its loss by dipping into income through depreciation, obsolescence, depletion. But the human vitality, health and strength lost in earning salaries, fees and similar compensation cannot be deducted as depreciation, obsolescence or depletion from the income of the earner.

The ideal solution would be a flat tax on earned income, regardless of amount. We are not prepared to advocate this, however, for we are aware of the difficulties of distinguishing between earned income and income produced by the use of capital, either in the form of money, reputation or good will. The practical difficulties are insurmountable to us at this time.

We suggest four things for consideration in this connection: *First,* the rate of surtax on incomes within the range of substantial earnings should be brought in line with the rates below and above those limits; *Second,* the increase in rates should occur less frequently. Instead of increasing at intervals of $2,000, the spread in income might be $5,000 between each change in rate. In that way the effect of fluctuation of income from year to year would be reduced in some degree; *Third,* some provision might be made with respect to earned income analogous to that of capital gains, that is where the taxpayer receives income in one year as the result of several years of labor the capital-gains rate might apply; *Fourth,* the averaging of all incomes over a period of three years would minimize the present effect of sporadic, occasional, fluctuating earned income.

NORMAL AND SURTAX

We have discussed the question of tax rate above (see p. 42). The desirability of a single tax instead of two graduated taxes, one superimposed on the other, is manifestly in the interest of simplicity.

The limitation on surtax expressed in Section 211 is little below the maximum rate and has no effect unless the gross receipt exceeds $64,000. The saving of tax when the selling price is $100,000 is only $860; on $1,000,000 it is only $36,800. The provision served a useful purpose when surtax rates were almost confiscatory. It is now devitalized and in a subsequent revision consideration might well be given to its entire omission.

Net Income Defined

Subdivision (b) of Section 212 is inappropriately placed under the heading of "net income of individuals defined." It should bear a heading more descriptive of its contents, or it might properly be transferred to the section on returns. Subdivision (c) would naturally find a place in Section 207. It is of interest primarily to the taxpayer who contemplates establishing a fiscal year.

Installment Sales—Casual Sales

Subdivision (d) of Section 212 deals with an accounting method. It is hidden under the heading "Net income of individuals defined."

This committee is of the opinion that the statutory language relating to installment sales and casual sales should be general in its terms and not attempt to enunciate a definite rule. A general permission to the taxpayer to report on a cash basis, an accrual basis, a combination of both, or on any other basis of good accounting which clearly reflects his income, would leave such questions as these to be worked out under regulation of the Commissioner and decisions of the courts. These questions come under the general heading of methods of accounting. Under general statutory rules, methods of accounting can be developed satisfactory to taxpayer and Government. A specific statutory rule raises a barrier to free development, along lines which have been so successful in the development of the common law.

This committee has received a number of criticisms of this provision. Among them are the following:

The sale of real estate on the installment plan should be treated precisely the same as the sale of personal property.

Contracts for the sale of real estate, where neither title or possession passes until full payment is received, should not be treated as installment sales.

The requirement that payments on real estate sales shall not exceed 25% during the taxable year is an unnecessary and unjust discrimination against real estate dealers and one which tends to complicate income tax procedure, as it compels the vendor to wait until the end of the year to ascertain whether or not he may treat the transaction on his books as an installment sale.

The chief complaint and one with which this committee is in entire sympathy is the double taxation of income resulting from changes from an accrual basis to the statutory "installment sales" basis. A rule which requires a taxpayer to include the same net income in his return for two years requires consideration in any revision of the law.

GROSS INCOME DEFINED

Section 213 can in our opinion be greatly simplified. The general definition of gross income should not be burdened with the exceptional statements regarding the salaries of the President, federal judge and other officers and employees of the United States. Such special provisions should be segregated at the end of the law under appropriate headings.

The remaining language of subdivision (a) is capable of improvement. Its phraseology has come down to us from the Revenue Act of 1913. It is tautological and might be replaced with simpler, comprehensive terms adopted from the language of the Supreme Court, which on several occasions has defined net income.

Subdivision (b) we consider bad from several standpoints. Gross income is defined in the preceding subdivision, in conformity with the general accepted meaning of that term, but in (b) the definition is distorted from all semblance to the general acceptation. Subdivision (b) should be divided into three sections. One should enumerate items which actually are not income, the second should state items not within the power of Congress to tax, and the third should be headed " Exemptions from tax." We have in this subdivision exemptions based on international comity, exemptions granted to federal beneficiaries, partial exemption of interest or dividends from building and loan associations, an exemption to a minister of the gospel, exemptions to residents of China on certain dividends, and the exemption extended to non-resident American citizens on earned income. The listing of these exemptions under the heading of gross income is inaccurate and misleading. Their position makes them difficult to find. We believe they should be listed under the heading of exemptions and be segregated from the general definition of gross income.

Subdivision (c) might well be consolidated with Section 217 (a).

DEDUCTIONS ALLOWED INDIVIDUALS

Expenses. General complaint has been received by this committee of the phrase " ordinary *and* necessary expenses " in Section 214 (a). The conjunction " and " can be, and has been, construed to be a statutory requirement that the item of expense be not only necessary but also ordinary, in the sense of recurring with some regularity. Items of expense occur sporadically as well as regularly. We are of the opinion that the test of deductibility should be the propriety of the deduction for the purpose of determining annual income, and that the combined test of " ordinary *and* necessary" is narrow enough to support a narrow construction detrimental to the taxpayer. The phrase "all actual expenses pertaining to the production of the net income of the taxpayer" would exclude improper divestments of income and yet leave the administration officers unhampered by arbitrary statutory tests. Any fear that this might authorize the deduction in one year of items which should be depreciated over a period of years, or similar items, is dissipated by the inclusion in the statute of special provisions covering such items.

Salaries. The clause "including a reasonable allowance for salaries" places the administration officers in the position of arrogating to themselves power to determine the reasonableness of salaries, and has often resulted in extended argument on the question of reasonableness of large payments. In the case of an individual employer the necessity of reasonableness in amount is not deemed to be so important as in the case of corporation employers. The reason for this is that a corporation with few stockholders who are active in the business may cover up dividend payments under the guise of salaries. The temptation to do so was great during the period of the excess profits tax, and will exist so long as the tax on corporations is out of line with the tax on individuals. The correction of this state of affairs lies in the reduction of the corporation tax to its proper rate in relation to the tax on individuals—or the abolition of the corporation tax under the plan we advocate.

Of course, there are instances where so-called "salaries" serve to disguise payments of a different nature, as for instance, in the case of the purchase of a business where the former head may be paid a salary for several years without rendering service to the new owner. Such payments are often part payment of the property acquired or for the purchase of the former owner's good will during the period of transition. The administrative officers should be fully empowered to question such payments or the actuality of any payments of salaries. But the reasonableness of salaries paid in good faith should not be a matter of administrative review.

Inheritance Taxes. We are of the opinion that estate, inheritance, legacy and succession taxes should not be continued as a deduction in the future revisions of the law. Such taxes have nothing to do with annual income. Their effect is to reduce the legacy or inheritance; they do not reduce the taxpayer's ability to pay tax on his regular income.

Stock Sales. With the introduction of reasonable and steady surtax rates, in combination with an appropriate tax on capital gains, we believe the necessity which called into existence the rule that no loss can be claimed on the sale of shares of stock or securities, if the taxpayer has acquired or acquires substantially identical property within thirty days will cease to exist. This provision, therefore, may well be eliminated in a new law.

Worthless Debts. That debts may be deducted only if **ascertained** to *be* worthless *and* if charged off in the taxable year is open to a very genuine criticism. Frequently a taxpayer charges off in one year debts which he ascertained to be worthless, only to find that the administration, on good grounds, determines the debt to have become worthless in another year. In such cases the taxpayer is deprived of the deduction, through the mere accident of charging off the item on his books in the wrong year. Worthless debts are genuine losses. They should be allowed as deductions, whether properly charged off or not. The general rule that taxpayers must keep proper records covers the purpose of the words "and charged off." These words should therefore be omitted from paragraph (7), Subdivision (a), Section 214.

Contributions. Contributions are enumerated as a deduction from gross income in order to arrive at net income. This we regard as incorrect. The allowance should be labeled as an exemption, which it is in fact, and should be classified with other exemptions, under an appropriate heading. We advocate a general plan of reporting net income in such manner that the true net income of the taxpayer is first shown on his return, after which deductions may be made for exemptions and "credits." We are doubtful of the wisdom of continuing to allow amounts paid out as contributions, as a deduction from taxable net income. We fully recognize the need of that provision when the income tax rates were suddenly increased to such high rates that the margin left to the taxpayer was often insufficient to permit him to divert any of it to charitable uses. Under those circumstances Congress was compelled to recognize the public interest in maintaining certain quasi-public organizations. But as a general proposition, in normal times and under normal rates, we see no justification in permitting taxpayers to divert fractions of the revenue to quasi-public organizations. A taxpayer may divert a part of his net income to many commendable charities and to many laudable public interests without allowance therefor on his income tax. It is only when the gift is made to certain classes of organizations that a deduction may be taken. The statutory provision is an indirect subsidy to the specified organizations. The vice of tax exemption is the tendency to enlargement. The list in Section 214 (a) (10) is proof of this. It has grown with almost every revision and new groups of organizations will always arise and clamor for inclusion. The organizations favored by this provision will no doubt stress the inducement to contribute aroused in the mind of the taxpayer by the prospect

of the consequent reduction in his tax. We feel the answer is that inducement to contribute to endless laudable purposes can be stimulated by the pressure of favorable legislation, but a taxing statute is no more the place for such legislation than it is for the punitive legislation attempted in connection with child labor. A taxing statute has the serious purpose of taking property for the general good. The expenditure of the revenue should be limited to necessary governmental purposes, and until our Federal Government enters the field of paternalism to the extent of supporting all organizations for religious, charitable, scientific, literary, educational and the other purposes, with funds collected from every taxpayer, we see no reason why some taxpayers should be permitted to divert public funds to some such organization in the amount of tax withheld from the Government, by reason of the deduction for contributions. Checking the contributions of taxpayers entails a considerable amount of administrative work. The elimination of the deduction is a step towards simplicity in administration.

Casual Sales. The problem of the casual sale of real property is perplexing. Such provisions as Section 214 (a) (11) should be avoided wherever possible. The giving of a bond by the taxpayer on each sale and the necessity on the part of the Commissioner to follow up the transaction and check it at some future time are both complexities to be avoided. This committee, however, has been able to evolve no suggestion on this point.

Subdivision (b) of Section 214 should be transferred to Section 217, under the heading of "Net Income of Non-Resident Alien Individuals," where naturally it would be first sought by anyone interested in that subject. The last sentence of this paragraph, which is effectually hidden by the preceding language on a different subject should be transferred to Section 262.

CREDITS ALLOWED INDIVIDUALS

This title and the title of Section 222, namely, "Credits for Taxes in Case of Individuals," are confusing. Attention might well be given to the phrasing of different headings for both sections. The word "credit" is not used in the popular sense and to the average individual both headings are obscure.

We think (a) of Section 216 might be placed under the heading of dividends, (b) under the heading of interest and the remaining paragraphs under the heading of "Personal Exemption," a phrase used in the earlier laws. In short, we advocate a rearrangement of the statutory provision so that all provisions affecting interest or dividends or any other subject will be found grouped together for convenient reference. The taxpayer's index word is the name of the thing he is concerned with. If he is curious about any phase of the tax as it applies to dividends he looks for dividends and close proximity of all provisions affecting that subject assists him in his search. The present form of the statute is arranged to group provisions under headings dealing with phases of the law. We believe an objective grouping would be simpler and would avoid much repetition.

Personal exemption. We believe simplicity would be achieved, as well as a greater uniformity of effect, if the personal exemption were stated in terms of tax rather than in terms of income. That is, require the taxpayer to compute his tax without reference to the personal exemption and then permit him to deduct certain amounts of the tax as exemptions for his single or married state and his dependents. The personal exemptions should primarily be for the benefit of the individual of small means. At present it confers larger benefits on the taxpayer of large means. If measured in terms of tax it would grant the same reduction in tax to all taxpayers similarly situated.

NET INCOME OF NON-RESIDENT ALIEN INDIVIDUAL

This heading is misleading, as the section opens with the statement that its provisions apply to non-resident aliens and citizens entitled to the benefit of Section 262. The reference to citizens can be omitted if the last line of Section 214 is transferred to Section 262.

The taxation of non-resident individuals is in a complicated, unsettled and obscure state under our laws. We suggest the most careful revision of this section but have no specific suggestion to offer, except in the way of criticism of the present form. Subdivisions (a) (1) and (a) (2) are composed principally of negatives of the opening statement. A recasting of this language in positive form would make it more readily understandable. Perhaps a recasting of paragraph (e) would make it look less formidable. Paragraph (f) should, if possible, be relegated to that section in the back of the law which should contain so far as possible all necessary definitions of words and phrases used in the statute.

ESTATES AND TRUSTS

The general dissatisfaction with this section of the law arises from the complexity of the administration. It is suggested that simpler forms and simpler requirements on fiduciaries are possible.

A general protest is made against the rule laid down by the Court of Claims that an executor's basis for determining gain or loss is the decedent's cost. The Board of Tax Appeals has failed to follow the Court of Claims in another case. The trustee in the same estate or a beneficiary uses the market value at the date of

decedent's death. The statutory rule is expressed in Section 204 (a) (5) and provides that the basis on the sale of property acquired by bequest, devise or inheritance shall be the fair market value at the time of such acquisition. The time of acquisition may be different for each of the following persons:

    a. Executor
    b. Trustee under will
    c. Beneficiary
    d. Remainderman with contingent interest
    e. Remainderman with vested interest.

In view of the peculiar responsibilities of fiduciaries we suggest that consideration be given to the advisability of expressing in the statute the basis for each of these classes of taxpayers.

PAYMENT OF INDIVIDUALS' TAX AT SOURCE

We approve of the withholding at the source of the tax on income paid to non-resident aliens. We recommend for consideration the practicability of a special flat rate of tax greater than the normal tax on non-resident aliens, to be withheld so far as possible at the source, and to be in lieu of normal and surtax, as in the case of the capital gains tax. There is much to be said for not imposing graduated surtaxes on non-resident aliens not engaged in business in this country, and the imposition of a compensating flat tax collected through withholding at the source.

The provision relating to withholding tax on tax-free covenant bonds is an excrescence on the law and should be eliminated. It is a special provision retained by the influence of special interests for a special purpose. The provision creates complication and has no place in any plan for simplication.

Furthermore it is capable of compelling a corporation to pay sums of money into the federal treasury that are in no sense taxes, in cases where the taxpayer is only subject to a normal tax of $1\frac{1}{2}\%$ and yet the corporation is required to pay at the rate of 2%. The requirement that withholding against non-resident aliens shall be only at the rate of 2% on this class of securities when it is 5% on all other fixed income is an unwarranted interference with the operation of a contract between private individuals. The naive assumption of the law that bondholders will go to the trouble of claiming the benefit of their personal exemption or notify the corporation that they are subject to only the $1\frac{1}{2}\%$ normal tax is amusing.

INDIVIDUAL RETURNS

Our principal recommendation regarding returns is made above (p. 21). We believe there should be no option on the part of husband or wife to make joint returns. The return should either be joint in all cases or separate in all cases (see p. 66). Joint returns are never filed, where separate returns are more favorable, and *vice versa*. Through the alternative provision the husband may (by filing separate returns) avoid the inclusion of a profit on property given to his wife and sold by her and (by filing a joint return) obtain the benefit of a loss on any property sold by his wife where the incomes of the husband and of the wife show a wide disparity. The saving in surtaxes by this method of avoidance may be quite substantial.

CONDITIONAL AND OTHER EXEMPTIONS OF CORPORATIONS

The committee regards Section 231 as fairly crying aloud for improvement in language. It reiterates its statement that exemptions should be avoided so far as possible in a tax law. This section would be of little interest if the plan of taxing corporations only on undistributed income is adopted.

GROSS AND NET INCOME OF CORPORATIONS DEFINED

In a logical rearrangement of the statute these provisions (Sections 232 and 233), could be omitted.

DEDUCTIONS ALLOWED CORPORATIONS

In addition to the applicable comments made with respect to Section 214 (p. 81), the committee believes:

The requirement that dividends received by a corporation shall be reported in its gross income and be deducted in arriving at its net income should be replaced by a single requirement that the amount of dividends received during the year should be stated in the return, but not included in gross income. This is in accordance with its recommendation that the calculation of net income in the law should be restricted to true net income, leaving adjustments of an extrinsic character to be made after net income is arrived at. By this means statistics would be more easily collected and be more accurate.

The provision with respect to insurance companies should be stated in separate sections under appropriate headings.

CREDITS ALLOWED CORPORATIONS

The requirement for the inclusion in gross income and the permission to deduct as a credit, interest on certain obligations of the United States seems to us to be a duplication of work. Such tax-free interest could be stated separately in the return.

The specific credit of $2,000 allowed only to corporations having a net income of $25,000 or less, has the same effect as a gradation of rates. We are of the opinion that graduated rates of tax should not be applied to corporate incomes, and that discriminations in the specific credit should also be avoided. Under the plan of taxing corporations proposed herein, this provision would be unnecessary.

PAYMENT OF CORPORATION INCOME TAX AT SOURCE

We believe this section (Section 237) is out of place at this point in the law. It should be placed under the heading of foreign corporations. Our recommendations on withholding at the source are stated above (p. 89).

CREDIT FOR TAXES IN CASE OF CORPORATIONS

Section 238 deals with the difficult case in which a domestic corporation is subject to taxes in a foreign country as well as in this country. It is necessary, so long as the corporation rate remains high and corporations are taxed as separate entities and not treated as conduits of income. If the suggestion we made above (p. 44) is adopted and corporations are taxed only on undistributed income, any tax paid in a foreign country would be treated as a deduction, for the purpose of arriving at the undistributed income. If the present method of taxing corporations is continued this provision should be contained in the revised law. We recommend, however, a revision of the language with a view to its simplification.

CORPORATION RETURNS

We believe this section (239) should be clarified in several respects. The requirement in the case of foreign corporations should be stated under the heading relating generally to such corporations. The provisions relating to payment of tax by receivers, trustees in bankruptcy and assignees should not be under this heading but should be set forth under a heading referring to such persons. Other changes would follow from a rearrangement of the provisions of the law. Tentative reports should be provided for as set forth above (p. 21).

CONSOLIDATED RETURNS OF CORPORATIONS

It is generally believed that the requirement of Section 240 that 95% of the stock shall be owned is too strict. In many instances of genuine consolidation the actual ownership is less than 95%. This committee recommends consideration of a more flexible rule—a lower percentage of ownership, combined with actual intercompany relations which require consideration in arriving at true net income. The present high percentage of ownership required by statute renders the administrative officers powerless to consider cases other than those in which the ownership is practically complete. The present law excludes from the test of ownership all "nonvoting stock which is limited and preferred as to dividends." The position of preferred stockholders, whether having voting powers or not, is in some respects analogous to that of creditors in the distribution of profits; their share is not primarily affected by the amount of taxes paid; their interest in consolidation is very slight, if any. Furthermore, the right of preferred stock to vote is often a limited and exceptional one, so that it is "non-voting" in some years and "voting" in others. On the whole, we believe a step toward simplification lies in the elimination of the word "non-voting" in Section 240 (d), the effect of which would be to exclude all preferred stocks from consideration in determining affiliation.

ADMINISTRATIVE PROVISIONS

Beginning with Section 254 and ending with Section 259 is a series of provisions labeled "Administrative provisions." Among these provisions are a number which are inappropriately placed under this heading, if we regard the term "administrative provisions" as referring to those provisions which are intended to define the powers and duties of administrative officers. Similarly scattered through the law are other administrative provisions. For example, much of Part V and all that part of Title XI which refers to the manifold duties and powers of the Commissioner should be collected under one heading, to form a code of administrative rules for the guidance of the Commissioner, his assistants, and the collectors of internal revenue. There is much uncertainty today regarding the procedure in the Bureau of Internal Revenue and some conflict between the powers of the Commissioner and the collectors. A complete revision and codification of all administrative provisions would for the first time present a clear and consistent outline of procedure in the assessment and collection of the tax. Such codification would serve also to point out the inconsistencies of the statute in many respects.

DEFICIENCY IN TAX

We believe the language of Section 273 can be simplified. A deficiency is the additional tax which the Commissioner finds to be due from the taxpayer for any year. If the Commissioner finds the taxpayer has paid more than he should, the result should be defined as an "over-payment."

Most of the definition of deficiency is matter to be embodied in an administrative provision directing the Commissioner to make due allowances for previous assessments or collections, and abatements, credits and refunds.

Section 274 can be divided into three parts — one consisting of those provisions primarily of interest to the taxpayer, the second, of those affecting the Commissioner, and the third, of those which

11

should be relegated to the head "Payment of tax" or the head "Interest."

Similarly Section 275 and Section 276 should be consolidated with other provisions relating to penalties so that all penalty provisions may be read at one time. Such consolidation would do much to clarify the penalty provisions of the statute.

PERIOD OF LIMITATIONS

We have stated above (page 32) our recommendation regarding the period of limitations. In the next revision of the law we suggest a statement on this subject affecting that law alone. Section 277 is confusing, as it prescribes varying rules under prior laws.

TAXES UNDER PRIOR ACTS

Section 283 contains a series of special provisions which should be omitted from the body of the income tax law and segregated under the head of "temporary provisions," if necessary at all in a permanent revision.

CLOSING BY COMMISSIONER OF TAXABLE YEAR

We are of the opinion that Section 285 should be combined with the provisions relating to jeopardy assessment, with the purpose of consolidating all such special provisions under one general head.

BOARD OF TAX APPEALS

All provisions relating to the Board of Tax Appeals should be embodied in a separate act, or at least in a distinct and separate part of the income tax act. The provisions of Sections 900 to 1005, inclusive, are largely concerned with the creation of the board and its internal affairs. These provisions are not of interest to the taxpayer and should be segregated from those provisions which affect the taxpayer's relation to the board on appeal. Only the latter should be made a part of the income tax law.

This committee considers the Board of Tax Appeals as a necessary and desirable part of our income tax system. We recommend the following changes in the provisions relating to appeals to the board.

The taxpayer should be allowed ninety days instead of sixty days to file his appeal. The present period is not always sufficient to consider the matter of the appeal and we believe a longer period will result in more carefully prepared petitions to the board.

The right of the taxpayer to elect to appeal to the board or to pay the tax and sue for a refund in the District Court or the Court of Claims should remain unchanged. Such election will tend to expedite the settlement of cases, by permitting the taxpayer to choose the court which has the lightest docket. Furthermore, in certain cases, local courts may be more familiar with the subject matter of the action—as for example; cases involving mining or patent valuations or questions relating to the local law governing estates.

In addition to the above, we recommend that the taxpayer be given the right to file a claim for refund and institute suit for the recovery of taxes within the period of limitation otherwise provided, notwithstanding the fact that an appeal may have been filed with the board for that year. This right should be limited to questions that have not been decided by the board or courts in his case. Section 284 (d) should be changed so as to preclude the taxpayer from filing a claim or instituting suit for the recovery of taxes, based upon any question which has been decided by the board or courts in his case.

We believe that the adoption of this suggestion will greatly relieve the congestion of cases before the board and put the taxpayer more nearly on par with the bureau in the settlement of cases within the bureau. Under the present procedure of the bureau, the taxpayer is at a great disadvantage in endeavoring to settle a case within the bureau. His first opportunity to discuss his case is after the sixty-day letter has been issued. The bureau has naturally decided all doubtful points against him. In his discussions with the bureau, it develops that there are some points which the conferee is willing to concede and others, perhaps dependent upon some pending case, which the conferee is not willing to allow. It almost invariably happens that the sixty-day period has expired and the appeal has been filed before the final decision of the bureau can be approved. The taxpayer is then confronted with the alternative of either accepting the bureau's offer to settle the questions which perhaps should never have been decided against him and forever losing his right to benefit from the doubtful questions, or of continuing his appeal and adding one more case to the overburdened docket of the board. The majority of taxpayers very naturally choose the latter alternative.

Under our recommendation, the taxpayer could accept the settlement proposed by the bureau, pay the remaining deficiency, and take advantage of the subsequent decision, by means of a claim for refund, which could be adjusted in the bureau without further burden on the board or courts. In the case of a doubtful question, which was not dependent upon some pending case, the taxpayer could bring suit for it in the usual manner. This would tend to divert to the Court of Claims and District Court part of the cases that are now burdening the docket of the board. Many of the doubtful questions which are now carried through the board, would undoubtedly be dropped altogether, for in bringing suit to recover taxes, the taxpayer must himself take the initiative. He will consider well the merits of his case before committing himself to the expenses of such a suit. If the taxpayer believes in his case strongly enough to make the necessary expenditure he is certainly entitled to a hearing.

Those cases where a taxpayer would bring a second suit on some question not covered in the first decision, would, we believe, be extremely rare and would be more than offset by the elimination of cases which go to the board for decision under the present procedure.

We suggest consideration of the proposition that the board be authorized to assess costs not exceeding $500 against either the taxpayer or the Bureau of Internal Revenue, or apportion such costs between the two, as a means of encouraging the settlement of as many questions as possible before appeal is taken.

The board should consider the introduction of the practice of hearing questions of law before the introduction of evidence as to facts, in cases where the settlement of a point of law would dispose of the case. The necessity of proving the facts in all cases before the question of law can be raised results in expense and delay to the taxpayer.

We suggest consideration of the proposition that the board be permitted to appoint special masters for taking testimony and finding facts in long and involved cases.

The formal finding of facts should not be compulsory in cases where an opinion or a memorandum decision is written.

The burden of proof should be on the commissioner in case of fraud and in cases of decedents.

RULES AND REGULATIONS

We recommend the discontinuance of the publication of the Treasury Bulletins and a limitation on the publication of regulations to such as are necessary for the administration of the law. We believe the extensive publication of opinions of the Bureau of Internal Revenue has not been conducive to the settlement of cases, but has on the contrary stimulated taxpayers and administrators alike to lay undue emphasis upon technicalities in the statements issued by the chief administrative officers. In the great mass of opinions and rulings issued by the bureau are many which have been reversed or superseded and which are therefore misleading and far from helpful. We believe a single statement of general rules is sufficient for administrative purposes and will tend towards more efficient work on the part of subordinates in the bureau.

GENERAL ADMINISTRATIVE SUGGESTIONS

Simplification is not only a matter of statutory revision. It embraces also the practice of administrative officers. We regard the present system within the Bureau of Internal Revenue as too informal in one respect and too impersonal in other respects, to accomplish the steady settlement of cases. At present the opinion of the auditor who examines the case and reaches his own conclusion as to facts and law in the first instance often permeates the entire subsequent procedure and tinctures the opinion of all others who may be called upon to consider the case. A natural reluctance to overrule a subordinate with dogmatic disposition and positive attitude, often hampers an unprejudiced consideration by superiors. The practice of having cases reviewed by persons who have had no contact with the case and have heard no argument on behalf of the taxpayer has led to unsatisfactory results.

We suggest consideration of a procedure whereby facts can be proved in such manner that the bureau may rely thereon, in appeals before the board, thus increasing the likelihood of stipulations with the taxpayer instead of putting him to proof on appeal.

FINAL DETERMINATION AND ASSESSMENTS

We consider Section 1106 (a) in great need of clarification. It should unequivocally state that the running of the statute is a complete bar to the collection of the tax and any tax assessed after the statute of limitations has run on assessments or paid after the statutory period has expired, should be refunded on that ground alone.

The agreement provided for in Section 1106 (b) which precludes reopening of the case, except for fraud or misrepresentation, should be made available at the time of settlement of the case, instead of after payment of the tax or acceptance of credit or refund. The statute should provide that the Commissioner shall request such agreement from the taxpayer upon final closing of any case without appeal. The present rule requires the taxpayer to take the first step to obtain such agreement and this necessity for affirmative action on his part has prevented the execution of such contracts in many cases.

LIMITATION OF ASSESSMENTS AND SUITS BY THE UNITED STATES

Section 1109 should be consolidated with the complementary provisions in other sections of the law, in order that all provisions relating to this subject may be conveniently read at one time. Our recommendations on this subject are stated above (p. 32).

LIMITATION ON PROSECUTION BY THE UNITED STATES

Section 1110 is in great need of clarification. It contains no less than five provisos. One proviso is limited to acts which were not barred by law at the time of the enactment of the Revenue Act of 1924; another proviso excludes from the operation of the section all offenses committed prior to its passage. The intent of Congress is very obscure.

DECENTRALIZATION

This committee is not in favor of decentralization—at the present time. Local determination of taxpayers' liability, under central control, would go far toward expeditious closing of cases, but until all employes of the Bureau of Internal Revenue are placed under civil service and until proper salaries and permanent tenure have been established, decentralization presents problems which are insurmountable. Carelessness, favoritism and sectional prejudices, as well as differences of opinion would flavor the local administration of the law by political appointees. If decentralization is desirable, as we think it is, it should be introduced slowly and cautiously, through the agency of men trained at Washington, with a national viewpoint, and having confidence that work well done will lead to higher positions and commensurate salaries. Not until the collection of revenue is recognized to be a highly specialized, technical profession, an honored, permanent, important and well-paid occupation, suitable to the abilities of men capable of achieving success in professional or business careers, will decentralization be desirable or effective.

We urge the creation of strictly non-political civil service status for all employees of that branch of the Government concerned with the collection of revenue.

FIELD FORCE

This committee is of the opinion that great economies can be effected and efficiency furthered by consolidation of the offices of collectors and revenue agents. The law should also clearly state the relation of all field officials to the Bureau of Internal Revenue. There should be no question about the complete authority of the Commissioner over collectors, in all matters pertaining to the collection of the revenue.

Necessary limitation to the length of this report has precluded us from a full discussion of propositions we have herein advanced; and shortness of time has prevented consideration of many worthy suggestions which have been brought to our attention. We have been deeply impressed with the very general opinion that the need for a thorough revision of the statute and improvement of administration is urgent and pressing; that a partial revision, looking to improvement of the present structure, is inadequate to meet the needs of the situation and should not be substituted for a thorough renovation of our income tax system; and that the existence of the Joint Congressional Committee should be extended for as long a period as may be necessary to fully consider the manifold aspects of the subject, in order that a new system of income taxation, simpler in its terms, sounder in its concept and more flexible in its operation may spring from the experience of the past.

> GEO. E. HOLMES, *Chairman,*
> DONALD ARTHUR,
> HENRY H. BOND,
> F. MORSE HUBBARD,
> ALBERT E. JAMES,
> ROBERT N. MILLER,
> HUGH SATTERLEE,[4]
> CHARLES B. McINNIS, *Secretary.*

[4] On account of his absence Mr. Satterlee has not read the report in its final form, but his approval of the position taken by the committee in large has been indicated.

CHAIRMAN ALEXANDER: Now, I am intending to throw the meeting open for questions and discussion, but I want it thoroughly understood that this is a closed season, so far as I am concerned. Mr. Holmes is here. Any questions that you have to ask I want directed, perhaps through me, or direct, to Mr. Holmes, and I am very sure that he will be glad to answer anything which you may ask with respect to the report, to the best of his ability.

On the other hand, with respect to the discussion, I am sure that he and the other members of the committee who are present here will be very glad to receive your views.

I do want to say this, however, that I think it would be a great aid to the reporter of this meeting, and I am sure it would be a great aid to me, if you will, in asking a question or in seeking recognition for discussion, state your name, in order that there may not be any confusion on the record.

The meeting is open for discussion or questions.

PHILIP ZOERCHER (Indiana): Mr. Chairman, on the 10th recommendation, I should like to ask Mr. Holmes why in that recommendation one year would not be sufficient instead of three years. Why should a taxpayer who makes out his report wait three years for the final passing by this board? Why shouldn't it be passed on in the year in which it is filed?

MR. HOLMES: The committee did not feel that in the final analysis it should determine questions of absolute period of time because that, after all, is something which Congress, or, rather, the Bureau of Internal Revenue, will have to work out as a matter of experience. The question is whether the government, especially as it is now situated, having a central office for administration in Washington, and having to examine all the letters in Washington, could do it within a year. Perhaps under a simpler law we might find that that period could be cut down to two years or even one year. The present rule is about three years, and we felt that it would be well not to disturb that present period until new experience under a revised law should indicate the wisdom of a shorter period.

RUSSELL BRADFORD (New York): I endorse Mr. Holmes' point of view that one year is too short, that a complicated subject like the income tax may not be administered by any administration, however intelligent the officials or bureau may be, within one year. I agree that three years is an appropriate period.

However, I am interested particularly in two phases of the report. I am interested in two phases of this law, isolated, so to speak, from the other phases of it, and those are with respect to the administraion of estates, the taxation of income from estates, and the bases now employed for the calculation of capital gains upon the sale of property received by gift.

The basic valuation, as the law now stands, on the sale of property by an executor who must administer the estate in order to turn over cash to legatees or beneficiaries—I speak now particularly of Treasury Decisions 4010, 4011 and 4012—is not the price at which the executor receives the property, not the valuation for the purpose of inheritance tax or death duty, but the value at which the decedent purchased the property. Let us analyze that for a moment:

A buys property (we will say United States Steel, to take a generally marketable subject) at $100 per share; A dies; B is the personal representative, the executor; C is a legatee. B has got to pay as executor for A's estate the debts, administration expenses and other obligations of the estate. The stock at the time of A's death is worth $200 per share. I don't care what value you give to it,—yet B must have gotten that stock at a new valuation. Because why? Two reasons: One is that the Federal Government or state government in each particular instance has given a new value to it for death-duty purposes. Another reason is that B, the personal representative, does not carry on what A has done. What B does is to obtain new assets, in part at least, for the purpose of transmitting them to the legatees or beneficiaries of the estate. Thus B, the executor, is a new owner, and by the law is made a separate taxable entity. The Federal Government says that when B, the executor, sells United States Steel, which has cost A twenty years ago $100 and is now at $248 or $250 per share, he must pay a profit on the difference between $100 and $250. Yet B got the property at a value of $200. Am I getting over what I am trying to say? Analyze it for just a second in your own thought. This is it:

The Government, for death duties, has said it is worth $200 per share. It has imposed an advalorem tax, measured by a value of $200 per share, yet it says, in addition to that you must pay an income tax because it was not worth $200 when this particular seller, that is, the decedent, transferred it to this particular sellee, that is, the executor. It was worth only $100.

That is not so. It is not a fact. Congress has undertaken to legislate a fact. I want to say this, that when adoption by congress is recommended of a report that gives to a basic value a value that is not basic, it is a wrong report. When the report does as this report does,—recommends to congress giving to the basic value a value that is a value,—we have a different proposition.

May I interpolate just a second, by saying that all values are arrived at by due process of law; that determination of values is and must be a judicial function. That is, the legislative department may not find values as facts; that is essentially a judicial function. Neither the executive department nor the legislative department has anything to do, under our constiutional system, with finding of facts. The fact is or it is not. If it is, under competent evidence, the judicial department of our Government will find that it is. If it is not, the legislature may not make it so; and of course the executive department may not make it so.

So far as this report is concerned, I endorse it. But I think the law in this respect raises very serious questions in the effect upon estates. An executor or administrator, when he sells property belonging to him as such, which formerly belonged to a decedent, but which has come to him by process of law, necessarily sells the same charged with the value as of the date of acquisition by him. That a new valuation starts at the date of acquisition by him is obvious, or should be obvious. Why?

For two reasons, as I said before, because the Government has made a new valuation for that asset as of the time the executor gets it, and further because he is a new owner. In that respect I endorse the ercommendations of Mr. Holmes' committee.

Now, another phase of law reads viciously, I think. I use the word "viciously" in its nicer sense, not in a bad sense. The law now reads viciously, that when a man makes a gift to another, and the donee sells, he is charged, so far as income tax purposes are concerned, with the value of the property as it was in the hands of the donor. That is the law. Let us analyze that just briefly—because I can only speak briefly—its equity and its legal effect.

Its equity is this: A turns over property to B—it may be his wife, maybe his son-in-law; it may be a wedding present; it may be a birthday present. B gets property at that moment charged with the value of the thing he has got. He has not at that moment received income, or any appreciation of capital while possessed of such capital. He receives merely property — an asset — worth so much at the time he receives it.

Under our constitutional system we cannot take the property away from B that A has given him.

I am not talking about theory right now. Theoretically, all property laws are within the state's power; the state has the power of regulation of property; the Federal Government has no control over property rights. That power is reserved to the states under the Tenth Amendment to the Constitution of the United States. The state may say, " You may not do this." So far, so good. As I said, I am not speaking theoretically, as to whether or not a complete prohibition by the state might not cause a revolution. I wish to analyze only the condition as it now confronts us and not necessarily the theory. A gives property to B, his wife, son, daughter or daughter-in-law. B gets it; at that moment what is its value, that is, what is the value of the net asset belonging to B? Why, its value at that time, and no other. B wants to sell it, B, the daughter or the wife. How did she get the property? What is the profit to B? The profit clearly is the difference between the value of the thing at the time it is given and the price received for the same upon the sale thereof. That is alone the profit.

When the law undertakes to say that it is going to charge B with taxation, and that he must pay a tax upon the accumulated appreciation in the hands of another taxpayer, a separate taxable entity, because of economic conditions, the ebb and flow of which no man can control, which have given an appreciated value to the property and increased the value of the gift in the hands of A, then the law is taxing B upon A's income or appreciation. This can no more be done rightfully, and as I think, legally, than that I may be taxed upon my house, for a real property tax, measured by the value of your house which may be a hundredfold more.

Any law is vicious and wrongful that attempts to exact contribution for the support of government because of A's generous instinct in doing the natural thing of making a gift to his daughter or son or wife—and such a law, in effect, undertakes to penalize generous impulses and dam the natural, normal flow of paternal and family acts. In effect, the law says, if you do the natural, normal sort of thing, that sort of thing shall be penalized by the imposition of a tax upon you.

Weigh the full import of these observations. All I am intending to do for the few moments I am going to talk here is merely to suggest these thoughts in order that you may weigh them.

The second point, aside from the equity of it, is the legal consequence of it. The legal consequence of it is that you may impose the tax, and the United States Supreme Court has upheld it, in Goodrich v. Edwards, and Brewster v. Walsh, that is, that a capital gain is subject to the tax. We happen to be isolated and unique, in so far as taxation upon capital gains is concerned. No other country in the world imposes or has ever undertaken to impose a tax upon the appreciation of property upon its sale. Italy did advocate the same thing about two or three years ago, and it abandoned the advocacy of it even under such a dictatorship as Mussolini's. Australia considered it with much more seriousness than Italy did, but Australia did not adopt the taxation of capital gains as income. Income, as the United States Supreme Court said in the Macomber case, is the thing that flows from, is received out of, emerges out of capital. Analyze that. Does capital gain emerge out of, come from, develop out of, anything?

The asset is the same thing, merely developing. The same thing reaches one particular point. If it is sold it is income. The Supreme Court said it is. That settles it. The Supreme Court of the United States has said so, so that settles it. But, nevertheless, as a logician—and just for the moment I am assuming that I am one— it is not income, the tour-de-force reasoning of the United States Supreme Court to the contrary notwithstanding.

I say, therefore, that when the donee gets his particular property, the donee gets what? He gets a ring worth $200; he gets stock, thousands of shares, worth $200,000; he gets a house, a home, a farm, worth $100,000; he gets a piece of paper for stock, another piece of paper, a bond, worth $10,000. When does he get it? He gets it at the moment of gift. He sells it. Shall he, the person who owns the thing, and sells it, be penalized with what has happened to the person who happened, chancefully, as a mere sport of fortune, to give it? Shall he, the seller, be penalized for what A has done or because A has been generous? Can burdens of taxation be arbitrarily shifted from A to B by mere legislative action?

My point is this; so far as the report recommends that the price in the hands of the donee shall be the price in the hands of the donee, it is correct. The federal law of the United States so far is wrong. So far as an estate is concerned, when the executor sells, he sells, or should be considered to have sold, property charged with the value as of the date of acquisition by him. When that value is increased by a statutory or legislative fiat, it is one of two things, unconstitutional or unjust. If it is unconstitutional, that settles it. If it is unjust, the legislature ought to correct it. The courts will settle the constitutional question; the legislature ought to settle the facts, the equity of the situation.

Those are the things I am interested in. May I say this, just in closing: I approve of practically all the report, so far as I have seen it. This report was handed to us this morning. How many of you have read every word and analyzed and studied and considered the consequences of the report, the projected force of the report?

In New Orleans two years ago we had an inheritance tax report. It was presented to us one evening and was to be adopted by this convention the next afternoon. I like to think I know something about inheritance taxation, and I do. But I did not know the full import, after a day's study of that report two years ago at New Orleans.

I endorse practically everything that Mr. Holmes has said. There is no person here, male or female, that bows with more deference or doffs his hat with more respect to Mr. Holmes than I do; yet I advocate, and say to this association, that without opportunity to study the import, the significance, the purport of what this report recommends, suggests, intimates, don't let us adopt it. Let it rest just where it is. I think it is worth while. I think it is highly worth while. Personally, I endorse it. Personally, I approve it. Personally, I am for it. Undertaking just for the moment to advise you, I say that as a body politic we should not adopt any report we have not had a chance to study. We will not have a chance to study it. Let it stay where it is. I oppose the adoption of any report of that significance, of that force, of that power, at this time.

CHAIRMAN ALEXANDER: Any other person desire to speak?

EDWARD F. DOYLE (New York): The Real Estate Board of New York, and, I think, the National Association of Real Estate Boards, submitted some questions to the committee on the simplification of the income tax in regard to problems of real estate. One you took care of. Another was the installment sales proposition.

VOICE: Can't hear you.

MR. DOYLE (continuing): I always feel a great diffidence in addressing a collection of hard-boiled tax experts, who spend all their time trying to find some way to get some more money out of the taxpayers whom I represent, and who know more about tax matters in a moment than I ever will know; consequently, it is rather difficult for me to properly express myself. I am in the position, more or less, of the Baptist convert—I may have told you this before— that stood on the banks of a cold and icy river, and got cold feet when he saw the others being immersed; so he said to the parson, " Parson, I doesn't need to be baptized." The parson said, " Why not?" He said, " I have been baptized." The parson said, " Where were you baptized?" He said, " I was baptized in the Methodist Church." " Oh," the parson said, " that was not baptism; that was merely dry cleaning." He was not a regular Baptist, and I do not feel like a regular tax expert.

We submitted three or four questions to the committee. One you took care of. One is in regard to installment sales of real estate. If a piece of real estate is sold for $100,000 and a $25,000 mortgage is taken back, or $25,000 cash is received and a $75,000 mortgage is taken, of course we considered that a closed transaction and willingly paid on the profit on it. But during the last three or four years there have been tremendous subdivisions of real estate, valued perhaps at millions of dollars—I have one in mind where I was interested, where the property was valued at six millions of dollars—and the way that is sold is this: A lot is sold for $1000; the first payment is $150, then the purchaser is supposed to pay $10 a month; that would make $270 in one year, or more than the 25 per cent, making it a closed transaction; but the commission runs from 30 to 35 per cent, and 65 per cent of all the money that comes in is withheld until the commission is paid; so that when the Government insists upon calling that a closed transaction and making you pay on the estimated profit — and as you know, they figure the profit whether you have sold all the property or not — it makes it pretty hard, extremely hard, for the man who owns the property to make his payments, especially when he has to pay on a mortgage and pay for all the other things.

We thought we had pretty well taken care of the finance committee of the senate and the ways and means committee; both agreed to take care of it; but they were persuaded not to put the amendment we asked in the bill; and from what was said we considered that they would take care of it in the regulations, but they never did; and we asked you to consider that. I don't know whether you did or not.

Mr. Holmes: That has been referred to on page 78 and 79.

Mr. Doyle: Is it taken care of there?

Mr. Holmes: Yes.

Mr. Doyle: I beg your pardon.

Another point was differentiating between an investor and an operator. Now, all real estate operators are really investors, — I mean; they buy a piece of property and base the amount they pay on what that property will return, naturally, if they have any sense. It may be that they will sell that property within three or four months; maybe they will hold it for ten years, but the Government now taxes them if they sell it within two years, as though they sold ordinary merchandise which can be inventoried and which is not subject to local taxation in our state the way real estate is. We don't think the Government should differentiate between two classes of holders of real estate. Did you do anything about that, Mr. Holmes?

Mr. Holmes: With reference to installment sales, we are of the opinion that the statute ought not to contain any restriction as to the treatment of installment sales. There should be a general permission in the statute to the taxpayer to report on a cash basis, accrual basis, a combination of both, or any other basis of good accounting. Restrictive provisions in the statute hamper the ad-

ministration of the law.   We also call attention to the fact that we
have received a number of criticisms of the installment provision,
among which are that a sale of real estate on the installment plan
should be treated precisely the same as a sale of personal property.

Mr. Doyle: That is what we ask, and that is what they agreed to.

Mr. Holmes: And that contracts for the sale of real estate, with
the entire title passing or full payment received, should not be
treated as installment sales, and that the requirement that payments
on real estate sales must not exceed 25 per cent in the first year, is
an unjust discrimination, for the reasons you have stated, namely
because in cases where the initial payments exceed 25%, there are
nevertheless certain expenses against them which reduce the net receipt of the seller; and that it tends to complicate the income tax
procedure.   For one thing, it compels the vendor to wait until the
end of the year to ascertain whether or not he may treat a transaction on his books as an installment sale.

We recommend no mention in the law of requirements governing
installment sales, but a general provision in the law permitting the
taxpayer to report on a cash basis or accrual basis or a combination
of both, as most taxpayers now do, or any other recognized basis
of good accounting which will show net income.

Under such general rules it will be a matter of simple evolution
to work out methods of accounting that will be fair to taxpayer and
Government alike; and those methods, if not fair, will be the subject of judicial scrutiny; but, as the statute now stands, if these
cases came up for judicial scrutiny, the judge would have to hang
on the meaning of the statutory words, rather than on common sense.

We think any provisions such as those relating to installment
sales, or any other special provisions in the statute which intend
to restrict or limit the freedom of action of the administrative officials, should be dropped.   The statute itself should be in broad
terms, permitting a common-sense administration of the act.

Mr. Doyle: That is entirely satisfactory.   Several of the gentlemen and myself submitted a similar proposition in Washington a
few months ago.

There is another matter, and that is where three or four pieces
of real estate are held by a corporation and they have not been able
to sell it or manage it properly and they decide to abandon the corporation and take the property back, each one taking his own piece
back.   We feel that the Government ought not to tax that.   Now
they have it appraised and tax it.   I don't think you have covered
that.   I have not had a chance to read the report.

Mr. Holmes: We admit that is a perplexing problem, and the
committee did not have any solution to present.

MR. DOYLE: Three or four men own three or four pieces of property, and for a time it seems it would be to their advantage to incorporate; after a while they find it is not, and then they want to return the property to the owners, taking back the stock and dissolving the corporation. They don't think they should pay a tax because there was no real exchange.

MR. HOLMES: The committee has not acted on that.

MR. DOYLE: From what you said, Mr. Holmes, I think the National Association of Real Estate Boards, and of course the Real Estate Board of New York is entirely in favor of the recommendations of the committee.

CHAIRMAN ALEXANDER: It has been called to my attention that last night here at the meeting there was a limitation placed for the period of this conference of seven minutes on any one discussing from the floor. I shall expect you gentlemen to confine yourselves to seven minutes, although I think I have given a little leeway to one or two of the speakers, due to the fact that I did not know that that period of time had been fixed upon by the meeting last night.

Does any one desire to discuss any of these matters further, or to ask any questions of Mr. Holmes?

CARL C. FLEHN (New York): I have read carefully only some fifty pages of the report, and glanced at the rest of it. There seem to be three or four very fundamental questions or principles, one might almost say premises, underlying the report, to which it would be desirable to direct our thought and attention before we go into the multitudinous details which are always suggested by a report on a tax so comprehensive as this.

The first of these is the assumption in the report that the method and principle of self-assessment is to be continued. I notice, however, towards the end of the report, on page 103, a paragraph regarding decentralization of the administration, which involves indirectly a possibility that the committee contemplated ultimate modification of the method and principle of self-assessment.

I should be glad if Mr. Holmes would correct me, if, owing to the haste with which I had to read the report, I unintentionally make any misstatement regarding the attitude of the committee.

It appears, however, to me that in all the first part of the report it is at least assumed that for the time being, the principle of self-assessment should be continued.

Most of you gentlemen are accustomed to the administration of the property tax and to its interpretation, and you are quite aware that we should land in great difficulties if we left the assessment to the taxpayer, even temporarily. You are quite aware that in practice the assessment is an official one; that the assessment roll is written up, equalized, scrutinized, audited, and a great many other things done to it, before the taxes are charged to the tax collector.

And you are quite aware that unless that assessment roll is perfeet and complete in all details, no tax is due or payable. You know that such trifling errors as the omission of a dollar-mark will invalidate the assessment roll or invalidate any one assessment thereon; and it is really one of the most ancient traditions of the Anglo-Saxon race that no warrant exists for the collection of a tax until an assessment has been made.

Now, owing to the exigencies of war and for other reasons of haste when we inaugurated the federal income tax, we had to get the money in as quickly as we could, and no time was available for organizing an orderly and proper assessment of incomes, and we resorted to the principle of self-assessment.

Thanks, too, to the patriotism of the American people, the method of self-assessment has worked very well, but we have to remember that the excitement of war and the high tension of that period and the moral exaltation of that period have gone by; and may we not discuss carefully the advisability, if the income tax is to continue, of going back to the fundamental principles of an official assessment, before any tax is due or payable.

Just stop to think how that would clear away a vast number of these difficulties which the committee so carefully and so shrewdly and so wisely discusses. If the assessment were finished before the tax was due and payable and all questions as to what the income is, and its amount, and the tax properly extended by a proper auditor, you would have relief from a great many of these serious difficulties.

If you are going to regard the income tax, however, as a temporary expedient that is likely to be repealed, then well enough, let us go on and patch up the old system without so radical a change.

Most of you are also aware that the British have proceeded on the other principle: that they have an official assessment before any tax is due and payable; that they, moreover, afford the taxpayer ample opportunity for immediate hearing upon the assessment before a board of local gentlemen, who are authorized to revise and hear his complaint. I leave that because I have to hurry on to get within the seven minutes.

Another very interesting matter is discussed by the committee, and that is the double taxation of dividends. The committee goes at some length into the details of the explanation that income derived from dividends, where the taxpayer's income is small, is taxed approximately 13½ per cent, whereas, perhaps, a neighbor, whose income is of the same amount but from some other source, may be taxed at a very much lower rate; and it constitutes, of course, in those instances, double taxation. I may have overlooked it, but it

seems to me the committee might, in passing, have called attention
to the fact that the taxpayer whose income is entirely within the
exempt class—too small for any tax, but who derives some income
from dividends—is taxed 13½ per cent on that part of the income,
whereas a neighbor, with like income, may pay no tax whatsoever.
I think that is a subject for very careful consideration and discussion.

Another very interesting suggestion in the report relates to the
permanency of the rates, and I can see at once the enormous administrative advantage, and the advantages to the taxpayers, of
steady rates for the income tax.

This matter of the changing of dates and of getting your loss in
on this year or on the other year, or of getting your big income in
when the rates are low and out of the years in which it was large,
cuts an enormous figure in making the returns and determining how
much one has to pay; and the committee has made a number of
exceedingly wise recommendations with reference to that.

On the other hand, gentlemen, should we not discuss or consider
whether the Federal Government does not need an elastic element
in its revenue system and whether, of all the possible elastic elements, the income tax is not the best one; that that should be the
tax which should move up and down with the changing needs of
the Government.

The committee seems to think, though, so far as I have gone—
and please realize that I have not read it all—that there are other
sources which might be the fluctuating element.

I have cast about hurriedly for other sources. You cannot change
the customs duties up and down, with the needs for revenue, because that affects a great many other things besides revenue; nor
have we at the present time, since we lost the liquor taxes, any
other large element that we can move up and down in rates to
meet the varying needs of the Government from year to year. I
wish the committee had been a little more specific upon those other
sources.

Here and there I see that the committee is quite in doubt as to
the identity of all kinds of gains and profits with income; that here
and there they have indicated that they might feel that certain
forms of certain so-called gains and profits are not income, in the
sense in which the ordinary man uses the term "income," and
therefore should not be taxable; they have not gone very far in the
direction of identifying taxable income with what the ordinary man
considers income.

Now, what do we ordinarily consider income? We consider as
income current receipts which are spendable, without impairing
one's future income receipts. And there are a good many items taxable under the federal income tax law that the ordinary business,

12

or the ordinary householder does not consider income. That is a large field for discussion, and comes under the provisions concerning the definition of income.

There are a vast number of other minor points, but those four big points seem to me to be worthy of very careful consideration.

I notice in one of the recent bulletins of the association that my colleague in California, Professor Lutz, suggested that one way of simplifying the income tax would be the abolition of the normal tax, leaving, I assume from his argument, the surtax.

In closing, perhaps not too seriously, gentlemen, I would suggest that the best way of simplifying the income tax is to repeal the tax.

CHAIRMAN ALEXANDER: Gentlemen, that was a very short seven minutes. We now have another seven minutes open for any one of you who wishes to speak.

MILLBANK JOHNSON (California): I should like to ask Mr. Holmes if he has given any consideration, or if the committee has given any consideration to the averaging of income for a period of years upon which to base the tax.

MR. HOLMES: The committee gave a good deal of consideration to that, and suggests that as a proposition for consideration, particularly with respect to the earned income. The committee was a little bit in doubt as to the feasibility of averaging income over a period of years, being swayed, perhaps, to some extent by the fact that England has recently dropped the averaging of income on grounds with which we are not familiar, and did not have time to become familiar before this report was made, but which, we understand, might relate more to the complications of the English system and their method than to ours, and might not be an objection under our method.

We do recommend, for instance, consideration of the averaging of net income in that portion of our report which deals with earned income. We call your attention to the fact that the present earned income credit is so niggardly as to be of no real advantage to the taxer, and the methods of collection are so complicated that almost universal objection is voiced to it. We do say at the end of that division, on page 77, that we suggest four things for consideration in connection with earned income; first, that the rate of surtax on incomes within the range of substantial earnings should be brought in line with the rates below and above those earnings. The rate in the revenue act of 1926 is a little lower than the rate in the act of 1916 on very small incomes. In 1916 a married taxpayer with two children paid $120. In 1926, with the same income, he pays only $111, and has an earned income credit which brings that down. The large income taxpayers have had their surtaxes reduced from a maximum in 1918 of 70 per cent to a maximum of 20 per cent, but the great brackets in between 20,000 and 60,000 have not been materially reduced, and are still six times as high as in 1916.

One thing for consideration would be the amelioration of the burden on those whose incomes fall in the intermediate brackets.

Our second suggestion is a less frequent graduation than under the present law. Under the present law the surtax rate goes up one per cent for every $2000. Perhaps one per cent for every $5000 would be better, because it would not then show so marked a difference in the tax, in the case of extraordinary receipts of income in one year as against another; and this is a tendency towards the principal purpose of the average over three or five years which is to smooth out the income curve, take out the peaks, remove the depressions, and get as nearly as possible a straight line.

Our third suggestion is that in the case of extraordinary receipts of earned income some provision analogous to that which now applies to capital gains might be adopted; that is, if the receipt is in payment of services that have been rendered over a period of more than two years, the application of a flat rate to that receipt.

Our fourth recommendation is that the averaging of incomes over a period of three years would minimize the present effect of the surtax on abnormal receipts of occasional, fluctuating earned incomes.

The committee prefers at this time not to be too dogmatic about the averaging of the rates. England has had some trouble with it. Perhaps that trouble has been due to the peculiarities of the English system. One difficulty in England in the averaging of incomes has been that the taxpayer has a relatively large tax over a period of three years, where a large receipt comes into the first of those three years, and by the time he comes to pay his tax for the second and third year, he has spent his money and feels the burden of the assessment that much more; while if he pays the tax in the year he receives the money it is not so painful to him, because he still has the extraordinary receipt in mind.

ROY G. BLAKEY: I do not wish to make a speech. There are a number of things I should like to ask questions about, but I am going to close with one question which Mr. Holmes may answer or may not.

I do want to emphasize the point made by one of the speakers a while ago. It seems to me the committee has passed the buck, if you will allow a slang expression, on the changing of rates on some other tax. What other tax? I want to emphasize that point.

Another speaker has referred to the question of capital gains, whether they should be taxed or not, and how are they treated in England. Let me remark, that in that case you ought, at the same time, to see how they treat depreciation in England. We allow for depreciation but they don't allow for it. If we should do away with capital gains we should also have to do away with depreciation to a large extent.

One other thing I wanted to speak of might be referred to in this way. You have heard it said that the grass on the other side of the fence is always the greenest, or heard the saying that misery likes company. I have just been reading a book by an Englishman, comparing the American and English income taxes, and I want to quote a paragraph or two from this book, which came out this year, by Mr. H. B. Spaulding on this comparison. With that I will sit down, except the one question. (Quoting:) " Until 1918 the British Income Tax Law was contained in the Act of 1842 and a great number of amending acts. In 1918 the law of income tax was collected into one statute — the income tax act, 1918. Each year's finance act adds amendments, so that already the income tax law is contained in eight different statutes. Not only is it necessary to consult a number of statutes, but the income tax act, 1918, was little more than a consolidation of the previous acts; it was in no sense a codification of the law. This is most unfortunate, for never was so important a law in such need of codification. It lacks logical arrangement, many of its provisions are obscure, and in many cases the practice under the act is the exact opposite of the rules laid down therein. The sections of the law which actually define taxable income, and provide the rules under which various kinds of income are to be assessed, are not, properly speaking, in the act at all. They are collected in schedules and placed in a sort of appendix to the act. The reason for this arrangement is that the proper place for a schedule is at the end of an act. It seems almost unbelievable that in over a hundred years no one was able to devise a plan which would permit the principal part of the income tax law to be placed in the act itself. It remained for the 1920 Royal Commission to offer a solution by the suggestion that the word 'part' be substituted for the word 'schedule' in order that the subject matter of the present schedules might with propriety be placed in its fitting position in the body of the act."

Up to the present time, however, the suggestion of the Royal Commission has been ignored.

"It must be a difficult matter for any one who is obliged frequently to consult the British income statutes to observe restraint in his comments. As Lord Summener has said: 'It is a most wholesome rule that in taxing the subject the Crown must show that clear powers to tax were given by the legislature. Applied to income tax, however, this is an ironical proposition. Most of the operative clauses are unintelligible to those who have to pay the taxes, and in any case derive such clarity as they possess from the judges who have interpreted them.' "

Brown vs. National Provident Institution (1921), 2 A. C., at page 257.

One other paragraph: In other words, they have experiences of over one hundred years. See what is said now of us, we having experience of thirteen or fourteen years:

"The enactment of an entirely new income statute every few years has great advantages. It keeps the law of income tax in one convenient statute; it permits of minor improvements in drafting without the necessity for a separate act; and it frees the legislators from the inertia inevitable where an entirely new income tax act occurs perhaps only once in a century. The result is that the United States income tax is a modern, carefully drafted, and logically arranged statute, whereas the British law is antequated, ill-arranged, and obscure and ambiguous in its provisions. It is unfortunate that the British law was not thoroughly revised and codified in 1918 when all the income statutes were consolidated. There is no possible excuse for any further delay in this most important work of codification. It is, of course, under modern conditions of business and finance, impossible to make any income tax law a simple matter, but certainly everything possible in that direction should be done. This must not be taken, however, as a plea for the enactment of a British income tax law in such detail as is found in the United States statute. In the United States the taxpayer is obliged to assess himself, and it is therefore necessary that the law be clear and detailed. In Great Britain much more responsibility and discretion are given to the administrative officers and less to taxpayers. Accordingly, the British law may remain fairly general in its terms and yet be regarded as satisfactory in this regard. But even within these limits there exists the most urgent necessity for clarification and systematic arrangement of the British law. This necessity was recognized by the 1920 Royal Commission, which strongly recommended that steps should be taken to prepare a bill containing the whole law on the subject in the most modern and approved form. The Commission urged a real codification so that the suggested new act would embody not only the present statutory provisions, but all decisions of principle which have been laid down by the courts. Clear definitions of taxable income and allowable expenditures were recommended and suggestions were made for improvements in form and arrangement. Finally, it was suggested that the schedules be reduced from five to three, and that income be reclassified under the three new schedules."—(Report of the 1920 Royal Commission, Cmd. 615. p. 89. See Chapter XVI for a discussion of the British schedules.)

It is unnecessary to go any further. This is really to point out that there are others who have troubles.

One other thought; in this report it is suggested that the first and most essential thing to do is to demolish the law. Now, it seems to me that most of this is not that, but it is patchwork on what we have now. What I should like is for Mr. Holmes' committee to write the law they want.

CARL C. FLEHN (California) : I have been carrying Spaulding's book around, trying to write a review on it on the very points the gentleman refers to—the simplicity of our law as against the complexity of the British law. I am going to venture to say in that review that the last law is not in itself comprehensive enough. With the 1913 statute more or less in effect still, with a body of regulations, with a body of decisions, with a body of the Lord knows what not, piled on top of it, the whole confounded thing since 1913 all more or less in effect, we haven't wiped out anything. The British never make a revision but wipe out something.

CHAIRMAN ALEXANDER: At any rate, Professor, I am pleased to find that this great indoor amusement of the American people is not confined only to the American people on the making of laws and rules and regulations for the income tax.

MR. HOLMES: I would like to say first that the author of the book which we have been discussing for the last ten minutes was sitting beside me, until a little while ago. He must have had a premonition of what was coming. He left, saying he was going back to his office to tend to business. Mr. Spaulding was in a splendid position to write that book. He had some four or five years' experience, which happened in my office in New York, under the American act; then he went to England and spent two years studying the British act and wrote the book to obtain his Doctor's degree.

While he states that the American act is simple, as compared to the British, which I think any student will admit, he does not admit that the American act is as simple as it could be; and I have heard him use some very vigorous language at times as to the obscurity of our law and the difficulty of determining a question under our law.

To refer to the questions that have just been asked: When the committee says that it feels that the rate of tax ought to be steady and uniform and unchanged from year to year, and that necessary revenue from time to time should be made up from other sources, it has this particularly in mind: it does not feel it is a good thing for the Government to rely entirely on one source of revenue. It ought to have as many sources of revenue at its command as is consistent.

We talk a good deal about nuisance taxes, and all that sort of thing. They are not so great a nuisance, after all. In a prosperous country such as ours, it might be perfectly proper to keep the manufacturer's tax on automobiles, for instance. That is a rather direct tax, paid by the man who buys the car, for the use of roads, a large part of the cost of which is defrayed at federal expense. There are many other taxes which the Government should keep alive. It should have some sort of nucleus of an organization, so that if an occasion comes, a crisis arises, it does not have to fumble about for a year or two, before it can get such special taxes into operation.

While the committee is quite dogmatic on keeping the rate unvaried from year to year, that might perhaps be taken with a grain of salt. There might be a very slight increase in rate from time to time, but as rarely as possible. Perhaps just a little bit higher rate than might be necessary this year, rather than paring the rate down as low as possible, and boosting it next year, would be preferable. The uniformity of it is the important thing. A taxpayer should feel that it makes as little difference as possible whether a transaction falls as a taxable item into one year or another year. When we get that, when we get the feeling that the tax is going to be about the same four or five years from now as it is today, we are going to have much less wrangling about annual deductions for depletion, depreciation and things of that sort; we are going to have much less resort to unusual, artificial forms of transactions which will spread the income over a period of time. Even the tax on installment sales will not be so important where the rate does not vary.

An analysis of our law and the administration over the past ten years will show that a very large proportion of the difficult and exasperating questions, that have kept cases hanging and kept them from being settled, have revolved around the time element. Was this worthless debt actually ascertainable to be worthless in 1920 or 1921? Should this allowance be made in 1921 or 1922? Naturally the taxpayer will strive to get all of his deductions in years of high rates and bring about all of his receipts in years of low rates; and naturally the Government will attempt the very opposite. That is what we want to remove as far as possible by uniformity of rate— steady rates; or if the rate must be changed, changing it as slightly as possible and as infrequently as possible, will do a great deal towards simplification.

The committee is very strongly of the opinion that the United States government should not rely solely on the income tax. Other objects should be subject to tax—perhaps a very low tax but some tax, to keep the organization in the Treasury Department going, so that in case of national crisis it can fall back on six, seven or eight or ten sources of revenue, instead of at that time devising new means of raising taxes and going through all the temporary paralysis that comes with the inauguration of an entirely new form of tax.

Question has been raised as to why capital gains should be taxed; why we should not abolish the tax on capital gains.

If you recall, the committee is in favor of abolishing the tax on capital gains. It does not feel that capital gains and profits should fall in the same category as current income, but practically, it cannot surmount the difficulties of distinguishing between current income and capital gains; of so framing the statute that the taxpayer will be prevented from shunting current income into the form of capital gains. So long as that distinction cannot be made, we feel that the tax should remain on capital gains at a moderate rate, perhaps at one rate where the property has been held for two years, and at a lower rate where it has been held for five or more years; but there should be some tax on capital gains, to destroy the incentive to shunt current income into the form of capital gains, which incentive would be great, if there were no tax on one form of income and a substantially heavy tax on the other form.

When we speak of demolishing the law, what we mean is breaking away from the present form of the law and erecting an entirely new statutory structure, making that simpler, more flexible, sounder in its concept of net income, and leaving it more to administration and the courts to treat the unusual cases. I think the provision in the law of today regarding installment sales is very bad. The law ought not to deal with installment sales. The question of installment sales is a method of accounting and should be an administrative problem. The method of accounting for annual income ought to be the soundest method that can be devised, and installment sales ought to be treated and accounted for in that way which produces a statement of true net income or as near as we can get any statement of income, as an estimate. One of the difficulties we have had is that Congress has not regarded the amount of income reported as an estimate but has treated the subject more as a mathematical problem that could be figured to the last cent.

I am informed that splendid work is being done in Washington looking towards the reforming of the statute, and that perhaps at some time later in the fall a report will be issued by the Joint Congressional Committee which will embody some features very far in the direction that we are urging. We have inadequate language, obsolete phrases, repetitions, absolutely meaningless phrases in the statute; what we urge, instead of a patchwork amendment, changing a section here and there, and perhaps adding a few words to it and making it a little more difficult to understand, is that we ought to revise and revamp the whole law, cutting out the old language of doubtful meaning, keeping in what is good, based upon our experience of the last thirteen years, and frame a simple, direct, understandable statute. I think we will probably find that the committee at Washington is doing a great deal of work along that line, and that it will have some sort of a report this fall that will be of considerable interest to every student of taxation.

OSCAR LESER (Maryland) : I wanted to ask the committee whether they gave any consideration to a flat rate on all incomes, regardless of size; then I want to ask also whether they considered a reform in the administrative feature which will require people to report all their income whether it is taxable or not taxable. I do not mean that they should be taxed on the exempt income, but as a check.

We constantly read statistics of the income of the American people, and we speak of it as taxable income. That is all we know about. Personally, part of my income is exempt from taxation. I always make it a point to report it in parenthesis, so that the Government won't think I am entirely a pauper; but I do believe there are a good many people who form their own judgment as to whether or not income is taxable or exempt. That is a matter that ought to be left to government authority.

As to the legal right to do it, I have no question, since the decision of the Supreme Court that you can call one-half of one per cent of alcohol intoxicating.

E. M. TROWERN (Ottawa) : As I became a member of your association this morning and had the pleasure of looking at your report, I feel that I must congratulate your committee upon the report, and I thought probably you might like to know something about how the income tax operates in Canada.

We have a population here of a little over 9,000,000 people, with a territory larger than the United States, and if we flopped Canada over onto the United States it would still cover Great Britain, Ireland and France, and then we would have enough ice left to fill every ice-box in the United States.

We have a large country, with a little over 9,000,000 people, and we have been studying this income tax. It is a bad egg, and I never knew of anything in my life that would ever make a bad egg a good egg.

We have come to the conclusion in Canada that the best way to deal with the income tax is to cut its tail off right behind the ears.

We have quite a propaganda in Canada, and we have had it for the last two and one-half years—addresses all over this country, from one end to the other, putting out thousands of pamphlets, copies of which we shall be glad to give you. We have, as I stated before, come to the conclusion to ask the Government to abolish it entirely.

I am living here, and 200,000 people in Canada paid an income tax, out of 9,000,000. Now, the problem you have to solve and the problem we have to solve is, how are you going to get people to assess themselves honestly? I consider that 200,000 people in Canada being assessed for income tax is an insult to the country. This is a great agricultural country. Now, how are you going to get income tax out of farmers? I am not reflecting on their honesty. I am simply saying that it cannot be done. If I were a farmer and I had to pay income tax, which our farmers have got to do, instead of turning in cash I would drive down some geese and some calves and a few things and make them take it in kind, because that is the only way you can get anything out of a farmer; let them take it in kind.

Now, what sort of a system is that? Do you think that human nature is of such material, that they will honestly put down what they make every year? You cannot tell what income you make, and yet the assessor comes up to you and says so and so. They are making liars out of the people.

W. E. Gladstone said that. He said that before Parliament; that by that system of taxation you are only going to make liars out of the people.

Now, gentlemen, we want to join with you, and we are pleased with all this information, this magnificent information. The committee ought to be congratulated, because, it all comes down to one thing; it is a difficult, insolvable problem. No one knows yet how to handle it. We say, abolish it.

Now, why abolish it? We are all neighbors and friends here. I have a 'boy in your country. He is doing fine, and I am glad of it. He says you are taking care of him all right. We are all working on this problem together; we have to solve this problem. You go along on your lines, and we are going along our lines, but the public are beginning in Canada to understand that this thing cannot be fixed. You cannot repair it; it has gone beyond repair.

Now, our proposal simply is: abolish it, get rid of it. Remember, they have an organization in Great Britain the same as you have, trying to solve this problem, and surely out of the brains in the United States and in Canada and in Great Britain we can come to some system whereby we can collect our taxes without a man coming along and slipping a paper to the assessor, who knows when he hands that in that it is a lie. We don't want liars in this country. We want to give all an opportunity to do everything possible, to have taxes so that they will be collected honestly, honorably and freely. I thank you.

MEYER D. ROTHSCHILD (New York): Mr. Chairman and Gentlemen: Mr. Holmes raised a point, which I should like to dwell on for a minute and, if I may be permitted, to give some tardy suggestions.

I was invited by that committee, as probably most of the members were, to make suggestions. I was unfortunately abroad for six months and was not able to respond.

The question of a flexible tax which could be used in an emergeney to make up any deficiency seems to me to be a very simple one.

Mr. Holmes, in answer to a question, stated that such a tax as the manufacturers' tax on automobiles might be retained; and possibly he had in his mind some other of the nuisance taxes which are still on the statute books. In an emergency, possibly, if nothing else, that might be fine, but when we remember how these so-called luxury taxes were placed on certain articles of merchandise in the midst of war and war excitement, I think that every American citizen should be thankful when the last of those taxes disappears from the statute books.

There is no warrant to take any article of merchandise and tax that and leave all other articles, especially other articles of the same general nature, untaxed. That was the kind of luxury taxation which Congress placed during the war. They served their purpose; most of them have disappeared, and I sincerely hope, with the present large surplus, that those that are still on the books will promptly disappear in the next session of Congress.

My suggestion to the committee is a very simple one, a very workable one, and one that I verily believe will finally result in a gradual reduction of the unfair parts of the income tax, and will assist the Government and will assist this body and all tax students in arriving at a conclusion which will make our tax system workable, honest and effective. That is the inauguration of a very, very small gross turn-over tax—one-tenth of one per cent, if you please. There you have the nucleus. There you have probably three or four hundreds of millions of dollars a year to start with. If that is too much you can reduce it some more. When the time comes when you have the necessity for larger taxation, when such a time should come again, and I hope it will not come in my lifetime, as in 1917, when large amounts are necessary, the rate can readily be raised to one per cent, and you will have three or four billions of dollars of taxation, every dollar of which can be collected. No man is going to falsify his books for one-tenth of one per cent or one per cent on his turn-over. The cost of the collection of that tax has been demonstrated to be very, very small. Tax officials, tax people who had it up with the sales tax division, have all been in favor of it, have all stated and testified that even under the unequal conditions under which it was levied, it was workable and was generally paid without any default.

Now, that is a suggestion to the committee. If you should have any occasion to amend the report or change it, I trust the committee will take that under consideration. A note has been raised here today which I trust may bear some fruit, and that is the impossibility, or rather, the difficulty, of asking a body of men of this class, this group, to pass on such a very, very important report, that is, to try to bind the conference by a vote on the report when there has been opportunity for us to read the report; not even, let us say, in a slighting manner.

I suggest to the officers of the organization that when such a report as the admirable one made by Mr. Holmes and his committee, and such a one as was made two years ago, which created some little disturbance in New Orleans — when such a report is ready there should be an effort made to have that report in print at least a month before the conference. An effort should be made to have such a report in the hands of every member of the National Tax Association and of every delegate if it could be done. It possibly could not have been done this time, but if that could have been done I do not think any plea could have been raised as to the impossibility of voting intelligently on the subject when the question for a vote should come up.

NATHAN B. WILLIAMS (District of Columbia) : Some thousands of years ago a distinguished writer of fables, one Æsop by name, recounted a convention of mice, who determined on, or at least debated for several hours, the feasibility of killing the cat.

The cat in this instance is the income tax law. The distinguished gentleman from Ontario says the way to do it is to clip its tail off just behind its ears. The distinguished gentleman from New York suggests that the way is to set up another cat, and call it a gross turn-over tax. And other gentlemen suggest that there are other features of the idea, and even go so far as to refer, to prove our hyprocisy in the United States, to finding anything as intoxicating as one-half of one per cent. But, we have one-half of one per cent in the Constitution of the United States, just like we have the income tax law; so it is not a theory which confronts this convention, to see if the cat rebels, but it is a practical fact, of the necessity of something being done to make it easier to administer the laws of the United States to raise the necessary funds to discharge the obligations of a growing Nation, and also to meet the political exigencies of a Congress that likes to spend money.

Now, all facetiousness, or all attempts at facetiousness aside, the report brought to this conference by Mr. Holmes and his committee is an admirable document. I am willing to admit that, because I at least voted on some of the ideas that are contained in it. Probably several other hundred people have the same notion, that we contributed some of the suggestions. We like to find people agreeing with us.

There are other suggestions that were made, of which I have knowledge, that the committee has not yet seen proper to make recommendations upon.

I represent the law department of the National Association of Manufacturers. We have a committee in our association on that subject. I carry in my hand a typewritten document of a number of subjects on which we have reached at least tentative conclusions, but the practical suggestion, gentlemen, is this:

The Joint Congressional Committee, created by the last act of Congress, the 1926 act, after taking a year and a half to get organized, and having only two years in which to report, are at work on a report. Some sort of a report will come forward.

I agree thoroughly that the work of that committee must be continued, but in my opinion the way to bell this cat is to get George Holmes' committee to write the statute, and then we could take shots at it and criticize it among ourselves for a convenient length of time, and then everybody could get behind their final conclusions and tell Congress that we want that written into a law.

The fact that they suggest putting a new statute in the front, effective on a future date, I think is one of the soundest things there is in the report. They have not got all the questions that would come up, that would arise in their own minds with respect to the drafting of an income tax law, in this report. They would and could and ought to receive and give considerations, and if they did write a statute a lot of questions would arise.

So, it is a question again of how we are going to bell this income tax cat. We are not going to do it by holding a mice convention. We have to reach some determination upon just the particular individual or group of individuals upon whom we are going to lay the responsibility of getting the bell squarely fastened around its neck; and when we have done that the National Association of Manufacturers, and the thousands of other business organizations, the thousands of other organizations of other kinds that are interested, may be expected to accept the work of such a committee, of which this is such a proud example, and get behind it and ask Congress to write it, and not to run in to Congress for our special, particular pet notions, when a committee of self-sacrificing and patriotic, comprehensive and thoroughly informed gentlemen bring forward such a result. But this is not an income tax law, it is only a working basis for a starter. I thank you.

CHARLES D. ROSA (Wisconsin) : I think I can make the audience here hear; if not I will move forward.

I just want to make several little suggestions. In the first place, in my judgment an income tax law cannot be simplified. It may be simplified a little more than the federal income tax law, but income is as complicated as human life, and when you attempt to tax it, as has been our experience in Wisconsin since 1911, you will not find it a simple thing.

Probably like fools who rush in where angels fear to tread, Wisconsin rewrote its income tax law during the last session of the legislature, and in spite of the fact that England has discarded an average basis, Wisconsin has put the taxation of income upon a three-year average basis. Perhaps we shall be wiser in four or five

years, but there is at least one thing we know in Wisconsin, and that is that it is not possible to go very far in the simplification of an income tax.

Our friend and host over here, from Canada, seems to think some other method of taxation is a simpler thing.

I want to call your attention to what we are up against in Wisconsin in the property tax line. For fifty years, almost, the rule laid down in our statute for the assessment of property is that real estate must be assessed at the full value at which it will ordinarily sell at private sale. How, then, are you going to assess the great manufacturing plants in the State of Wisconsin that never sell as going concerns? And in a recent case our Supreme Court has said that our State Engineer is an incompetent witness to testify to the value of those plants.

It is not a simple thing to administer the property tax on the basis that you hope to have it administered.

I wondered, when Mr. Holmes was suggesting that a taxpayer be allowed to report his income either on a cash or an accrual basis, or any combination that he wished, if the committee would also suggest that they would allow him to change it every time he saw fit. We have had our experience in Wisconsin along that line. Finally the commission had to lay down the rule that we only knew of two methods of accounting for income; one was on the cash basis, and one was on the accrual basis; and we assessed a couple of concerns on that basis, and the Supreme Court sustained our finding.

We are probably in Wisconsin not so much interested in what the Federal Government does with its income tax. We have sort of a fellow feeling of sympathy in their endeavor to administer that tax. We ourselves are always aiming to progress and to simplify and to make the tax a more equitable and just one. In Wisconsin, of course, it is not the sole tax, although our income tax yielded last year in the neighborhood of $17,000,000, which is frankly known and admitted there to be an additional or supplemental tax to the property tax; and the people of Wisconsin universally, I think, would not discard it; and most people who have studied the subject there realize that in a vast majority of cases it is a leveling-up of the burden of taxation.

COLEMAN SILBERT (Massachusetts) : I should like to make one observation and also ask one question. I recently read a little pamphlet put out, I believe, by the Bureau of Business Research associated with the University of Indiana, which gave rather comprehensive statistics about the working of the income tax in the various states, both corporate and personal, throughout the United States. It pointed it out to be a fact that perhaps every state which has had to pass within recent years on the question as to whether it should have an income tax, either by way of amendment or referendum, had defeated it overwhelmingly in most cases, in any event defeated it in all states, and there was added at the very end of the pamphlet this rather significant note: it said that the United States should get down to the situation that it is not enough for tax experts to get together and decide what is a just and equitable tax and what is a relatively easy one to administer, but we have to take the people into consideration; we have to take the business man into consideration; we have to put forth a tax that is not only just and equitable really, but one which the people think is just and equitable.

I venture the suggestion that one of the reasons, perhaps the principal reason, why the states defeated the income tax was because they had back in their minds the workings of the federal income tax, and if any of us believe in the principle of the income tax for the states, I venture the suggestion that we shall go a long way towards getting that sooner than we otherwise would, the sooner we simplify the federal income tax. The sooner we make the people accept the federal income tax as a just and equitable tax, the sooner we can make them accept it in the states.

The question I wanted to ask was on administration; whether the committee had gone into the question of whether the burden of proof in suits before the board of tax appeals should rest on the Government, rather than on the taxpayer. I take it that once the Government sends out the proposed notice of assessment and the taxpayer takes an appeal to the board of tax appeals, that is an entirely new cause, as if there never had been anything done, and then the entire burden from that time on is on the taxpayer both as to the law and facts; but what does Mr. Holmes think as to how far we can go in having a sufficient part of the burden rest on the Government, rather than putting the taxpayer to the entire expense of going down to Washington and putting in his case without the Government having to do a single thing.

CHAIRMAN ALEXANDER: Can you tell us who is the criminal in that case?

MR. HOLMES: I have noted down seven questions that I suppose I am called upon to answer. I will work backwards.

We gave a great deal of consideration to the proposition of whether or not the Commissioner should bear the burden of proof, in cases before the Board of Tax Appeals. We recognize the fact that the Bureau of Internal Revenue is not doing what it should do, to help the Board of Tax Appeals settle cases. We did go so far as to make a definite recommendation that the burden of proof should be on the Commissioner, in the case of fraud and also in the case of deceased persons. It is not that now, even in the case of fraud, which is contrary to all usual rules of trial and procedure.

We make another suggestion, which we hope is a step in the right direction; that the Board of Tax Appeals be permitted to assess costs, perhaps even to the extent, at times, of very considerable amounts, against either one or both parties, in the hope that the possibility of costs running perhaps as high as $500, might be a deterrent to the taxpayer and Government alike, in the conduct of the case.

In the past we know that many cases have been sent to the board to merely "pass the buck," because the Bureau did not want to take the responsibility of settling the particular point.

Then we go one step further. We call attention to the fact that in our opinion the entire procedure of settling cases in the Bureau is wrong. It is too informal in some respects, and too impersonal in others. What ought to happen when a case is taken up by the Bureau for consideration is, first, a finding of facts. The auditor or engineer or other man in the Bureau who gets the case in the first instance ought to be concerned solely with the finding of facts. That is not true now. The first thing he does now is to find the conclusions, and you have got to stir him out of those preconceived conclusions with a bombardment of facts and argument. Very often he does not listen to your facts. The first thing that ought to be done in the department is to find the facts. The man that finds those facts ought not be called upon to reach any conclusion of law. Now, a case is often tinctured with the prejudice of the auditor who first got it. His immediate superior approves more or less, as a matter of form, the finding of the auditor; the head of the section approves the findings of his two subordinates. If it finally gets to the general counsel's office, it is charged with the approval of four or five subordinates underneath, and it makes it ten times as hard for the lawyer who considers the case to reach an independent conelusion, because he is, to an extent, bound by the prior findings. He does not like to reverse men who have worked on the case; and so we often find the prejudice which first attached to the case in the mind of the auditor coloring consideration of the case by the final Bureau authority.

If the department had a system whereby facts were found and proved in a way that could be relied on, it would be a relatively simple thing for the general counsel's office to enter into stipulations of fact with the taxpayer, instead of making general denials to almost all the statements in the petition.

It is a difficult thing—that question of burden of proof—because if the burden of proof were thrown entirely on the Commissioner he would need ten times as many employees as he has, to conduct the cases. It would mean the creation of a tremendous legal department.

We are hopeful that some plan can be worked out, whereby there will be greater cooperation between the department and the board, more of a readiness to concede and stipulate things, about which there should be no argument, and to get right down to the crux of the matter; and in that connection we strongly urge that the Board of Tax Appeals should adopt a modification of its present procedure and permit the testing out of questions of law before the facts need be proved.

Very often a tremendous amount of time has to be spent in proving facts — and the Board does require the most careful sort of proof — only to find that it was unnecessary to prove those facts after all, because the case goes off on a point of law. We ought to have a procedure before the Board, where a case may be tried on points of law, somewhat in the nature of a demurrer, or some other procedure that will not require the proving of a great many facts until it is absolutely necessary.

As to the remark made by the gentleman from Wisconsin, Mr. Rosa, I wish he should modify that statement, not make it quite such a strong statement; that the tax cannot be simplified. We admit it cannot be simplified to very simple terms. Simplification, after all, is a relative thing; but the committee feels that, relatively speaking, there is great room for simplification in our federal tax system.

There will always be some degree of complication, complexity, difficulty, and I think Wisconsin has very ably tackled those problems of administration and is an outstanding example of what can be done by way of efficient administration. His remarks that income taxes cannot be simplified deserve great weight. It is a statement that is admitted, in its absolute sense, by the committee, but after all the term has a relative sense, too.

The suggestion of Mr. Williams that the present committee write the law is received with gratitude, but attention is called to the fact that we are all concerned with our own everyday business, and that a job like that would probably take a year's time or more. On the other hand, we are thoroughly in sympathy with anything this conference feels might be accomplished in that line.

The National Tax Association did at one time draft a model state income tax law, which I think has had some influence on state legislatures.

On the question of self-assessment, which Professor Plehn raised, we regard self-assessment somewhat as a necessary evil, at least until there is complete decentralization. If you are going to have assessment by officials, you will have to divide your taxing areas into very small units; so small that the assessor can either personally see each taxpayer and interrogate him, or be very closely in touch with him—or you will have to fall back on what, after all, is not a very satisfactory procedure, but which is followed, at least to some

13

extent, in England; and that is just putting an arbitrary assessment on the individual each year. If he does not object, it stands; if he objects, you have to cut. If he does not object, the assessment is raised a little next year, and it is finally brought up to a point where he does object. But that procedure does not satisfactorily meet the situation, so long as there is fluctuation in incomes.

So long as incomes fluctuate there should be fluctuating amounts of tax due from individuals. We do not see how that can be accomplished except by filing returns. Self-assessment is to some extent, and in one sense, an administrative matter. It means that the taxpayer figures out the amount of tax and so relieves the Government of that much clerical work. I know that is not the fundamental distinction, but it is one of the labor-saving effects of self-assessment.

What we recommend is something not so much in the nature of a complete assessment as we have had thus far. We recommend that the taxpayer shall report the amount of income which he concedes is taxable. With respect to that on which he does not concede he is taxable, he should give due and sufficient notice to the Commissioner that he has received the money, by stating, to whatever extent he deems proper, the reasons why he does not report it. He should give sufficient notice to call the facts to the attention of the Commissioner.

We regard as bordering on the reprehensible the action of some taxpayers in omitting from their returns transactions and items which they themselves have decided are not taxable, and not giving the Commissioner any notice, sometimes, perhaps, in the hope that the omitted item will never be found. We think it is the primary duty of every taxpayer to make a full and frank disclosure. Having done that, the statute ought to run as speedily as possible, and all doubtful points ought to be decided somewhat in the taxpayer's favor.

OSCAR LESER (Maryland) : Do you require a report of all the income, Mr. Holmes?

MR. HOLMES: I am coming to that. With respect to the two questions that Mr. Leser asked, first, why didn't we recommend the flat rate of tax on all incomes, and, secondly, what does the committee think of the proposition of citizens reporting all their income, whether taxable or not, we felt for one thing that a flat rate of tax would probably not meet with favor, because the theory of ability to pay has been generally understood to imply a graduated tax; and secondly, that a flat rate of tax might of necessity be so high that you would have to have a graduation downward or retrogression at the beginning to take care of the man of very small income. In order to raise a sufficient amount of revenue we would need a higher rate than could be properly applied to everybody. There are a great many taxpayers of small means who have large personal requirements—large families to feed, and all that sort of thing—and we would find it necessary to step the rate down in the beginning in some way; and the moment you do that you get away from the flat tax.

We did feel, however, that the maximum rate in a graduated tax ought to be reached rather quickly, and perhaps with very few gradations, instead of by very numerous gradations as we now have it.

As to the reporting of the income, that question divides itself into two phases. If by reporting all income is meant exempt income as well as income which might be taxable if large enough, the committee did not give any special attention to the question. That is one of the questions which we must admit we did not have time to consider, because of the limited amount of time at our disposal.

We state in the last paragraph of our report: "Necessary limitation to the length of this report has precluded us from a full discussion of propositions we have herein advanced; and shortness of time has prevented consideration of many worthy suggestions which have been brought to our attention."

As to taxable income, we do feel that perhaps a very large number of small taxpayers avoid paying a tax now which should properly be due from them. We make reference to it in a footnote on page 21 of the report.

A taxpayer now — a single person with no dependents, for instance—is not required to file a return, unless his net income exceeds $1500 or his gross income exceeds $5000. There is a spread of $3500. He may receive $4999 gross income. He is then permitted to decide in his own mind, without any check, what his deductions are, and if he decides mentally that he has sufficient deductions to reduce his income to $1499, he is under no obligation to file a return. There is a very large field in there. The question is, at what point fhould returns be required?

Mr. Henry Bond of Boston, who unfortunately is not present, or he would be answering this question, has had a great deal of experience as an administrator, and he was very strongly opposed, as were one or two other members of the committee, perhaps in lesser degree, to a requirement that returns be filed by individuals of small incomes, where no tax, or very little tax was likely to be found due. Bond says very strongly that he thinks compelling people of small means or small incomes to file returns, to go through all the annoyance of making up a return and signing it, or consulting some one to find out if they are taxable, has a tendency to create Bolshevism and general disgust with the Government. He feels that that is one reason why returns on very small incomes should not be demanded.

The other is a practical proposition. How far should the administrative officers go to check up; how far is it up to them to go; at what point of time is the detail and the annoyance of handling small returns offset by the amount of tax collected? The entire committee was in favor of an occasional general check-up, perhaps the filing of returns by everybody once every four or five years. We do not have a general check-up under the present administration. The filing of income tax returns is, to a great extent, especially among people of small incomes, an entirely voluntary thing, and is very often disregarded, where the individual thinks the United States Government cannot check him or her up, especially in cases of individuas who receive their incomes from several sources during the course of the year. .

Some check ought to be devised to apply to that group of individuals, but the committee is not convinced that returns on a much lower basis than at present should be demanded.

Some of the members are inclined to think that a report of gross income of $2000 for a single person, and $4000 for a married person might produce some very decided results in revenue.

It would be an ideal thing for the sake of national statistics, to have exempt income included in returns. But the moment you go that far, you open up a whole field of questions as to how far the United States should dip into the private or more or less private affairs of the individuals.

CHAIRMAN ALEXANDER: The suggestion has been made to me that Wednesday afternoon is vacant, and that if some of the income tax sharks, a group of them, desired to meet tomorrow afternoon for further discussion of this report, after they have had an opportunity to read it over night, possibly that could be arranged. Would it be possible for you to be here?

MR. HOLMES: I think, Mr. Chairman, that ought to be a thing to be decided by a rising vote of the audience. I may not find it possible to be present, but Mr. Hubbard and Mr. Arthur, both members of the committee, are here.

CHAIRMAN ALEXANDER: So there would be representation of the committee possible. Now, there is that suggestion, and if any number of the members here desire to take advantage of the further reading and further discussion tomorrow afternoon, I am sure that can be arranged. If you desire to do so, signify by rising.

(Rising vote)

CHAIRMAN ALEXANDER: Apparently the discussion here has been so free and so clarifying that no one desires to discuss it further tomorrow afternoon, Mr. Holmes.

Is there some one now who wants to discuss this further this evening?

C. L. TURNER (Pennsylvania) : First I want to say that I think the work which has been done on this attempt to simplify the income tax is very fine. I think the main thing which must be done to simplify the income tax is to omit a lot of definitions of income, and a lot of ambiguous phrases, and also to omit a lot of the language in the law which attempts to define what is income. It causes a lot of trouble.

I should like to direct your attention to one of the things that is a mooted question, and that is income on exchange. The committee has covered it in a general way, but made no specific recommendations, except in case of reorganizations, but I call attention to an exchange of one kind of property for another kind of property.

On a straight exchange the position of the taxpayer is the same as it was before the exchange. He has not received any cash, he has no more liquid assets than he had before, and he has nothing with which to pay a tax. For example; supposing a taxpayer desires to exchange a piece of real estate in Philadelphia for, we will say, a piece of real estate in Atlantic City, as a good many of them are doing, certainly if it is a straight exchange the values must, in the minds of the two parties to the transaction, be the same, and it is my opinion that the Government should not attempt to exact any tax in a transaction of that kind, until the property received has been turned into cash.

Another exchange that causes considerable trouble is exchange of cash and property for other property. For example; suppose a taxpayer has some securities, or other property, which cost him $50,000 several years ago; suppose he now makes an exchange with another party for $50,000 of cash and $50,000 supposed value in other property, the income tax law provides that this taxpayer must report as income the $50,000 that he receives in cash. In other words, the Government says the cash must be applied first against the property. Then maybe in four or five years, or three years, or two years from the date that they make this exchange, the taxpayer decides to sell the property he got in exchange, and it may bring $10,000 instead of $50,000. He has sustained a loss, which is deductible, if he has enough capital gain to offset it. That is expressly covered by the committee in a suggestion on carrying forward the loss against capital net gain of the succeeding year. If the transaction would work out within the three-year period, he might be able to adjust his tax situation; otherwise he would not.

The committee has suggested that the definition of the term " net losses " be simplified, with which I agree. As it is now, the law provides that only net loss sustained in trade or business can be deducted. Any net loss, whatever it may be from, should be allowed to be carried forward and deducted.

I only have another minute. One other point the committee

covers is contributions, and the committee says it is not expense. I desire to take issue with them, because it is expense. It is something corporations are having to pay every day, and they cannot get rid of it, if they want to do business on a fairly competitive basis in their locality. I think the corporation should be allowed to deduct donations, as well as an individual, with a limit of some percentage of gross income, corresponding to the limit allowed individuals.

RUSSELL BRADFORD (New York) : I am not going to take much time of this association, because I think it is getting quite late, as it is. Further than that, I think we are almost discussing academic questions, if I may say so. Let us clarify just what we are doing.

Here is a report made by the most eminently learned men on this question in the United States. There may be others who are just as eminently learned, but these gentlemen are those who know the subject thoroughly. They have reported to this association, a report that I have opposed the adoption of. I always shall oppose the adoption by this association of any report—I do not care what it is, or how perfect, how correct or absolute in its terms it is—that all of the members have not had an opportunity to study and to analyze.

Here is another situation. It has been suggested that the income tax be abolished. The Federal Government needs approximately $3,800,000,000 for its operations during the fiscal year ending June 30, 1928. From the income tax, including the income from corporation taxes, at 13½ per cent, the Government gets revenue of from about $1,900,000,000 to $2,100,000,000. We get from tobacco taxes approximately—I use 1922 terms—$342,000,000. From estate tax, that is the death duties, the largest the United States has ever gotten from that was $157,000,000 in 1920, which was a reflection of the 1918 tax, which was an extortionately high tax. The operation of the estate tax returns approximately $100,000,000. There have been no statistics either by the Treasury or any other official body since the 80 per cent credit clause was adopted, but at the present rate it ought not exceed about $40,000,000. Taxes from liquors, fermented and distilled, in 1919, the last year in which the Federal Government collected the tax, were about $565,000,000. In 1925 it was about $26,500,000 — about $25,000,000 for distilled liquors and about $1,150,000 for fermented liquors.

Now, under our constitutional system, when anybody talks about collecting revenue of $3,800,000,000 for the operation of the Government from any source as a body, I mean the base of the revenue or tax system, other than the income tax, they have not studied the subject, that is all, because that is the basic tax; that is the source from which we get most of our revenue. It stands at the very base of our fiscal system.

We got in 1925 from imports—there can be a barrier on imports until there can be no revenue, I don't have to explain that—about $575,000,000. That is the Government, from the tariff imposed upon importations into the United States, received revenue of about that sum. In the reduction of taxes here is a branch to which the pruning knife may be applied liberally with highly beneficial results.

Now, can we simplify the law, can we remedy the inequalities, so that the average man, the ordinary normal citizen, can meet the income tax law and the income tax regulations so that Mr. Holmes, or any other person here, can make his return accurately, without paying a penalty or a premium to a lawyer, because of his specialized knowledge, or paying Mr. Holmes, because of his specializzed knowledge of the subject. That is the question down in A-B-C language. All of us understand that.

Now, Mr. Holmes' committee and Mr. Holmes have recommended a change from the present law. They are recommending something for the present law that will simplify this. You remember that when I had an opportunity to speak before, I said I had not had an opportunity to study it, but so far as I have read it I approve of most of the points made, but I oppose the adoption of any report or anything anybody says, so far as I am personally concerned, until I have had a chance to analyze it, and I have had no chance to analyze this, and I do not believe the rest of you have.

So I say this: Let us accept the report. It is a good report. Whoever appointed them appointed as liberal-minded, intelligent and analytically-minded men for the committee, so far as I know—and I think I know something about it—as could have been gotten. My suggestion to you is, and I say it with deference, when I suggest anything to a body of men who know a great deal more about the affairs of life than I — I suggest to you nevertheless, let us accept the report without adopting it.

There are lots of things in the report that need study. We cannot change laws. Our action will not do that. We cannot change the report. It stands for itself. In New Orleans in 1925 a report was adopted, I am aware, but it didn't make any difference whether it was or not, for the report was already before Congress and had received its tacit approval, and had whatever effect its merit justified or its reasoning persuaded, but don't let us again adopt so significant and important a thing, without full study and mature consideration. Accept it. Accept it, why? Because its study and recommendations merit consideration and are worth while. They are stimulating to the study of this highly technical and, in many ways, intricate subject. I doubt that we add force or vigor to our resolutions if they are adopted without a full study of the subjects covered or recommendations made.

Taxes have got to be imposed. The Federal Government needs

big revenue. We all recognize that. They ought, of course, constantly to decrease; that is the reason I am opposed to the flat-rate plan of taxation. I am opposed to the flat-rate plan because we cannot tell, and nobody will be able to tell, when you try to pick up, after a flat-rate imposition, the necessary revenue for the Government from other sources, that is, from excises, whether you are going to overdo one excise and underdo another excise, or what the needs of Government may be. Such a tax system lacks flexibility, and is too standardized and inelastic to meet properly changing economic conditions.

I now take the liberty, and I do it with much more deference and hesitancy than most of you will think, of moving, Mr. Chairman, that this association accept — I use the word "accept" advisedly—this report.

CHAIRMAN ALEXANDER: Is there a second to that?

(Motion duly seconded)

CHAIRMAN ALEXANDER: It has been moved and seconded that this association accept the report of this committee.

MR. NATHAN B. WILLIAMS (District of Columbia): I move this as a substitute—I will attempt to formulate it:

Moved that the report of the committee of the National Tax Association on the Simplification of the Income Tax be accepted, and that the committee be continued, with direction to maintain its cooperative relations with the Joint Congressional Committee and with committees or other associations interested in the same subject, with a view of urging upon the Joint Congressional Committee the earliest report possible, in the interest of simplification in income tax laws. That is a bit crude.

RUSSELL BRADFORD (New York): I accept the amendment, provided — I am saying this with utter respect — provided there is a draftsman of the resolution. I have no objection to the amendment, providing somebody puts it in proper language. Mr. Williams will not misunderstand this suggestion.

CHAIRMAN ALEXANDER: Is there a second?

(Motion to substitute duly seconded)

CHAIRMAN ALEXANDER: Now, as I understand it, there has been a motion with a second, which I will ask the reporter to read.

DELEGATE: I rise to a point of order; isn't this in the nature of a resolution that should be submitted in writing and referred to the resolutions committee?

CHAIRMAN ALEXANDER: I understand this is with respect to the acceptance of the report and the request that this committee kindly continue its relations with the Joint Congressional Committee and other committees. I think it might be clarified if we had that substituted motion read by the reporter. I should hate to try to state it over again.

(Record read as follows:)

"MR. NATHAN B. WILLIAMS (District of Columbia): I move this as a substitute—I will attempt to formulate it:

"Moved that the report of the committee of the National Tax Association on the simplification of the income tax be accepted, that the committee be continued, with directions to maintain its cooperative relations with the Joint Congressional Committee and with committees of other associations interested in the same subject."

CHAIRMAN ALEXANDER: Does the second accept that?

VOICE: Accepted.

CHAIRMAN ALEXANDER: Are you ready for a vote upon the substitute amendment as read?

(Call for the question)

(Ayes and Noes)

(Motion on substitute amendment as read was carried)

CHAIRMAN ALEXANDER: It is a vote. That disposes of the proposition.

It is now ten minutes of six. Shall we adjourn?

(Adjournment)

FOURTH SESSION

CHAIRMAN MATTHEWS: It is past the hour when the evening session was to be opened. If the members will take seats we will endeavor to get started.

The first subject this evening is State Taxation of Federal Public Lands, by Professor H. L. Lutz, Leland Stanford University, Chairman of the committee of the National Tax Association, who will present the report of his committee at this time.

HARLEY L. LUTZ (California): Mr. Chairman, Ladies and Gentlemen: I have felt from the beginning that the title of this committee is a little misleading. I wanted to protest to the secretary about it, but it was too late. The program was printed before I was really aware of it. I did not consider that this is a committee on the state taxation of federal public lands necessarily or solely. I have labeled the report simply " Report of the Committee on Revenue from Public Lands." It may be through taxation and it may be in other ways. It is, in a way, a report of a committee by courtesy only. There were three members of the committee, one in Washington, D. C., Mr. T. C. Havell of the Land Office, Mr. William Bailey, Nephi, Utah, and myself in California. Neither Mr. Bailey nor myself have ever met Mr. Havell. I have had some correspondence with him.

I was fortunate enough to see Mr. Bailey once or twice during the summer. A first draft of the report was read by Mr. Havell and I have his comments, but the report as it stands, while I think it fairly represents the views of the committee, is a draft upon which they have not been able to pass final judgment.

Now, this is a very long report, and I do not intend to inflict all of it upon you. I do want to read certain passages, and I will indicate the general character of the remainder of it.

The report falls into two parts. In the first part I have assembled some information about the public lands situation from easily available sources which did not involve any particular research, but I thought it worth while to bring together certain facts about the area of federally owned lands, where it is located and the classification of it, because the resolution implies that it is all one thing.

As a matter of fact there is forest land, vacant and unappropriated domain, that grasshoppers do not customarily make a living on, to say nothing of human beings; there are the national parks and

(202)

monuments, and there are oil and mineral reserves, and then in addition, tribal Indian lands, which are not properly federally owned lands, but regarding which the Federal Government has certain responsibilities.

Then I have given a table showing the course of the cost of government, as shown by taxes collected in the public land states, and certain other facts of a general nature that would help you to size up the background of the situation.

I am going to pass over that .part of the report, in order to give such time as the chairman will permit, to a discussion of certain of the controversial aspects of the situation.

The resolution under which this committee was created, I think it is fair to say, was an outcropping of the perennial controversy between the Federal Government and the public land states. As you know, there has been this controversy between the Federal Government on the one hand and those who wanted to exploit the public lands or own them or do something with them, ever since the opening of public domain, in one form or another; and the course of that controversy has moulded the course of our public-land policy to a certain extent.   The critical stage of this controversy at the present time has been precipitated by the recent proposals of the general land office in the Department of the Interior to withdraw the remaining public lands from entry and substitute some sort of system of controlled use of the public domain.

President Coolidge has spoken of that development, the need of some system of controlled use, to put an end to the chaotic condition of affairs in public lands.

The committee did not undertake to go into the whole controversy over conservation and withdrawal from use, and so on. There are many important aspects of that question of which the financial matter is probably the least important; but I do want to summarize some of the arguments that have been advanced.   The committee did not attempt to express an opinion on many of these arguments, but you ought to know some of the things that are being said.   I cannot tell you all the things being said on both sides of this, because out west they are saying some things that it would not be polite to repeat, and perhaps some things that are not wholly accurate.   I don't know what they are saying in Washington, but the first argument put forward by those who oppose the withdrawal of public lands from further entry, and who oppose all forms of conservation is that it is unconstitutional.

The Federal Constitution has this provision relative to the public domain:

> " The Congress shall have power to dispose of and make all needful rules and regulations respecting the territory or other property belonging to the United States; and nothing in this

Constitution shall b construed as to prejudice any claim of the United States. c of any particular State."

The constitutional ar⌐ment turns around the meaning of that phrase "to dispose of.' Of course the earliest practice was to dispose of it, sell it. gi⟍ t away, get rid of it in any fashion that you could, but alienate it⟍ some manner; and the argument is that that early practice estab⌐hed definitely the meaning of "to dispose of," and meant that Co⌐ ress was to get rid of it. Of course the Constitution does say th. Congress shall have power to dispose of it, but it does not say ⟍vthing about a constitutional mandate to dispose of it, and there t matter stands today.

I think some person⟍ the West insist that if this matter came to the Supreme Court. t court would rule that "to dispose of" meant a mandatory obli⌐.ion to dispose of, and therefore any refusal to dispose of it w⟍ contrary to the constitutional intent. Of course a proper battlegre⌐nd for all these matters is the courts, and the committee has natur⌐ v no opinion to express on it.

Another argument i⟍ ⌐at this withholding of the land from settlement is an invasion ⌐nd impairment of the sovereignty of the states. The legislature ⌐ Wyoming sent a long memorial to Congress in December. 192⌐ I will read one or two paragraphs:

"Whereas, we se⟍h in vain for any clause of the federal constitution which ⌐ hibits to the states the exercise of any power connected w⌐it the public lands, and the control asserted by the federal gov⟍ ment is a growth of a system nowhere even contemplated ⌐ the founders of our government and in violation of a sover ⌐nty of states which came into the federal union on an e⟍ l footing with the original states in all respects whatever;

"Whereas, of the rty-eight sovereign states the inhabitants of thirty-seven own ⌐ l have always owned all their lands and their state sovereig⌐ and authority cover every natural re-source within their orders, thus placing the eleven states aforementioned on ⟍ unequal basis with other states to the untold financial inju of the inhabitants thereof."

There are certain ratl sweeping statements in those resolu-tions, some inaccuracies statement, but a good many people in the West believe that the even public domain states, in which the Federal Government ow⟍ a certain portion of the area, are de-prived of their sovereig⌐ and are not really on an equal basis with the other states.

Another argument whi is a corollary to this argument of im-paired sovereignty is that ⌐ey are deprived of revenue. There is some amount of federal ⌐⌐d which they may not tax, and conse-quently there is a loss of r enue. Their feelings are hurt because

id **their pocketbook** is hurt in case
this **federally** owned land.   They
.ing **act, under** which every one of
.:1, **expressly** provided that the fed-
.:; **that had not been** settled, had not
remain **exempt** from taxation until
d. **but they say** that they agreed to
: **the exemption** was temporary and
Government **would** give up its hold-
id **so withdraw** from the land busi-
: **conservation movement, the** with-
:rly, **because they see** in it the very
that **the Federal Government** will
t it **is indefinitely postponed.**   Conse-
they **will have acquired sovereignty,**
id, **is indefinitely postponed.**
:nen, **or near** enough laymen so that
:1 **these** weighty questions of consti-
:1 **invasion of the sovereignty of the**
ice **this, that** some of these persons
r attack **on the** federal invasion of
illing **to compromise the** sovereignty
:al **purposes; and so, in view of that**
lo **not feel** that the sovereignty issue
se **as** it might be.

I question of state sovereignty is at
rom the Federal Government should
That is evident.   But it is interesting
ion, at least, whether federal owner-
really involve the question of sover-
serve my status as a layman I cannot
ions.

itimates of the value of the federally
nge anywhere from $150,000,000 to
: State Tax Commission reported in
iment owned land, appraised by the
)00,000.   The Massachusetts tax com-
iat the federal real property in that
ike $146,000,000.

at those **figures** represent a smaller
of the real property in those states,
land in California represents in that
st the Federal Government own in a
om local taxation, before you get this
y?

I am not arguing it at **all**; but when

Constitution shall be construed as to prejudice any claim of the United States, or of any particular State."

The constitutional argument turns around the meaning of that phrase "to dispose of." Of course the earliest practice was to dispose of it, sell it, give it away, get rid of it in any fashion that you could, but alienate it in some manner; and the argument is that that early practice established definitely the meaning of "to dispose of," and meant that Congress was to get rid of it. Of course the Constitution does say that Congress shall have power to dispose of it, but it does not say anything about a constitutional mandate to dispose of it, and there the matter stands today.

I think some persons in the West insist that if this matter came to the Supreme Court, the court would rule that "to dispose of" meant a mandatory obligation to dispose of, and therefore any refusal to dispose of it was contrary to the constitutional intent. Of course a proper battleground for all these matters is the courts, and the committee has naturally no opinion to express on it.

Another argument is that this withholding of the land from settlement is an invasion and impairment of the sovereignty of the states. The legislature of Wyoming sent a long memorial to Congress in December, 1926. I will read one or two paragraphs:

"Whereas, we search in vain for any clause of the federal constitution which prohibits to the states the exercise of any power connected with the public lands, and the control asserted by the federal government is a growth of a system nowhere even contemplated by the founders of our government and in violation of a sovereignty of states which came into the federal union on an equal footing with the original states in all respects whatever;

"Whereas, of the forty-eight sovereign states the inhabitants of thirty-seven own and have always owned all their lands and their state sovereignty and authority cover every natural resource within their borders, thus placing the eleven states aforementioned on an unequal basis with other states to the untold financial injury of the inhabitants thereof."

There are certain rather sweeping statements in those resolutions, some inaccuracies of statement, but a good many people in the West believe that the eleven public domain states, in which the Federal Government owns a certain portion of the area, are deprived of their sovereignty and are not really on an equal basis with the other states.

Another argument which is a corollary to this argument of impaired sovereignty is that they are deprived of revenue. There is some amount of federal land which they may not tax, and consequently there is a loss of revenue. Their feelings are hurt because their sovereignty is impaired, and their pocketbook is hurt in case they cannot get the tax from this federally owned land. They admit, of course, that the enabling act, under which every one of these states came into the Union, expressly provided that the federally owned lands and the lands that had not been settled, had not been patented to settlers, should remain exempt from taxation until such time as they were patented, but they say that they agreed to that, because they assumed that the exemption was temporary and that sooner or later the Federal Government would give up its holdings to settlers or purchasers and so withdraw from the land business; and so they denounce the conservation movement, the withdrawal progr ım, the more bitterly, because they see in it the very likely possibility or probability that the Federal Government will never give up that land; at least it is indefinitely postponed. Consequently, the question of when they will have acquired sovereignty, so to speak, over all of their land, is indefinitely postponed.

All of the committee are laymen, or near enough laymen so that we had no opinion to express on these weighty questions of constitutional law, what constitutes an invasion of the sovereignty of the state and so on; but I did notice this, that some of these persons who are rather strong in their attack on the federal invasion of state sovereignty seem to be willing to compromise the sovereignty issue for larger revenue for local purposes; and so, in view of that willingness to compromise, I do not feel that the sovereignty issue is as strong a factor in the case as it might be.

As a matter of fact, if the question of state sovereignty is at stake, no amount of subsidy from the Federal Government should be allowed to close the issue. That is evident. But it is interesting to know, or to raise the question, at least, whether federal ownership of land in a state does really involve the question of sovereignty, and while trying to preserve my status as a layman I cannot resist raising one or two questions.

For example, the various estimates of the value of the federally owned land in California range anywhere from $150,000,000 to $300,000,000. The New York State Tax Commission reported in 1915 that the Federal Government owned land, appraised by the assessors of that state at $200,000,000. The Massachusetts tax commissioner reported in 1926 that the federal real property in that state amounted to something like $146,000,000.

I will admit, of course, that those figures represent a smaller proportion of the total value of the real property in those states, respectively, than the federal land in California represents in that state; but how much land must the Federal Government own in a state and have it exempted from local taxation, before you get this question of invaded sovereignty?

I merely ask the question. I am not arguing it at all; but when you consider the amount of real property the Federal Government owns in every state, it seems to me that if the sovereignty issue is raised—in our own state it is raised—if it is an issue in the public-land states it is an issue in every state of the Union, and they are all in the same situation. Consequently, the rights of one particular state, whether it is a state in the Rocky Mountain district or a state in New England, are not impaired any more than the rights of any other state.

Another argument against federal ownership or management of the public domain is that so much of this land is of such little value that it is really unwise for the Federal Government to continue to hold it and manage it, and therefore it should be ceded to the states. But of course that argument, when you look into it, loses a certain amount of its force, because if the land is of so little value that the Federal Government cannot afford to administer it, one wonders just what the state is to gain by taking it over and assuming the cost of administration, and just where the state would get the revenue that would pay those costs, because they admit there is a burden of cost there.

Of course, I think we may speak as among friends here and speak out rather frankly in meeting, and say that everybody knows that there are certain worthless lands about which there is no quarrel. The states do not care very much about who owns those lands. The Federal Government may keep them, but the real issue is over the lands that have wealth in some form — oil, minerals, timber, what-not. And I suspect that there would be rather general agreement that the whole problem would be considered closed and satisfactorily solved if the Federal Government were willing to cede all valuable lands to the states but keep those that had no value, but the argument has to apply, of course, to all of them. They cannot be quite as frank as that in their demands.

There is another suggestion, that the Federal Government authorize the local taxation of these federally owned lands.

The California Farm Bureau Federation adopted this resolution at a recent meeting:

> "Whereas, if the contemplated plan of the Department of the Interior should become effective [i. e. the withdrawal of all remaining lands from entry] one-half of the land area of the state would be forced to forever sustain the whole state, thus casting an ever-increasing burden on the agricultural interests already over-taxed:
> "Now, therefore, be it resolved by the California Farm Bureau Federation in annual conference assembled
> "That it protests against any further or additional withdrawals of public lands in the state, unless provision is made in such withdrawal orders or laws to reimburse the counties

affected, by payment to each of them annually of the sum of money they would receive if such lands were in private ownership and subject to tax; and be it further

"Resolved, that the Congress of the United States be and is hereby requested to enact at the next session proper and requisite legislation whereby the several counties of this state as well as any other western public-land state be reimbursed annually on the same basis of monetary return as such counties would receive were all the present withdrawn lands taxed at the same rate as privately owned lands similarly situated."

I must confess that I am in some doubt how to understand just how the general farming interests of the State of California are penalized by the existence of federally owned lands in the state, or how these interests would be materially benefited by the authorization of a tax. That is, you could not do it without a constitutional amendment and radical changes in the California system of state and local taxation.

The only beneficiaries of the scheme advocated in these resolutions would be the property owners in such counties as happen to contain forests, oil, mineral or other valuable reserve lands. Much of the vacant land in California has little or no value and would yield but little or no tax return. Since the state does not tax real property for state purposes, general farming interests could not, so far as I can see, benefit in any appreciable degree from the plan proposed.

These resolutions are misleading, furthermore, in that they imply that the valuable federally owned lands in California are now contributing nothing to the counties in which they are situated.

Part 1 of the report gives some figures on the distribution of the revenue from the forests and the oil land and mineral royalties, and of course many of you know that there is a distribution of a substantial proportion of that income.

The question has come up in these states, and in Oklahoma also, of the exchange of cut-over land for timber cutting sections in the national forests. The owner of cut-over land having skinned his land by a process of forest exploitation is interested to continue timber-cutting, but he has no more standing timber himself, and he cannot wait seventy-five years for a crop; so by reason of the national forest he may trade his cut-over land for an equivalent in value of timber ready for market within the national forest.

Of course, the exploitation process is stopped. He cuts the timber in the forest under regulation and control, but the Federal Government gains by having the timber marketed by a man who is in the business of cutting and marketing timber, at the time when the crop is ready, and it gains also by being able to use this timber,

...ecesses of long destructive marches to the

...made in Utah, Mr. Bailey and others told ...which indicated that there were parts of the ...could be sunk that would supply water ...for irrigation—that is not necessary—but ...grazed there;

...where, it wells prove impractical, reser-... strategic points which would catch the drain-... considerable size, from the winter rains and ...an available water supply for stock purposes. ...roughly in accord with the idea that the ...ment of the range, the restoration of its graz-... everybody admits is below what it once was, is ...true reclamation work as it is to build expen-... for intensive farming. Much of this range ...possible for any other kind of economic ...and the grazing capacity, the grazing useful-... forage crop and on the water supply available

...conception of reclamation needs over-hauling, ...ened to the extent of including the range; ... made as it were—it is quite possible that we have ...reclamation idea a little further than it needs ...and that some of our energy in the past ...into a study of the range problem and a con-... of the open range. A policy of this sort, ... and carried out, would give stability to the ...the west, and so would sustain and develop ...for which some of these states are pecu-... to the states would be indirect, through the ...the possibility of deriving public revenue ...this wealth, but it would be a real and sub-... should prove productive of the possi-...in it. If this experiment should fail, the ...the range country as having large economic ...been adequately demonstrated.

...thought was that the first use of the revenue ...this fund should develop the possibilities of sink-... in other ways, and of the other improve-... necessary, and after that improvement had ... ...with the ... ...ld be

f controlling the range, because in the first place, so far
d gather, the sentiment in the west is not universally in
ession, and even if the lands are ceded to the states,
not solve the sovereignty question, because there would
e 68,000,000 acres of tribal Indian lands scattered through
of states. We could not cede those lands to the states,
out of the jurisdiction of the states and always will be in
not taxable. The state hasn't even any police jurisdic-
hem. We could not turn those over to the states without
rayal. That does sound funny because of the thousands
which we have betrayed the trust of the Indian—but
further or even grosser betrayal of the trust reposed in
It would be greater than it ever committed in the
ny rate, the sovereignty question would still exist, as in
s there are tribal Indian reservations.
ore, the character of the problem is such that it resort of integrating agency for its solution. The range
bserve state boundary lines. It runs here and there,
ve a district in which the problem is less homogeneous,
would require that it be dealt with as a district, regard-
her it is in this state or that or in three or four states.
tacle of the power and after-flow discussion down
Colorado was regarded as an indication, in the minds of
ee, of what we might expect if we relegated to the
ed, the disposition of some of these economic and ad-
problems, which, as I say, are not respecters of state
es but simply follow the configuration of the country.
than have a repetition of the Colorado River dispute,
s involved, we thought it best to leave the matter where
resent, in the hands of the Federal Government.
not undertaken to formulate a plan of control. Any
ntrol that is introduced must be one which will safe-
hts of the sections involved, the west itself, promoting
ime the larger objective. The details of this system
tten in Washington. They cannot be written in the
after the most careful consideration of the relative
ocal settled communities by stockmen who operate on
s well as those who operate on a large scale.
al objections which the committee has seen in the
thorize the local taxation of public lands are these:
ce, while it is conceded that such action could readily
complished through federal legislation, a difficulty
of the permissive legislation. Such a law
its scope, conceding the constitutional
apply specifically to the public land
of federal property.

that is, the sale of the standing timber, in the acquisition of lands that are suitable for incorporation into the forest reserves.

The rub comes in the fact that this cut-over land, when incorporated into a national forest is withdrawn from the local tax rolls. It becomes exempt from local taxation, and the counties affected naturally lose for the time being a certain amount of revenue. But, I think it is rather short-sighted to criticize that policy entirely on that ground.

In the first place, cut-over land, which is simply cut-over land and producing nothing, has ordinarily a rather low value per acre or per 100 or per 1000 acres. It would be assessed at a very low figure, even if it were privately owned. The tax which it would produce is a rather small sum. Therefore, the tax loss to the counties in which it is situated is not a tremendous amount.

On the other hand, there is this gain through the continuance in business of the lumbering interests in the community. They are able to continue to operate in that section; they bring a certain amount of wealth into the section; the timber that is harvested is added to the general wealth of the community and may some time or other, somewhere or other, be subject to taxation.

Most important of all, this is one of the most promising ways in which the land that is adapted chiefly for timber-growing can be put back under cultivation, so to speak, can be reforested, because the timber owner is not likely to make use of it in that way. The Federal Government is one of the agencies which will undertake that long-run job of reforestation.

The remedy which some of the less extreme-minded of those who consider the problem have looked upon with favor, is that the Federal Government should proceed with this policy of control of vacant lands with a view to applying to the lands a policy of development and conservation, similar to that which has been applied to the national forests.

This is apparently the plan that the general land offiee has in contemplation. The argument for such a policy is that we shall do away with the free and unregulated use of the open domain, especially in the range country, and substitute for it some kind of controlled use, with a system of fees and so on.

The argument is that that policy is necessary, if the resources of the range are to be preserved and developed. The system of competitive, unregulated use of the open range has greatly reduced its value. for grazing purposes, and in some places the loss and destruction have been such that a long time will be required for its recovery.

A gentleman in Utah who has become thoroughly conversant with the range situation has written this on the question of the range:

"Even though by 1900 the western states found they were

grazing a sufficient number of cattle, horses and sheep to fully occupy all the grazing ground available, while the ownership was a very small percentage, the grazing practices under these conditions were not corrective. The rush in an attempt to establish a seasonable priority on the best grazing ground led to the practice of damage and killing out much valuable forage, and with the elimination of the forage, erosion tremendously increased. This method depleted the range and rendered the carrying capacity very much less than it normally should have been. Much of the otherwise economic forage has been replaced by poisonous and useless plants. Thus the struggle has been made all the more intense."

In other words, federal control has been rendered necessary for the open range for very much the same reasons that it was made necessary in the case of the forests, in the case of the salmon, in the case of the oil and mineral reserves; and Mr. Bailey reports to me that a combination of cattlemen, with which he has met and which he addressed last summer in Utah, was very strongly in favor of the proposition that some sort of control of the range was necessary, if they would have any range worth talking about left in the west.

The committee has considered these various proposals somewhat and while this report is in a way preliminary and tentative, in so far as we are disposed to make recommendations at this time, the committee inclines unhesitatingly to the proposition that the Federal Government should continue to control and develop the resources of the range; that is, as among the various alternatives—cession of the land to the states, local taxation of the land by the states, or a federal subsidy in lieu of taxes, and federal control and development of the range resources—the committee inclines to the last I have named.

The reasons for this attitude are in part positive, and I have given you a hint at what they are, and in part negative, in that they rest upon certain objections to various other schemes.

In the first place, in regard to the positive reasons for the system of federal control, it is apparent that the range problem is one that calls for a systematic long-run policy of control and development. The testimony is unmistakably clear as to the effect of the present policy of neglect and competitive use. The range should be dealt with as a long-run reclamation project, upon which systematic and extensive attempts should be made for the purpose of increasing and conserving the supply of forage and water for stock uses. The depleted grazing capacity of the range must be restored under a program of carefully controlled and restricted use, and steps must be taken to provide such a distribution of watering places for stock

14

as will obviate the necessity of long destructive marches to the water holes.

Some tests have been made in Utah, Mr. Bailey and others told me in Salt Lake City, which indicated that there were parts of the range at least where wells could be sunk that would supply water for stock, not on a scale for irrigation—that is not necessary—but for the cattle and sheep grazed there.

There are other sections where, if wells prove impractical, reservoirs might be built at strategic points which would catch the drainage of watersheds of considerable size, from the winter rains and snow, so as to put out an available water supply for stock purposes.

The committee is thoroughly in accord with the idea that the range and the development of the range, the restoration of its grazing capacity, which everybody admits is below what it once was, is just as much a part of our reclamation work as it is to build expensive irrigation projects for intensive farming. Much of this range country will never be suitable for any other kind of economic activity than grazing, and the grazing capacity, the grazing usefulness depends on the forest crop and on the water supply available for the stock.

So we hold that our conception of reclamation needs over-hauling, and it needs to be broadened, to the extent of including the range; and—this is on the side, as it were—it is quite possible that we have carried the intensive reclamation idea a little further than it needs to be carried just yet, and that some of our energy in the past might well have gone into a study of the range problem and a conservation of the resources of the open range. A policy of this sort, if properly conceived and carried out, would give stability to the live-stock industry of the west, and so would sustain and develop that aspect of agriculture for which some of these states are peenliarly fitted. The gain to the states would be indirect, through the growth of wealth and the possibility of deriving public revenue from the taxation of this wealth, but it would be a real and substantial gain, if the policy should prove productive of the possibilities which some see in it. If this experiment should fail, the futility of regarding the range country as having large economic possibilities would have been adequately demonstrated.

I should say that our thought was that the first use of the revenue collected in the way of fees should develop the possibilities of sinking wells, providing water in other ways, and of the other improvements that might prove necessary, and after that improvement had reached a certain stage the revenue could then be shared with the states, or any disposition that seemed proper at the time could be made of it.

In the second place the committee favored federal control of the range as against cession to the states, or relinquishment to the states of the job of controlling the range, because, in the first place, so far as we could gather, the sentiment in the west is not universally in favor of cession, and even if the lands were ceded to the states, that would not solve the sovereignty question, because there would remain some 68,000,000 acres of tribal Indian lands scattered through a number of states. We could not cede those lands to the states. They are out of the jurisdiction of the states and always will be in many ways not taxable. The state hasn't even any police jurisdiction over them. We could not turn those over to the states without a gross betrayal. That does sound funny, because of the thousands of ways in which we have betrayed the trust of the Indian—but without a further or even grosser betrayal of the trust reposed in the nation. It would be greater than that ever committed in the past. At any rate, the sovereignty question would still exist, as in many states there are tribal Indian reservations.

Furthermore, the character of the problem is such that it requires some sort of integrating agency for its solution. The range does not observe state boundary lines. It runs here and there. You will have a district in which the problem is less homogeneous, and which would require that it be dealt with as a district, regardless of whether it is in this state or that or in three or four states.

The spectacle of the power and water-flow discussion down around the Colorado was regarded as an indication, in the minds of the committee, of what we might expect if we relegated to the states involved, the disposition of some of these economic and administrative problems, which, as I say, are not respecters of state boundary lines but simply follow the configuration of the country.

So, rather than have a repetition of the Colorado River dispute, and all that is involved, we thought it best to leave the matter where it stands at present, in the hands of the Federal Government.

We have not undertaken to formulate a plan of control. Any system of control that is introduced must be one which will safeguard the rights of the sections involved, the west itself, promoting at the same time the larger objective. The details of this system cannot be written in Washington. They cannot be written in the west, except after the most careful consideration of the relative needs of the local settled communities, by stockmen who operate on a small scale as well as those who operate on a large scale.

The principal objections which the committee has seen in the proposal to authorize the local taxation of public lands are these: In the first place, while it is conceded that such action could readily enough be accomplished through federal legislation, a difficulty arises as to the scope of the permissive legislation. Such a law would be either general in its scope or, conceding the constitutional difficulties removed, it would apply specifically to the public land states and to that particular form of federal property.

Of course, if it were general permissive legislation, it would open to all the forty-eight states, federal property everywhere, and that would mean that every post office and every custom house and every military post would be subject to taxation, and it would simply mean lifting ourselves by the boot-straps, because the federal tax would have to be high enough to pay that bill to the states; nothing in particular would be gained by it, except possibly a shuffling of the tax burden in different sections. That is obviously an objectionable way in which to do it.

We have no information on this, but if it were constitutionally possible to secure special legislation, applicable simply to the public-land states, the practical result here would be a form of subsidy to these states, because a certain part of this public domain is either mountainous or desert and would yield no local revenue. If it were now in private ownership it would be sold for taxes. On the first installment of a levy that went against it, it would be defaulted for the tax title. And so, if you say the Federal Government shall pay a tax similar to local land, it would simply mean a subsidy; and I need not remind this organization of the arguments against the further extension of the subsidy principle.

In the second place, if you authorize the local taxation of federal land in these states, and if you accompany that authorization by such safeguards as you would need to have, in order to assure equitable taxation, you would have a degree of federal interference and federal control over local assessment administration that many would regard as intolerable. I say that because I do not believe it would be wise even for Congress to authorize the local taxation of these lands in a number of states, without some sort of safeguard as to equalization and review of assessments. This is the more necessary because we know that the machinery for equalization in some of these states is not functioning as satisfactorily as it should. In the third place, it would not do much, in the opinion of the committee, to relieve the general local tax burden in these states. That local tax burden is intra-county, for the most part. California has no state tax on property, and in the other states constitutional or statutory—mainly constitutional—restriction keeps the rate to a low figure.

The bulk of the tax burden, 75 to 80 per cent, in these states as in the other states of the Union, is local—county, school district and municipal—and if you had local taxation of the land in the county in which it is situated, it would simply benefit the counties which now have the high proportion of federally owned lands; and in every one of these states there are counties that have comparatively small amounts of federally owned land, and therefore counties in which there would be very little relief to the local taxpayer.

Here is Gila County, Arizona, that has 3,000,000 acres roughly.

2,915,000 acres are owned by the Federal Government, leaving only 92,000 acres, or 3 per cent of the area, in private ownership and subject to state and local taxation, out of 3,000,000 acres.

On its face it looks like an urgent case for relief, but consider what would happen if you authorized state taxation of federally owned land. Gila County would become the taxpayer's Paradise, because private property owners in Gila County would find their taxes approaching the vanishing point, or else there would be an orgy of local extravagant expenditures, because of the enormous tax base they would have.

In the State of California, there are a number of counties in which there are no federally owned lands whatever, and as long as those counties are taxing property for local purposes only, it would mean that such counties, having no federal lands within their borders—no public domain so-called—simply would not gain anything by local taxation.

The mountain counties, the public land counties, would gain the benefit, but what would the people in San Francisco County gain? Their argument would be, if it is proper to tax Yosemite Park where it is located, it would be proper to tax the Presidio, or the Customs House and Post Office, and so forth.

I must stop without covering even all the matter that we have assembled. I may refer to one other thing here, the consideration of certain parallel arguments, precedents of state authorizing localities to tax their property. New York permits county taxation or local taxation of state-owned forest lands, Pennsylvania does the same thing, under certain conditions, Massachusetts has a grant in lieu of taxes. The committee has considered those and has come to the conclusion that they are not precedents.

We have considered also the case of the tax refunds in the case of the Oregon & California Railroad Company's defaulted land grants. There are special considerations there which prevent them from being a precedent. But, we hold that these cases of local taxation of state lands are not adequate precedent here because, in the first place, there is no conflict of jurisdiction. The state may do what it pleases with its own subdivisions, and if the state carves out a watershed boundary and interferes with those old established boundary lines, it may say, " Very well, these shattered, these bleeding remnants of counties may tax the state or not, we will pay the bill. they levy the tax and we will pay the bill." That is one way of dealing with a problem of local administration.

Another way of dealing with it would be to wipe out those fragments of counties and regroup them, and establish new units, capable of carrying the load, and let the state carry the load of whatever administrative costs are involved in the case of its own state land. I say the state is free to do that, and the jurisdictional problem does not enter in, as it does in the case of Nevada, where the Federal Government owns upwards of 85 per cent of the land. We cannot blot out the State of Nevada and say we will forget that state. We have gone too far for that.

So, you have jurisdictional questions involved between the Federal Government and the states in this matter of tax jurisdiction, that you do not have in the case of a state dealing with its own subdivisions.

But, the report concludes with this suggestion, which I think is well advanced in this connection. It is not a very satisfactory suggestion, so far as the solution of the problem goes, simply the idea that a good deal of this cost of government about which they are complaining in the public land states, as in the other states, is due to the excesses that they have committed in over-organizing their local governmental units. We have too much local organization. We have done it for sentimental reasons and political reasons, and so on. The result is that we have piled up an enormous number of all sorts of administrative units, with the power to levy taxes, with their inevitable overhead, and if you examine any of the figures relating to the cost of government, you will find that the great bulk of the burden is due to the cost of local government, not state government; and our suggestion is—you may say, giving them a stone when they ask for bread—that we reconsider some of these moves we have made in the way of this excessive development of our local organizations, and perhaps the problem will solve itself.

In that connection I ran through the census report of 1922, in which they listed the various kinds of administrative districts which had the power to levy taxes, and so that I will not be accused of partiality and discrimination, I will take my own state of California. I will read you the list of districts in California which have the power to levy taxes:

Counties, incorporated places, school districts, drainage districts, irrigation districts, levee districts, road districts, library districts, lighting districts, fire districts, mosquito-abatement districts, sanitary districts, water districts, cemetery districts, junior college districts and reclamation districts.

Can you beat it? Those are the local subdivisions in the State of California which have the power to levy taxes. All those want to levy taxes on the federally owned lands. The point is this, they want to do the same thing in the other states, although California heads the list with the greatest variety of local governmental units.

We have got somehow to face that problem of local governmental organization and correct a lot of mistakes made in the past, because there is where I think we could do some of our most fruitful work in controlling the increase in the cost of government. We simply bring this in, in order to bring it to the attention of the public land states. They are no worse than the other states, but here is an aspect of the problem which has probably not been adequately considered, in a program set forth for taxing federal lands.

I am sorry I have made the report so sketchy, but, as you see, it was a matter that could not be covered very briefly. At that, I must remind you again that the committee considers this as a preliminary and tentative report, because we have not been able to study the problem with sufficient thoroughness to feel that we have anything like an adequate solution in all of its aspects, or that we are on solid ground in offering recommendations on a large scale; and therefore we submit this as a tentative and preliminary report on the problem of revenue for local purposes from federally owned lands.

REVENUE FROM PUBLIC LANDS

REPORT OF COMMITTEE OF THE NATIONAL TAX ASSOCIATION

HARLEY L. LUTZ, *Chairman*

Leland Stanford Jr. University

I

The resolution under which this committee was appointed laid on it the task of studying the problem presented by the federally owned lands, for the purpose of ascertaining whether some suitable method could be devised whereby the states in which these lands are located might secure an increased revenue therefrom. The problem has proved to be so extensive, and has involved not only so large a range of factual material but also the consideration of so many points of federal and local policy that the committee has been unable, in the time available, to make the thorough study which the situation demands. This report must therefore be regarded as preliminary and tentative.

Before a judgment can be reached as to the merits of the suggestion that the public land states should receive a larger revenue from or on account of the public domain within their borders, it is necessary to consider some of the facts in the whole situation, such as the character and location of the remaining federally owned lands, the recent changes in the cost of state and local government in the public land states, and the relations between these states and the Federal Government, as shown by the grants and contributions which have been made, and are now being made, for local use. It is necessary to consider also some of the contentions that have been advanced in connection with the proposal to provide a larger revenue from the public domain for local use. This report falls, therefore, into two parts. In the first part is presented some material from readily available sources, for the purpose of depicting the general setting of the situation. The second part of the report deals with the various aspects of the present stage of the controversy between the public land states and the Federal Government, and with the remedies which have been proposed in settlement of this controversy.

The public domain of the United States, which at one time or another has included practically all of the land west of the Mississippi River except the State of Texas, has dwindled to about 400,000,000 acres. Remnants of the original public domain are to be found in twenty states, but the bulk of these holdings is now located in eleven western states. The expression " federally owned lands " is frequently used, as if there were but one homogeneous class of such lands. As a matter of fact, there are now several classes, the classification depending in part on the different characteristics of the land, and in part on the differences in policy which have emerged with respect to the use, control and disposition of the remaining lands. The area of the public domain by main classes, and of the amount thereof located in the public land states, are given in the table which follows:

TABLE I

CLASSIFICATION, AREA AND DISTRIBUTION OF THE PUBLIC LANDS, INCLUDING TRIBAL INDIAN LANDS [1]

Class	Total Area (Acres)	Amount in the Public Land States (Acres)
Vacant and unappropriated	196,056,747	195,079,284
National forests	134,834,702	131,079,316
Oil and mineral reserves	46,989,595	40,160,713
National parks, monuments........ ..	6,077,681	6,061,756
Power site reservations........	2,500,000	2,500,000
Total	385,458,725	374,845,069
Tribal Indian lands..............	68,241,450	39,280,623
Grand Total	454,700,175	414,125,692

The lines of demarcation between these several classes of public domain are no doubt sufficiently clear. The tribal Indian lands are, for the time being, regarded as the property of the occupants, who

[1] Figures supplied by the General Land Office.

become the joint owners of any unusual sources of wealth that happen to be discovered in the land allotted to the tribe. These lands are included here, since they are exempt from local taxation and from local administrative jurisdiction, quite as completely as the other classes of the public domain. The only lands in the above table that are at present yielding a revenue from operation or use that could be assigned to or shared with the states are the national forests and the oil and mineral reservations, and a substantial proportion of the gross revenue from these sources is, in fact; distributed to the states of origin. The fees collected for admission to the national parks and monuments are applied to the upkeep and operation of these reservations. The vacant and unappropriated land yields nothing. It has remained vacant and unappropriated to the present, largely because there were no prospects of making a living on such land or of getting wealth from it.

Some idea of the significance of the public-land problem in the western states may be gained from the following statement of the proportion of the total area of each state included in the National Forests and in the vacant and unappropriated domain.

TABLE II

AREA OF EACH PUBLIC LAND STATE,[2] AND AGGREGATE AREA OF THE
NATIONAL FOREST RESERVE AND VACANT PUBLIC DOMAIN [3]

State	Total Area (Acres)	Total Area, National Forest and Vacant Domain (Acres)	Per cent of Total Area in National Forest and Vacant Domain
Arizona	72,838,400	30,397,048	41.7%
California....	99,617,280	44,881,735	44.9
Colorado	66,341,180	22,138,921	33.3
Idaho.....................	53,336,560	31,494,977	59.0
Montana	93,523,840	25,570,981	27.1
Nevada	70,285,440	59,170,057	84.1
New Mexico	78,401,920	26,347,245	33.5
Oregon	61,188,480	28,838,373	47.0
Utah	52,597,760	34,865,758	66.2
Washington	42,775,040	12,256,212	28.5
Wyoming	62,430,720	28,622,140	45.7
Totals..............	753,346,560	344,683,447	45.7

[2] From U. S. Census of 1920.
[3] From Report of General Land Office.

With respect to the proportion of their area owned by the Federal Government, the above states fall into certain rather distinct groups. In one group are Colorado, Montana, New Mexico and Washington, with one-third or less of their area under federal control. In another group are Arizona, California, Oregon and Wyoming, with federal ownership ranging from 42 to 47 per cent of the area. Idaho and Utah constitute another group, in which federal ownership extends to 59 per cent and 66 per cent, respectively; while Nevada is distinctly outside any of these groups, with 84 per cent of its area under federal ownership and control. The committee has not been able to make the local investigation necessary· to ascertain whether or not the urgency of the need for additional local revenue varies with the proportion of federal ownership in these states.

The increase in the cost of government in the public-land states cannot be shown in its entirety, for lack of comparable statistics. The special Census reports on Wealth, Debt and Taxation for 1903, 1912, and 1922 have supplied the material for the following table, which will throw some light on this aspect of the problem.

TABLE III

TAXES COLLECTED IN THE PUBLIC LAND STATES,. FOR THE USE OF THE
STATES, THE COUNTIES, AND THE INCORPORATED PLACES [4]

Governmental Unit	Year		
	1903	1912	1922
States	$17,505,000	$45,185,000	$115,221,000
Counties	29,280,000	89,706,000	144,143,000
Incorporated places	....	121,659,000	131,134,000
Total	$46,785,000	$256,500,000	$390,498,000

Since these figures do not represent all taxes collected by all subdivisions, they understate the real situation; but on the basis of the facts presented here, it appears that in the year 1922 the cost of the state governments was responsible for 22.6% of the taxes collected, while the various subdivisions of local government required 77.4% of the total taxes collected. In these states as in the remainder of the country, the aggregate cost of local government greatly exceeds the cost of the state government. The burden on the taxpayer is produced mainly, therefore, by the cost of the various forms of local

[4] From U. S. Census Reports on Wealth, Debt and Taxation.

government, and the situation which has led to the demand for larger revenues is the product chiefly of the growth in the variety of local subdivisions and the cost of operations which they have assumed.

The figures which have been presented in Table III indicate a rapid increase in the cost of government in the public-land states, and, when taken in conjunction with the facts relating to the proportion of the area of these states which is owned by the Federal Government and exempt from state and local taxation, seem to present a situation which demands relief. If we turn to the other side of the case, it becomes necessary to consider the relations of the Federal Government with the public-land states, in order to ascertain what has been done, and what is now being done, by way of recognition of the Federal Government's obligation toward these states. While there has been no official or formal statement of the Federal Government's position or policy, various federal agencies, including the Department of the Interior, the Forestry Service and the General Land Office, have cooperated in supplying data which indicate that the Federal Government has dealt with and is dealing with these sparsely-settled states in a spirit of liberality.

This liberality has been manifested not only in the relatively larger land grants made to the western, as compared with the eastern states, but in the allotment to the public-land states of a substantial proportion of the gross revenues collected in the form of grazing fees and oil and mineral royalties. The increasing burden on their taxpayers has engendered the feeling in these states, however, that still larger local revenues must be obtained in some way or other from the federally owned lands which constitute so large a proportion of their area. Just how much more revenue they feel that they should receive has not been indicated. It is impossible, therefore, to undertake an accurate balancing of the account, but in order to shed as much light as possible on the financial aspects of the situation such data and suggestions as have come to hand will be presented.

The contributions from the Federal Government to the states fall into two main classes; first, grants of land, mainly for educational and highway purposes, and second, grants of money, either in the form of allocation for local use of a part of the revenue derived from the public lands or in the form of appropriations, mainly for highways, under general laws. The facts regarding certain of these contributions to the public-land states will be briefly summarized.

At the close of the fiscal year 1924 the total land grants to all of the states amounted to 202,387,483 acres. Of this area, the public-land states had received the amounts shown below:

TABLE IV

AMOUNT OF LAND GRANTED TO CERTAIN STATES [5]

State	Total Amount Land Granted States (Acres)
Arizona	10,489,236
California	8,422,664
Colorado	4,433,378
Idaho	3,631,965
Montana	5,869,618
Nevada	2,723,647
New Mexico	5,700,364 *
New Mexico	6,705,662 †
Oregon	4,352,132
Utah	7,414,276
Washington	3,044,471
Wyoming	4,138,569
Total	66,925,982

* Act of June 21, 1898.   † Act of June 20, 1910.

It appears from this tabulation that the eleven public-land states have received 33% of all lands granted to the states by the Federal Government for all purposes. The great bulk of these lands were given for educational purposes, but the figures above include also the swamp and salt-spring lands, and in the western states, the grants for institutions to care for defectives and delinquents, as well as for various miscellaneous activities. Larger amounts were naturally enough given to these states, since they contained so large a part of the available public domain. But the broadening generosity of Congress is seen in these more liberal grants. The Arizona and New Mexico Enabling Act alone granted to each of these states four sections in each township for school purposes, instead of the two sections which had been given to many of the older states. The latest change in this connection is the Act of January 25, 1927, whereby the earlier policy of withholding numbered school sections of known mineral character and giving indemnity therefor was abandoned, and the numbered school sections were given to the state, even if known to contain minerals. The effect of this legislation will be to enhance very considerably the school resources of certain states.

The greater liberality of the most recent grants is effectively realized when presented as a comparison with the terms of the Ohio Enabling Act. Ohio was required to refrain from taxing public

[5] From mimeographed Circular 8304 (1924) issued by the General Land Office.

lands for a period of five years following their sale, while Arizona and New Mexico may exercise the tax privilege when complete equitable title has passed from the Government. They may even tax, prior to patent. Ohio was allowed five per cent of the public land sales, after deducting all expenses of survey and sale from the proceeds, while in Arizona and New Mexico survey is made without cost to the states, and each receives, either directly or through betterments in the form of reclamation of their arid lands, practically all of such proceeds.

Concurrently with the development of the conservation policy and the withholding from private entry of the more valuable remaining lands, the Federal Government has developed the policy of sharing with the public-lands states the current income obtained from the reserved lands and resources. Indeed, this policy was inaugurated as early as the Ohio Admission Act, when 5% of the proceeds of public-land sales was given to the state in which the land was situated, for educational and highway purposes. The Reclamation Act of 1902 provided that the remainder of the proceeds of the land sales should be paid to the reclamation fund. An Act of May 28, 1908 (35 Stat. 260) amended, June 30, 1914 (38 Stat. 441) provided that 25% of the money received from each forest reserve during any fiscal year should be paid at the end of that year to the state in which the forest reserve is situated, to be expended as the state legislature may prescribe, for the benefit of the public schools and public roads of the county or counties containing the reserve. An Act of March 4, 1913 (37 Stat. 843) provides that an additional 10% of the receipts from the national forests shall be set aside for the construction of roads and trails within the forests, in cooperation with local authorities. The mineral leasing Act of February 25, 1920 (41 Stat. 437) grants 37½% of the royalties to the states in which the royalties are collected, and 52½% to the reclamation fund. Since the great bulk of the reclamation projects have been in the public-land states, it appears that 90% of the oil and mineral royalties have been returned to this section as a whole.

The loss of local revenue, on account of the exemption of the public domain is offset, indirectly, at another point also, by the fact that the forest-leasing policy facilitates the maintenance in these states of larger numbers of cattle and sheep. If this property is efficiently assessed, the local tax duplicate is correspondingly increased.

Finally, it should be pointed out that the revenue received by the public-land states from the public domain is a clear net revenue, since the Federal Government pays the entire cost of the forest administration, and is carrying, in addition, certain administrative costs on account of the other divisions of the public domain. The gross forest revenue and the gross revenue from mineral royalties are shared with the states. The following table, compiled by the Department of the Interior, presents the amounts expended on account of the maintenance and administration of the public domain.

TABLE V

AMOUNTS EXPENDED IN CERTAIN STATES, ON ACCOUNT OF THE MAINTENANCE AND ADMINISTRATION OF THE PUBLIC DOMAIN [6]

State	Fiscal Year 1926	Total for Years 1917–1926 inclusive
Arizona	$108,865	$1,297,381
California	135,715	1,773,576
Colorado	161,181	2,059,569
Idaho	98,679	1,335,977
Montana	125,445	2,616,137
Nevada	70,015	843,924
New Mexico	136,018	1,883,396
Oregon	152,446	1,426,846
Utah	130,157	1,403,456
Washington	79,328	1,092,600
Wyoming	120,656	1,642,348
Total	$1,318,632	$17,375,214

The public domain is not entirely a dead weight, as these figures indicate. While the states are losing such tax revenue as might be collected if the land were privately owned, the fact remains that they are now receiving some revenue on account of these lands, and the Federal Government is paying, in addition, certain administrative costs which would constitute an obligation of the states if the land were ceded to them. Further, the services of the Federal Forestry Service are of considerable indirect benefit to the private timber owners and to the states as a whole, through the assistance which this organization renders, in controlling pests and diseases which menace the forests, public and private; in fire prevention; in maintaining the flow of water in streams, and in other ways. The value of these services is not easily reduced to a financial basis, but it is clear that they are advantageous to the states in which the national forests are located, and that account should be taken of them in considering all of the pros and cons of the problem.

The rapid development of the highway network and the corresponding increase of the expenditures for highway construction and

[6] From Circular issued by the Department of the Interior, 1927.

maintenance, present a situation of which some aspects are favorable to the public-land states, while some others are unfavorable. In the first place, Congress has made various special appropriations for the construction of roads in the National Forests, the aggregate since 1916 under this head being $19,000,000. In the second place, the entire area of the state, including the public domain, is used in apportioning highway funds according to, area, and the mileage of post roads on the public domain, if any, is included in determining the distribution according to this factor. Further, the limitation on the amount and proportion of federal aid provided for in the Highway Act of 1921, namely, a maximum of $15,000 per mile and 50% of the cost, are increased on a sliding scale, depending on the percentage which the unappropriated public land and the non-taxable Indian lands bear to.the entire area of the state. Within Indian Reservations the federal aid may be increased to 100% of the cost on projects or portions of projects along which the adjacent lands are tribal, or trust patent, the fee simple with the full right of alienation not being vested in individual Indians. Under this provision the public-land states are receiving the following percentages of the cost of federal-aid highways:

TABLE VI

PERCENTAGE OF THE COST OF FEDERAL AID HIGHWAYS
RECEIVED BY PUBLIC-LAND STATES

State	*Percentage*	*State*	*Percentage*
Arizona	72.34	New Mexico	63.43
California	60.05	Oregon	62.25
Colorado	56.08	Utah	78.90
Idaho	59.75	Washington	54.38
Montana	56.46	Wyoming	64.20
Nevada	87.72		

NOTE.—The states bear the preliminary engineering costs, and some other items, which operate to reduce the actual percentage of cost borne by the Federal Government. Chairman Henry H. Blood, of the Utah Highway Commission, estimates that the proportion of the total cost of federal aid highways in Utah actually met by the Federal Government is about 60%.

On the other hand, there are certain disadvantages encountered by the public-land states in the execution of the highway problem, viewed as a long-run enterprise. The area of the National Forests is not included in ascertaining the percentage by which the maximum amount and proportion of federal participation in highway construction are determined. If it were, obviously the proportions of the cost of all highways borne by the Federal Government in some of these states would be materially increased above the percentages shown above. While the earlier highway acts required local participation on an equal basis to supplement federal appropriations for highways in the National Forests, the Act of 1921 permits, but does not require such cooperation. The practice, as outlined by the San Francisco District Forester, is to judge each national forest-road project separately, and to invite local participation, if and when a local benefit is clearly demonstrable. The point has been made by some critics of the Forest Administration, that the practice has been to use the available funds for the construction of forest roads in those districts in which the local authorities were able and willing to contribute toward the construction. The forests in the poorer counties, it is said, lack adequate roads for fire control, and instances have been cited of serious fire loss, which might have been prevented, had the road program been carried out on a different basis. The committee has had no opportunity of investigating this aspect of the question, and has no opinion to express with respect to these questions of forest administration policy.

The point at which the public-land states may be most seriously burdened by the present highway program, in the long run, is in the cost of maintenance. While it is customary for the Federal Government to maintain the highways in National Forests, for two years after construction, the law requires that all roads built with the aid of federal funds be maintained thereafter by the states. This includes all highways built across the vacant and unappropriated domain, and all forest highways, after the two-year period has elapsed. The main highways across federally owned lands, forest, or other, will be chiefly of an arterial or interstate character, and while there is unquestionably an element of local benefit in these roads, the completion of the national highway system will eventually involve a considerable burden on the western states for the maintenance of roads which are situated on federally owned lands. In view of the fact that these lands are not open to entry, and are exempt from local taxation in support of roads, it seems appropriate to suggest that the Federal Government should assume a part, at least, of the cost of maintaining the federal-aid highways that are constructed in the National Forest or across the other forms of the public domain. A detailed recommendation on this point would require further investigation as to the probable mileage eventually to be constructed and the total burden of maintenance which will be involved. Cession of the public land to the states, the extension of the right to tax these lands, or a grant in lieu of taxes would in equity require that all federal highway funds in the future be distributed on a 50-50 basis. The public-land states would have no further basis for the privileged treatment they are now receiving, in the apportionment of highway-aid funds, nor would there be a valid basis for the suggestion that has just been made relative to federal participation in the maintenance of these highways.

II

The public domain has been a fruitful source of controversy from the beginning. Whatever the particular form of dispute, the issue has usually been between the Federal Government and those who wished to occupy, use or develop the resources of the land, and our national land policy has been molded in part by these controversies. Throughout the evolution of this policy, the most fundamental change has been the shift from an emphasis upon alienation to an emphasis upon reservation and conservation. These viewpoints have not been mutually exclusive, for it is possible to show that some, at least, of those who were most active in promoting alienation realized fully the need and importance of a wise development of the resources; and it is likewise true that there has been some alienation during the period in which the conservation policy has been developing. It is fairly accurate, however, to say that the major emphasis of our public-land policy to the end of the 19th century was upon alienation, while the major emphasis, thus far in the 20th century, has been upon reservation and conservation. This change of emphasis, which is so decided as to constitute, for practical purposes, a change of policy, is at the bottom of the whole question. The resolution under which this committee is acting is an outcrop of the latest phase of the controversy between the public-land states and the Federal Government over the public-land policy of the present and the future. The critical stage of this controversy has been precipitated by the recent proposal of the General Land Office to amend various public-land laws and withdraw all remaining public lands from entry, introducing at the same time a leasing system for grazing and other purposes, similar to that now in effect for the national forests and the reserved oil and mineral lands. In his annual message to Congress in December, 1926, President Coolidge referred to the chaotic condition that prevailed with regard to the use of the vacant public lands, and suggested that a study be made of it and of the means whereby a more orderly administration of the use of the public lands might be secured.

The full discussion of the conservation controversy would carry this committee far beyond the proper limits of the subject assigned to it. The issue raises weighty questions of public policy, of which the merely financial aspects are probably among the least important. If it were feasible to separate sharply the financial from the larger aspects of the situation, this report would be confined to a consideration of the financial query propounded by the resolution. Such separation is not possible, and it is therefore advantageous to summarize the contentions which are being advanced in support of the attack now developing against the federal public-land policy.

The first argument put forward by those who oppose the policy of reserving the public lands from entry, in order to promote forest,

15

oil, mineral or other forms of conservation is, that such action is unconstitutional. The course of the argument will be briefly set forth, although the committee does not presume to express an opinion on the merits of this contention. The Federal Constitution contains the following provision relative to the powers of Congress with respect to the public domain:

> " The Congress shall have power to dispose of and make all needful Rules and Regulations respecting the Territory of other Property belonging to the United States; and nothing in this Constitution shall be construed as to prejudice any claim of the United States, or of any particular state." (Art. IV, Section 3, Par. 2.)

Much of the constitutional discussion turns round the meaning of the expression " to dispose of." Since the earliest practice of the Federal Government, in the administration of its immense public domain, was to sell the land to anyone who was able to pay for it, it is contended that a definite meaning was thus given to this expression by the original sales policy. To dispose of, means to sell, or at least to alienate in some manner, and the grant of authority in the Constitution carries with it, so the argument runs, the mandate to get rid of the public lands by sale or other process of alienation. But the Supreme Court of the United States has said in more than one case, that the United States, like any other landed proprietor, was free to sell its lands or to withhold them from sale.[7] cited passage from the Constitution has never been fully construed by the Supreme Court, and he has expressed the opinion that when it is brought to the test, the court will adhere to the earlier view. The proper battleground for the constitutional argument is the courts, although so far as the committee is aware, no steps are being taken at present to force a judicial determination of the issue.

A second argument against the present and proposed public-land policy is that it is said to constitute a violation and impairment of the sovereignty of the states. A memorial presented to Congress by the legislature of Wyoming in December 1926, contained the following statements:[9]

---

[7] See Camfield vs. United States, 167 U. S. 521; United States vs. Midwest Oil Company, 236 U. S. 459.

Governor Hunt[8] of Arizona has recently asserted that the above-

[8] See his open letter to President Coolidge, in *Congressional Record*, 69th Congress, First Session, p. 7362.

[9] This Memorial is in the *Congressional Record*, 69th Congress, 2nd Session, p. 4648. The Wyoming legislature urged federal action looking to the immediate return of all public lands to the states in which these lands were situated. At the same time another Memorial was submitted, asking that the terms of the 640-acre Homestead Law be modified to permit entry upon 2,560 acres of grazing land and that the terms of entry be liberalized. *Ibid.,* p. 4649.

"WHEREAS, We search in vain for any clause of the Federal Constitution which prohibits to the States the exercise of any powers connected with the public lands, and the control asserted by the Federal Government is a growth of a system nowhere even contemplated by the founders of our Government and in violation of the sovereignty of States which came into the Federal Union on an equal footing with the original States in all respects whatever;

"WHEREAS, Of the 48 sovereign States, the inhabitants of 37 own and have always owned all their lands and their State sovereignty and authority cover every natural resource within their borders, thus placing the 11 States aforementioned on an unequal basis with other States to the untold financial injury of the inhabitants thereof."

Various writers have given expression to similar views, although it is doubtful if any of these persons would be generally regarded as authorities of the highest rank on matters of constitutional law. Governor Hunt voiced his opposition to the encroachment of federal control over the rights of the states as manifested in the reservation policy, in the open letter to President Coolidge already mentioned. During the past summer he has been urging the State of Arizona to adopt certain amendments to its own constitution which, he holds, will enable it lawfully to tax federal property or undertakings within the state.

Another argument which is corollary to the contention of impaired sovereignty, is that the states are being deprived of revenue, through this withholding of public lands from private ownership. Each state, from Ohio in 1803, to Arizona in 1912, as it was admitted, accepted the stipulation that public lands were to be exempt from local taxation until these were patented; but it is contended, with some measure of correctness, that this condition was accepted the more willingly, since it was assumed that the exemption would be but temporary and would lapse as soon as the public lands within the state were settled and the titles had been issued to the possessors. The reservation of lands, an expression of the broader policy of the conservation of resources, is the more bitterly denounced as a violation of the spirit of the agreement between the Federal Government and the several public-land states, in that it delays indefinitely the time when these states may tax a certain part of the lands within their boundaries. Since the power to tax is an attribute of sovereignty, the alleged loss is a double one—the state is deprived of the opportunity of collecting revenue from certain property within its jurisdiction, and this deprivation constitutes an impairment of the powers guaranteed to each state under the Constitution.

We shall leave to one side the legal and constitutional aspects of the controversy, except for one or two queries which even the layman may propound. It is difficult to regard these aspects of the case as tremendously impressive, in view of the readiness with which some who advance them appear to be willing to compromise on a larger revenue return. If the principle of state sovereignty is really at stake, no amount of subsidy from the Federal Government should be allowed to compromise or close the discussion. As a matter of fact, however, the Federal Government owns real property in all of the states, and this property is everywhere exempt from local taxation. This has been the situation from the beginning. It seems proper to ask how much property the Federal Government may thus own and exempt from local taxation before the matter assumes the importance of a question of principle, involving the sovereignty of the states. While the eleven public-land states do contain the bulk of the federally owned lands, there are at least nine others in which remnants of the vacant, unappropriated and unreserved public lands are to be found. In 1926 the aggregate of such lands in these nine states was 977,463 acres. Was this sufficient to present the constitutional issue in any or all of these states? The Wyoming Memorial inaccurately declares, in the passage quoted above, that the inhabitants of the thirty-seven other states had always owned all of the land within their respective boundaries, and that these states had accordingly attained full sovereignty, while the eleven public-land states were deprived of their privileges guaranteed under the Constitution. Many of these thirty-seven states were organized out of the public domain and at the time of their admission, as well as for a long time thereafter, the Federal Government continued to hold title to vacant and unappropriated lands within their borders.[10] It holds a considerable amount of land in nine of them at the present time. Nevertheless, the state of mind

[10] The problem of tax-exempt public land was vastly more aggravating for Ohio, at the time of admission, than it is and has been for Arizona and New Mexico. Ohio was given one section in each township for common schools and nothing for higher education, while Arizona and New Mexico were each given four sections to the township for common schools, and magnificent grants for universities, normal schools and other state institutions. At the time of the respective donations the cash value of the Ohio lands was much less, acre for acre, than those given to Arizona and New Mexico. In 1802 the demand for wild lands was small and competition was at its maximum. The thirteen original states, having succeeded to the rights of the British Crown to all of the waste or undisposed-of lands within their respective borders were busily engaged in selling and settling such lands. Moreover, Massachusetts was then actively parceling out the areas now constituting the State of Maine; North Carolina, those in the State of Tennessee, and Virginia, was busily occupied in settling Kentucky. To the north of us, Great Britain, and especially to the south and west, Spain and France, were offering attractive inducements to the colonizer. The prospects, therefore, were not bright in 1802 that at any time in the near future the government-owned lands in the State of Ohio would be rendered subject to taxation through their sale and disposition.—Comment by Mr. T. C. Havell.

of some extremists is such that they are making statements which have little foundation in the facts of the case. One writer declared, for example, that the eleven public-land states were provinces of a central power, and not sovereign states, on an equality with the others.

It is interesting to state this phase of the question qualitatively rather than quantitatively. The estimates of the value of the federally owned lands in California vary from $150,000,000 to $300,000,000. In 1925 the Federal Government owned real property in New York State valued by the assessors at $200,460,000 (*Report,* N. Y. Tax Comm., 1925, p. 140). In Massachusetts, in 1926, the valuation given by assessors to federally owned real property in that state was $146,000,000 (*Report,* Mass. Tax Com'r, 1926, p. 127). While these totals are, in each state, a much smaller proportion of the entire taxable wealth than the public domain in California is of the total wealth of that state, the fact remains that, measured in values, there are large amounts of federally owned land exempt from taxation and from local jurisdiction in other ways in these and other eastern states. If the issue of the constitutional rights of a state is presented by federal ownership of real property in one instance, it is presented in every case, and all of the states are in the same position. All suffer an invasion of their sovereignty, if any one of them does. It has not yet been determined judicially whether the problem of constitutional rights is presented more sharply in terms of acreage or in terms of value.

Still another argument against the reservation policy is the eriticism of the improvidence of the Federal Government in continuing to hold and administer, at great expense, these large tracts of low-value lands so remote from the seat of the Federal Government. The Wyoming Memorial states that "the value of that portion of the public domain still remaining vacant is such as not to warrant further administration by the Department of the Interior, and is insufficient, even in 640-acre tracts, to justify homesteading under the requirements of the 640-acre Homestead Law." The conclusion is that these vacant, low-value lands should be ceded to the states in which they are situated, in order to make good the loss of revenue now being incurred through their exemption. It is difficult to reconcile this contention with some of those which have already been set forth, for, by the admissions regarding their value which the advocates of cession advance, much of this land would be a liability rather than an asset to the states which happened to receive them. That is, the states would be compelled to assume the costs of administration now being borne by the Federal Government, and they would have but little prospect of securing revenue from much of this low-value land. The real issue is not, however, over the vacant lands of little or no value, but over those lands which have been reserved on account of the natural wealth which they contain. Doubtless the public-land states would be content to receive the valuable lands, leave the worthless lands in the possession of the Federal Government, and say no more about the matter of state sovereignty; but since they can hardly propose such a course, it is necessary to demand that the worthless lands be çeded, along with those of high value.

Finally, it is suggested that the experience of certain states with the management of their public land, notably Minnesota and Texas, is a satisfactory demonstration that the other states could and would manage their lands with equal efficiency and equity. This kind of argument is beside the point since the federal conservation policy is not based entirely on the assumption of state incompetence.

Various remedies are proposed to correct these evils and difficulties which the federal land policy is said to have evoked. Although the critics of the Federal Government are substantially in accord as to the bill of indictments which they would draw, they are by no means unanimous as to the proper remedy to be applied. The "bitter-enders" demand immediate cession of all federally owned lands, reserved and unreserved, to the states in which these lands are situated. This is requested in the Memorial from the Wyoming legislature, and in various bills that were introduced in recent sessions of Congress by the late Congressman Raker of California and others. Some less extreme advocates of this general solution would make an exception of the National Parks and Monuments (e. g., Congressman Winter of Wyoming. See *Cong. Record*, 69th Congress, 2nd Session, p. 1439), while none of them are definite as to the action to be taken with regard to the tribal Indian lands.

This solution is obviously the only one which would be accepted by those who concern themselves chiefly with the constitutional questions involved. If permanent withdrawal of the remaining public lands from private ownership does in fact constitute a serious violation of state rights and state sovereignty, the only satisfactory solution would appear to be a policy whch looked ultimately to the surrender of this control.

Nevertheless, some of those who make use of the constitutional arguments are evidently willing to compromise their position for a larger amount of revenue for state and local purposes. A suitable remedy, in the minds of these persons, would be the assignment to the several public-land states of all the royalties and fees collected from the public domain within the state. As has been shown in Part I of this report, a very substantial proportion of these revenues is now being paid directly to the states or is being used in reclamation or other improvements which are of benefit to the public-land states. Whether or not an increase is made in the proportion of

the public-land revenues that is paid directly to the states, the re-
reipts of the states from these sources could be increased by the
upward revision of the rates of fees and royalties that are collected.
Such a suggestion rouses instant and determined opposition, however, from those who are engaged in using the public lands and
paying the fees or royalties in question, and especially the cattlemen. If the states owned these lands, however, the only way in
which the revenue return could be materially increased would be by
an advance in the rates charged for grazing or other uses. If the
lands were sold to individuals, these owners would find their operating costs increased by the taxes which the states or their subdivisions would impose on the land as well as by the interest charges
on the investment.

Another suggestion is that the Federal Government authorize the
local taxation of the federally owned lands in each of the public-
land states. Governor Hunt is said to be sponsoring a proposal for
taxing the Colorado River Dam, when built, for state purposes.
The California Farm Bureau Federation had before it, at a recent
meeting, the following resolution:

> "WHEREAS, If the contemplated plan of the Department of
> the Interior should become effective (i. e., the withdrawal of
> all remaining lands from entry) one-half of the land area of
> the state would be forced to forever sustain the whole state,
> thus casting an ever-increasing burden on the agricultural in-
> terests already over-taxed; Now THEREFORE BE IT RESOLVED,
> by the California Farm Bureau Federation in annual confer-
> ence assembled,
>
> "That it protests against any further or additional with-
> drawals of public lands in this State, unless provision is made
> in such withdrawal orders or laws to reimburse the counties
> affected, by payment to each of them annually of the sum of
> money they would receive if such lands were in private owner-
> ship and subject to tax; and be it further
>
> "RESOLVED, That the Congress of the United States be and
> is hereby requested to enact at the next session proper any
> requisite legislation whereby the several counties of this State
> as well as other western public-land states be reimbursed an-
> nually on the same basis of monetary return as such counties
> would receive were all the present withdrawn lands taxed at
> the same rate as privately owned lands similarly situated."

It is difficult for anyone familiar with the California revenue
system to see just how the general farming interests of the state are
now being penalized by the existence of federally owned lands, or
how these interests could be materially benefited by the attainment
of the demands set forth in the Farm Bureau Federation's resolution quoted above, without the adoption of a constitutional amend-

ment introducing radical reforms in the system of state and local taxation. Indeed, the only beneficiaries of the scheme advocated in these resolutions would be the property owners in such counties as happened to contain forest, oil. mineral or other valuable reserved lands. Much of the vacant land in California has little or no value and would yield little or no tax return to the county in which it is situated. Since the state does not tax real property for state purposes, the general farming interests would not, and could not, benefit in any appreciable degree from the plan proposed.

Those resolutions are misleading, furthermore, in that they imply that the valuable federally owned lands in California are now contributing nothing to the counties in which they are situated. On the contrary, as is shown in Part I of this report, the counties containing National Forests, oil and mineral lands, are receiving every year fixed percentages of the timber sales, grazing fees, and the oil and mineral royalties, while the remainder of these revenues is being used for the general development of the West, through reclamation, reforestation, fire prevention and in other ways.

The late Congressman Raker suggested, in his remarks before Congress on one occasion, that there were many owners of cut-over lands who found it difficult to realize enough revenue from their lands to pay the taxes now being levied, and that these owners would be glad to have the lands taken over by the Federal Government by incorporation into the forest reserves, in order to be relieved of the current tax burden. He held, however, that the counties ought not to lose the revenue, and that the Federal Government should therefore contribute to those localities an amount equal to the taxes which would have been assessed against the former owners.[11] Stated thus, the proposal becomes virtually one to subsidize the local treasuries and at the same time to relieve from further carrying charges the landowners who have skimmed the cream from their lands, thus increasing the premium for pursuing a policy of ruthless exploitation and destruction of forests and other resources. There are doubtless landowners in other states who would not be averse to a similar arrangement.

It is true that the owner of cut-over lands is relieved from local taxation in the case of the exchange of such land for timber-cutting concessions in the National Forest. Cut-over lands, so situated as to be desirable additions to the forest holdings, are sometimes accepted at their fair value in exchange for standing timber ready for market. The lands thus traded are incorporated into the forest reserve, but the object of such exchanges is the promotion of the objectives of the forest reservation policy, and not the relief of property-owners from taxation on their cut-over lands.

[11] See *Congressional Record*, 68th Congress, 2nd Session, p. 6506.

While the lands thus acquired for national forest purposes are withdrawn from the local tax rolls, it is rather short-sighted to contend that this withdrawal constitutes a permanent loss to the community. Cut-over lands usually have but little value, and would yield only a small tax per acre. Further, the use of such land as a means of paying for standing timber, facilitates the harvesting of the National Forest timber crop, and enables the lumberman to continne in business, thereby sustaining or adding to the taxable wealth of the community. Most important of all, the incorporation of the land into the forest is the most promising means whereby reforestation can be accomplished, in the case of the greater part of this acreage. In the long run the community tends to gain rather than lose through such a policy.

The contention that the states have been losing, or would potentially lose tax revenue, through the withdrawal from entry of the remaining vacant public lands rests on the assumption that all of these lands have value and would be capable of being used in such a manner as to produce the taxes. It is well known that millions of acres of the vacant and unappropriated public lands are either desert or mountainous, and are incapable of supporting any economic activity. They have not been settled, because no settler could make a living on them. If they were given away tomorrow, they would be sold to the state in settlement of the first installment of taxes levied against them. Some other vacant public lands are of great value and would yield handsome profits to the exploiters, as well as substantial taxes to the assessing districts in which they are located. The proposal to withdraw all remaining public lands from entry involves the general policy of conservation and of the administration of the public domain upon which the Federal Government has embarked. So far as the demand for tax compensation is concerned, it is clear that there is no valid ground for demanding a federal subsidy in lieu of taxes, with respect to those lands which would yield no income and no taxes if they were relinquished to private possession. The question of local taxation of the domain is discussed more fully at a later point in the report.

Another remedy which should be acceptable to those who take a less extreme position on the whole matter of the relationship of the Federal Government and the public-land states is the continuation and extension of federal control over the vacant lands, with a view to applying to these lands a policy of development and conservation similar to that which has been applied to the National Forests. This is apparently the plan which the Department of the Interior has in contemplation. The argument for such a policy is that it is necessary, especially in the grazing country, if the resources of the range are to be preserved and developed. The system of competitive, unregulated use of the open range has greatly reduced its value for grazing purposes, and in some places the loss and destruction have been such that a long time will be required for its recovery. On this matter a man thoroughly conversant with conditions in Utah has written as follows: [12]

> "On the unrestricted and uncontrolled public domain many thousands of dollars have been wasted in attempting to establish a grazing privilege without ownership by trying to set up a seasonal priority, both in reference to spring range and winter range. While many of the actions under this controversy have been personal and individual, the results generally have not been what would be classified as an orderly procedure.
>
> "Even though by 1900 the western states found they were grazing a sufficient number of cattle, horses and sheep to fully occupy all the grazing ground available, while the ownership was a very small percentage, the grazing practices under these conditions were not corrective. The rush in an attempt to establish a seasonal priority on the best grazing grounds led to the practice of damaging and killing out much valuable forage, and with the elimination of the forage erosion tremendously increased. This method depleted the range and rendered the carrying capacity very much less than it normally should have been. Much of the otherwise economic forage has been replaced by poisonous and useless plants. Thus the struggle has been made all the more intense."

In other words, federal control has been rendered necessary with respect to the open range, for the same reasons that made such control necessary in the case of the forests, the salmon fisheries, the oil and minerals. A convention of cattlemen in Utah in the summer of 1927, addressed by Hon. William Bailey, a member of this committee, endorsed the proposition that some kind of federal control and regulation of grazing was necessary to the preservation of the range.

On the basis of such consideration as the committee has been able to give the different suggestions that have been advanced, namely cession to the states, local taxation and federal control and development, it gives its approval unhesitatingly to the last-named—federal control and development, with such arrangements for using and sharing the increased revenue yield as may be determined upon. The reasons for this recommendation rest in part on the positive advantages of such a solution, and in part on the objections that may be urged against some of the other proposals, especially local taxation of the public lands.

In the first place, it is apparent that the range problem is one

[12] William Peterson, Director, Utah Agricultural Experiment Station and U. A. C. Extension Service, Logan, Utah. Address at American Livestock Association at Salt Lake City, Jan. 25, 1927.

which calls for a systematic long-run policy of control and development. The testimony is unmistakably clear as to the effects of the present policy of neglect and competitive use. The range should be dealt with as a long-run reclamation project, upon which systematic and extensive attempts are made, for the purpose of increasing and conserving the supply of forage and water for stock uses. The depleted grazing capacity of the range must be restored, under a program of carefully controlled and restricted use, and steps must be taken to provide such a distribution of watering-places for stock as will obviate the necessity of long destructive marches to the water-holes. Some tests that have been made in Utah indicate that wells can be sunk that will supply water. In other places storage reservoirs might prove feasible, in which the surplus waters of winter rains and snow might be accumulated. The first use of the grazing fees collected would properly be the construction of these improvements. If the receipts from fees were not at first sufficient, it is submitted that this sort of improvement of the grazing range is a form of reclamation that is as deserving of a place in the general reclamation scheme as the expensive irrigation projects that have been launched to promote intensive farming.

A policy of this sort, properly conceived and carried out, would give stability to the livestock industry of the West, and so would sustain and develop that aspect of agriculture for which some of these states are peculiarly fitted. The gain to the states would be indirect, through the growth of wealth and the possibility of deriving public revenue from the taxation of this wealth, but it would be a real and substantial gain, if the policy should prove productive of the possibilities which some see in it. If this experiment should fail, the futility of regarding the range country as having large economic possibilities would have been adequately demonstrated. After the development of the range had reached a point beyond which a further large reinvestment of the proceeds from fees was unnecessary, it would be possible to share these fees with the states, in any proportion that the circumstances seemed to justify.

In the second place, the committee favors federal control, rather than cession to the states, with a view to permitting the several states to undertake the necessary development. The sentiment of the West is by no means unanimous in favor of cession of the public lands to the states.[13] Such action, if taken, would not wholly dispose of the question of federal invasion of state sovereignty, for the Federal Government would continue to be under the obligation of supervising some 68,000,000 acres of tribal Indian lands, which clearly could not be ceded to the states, without a gross betrayal of

[13] Mr. Asplund, of New Mexico, writes that the people of his state would not, in general, favor the cession of the public lands to the states.

the trust that has been assumed on behalf of these wards of the Nation. Further, and more important, the character of the problem is such that federal control, at least for the present, is demanded. The Federal Government has accumulated some experience in handling such matters; it is free from local influences in the establishment and execution of its policy; and the fact that the range does not conform to state boundary lines renders it necessary that there be some authority that would be able to integrate the various district projects. The spectacle of the seven-state squabble over the division of the flow of the Colorado River illustrates what might be expected if the states undertook to launch cooperative projects for range reclamation and development.

The committee has not undertaken to formulate the details of a plan of control. It is clear, however, that any system of controlled use of the range that may be introduced should be one which will most fully safeguard the rights and interests of the sections involved, while it promotes at the same time the larger objectives of the program. The details of this system cannot be written in Washington, nor can they be written in the West, except after the most careful consideration of the relative needs of the local settled communities, and of the stockmen who operate on a small scale, as well as of those who operate on a large scale.

The principal objections which the committee sees in the proposal to authorize local taxation of the public lands are the following:

In the first place, while it is conceded that such action could readily enough be accomplished through federal legislation, a difficulty arises as to the scope of the permissive legislation. Such a law would be either of general application, or, assuming no constitutional barriers, of special application to the public-land states. That is, the taxation of all federally owned real property, wherever situated, and for whatever purposes used, would be authorized, or the legislation would apply specifically and solely to the designated forms of the public domain. If the former alternative were chosen and a general permissive taxation statute were enacted by Congress, the result would be the local taxation of every post office, federal office building, military post, etc., and the payment of these taxes throughout the nation would simply necessitate a heavier levy of federal taxes to meet the bill. Assuming that the constitutional obstacles to special legislation applicable only to a certain number of states could be overcome, the practical result would be a form of subsidy to these states, since some parts of the public domain are mountainous or desert, and would yield no local revenue, even if ceded outright to the states in which they are situated. Many reasons have already been presented, in previous discussions before this association, against further extension of the federal-subsidy principle. In view of the record of federal liberality to the public-land states, the question may well be raised whether there is adequate warrant for an extension and continuance of the subsidies being given to these states, with the possible exception of the highways on the public domain.

In the second place, local taxation of the public lands, if authorized, and if accompanied by such safeguards as are essential to the assurance of equitable taxation would involve a degree of federal interference with and supervision over local assessment administration that would be very unpalatable to those who now object to such interference. The proposal to tax federally owned lands usually involves the assumption that such lands would be assessed on a basis similar to that used for privately owned lands of similar character. It would be folly for Congress to authorize such action in a number of states, without providing for some kind of federal review or equalization of assessments, especially in view of the fact that in most of the public-land states a highly qualified and competent assessment and equalization organization is lacking. If the people of the West find the existing measure of federal administrative control irksome, they would find that which would be involved in a federal review and equalization of local assessments vastly more so. We have one example of the complications that may follow an attempt by Congress to enact permissive taxation legislation in the case of the national banks. The members of this association need no further warning to keep clear of such entanglements in the future.

In the third place, local taxation of the public lands, if authorized, would accomplish but little for the relief of the general local tax burden in the public-land states, without radical changes in the tax system of most of these states. The form of relief which would operate most widely would be that secured by a reduction of the state tax on property, through an increase of the property tax base subject to state taxation. But California levies no state tax on property, and in most of the other states the levy for state purposes is restricted by constitutional provision to a rather low rate. In all of these states, as shown in Part I of this report, the bulk of the tax burden is occasioned by the cost of county and city government, schools, and other distinctly local affairs. It is the cost of local government, rather than the cost of state government as such, that is oppressing the taxpayer. But local taxation, that is, intra-county taxation of the public lands, would benefit only those property-owners in the counties containing public lands, while the relief from the burden of local taxation in the case of counties in which the land is in large degree or wholly, privately owned, would be little or nothing.

On the contrary, the counties or districts in which there happened to be a relatively large quantity of public land would enjoy the same privileges in the matter of low tax rates that tax colonies everywhere have enjoyed. Consider the case of Gila County, Arizona, for example. This county has an area of 3,007,360 acres, of which 2,915,279 acres are owned by the Federal Government, leaving only 92,081 acres, or 3% of the area in private ownership and subject to state and local taxation. From one standpoint, here is an urgent case of need for relief; but if local taxation of the public domain were authorized, the fortunate owners of the 92,081 acres would see their taxes approach the vanishing point and Gila County would become a "Taxpayers' Paradise," or else the county would be plunged into an orgy of extravagant expenditure for all manner of useless local undertakings. Under the California revenue system it is difficult to see how the citizens of San Francisco could secure any relief from their city and county taxes, by any plan of local taxation of the National Forests, Yosemite National Park, or the sandy desert of Death Valley. Their logical reply to the intra-county taxation of these lands would be the demand to tax the post offiee, the custom house, the Presidio, and other federally owned lands within their own jurisdiction, and it would be rather difficult to present a convincing reason why they should not enjoy this privilege, if it were extended to the public-domain counties of the state.

A few instances have been cited which, by a parallel of reasoning, may be regarded by some as sustaining the argument for the local taxation of federally owned lands. One of these cases is the action taken by Congress for the relief of certain counties in the states of Oregon and Washington, in which were situated lands originally granted to the Oregon and California Railroad Company. By an Act of 1916 (June 9, 1926, 39 Stat.) these lands were re-vested in the United States, on account of certain violations of the terms of the grant. Section 9 of this Act provided for the payment by the United States of accrued and unpaid taxes on the defaulted lands. Section 10 provided that all moneys received from the sale of these lands, or from the timber thereon, should be deposited in a special fund, to be disposed of, first, for the settlement of any just claims for balances due, which the railroad company might have, under the terms of the original grant, and second, for the reimbursement of the United States for taxes paid. If the receipts into the fund were not sufficient to pay the railroad company's balance in full in ten years, the remainder was to be paid by an appropriation from the Treasury. The Act of July 13, 1926, brings the matter to date by authorizing payment of the taxes which would have accrued had the lands remained in private ownership during the years 1916 to 1926 inclusive, and authorizes an annual payment of the taxes accrued against these lands, until all charges against the special fund have been liquidated. Section 4 of the Act of 1926 provides that all proceeds realized from the sale of land or timber shall be placed to the credit of this fund until all sums charged against such fund are fully and completely liquidated, and until the United States has been reimbursed for the taxes advanced, no distribution of the proceeds shall be made as provided in the Act of 1916.

It is evident that the special circumstances attending this action for the relief of the counties affected cannot be regarded as a precedent for extending the general privilege of local taxation of federally owned lands. As a matter of fact, the Federal Government is simply undertaking to make an annual advance, equal to the taxes assessed in 1915, until such time as the sales of land and timber have amounted to a total sufficient to repay the railroad company and to reimburse the Federal Treasury for the taxes advanced. The usual provisions for the allocation of the proceeds of land and timber sales are suspended in this case, in favor of the special purposes of meeting the claims of the railroad company and paying accrued taxes. Whenever the special fund shows a balance for distribution, according to the provisions of the Act of 1916, the payment of accrued taxes by the Federal Government will cease, unless this arrangement is extended by future legislation. The amounts credited to the special fund may never equal the charges against it, but the existing legislation does not in terms contemplate an indefinite period of payment of the accrued taxes.

Certain states have authorized their subdivisions to levy taxes against the property which the state has acquired for forest or other purposes. New York permits the counties in which any part of the state forest and watershed preserves is located to assess such lands on the same basis as adjoining lands and to bill the state for the amount of tax thus determined to be due, on account of the withdrawal of the lands from private ownership. Massachusetts authorizes a payment in lieu of taxes to the localities in which state-owned lands are situated, upon a quinquennial valuation, ascertained by the state tax commissioner, and Pennsylvania permits counties or townships to assess taxes upon lands acquired by the state for water conservation or for the prevention of flood conditions, upon the valuation for which such lands were assessed at the time of their acquisition. Somewhat similar provisions may be found in the tax laws of other states. They have been one phase of the recent uprising against the earlier loose practices in the granting of tax exemptions.

None of these cases are regarded by the committee as an acceptable precedent for the state taxation of federally owned lands. The jurisdictional conflict, which looms so large in any attempt at federal permissive tax legislation, is lacking in any arrangements between the state and its own subdivisions. In every instance the authorization to assess state-owned lands, or the grant of a sum in lieu of taxes on land withdrawn from private ownership, seems to be simply a more convenient and expedient way of meeting the difficulty created by the erection of state properties, than it would be to reorganize local boundaries to take account of the changed conditions. If New York establishes a state forest or a watershed district, and prefers to keep intact the remnants of townships or counties that are left, after the state property lines have been carved out, rather than effect a reorganization of the privately owned lands into new districts, we concede her this privilege. It may be simpler and less troublesome all around, than to face the problem of local consolidation and reorganization. Tax exemption has assumed in every state the proportions of a major problem, and must be dealt with as such. Local taxation of state-owned land may or may not be the solution, but whatever its usefulness within the limits of a state which is free to deal with its political subdivisions as circumstances may require, we cannot regard such a practice as a precedent for establishing the principle of state taxation of federal property or federal agencies located within the states.

Finally, while the taxation scheme would solve the one difficulty of providing certain favored localities with the desired additional revenue, it is objectionable, in that it misses the main element in the problem, namely, that a long-run reform must be one which looks to the improvement of the economic usefulness of the federally owned lands. The object of federal forest management is to put the forests on a crop basis and to assure a yield of timber from these forests throughout an indefinite period. The object of any program which is undertaken with respect to the vacant domain should be, similarly, to develop and to assure a grazing territory for the stock-raising states for an indefinite future. It would be very unwise to sacrifice the long-run possibilities of development for any course, however attractive otherwise, which looked simply to the relief of an immediate situation, and this the taxation proposal would do.

It may not be amiss to suggest in concluding this report, that one reason for the heavy proportion of the cost of government being local in character is due to the over-organization of the states, from the standpoint of local government. This criticism does not apply simply to the public-land states—it is generally true of the American states. Its validity is recognized by the fact that various consolidation movements are under way, in school administration, in the combination of city and county governments, and in other ways. The discussion at the 1926 conference of this association (pp. 298-302) brought out the point that there is no logical or *a priori* ideal local governmental unit, and that the tendency to create a great number of such units for sentimental or political reasons, tends to break down efficient tax administration, as well as to increase the cost of local government.

In connection with the figures which were presented earlier in this report to show the increase in the cost of state and local government in the public-land states, it is interesting to note the extent to which local subdivisions have been created, with the authority to levy taxes or special assessments. The Census Report on Taxes Collected for 1922 lists for all of the states, the various subdivisions which reported receipts from taxes in 1922. The situation in the public-land states was as follows:

Arizona—counties, incorporated places, school districts, drainage districts, irrigation districts, fire districts and electrical districts.

California—counties, incorporated places, school districts, drainage districts, irrigation districts, levee districts, road districts, library districts, lighting districts, fire districts, mosquito-abatement districts, sanitary districts, water districts, cemetery districts, sewer districts, junior college districts, promotion districts and reclamation districts.

Idaho — counties, incorporated places, school districts, road districts, lighting districts, irrigation districts and drainage districts.

Colorado—counties, incorporated places, school districts, drainage districts, and irrigation districts.

Montana—counties, incorporated places, school districts, drainage districts, irrigation districts, road districts, and fire districts.

Nevada—counties, incorporated places, school districts, drainage districts, and irrigation districts.

New Mexico—counties, incorporated places, school districts, irrigation districts, and drainage districts.

Oregon—counties, incorporated places, school districts, road districts, port districts, water districts, irrigation districts, and drainage districts.

Utah—counties, incorporated places, school districts, drainage districts, irrigation districts, and conservation districts.

Washington—counties, incorporated places, school districts, townships, drainage districts, levee districts, road districts, port districts, park districts, water districts, irrigation districts, and commercial waterways districts.

Wyoming—counties, incorporated places, and school districts.

In an earlier generation there may have been a certain justification for many local subdivisions, on account of the distances and the inadequate means of transportation and communication. This justification is now largely removed, with the universality of the automobile, the improved highway, the railway network, the telephone, the telegraph and the radio. Yet the pressure for further subdivision continues in some of the public-land states. New Mexico started statehood with four counties; she now has thirty-

16

one, and each legislature is confronted with the question of creating still others, by further subdivision. Each additional county means the usual governmental framework, with the standardized list of jobs and expenses, and a heavier tax rate on a relatively smaller tax duplicate. Mr. F. N. Fletcher, of Nevada, stated before the conference of the Western States Taxpayers Association at Santa Fe in September, 1927, that Nevada had seventeen counties and required only ten.[14] When one considers the plight of Gila County, Arizona, referred to above, it seems pertinent to inquire whether, under such circumstances as exist there, a real justification can be given for a separate county organization. The State of Maine solves its problem of vast stretches of unsettled country, by leaving it in an unorganized condition. A rational policy of reorganizing local boundary lines in the public-land states, excluding the large compact areas of the public domain as unorganized territory, and re-grouping the settled areas into counties of considerable size, geographically, might effect a very important reduction in the cost of local government, and so, a very significant reduction in the tax burden of the local property-owners, without any very serious losses, other than those which might be involved in the number or the distribution of offices and jobs. The committee has undertaken no studies which would enable it to offer specific recommendations for any given state, in this matter of local reorganization, but in view of the growing feeling that the local governmental organization has been rather over-done and that some sort of retrenchment, through consolidation or otherwise, is necessary, the suggestion is offered as bearing on the problem of the local tax burden in the public-land states.

VIRGIL H. GIBBS (Ohio) : Mr. President, we have with us the Governor of Iowa. I am sure we should be glad to hear from him.

CHAIRMAN MATTHEWS: I am sure the convention would.

HON. A. J. HAMMILL (Governor of Iowa) : Mr. President, Ladies and Gentlemen: I just dropped into the conference yesterday and today with the idea that I might sit here and hear your various discussions and learn of the plans that this organization had in

[14] The history of the changes in county boundaries has been traced for some of the public-land states. By the end of the territorial period, Colorado has been organized into 26 counties. In 1905 this number had increased to 55.—Paxson, F. L., " The County Boundaries of Colorado," in *University of Colorado Studies*, Vol. III, pp. 197-205, August, 1906. In 1850 California was divided into 27 counties. Successive subdivisions had increased the number to 58 in 1907, and almost every legislature since then has encountered further proposals for subdivision.—*Cf.* Coy, O. C., *The Genesis of California Counties*, published by The California Historical Survey Commission, Berkeley, 1923. See also Coan, C. F., " County Boundaries in New Mexico," in *Southwestern Political Science Quarterly*, Vol. III, December, 1922.

mind. Up to the present moment I have enjoyed the presentation of the various subjects that have been before this body. I enjoyed the discussion this afternoon, which, to my mind, resolved itself into a problem of the revision of our national income tax laws, simplifying them, making them more definite and certain, and inaugurating a program in connection therewith that the ordinary man might read the law and correctly understand what his assessment might be, and be prepared to make a report accordingly and be assessed upon that basis, as distinguished from the present-day uncertainty as the law is now being administered.

To my mind this organization could no no greater service to the people of the country generally than to inaugurate a definite program and recommend it, with a definite idea and definite hopes in mind.

I have enjoyed the discussion tonight here. I was carried along with a great deal of interest.

During the Governors' conferences we have had much discussion from Governor Dern and other governors, but particularly Governor Dern, and I presume you people have read his discussion of this question, because he circularized the country generally with his presentation of his ideas in connection with what he terms the states' property rights, as distinguished from the National Government. I sincerely hope that this body will never commit itself to a program admitting of subsidizing the rest of the country with an idea of trying to rehabilitate in those particular states where they have small units of government that are costly, and thus adding an additional burden to the rest of the country generally.

To my mind a plan of that kind would be simply treating the symptom and not the cause; and if there has been any fault or criticism in the general administration of our various departments of government, in the matter of our taxation policy, it is because we have thought in many cases we have attempted to treat the symptom and not the cause. I am mighty glad to know that the committee does not suggest the creation of a subsidy, but just casually referred to it. To my mind in those particular cases the government reserved those rights when those places were admitted as states.

Our various departments of government, just as the chairman of this committee has said, have attempted in many cases, because of self-pride or other imaginary reasons, to create many departments of government that have become costly.

Now, men and women, we must begin to look at that situation squarely and observe just exactly where we are drifting on this very proposition.

We had a measure before our last session of the legislature in which some of the counties said they were unable, with the limit of levies that they have, to carry on the departments of government as they thought they should. I said to those men, "Have you attempted to budget your system; have you attempted to bring your cost of administration of government down?" "No," they said, "we have not particularly done that, but we feel that we must have this additional fund for the purpose of carrying on the administration of government, of these particular counties." And I said to them, "You are already levying as much as the people in that particular county can carry, and you must bring your expenditures within the funds that are available to carry on that department of government, as distinguished from spreading an additional levy all over the state for the purpose of helping out that situation."

To my mind, with respect to many of these departments that I am speaking of — I know in many places this is not going to be popular, gentlemen—it is a question of common sense; if you have a small county organized years ago, when matters of transportation were entirely different from what they are now, when communication was entirely different from what it is now, instead of maintaining two departments of county government, we must have in many cases one department of county government; and perhaps in some cases where we have five departments of government, have two or three, as the case may be.

In other words, we must apply to the administration of our various departments of government that same common sense that a splendid business man applies, if he is carrying on a particular business of his own and he sees that he cannot make good. If there is some way to consolidate or coordinate that business, he will do it, rather than have an additional burden or rather than go out and simply add a subsidy, for the purpose of carrying on, which in the end would only result in a situation that would be disastrous.

There is another fault in connection with this taxation matter, to my mind. I thought when the matter was up this morning, when the last speaker was presented this morning, that the question in that paper was practically a new means or way of raising money in an indirect way, if you please, rather than by direct taxation. That probably was not the way it was stated, but that was the thought.

I am not going to discuss the question from the point of view of new means of revenue for the purpose of giving a department of government more money to expend, but here is our situation:

In many businesses we are finding the burden is already as heavy as the people can carry, and I am referring not alone to industry but to agricultural activities, one just as well as the other, with burdens which are absolutely destroying them in many cases, making the cost of business in our agricultural field so great we can hardly meet the situation. The question naturally arises, what can be done to relieve that situation.

Now, we must have good schools, we must have good government in all of our activities. The question naturally arises, how can we continue to give that same good government and not increase taxation in the operation of our various departments of government? Of course, you must study how to do this. We must give more, if you please, for the money that we have for expenditure, we must get more results for the moneys we have; we must apply better business methods in connection with the operation of our activities. If we have a lot of farms, in connection with our educational institutions, we must have business methods in connection with them. If the production upon those farms is greater, so as to relieve the general burden of taxation, providing more moneys or more products, if you please, it operates indirectly to the relief of the general taxpayer in that connection.

To my mind there is another thought we must keep in mind, and that is this, it has been my observation that commercial organizations and other organizations conceive the idea that they want some particular improvement. They start in boosting that activity; they never ask what it is going to cost; that is secondary, as far as they are concerned. The whole thought is for setting in motion that activity.

Men, we ought to begin to study all of these questions and to analyze them. You know that the benefits to be received from an improvement ought to be the element in determining the spirit of the moving organization for the acquisition of that improvement. We ought to weigh one with the other, if we are going to solve this problem.

It seems to me, men, the problem comes down to one of common sense, of good business. We are getting too much complex government. There is no question about that. It has been the tendency, not alone of our National Government, but of our state governments as well, to further branch out into too many complex activities; too much supervision; too much inspection; too much regard for what somebody else is doing. Those things all cost money, and we must begin to come to a realization of the fact that there are certain things we desire, certain things we must have, and certain things we can pay for. We must make progress, we must make growth and development, and we cannot have a retarding influence, but we must keep going on. Now, to do that we must put into our departments of government that same business activity that a good business man must do. We must, if you please, begin to treat the thing, as I said in the beginning, in the cause and not the symptom.

In speaking of this address this morning, I do not know how far the speaker intended to go in saying, in connection with our universities and colleges and our schools, that the individual pupil should contribute to his maintenance there. I think there should be some contribution, perhaps more than is now being made; but I do believe, however, that society owes an obligation to the young men and young women of the state and of the nation, to give them an opportunity for an education. While they should pay a substantial sum for that service, we must not be unmindful of the importance of education, but give every boy and girl an opportunity for higher education, if they desire, letting them, as I said, contribute a fair share, too.

Of course, naturally the taxpayer is going to be called upon, and should be called upon to my mind, to make up a contribution. Every man owes that to society in order that it may be carried on.

Ladies and gentlemen, I am pleased to have been with you, pleased to have had this opportunity to enjoy your discussions, and I hope the same high-minded purpose and the same able discussion will continue throughout this meeting. I thank you.

CHAIRMAN MATTHEWS: Any of the members desire to discuss the report of the committee?

WILLIAM G. LITTLETON (Pennsylvania): I have been interested very much in the report of this committee. It has seemed to me, however, that it is dealing with this public land question, about which I know nothing whatever, somewhat in the same way in which the tax experts some years since attempted to deal with state and municipal bonds.

We had propaganda throughout this country which if it had been successful, would have deprived the states of the union of the power over the pocketbook. If the bonds that were issued by the states and by the municipal divisions of the states had been subjected to federal taxation, we should have had the states reduced to the position that the counties found themselves in in England, and the old satrapies or the provinces of the Persian and the Roman Empires, had with regard to central authority.

Now, it seems to me, without knowing very much about the land question, that the principle is somewhat the same. You propose to introduce into the state, by perpetuating the federal control over the lands and by enabling the Federal Government to issue regulations. to erect within the limits of the sovereign state another sovereign jurisdiction, and a sovereign jurisdiction which Chief Justice Marshall pointed out in McCullough vs. State of Maryland, is a superior and stronger sovereign jurisdiction.

Now, are we not, in doing something of that kind, violating the fundamental principle which you will find laid down in Brice's *American Commonwealth*, that the Federal Government should be supreme in national and federal affairs, but in local affairs it is the state and the local government.

Now, you may say these are federal lands. but, gentlemen, if you permit federal jurisdiction to come in, you are introducing into the state a superior sovereignty; and I can well sympathize with the executives of those eleven states when they say they are deprived of their sovereignty; and, furthermore, it has always been the feeling of the Anglo-Saxon race that local affairs must be protected from the centralizing power.

It was so in England in the old days, when the different portions of the Kingdom contested vigorously as against the royal prerogative in the preservation of their own privileges and their own rights, and so here, if the ownership of the federal lands is to be followed by federal regulation, these states where these properties are will have but a shadow of sovereignty.

Now, in regard to the Colorado, I don't know the exact facts that the gentleman has in mind in regard to the Colorado River case, but I do know this one thing, that in the controversy in the Supreme Court between the states of Colorado and Kansas, President Roosevelt ordered his Attorney General to file a brief in the Supreme Court claiming that the Federal Government, by the right of inherent sovereignty, had a right to interfere in this controversy, and the Supreme Court said that the Federal Government had no inherent sovereignty, it was a body to whom powers were delegated by the states. Within those powers it was absolute. Without those powers it had no existence. And so, gentlemen, let us not sacrifice constitutional government for the sake of efficiency; and while these errors have been made in the local jurisdiction, if liberty is to be preserved, the cure must come from within and not from without. In other words, the voters, the citizens, of these jurisdictions must correct their own errors, and they must not be corrected from Washington.

CHAIRMAN MATTHEWS: Is there any further discussion? If not, we will proceed with the next paper, " Taxation of Commercial Motor Vehicle Transportation," by Professor Frank R. Hunt, Lafayette College, Pennsylvania.

FRANK R. HUNT (Pennsylvania) : Mr. Chairman and Ladies and Gentlemen of the Tax Association: I wish at this time to thank the various members of the state tax commissions and the tax officials of the various states for their hearty cooperation with me in furnishing me material with which to prepare this paper. Your cooperation was very splendid, and I assure you it is very greatly appreciated.

Now, this evening before I take up the subject of taxing commercial motor vehicles, I want to review very briefly a few of the principles of taxation of motor vehicles in general. I think that will be helpful to us in arriving at a conclusion and making clear some of the suggestions of this paper.

THE TAXATION OF COMMERCIAL MOTOR VEHICLE TRANSPORTATION

FRANK R. HUNT

Lafayette College, Pennsylvania

The number of motor vehicles used to transport passengers and property for hire has increased rapidly within the past few years. The establishment of bus and truck lines has been due to a desire for a more convenient means of transportation. The ability of the motor vehicle to stop at any point for passengers and the frequency of operation between centers of population has made the motor-bus the favorite means of travel for short distances and has all but displaced local passenger service on many railroad lines. The quicker service and the elimination of unnecessary handling of freight at terminal points has been responsible for the establishment of many trunk lines between cities. This commercial use of the highways is possible because of the movement for improved roads which started several years earlier, chiefly in response to the demands of pleasure vehicle owners.

A better idea of the important place commercial motor transportation has already reached may be had by recalling that during 1927 over 270,000 miles of bus lines are being operated in the United States. This vast mileage of bus lines, greater than that of the railroads of the country, is not confined to any particular section.

Many of the leading railroads are using motor trucks in various capacities. Their use in terminals and for store-door delivery has been common for some time, but at least eleven railroads of importance are using trucks to replace portions of their local freight service.

Along with these changes in the methods of transportation—this tendency to shift from rails to roads—have come many problems of public interest, not the least of which is the taxation of the vehicles engaged in the movement of passengers and freight for hire.

Before we consider the actual taxation imposed on vehicles engaged in regular commercial pursuits, attention will be given to the principles underlying the taxation of motor vehicles in general. This will help explain some of the tax laws in existence and will be useful in arriving at a conclusion as regards the best methods of assessing taxes against motor vehicles.

The demands for improved roads has led to enormous expenditures by the states and local communities. It seems to be the intent of the people, as expressed by legislative acts, that a considerable portion of the costs of construction and maintenance shall come from those who use the roads and thereby receive direct benefits. As a result, the owners of motor vehicles are subject to certain fees and taxes for the purpose of providing revenue for the construction and maintenance of improved roads. Of course the proper registration of a motor vehicle and the purchase of license plates serve other important purposes, but the occasion of registration is being used today chiefly to secure revenue.

In determining the amount of such fees and taxes one motor vehicle owner should pay, in comparison with another owner of a different kind of vehicle, nearly every state has tried by some means to fix a schedule of license fees which will be in proportion to the amount of damage the vehicle will likely do to the roads. If the license fees and other taxes are to be fixed according to the use and damage a vehicle does, how shall the probable use and damage be measured? There are many factors entering into the measurement of road use and damage, but at least four factors are outstanding. They are:

1. The number of *miles* the vehicle will be operated.
2. The *speed* at which it will be operated.
3. The *gross* weight of the vehicle.
4. The *type of tire equipment.*

No license fee payable in advance at the beginning of the year can cover all these factors, especially the first two—distance and the speed of operation. To overcome this difficulty the gasoline tax has been adopted by 46 states to measure certain elements of road use and to tax accordingly. The amount of fuel consumed will be a pretty accurate measure of the miles traveled; not a perfect one, of course. The driver, the condition of the car, the roads, the load, and many other factors will affect the distance a motor vehicle will travel on a given amount of fuel. In spite of these conditions the number of gallons of fuel bought will be a pretty reliable indication of the distance traveled. Not only is the gasoline tax a good one to measure the use made of the roads, but it is the only one. A license fee payable in advance cannot be used.

A tax on gasoline will also measure the damage done by operating a vehicle at excessive speed. A vehicle driven at high speed injures the road surface more than one which travels more slowly. This is partly true because, at the higher speeds the weight comes into contact with the road surface with greater suddenness. It also is true that the impact of a wheel is much greater when traveling at a high rate of speed. By impact is meant the force with which a moving body strikes another body. If a wheel-load of one ton comes into contact with the surface of a road very gently the impact will be one ton, but if it drops from an obstruction at high speed the impact will be much greater. How much greater, will depend on the height of the fall, the kind of tire, characteristics of the vehicle and the speed. Tests made some years ago by the United

States Bureau of Public Roads indicate that, other factors of the vehicle being constant, the impact may increase with the speed as follows:

> For solid tires from 10–100%.
> For cushion tires from 10–75%.
> For pneumatic tires from 0–10%.

This is merely the range within which impact may increase with increasing speed and is not intended as an average of what will happen under all conditions. It is sufficient to say that it proved that increasing the speed of a vehicle beyond a certain point increases the possibility of damage to the roads, by causing heavy impact.

While high speeds will cause damage to the roads, it also happens that more fuel is consumed at the higher speeds. A popular notion exists that less fuel is consumed the faster a vehicle is driven. This is true up to a point of maximum efficiency. Any speed higher than this will consume more fuel, thereby incurring more tax to pay for the damage caused by high speed.[1]

The third factor in road damage—gross weight—is also partially covered by the tax on gasoline. The heavier vehicles will as a rule do more damage to the roads than lighter ones. At the same time they will consume more fuel than the lighter vehicles. The damage done by a heavy vehicle is likely to be out of proportion to its weight, because the heavier vehicle may strain the road surface to the elastic limit. At certain seasons of the year a heavy vehicle may approach or exceed the limit of the road and thus cause damage entirely out of proportion to weight.

Gasoline consumption is greater for the heavier vehicles than for the lighter ones, but does not increase in proportion to weight. For example, a vehicle weighing one ton will travel a given distance per gallon of fuel. Another vehicle weighing seven tons will of course consume more gasoline in traveling the same distance as the first vehicle, but it will not be seven times as much. Even if the second vehicle did consume seven times the amount of fuel as the first, the fuel consumption would not likely be in proportion to the damage done by the heavier vehicle. Comprehensive tests made by engineers show that a seven-ton vehicle will consume less than four times as much fuel as one weighing one ton. It follows from this that the tax on gasoline will not be sufficient to compensate for the damage which may be done by weight of the vehicle. Since a car must be registered for police purposes, a license fee based upon the gross weight of the vehicle can be collected at the same time.

[1] For further engineering data on this subject see *Taxation of Motor Vehicles and Its Relation to Highway Finance* by the author of this paper, published by the Ohio Good Roads Federation, Columbus, Ohio.

This license fee according to weight will then serve to supplement the gasoline tax and the combination of the two will be in proportion to every element of road use and damage except the type of tires.

The fourth factor in road damage—type of tire equipment—is a fact which is easily ascertained at the time of registration. Allowance can be made for the different destructive effects of tires, by having two schedules of license fees; one to apply to the pneumatic and the other to solid tires. The difference between the two schedules of fees for pneumatic and solid tires should be fixed in proportion to the damage each kind of tire will cause. The United States Bureau of Public Roads published in June, 1926 some data relative to the effect of tires and other truck factors on impact. From these data it appears that all other factors being equal, solid tires will on the average cause an impact about twice that of pneumatic tires. Further investigation into the destructive effects of impact is now in progress and when completed will give a basis for the relative destructive effects of different kinds of tire equipment. Up to January 1, 1927 only 18 states had made any distinction in license fees, on account of the type of tire. Of the 28 states which have special license or franchise fees for motor trucks operating as common carriers, only 12 have made any differentiation in fees on the basis of tires.

Thus in brief we have presented what in the light of scientific investigations appears to be the logical method of taxing motor vehicles in general.

First, a gasoline tax which will be paid according to the use made of the highways and which will vary in such a manner as to cover the damage due to operation at excessive speed. Second, a license fee based on gross weight of the vehicle and the type of tires. The fee according to the gross weight will serve to supplement the gasoline tax, since motor vehicles do not consume fuel in proportion to their weight and the damage which they may cause to the highways. The difference in the amount of the fee according to whether the vehicle uses solid or pneumatic tires should be in proportion to the destructive effects of each type.

Of all the taxes on motor vehicles the tax on gasoline covers more items of road damage than any other single tax. It measures the distance traveled or the amount of the use. It varies in a manner which will cover the effects of excessive speed and it covers part of the damage due to the weight of the vehicles. When supplemented by a graduated license fee on weight and tire equipment each element of road use and damage is measured and paid for by some part of the combined taxes.

There are some other factors, in addition to the four major factors, which may well be given some consideration in fixing a schedule of license fees for common-carrier motor vehicles. In tests made by the Bureau of Public Roads it was found that a heavy vehicle on four wheels produced twice the stress on the surface of the road of a similar vehicle, which had six wheels. In each case the total load was the same, only in the latter case the load rested on two rear axles instead of one. Later tests made by the same bureau show that the four-wheel truck gave twice as great an impact as the six-wheel, when tested over the same obstructions and with the same total load.

This indicates that a heavy vehicle having four drive wheels should not be charged as high a fee as a vehicle of equal weight having but two drive wheels.

Another factor is the ratio of sprung to unsprung weight. The sprung weight is that part of the total load which is supported by the springs of the vehicle, while the unsprung weight includes the axles, tires, wheels, and springs. It has been found that vehicles having heavy unsprung weight will give higher impact than those with lighter unsprung weight. As this is not a controlling factor in impact no recommendation is made at this time in regard to recognizing this feature in fixing license fees.

Having very briefly reviewed the fundamentals of motor vehicle taxation in general, the remainder of the discussion will be confined to the actual taxation of these motor vehicles which operate as common carriers of passengers or freight for compensation between fixed termini or over a regular route. A common-carrier motor vehicle is one employed by the owner for the transportation for hire of all persons or all property indiscriminately, under general conditions of agreement applicable to the whole public. Practically all motor buses are common carriers. However, a motor truck may operate regularly between fixed termini or over a regular route, hauling goods on contract for one or more parties, and thus it is not a common carrier in the legal sense of the term. Since both classes of operation are essentially alike, both being regularly conducted business enterprises for profit, the operators who haul on contract should be included with common carriers. Such is now the practice in a number of states where common-carrier vehicles are subject to higher license fees than private vehicles of similar size and equipment. This is a desirable way of preventing evasion by those who plan to use the highways regularly, as a part of their business equipment. Therefore, we shall refer to common-carrier motor vehicles and include in addition those vehicles operated regularly on contract for one or more parties.

A study of the tax laws applying to common-carrier vehicles indicated that the lawmakers of the various states had in mind one of two principles. The first is that each vehicle should pay fees sufficient to cover all damage done to the road. Acting on this prin-

ciple, common-carrier vehicles are charged a franchise fee, in addition to regular fees, because it was believed that such vehicles made
more use of the roads than a similar vehicle privately operated.
The franchise fee is usually based on some feature which will indicate the amount of use made of the highways, such as capacity,
capacity-miles, gross receipts, or miles traveled. The state, in acting upon this principle, assumes a role not unlike that of a keeper •
of a toll road who maintains a road and charges each user an amount
which will approximate the damages attributable to him.

The second principle looks upon commercial transportation as a
business enterprise, entered into and carried on for profit. The
state in furnishing the highway has supplied a vital part of the
business equipment and has become a silent partner in the undertaking. The state is entitled to reimbursement for all costs of highways incurred in behalf of the common-carrier vehicles and in
addition, a share in the profits of the business. A state in following this latter principle may impose the same kind of taxes as those
already mentioned in connection with the first principle, but at such
rates as to more than cover the damages done by the common-
carrier vehicles and thus secure a share in the profits of the business. Doubtless these principles have not been phrased in terms
used here but they are the logical conclusion to be drawn from the
tax legislation in existence.

In order that actual taxes paid by common-carrier vehicles in
different states may be discussed more clearly, two motor vehicles—
a bus and a truck—have been chosen as representative of their class.
Actual specifications of the manufacturers were followed as closely
as possible and actual cases of operation were chosen, in order to be
near real conditions. For the motor-bus the following conditions
were assumed to prevail: Horsepower, 25; unladen weight, 7,200;
seating capacity, 15; tires, pneumatic; value, $5,500; operated 36,000
miles; annual gross receipts, $10,000; annual gasoline consumption,
4,000 gallons. Certain of these assumptions or combinations of
them were necessary, in order to determine how much tax each
state would levy on the same vehicle.

The result of the computation of the license fee for this vehicle
·in each state showed a wide variation as between states. There are
44 states which make a definite provision for the separate registration and taxation of such vehicles. The other four states [2] tax
them as private passenger cars. In the 44 states the license fee
varied from $40 as the lowest, to $675 per year as the highest, while
the average fee for this motor-bus was approximately $204. If we
consider the other four states, in which no provision is made for
special taxation, the lowest tax for this vehicle would be $15 per

[2] Delaware, Missouri, New Hampshire, and Montana.

year, a range of license fees from $15 to $675 per year, for the same car operated under the same conditions.

It might be expected that the gasoline tax will tend to overcome the wide variation in license fees. This is not always so. A state which has a low license fee may or may not have a high tax on gasoline. Two states [2] have no gasoline tax. When the gasoline taxes in the various states are added to the license fee, the total of the two ranges from $43 as the lowest to $815 as the highest cost per year, for the privilege of operating a motor-bus for hire. The average of license fees and gasoline taxes on this vehicle is $322 per year.

Nor is this the whole burden which the owner of the above vehicle is called upon to pay. Thirty-four states tax automobiles as personal property. Because of the variation in rates from state to state, the general property tax has not been computed per bus. Another reason for not including it is that the money raised in this manner does not find its way into the highway funds except in an indirect way, through an appropriation by the legislature for highway purposes, or a special road levy on all property. It is a part of the general property tax and therefore not connected with this paper. If other forms of personal property are taxed, then this form should not be an exception. It must be remembered, however, that a motor vehicle is not easily concealed and is more likely to be assessed at a higher per cent of its true value than other forms of personal property, and therefore motor vehicles as a class may bear more than their share of the general property tax.

Municipalities and local subdivisions of Government have in some states been given power to tax motor vehicles locally. It was not possible to determine how much additional tax must be paid because of this decentralization of the taxing power but in some states it might amount to a rather large percent of the total.

In case a bus line is doing an interstate business it may be called upon to pay full license fees in each of the states in which it operates. A bus operating in two states, each of which determines its license fees on the basis of seating capacity, would be liable for the full license fee in each state.

Thus, in addition to the average license fee and gasoline tax of $322.14 per bus, the owners may pay a property tax, a local tax, and extra license fee, if operating in interstate commerce. There is also a possibility of having to pay an income tax.

In assessing the license fees on buses, more than one feature of the vehicle is usually made the base of a tax. Many states require the regular license fee of a private passenger car and in addition another fee, usually based on some feature of the vehicle which will

[2] Massachusetts, and New York.

LICENSE FEES AND GASOLINE TAXES ON A PASSENGER BUS OF 15 SEATING
CAPACITY IN 44 STATES WHERE BUSES ARE LICENSED SEPARATELY
FROM PRIVATE PASSENGER CARS

State	License Fee	Gasoline Tax	Total	Basis of License Fee
Alabama	$60.00	$160.00	$220.00	Seating capacity
Arizona	270.00	120.00	390.00	Capacity—miles
Arkansas	255.38	200.00	455.38	Gross receipts
California	425.00	80.00	505.00	Gross receipts
Colorado	270.00	120.00	390.00	Passenger—miles
Connecticut	361.00	80.00	441.00	Gross receipts, capacity
Florida	292.50	160.00	452.50	Seating capacity
Georgia	75.00	140.00	215.00	Flat rate
Idaho	204.00	200.00	404.00	Seating capacity
Illinois	113.50	....	113.50	Gross weight
Indiana	90.00	120.00	210.00	Seating capacity
Iowa	518.25	80.00	598.25	Ton—miles
Kansas	184.00	80.00	264.00	Seating capacity
Kentucky	219.25	200.00	419.25	Seating capacity
Louisiana	68.00	80.00	148.00	Seating capacity
Maine	48.50	120.00	168.50	Horsepower, weight
Maryland	300.00	120.00	420.00	Capacity—miles
Massachusetts	75.00	....	75.00	Seating capacity
Michigan	111.60	80.00	191.60	Unladen weight
Minnesota	550.00	80.00	630.00	Value
Mississippi	100.50	160.00	260.50	Seating capacity
Nebraska	130.00	80.00	210.00	Seating capacity
Nevada	100.00	160.00	260.00	Seating capacity
New Jersey	540.00	80.00	620.00	Miles traveled
New Mexico	70.00	120.00	190.00	Seating capacity
New York	43.00	....	43.00	Seating capacity
N. Carolina	75.00	160.00	235.00	Seating capacity
N. Dakota	241.90	120.00	361.90	Seating capacity
Ohio	140.00	120.00	260.00	Seating capacity
Oklahoma	159.50	120.00	279.50	Miles traveled
Oregon	502.00	120.00	622.00	Capacity—miles
Pennsylvania	60.00	120.00	180.00	Seating capacity
Rhode Island	60.00	40.00	100.00	H. P. plus gross weight
S. Carolina	108 00	200.00	308.00	Capacity—miles
S. Dakota	310.00	160.00	470.00	Gross receipts
Tennessee	43.50	160.00	202.50	Seating capacity
Texas	130.63	160.00	290.63	Seating capacity
Utah	675.00	140.00	815.00	Passenger—miles
Vermont	95.00	120.00	215.00	Gross weight
Virginia	135.00	180.00	315.00	Capacity—miles
Washington	194.20	80.00	274.20	Seating capacity
W. Virginia	360.00	140.00	500.00	Capacity—miles
Wisconsin	211.00	80.00	291.00	Ton—miles
Wyoming	40.00	120.00	160.00	Seating capacity
Average	$203.96	$124.63*	$322.14	

* Average of 41 states.

indicate the use of the roads or the amount of damage it is likely to do. The regular license fee of a private passenger car in the various states is based on horsepower, weight, value, a flat rate, or some combination of these. The license fee which buses must pay, in addition to the regular fees, or in those states where buses do not pay the regular fee, is levied as follows:

> 22 states fix the payment according to seating capacity.
> 8 states determine it according to capacity-miles.
> 4 states levy it on gross receipts.
> 2 states according to gross weight.
> 2 states according to ton-miles.
> 2 states according to miles traveled.
> 1 state on each of the following bases: flat rate, unladen weight, horsepower and unladen weight, and horsepower and gross weight.

The first of these—seating capacity—when reduced to final terms, is nothing more or less than a licene fee based on the load which the vehicle will carry. The greater the seating capacity, the greater the weight of the vehicle and the more likelihood of it doing damage to the roads. Thus, seating capacity is taken as a rough measure of weight and the principle of taxing heavier vehicles more than lighter ones prevails. Moreover, a careful examination of the statutes shows that in some states the greater the seating capacity, the higher the rate per seat. This is true in only a few states but it is a sound principle of taxation according to weight, as has already been mentioned, and should find a more general application if license fees are to be based on seating capacity.

The second basis for taxing motor-buses—capacity-miles—measures both weight and distance. In this respect it operates like a license fee on weight and a tax on gasoline. In states where the gasoline tax is in force, to tax on the mileage basis is to tax the distance traveled twice.

The third basis for motor-bus license is gross receipts. The receipts are an indication of the amount of business, and as the place of business is the public highway, gross receipts indicate highway use. It is therefore somewhat similar to a tax on mileage. Where the gasoline tax is low, such a tax may serve as an additional charge for the use of highways.

The limitations of this paper forbid a separate discussion of the other miscellaneous methods of taxing motor buses.

The remainder of the paper will be concerned with the taxation of motor trucks operating as common carriers. While 44 states impose special taxation and registration on motor buses, only 28 states do the same for trucks operated regularly for hire. This is largely due to the more recent development of the freight truck lines.

As was done in the case of the motor bus, a specific example of a freight carrier was taken as follows: capacity, 2½ tons; unladen weight, 6500 pounds; tires, solid; total width, 26 inches; horsepower, 29; annual mileage, 18,000; annual gross receipts, $9,000; annual gasoline consumption, 3000 gallons; value, $4,000. From these facts the license fee and gasoline tax were computed for each state. For the 28 states which provide for special taxation and registration, the fee was computed on the truck as a privately-owned vehicle operated as above; then as a common-carrier truck. The difference between the two fees is the franchise fee, a payment for the privilege of carrying on a business and making use of the highways.

It was found that if a truck of this size is operated privately, the average license fee would be approximately $59 per year. If operated as a common carrier, the average license fee would be $203. The difference, or $144, represented the franchise fee. It will be noted that the same vehicle, when operated as a common carrier pays about 3½ times as much license fees as when operated privately. While the average of license fees and franchise fees is $203.15, the range is from $75 as the lowest, to $607.50 as the highest. When the gasoline tax is added to the commercial license fee, the range is from $137.50 to $667.50, with an average fee of $295.

Having before us the total amount of gasoline taxes and license fees paid by common-carrier vehicles, it may be well to briefly compare the burden of taxation now resting on commercial motor transportation with that borne by the railroad industry.

Under the conditions of our example, the gasoline tax and the license fees of a common-carrier truck amount on the average to 3.3% of the gross receipts. In some cases they amount to as much as 7½% of the gross receipts. In the case of the motor bus the same taxes will, on the average, amount to 3¼% of the gross receipts and to take the extremes this will vary from .4 of 1% to as high as over 8% of the gross earnings. The railroad industry during the five-year period from 1921-1926 paid taxes equal to slightly more than 5½% of the gross receipts. During 1926 the railroads paid over 6% of gross earnings in taxes. While the percent of gross receipts paid by the motor transportation industry appears smaller than that paid by the railroads, it must be remembered that only gasoline and license taxes are being compared with the total taxes paid by the railroads. When personal property taxes, local taxes and possibly income taxes are computed and added to the gasoline and license fees, the competitive conditions between the railroads and the motor transportation industry are not so unequal, as far as taxation is concerned, as is usually supposed to be the case.

There is great diversity of methods in assessing license fees on common-carrier and private trucks. The majority of the states attempt to use some feature of the truck which will indicate weight.

17

Of the 28 states which we are considering in this paper, the fees for private operation are based on:

LICENSE FEES AND GASOLINE TAXES ON A 2½-TON TRUCK IN 28 STATES
WHERE PRIVATE AND COMMON-CARRIER MOTOR TRUCKS
PAY A DIFFERENT LICENSE FEE

State	License Fees		Franchise Fee	Gasoline Tax	Total License Fees as a Common Carrier and Gasoline Tax
	Private Carrier	Common Carrier			
Arizona	$15.00	$90.00	$75.00	$90.00	$180.00
Arkansas	135.00	315.00	180.00	150.00	465.00
California	33.00	450.00	417.00	60.00	510.00
Colorado	25.00	225.00	200.00	90.00	315.00
Idaho	65.00	277.00	212.00	150.00	427.00
Illinois	22.50	137.50	115.00	....	137.50
Iowa	90.00	607.50	517.50	60.00	667.50
Kansas	37.50	117.50	80.00	60.00	177.50
Maryland	225.00	217.50	192.50	90.00	307.50
Michigan	81.25	146.25	65.00	60.00	206.25
Minnesota	96.00	400.00	304.00	20.00	460.00
Mississippi	75.00	112.50	37.50	120.00	232.50
Nevada	34.50	75.00	40.50	120.00	195.00
New Jersey..........	45.00	315.00	270.00	60.00	375.00
New Mexico	31.25	75.00	43.75	90.00	165.00
North Carolina	100.00	150.00	50.00	120.00	270.00
North Dakota........	55.90	98.40	42.50	90.00	188.40
Ohio	65.00	80.00	15.00	90.00	170.00
Oklahoma	80.00	116.00	36.00	90.00	206.00
Oregon	65.00	110.00	45.00	90.00	200.00
South Carolina	120.00	225.00	105.00	150.00	375.00
South Dakota........	35.00	360.00	325.00	120.00	480.00
Utah	65.00	300.00	235.00	105.00	405.00
Virginia	40.00	180.00	140.00	135.00	315.00
Washington	63.50	153.50	90.00	60.00	213.50
West Virginia........	75.00	112.50	37.50	105.00	217.50
Wisconsin	20.00	157.00	137.00	60.00	217.00
Wyoming	60.00	85.00	25.00	90.00	175.00
Average	59.12	203.15	144.03	95.00*	294.75

* Average of 27 states.

LICENSE FEES AND GASOLINE TAXES ON A PASSENGER BUS OF 15 SEATING
CAPACITY IN 4 STATES WHERE BUSES ARE NOT LICENSED
SEPARATELY FROM PRIVATE PASSENGER CARS

State	License Fee	Gasoline Tax	Total
Delaware	$36.40	$120.00	$156.40
Missouri	16.50	80.00	96.50
Montana	15.00	120.00	135.00
New Hampshire	54.00	80.00	134.00
Average	$30.48	$100.00	$130.48

LICENSE FEES AND GASOLINE TAXES ON A 2½-TON TRUCK IN 20 STATES
WHERE PRIVATE AND COMMON-CARRIER MOTOR TRUCKS
PAY THE SAME LICENSE FEE

State	License Fee	Gasoline Tax	Total
Alabama	$75.00	$120.00	$195.00
Connecticut	60.00	60.00	120.00
Delaware	46.00	90.00	135.00
Florida	230.00	120.00	350.00
Georgia	37.50	105.00	142.50
Indiana	35.00	90.00	125.00
Kentucky	85.00	150.00	235.00
Louisiana	34.72	60.00	94.72
Maine	73.33	90.00	163.33
Massachusetts	57.50	....	57.50
Missouri	18.00	60.00	78.00
Montana	37.50	90.00	127.50
Nebraska	52.50	60.00	112.50
New Hampshire	92.00	60.00	152.00
New York	48.00	....	48.00
Pennsylvania	70.00	90.00	160.00
Rhode Island	64.75	30.00	94.75
Tennessee	34.50	120.00	154.50
Texas	97.08	120.00	217.08
Vermont	86.25	90.00	176.25
Average	$66.73	$89.17*	$146.98

* Average of 18 states.

Tons capacity in .... 16 states
Gross weight in .... 4 states
Unladen weight in .... 3 states
Flat rate .... 1 state
Flat rate plus capacity .... 1 state
Value, horsepower, weight and capacity .... 1 state
Value .... 1 state
Total width of tires .... 1 state

In the 28 states which have a franchise tax for common-carrier trucks the bases of the franchise are as follows:

    11 states base the franchise fee on capacity
    10 states base the franchise fee on ton-mileage
     2 states base the franchise fee on gross receipts
     2 states base the franchise fee on miles traveled
     1 state on gross weight, unladen weight, and value.

It will be noted that the bases of the franchise fees on trucks operated as common carriers are, for the most part, intended to measure the use which the vehicle will make of the highways. The first four—capacity, ton-mileage, gross receipts, and miles traveled—are all indications of the amount of use made of the roads, the first three indicating weight as well as mileage.

The same comment may be made here as was made in the case of motor buses. If these vehicles, when operated privately, are paying a license fee and a gasoline tax, then another tax on weight and mileage is taxing the same element of road use and damage twice—a duplication of taxes.

It is certainly the aim of all states today to charge each road user an amount which will compensate, in proportion to the damage which he causes. A license fee on the proper features of the vehicle and a gasoline tax will do this, regardless of the purpose for which the vehicle is operated. Of course the gasoline tax must be high enough to accomplish the purpose intended.

If it is the intention to tax each road user an amount sufficient to cover all damages done by reason of use of the highways, then a gasoline tax and a graduated license fee based on the gross weight of the vehicle and the type of tire equipment will accomplish the results desired. Furthermore, it will not matter whether the vehicle in question is operated privately or as a common carrier. If the common carrier uses the roads to a greater extent, as it probably will, it will pay more in the form of a gasoline tax. However, if the intent of the people is to tax the profits of the motor transportation industry, in addition to taxes which will cover damages, this can be done in other ways than by imposing a fixed license fee which will not vary with the volume of business done. It is offered as a suggestion that all common carriers of property and persons pay the regular license fee on weight and type of tire, the regular gasoline tax, and a percent of the gross receipts. The only difference then between the taxation of common-carrier vehicles and others of the same kind operated privately is that the former will pay, in addition to regular taxes, a percent of gross receipts. This latter tax will enable the state to share in the profits of the industry, in proportion to the amount of business done.

What are some of the advantages of this combination of taxes in preference to some of the systems in use at the present time? In the first place, the tax on gasoline and a graduated tax on the gross weight and tire equipment will conform to scientific measurements of road damage. Some of the present attempts at taxing motor vehicles are almost without relation to either the amount or kind of usage. For example, value, flat rates, and horsepower are of little or no value in indicating the amount of damage done by the type of vehicle operating.

In the second place, motor-vehicle licenses would be much simpler and would be more convenient to the payer. Some of the systems in use for taxing common carriers are complicated almost beyond belief. For example, one state taxes a common-carrier vehicle on bases of weight, value, horsepower and seating capacity, in addition to the gasoline tax and stated fees to be paid the public service commission. The proposed system, on the other hand, calls for a license fee according to weight and the type of tire applicable to all vehicles of a given class. Both of these facts are easily ascertained and are of great significance in determining road damage. The gasoline tax is paid currently, as the vehicle is operated. Doubtless it is the most convenient and least burdensome of all. The tax on the gross receipts may be called a franchise tax for the privilege of conducting a regular business enterprise on the public highways. It will vary with the amount of operation and will measure the use made of the roads in those states where the gasoline tax is low or non-existent. The amount to be paid will vary with the volume of business and the payments can be made at the end of such fiscal periods as will be most convenient and economical for both the state and the operator.

CHAIRMAN MATTHEW: Is there any discussion on the subject of this paper?

WILLIAM J. SHULTZ (New York): Mr. Hunt's paper has drawn into my mind some ideas that have been there for some time. I had occasion recently to go over the motor vehicle license changes and review them, and to attempt to reduce them to any common denominator is like answering the question with straight lines to show the distance between two points. There is no possibility of bringing them together. And, it seems to me, that in an attempt to arrive at abstract justice the legislatures have overshot themselves. In some cases, particularly when they made the basis of a charge that of mileage covered or that of gross receipts, they brought into the tax a large possibility of evasion. They made it a nuisance tax, one that is obnoxious to the common carriers, to which those charges apply and which they do not see themselves in conscience bound to follow.

A qualification that I think should be made to Mr. Hunt's paper is that the motor vehicle revenue is not intended solely to maintain the roads or repair damages, but is being used today to construct roads, and the rather finely spun qualifications to make damage the basis of the charge loses its ideal of justice when you are making automobiles not only pay the damage to the roads but pay also for the construction of new roads.

I have felt that a practical approach to this problem would be to throw overboard an attempt to refine upon refinement and broadly use the gasoline tax as a basis of motor vehicle taxation. Then, in the case of common carriers there is an item of privilege entering in, which could and should be reached.

Now, one automobile that is left out entirely by this system, and which Mr. Hunt did not cover, was the electric vehicle. You have to make some special charge upon some independent basis to reach that. It is, perhaps, a step back to go from the refined down to a simple broad basis that way. I think it would eliminate a good deal of the feeling of dissatisfaction that I know from conversation is prevalent, particularly among the larger companies that use automobiles in their business. They feel that the automobile charges are getting to be such complicated matters that it requires as technical an accounting staff as the income tax, and do not see why it should be so. A simpler system would in a general way cover the elemental demands of justice that I think enter into the motor vehicle taxation idea, eliminating those elements which cause dissatisfaction.

CHAIRMAN MATTHEWS: If there is no further discussion I have one announcement to make. It is reported from the registration desk that only 130 railroad certificates have been turned over. They say that unless 120 additional certificates are delivered at the desk it will be impossible to secure return tickets at one-half fare. It behooves all holders of certificates to hand them to the registration desk.

If there is no further discussion of the papers the meeting will be adjourned to tomorrow morning.

(Adjournment)

FIFTH SESSION

WEDNESDAY MORNING, OCTOBER 12, 1927

CHAIRMAN MATTHEWS: The convention will come to order. I will at this time announce as the chairman of the resolutions committee Harry P. Sneed of Louisiana. I will also ask Mr. W. H. Blodgett, the State Tax Commissioner of Connecticut, to preside at this session.

(A resolution was presented, read, and passed to the resolutions committee for consideration.)

(W. H. BLODGETT presiding.)

CHAIRMAN BLODGETT: The first item of the program this morning will have reference to the valuation of railroads. This question has disturbed all the railroads of the country for a number of years. I am sure we shall be interested in what may be said in reference to that subject, and, furthermore, we shall be greatly interested in having a paper from Mr. G. G. Tunell, Tax Commissioner of the Atchison, Topeka & Santa Fe Railway. Mr. Tunell.

VALUE FOR TAXATION AND VALUE FOR RATE MAKING

GEORGE G. TUNELL
Tax Commissioner, Atchison, Topeka & Santa Fe Railway

I shall discuss the question as to whether value as defined by law for taxation, and value as defined and ascertained by the Interstate Commerce Commission for rate making are one and the same thing.

If legislatures, tax commissions and courts were informed as to what the Interstate Commerce Commission has been doing, there need be no uncertainty or misunderstanding. The commission is not responsible for the confusion that exists, but as legislatures, assessing bodies and the courts have not taken the trouble to find out what the Interstate Commerce Commission is actually doing under Section 19-A and Section 15-A of the Interstate Commerce Act, there appears to have been reason enough for placing the subject assigned to me on the program.

To prevent misunderstanding I shall at this point state that I am now speaking of value as found by the commission. I am not speaking of the definitions of value that have been urged upon the

(263)

ing them together. And, it seems t ne, that in an attempt to arrive at abstract justice the legislature: iave overshot themselves. In some cases, particularly when the) ade the basis of a charge that of mileage covered or that of gro receipts, they brought into the tax a large possibility of evasion. They made it a nuisance tax, one that is obnoxious to the cc non carriers, to which those charges apply and which they do t see themselves in conscience bound to follow.

A qualification that I think shoi be made to Mr. Hunt's paper is that the motor vehicle revenue not intended solely to maintain the roads or repair damages, but being used today to construct roads, and the rather finely spun (lifications to make damage the basis of the charge loses its ideal justice when you are making automobiles not only pay the dam e to the roads but pay also for the construction of new roads.

I have felt that a practical appi ch to this problem would be to throw overboard an attempt to rc e upon refinement and broadly use the gasoline tax as a basis of)tor vehicle taxation. Then, in the case of common carriers ther s an item of privilege entering in, which could and should be rea ·d.

Now, one automobile that is le)ut entirely by this system, and which Mr. Hunt did not cover, w the electric vehicle. You have to make some special charge upo ome independent basis to reach that. It is, perhaps, a step back go from the refined down to a simple broad basis that way. I tl < it would eliminate a good deal of the feeling of dissatisfaction it I know from conversation is prevalent, particularly among th(irger companies that use automobiles in their business. The) ·el that the automobile charges are getting to be such complicat(matters that it requires as technical an accounting staff as the ome tax, and do not see why it should be so. A simpler system)uld in a general way cover the elemental demands of justice tl I think enter into the motor vehicle taxation idea, eliminatin· hose elements which cause dissatisfaction.

CHAIRMAN MATTHEWS: If th(is no further discussion I have one announcement to make. It reported from the registration . desk that only 130 railroad ce icates have been turned over. They say that unless 120 additio certificates are delivered at th(desk it will be impossible to sec' return tickets at one-half f·' It behooves all holders of certifi es to hand them to the re?' tion desk.

If there is no further discuss of the papers the me/ be adjourned to tomorrow morni

(Adjournment)

FIFTH SESSION

WEDNESDAY MORNING, OCTOBER 12

CHAIRMAN MATTHEWS: The convention will
will at this time announce as the chairman of
mittee Harry P. Sneed of Louisiana. I will
Blodgett, the State Tax Commissioner of Conn
this session.

(A resolution was presented, read, and pass
committee for consideration.)

(W. H. BLODGETT presiding.)

CHAIRMAN BLODGETT: The first item of the
ing will have reference to the valuation of
tion has disturbed all the railroad of the co
years. I am sure we shall be interested in
reference to that subject, and, furthermore,
terested in having a paper from Mr. G. G.
sioner of the Atchison, Topeka & Santa Fe R

VALUE FOR TAXATION AND
RATE MAKING

GEORGE TUNELL
Tax Commissioner, Atchison Topeka & S

I shall discuss the question as whether
for taxation, and value as define and ascer
Commerce Commission for rate king are
If legislatures, tax commission and cour
what the Interstate Commerce mmissic
need be no uncertainty or mist lerstandi
not responsible for the confusi that ex
assessing bodies and the courts h
what the Interstate Commerce
Section 19-A and Section 15
there appears to have been
assigned to me on the progra
To prevent misunderstand
now speaking of value as
speaking of the definitions of

r deals with a
e the property

ie group in my
terms that are
erms set up in
fact no con-
ie courts have
same thing.
lroad Company
s said:

l for the claim,
sments, whether
equalization, are
equires all prop-
i taxation, at its

re than what the
qualified direction
the duty of ascer-

pressed itself upon
k, the court speak-

value,' 'cash value,'
ing officers, all mean
the same purpose."

or the assessment of
The term "value" as
rty sold for, or would
intary sale.
t there is nothing un-
as formulated in tax
iuse the definition of
in the business trans-
wayfaring man

commission for adoption. After I have presented my material on the question of what is the value for taxation and after I have presented the views of the commission, as to what is value for rate making, I shall try to give you some idea of the significance of the subject assigned to me for discussion. I shall try to do this by con-. crete examples, and then if time still remains I shall try to give you an idea of the confusion and contradiction found in the very recent decisions of the courts.

Until very recently, strange to say, the courts in their decisions made no attempt, either to harmonize or to differentiate value for taxation and value for rate making. In order to make sure that my own position shall not be misunderstood, I shall state that I believe the term " value " should always mean power in exchange and that the term should not be used to express utility, or cost, or esteem. I shall have something to say respecting value for taxation.

By the laws of our states the assessing officials are directed to assess property at its value, at its real value, at its actual value, at its cash value, at its fair cash value, at its fair cash market value, at its true value in money, or at its value, with qualifying words of similar import to those just given; and in order that none need go astray, a guide or rule for the valuation of property for assessment was also set up.

For more than fifty years assessors in Illinois have been explicitly directed by the constitution and acts of the legislature regarding the discharge of their duties. The law has stated that " all personal property . . . shall be valued at its fair cash value," and that " real property shall be valued at its fair cash value, estimated at the price it would bring at a fair voluntary sale."

The constitution of the state of Oklahoma declares that " all property which may be taxed ad valorem, shall be assessed for taxation at its fair cash value, estimated at the price it would bring at a fair, voluntary sale."

Mr. Cornelius Roach, first chairman of the Missouri State Tax Commission, in notable language summarized the instructions of the tax commission to the local assessing officials of Missouri in saying:

" There is nothing uncertain about the meaning of ' actual cash value,' ' its value,' ' its true value in money,' " these being the terms used in the laws of the State of Missouri, " or the method of determining it. It is not necessarily what was originally paid for the property, or what it would now cost to reproduce, or what it would sell for in some other locality or at forced or auction sale, or in the aggregate with other properties in the community; it is not necessarily to be determined from the income it produces, or the pleasure it gives its owner, or the price he may demand for it. It is the usual and customary selling price at private sale, under nor-

mal conditions, when a ready, willing and able seller deals with a
ready, willing and able buyer in the community where the property
is located at assessment time."

I recently heard a man who was employed by a civic group in my
home town of Chicago declare that these different terms that are
used as a guide for the assessment of property, the terms set up in
the laws, introduce great confusion. As a matter of fact no confusion need exist in regard to these terms, because the courts have
over and over declared that these terms all mean the same thing.

Long ago, in the case of Illinois & St. Louis Railroad Company
vs. Stockey, Collector, the Supreme Court of Illinois said:

> "There is no claim, nor is there any ground for the claim,
> that the provisions of the statute governing assessments, whether
> made by town assessors or the state board of equalization, are
> in conflict with the constitution. The statute requires all prop-
> erty to be valued and assessed, for purposes of taxation, at its
> ' fair cash value.' "

And the court adds:

> "This requirement, however, is nothing more than what the
> law would imply without it, for a simple, unqualified direction
> to value property, by its very terms imposes the duty of ascer-
> taining and declaring its cash value."

Long ago the United States Supreme Court expressed itself upon
the same subject in Cummings vs. National Bank, the court speaking thus:

> "The phrases ' salable value,' ' actual value,' ' cash value,'
> and others used in the directions to assessing officers, all mean
> the same thing, and are designed to offset the same purpose."

The basis set up in the laws of the land for the assessment of
property for taxation has been presented. The term " value " as
defined in tax laws means the price the property sold for, or would
have sold for on assessment day at a fair, voluntary sale.

Perhaps it has already occurred to you that there is nothing unusual or special about the definition of value as formulated in tax
laws, and such is the case. This is true because the definition of
value set up in our tax laws is interwoven in the business transactions of mankind from time immemorial. The wayfaring man
says a thing is worth what it will bring; the economist defines value
as power in exchange, and more concretely, as a price which has
been or which can be actually obtained.

Value as an economic term is likewise defined by the dictionaries.
In Brooks-Scanlon Corporation vs. United States, decided May 12,
1924, which was a suit brought to determine the value of a contract
with a shipbuilder for a vessel in process of construction, expro-.

priated by orders of the Emergency Fleet Corporation, the Supreme Court of the United States held:

> "It is the sum which, considering all the circumstances—un-- certainties of the war and the rest—probably could have been obtained for an assignment of the contract and claimant's rights thereunder; that is, the sum that would in all probability result from fair negotiations between an owner who is willing to sell and a purchaser who desires to buy."

The word "value" as used by economists has long had a very definite, limited and clear-cut meaning, and unless qualified, always has that meaning when employed by them.

On the very first page of his book on *Leading Principles of Economics*, J. E. Cairns, one of the great authorities on economic theory, said:

> "The sense proper to value in economic discussion may, I think, be said to be universally agreed upon by economists, and I may therefore at once define it as expressing the ratio in which commodities in open market are exchanged against each other."

A quotation in greater length from *Principles of Economics*, by Alfred Marshall, will also be submitted. On page 8 he says:

> "There is another word of which some account should be given here; because it will often occur in this preliminary survey; and confusion might arise from the want of a proper distinction between the different senses in which it is commonly used.
>
> "The word 'value,' says Adam Smith, 'has two different meanings and sometimes expresses the utility of some particular object and sometimes the power of purchasing other goods, which the possession of that object conveys. The one may be called value in use; the other, value in exchange.' In the place of 'value in use' we now speak of 'utility'; while instead of 'value in exchange,' we often say 'exchange value' or simply 'value.' 'Value' by itself always means value in exchange.
>
> "The value, that is, the exchange value, of one thing in terms of another at any place and time is the amount of that second thing which can be got there and then in exchange for the first. Thus the term 'value' is relative, and expresses the relation between two things at a particular place and time.
>
> "Civilized countries generally adopt gold or silver, or both, as money. Instead of expressing the values of lead and tin, and wood, and corn, and other things in term of one another, we express them in terms of money in the first instance, and call the value of each thing just expressed in price."

Marshall rightly emphasized the importance of place and time, and by so doing fixes attention on the fact that value is not permanent and unvarying. The price of wheat in London generally differs materially from the price in North Dakota, and the price of one day may differ materially from its predecessor or successor. Value, in the very nature of things, is in constant flux. Value does not inhere in things, but is a result of the bargaining of buyers and sellers. It is nothing more than the agreed price of closed transactions. Value is not intrinsic. If value inhered in things, there would be no change of value, except as things changed. Successful business men are acutely alive to the fact that place and time are of utmost importance.

Judge Cochran, in Louisville & Nashville Railroad Company vs. Bosworth, very truly said:

> " But in case of real estate, which has been sold at a fair voluntary sale, the test of what it will sell for is no longer needed. The price at which it actually sold fixed its fair cash value, in the absence, at least, of any exceptional circumstances."

Value by definition is power by exchange. It is concretely expressed in a closed bargain, but may take new expression with each sale. Of the past it is thus possible to speak with certainty, but what the morrow will bring forth, no man knows.

Without sales there can be only guesses, conjectures or estimates of value, depending on the character of the data available for estimating the price obtainable. The fundamental considerations of the nature of value are often imperfectly comprehended or overlooked or disregarded. Sometimes entirely novel definitions are set up. No question of morality or justice has a logical place in the discussion of value. What the property ought to sell for, because of the labor and money expended in its production, or because of its utility, is beside the mark. The assessor's only concern under the law is to determine the price the property he is assessing did sell for or would sell for at a fair voluntary sale. The law lays upon him but one command. His sole duty is to determine the price for which property was sold, or for which, in his judgment, based on all relevant facts, it could have been sold at assessment time.

The question as to whether the term " value " has the same meaning in rate regulation as that given to it by business men and economists was denied long ago by Mr. Eschleman, President of the Railroad Commission of California. On page 72 of Volume 5 of the Opinions and Orders of the Commission, in his concurring opinion in the case of Town of Antioch vs. Pacific Gas & Electric Company, decided July 6, 1924, he said—and what he has to say I think is one of the best things that has been said upon this question as to whether value for taxation and value for rate making are one and the same thing, or whether exchange value and rate-making value are one and the same thing:

" To fix rates we are told we must know the value, but the final beneficial value to the owner of such property cannot be known or even exist until after the rates are fixed. Therefore, of very necessity the first value which must be known before rates are fixed cannot mean the same as the resultant, and we must find it by other rules. The courts have called it ' fair value.' . . . That the confusion existing with reference to the proper basis for determining this so-called value is due to the fact that it is misnamed, I have often heretofore pointed out. . . . Value . .. in its commercial aspect . . . we have made . . . dependent primarily upon the earning power of the property valued. Value as thus understood, and as blindly sought after in all these rate inquiries by the utilities and many commissions and courts is something that cannot be of aid in the fixing of rates."

I have now come to the valuation provisions of the Interstate Commerce Act.

By the provisions of Section 19a, commonly called the valuation amendment, the Interstate Commerce Commission is directed to " investigate, ascertain and report the value of all the property owned or used by every common carrier subject to the provisions of this act."

As the first step in this undertaking, Congress directed the commission "to make an inventory which shall list the property of every common carrier subject to the provisions of this act in detail and show the value thereof as hereinafter provided."

The instructions for showing the value, that followed were:

" (1) The commission shall report in detail as to each piece of property, other than land, . . . the original cost to date, the cost of reproduction new, the cost of reproduction less depreciation, and an analysis of the methods by which these several costs are obtained, and the reasons for their differences, if any,"

and

" (2) in like manner ascertain and report separately, other values, and elements of value, if any, of the property of such common carrier, and an analysis of the methods of valuation employed, and of the reason for any differences between any such value and each of the foregoing cost values."

By the act as amended the commission was directed to report the original cost and present value of all lands.

Except as otherwise provided in the amendment, the commission was given the power " to prescribe the method of procedure to be followed in the conduct of the investigation, the form in which the results of the valuation shall be submitted, and the classification of the elements that constitute the ascertained value."

A preliminary finding is designated " a tentative valuation," and

-ultimate findings are designated "final valuations," and "final value." It is declared that "All final valuations by the commission . . . . shall be *prima facie* evidence of the value of the property in all proceedings under the act to regulate commerce as of the date of the fixing thereof."

This announcement is important. It declares the use to be made of the results of the commission's labors.

The amendment directs the commission to report three cost findings, namely, original cost, cost of reproduction new, and cost of reproduction less depreciation. It then directs the commissioner, unmindful that only cost findings have been provided for, "in like manner" to ascertain and report other values and elements of value if there be ány, but in no way so much as suggests what these values and elements of value may be.

There is no definition of value in 19a. The commission was left by Congress to work out its own salvation. It was explicitly directed by Congress to find and report "costs," "values," and "elements of value," and from these it was expected it would determine final values, but the job of selecting, weighing and combining these elements was left to it for decision.

Congress assumed that the commission would look to the decisions of the Supreme Court for guidance, and that help could there be found.

By Sectoin 15a, which was added to the Interstate Commerce Act February 28, 1920, Congress directed the commission to adjust rates, ascertain the value of railway property, and recover and place in a reserve fund one-half of the net railway operating income in excess of 6 per centum of such fortunate railways as earned more than 6 per centum.

To ascertain the "value" and "aggregate value" of the railway property, Congress further directed that:

> "4. For the purposes of this section, such aggregate value of the property of the carriers shall be determined by the Commission from time to time and as often as may be necessary. The Commission may utilize the results of its investigation under Section 19a of this act insofar as deemed by it available, and shall give due consideration to all the elements of value recognized by the law of the land for rate-making purposes, and shall give to the property investment account of the carriers only that consideration which under such law it is entitled to, in establishing values for rate-making purposes. Whenever pursuant to Section 19a of this act the value of the railway property of any carrier held for and used in the service of transportation has been finally ascertained, the value so ascertained shall be deemed by the Commission to be the value thereof for the purpose of determining such aggregate value."

By this paragraph a " final value " found pursuant to Section 19a *ipso facto* becomes the " value " and " aggregate value " for the purposes of Section 15a. But there is nothing added or taken away in express terms that clarifies the meaning of the term "final value" or the procedure to be followed to find it. The paragraph does, however, direct that before " final values " become available, the commission shall, in making emergency valuations, give due consideration to all elements of value recognized by the law of the land for rate-making purposes.

The construction placed upon the provisions of the valuation act by the Interstate Commerce Commission and by its director of valuation will now be presented.

Soon after Congress passed the Valuation Act, the Bureau of Valuation was organized by the commission, and Judge Charles A. Prouty, who resigned from the commission to take charge of the work, was made director. This Bureau of Valuation has done the work.

The interpretation of the Valuation Act by Judge Prouty, the director of the Bureau of Valuation, will first be presented. In 1917 he submitted a memorandum to the commission on the " Valuation of the property of the Texas Midland Railroad." On pages 3 and 4 he outlined his construction of the Valuation Act.

" Rate-making value," said Judge Prouty, " is a thing which has come into existence in connection with the regulation of public utilities. It has never been defined by any economist or dictionary maker. It has been *described* by the courts and is *that sum upon which, under all the circumstances and upon a fair consideration of all the facts and elements to be taken into account, a fair return should be permitted.* I doubt if any definition can ever add to this description of the thing itself.

" This value, as already said, is not exchange value, nor can exchange value be of much weight in determining rate-making value, for the patent reason that exchange value depends upon the rate which the utility is allowed to earn, and that rate cannot be determined until the rate-making value is known."

You have seen from this that from the very outset Judge Prouty, who formulated the plans of the Interstate Commerce Commission for the valuation, so-called, of the railroad properties, declared that the thing sought by them was not exchange value.

Early in 1920 Director Prouty submitted another statement of his views and contentions to the Interstate Commerce Commission, in a paper entitled " Memorandum upon Final Value." On page 2 he reaffirms he fundamental contention of his memorandum of 1917. He said:

" In a memorandum filed with the Commission upon the first

valuation hearing I stated that this value to be fixed by the Commission was not the exchange or condemnation value, so-called, but was rather that sum upon which, giving due consideration to all relevant facts, a fair return ought to be allowed. Nothing which has transpired in all the elaborate discussions then and since, has in any wise tended to alter that opinion."

He could well speak of elaborate discussion and extended opinion, for literally there had been tens of thousands of pages of printed matter put out on this subject since the valuation act was passed.

Having reaffirmed his position of 1917, and having declared that his position had been in no wise altered by the elaborate arguments that had been submitted to the commission, Judge Prouty outlined his own plan of valuation. He is being quoted at some length, as his views appear to have greatly influenced the commission. Judge Prouty said:

"In no one of the cases which have come before the United States Supreme Court has the claim that exchange value ought to determine the rate-making value, been approved. There was in the original Smyth-Ames case a suggestion that the market value of stocks and bonds should be considered, but that suggestion has been repeated in no subsequent case and never has been acted upon in any case.

"The whole proposition involves a legal absurdity. A rate-making value is to be stated for the purpose of determining a fair rate. Commercial value is determined by the rates actually in effect. If, therefore, commercial value is to determine rate-making value, and rate-making value is to determine the rate, then the present rates must be right.

"It is confidently believed that the Commission must reject value as determined by earnings or exchange value as a measure of the rate-making value which is to be stated."

We now come to the position of the Interstate Commerce Commission itself.

The position of the commission on the question as to whether there is but one "value" for all purposes will first be shown. In discussing its report for the Salt Lake Railroad the commission said:

"It is quite evident that in enacting paragraph 15a of the Act, Congress intended that one of the purposes for which we should ascertain and report the value of the property of common carriers was to arrive at a base for determining the fair return to which the carriers were declared to be entitled, and the amount of excess, if any, in their earnings which it became our duty to recover.

"It is our conclusion, therefore, that the final single-sum value which we shall ascertain and report in this case is the value for rate-making purposes. Having reached that conclu-

sion, it is unnecessary for us to detemine now to what extent
or in what manner values for other purposes may differ from
values for rate-making purposes.   Our present problem is to
discover and apply the principles which must control in the
ascertaining of a value for rate-making purposes."

In discussing its report for the Atlanta, Birmingham & Atlantic
Railroad, the commission said:

"Section 19a of the Interstate Commerce Act provides that
we shall ascertain and report the various costs enumerated with
respect to the property owned or used by each common carrier
for its purposes as a common carrier. We are then directed to
show separately the property held for purposes other than those
of a common carrier. It is clear that by this direction Congress
intended that we should ascertain a value for rate-making purposes. The amendments of the act embraced in the Transportation Act, 1920, particularly those contained in Section 15a of
the Interstate Commerce Act, direct that the values so found
shall be used in establishing rates that will yield to the carriers
'a fair return upon the aggregate value of the railroad property of such carriers held for and used in the service of transportation.' The value we are required to establish, therefore, is
a value determined for the specific purposes of governmental
regulation under the Interstate Commerce Act. That value
must embrace all of the property used by the carrier for purposes of transportation, whether owned by it, or leased from
others, and must include any intangible value that inheres in
the property because of its use."

And then it concludes:

"We are not concerned with a value for purposes of sale or
of condemnation, which in either case might well be something
different from the value of the same property for the purpose
of governmental regulation."

In discussing its report of March 4, 1924 for the Kansas City
Southern Railway the commission said:

"Whatever the limitations may have been upon the original
meaning of the term 'value' it is certain that at the time the
Valuation Act was passed the term was generally used with
recognized but widely varying meanings. Valuation for capitalization, consolidation, taxation and rate-making purposes and
estimates of exchange value cannot all be made upon the same
basis."

And on the following page, after quoting parts of Section 19a
and 15a, the commission closed the discussion of this point by
saying:

"We conclude that a valuation under Section 19a should be
one that would serve for rate-making purposes."

In order that an idea may be formed of the effect the substitution of the cost of reproduction values of the Interstate Commerce Commission for fair cash value, as the basis for assessment of railways, I shall introduce two actual examples for which all the facts are in my possession.

The final value for rate-making purposes of a small Western railway having a mileage of something more than 100 miles was placed by the Interstate Commerce Commission at $1,365,000 as of June 30, 1916, and would, of course, be much more if wages and prices now prevailing were used. For the year 1925 this railway was assessed for $231,400; and for the year 1926 for $406,450. Just before the assessment for 1926 was made, this road was sold at a voluntary sale for the sum of $700,000. The substitution of the Interstate Commerce Commission's final value, based on the so-called normal unit prices for the five-year period 1910-1914, for the sale value would have nearly doubled the taxes of this struggling little railway.

There is a little bit of interesting history in connection with the assessment of this railway. When the Interstate Commerce Commission reported its value for this railway, the State Tax Commission of the state in which it was located fixed its assessment accordingly. The railway promptly instituted a suit in the Supreme Court of the state. This brought reconsideration by the tax commission and reduction of the assessment to that of the previous year.

I will also add that in the state in which this railroad was located, by law the State Tax Commission is directed to assess railroads on the basis of the findings of the Interstate Commerce Commission, so the tax commission was only attempting to carry out the provisions of the law. It was, of course, seen that the railroad could not stand this assessment, and the tax commission, when the matter was properly called to its attention, realized the situation, but there was the law. The tax commission appealed to the attorney general for an opinion, as to how it should proceed, and the opinion of the attorney general is certainly, to say the least, a very interesting document. He showed the commission how it could avoid following the provisions of the law.

VOICE: What is the name of the state?

MR. TUNELL: I think we'd better not give that. The state happens to be represented here, so I would prefer not to name the state.

CHAIRMAN BLODGETT: Secret state.

MR. TUNELL: I will show you that this case is not an extreme case. After the publication in the *Journal of Political Economy* of February, 1927, of my paper entitled " Value for Taxation and for Rate Making," a friend of mine, who is a tax commissioner of a railroad in another section of the country, wrote me a letter and

18

told me he knew of something worse than that which I had reported, and if you are interested I will read a paragraph of his letter.

VOICE: Read it.

MR. TUNELL (reading letter):

"On June 5, 1925, the Interstate Commerce Commission issued its valuation as of June 30, 1916, in respect of a little subsidiary of ours in . . . , stating the value at $540,000. The property was operating continually at a loss. In 1923 the State Tax Commission assessed the property for taxation at $56,400. In 1924 it placed a tentative assessment of $94,000 against the property. We had been trying for some two or three years to sell it for $50,000 and had been unsuccessful. I offered it to the state of . . . . for $25,000." Whereupon the tax commission put the assessment back to $25,000, a highly commendable act. "We finally sold the property in 1925 at a *bona fide* sale to an outsider, for $25,000."

Here we have an actual sale of property at $25,000. The so-called value put out by the Interstate Commerce Commission was $540,000.

I can show you some other interesting facts, but I venture to say that I have more than exhausted my time.

I will give you some information showing how, and the extent to which value, as I know it, by which I mean, of course, exchange value, and the cost of reproduction, which is substantially what the I. C. C. is finding, varies, and how they move sometimes in different directions. I am going to give you the facts for a railroad of which I have some knowledge.

I will show first of all the value based upon the high and low stock-market quotations and the high and low of each month averaged for years. The first year that I shall quote, for which I shall give you values, is the year ending December 31, 1914, which was before the war, so to speak, and I shall only read figures for the millions. In that year the stock-market value of this property was $589,000,000. The next year it went up to $620,000,000. In 1916 it raised to $629,000,000. And in the year 1916 that railway had its highest net operating income for any year down to the present time, except the years 1925 and 1926. About 1916 the effect of the higher prices for materials and higher wages began to show, and the net railway operating income of the company dropped, and conditions in the railroad world were generally unfavorable. For 1917 the market value based upon the stock quotation fell to $565,000,000; in 1918, $546,000,000; in 1919, $538,000,000; 1920 to $501,000,000, a fall of nearly 20 per cent from 1914.

By 1920 things began to look a little better in the railway world

and the prices of stocks and bonds began to go up. In that year
the Transportation Act was passed, which helped matters considerably. In 1921 the stock-market value rose to $525,000,000; 1922,
$595,000,000; 1923, $579,000,000; 1924 to $598,000,000; in 1925 to
$647,000,000.

After 1916 the net railway operating income fell, and the prospects in the railway world looked bad. Investors did not care for
stocks and bonds and the stock market fell steadily; fell to 1920.

Now, during this period costs of reproduction steadily increased,
and by the data contained in the records of the Bureau of Valuation of the Interstate Commerce Commission, by 1920, the year in
which the stock-market quotations had gone down to the very bottom, cost of reproducion had more than doubled.

On the basis of cost of reproduction, this property should have
been worth more than twice what it was worth on the stock market.

I leave it to you which value came more nearly conforming with
actual conditions. I thank you.

CHAIRMAN BLODGETT: It is not to be wondered that you like this
paper; that you maintained such perfect interest in it. Its greatest
value is that to be gained from having it in our respective offices,
as part of the proceedings of this conference.

Before we proceed any further we ought to come to an understanding about this question of discussion. I borrowed Professor
Fairchild's watch, which keeps accurate time, and he loaned it to
me on the consideration that he might be permitted first to just
make some comments about this paper. The rules prescribe that no
one discussing these papers may take up more than seven minutes.
This paper was given fifty minutes in the entirety.

I notice there are three items on here. Giving fifty minutes to
each, we cannot have very much discussion under the seven-minute
rule.

I call your attention to this, so that you will understand it, because there is great interest in this subject of valuing property, and
the entire program this morning is devoted to that subject. I am
going to call any one to order who exceeds seven minutes, and there
will be room now for two people to discuss this, and in order to
keep faith with Professor Fairchild I will permit him to talk.

FRED R. FAIRCHILD (Connecticut): Mr. Chairman, we regard
Mr. Tunell's paper as one of the most refreshing contributions ever
offered in the long series of these conferences. It ought to go a
long way to clear up the muddy waters in which we have permitted
the discussion of tax assessment to become submerged.

The economists do not agree on everything, Heaven forbid; but
if you will examine the writings of the authorities of economic
science on the subject of value, you will have no difficulty whatever

in confirming the statement with which Mr. Tunell began his paper; that there is practically unanimous agreement upon the meaning of value.

By "value" we mean what you could get for something in exchange; what it would sell for, assuming that the seller has full opportunity and time to find the best possible buyer, the buyer who will give the best price. That definition; that concept, is in agreement wih the popular idea of the man on the street, and is, I submit, what we all think of when we think of value.

In our forty-eight states and the District of Columbia there are forty-nine tax laws. They are not in identical language, obviously, but a study of those laws will show that they all mean the same thing essentially by the term "value." By "value" they mean what the economist means; they mean what the man on the street means; they use certain qualifying phrases, "fair," "true," "just," and so forth. These words are used for nothing more than emphasis. If the legislature had neglected to say "fair," would the law have implied unfair value? If it had neglected to say "true," would the law thereby mean false value? Nothing is added to the concept of value, except a certain emphasis, by these qualifying terms; and when they go sometimes still further and say the value shall be the market value, they are not introducing another kind of value, they are simply trying to make doubly clear the notion that value does not mean a forced value, in which the seller has not had full opportunity to make the best sale he can. The Connecticut law says this in practically so many words: Assessors and boards of relief shall deem the true and just value to be the fair market value and not the value at forced or auction sale. So, we get down to the conclusion that value in the tax law means just what it does in the writings of economic science and in the idea of the man on the street. .

We hear a great deal about the difficulties of the property tax. We have heard lately much talk to the effect that the difficulty comes from nobody knowing what is meant by value. I submit that the whole question can be cleared up only when we recognize that this is not the difficulty. The rate-making authorities have been frank in admitting that value in their field does not mean value in the economic sense. The only unfortunate thing is that they have not thrown overboard the word "value" and got another term, which would mean what they are talking about. There is no reason for our thinking that there is inconsistency or fraud, when a railroad corporation has one value for rate-making purposes and another for taxation, and we should never have fallen into that confusion were it not for the fact that the word "value" is used in two different senses. Whereas the term value is used in taxation in its accepted sense, the same word in rate making is used to mean something quite different. Mr. Tunell has demonstrated that, it seems to me, absolutely.

Now, the situation is that the legislatures have commanded the assessors to determine and record the true value of every taxable piece of property. Every one knows that for many kinds of property this impossible; for all kinds of property it is difficult. The law has a comforting principle, every now and then pronounced, to the effect that "the law never commands the impossible." This is like that other pleasing principle, that of course "a man must live," pronounced, in spite of the fact that at all stages of history men have been dying, from starvation and other causes. Our tax laws have directed the impossible. When our assessors find themselves struggling against this insuperable problem, do not tell them that their difficulties arise from the fact that nobody knows what value is. Let us be honest and face the fact that no man on God's earth can find out the value of ninety per cent of taxable property. If we are going to make this property tax work, we shall have to recognize that in many, if not in all cases value is an impossible tax basis. This was recognized long ago in Europe, where they have generally abandoned all of the general property taxes except the tax on land where they thought the difficulty was not so serious as to be insuperable.

CHAIRMAN BLODGETT: I wonder if there is anyone in the audience who desires to find fault with any part of the paper that has been read. If so and I can recognize him, I will do so.

THORNTON ALEXANDER: I don't know but what this is getting the floor under false pretenses. It is not so much that I want to criticize anything Mr. Tunell said, because I thoroughly agree with everything he has said, but I should like to ask him one question, and that is this:

Assume that a railroad actually for any given year made the full return upon the I. C. C. value for rate-making purposes, would you then say it should be taxed upon the Interstate Commerce Commission's valuation, or, in other words, would the commission's valuation necessarily conform to the market value or tax value of the property?

MR. G. G. TUNELL: I should be glad to answer that, and I shall answer it with perfect frankness. I have answered it on many occasions on my appearances before the tax commissions of the states in which the Santa Fe Railroad operates.

I should say that where the net railway operating income is such as consistently to produce a fair return upon the so-called value found by the I. C. C., that that value may properly be used as the basis for the assessment of the property in that state. Of course, if the property generally is assessed on a 50 per cent basis, as it is in some states, that fact should be recognized.

MR. ALEXANDER: Then the implication of your answer would be that without regard to past history, or the prospective future earning capacity of that road, or without regard to whether the return fixed by the Interstate Commerce Commission would assure the sale of that property, if sale was desired, at the commission's value, the road should then necessarily be taxed upon that value?

MR. TUNELL: As a practical question it seems to me that many of the states have followed a good course. The state must have a stable basis, or a relatively stable basis, for deriving its revenue, and it cannot move things up and down with wide variation; so in most of the states with which I am familiar the five-year basis for assessing the property for taxation has been adopted.

ARTHUR S. DUDLEY (Wisconsin): I, too, have been called upon to answer this question before many state boards. I do not think I should answer the question propounded in just the same way Mr. Tunell has.

As I understand the question, it is: if the reasonable return has been made for a single year, whether that would be the assessment of that year. It is true that when the present and prospective, the actual and the anticipated earnings, using the phraseology of the Supreme Court, are such that we may count upon a continuance of this fair return upon the rate value, then the rate value and the tax value will probably be identical, because then the market value, which is dependent mainly upon the present and prospective income of the property, will be identical with the rate value, but it is a matter simply of coincidence. The rate value does not then become the tax value, but the rate value, an independent thing, becomes practically the same as the tax value. Mr. Tunell did not take into consideration the fact that the earnings of a single year, or the earnings of the past, might not be the prospective earnings.

MR. TUNELL: Of course actual sales are the best evidence of value, but if the going return were realized, then probably the market value would coincide with the I. C. C. cost of reproduction. I think I tried to emphasize that point without any appearance of evading the question. I tried to emphasize the point that the return must be what is regarded by investors as the going return upon money, and if it was and the prospects were that it would continue to be the going return upon money, then the stock-market value would approximate the cost of reproduction.

MR. DUDLEY: It would be a stable return.

CHAIRMAN BLODGETT: Unless the Chair obtains a motion, the

discussion of this paper will have to close, if we are going to adhere to the rules and to the program which is outlined for this morning's session. As I said before, this question is extremely interesting. I wish we could devote vastly more time to it; but unless there is a motion made, I shall now call the debate with respect to this paper closed, and we will take up the next subject, which is really a continuity with respect to much of the discussion we have already had.

Not hearing any motion, I announce the next subject, "A Survey of the Problem of Valuation." The discussion of this subject will be by Mr. J. C. Bonbright, Columbia University. Mr. Bonbright, come forward.

MAY THE SAME PROPERTY HAVE DIFFERENT VALUES FOR DIFFERENT PURPOSES?

J. C. BONBRIGHT
Columbia University

The admirable and convincing analysis that Mr. Tunell has just made of the nature of tax valuations, as contrasted with valuations for purposes of rate making, raises a question that is every day becoming more and more insistent, with the growing number of valuation cases that are brought before our various administrative bodies and our law courts. That question is whether "value," as the term is used by courts and legislatures, always means the same thing for all purposes; whether it has a meaning as definite for economics as has the watt and the ohm for physics; or whether it has the color of a chameleon, changing its hue to suit its environment. Either of these points of view can be supported by chapter and verse from judicial opinions. To the federal District Court for Southern California the valuation of the Los Angeles and Salt Lake Railroad Company [1] by the Interstate Commerce Commission was an improper valuation, because it "was based upon the view that the property of the railroad company in question has more than one kind of value." To another federal district court, speaking in a tax case involving the valuation of railroad property, "where the effort is to ascertain a fair value for rate-making purposes and a fair value for taxation purposes, cases may and often do arise where there are differentiating considerations." [2] Opinions of the United States Supreme Court are both confusing and conflicting. In public-utility rate decisions the court has frequently reiterated its dictum in Smyth v. Ames, to the effect that a public utility is entitled to earn a reasonable return on the " fair value of the property being

[1] Los Angeles and Salt Lake Railroad v. United States, 8 F. (2d), 747, 756.

[2] (1924), 294 Fed. 742, 749.

used by it for the convenience of the public," [3] and this statement has been made with the implication that the phrase " fair value " has such a definite and well-accepted meaning in current usage that it should of itself set the criterion by which to test the fairness of a rate schedule. But the same Supreme Court, and even the same judges who have most religiously chanted the incantations of Smyth v. Ames, have accepted different principles in a rate-making valuation from those that are applicable in an appraisal for taxation, for condemnation in eminent domain, and for compensation in damage cases.

Before attempting to answer the question whether and to what extent value may vary with the purpose of the valuation, we must make clear just what we mean by the question that is raised. Do we mean to ask simply whether the same property can have more than one value, as that term is used by economists, or by the dictionaries? Or do we mean to ask, rather, whether " values " or " valuations " as the terms are loosely used in statutes, in the court rooms, and in the market place must always mean the same thing, regardless of the purpose for which the valuation is being made? Clearly it is the second rather than the first question that we are interested in answering. And it is highly unfortunate that many of the discussions of judicial valuation have completely dodged the real economic issues by quoting the economists' definition of value— a definition developed with reference to a specific type of problem which the classical economists were interested in discussing—and by deriving their whole conclusion as to a proper tax base, or a proper rate base, from a deduction from this definition.

It may be well, however, to start with the economists' definition of value, if only to reject it, where it does not happen to suit the practical purposes for which so-called property valuations are being made. To the economist, as is well known, value—when used without an adjective—means market value, or market price. " The worth of a thing is the price it will bring." Cost, whether original cost or cost of reproduction, is irrelevant. It is irrelevant, that is, except that under competition there is supposed to be a rough tendency for the market value of a piece of property to approximate its cost—a tendency that is always being more or less defeated by various factors which throw prices out of stable equilibrium.

As thus defined by the economists, value is indeed a far more definite and less variable term than would be indicated by the many uses to which the term is put by the accountant, the business man, and the judge. And yet it would be going too far to say, as some writers on valuation have said, that even as used by the economists, value is perfectly definitive, like a unit of measure in electrical

---

[3] (1898), 169 U. S. 466, 546.

science. For may there not be more than one *market* value for the same property, depending upon one's assumptions as to the nature of the market? What is the market value of a piece of real estate? That may depend on the time element. If sold quickly, at what is called a forced sale, the price may be one thing; if sold deliberately, another thing. Again, what is the market value of a certain share of a stock? If offered along with ninety-nine other shares, in a hundred-share lot, the price may be par. If sold as a single share, or in an odd lot, it may be 99⅞; if sold with several thousand other shares, in an oversized lot, the price may be very much less than par, because the market may break, or it may be very much more than par, because some group of capitalists is willing to pay a premium for a controlling interest. These difficulties are familiar enough to the tax assessor in capital stock cases. They simply show that not even the economist's definition of value is as precise or as exclusive as many people, including, I fear, some economists, seem to think. And it therefore follows that it is possible to place two different valuations on the same property, at the same time, and yet to maintain accurately that both valuations represent the market value of the property. So, for example, a certain railroad might be reorganized through foreclosure sale at a judicially fixed upset price of $100,000,000, representing a liberal estimate of the market value of the property, in the sense of its forced-sale value; yet, immediately thereafter, the same railroad might be assessed for taxation at $150,000,000, representing a more normal market value, as measured by the current prices of the newly issued stocks and bonds.

But while it is true that there may be different values for the same property, even in the restricted sense in which value is used by the economist, it is still more significant that there are other " values " in the loose and perhaps unfortunate sense in which the term is used in legislation and in legal language, which are entirely different from market values under any reasonable interpretation of that term.

As bearing out the fact that value, in this looser and vaguer sense, may mean different things for different purposes, I propose to consider four of the more important objects for which adminis_ trative commissions and courts are called upon to fix a property valuation, noting in each case how the " value " arrived at may differ with the differing purpose for which it is made. Let us turn first, to valuation for public utility rate control; second, to valuation for a property tax; third, to valuation for compensation under the right of eminent domain; and fourth, to valuation for the setting of an upset price in a corporate foreclosure sale.

Value As a Basis of Rate Control

According to the famous dictum of Smyth v. Ames, railways and other public utilities have a constitutional right to charge such rates as will yield them, under reasonable management, a fair return on the " fair value " of their property. As economists and others have long since pointed out, however, this " fair value " cannot properly mean value in the ordinary sense of commercial or market value. For the commercial value of a public utility is simply a capitalization of the expected net earnings, and it is precisely the fairness of the net earnings that is the subject of dispute in a rate case. It is now many years since the vicious circle involved in the attempt to base rates on commercial values was clearly brought to public attention. The persistence of the fallacy down to this day, not merely on the part of company attorneys, whose object is obfuscation, but on the part of judges, whose object is presumably truth and light, is one of the most striking examples of the slavery of the human intellect to the magic of words and phrases. One can only hope prayerfully for the time when this incubus overlying most of the current judicial thinking on public utility valuation will be once and for all exorcised, and when the lawyer who insists in arguing a rate case on the assumption that rate-making value means the same thing as value for other purposes, will be laughed out of court.

The question as to what basis of valuation should be accepted for purposes of rate control, in lieu of commercial or market value, is too vast a problem, and would take us much too far afield to warrant discussion at the present time. Students of public service regulation are generally agreed, however, that the basis must be some form of cost. As to whether this cost should be original cost or cost of reproduction, opinions differ sharply. But in any case it is cost rather than value, in any accurate sense, which must govern in a rate case. And the growing practice of speaking of the " rate base " instead of speaking of a " value " or " valuation " for rate making, has much to be said in its favor.

Tax Valuation

In striking contrast with the principles underlying valuation for rate making are those underlying valuation of property for taxation. With Mr. Tunell's contention that the two types of valuation should be distinguished the present speaker is in complete agreement. The distinction is due to the fundamentally different purposes of the two types of proceedings. In the rate case the object of a public service commission is not to *find* the value of the property but rather to *fix* the value. It is not merely to discover how much the property is earning but rather to decide how much the property *should* earn. But in the tax case the situation is quite the reverse. Here the attempt is, not to *control* earnings nor to *fix* values but rather to *discover* the earnings and to *find* the values. For the amount of the tax is supposed to depend on the economic power accruing to the owners of the property in question, under the circumstances that actually prevail as to the prosperity of the company. If a railway or a public utility, for example, has a so-called valuation for rate making of $10,000,000 but if its earning power, due to over-competition, or to restrictive rates, or to any other reason, gives it a commercial value of only $1,000,000, then it is this $1,000,000 which is the proper basis for a property tax, simply because it is this $1,000,000 which represents the wealth, the economic power, of the investors in the railway. Conversely, if this same railway is unusually prosperous, due to excellent management, or to lack of severe competition, or to ineffective regulation of rates, or to any other cause whatsoever, with the result that its commercial value exceeds its rate base, then it is the higher figure and not the rate-making value which should be the basis of the tax. Any other policy simply defies the whole principle of ad-valorem taxation.

I conclude, therefore, that the tax base and the rate base are properly to be distinguished, in that the former should be measured by commercial value rather than cost, whereas the latter should be measured by cost rather than by commercial value.

There is a further aspect of the problem of tax valuation which I propose to discuss in this place—an aspect involving a different set of distinctions from the one between cost and commercial value. I refer to the question raised by my associate Mr. Rifkind at the last year's conference of this association, as to whether the proper basis of a property tax is sale price on the one hand, or value to the owner on the other hand.[4] Let me cite a pending piece of litigation which brings out this problem in a very dramatic way. The New York Stock Exchange, as is well known, owns a very expensive and very elaborate building on the corner of Wall and Broad Streets. The building was erected in 1900-3 at a cost of $3,300,000, and its present cost of reproduction has been estimated at something under five millions. An assessment was placed on the building of $2,050,000. From this assessment the stock exchange appealed to the New York courts, on the ground that the proper basis of a tax assessment is the market or sale value of the property, and not the value to the owner. Testimony was offered to show that no other purchaser could be found for the building, because of its peculiar construction. And hence it was argued that no tax should be imposed save on the value of the land without any improvement. This case has already been decided against the stock exchange by the Appel-

[4] National Tax Association, *Proceedings of the 19th National Conference,* 1926, p. 305.

late Division of the New York Supreme Court,[5] but an appeal to the Court of Appeals is still pending.

When Mr. Rifkind discussed this problem last year, he pointed out that the Wisconsin Supreme Court has taken a position squarely in support of the use of sale value, even when that value is much less than the value of the property to its existing owner. He also noted that other courts were in more or less disagreement with the Wisconsin position. But, being not only a trained lawyer but also a tax specialist, Mr. Rifkind refused to express an opinion of his own as to the merits of this controversy. Not being either a lawyer or a tax specialist, I make bold to step in where Mr. Rifkind declined to tread, and to take the position that, where property has a distinct value to the owner, over and above the price for which it can sell on the market, this value should clearly be included in the tax appraisal.

In making this assertion, I venture no opinion as to whether the Wisconsin courts were really obliged by the distinct wording of their tax statutes to take a contrary position. One thing, however, seems to me clear, beyond reasonable doubt—that, judged from the point of view of fairness in taxation, the Wisconsin rule is an economic absurdity. Why under heaven a building or any other structure that is especially adapted to the use of one particular owner, should be taxed on the basis, not of its value for that particular use, but rather of its much lower value for some other use, is beyond my comprehension. If the purpose of an appraisal of property for taxation is to measure the economic power, the economic wealth, of the owners of that property, why should not the value of such property to the owners be accepted as the criterion, even though it may exceed the value to any other owners? To this question I have so far seen only one attempted answer. It is to the effect that administrative convenience requires the use of a definite and objective standard of tax appraisals, and that such a standard can be found in sale value, which can be estimated by observing sales of similar property, but cannot be found in the value to the owner, which involves assumptions as to the owner's state of mind. Some such defense, indeed, has been made by the Wisconsin Supreme Court in upholding the Wisconsin rule. The point of objectivity is important if true. But is it true? Suppose we accept the Wisconsin position that a building, peculiarly adapted to the needs of its present owner, must be valued at the price for which it might be sold to an outside purchaser. How is that price to be estimated? Clearly it can be estimated only by making some highly speculative assumptions, first as to the type of buyer that would find the building most usable for the purpose that he has in mind; second, as to

[5] Peo. ex rel. N. Y. Stock Exchange Building Co. v. Cantor et al., 223 N. Y. Supp. 64.

the cost of readapting the building to that new purpose; and third, as to the price that the prospective buyer would be willing to pay for the building, rather than to put up or purchase some other building more nearly adapted to his particular needs. I fail to see how anyone could claim for such a procedure the merit, claimed for the sale-price standard by the Wisconsin Supreme Court, of eliminating "in as large a measure as possible . . . the mere judgment of the assessor, and enabling the owner or the assessor, as the case may be, to prove the valuation by facts which he has no part in establishing. . . ." [6]

But other courts, as has already been noted, do not agree with the Wisconsin ruling to the extent of excluding entirely the owner's valuation where the property is especially adapted to his needs. These courts, such as those of New Jersey and possibly of Massachusetts, while still adhering verbally to the doctrine of the market value as the basis of tax appraisal, in fact take more or less account of the owner's valuation, by conjuring up that very convenient but almost meaningless notion of the willing buyer and willing seller. By means of this *deus ex machina,* the market value of a piece of property is interpreted to mean, not what the property *can* be sold for, but rather what it *could* be sold for, if only there existed persons who, oddly enough, happened to need just the type of property which is peculiarly adapted to the uses of its present owner. So in the case of a stock exchange building, which nobody else in real life, other than its present owners, wants, except as a tear-down proposition, or of a golf course, which no one would buy except for meadow-land use, or of an insurance company building, which no other business could use, save after making extensive alterations, those courts that resort to the willing-buyer device would assume, directly contrary to the facts of the case, that other stock exchanges, other golf clubs, and other insurance companies are in the market, willing, but not too eager, to buy the property in question. The price that these hypothetical buyers are presumed to offer is called " market value "; yet it is clearly not market value, in any accurate sense of the term.

You may not like this judicial abuse of the English language. But you must at least sympathize with the courts in their dilemma. For on the one hand, many of the tax statutes insist that the basis of tax appraisal shall be the market value of the property; on the other hand, the literal acceptance of market value leads to results that are unfair to the point of being ridiculous. Hence the resort by many courts to the legal fiction of willing buyer and seller—legal fiction, being another name for gentleman's lie. And between being

[6] State ex rel. Northwestern Mutual Life Insurance Co. v. Weiher, 188 N. W. 598.

ridiculous, like the Wisconsin courts, and being gentlemanly liars, like the other courts, I leave the choice to this convention.

I have mentioned in this paper two characteristics of tax appraisals that distinguish this from certain other types of property valuation. These two features, however, by no means exhaust the list of distinctions. Two or three other peculiarities of tax valuation have been briefly noted in a more extensive discussion of this whole problem of valuation published in the issue of the *Columbia Law Review* for last May. But I must pass them by here in order to continue with a discussion of other types of valuation.

VALUATION FOR CONDEMNATION UNDER THE POWER OF EMINENT DOMAIN

The third in our list of purposes of judicial valuations is condemnation, under the power of eminent domain. The Government, or a public service corporation, institutes proceedings to take over land and appurtenances necessary for some public purpose. What shall be the compensation to the owner of this property?

One may note first that, in principle at least, the nature of the valuation in this case resembles the tax appraisal far more than it does the rate-making valuation. For here, as in the tax case, it is the commercial value of the property and not its original or replacement cost that is to be used as the measure. Cost of reproduction, to be sure, is relevant, but only as evidence, subject to disproof, as to what the property is really worth at the time of the taking. Nevertheless, the principles of valuation for eminent domain, though they are similar, are not identical, for the peculiar nature of a condemnation case raises problems that are not germane to the ordinary tax situation.

The first distinguishing feature to be noted is that condemnation, while it requires a commercial valuation—a market value in the loose sense of that phrase—nevertheless assumes a market with one of the purchasers—and that the most eager and insistent purchaser— left out. I mean that the valuation is not supposed to include the peculiar value of the property to the body which is taking it over. What the value was to the owner, and not what it is to the taker, is the desirable criterion. Even if the property, prior to the taking, should change hands at high prices, in a speculative market which capitalizes the hope of high compensation, when the property is to be condemned, still that higher value—though undoubtedly it represented market value in the strict sense of the term—would probably not be judicially recognized as justifying an enhanced award. For the very object of eminent domain is to permit property to be taken for a public use without the payment of the peculiar value of the property to the public agency. We have, then, in eminent domain, another kind of hypothetical market value, the hypothesis being that the most important demander for the property shall exercise no bullish influence on market price. I hasten to add that these principles of valuation for condemnation are said to be constantly disregarded in practice by juries and commissions, and that not even the courts in their directions to the juries, are in unison as to the principles themselves. In fact, judicial utterances in the field of eminent domain are almost as chaotic as judicial pronouncements in the field of valuation for rate control. But the point of the present paper will be served if it is clear that the peculiar purpose of valuation for condemnation may have a decided influence on the principles accepted in measuring the values.

, There is still another aspect of valuation for eminent domain which is sharply to be distinguished from tax appraisals. I refer to the different principles to be accepted in the valuation of a portion of a whole property. For example, if one-half of a building lot is expropriated by the Government, the loss imposed upon the owner may be much greater than half the value of the whole lot, because of the fact that the remaining piece of land may be too small or be otherwise unadapted for building purposes. Fairness to the owner, then, may require that the compensation for the taking of either half of his property be much greater than half its total value. On the other hand, in a tax appraisal, where the problem of valuing a portion of an organic whole arises, the rule of apportionment should be such that the sum of the values of the parts is equal to the value of the whole. The problem suggested here is the difficult problem arising under the unit rule, as applied to interstate railways and other public utilities. I mention it here, not to discuss it, but simply to emphasize again the important influence which the purpose of a valuation must have on the principles to be applied in determining the values.

Upset Price in a Corporate Reorganization

The fourth and last type of valuation to be mentioned in this paper is a valuation made by a court for the purpose of fixing an upset price on a corporate property that is about to be sold at a foreclosure or other judicial sale, as for example, the upset price fixed by Judge Wilkerson in the recent sale of the St. Paul railroad system.

Here, as in the condemnation case, the basis of valuation resembles the tax appraisal more than the rate-making value, in that it rests on a commercial valuation, rather than on actual or reproduction cost. But there is a difference as well as a similarity. For the upset price is in the nature of a forced-sale valuation, whereas the tax appraisal is in the nature of a more ordinary and deliberate sale. The peculiar nature of the upset price arises from the purpose which it serves in the procedure of a reorganization. It is designed to protect the minority interests in the reorganization by means of a rock-bottom price, below which the majority may not buy out their claims. But in fixing this rock-bottom price, the judge, if he is convinced of the fairness of the reorganization, will not wish to set it so high as to tempt many security holders to remain in the minority and take cash, rather than join with the majority in taking new stocks and bonds. Consequently, the upset price must be designed frankly to give the assenting security holders more favorable treatment than the dissenters. In short, it is not a full valuation but rather a deliberate undervaluation.

Conclusions on Valuations for Different Purposes

The four types of valuation that have been mentioned in this paper by no means exhaust the list of purposes for which our law courts and our administrative commissions are called upon to value property. They may serve, however, to show how useless it is to speak of the value of property without reference to the purpose for which the valuation is being made. For value is a word of many uses and many meanings. Even the definition of the economist is by no means as precise and definite as is frequently supposed. And as used by legislatures, by courts, by accountants and by business men, the meanings of the term far transcend any definition that the economists or the dictionaries have placed upon it.

Because of these multifarious meanings of the word, it follows that no rational conclusion can be reached as to the proper nature of a tax base, or of a rate base, or of any other so-called property valuation, by a mere deduction from some preconceived meaning of the term value. I often hear it said that the great problem which you tax administrators face is to discover what value really means. With all due respect to the makers of this remark, I submit that this is not your problem at all. It is to discover, not what value means— for value means whatever you want it to mean—but rather what a fair and proper tax base means. It is the problem of deciding, not whether the New York Stock Exchange building has any value, but rather whether it ought to bear any tax. And in making this decision you will get only a limited and qualified aid from those so-called principles of value that are applied to other purposes, such as rate-making or condemnation or reorganization. To follow the other policy — to deduce a basis of tax appraisal from traditional definitions of value, is to be guilty of that serious intellectual vice which some of my friends at Columbia University are fond of terming the vice of conceptualism.

In concluding, I should like to revert once more to the paper that has just been read by Mr. Tunell. As to his main thesis, to the effect that the rate-making value that is placed upon a railway is not necessarily the proper basis for a tax appraisal, I am of course in entire accord. But it should never be forgotten that, for the prevalence of the contrary view Mr. Tunell has to thank his own fellow associates, the railway attorneys, more than any other group of individuals. These astute gentlemen, in their concern to secure for the railways a rate base inclusive of all conceivable kinds of value, however mutually inconsistent these different kinds may be, have constantly reiterated and insisted that valuation for rate-making purposes is of the same nature as other types of judicial valuation, such as valuation for eminent domain and for taxation. Perhaps the valuation counsel were not completely aware, in taking this position, that they were forging a two-edged sword which might be used against them in tax cases, or perhaps they were aware of this fact, but were willing to accept the danger of higher tax assessments in order to gain the much greater benefit of permission to charge higher railway rates. However this may be, I trust that Mr. Tunell will forgive students of railway valuation, like myself, if we derive a certain amount of amusement from the dilemma in which he, as a railway tax commissioner, has been placed by the unreasonableness of his own associates. And I am sure that everyone here will wish him the best possible success in his laudable home-missionary endeavors to bring his friends of valuation counsel back to their senses and to show them that this unreasonableness may in the end react against the interests of their own clients.

CHAIRMAN BLODGETT: I have a couple of notices which the secretary has given me. I will read them.

(Announcements with respect to garden party and drive around the City of Toronto.)

CHAIRMAN BLODGETT: We have remaining fifteen minutes of time for this paper, each person being given seven minutes. Will you proceed with the discussion?

DELEGATE: What would the stock exchange do, if it had no other assets and could not sell its buildings and presumably, therefore, could not raise the mortgage nor pay taxes?

MR. BONBRIGHT: "Presumably, therefore, they could not raise the mortgage" does not follow from the fact that it could not sell its building. Mortgages are constantly being placed on property which cannot be sold as an ordinary piece of real estate can be sold, to an outside purchaser. Great railway systems are constantly placing great mortgages on their systems when it would be quite impossible to sell the railway property for even the amount of the first mortgage; but as to the question, it seems to me to imply an utter disregard of the nature of a tax valuation. In valuing a piece of property for ad-valorem tax purposes, you do not hang it on the

19

basis of the amount of ready cash that you suppose the owner has on hand with which he can pay this year's tax or the next year's tax; you value it on the basis of the entire economic value of the individual, and then you leave it to him to secure in some way or other the tax or the money in bank with which to send a check to the tax commissioner.

Mr. G. G. Tunell: Mr. Chairman, may I say a word with respect to one of the remarks made by Professor Bonbright?

I, of course, have had conferences with members of our legal department since the passage of the valuation amendment. I think their views have grown out of the decisions of the courts. There cannot be greater confusion than exists in the decisions of the courts, including the highest court of the land. I believe that a correct view of this situation would be helpful to the railroads and not harmful to them, and this is the reason I have been working to bring about a correct view.

Charles W. Gerstenberg (New York): I apprehended, as Mr. Bonbright was speaking, that we might be up against this difficulty: If a corporation owning a piece of property was earning less on that property than somebody else could earn, the question would arise whether the tax-valuers would assess that property at less than its sale value. Mr. Bonbright gave us the converse of that, and I think he took an extreme case in the stock-exchange example.

Let us suppose, for example, that a piece of property on a corner is being used for some purpose for which it is not really appropriate, and the people using it are not able to make enough out of it to have the property valued at what somebody else, who could use it for an appropriate purpose, could pay for it. I am quite sure tax assessors would not agree to value it at less than its commercial value though it would see at first blush that such a position, assumed by the taxpayer, would have to be agreed to; but if you think it through I think you will agree with me that the assessor does not have to take the position that the earning power of the particular occupant of the land is the criterion of value.

The difficulty is that the taxpayer is not applying sound principles of accounting and finance to his business. Every corporation should charge against its property on the basis of its investment in such property a fair return, of say 6 per cent. If the corporation charged against its income a fair rate of return, 6 per cent on the value of that property, which value is determined by what the corporation could get for it, then it would be apparent that the corporation is not making money—not making enough to pay 6 per cent, to pay operating expenses and yield a fair return for the managerial ability which is being put into the business. The result is the corporation ought to give up, for they are not doing business at a profit, and we cannot assume that in the ordinary course of events they would continue. The best thing to do is to sell the property and go to some other place where they can charge 6 per cent on their investment, get their operating expenses and get a fair return; so that, in every case, property should be valued on the basis of earnings; not of a particular occupant, but on the basis of the average occupant who could use the property to best advantage, and who therefore sets the commercial or sale value of the property.

After all, it seems to me it gets down to the question of what is the property worth to anybody on the basis of what they can get out of it. That is what we pay for when we buy property. We buy future income and pay for it its discounted present worth.

The best example of that is the bond. Take a 5 per cent bond that has, we will say, one thousand years to run. It has one thousand coupons. The popular idea is that the principal is worth $1000 and the coupons are something attached. As a matter of fact, if you will put in one pile the first fifteen coupons, and in another pile put the 985 subsequent coupons, plus the principal of the bond, you will be ahead by taking the pile containing the first fifteen coupons, because the first fifteen coupons are worth more today than the principal of the bond itself, plus the last 985 coupons; if you calculate the present worth of the bond itself, without the income represented by the coupons, you will find that the principal shrinks in value, so that a $1000 bond payable one thousand years hence [1] is worth practically nothing today and the coupons, that is, the income, are worth just what you pay for the bond and its coupons—$1000.

That, to my mind, clearly indicates in a theoretical way that every piece of property is worth what it will earn; the coupons being the representation of the earning power, clearly indicate that that is what you pay for when you buy a bond. You do not buy the principal of the bond, you buy those coupons.

There is the old story of Dr. Samuel Johnson, who was asked what he thought a brewery was worth when he was selling it to settle an estate. He replied: "I am not about to sell a parcel of vats and boilers, but the potentiality for growing rich beyond the dreams of avarice." Here we have a clear statement of what property is actually worth. It is worth what can be gotten out of it. If the owners cannot get a fair return out of it they certainly should quit and go some other place, so somebody else can have the property who can earn a fair return from it.

THOMAS W. PAGE (District of Columbia): Gentlemen, I think these two papers we have listened to this morning are two of the very best papers I have heard read before this association. They

---

[1] The exact value of the principal is $.000,000,000,000,000,0006456.

are suggestive, they are clear, and they analyze the subject that they dealt with in such a way as to get their meaning across to all the people here.

Unfortunately, however, there are some points of disagreement between the gentlemen who read these papers, and they did not seem to be altogether in accord with Professor Fairchild. I am wondering, therefore, whether those of us who are interested in the practical problems of taxation, and particularly in the matter of assessment, will go home feeling that we are very much enlightened and know better what we ought to do, by reason of having heard these most excellent papers.

The difficulty seems to arise over the question as to what is value. These gentlemen seem to be more or less in agreement that there is such a thing as value. Although amongst them they enumerate at least fifty-seven different kinds of value, yet somehow or other they all get back to the idea that value, as the first speaker said, is power in exchange; so here we have the rather confusing problem of fifty-seven in one.

Now, what after all is value for taxation? It is whatever the appraiser says it is. He is supposed to take into consideration a great many things, some of what have been specified by the Supreme Court in the Minnesota rate case and many other cases, and some which the court admits but does not specify. He must also weigh with care one to which the court made no reference whatsoever, and that is the important consideration: What will the owner of a piece of property probably stand for in the way of assessment?

If we accept the definition of value that seems to be most popular among these speakers, namely, that value is power in exchange— so that we really have in mind only market value—we meet with trouble, because there are a great many classes and kinds of property for which there is no market. You cannot sell such property. There are no buyers for it. For example, you can sell shares in a railroad, but a great railroad system cannot be put up and a market found therefor of the kind described by Mr. Tunell and Mr. Bonbright, and implied by Mr. Fairchild. Therefore, the property tax law requires you to get as " value " something that does not exist. There are many forms of property that have no market value, because they have no market.

The use made of this thing called value is as precarious as the thing itself. It is supposed to be used to measure the ability of a taxpayer to pay taxes. It presupposes a tax system that aims to apportion taxes in accordance with the ability of taxpayers to contribute to the public revenues.

In practice, however, as you are all well aware, there are other things besides ability to pay that every legislature takes into consideration in enacting a tax law. For example, no legislature ever lays aside altogether the thought of what benefit from the expenditure of the money raised under the law is going to accrue to certain classes of the population. Therefore, in shaping the law the legislature takes into account, not only the ability of different classes to pay, but likewise the benefit to particular classes from the expenditure of the money collected. Again, taxes are sometimes levied that appear really to aim at a redistribution of wealth. Inheritance taxes, for instance, sometimes ignore ability to pay and are assessed so as to redistribute the amount of wealth in private ownership. There are other purposes of taxation which, following the example of the Supreme Court, I will not attempt to enumerate.

What the law really does, therefore, when it asks for the value of property is to require assessors to get something that does not exist, to be used for a purpose which there is no intention of carrying out! That creates a very difficult situation for the tax administrator.

Ever since this association has been in existence we have been striving and fishing around, trying to find out whether there isn't some sort of mechanical device, some mathematical formula, something that we can use to measure this fleeting, elusive, and sometimes non-existent thing called value. We have been trying to find some way to keep the tax assessor out of difficulties and to satisfy the public that somehow justice is being rendered.

Well, we cannot find it. Nevertheless, we have got to bear two things in mind; in the first place, as Professor Fairchild has said, value is no proper basis for taxation, but, in the second place, whether it is a proper basis or not, we cannot get rid of ad-valorem taxes in this country for many years to come. We are going to have the property tax, and we are going to require the value of property to be assessed as a basis of that tax.

As long as we have the property tax, it is just as well to have the law read very much as it does now. It matters very little how the definition of value is phrased. It may be called market value, or fair market value, or fair market value in money, or the law may add any number of descriptive terms. In any event the practice in taxation will continue to be something very different from what the law seems to mean.

(Speaker advised by Chair that his time for discussion had expired.)

DELEGATE: I move Dr. Page be allowed to continue, that the time be extended.

CHAIRMAN BLODGETT: This is a suspension of the rules and requires a two-thirds vote.

(Motion put and carried, extending the time of Dr. Page.)

THOMAS W. PAGE (continuing) : I appreciate your kindness. I was saying that this term "value" that is now used in the law might just as well be retained. I could suggest far more modern terms that I think would be equally applicable, such terms, for example, as "blah," or "bologny," or "applesauce." The only thing important is that tax practice shall conform to the true spirit of the law. Unfortunately there is uncertainty about the quality and the character of all our "spirits" in the United States, and the spirit of our tax laws is not always apparent. Accordingly, public officials who are charged with the duty of apportioning taxes must take into consideration ability to pay, the allocation of benefit, the intention of promoting social reforms, and other objects of the tax laws. It follows that for carrying out the spirit and intent of the law, there is no mathematical formula. Certainly market value of the kind that is contemplated by economists and accountants can be of little aid to tax officials in discharging their duty.

We are, therefore, compelled to rely, as we are in practically all activities of life, upon human honesty and human wisdom. We have got, in other words, to try to impress upon the public in this country the necessity of having as the head of our tax administration in the states a qualified, competent, well-trained and trustworthy tax commission, with wide powers, to supervise assessments and allocate taxes amongst different classes of the population. That is the only solution of the problems that confront us. Justice will depend, so long as we have ad-valorem taxes, much more upon competent administration than upon phraseology of the law.

CHAIRMAN BLODGETT: We have exhausted all the time that may now be devoted to this subject, if we are to finish the morning's program as outlined. Before we leave this subject, I have the pleasure to announce to you that Mr. Tunell has a few copies of a pamphlet entitled "Value for Taxation and for Rate Making," which he, if you will write to him or communicate with him, will mail to you. I understand the number is limited. This is a manuscript published in the *Journal of Political Economy* of February, 1927.

The next subject has a very close relation in thought to the maters which have been under discussion this morning. It is a troublesome question to every person who has to deal with assessments, particularly in our industrial sections of the country. I have the pleasure to introduce to you, to discuss the subject of Valuation of Commercial and Industrial Properties for Taxation, Mr. W. F. Connelly, Tax Commissioner of Bridgeport, Connecticut. Mr. Connelly, come forward, please.

W. F. CONNELLY (Connecticut) : Mr. Chairman and Gentlemen of the conference: My hope was that it would be the sense of the conference to permit Dr. Page to continue. As Dr. Page talked I recognized in him a kindred spirit, and I got a lot of consolation out of what he said.

We tax assessors are usually without honor in our own community, and I am no exception to that rule. We are very much like the white missionary who ventured into black territory, where the white men had a very bad reputation and of course were very much disliked. This white missionary happened to meet up with a colored clergyman and made friends with him to such an extent that he was invited to come to his colored church and see his colored congregation, which he did. The congregation came in, and they were very much disturbed and alarmed to see this white person in their midst. The colored parson very quickly reassured them, and said, " Brethren, this man who is with us today, it is true, has a white face, but, brethren, he has a black heart." And so it is with us.

THE VALUATION OF INDUSTRIAL AND COMMERCIAL PROPERTIES FOR TAXATION

WILLIAM F. CONNELLY

Tax Commissioner, City of Bridgeport, Connecticut

The statutes of the various states relative to the taxation of real property are virtually the same. Differences in terminology may be noted but a brief consideration would suffice to show that the laws are essentially identical in meaning. Fair market value, fair cash value, full cash value, etc.; all have the same significance.

It is not hard to understand that in the early days of our community, when property was small in amount and property types relatively few and simple, a statute directing assessments to be levied on fair market value was reasonably specific. It could be carried out without injustice since, due to more intimate community association, the value of the existing property was almost common knowledge; when transfers took place the surrounding circumstances were generally known and the basis for comparing other like properties was thus kept up-to-date.

The tremendous economic growth of the last half-century has wrought changes. Newer and more complex forms of construction appeared; life became less intimate; sales negotiations were covered; combinations of trades and leases became a part of the sale and nominal sale prices meant little. The result, of course, made the establishing of a fair market value by sales and comparisons unreliable. The law, which, under simple conditions, might function satisfactorily became less and less adequate, as our economic activities increased in variety and complexity. The law lags progress.

Reference to the fundamental conditions existing in the early days is not useless. It would appear to be significant, in that it helps us to understand the intent of the law. There is no doubt in my mind that the term " fair market value " was designed to be a common yardstick for measuring tax contributions; the intent was to treat all taxpayers alike. No other conclusion would seem reasonable. In other words, our tax statutes in this respect contemplate equalization. Equalization is today only possible through the uniform application of valuation methods. Uniformity of valuation methods, to my mind, is in accord with the spirit of the statutes as they stand.

It is possible to argue on this matter in an academic way, but with the tax assessors of the country the problem of establishing a fair tax base is very vital and pressing. Drifting in this respect produces chaos. Tax assessors must take the law and adapt it to present.conditions; they must work out practical methods that will carry out the original intent of the law. Many so-called scientific systems of assessment have been developed in our cities; the outstanding principle in each one is uniformity. It is the only means to secure equity.

We have just completed a revaluation of Bridgeport, Connecticut. Bridgeport is a city of about 175,000 people and contains almost every type of property, ocean frontage, harbor and river frontage, city lots and farms, factories, apartments, offices, hotels, and all classes of dwellings. It was necessary, of course, to classify these properties before attempting to apply valuation methods. We are not concerned here with the assessment details of all the various types but will confine the discussion to a consideration of industrial and commercial properties.

It is necessary first of all to develop a basis which is workable and which complies with the spirit of the law. Our basis we might call " constructive market value." In the case of ordinary dwellings there might be enough *bona fide* sales to aid in establishing a basic value. Sales of industrial and commercial properties are comparatively rare. When industrial properties are sold, the selling price is usualy influenced by factors which have no bearing on the physical value of the property. If the concern is prosperous, it seldom wishes to sell; if it does sell, the price includes capitalization of profits or good will, which is hard to segregate. If a concern is bankrupt it has a buyer who will give a fair price. Such sales are usually far below a fair price. And even if this kind of property did sell at a fair price, each parcel is usually so different, that prices established through the process of comparison would be extremely unreliable. Each structure is a problem in itself.

Frequently, one hears in assessment work that " value is a matter of judgment." This always appears to me as an excuse for lack of method. Judgment, of course, is an essential quality, but judgment alone will not produce equalized values. Judgment cannot be entirely eliminated but it should be used only where concrete methods fail. Without a method the valuation of special properties would try the knowledge and judgment of Solomon. And no Solomons arise to help the assessor.

It is desirable in attacking the problem to segregate the land from the buildings. There is no serious difficulty in arriving at an equitable value for land. Land value is common knowledge, and since land is contiguous, reasoning from comparison is satisfactory.

In arriving at an equitable basis for assessment of buildings, we start with cost of reproduction; this represents a value, definite, ascertainable and uniform. From this figure must then be deducted an allowance for physical depreciation. One might calculate the same value by starting with original cost, making adjustments for variations in the construction price index and deducting an allowance for depreciation. This is a more difficult process, without any compensatory features. The first method is usually preferred.

Leaving aside for the moment the question of functional depreciation or obsolescence, if this value, reproduction cost less depreciation, is applied on all properties they will bear a proper value relationship to one another. It is not a matter of doubt that cost of reproduction is the highest value which can be substantiated for new buildings or, in the case of old buildings, cost of reproduction less depreciation. This is true, of course, providing other things are equal, such as availability of time, location, etc. No one would pay more for a structure than it would cost him to build one just as suitable. As a practical matter he probably would pay somewhat less than reproductive cost, less depreciation, due to the factor of obsolescence which may be present. This factor must be considered in establishing a constructive price and we make a special allowance to cover this contingency in practice.

Cost of reproduction, as I have indicated, is not difficult to ascertain. The establishment of the amount of accumulated depreciation and obsolescence, however, calls for careful observance and study of conditions in each individual case. Tables showing structural depreciation on different types of buildings are plentiful but they are, after all, an average of estimates. It is hardly necessary to show how two identical buildings of the same age, if put to different uses, may depreciate at different rates. One, for instance, may be subjected to excessive vibration, due to heavy machinery, while the other might be used for dead storage; under such conditions the first might last twenty-five years and the latter fifty years or more.

Frequent and substantial replacements and prompt repairs might keep a building standing almost indefinitely. Remodeling of parts of a structure is in the nature of a replacement and affects the

physical life. One can see in any city old buildings which, by virtue of proper maintenance are in far better physical condition than newer ones. Condition is an important factor in judging accumulated depreciation; age alone is not a fair index.

Functional depreciation or obsolescence may or may not be present in a situation. It is extremely difficult if not impossible to gauge accurately. Theoretically, obsolescence is loss of value, due to lack of utility or out-of-datedness. It may be present actually in some instances, only impending in others. Every improvement tending toward reduced cost or increased efficiency, benefit or comfort produces a certain amount of obsolescence in existing structures of the same type. The loss in dollars is purely a matter of opinion.

There is of course a difference in the character, construction, use and marketability of commercial buildings, as distinguished from industrial buildings. And yet we can apply the same basic methods to them with more equity than is possible by other means. . Commercial buildings, especially those producing revenue, probably have a readier market than other special structures. If we adopt income in revenue-producing buildings as the basis of capital value, we must sacrifice the principle of uniformity established in all other cases. Furthermore, it would open up a number of questions that the tax assessor would be unable to settle equitably, because of the difficulty of getting pertinent facts. There are, too, a large number of so-called commercial buildings which are non-income-producing as such, including theatres, hotels, etc. where the income is primarily from a business activity. Income may be proper as an appraisal basis for specific appraisals of land and buildings combined, particularly where the appraisal is made for investment purposes. It is not desirable for tax purposes.

There is a great actual difference between an appraisal of an individual property made at the instance of the owner and a general tax appraisal. The first involves long study, not only of detailed physical factors, but of location, present and future needs, availability for growth, nature of business, etc. Assessors have no facilities for such research and it is doubtful if greater equity would result if they had.

Let us briefly examine the method of ascertaining cost of reproduction. To calculate this accurately, basic price schedules must be developed. These working schedules are prepared from tables of construction costs, divided into the three cost elements, material, labor and overhead. The tables can be prepared only by experienced estimators, who are constantly in touch with material and labor costs in the particular locality. These must be accurate; any errors are carried along and multiplied in the course of preparing the working schedules. Each minute part which enters into the construction of a building is priced in the basic tables according to the proper unit, lineal foot, square foot or cubic foot. For instance, a common brick foundation costs fifty-one cents per cubic foot for the material, forty cents for the necessary labor and nine cents for overhead, or a total cost of $1 per cubic foot. Again, joists and rafters cost twelve cents per lineal foot for yellow pine, four cents per lineal foot for erecting labor and two cents per lineal foot for overhead, a total of eighteen cents per running foot. And so it goes, for all the items forming a part of the structure.

The appraisers must get the measurements of all these items in lineal, square or cubic feet as the case may be. Usually the architectural and structural drawings will be available to show dimensions and sizes; if not, the data must be obtained by actual physical measurement. To make a detailed appraisal of every item in a building would take a long time; for our purposes a condensed form of appraisal is satisfactory. Minor items of machine foundation, underground piping, piling, etc. are eliminated; these, in many cases, would only be a matter of guess. Certain other items are definitely classed as equipment, such as furnaces, retorts, power plant, etc. and automatically eliminated. It is necessary that a definite understanding exist as to the classification of certain items, to insure uniformity.

For ease in applying prices we have found it convenient to build up group costs. For instance, if, according to our tables, twelve-inch common brick wall costs $1.10 per square foot, and painting inside five cents per square foot; then a wall painted inside would cost $1.15 per square foot. Other combinations of costs save much time in practical pricing.

It may clarify the discussion of this technical phase of the work by a concrete illustration. Assume we are to appraise a factory building 60 by 120 feet, with a basement and two stories. We must get full information as to the thickness and construction of foundation and exterior walls, story heights, etc., called vertical factors, and the amount of excavation, the area and type of floors, roof, etc., known as horizontal factors. Finally, general items, such as plumbing, lighting, heating, elevators, sprinklers, etc., must be added.

Priced and tabulated the cost, with certain assumed data, would appear as follows:

Vertical Factors:

Foundation walls and footings.... $12.87 per foot of wall.
Walls, 1st story .... 14.40 "   "   "   "
Walls, 2nd story .... 11.16 "   "   "   "

Total unit cost .... $38.43 "   "   "   "

360 feet (perimeter of building) by $38.43 .... $13,834

Horizontal Factors:

Excavation	.24	per square foot (8 ft. deep)
Floors: Basement	.20	" " "
1st floor	.54	" " "
2nd floor	.63	" " "
Roof	.39	" " "

Total unit cost .... $2.00   "   "   "

7,200 feet (area of building) by $2.00	$14,400
General items	5,475
Total...	$33,709

The total cost as tabulated is $33,709; the structure contains 230,400 cubic feet, or 21,600 square feet. The unit cost may be quoted as fifteen cents per cubic foot or $1.56 per square foot.

It can be appreciated that the results obtained from such a standard schedule are bound to be substantially uniform. Such detail is necessary, in order to account for differences in type, size, shape, etc. It is of course clear that differences in materials result in different costs; it is perhaps clear, too, that differences in size of buildings, influences cost. But it is not perhaps so evident that differences in shape of buildings may produce widely different costs; although containing the same area. For example, assume a ten-story building, one hundred feet long and one hundred feet wide; the usable area would be 10,000 square feet per floor. Assume that another building is five hundred feet long and twenty feet wide; each floor would contain also 10,000 square feet. But in the first instance, we have only 400 lineal feet of walls, while in the latter we have 1,020 feet, with a greatly increased cost. While this case is purposely exaggerated for illustration, it indicates that one cannot safely generalize in quoting building costs. There are other factors, such as difference in story heights, wall thicknesses, areas, etc., all of which influence unit cost.

It is true that we do not know that the properties in question would sell for that value calculated in this way; neither does anyone else. As I have previously pointed out, industrial and commercial properties differ so widely that no sound comparison of values can be universally made without definite methods. The method here outlined is uniform and substantially equitable. The courts which have tussled with assessment problems in the past have recognized the difficulty of taxing authorities, and have, on more than one occasion, voiced approval of the basis discussed. Will the doctrine of uniformity be universally accepted in courts? Time only will tell. One cannot help feel, however, that any court will listen attentively to the argument of assessors who employ uniform valuation methods in their work.

FRANCIS N. WHITNEY (New York) : I have been asked to present a resolution which, I understand, under the rules must be read and referred to the committee on resolutions without debate: (Reads resolution).

CHAIRMAN BLODGETT: Referred to the committee on resolutions.

CHARLES J. TOBIN (New York) : I want to take issue, if it can be an issue, with the last speaker. I do not think it should be accepted that replacement or reproduction value is the proper basis for tax value. I don't think we ought to go out of this conference and have it accepted as being the proper basis. The difficulty with reproduction value is that it is entirely built up on theory, and as instances of that I have in mind two cases in New York; two recent cases where engineers were employed on the basis of the value they would obtain. In the matter of overheads, in one case they built up 25 per cent, and in the other case they built up 20 per cent. One was an industrial plant, the other was a hotel property.

The courts of New York have entirely disregarded any such program or any such formula, and have held that reproduction value is solely an element to be considered by the assessor.

We have also got away from the old idea that you first ascertain the life of the property and then find out how much to take off in the way of depreciation. Instead of doing it that way, they say now that the assessors of New York must ascertain the condition of the property; they must find out what its condition is as of the date of assessment and disregard all this idea of depreciation. If it is in 50 per cent condition, it must be taken as of 50 per cent; if it is 60 per cent—the various parts of the property, that is, the brick structure, the foundation and the roof, whatever it may be—all those different elements, must be ascertained and in that way arrive at your value.

I have in mind a case at the present time, where a reproduction would be an absolute fallacy. This particular property is a water property, owned by a particular city, and is in the course of construction; not yet in use, not entirely completed. Reproduction value could not be used in that case as a tax value.

I think the best test of value and the best answer to this matter of reproduction is found in the case of Simpson et al. v. Shepard, 230 U. S. 352, where Justice Hughes said—this was the same as the Minnesota rate case—the ascertainment of that value is not controlled by artificial rules, it is not a matter of formula, but there must be a reasonable judgment, having its basis in a proper consideration of all relevant facts.

Further, in Standard Oil Company vs. Southern Pacific, 268 U. S. 146, the Supreme Court said it is to be borne in mind that the value is a thing to be found, and that neither cost of reproduction new, nor that, less depreciation, is the measure or sole guide. The ascertainment of value is not controlled by artificial rules; it is not a matter of formulas, but there must be a reasonable judgment, having its basis in proper consideration of all relevant facts.

I think that particular part of the Standard Oil case is really our guide today and should be our guide. I do not want to have it said or accepted here that reproduction value should be the test or the measure used in ascertaining the value for tax purposes, either in New York or in any other state.

FRED R. FAIRCHILD: While our chairman has my watch still in hock, I suppose I am still privileged to the floor?

CHAIRMAN BLODGETT: Certainly.

FRED R. FAIRCHILD: The last speaker has just referred to disagreement of 20 to 25 per cent between two engineers' estimates of overhead. I recently heard the evidence in a case in which the court was trying to find the true value of property, and competent assessors were put on the stand—competent appraisers—to testify to what in their judgment was the value of certain residence and connected real estate. The valuations sworn to by those competent appraisers varied from $40,000 to $145,000.

Now, we are not going to get protection in any kind of method, any kind of tax base, but to point out an error of five per cent, more or less, in one case, when faced with an error of 200 per cent or 300 per cent in this fair market value which the law prescribes, does not, I submit, make much of a case against reproduction value, or any other workable rule, which men charged with the duty of assessment are trying to introduce.

What I like about the session this morning is that it seems to have accomplished the purpose of these annual conferences; that is, it has brought together hardheaded, practical men, charged with the duty of administering our tax laws, and we academic theorists who dabble in the same subject.

I do not believe this association would ever have been organized, were it not with the hope on the part of its founders that those two groups could get together and be of mutual aid. Of all the popular slogans which rouse my ire, the worst is the one that this particular device is all right in theory but it won't work in practice. Theory may not stand the test of practice, but any theory that won't work in practice is not good theory, that is all.

By the same token, all of you men who are working by practical measurements to accomplish certain ends must submit your practical devices to the test of assessment theory, and if they are contrary to assessment theory, you are riding for a fall. Sooner or later your device will break down.

Mr. Tunell started things going. Mr. Connelly has clinched the nail.

Mr. Connelly is trying to substitute something for value in the assessment of industrial property. I seriously doubt if his device is legal, and that, I take it, is perhaps the point Mr. Tobin is making. If so, I think I am in agreement. But I have confidence that Mr. Connelly knows his business well enough to take care of himself on that matter. The fact is that he has something which is going to work; it is going to stand the pragmatic test of workability; and if he is permitted to go through and demonstrate by actual experience that it does work, then he will have gone one step further than the point which I made when I fraudulently obtained the floor an hour or two earlier.

In other words, he is engaged now in practical research, for the purpose of finding some tax base which we may substitute in place of value which will not work, and I believe he will find it for this particular class of property. When he does, my imagination is able to carry me to the point when the Connecticut legislature may amend its law and may say that industrial property shall be assessed upon the basis of reproduction cost less depreciation. When that is done, one class of property will be taken out of the realm of vague speculation and put on the sound basis of engineering and technical skill; and in the course of time other classes of property may receive the same treatment.

It is too early for us here to say how this thing is going to come out, but I am perfectly confident that our first great step will be taken when we recognize that value is for most kinds of taxable property not a workable tax base; and the next step will be the long, laborious, practical problem in which men like the tax assessor of the City of Bridgeport are now engaged, in finding what is a workable base for substitution.

FRED A. NEWMAN (Ohio) : I have listened to the various remarks this morning and to Mr. Connelly's remarks very attentively, and I have been very much interested, inasmuch as I have individually just completed a $100,000,000 appraisal of industrial properties in Summit County for taxation; and just thinking of Mr. Tobin's remark, I should like to know what basis Mr. Tobin would use, having ninety politicians with no engineering knowledge or experience, in appraising 250 parcels of real estate.

CHARLES J. TOBIN (New York) : My answer is this: What you are attempting to do and what Professor Fairchild attempts to do is to legalize an over-valuation in the assessment of certain real property.

The difficulties presented everywhere, not only in New York but all over the country, is that you use for the bulk of the property a particular basis of assessment—exchange or sale value—and then set up an entirely different basis for the more extensive property, the property that is not sold.

I say that until you establish a basis alike for all the real property on the roll, you are unfair and cause further inequality in the assessments. The plan tried in Mr. Connelly's location is to legalize over-valuations, that is, to value certain property on a basis which is not used for other property on the same roll.

It is advisable to have a basis that is a matter of actual calculation, but what about the instances in New York where 20 and 25 per cent were added solely to obtain big values, to make large fees for the engineers employed, they being paid on the amount of value found? Their actual calculation did not make a fair or equitable valuation. The overheads they added to the bare cost of labor and material were built up largely for the benefit of themselves. It is one of the elements that you will have to deal with in the problem.

Value is not tantamount to reproduction cost. We must use some basis that is fair and uniform, but do not let us pick out a particular class and leave the others untouched. What we need to do is bring them all under one rule, if it can be done. We are obtaining every day a better class of local assessors. Tax commissions are of high class and we should give them wide powers, big discretion, so that they may obtain assessments that are fair and take into account every element of value. When we attempt to use an exact formula as a basis of arriving at value, we are apt to go astray. It is excellent to have a mathematical calculation, so as to obtain certainty in valuation, but I do not believe you will ever make assessments of real property in that way. Any value of real property must take into account the human element, the owner's judgment, as against the assessor's judgment. What is the value of the property, irrespective of its present use, which takes into account its reproduction value, as well as every other element to be considered. When we do it that way we shall do justice to all taxpayers.

The wrong today is in picking out particular properties and measuring their value on certain fixed rules and leaving the rest of the property alone, not touching it at all. The taxpayer that suffers today is the large taxpayer, the man who is not able to sell his property, because there is no sale or exchange value for that particular class of property.

CHAIRMAN BLODGETT: It seems to me fair Mr. Connelly should be permitted to clarify one particular point he has raised here.

W. F. CONNELLY: Gentlemen, I think the gentleman from New York is laboring under a serious misapprehension. The fact that I only talked about one particular class of property was due to the limits set by the chairman of this convention.

As a matter of fact, to clear up this point that the gentleman from New York has raised, and to answer his main argument, we do assess all classes of property on exactly the same basis. We do not pick out industrial properties and put those on one basis, and other kinds of real estate on another. We differ in the method that we use, and that method is dictated by the administration. In other words, it is absolutely impossible to consider in detail the structural elements of every single dwelling, shack or lodge in any city of any size. What do we have to do then to carry out this principle of uniformity? We have to take those properties and classify them. We take dwellings and classify them into six or seven different classes and apply certain reproductive cost units to those classes, making little variations, where they do not absolutely conform with the class, and in that way it seems to me that the principle of uniformity still holds; that no class of property is discriminated against.

In the matter of land we use exactly the same methods of valuing land and of calculating lot and parcel values for industrial and commercial properties as we do for homes, and *vice versa*. Does that answer it?

CHAIRMAN BLODGETT: Mr. Walter Pollock of the Manufacturers Appraisal Association, of Philadelphia.

WALTER W. POLLOCK (Philadelphia): About three minutes is all I want. As a professional appraiser I have been very greatly interested in the academic and metaphysical discussion of the subject of value.

It seems to me out of the disharmony which seems to arise in the discussion of value from various points of view, there is an essential harmony, if it can be applied analytically. The valuation of land, as indicated by the Minnesota rate case decision, which was just quoted, was described to be by comparison with the value of contiguous and similar land. That is possible in any community and has been done in a great many communities. The value of buildings and improvements; of machinery in factories, can be appraised by uniform methods which will show the cost of reproduction new at a given time, and from which depreciation may be deducted, on a workable basis. The great trouble is in the application of depreciation judgment, and that can be analyzed, so as to show the separate judgment of depreciation for mechanical deterioration, obsolescence and lack of utility.

Now, if the taxable value arrived at in the way I have described, and as has been so well described by Mr. Connelly—if that is the taxable value uniformly, relatively, no owner can suffer from such a method if it has been properly applied.

If there be such a thing as going value or additional value to

20

utilities, by reason of the addition of some separate element that is not comprised in the physical value, then that can be added separately.

The appraisal of physical property is simple in theory, difficult in practice; and if the proper theory is determined, then it is possible to work out the difficulties of practice. I thank you.

CLEM W. COLLINS (Colorado) : The great difficulty in appraising real estate has always been the lack of some tangible uniform basis. Mr. Tobin says, in quoting the decision of the supreme court, that depreciation was relegated to the background, was not considered. I think he misunderstands the real intent of the thing, because I submit that no dependable judgment can be arrived at without somewhere along the line taking into account the element of depreciation.

Now, it is true, I agree, that physical valuation is not the sole factor to consider, not by any means, but I do submit that you must have, if you are going to have uniformity and equalization, some tangible basis to start with.

As an example, out in our state of Colorado we have the sugar plants, a rather difficult sort of industry to appraise on any sort of basis that seems acceptable to every party concerned. It has been attempted there to assess them on the slicing capacity while, if you are familiar with that line of business—it is similar in that respect to others—at certain seasons of the year, at the height of the campaign, they go far beyond their rated slicing capacity, and therefore the production actually is a great deal more than would be measured by the comparison of slicing capacity. They earn a certain amount of money on their investment, and it would seem, since they are a quasi-monopoly, that there should be something added to the physical value, but whatever that may be, there should be the physical value on the reproduction basis, taking into account depreciation and all the other factors necessary to arrive at that value as a basis.

I commend Mr. Connelly for the work that he is doing. I feel that men who are doing that sort of work, scientifically arriving at a basis on which you can add any other elements, such as goodwill, or monopoly value, or anything else—I say they are doing a great work for the United States.

CHARLES J. TOBIN: May I make a statement in correction : I don't want to be understood as saying that the Supreme Court of the United States has taken up the question of depreciation. I said the State of New York in its decision of the board of appeals, the decision of the Court of Appeals, in the Keeler case, in 238 N. Y., had substituted for the scheme of depreciation the observed condition of the property; they have said that the assessor should ascertain the actual condition of the property as of the date of assessment.

WALTER W. POLLOCK: Isn't that the same thing?

CHARLES J. TOBIN: Yes, and no. It is not exactly the same thing. It gets rid of a very awkward procedure. In other words, when the assessors go to make their assessment they find out what the particular condition of the property is—50, 60 or 70 per cent.

JOHN A. ZANGERLE (Ohio): Mr. Chairman and Gentlemen: As county auditor of Cuyahoga County, it is my function to appraise all the real and personal property of that county. That county has in taxable property as much as any one of about 35 different states of the Union. In other words, my county ranks with the states of the Union as about one-sixteenth. I am giving you that to give you a sense of proportion. We value real estate exactly as Mr. Connelly does.

As county auditor unfortunately I am on the board of revision, and as a member of the board of revision of three, I am called upon to revise my own assessments as county auditor. And then we get our work in as Mr. Tobin gets it in; then we have got to consider that our original work was a wholesale job, and was done in the only way that assessors can practically utilize. When the assessor begins to consider the utility of the property, the value to the owner, and so forth, it would cost instead of perhaps 50 cents per parcel, with three or four or five hundred thousand parcels, in a large city, three or four dollars per parcel. But when it comes before the board of revision and it is represented that your assessment on a piece of manufacturing property of $500,000 was all good and true, perhaps, on the basis that you established; but the owners are willing to sell that property for $250,000, and have been trying to sell it perhaps for a year and we cannot sell it. What is the board of revision going to do?

The board of revision then has to consider a lot of elements. They have to consider first and foremost, of course, the reproduction value less depreciation; they have to consider whether that property is salable in the market; the market may have entirely changed from the time that it was originally assessed; and the market in Cleveland now is considerably different from what it was a year ago.

Another thing, we have to consider the owner's own representation on his books. Now, I dare say that the owner's book value of a manufacturing concern is perhaps twice as much as our assessment, our assessment being based on a uniform basis. Whenever an owner comes in and complains about his value, the first thing we do is to look up what he says it is worth on his own books.

That is one way we have of checking these complainants that come in before the Board of Revision. But, I submit that Mr. Connelly's method is the first and proper method for an assessor, but I agree with Mr. Tobin that when the matter of the true value comes before a board of revision, which is called upon to make a particular assessment and not a general assessment, that they must consider all the elements and not merely one that is undoubtedly the best and the most convenient method of establishing it in the first place.

CHAIRMAN BLODGETT: Before we proceed any further with the discussion, the secretary has a resolution which he wishes to read.

(Reading resolution)

CHAIRMAN BLODGETT: Referred to the committee on resolutions.

SECRETARY HOLCOMB: May I intrude by saying that one state we should like to hear from is Michigan, in respect to its membership on the resolutions committee.

CHAIRMAN BLODGETT: I wish to announce this, that we have here from Mr. Burke, of the assessor's office of Buffalo, copies of their field sheets, which are employed there by men in gathering data with respect to buildings. These can be obtained if you are interested in them, and I have not seen anything better. They will be left right here, if you would like to take home with you copies of these sheets.

Do you know that it is past the dinner hour?

(Adjournment)

SIXTH SESSION

CHAIRMAN MATTHEWS: The delegates will take seats. There are two or three announcements to be made before we begin this evening.

It is suggested that the resolutions committee meet in this room after this evening's session, also the executive committee of the National Tax Association.

The following appointments have been made as the three members of the nominating committee of the National Tax Association, to serve with the past presidents who are present at the convention. They are Professor Carl C. Plehn of the University of California, Mr. Charles W. Gerstenberg of New York, and Hon. T. H. Thoresen of the Tax Commission of North Dakota.

The first subject on the evening program is The Problem of Tax Exemptions, upon which you will be addressed by the Hon. S. C. Mastick, chairman of the Joint Committee on Taxation and Retrenchment of the New York Legislature.

S. C. MASTICK (New York): As a preliminary to my remarks I will state that a good deal of what I have to say has its foundation in the preliminary report on tax exemptions in the State of New York, which is published and put in print by our legislature. Copies have been pretty widely circulated throughout the country, but if there are any here who wish copies and will give me their names I will see that my secretary sends them to you. Here is a copy for you to look at if you wish to examine it.

THE PROBLEM OF TAX EXEMPTION

SEABURY C. MASTICK
Chairman of the Joint Committee on Taxation and Retrenchment of the New York State Legislature

The problem of tax exemption is one concerning which much is said but little is done. Why is this? The answer is an easy one. The broad questions of taxation concern themselves with the problems of how to raise more money and how to distribute the resulting increased tax burden equitably. The question of tax exemption is submerged in this constant struggle. Then, from another point of view, every little exemption has a friend all its own, and this friend

(309)

and his friends use all the influence they possess to minimize the particular exemption desired or to obstruct or defeat any attempt to repeal laws under which exemptions have already been granted. The attempt to repeal tax-exempting laws has only a few sporadic supporters while the opposition always turns up in martial array, united and militant, strong politically and socially. Religious denominations, charitable institutions, benevolent societies, hospitals, educational institutions, cemeteries, patriotic societies, libraries and fraternal orders—all of the most diverse character, and possibly at swords' points with each other, unite as brothers, when any attempt is made to curtail their tax exemption.

Yet while all the opposition to reform in tax exemption comes from the sources enumerated, which may be broadly grouped as holders of privately owned tax-exempt property, the great mass of tax-exempt property is publicly owned, either by the Federal Government, the state or by the municipality, comprising the tax unit in question. It is obvious that no matter why the exemption, an increased tax burden is thrown on the remaining taxable property. This remaining taxable property may receive compensating advantages from the exemption but nevertheless it has to pay its share of the tax on the tax-exempt.

The reason why the opposition to reform in tax exemption comes from the holders of privately owned tax-exempt property is that such property is invariably the point of attack. Scarcely anyone considers the amount of publicly owned tax-exempt property. There is great confusion of thought and statement, and those who attack the problem, in order to make out a strong case, group all tax-exempt property together and reason from this total, in order to show the enormity of the problem. For example, in 1926 there was $3,828,000,000 of realty exempt from state taxes in the State of New York, as against $24,956,000,000 of taxable realty. Those attacking tax exemption therefore reason that 17½ per cent of all real property is tax exempt and infer that this is due to the privately owned tax-exempt property, while the fact is that 76.2 per cent of this is made up of publicly owned property, and but 23.8 or 4.2 per cent of the taxable realty is privately owned tax-exempt property. Although this percentage is relatively small, the amount is large, aggregating in New York in 1926 $913,000,000.

The question of tax exemption is broader than we usually think of it. Our minds naturally turn to the exemption of real estate, when we think about the subject, but there are exemptions of tangible and intangible personal property, the exemption of income derived from public bonds, the exemption of minimum incomes from income taxes, both federal and state, the exemption from state income taxes of incomes paid by the Federal Government and from the federal income tax, of incomes paid by the states or its subdivisions, etc. The whole subject is too large to discuss in any one paper and I shall therefore restrict my remarks for the most part to the most obvious phase of the question—the tax exemption of real estate.

While publicly owned tax-exempt property constitutes the greater part of tax-exempt realty, it scarcely comes into consideration for discussion because of the generally accepted belief that such property is held by the nation or the state or other governmental units, for the benefit of the whole and taxing such property would be but taking money out of one pocket and putting it in another of the same taxing unit. While this may be measurably true of federal property, it is not so clearly true of state-owned property. There are cases where state-owned property comprises so large a part of a tax unit that the burden of maintaining local government presses too hard on the remaining taxable property. This is particularly true with relation to local school and highway expenses. If the state-owned property is a public park there may be a compensating advantage in its presence, but if it is a prison or an asylum, for example, its presence may be a detriment, serving the particular community little or none at all, and not even contributing to the prosperity of the community through its purchases, which under modern practices are almost invariably made through some distant central purchasing agency.

County-owned property is in the same case with state-owned property. A county poorhouse or hospital is located in a particular town or township but serves the entire county and the local tax unit little or none. Yet the local tax unit not only has its tax receipts reduced because of the presence of the county institution but has to pay more than its share of the upkeep.

City-owned property located within the city; township-owned property located within the town; village-owned property located within the village, and school property located within the school district are the only examples which occur to me concerning which no question can be raised relative to the justness of the tax exemption.

It would seem to be a fair proposition that some tax should be paid or some allowance made towards local expenses on the part of the state to the city, town or other tax unit in which its property is located, and by the county to the city, village or township in which its property is located. This has been done in some instances where the injustice has been most glaring.

The problem therefore comes to the question of privately owned tax-exempt property. It is but natural that any narrowing of the tax base should be resented, because it is fully realized that the exemption of any one property throws a correspondingly additional burden on the remainder. Some of our tax exemptions are based on historical reasons, the reasons for the exemption having long since disappeared and only the tradition remaining. Some are based on relativity, not the kind Professor Einstein discusses, but the subtle kind that argues that the new request for exemption is so much like some old one that it too should be exempt. Some arise from a distorted sympathy for the purpose of the organization whose property is sought to be exempted, in that we have been led to believe that the special benefit sought is general, when in fact it is not. Sometimes a money-making proposition creeps in under the guise of a charity.

There is ample historical justification for the exemption from taxation of charitable institutions which perform without compensation a function which the state would have to otherwise perform or which the state has undertaken to perform, such as, the care of the poor, sick, demented, crippled, blind, deaf, impotent, the helpless, aged and young. *Per contra,* there is no historical basis for the exemption of benevolent institutions or institutions for mental or moral improvement which perform no function which the state would otherwise have to perform or which the state has never undertaken to perform.

Religious institutions fall within a different category. Although the United States stands today for religious liberty and complete severance of Church and State, such was not always the fact. Prior severance of Church and State, for the most part, was an integral part of the state, whether Congregational, Church of England or Dutch. But during the Revolution the Church in all the colonies was disestablished. There was thus cut away all historical ground for the exemption from taxation of religious institutions. But the old practice still continued, though the reason for it had vanished. Thirty of the states of the United States provide in their constitutions for the exemption of property of religious institutions, three have constitutional provisions broad enough to permit such exemption, and fifteen have no constitutional provision relating to the matter, one way or the other. Every state in the Union has passed statutory legislation providing for the exemption from taxation of religious institutions. Many of these statutes contain limitations as to the extent or use of the property to be exempted. No state, excepting New Hampshire, places a limitation of value on property exempted when used for purposes of religious worship, although most of them place a limitation on the value of parsonages. New Hampshire exempts the property of religious societies up to $150,000 although this limitation may be increased by appropriate action in town meetings or by the city government.

It is thus to be seen that, either for reasons of expediency or as a matter of public policy, the property of religious institutions in the United States is universally exempt, in greater or less degree, from taxation. The fact that it universally prevails indicates that it is in accord with public sentiment. Limitations of use, extent of acreage or of size of lot, or of value, may be imposed, without departing from the broad principle. Criticism is rarely directed against the exemption from taxation of property used solely for purposes of religious worship. Nor is there any criticism of the exemption of parsonages up to the several respective limitations of value. Most of the criticism is directed against the exemption of property of religious societies used for charitable or other analogous purposes. Large tracts of land may be purchased, of which only a small part is actually used or needed for the purpose in hand. Eventually some or all of this land is sold at a profit and the society either moves to cheaper land or uses the profit as an endowment. Having benefited by the unearned increment in value, without having paid any taxes, some think a portion of the increase should be repaid the community. The same state of affairs exists in the case of various eleemosynary institutions of a secular nature. It is not a problem solely of religious societies.

Most of the states have statutes exempting from taxation the property of educational institutions not conducted for profit. There is sufficient historical sanction for this exemption, although the question has been raised as to whether this sanction extends to parochial or religious schools. When the state provides education for its children at public expense the question has been raised as to whether it is also justified in subsidizing parochial or religious schools by granting them tax exemption.

Then there is the question of tax exemption of cemeteries. Some are conducted for profit. Should they be taxed? And what would happen if the taxes were not paid? In the vicinity of large cities there are many extensive tracts of land devoted to cemetery purposes. They can scarcely be called a benefit to the adjacent community, although the community must help support them through tax exemption.

It is unnecessary to refer to the lesser classes of exempt realty. Charitable, religious, educational and cemetery institutions comprise by far the greater part. In each of these instances we see that it is the abuse, not the use of the privilege which is causing criticism. And not only that, but in some cases there is an undue concentration of tax-exempt institutions in one community. Perhaps the community is adjacent to some great center of population or perhaps, because of its physical character, it is peculiarly adapted to some special use, such as tuberculosis sanitaria. In such cases the local community benefits little, if at all, from the presence of the tax-exempt institution, although it is subsidized for its support. This phase of the problem is not widely prevalent but it is serious where it does occur.

Some idea of the size of the problem may be obtained from a recital of conditions in the State of New York, with which I am most familiar.

For the fiscal year 1925-1926 the amount of tax-exempt real property, excluding new buildings in certain cities not exempt from state taxes but exempt from local taxes, was $3,828,000,000. This was distributed as follows:

Property of cities	$2,416,000,000
Property of United States	200,000,000
Property of New York State	155,000,000
Property of villages and school districts	76,000,000
Property of counties	45,000,000
Property of towns	23,000,000
Property of private owners	913,000,000

From the data in hand it is not possible to classify all the privately owned tax-exempt realty in one or the other of the various tax-exempt groups but a large part of it may be roughly classified as follows:

Schools, other than public schools	$53,739,000
History and art, including patriotic societies	7,589,000
Exhibition buildings and grounds of agricultural societies	1,939,000
Buildings and grounds used as places of religious worship	380,159,000
Property of religious corporation occupied by officiating clergy	7,775,000
Property owned by clergymen	1,935,000
Moral and mental improvement (religious)	43,313,000
Fraternal	4,414,000
Benevolent	37,429,000
Cemeteries	95,906,000
Property purchased with pension money	10,362,000
Miscellaneous, including universities, colleges, professional schools, libraries, hospitals, homes for children, etc	268,440,000
Total	$913,000,000

The total state and local taxes levied in the State of New York in the calendar year 1925 were $734,639,000. Of the total taxes levied, $547,517,000 was derived from the general property tax. In 1925, the equalized value of real property on which taxes were levied was $18,751,000,000, and the assessed value of personal property subject to taxation for state purposes was $265,000,000. The general property tax was levied on the total of these two items. As we are confining our attention to the tax exemption of real estate I shall exclude the personal property from my calculations. But 1.4 per cent of the total general property tax, or $7,665,000 comes from personal property. This leaves $539,852,000 to be carried in 1925 by $18,751,000,000 of realty.

If all the privately owned tax-exempt property was taxed in the same proportion as was the taxable realty, the total tax paid by such property in 1925 would have been approximately $26,000,000. The taxes paid by the taxable realty would have been reduced by approximately this amount, resulting in a saving of 4.7 per cent.

While the problem of tax exemption is of much importance, today we are even more interested in the tendencies towards increase, as our present difficulties are small compared with those we must face if we continue the lines of our present policy. This tendency towards increase must also be compared with the probable increase in the value of taxable realty, in order to get a true picture of the situation.

In 1905 in the State of New York, privately owned tax-exempt property amounted to $394,000,000; in 1915 to $661,000,000 and in 1925 to $913,000,000. This was an increase of 138 per cent from 1915 to 1925, and at the same rate of increase privately owned tax-exempt property in 1935 would amount to $1,260,000,000.

The total exemptions of real property of all kinds in the State of New York during these periods increased as follows: 1905, $1,389,000,000; 1915, $2,522,000,000; 1925, $3,828,000,000. If the rate of increase from 1915 to 1925 is maintained up to 1935, the total will then be $5,853,000,000. In this connection it is interesting to note that in New York City the total of tax-exempt realty of all classes in 1920 was $2,321,550,817; in 1925, $3,653,724,381, and in 1927, $4,340,213,236.

The assessed value of taxable real property in the State of New York during these periods increased as follows: 1905, $7,051,000,000; 1915, $11,336,000,000; 1925, $18,751,000,000. If the rate of increase from 1915 to 1925 is maintained up to 1935, the total assessed value will then be $33,564,000,000.

The percentage relationship between total tax-exempt real property and total assessed valuation in 1905 was 19 per cent; in 1915, 22.2 per cent, and in 1925, 20 per cent. In 1935 it would be 16 per cent.

This decrease in the proportional relationship between tax-exempt realty and taxable realty would be more significant were it not for the constant increase in the burden of taxation and the tendency of tax-exempt property to concentrate in certain localities. As real property bears by far the greater part of the tax burden, the increase in tax-exempt property tends to throw a still greater burden on the taxable property.

It is impossible to look into the future without realizing that the question of tax exemption is destined to become more important from decade to decade. Tax exemption of religious, educational and charitable associations is an inherited policy which has stood substantially unaltered from the earliest days of our government. Does this antiquity imply that the policy is unimpeachable? Does its vigorous survival indicate that it is ideally suited to present-day conditions? It does not seem so. The changes which have taken place since this important public policy came into existence have been so great that the older the policy is, the greater is the need for its re-examination and reconsideration.

The status of the Church has been revolutionized. It has been separated from the Government and is no longer supported from tax moneys. Its membership is entirely a personal matter and large parts of the population have no religious affiliation, where formerly membership was all but universal. Free public education has come into existence. Charities have been secularized and in considerable measure brought into the field of government work. Economic changes and the ease of travel have changed the situation, so that institutions which serve a community may be located in other districts, and institutions located in a given community may be of no local service. There has been a revolution in the relative burden of local taxation with the years and also a gradual development of the real estate tax as the one chief source of tax moneys. During the early days of tax exemption local government was inexpensive because local government furnished few services, and a large part of the taxes came from indirect sources and from sources other than real estate.

All of these changes have a distinct bearing upon the nature and the amount of tax exemption and the subject should be considered anew, in the light of present conditions.

In looking towards a program of reform we find that while there have been a number of public and private leaders who have taken occasion to study and criticize tax exemptions, no one has ventured to present a complete practical program. Carefully considered general principles have been enunciated and particular abuses have been attacked, but no specific plan has been outlined upon which it would be possible to secure any general agreement.

It has been suggested, for example, that all exemptions be forthwith abolished. But even the most ardent advocate of this plan realizes that there are insuperable practical difficulties in such a program, to say nothing of the public opposition which it would arouse.

It has been suggested that private property be left as at present but that all public property be made taxable. Should such a policy be adopted, without any consideration of the benefits conferred by the public properties?

It has been suggested that exemptions be confined to the improvements on the land, but that all land be taxed regardless of use.

It has been urged that exemptions be abolished, but requiring each taxing unit to make a subsidy appropriation exactly equivalent to the tax levied and collected from each institution now exempt. This compulsory subsidy would be continued for, say a period of ten years and would then become purely optional. While this would undoubtedly force each institution which is now exempt to justify its value to the community, would it not stir up more friction than the collection of the tax is worth?

These suggestions are not all which have been made but are merely illustrations of various plans which have been brought forth.

Like many other things we have to consider, it is much easier to state a problem than to answer it. I have endeavored to outline the problem, the complexities of reform, the objections which will be raised by the advocates of expediency and to set forth the subject in its true proportions. Real estate tax exemptions have a very healthy capacity for increasing. The most effective thing we can do pending a thorough reform is to maintain conditions as they are and do our best to stunt the growth of exemption.

NOTE.—In the preparation of the above paper acknowledgment is due to Hon. Mark Graves, one of the New York State Tax Commissioners, who has contributed many of the ideas advanced, and to " Tax Exemptions on Real Estate," published by the Westchester County (N. Y.) Chamber of Commerce, of which liberal use has been made.

CHAIRMAN MATTHEWS: Is Commissioner J. G. Armson of Minnesota in the room? I understand that he has an announcement to make.

J. G. ARMSON (Minnesota): Mr. President, Ladies and Gentlemen: Most of you, perhaps all of you, are familiar with some recent decisions of the United States Supreme Court, defining the limitation upon the states, in the taxation of national banks. Those decisions, three in number, affect the taxing system of Minnesota very seriously, as they do many of the other states of the Union.

As we figure, some thirty-odd states are affected by those decisions. Our legislature at a recent session, which adjourned in April, appointed a special tax commission or committee to study and report to the next session of the legislature, in 1929, such suggested amendments to our laws as might meet the situation.

I have had some correspondence with the different states, in the last few weeks, in an effort to summarize the methods of taxing banks and moneyed capital, chiefly moneyed capital in competition with national banks.

We have with us tonight the chairman of the special commission appointed by the legislature, Senator George H. Sullivan, who de-

sires to make an announcement and extend an invitation to you to
meet with us tomorrow morning in conference. Is Senator Sullivan
in the room?

(No response)

MR. ARMSON: Well, then, if the Senator is not in, I am going to
ask Mr. Youngquist, assistant attorney general of the state, to make
a statement of the purpose of the conference tomorrow morning.

(No response)

MR. ARMSON: Well, I better go at it myself. As I said just now,
some thirty-odd states of the forty-eight are affected by the recent
decisions of the Supreme Court in the taxation of banks. It is a
situation that the states must meet. Just how to meet it is the problem. In Minnesota we feel perhaps that the best way to meet it is
to secure an amendment to Section 5219, the section under which
we are permitted to tax national banks. However, regardless of
the best way to meet the situation, it is our desire to meet with
representatives from the different states affected, in a brief conference tomorrow morning in a room across the hall, just to the left
from where we are meeting today, our purpose being to make it a
brief session so that we shall be through with our conference before the general session meets at 10 o'clock tomorrow morning.
Meet at 9 o'clock.

Now, let me extend an invitation to every delegate, for that
matter, and particularly to the gentlemen representing the states
that are affected by these decisions. You are affected in Colorado,
Mr. Link, although you don't think so. California, I think, is more
seriously affected than any. Massachusetts is affected in another
way; Ohio is affected very much.

Here is Mr. Youngquist now. He was sitting there all the time.
Now, Mr. Youngquist, will you just explain briefly the purpose?

GEORGE A. YOUNGQUIST (Minnesota): I think everything has
been said that need be said. Something more than thirty of the
states of the Union are affected by the decisions of the Supreme
Court. The only effective way to meet those decisions is to secure
from Congress an amendment of Section 5219. That amendment
can be secured only by the concerted action of all the states affected,
and it is for the purpose of planning that action that we are asking
you to meet tomorrow morning in the room across the hall at 9
o'clock. A more complete explanation will be made then. It would
not be just to encroach any further upon this evening's program.

CHAIRMAN MATTHEWS: The subject of the Senator's address,
"The Problem of Tax Exemptions," is now open for general discussion.

FRANKLIN S. EDMONDS (Pennsylvania): Mr. Chairman, the Pennsylvania Tax Commission in the course of its four years of work found precisely the same conclusions for Pennsylvania that Senator Mastick has presented so well for New York. We found that the exempt realty ran from 12 to 20 per cent, that it was increasing rapidly. We had one class of exemptions which I think they have not in New York, namely, the realty used by public utilities in the actual exercise of their franchise. And we found also that this tendency to exempt institutions was causing a serious physical difficulty with some of our taxing units.

We set forth in our report 12 taxing districts in which the exempt realty was above 50 per cent, running as high as 85 per cent, which of course meant that the balance of the realty had to stand the entire expense of local government.

We put a reference in our report to a bit of correspondence between Benjamin Franklin and Robert Morris in the days before the Revolution, when Franklin was sent over to England to protest against the land of the proprietor in Pennsylvania being exempt from local taxation, and Franklin writes to Morris.

It seems to me that society is very much like a club, and every one who wants the benefits of society ought to be willing to pay the dues of the club. If he is not willing to pay the dues he might remove himself to some desert island.

Now, without going through a repetition of what has been so well said by the Senator from New York, I want merely to refer to three recommendations which were made in our report.

The first was that land owned by the state used for general state purposes should pay a contribution of 15 cents per acre to the local government for schools, and 10 cents per acre for highway purposes. A bill embodying that recommendation was approved by the legislature in both branches, I think unanimously, but was vetoed by the Governor, because there was no provision for the fund in the budget.

The second recommendation, following the lines of the law that I think Mr. Blodgett has introduced in Connecticut some years back, was that wherever there was a piece of exempt realty it must justify its exemption once every three years. We found several cases in which realty had been exempt originally for proper purposes, and when once marked exempt it stayed exempt, although the use of the realty might have changed. In order to plug up that hole that bill was suggested. It passed one branch of the legislature, failed in the second branch, and probably will come up again.

The third suggestion carried with it the strong recommendation of the commission, but we recognized that it was a complete change of the fiscal policy of the state, which was that all privately owned realty exempt from local taxation should have the exemption limited to the improvement alone, and that the land itself, the land value itself, should pay a tax at the normal rate of the district. That was for the purpose of meeting the situation where the exemptions are so bunched together as to seriously cripple the financing of the local district itself.

I merely present this experience from Pennsylvania because it is rather interesting to find that practically every sentence and every conclusion of the excellent address which the Senator has given us has been borne out in the experience of a neighboring state.

WILLIAM A. HOUGH (Indiana): I have listened with a great deal of interest to the very able paper that has been read on this subject. The exemption of property from taxation is one of the three great problems that must be solved. The growth of tax-exempt property is becoming a threatening menace, I think, in all of the states of the Union.

In our state we have twenty-six sections of the statute, each one of which exempts from taxation some particular class of property; and our legislature never meets, but what some group or other is there with their hands out asking to have some particular class of property exempted from taxation, with very plausible arguments, based upon the constitutional inhibitions which exist against laws which might be made by our legislature.

In 1921 there was a very harmless bill introduced in our legislature which provided that all of the property, both real and personal, owned by the Young Men's Christian Association should be exempt, and some thoughtful gentleman who was on the committee to which the bill was referred suggested that if property owned by the Young Men's Christian Association was exempt from taxation, property owned by the Young Women's Christian Association should also be exempt from taxation; and that waked up a little contingent in our legislature, which does not need anybody's guardianship in regard to financial matters, and forthwith there was introduced another amendment to the bill providing that all property, both real and personal, owned by the Young Men's Hebrew Association should also be exempted from taxation; and that awakened another group, and there was another amendment added to the bill which provided that all property, both real and personal, owned by the Knights of Columbus should also be exempted from taxation.

Well, they had about enough votes to pass a bill by that time. But talk about your club, my brother, there was a club in the face of the legislature with an enormous number of votes back of them, and they passed the bill exempting the property.

In 1925 the owners of orchards in our state came to the conclusion that they were engaged in a great and philanthropic enterprise; they were providing food for the people; it was a new industry in the great State of Indiana; they tacked an amendment on the bill in regard to the assessment of real estate providing that all real estate should be assessed without consideration of the value of growing crops and orchards located thereon. Just the year before that 52 acres of land in my county, 63 miles from my home town, had been sold for $47,000, and when the tax assessor went around to eliminate the value of the orchard on that farm, it was assessed for taxation at $9000. He left the orchard off.

We thought the bill was unconstitutional, and we took it up with the attorney general, and the attorney general was anxious to find whether the legislature, in passing the bill, really had some good purpose in mind, and he decided that the legislature really meant that the orchards should be assessed as personal property instead of real estate; so, having no other alternative, we proceeded to order a reassessment of all these orchards.

We found that peach orchards selling for $1000 an acre had been cut down to $100 an acre, and apple orchards the same; and we had many fruit growers in our office objecting to this terrible burden that was being placed upon the enterprise, people who were developing a new industry in our state, but we finally did get the orchards all assessed as personal property.

Now, we have this sort of a situation before us: A man sells his farm, we have got his orchard all assessed as personal property, but he cannot take the personal property off the farm when he sells it.

The same legislature passed another law exempting a large part of our property from taxation. It passed a law providing that no contract or lease, in which no obligation was placed upon the lessee, should be subject to taxation. They found out that they could sell a piece of real estate, get one-third paid down, and then take a provisory contract that if the man paid the balance down, with interest and assessments of all kinds, and insurance, without compelling him to do so by the terms of the contract, then he would have a deed to the property.

We had instances of this kind: A man would want to borrow $10,000 on a farm that was, maybe, worth $16,000 or $17,000—you know how willing farmers are to borrow money, if somebody will provide it for them—somebody would say, "Look here, we can save a little something on this transaction; you deed me your farm, and I will make you a contract that when you pay me back this money, with interest, and the taxes on the farm, and the insurance, I will deed you the farm back."

We had a case that was just decided this last week by the Circuit Court of Marion County, involving the taxation of these contracts, and the court held that the law was unconstitutional. Is my time up?

CHAIRMAN MATTHEWS: You have two minutes more.

21

WILLIAM A. HOUGH (continuing) : There is absolutely no property that ought to be exempt from taxation unless it is devoted to a public use. That is the rule. It is a simple thing to decide whether property is devoted to the public use.

I belong to the Mystic Shrine and the Scottish Rite and other organizations that have millions of dollars of property exempt from taxation, and none of that property is used for public purposes. That ought to be the measure of the exemption of property. I cannot agree with the author of the able paper this evening, that if a state owns property in my county, that it ought to pay taxes on it to the county, because if that law were enacted it would result in my county having to pay taxes on similar property in other counties, and after all it would amount to nothing. All property municipally owned ought to be exempt from taxation, in my judgment, and no other property, excepting such as is devoted to a public use and is open to the public. Thank you.

JENS P. JENSEN (Kansas) : We have heard this question of exemption being used to encourage industries. The Kansas legislature passed a bill permitting cities, if they wanted to, to exempt industries, to encourage them to locate. The Governor fortunately vetoed it, for reasons good and sufficient to himself. I wonder if anybody knows of any good case where such exemption really has encouraged the location of *bona fide* industries. Aren't we really facing some will-of-the-wisp where we are trying to get industries to locate by means of temporary exemption, whether it is an exemption of personal property in the way of merchandise or real property?

I had a student once who tried to get some information on that. I tried to help him. We wrote to some people in New York asking whether or not this housing proposition had done any good. Some said it did a lot of good; some said it had not done any good but all sorts of harm.

I cannot for the life of me find out any *bona fide* case where any good has been done. I wonder if anybody knows of such a case.

CHAIRMAN MATTHEWS: We have another subject to take up this evening. The time is getting away from us. The other item on the program is Standardization and Simplification of Business Taxes, the report of the committee of the National Tax Association, which will be presented by Charles W. Gerstenberg, chairman.

CHARLES W. GERSTENBERG: While these pieces of paper are being distributed I should like to say that we have prepared a comparison of the federal income tax, the New York State personal income tax, the model draft personal income tax, the model draft business income tax, and we have enough copies for everybody to take one. There is no necessity for passing those out now, but they will be all here, and you can get them after the meeting.

We thought that the way to get action tonight was to start some action and ask everybody to do something, so I am going to ask you all to take out your pencils and do some writing on this piece of paper.

First, let me say this: Resolutions were prepared hurriedly and brought here in this form, so that we should be sure to have them. The committee then went into conference and decided that the resolutions were not just exactly what the committee felt they should be, but I have had them passed out to you, and if you will just make these few changes you will have the resolutions. (Indicating changes.)

I have been a college professor for a great many years, and my memory is not as good as it should be; that is one of the prerogatives of the college professor; and all that is in spite of my youthful appearance. I may have told this joke before, but it is an appropriate one:

An evangelist was addressing an audience in one of the southern states, and a country lout called out, "I don't believe a word you say unless you perform a miracle." And the evengelist went right on, and the lout called out several times, "We want a miracle." Finally the evangelist got down from his platform, proceeded to the place where the lout was, took him by the back of the neck, led him to the flap of the tent, and planted a good kick, and said, "Did you feel that?" He said, "Indeed, I did." And the evangelist said, "It would be a miracle if you didn't." Then he came back and addressed the audience in this way: "Brothers and Sisters, the church may have lost the power of performing miracles, but it has not lost the power of casting out devils."

Last year we tried to do our share towards casting out some devils, and I am afraid this year we are trying to perform miracles; but we don't want to attempt that unless we get your cooperation and your consent, and so, at the end of this paper, as chairman of the committee, I am going to move a motion, and I hope that the rumpus will then begin.

STANDARDIZATION AND SIMPLIFICATION OF BUSINESS TAXES

Report of Committee of the National Tax Association, C. W. Gerstenberg, *Chairman*

Last year the committee on standardization and simplification of business taxes rendered a report that outlined the difficulties arising from the present chaos of diverse systems of business taxation and made certain tentative suggestions as to what should be done to remedy the evil. This present report is a report of progress and not of committee action. The members of the committee have been so scattered that conference meetings could not be held and the chairman of the committee, on whom naturally fell the task of preparing a report for conference, by correspondence, found it impossible to prepare a tentative draft early enough in the year to submit it to the members of the committee to get their views and incorporate them. It has seemed wise, therefore, instead of postponing a report for another year, for the chairman to prepare this document and submit it as a report of progress, rather than as an expression of opinion of the committee.

It appears that what is necessary at this time is to bring together the results of our past conferences; first, to save time in going over ground that has been covered in the past; second, to make available in compact form for future progress, the results of past discussion, and finally to lay the foundation for definite action. This procedure will also enable those who were not members of the association five years and more ago, to know what has previously been accomplished and thus the association may get from these new members, many of whom represent taxpayers, rather than administrators, the benefit of their views.

It will be recalled that at the tenth annual conference, held at Indianapolis in 1916, a resolution was passed calling upon the association to appoint " a committee to prepare a plan of a model system of state and local taxation." This resolution was probably prompted by a paper read by Professor Charles J. Bullock on " The State Income Tax and the Classified Property Tax " and the discussion thereon.[1] In 1917 the committee made a preliminary report [2] tentatively indicating that a combination of income and property taxes was desirable, as well as some separate form of business taxation. Dr. Adams read a paper on " The Taxation of Business " [3] which really should be included as an appendix to that preliminary report. In that paper Professor Adams advocated a separate income tax on business units, and proposed a division of the entire amount of net income of national businesses on the basis of property and pay-roll.

No action was taken on this report and apparently there was no discussion. On account of the war, no conference was held in 1918.

In 1919 a very complete report was rendered, although it was again called a preliminary report. The committee signing the report consisted of four members of state tax commissions, one university professor, one railroad man and Mr. Ogden L. Mills. Professor Adams, who did not take part in the deliberations of the committee, said of the report: " I regard this report as one of the

---

[1] For digest see Blakey's *Digest and Index*, p. 140.

[2] *Proceedings*, Vol. XI, pp. 183-4.

[3] *Proceedings*, Vol. XI, pp. 185-194.

wisest and most helpful statements ever published concerning the proper structure of the tax system of the American states." [4]

There seems to be no good reason why the present committee should not adopt this report and take it as a starting point. The report conforms with the recommendations made by the committee last year, and I may say that probably the conclusions and even the contents of that earlier report were not consciously in the minds of the members of the present committee when they made their report last year. It would appear therefore that the present committee is in substantial agreement with the earlier committee and that, as indicated above, what can best be done now is to bring before the conference a brief outline of this earlier report and the comments made upon it.

ANALYSIS OF THE REPORT OF 1919

The report was divided into eleven parts. In the first two parts general principles were laid down as follows:

A model system must meet these six requirements:

1. Yield sufficient revenue.
2. Be easy to administer.
3. Be adapted to our system of dual government.
4. Respect constitutional limitations or point to reasonable constitutional amendments.
5. Recommend itself as a basis for general agreement.
6. Conform to past experiences and present trends.

Three canons of taxation were expounded:

1. " Every person having some taxable ability should pay some sort of a direct personal tåx."
2. " Tangible property should pay for protection in the juris-diction where it is located."
3. " Business carried on for profit in any locality should be taxed for the benefits it receives."

The committee then proposed a system of three taxes, which taken together would satisfy these three canons:

1. A personal income tax.
2. A property tax.
3. A business tax.

It would seem that the present committee should confine its atten-tion to the third tax, the business tax. But this is impossible, just as it is impossible to understand the functioning of any part of our body, without considering the relation of that part of the body to the entire human anatomy.

---

[4] *Proceedings*, Vol. XII, p. 470.

These problems arise:

(1) Should there be a separate personal income tax, as well as a business tax?

(2) Should the separate business tax be one on net income?

(3) Should all businesses, however organized, whether individually owned, or owned by partnerships or corporations, pay the same kind of tax?

(4) Should there be a property tax where there is an income tax?

(5) If there is a property tax, should it be levied on tangible personalty as well as on realty?

It will be seen that all these questions affect what the present committee is considering—standardization and simplification of business taxation. The answers to these questions are given in the report that we have been analyzing — the report presented to the conference in 1919.

The principle of taxing each man who has tax-paying power was met by four possible methods, of which one was deemed superior. They were:

1. Poll tax. 2. Capital levy—that is a tax on a man's net fortune. 3. Presumptive income tax, measured by some such index as the rent paid. 4. Net income tax, which was declared superior. The nature of this tax was outlined and a model tax was later prepared.

The property tax on all tangible property was not clearly defined, but it is sufficient for our purpose to say that it was recommended that it be levied on all tangible property at the place where the property is located, though it was pointed out that in some states it may seem preferable to exempt all personal property. In passing, it may be noted that if this were done, in some states certain forms of personal property, such as paintings and other collections which yield no current monetary income, would escape all taxation and therefore bear none of the governmental burden of the cost of protecting it. On the other hand the owner of the property has no more ability to pay a tax because of his ownership of that property, but he would likely pay for its protection through his personal income tax.[5]

The older committee's report examined quite carefully the problem of the taxation of public utilities and of banks in relation to the problem of property taxation, but since we are to confine our attention to ordinary business taxes we may pass over that part of the report.

[5] This would be true only if the personal property were actually located in the same state in which the owner is domiciled.

BUSINESS TAXES

In introducing the question of business taxes the older report lays stress on the fact that a business tax is necessary " to reconcile in a satisfactory manner the legitimate claims of the several states of the American Union" and to prevent unjust double taxation, while at the same time giving weight to the just claims of the several state governments, first over the persons that owe allegiance to them, and second over the business operations to which they give protection and aid.

Eight possible business taxes were named and these were then classified into three groups:

(1) Taxes of fixed amount, which may be uniform throughout the state or be classified on the basis of the size of the town where the business is carried on. These taxes, illustrated by the occupation taxes of some of the Southern states, were regarded as inequitable, since they pay no attention to the varying sizes of businesses or the amounts of benefits received.

(2) Taxes based on external indicia of profits, such as gross receipts, rentals, number of employees or of machines used, amount of raw materials used or of goods purchased, were considered as being tolerably equitable, especially when used in combination, but were deemed objectionable from an administration standpoint, because to combine the indicia and thus achieve an equitable result would lead to confusion and trouble.

(3) The only tax left therefore was the tax on the net income of the business.

ADVANTAGES OF TRIPLE SYSTEM

This threefold system of taxation, it is pointed out, would have these advantages:

(1) It meets all the demands of the state and permits proper distribution of the tax burden on business carried on in different states.

(2) In the triple system, "such inevitable inequalities as arise in the working of any one tax may be, and to a considerable extent must be, offset or mitigated by inequalities arising from the others."

(3) The combination of property and income taxes places a heavier burden on funded income, where it belongs, without the cumbersome provisions that would be required to achieve the same result, were the income taxes to stand alone.

The report points out that the personal income tax is to be levied on all income at the place of domicile, and the business tax " should be levied equally upon all business carried on within the state, under whatever form of organization it is conducted."

The remainder of the report deals with administration. Before proceeding with this subject of administration, we may follow through the history of the report as it deals with the kinds of taxes to be imposed in the model system. The report was not commented on further in the Chicago convention of 1919 at which it was read, but the effect it made on the conference was indicated by the fact that a resolution offered by the resolutions committee to thank the committee on a model system, unlike most of the other resolutions offered at the same time, was adopted by a rising vote.[6]

Model Drafts

In 1920, at the conference held at Salt Lake City, a draft of the personal income tax which had been compiled in conformity with the previous report by Henry H. Bond, Esq., formerly an income tax deputy of Massachusetts, was presented in printed form to the conference and there explained and discussed. Unfortunately the draft is not available in the proceedings, and moreover it must be noted that the draft of the model personal income tax was the work of Mr. Bond, who did not have the benefit of conferences with the old or with any other committee on model taxation. However, a note in the *Proceedings,* Vol. XIII, p. 283, indicates that the committee subsequently worked on this model, and that as it was modified by the committee it appeared in the *Bulletin* for January, 1921. The draft was discussed at the conference in papers by Professor Lutz, by Commissioner Mark Graves of New York, by the State Income Tax Director of Massachusetts, Mr. Irving L. Shaw, and by Mr. Frank D. Strader, Auditor of Wisconsin returns. Questions of detail were discussed; it will be noted, however, that not the business tax, but the personal income tax was before the conference.

During the next interim between conferences, a model business tax bill was compiled by Mr. Bond and Mr. George Holmes. This, with the personal income tax model the old committee on model taxation had discussed, and their conclusions in the form of an original and amended draft, were printed and in the latter form were in the hands of the delegates at the 14th annual conference, held at Bretton Woods, New Hampshire, in 1921. The details of the drafts were discussed until 11 o'clock in the evening.[7] A committee which had been appointed to tackle separately the problem of allocation of business income among the states where a business was carried on among the states, merely reported progress and was continued.[8] In passing, it must be noted that up to this time prac-

[6] *Proceedings,* Vol. XII, p. 529.

[7] *Proceedings,* Vol. XIV, p. 101.

[8] The problem of allocation was, in fact, divided between two committees, one considering manufacturing and mercantile businesses, and the other interstate public utilities. Both committees were continued. *Proceedings,* Vol. XIV, p. 474.

tically no adverse word was said as to the general principles of the triple form of taxation. One dissenting voice was heard on the question of taxing all businesses alike, the argument being made that corporations should be taxed separately for the special privileges enjoyed.[9] As to this point it seems to us that if the corporation does have some special privilege, its value is undoubtedly reflected somewhat in its net income. We must not forget either that the benefit is not altogether on the side of the corporation. If governments did not create corporations, many businesses now in existence would never have been organized or developed and society would have lost the benefits of large-scale production, an item of much more importance than the taxes which the state could hope to collect on the privilege of limited liability.[10] Moreover, it will be noted that beyond discussing the drafts, the conference took no action.

WHAT HAS BEEN DONE WITH THE MODEL DRAFTS?

The model drafts again came before the 15th annual conference held in 1922 at Minneapolis. Only one person gave a careful analysis and that was directed at details.[11] During the discussion practically no objection was raised as to the principle of advocating a personal income tax law at the domicile of the person, a property tax on tangible property at its situs, and a business tax on net income of business where it is carried on.

At that same conference the committee on the apportionment between states of taxes on mercantile and manufacturing businesses made its report. This report and certain recommendations annexed thereto are to be found in the *Proceedings*, Vol. XV, pp. 198-215.

If we concede that a net income tax is the one correct business tax, then we must recognize that the construction of a proper allocation fraction to apportion net income of an interstate business equitably among the states is of prime importance. The committee on the allocation fraction in effect redrafted parts of the model business tax law dealing with the subject of allocation.[12] The re-

---

[9] *Proceedings*, Vol. XIV, p. 79.

[10] See " Business and Property Taxes " by E. Isaacs, *Yale Law Journal*, Dec. 1926, and Opinion of Justices, 138 Atl. 284, 286 (an opinion on proposed bills in the State of New Hampshire).

[11] *Proceedings*, Vol. XV, pp. 292-301; Blakey, *Digest and Index*, p. 143.

[12] " The problem of apportioning income derived by mercantile and manufacturing business conducted in more than one state has been greatly increased as the tax basis has been shifted from capital stock to income. States have not developed any complete plans of tax apportionment as yet. Different localities need different distribution systems. At the one extreme we find states where manufacturing predominates and the basis of a location of tangible property alone seems justifiable; at the other extreme are found

port was a carefully considered exposition of the principles and problems involved and was discussed at some length; it was highly commended by the chairman of the committee on model system, Professor Bullock. It is significant, however, that when a resolution was passed in reference thereto, the resolution did not urge the formula of the committee but urged " the adoption of a uniform rule by states, calculated to fairly and equitably apportion such net business income." In other words, the resolution did not achieve any definite concrete results. However, we may for the present consider this problem of allocation as one of detail in the proper administration of a net income tax on business as such, and so, for the present we will pass it with all other details.

We then come to the conference of 1923, that known as the 16th Annual Conference held at White Sulphur Springs. All that was done at this conference was the reading of a very able paper by Mr. A. S. James, which will be found digested in the Blakey *Digest* at page 144. In the main, Mr. James reiterated the principles in the original report of the model system committee and subscribed to them. Certain advantages in certain cases of a tax on personal property over tax on income were pointed out, and some changes in the details of the income tax law were suggested.

With 1923 the work of the model committee apparently came to an end. What, then, is the result?

1. A triple form of taxation was urged as a model and no dissenting voice to this plan was heard, except as to minor questions.

2. Two bills were drafted, one for a personal income tax and one for a business tax. The details of these bills were criticized and no conclusion drawn, so that we may say that this conference has never finally adopted and recommended model bills. No resolution of adoption was ever passed.

states where merchandising predominates and a basis of sales seems justifiable.

" It is essential to have a uniform method of apportionment in all states and, hence, a compromise system must be worked out. No correct method can be devised, as all results will be arbitrary. The commission recommends that a uniform mathematical formula for the apportionment of the net trading profit be incorporated in the statute of each state. Such a rule must consider both property and business, and the committee recommends a fifty-fifty basis, only tangible property to be considered. The business factor should be measured by the sums paid out by the taxpayers for wages, salaries and purchases, plus the amount of the receipts from the sale of the goods and products dealt in.

" No distinction should be made between resident and non-resident persons in regard to the business tax. It should be applicable to all trading profit of manufacturing and mercantile concerns. In regard to the personal income tax, the committee suggests an additional section to the model personal income tax, providing for a credit for taxes paid on activities outside of the state if they are taxed by said other state." Blakey's *Digest and Index*, pp. 127-128.

3. Parts of the model bills dealing with allocation were redrafted by a special committee. The redrafted provisions were discussed, but no resolution adopting these provisions on behalf of the association or of the conference was ever passed.

If agreement can be achieved on the general principles, and if a model draft of a personal income tax and of a business tax can be adopted, there would still remain some work to be done on the property taxes. It would probably be impossible to make any considerable progress in the direction of the adoption of uniform property tax laws. But certain relatively simple principles could be recommended by this conference, with the hope and expectation that they would be adopted by an increasing number of jurisdictions. The great and disturbing problems of property tax—those of valuation—affect tax administrators as a body more than they affect taxpayers as a body, and for that reason the administrator has given most attention to those problems. After all, however, taxpaying is the business of the taxpayer and his problems should be the subject of consideration. It is the effect of taxation on him that in the long run is going to determine the success of a tax system. If he is satisfied, administration of the system, whatever it is, will be relatively easier; if he is dissatisfied, administration is going continually to have to scratch its head and try to make progress with one leg tied to litigation in the courts.

It would seem, therefore, that the administrator should come from behind the tapestry where his work goes on and stand with the taxpayer on the other side to see the effect of his work. The present effect is that of confusion, lack of intelligent design. To remedy the situation a touch here and a touch there, while not as efficacious as a brand-new design, will do very much to bring about a more uniform result. For example, to reiterate what was suggested last year, the business man may reasonably expect these few principles to be applied to property taxation:

1. Intangible property should not be taxed, except as it is reached through the income taxes; to tax intangibles is to invite the confusion arising from the difficulty of trying to fix the situs of such property and to incur the risk of legalizing its location in several places.

2. All property should be assessed throughout the country as of a certain day, and should be payable within a certain period after that day; to do otherwise places a premium on window-dressing and complicates the taxpayers' problems.

3. All assessments of a given piece of property for all purposes should be made in a single bill in order that a single payment to a single individual may discharge the tax liability of that property. After all, every municipal entity is a division of the state; it should

be the business of the state to protect the people for whom these entities are created, against an unnecessary nuisance or detriment to which the existence of these entities may and does give rise.

Since the working-out of these principles is a matter of detail it would seem wise not to ask the conference to go on record with a resolution in respect to them at this time. They are reported here, that the members may have their attention directed to them, to the end that when some definite plan of putting them into operation is suggested, we may learn from the members the difficulties likely to be encountered and the means by which they best can be overcome.

What is to be Done Now?

It would appear that the time has come when this conference should, if possible, go on record as to general principles and should urge on all its members a study of the details of the model bills and a comparison with the laws of leading states, in order that we may definitely recommend to state legislatures a model system of personal and business taxation that will lead us to standardization and, through standardization, to simplification.

To this end the following resolutions are proposed as a basis for immediate action:

RESPECTING STANDARDIZATION AND SIMPLIFICATION OF BUSINESS TAXES

Moved (1) That it is the sense of this session of this conference that the states employ a system of taxation involving the elimination of all taxes except, (1) a personal income tax levied at the domicile, on all the income of the individual, subject to constitutional limitations; (2) property taxes on tangible property levied at the situs thereof; (3) a business tax on the net income of business carried on within the state, apportioned on the basis of a uniform rule to each of the several states where the business is conducted; (4) death duties, and (5) special taxes relating to financial institutions, public utilities and the extractive industries, as well as such special taxes as are specially adapted to the primary industries of a state or as are peculiarly suitable to the needs for which revenue is sought.

Moved (2) That at the next annual conference an entire day be set apart for a discussion of the several clauses of the model income tax bills, to the end that such conference may, if possible, agree upon model income tax bills *in toto*, or bills with alternative clauses suggested by minority votes of at least a reasonable proportion of the conference, the proportion entitling a minority to an expression of its views in a minority report to be fixed by said conference at the opening of its deliberations on this question.

There has been abundance of talking; what is now needed is *action*. In 1922 Professor Bullock said: "We did not take up that plan of a model system of state and local taxation until this association was nine years old, ... and until there developed among the members a very well-defined demand that the association do something to give articulate expression to the ideas of income and classified property and business taxation . . . . that had been engaging our attention at nine successive conferences." His committee, he pointed out, "was appointed in response to a spontaneous demand developed at the Indianapolis conference in 1916, that something be done to bring to a head all these things that we have been discussing year after year at our annual meetings."

Ten years and more have gone by. During the first six or seven years, as much was accomplished as might be expected, but in the past few years the work has again fallen into discussions of unrelated problems and there is danger that the work of the past will be lost in a maze of disconnected suggestions, rambling criticisms and discursive discussion. In order to retrieve it and to enable us to go forward in a scientific and well-rounded manner, this report has sought to refresh the memories of old members and to enlighten the minds of new members on what has transpired in our conferences looking to a solution of the problem of standardization and simplification.

CHARLES W. GERSTENBERG: Now I think our discussion can proceed a little bit more to the point. If I may be permitted at this time, may I say that in making this motion we are not binding the conference. The committee is merely trying to get the sense of the opinion of you members in your presence. If you think that this model system is a good system, the committee will be glad to go ahead and work on the details; but we certainly do not want to spend a year or, as the other committee did, three or four years to find at the end the principle is wrong and that you are going to turn our work into the waste-paper basket. We are glad to work on the details of any kind of a model system that you approve, but we are unwilling to give our time to chasing rainbows. You won't hurt our feelings one bit if you do not pass these resolutions as they are. If you think that some other model system is the correct one, why, tell us, that is what we should like to know.

We should like to have rather a unanimous vote, however, so that we won't run up against the absence next year of some of those who contributed to a majority vote at this time.

We do not commit any state to pass all the laws. We say the uniform principle of standardization and simplification would still be served if all of these exceptions were made.

The second part of that motion is merely to get some action definitely next time.

HENRY M. GOLDFOGLE (New York) : May I say a word on this excellently prepared paper on exemption? I fear my silence might be misunderstood, so I rise now to add my words of commendation to those expressed heretofore, as to the well-prepared and excellent paper read by Senator Mastick.

The City of New York is particularly interested in that subject. We have reached a point in New York City where we would call a halt upon the increase of exemptions. At the present time the total assessed value of exempted property approximates four and one-half billions.

In so far as the exemption under the act which provides for partial exemption of new buildings is concerned, we have reached the enormous figure of $916,000,000.

I am not going to discuss whether the bill providing for such exemption was altogether wise or unwise. Undoubtedly it stimulated building at the time it was passed. But, as Senator Mastick very wisely suggested, groups formed and were enabled to get into the bill a provision that exempted partially buildings of magnificent type, on the finest of streets and the best of avenues, so that buildings in which tenants pay for apartments as much as $10,000 to $20,000 per annum are partially exempted from taxation.

I want to join Senator Mastick in his declaration that we ought to find some way of calling a halt on legislation adding to exemptions, and creating thereby unequal burdens on the general taxpayer.

DELEGATE: I rise to second the motion of Dr. Gerstenberg on the adoption of these suggestions.

CHARLES W. GERSTENBERG: Perhaps, Mr. Chairman—I was just reminded—instead of having moved the adoption of those motions I should have done the regular thing and moved the acceptance of the report; so, I move the acceptance of the report.

CHAIRMAN GRAVES: We have two motions before us.

CHARLES W. GERSTENBERG: I withdraw the first one.

CHAIRMAN GRAVES: Do you consent to the withdrawal of the first motion?

SECOND: Yes, sir.

CHAIRMAN GRAVES: You have heard the motion of Dr. Gerstenberg that the report as read be accepted; is there any discussion?

(Call for the question)

(Ayes and Noes)

(Motion carried)

CHARLES W. GERSTENBERG: I now renew the motion.

CHAIRMAN GRAVES: This motion is now before the house. What is your pleasure? The subject is open for discussion. It occurs to me that this is a matter of sufficient importance to warrant some discussion. It rather seems to me that we should not adopt a motion in a perfunctory manner, on a matter of such importance as this.

MR. A. G. MACKENZIE (Utah): Mr. Chairman and Ladies and Gentlemen: Our state cannot approve at this time of items one and three of the amendment. I do not rise to discuss this question on its merits, but rather to express the undoubted sentiment of my state on these two points.

I want to say briefly that these suggestions have been before us in many ways. They have been proposed in our legislature several times, but have never passed either house. They have been submitted several times to a referendum vote of the people of the state, and have always been defeated. Not one governor of Utah, since these matters had been agitated there, has favored it; and in view of those circumstances our state must at this time record itself as opposed to those two recommendations, one and three.

CHAIRMAN GRAVES: Mr. MacKenzie, do you see anything fundamentally unsound in the two proposals?

MR. A. G. MACKENZIE: I did not rise to suggest that. I am simply endeavoring to convey to you the undoubted sentiment of our state on these points.

MR. CLEM COLLINS (Colorado): It seems to me that the temporary complication in your state legislature need not have any particular bearing on the position we may take on this matter at the present time. However, I am a little uncertain as to what is intended by the last clause of the last insertion here. It says: " as are peculiarly suitable to the needs for which revenue is sought." I wonder if that includes the gasoline tax?

CHARLES W. GERSTENBERG: It was intended for just that, and it was thought perhaps we better not put it in by mentioning it, but there you have a gasoline tax. That is peculiarly adapted to give us revenue for repairing roads. The two things are so closely tied up that certainly no business man could feel that he was subject to a hazardous lot of taxes in paying the gasoline tax.

We also felt as to the first part of that exemption that if some state has some industry such as a severance tax, a mining tax, or something of that kind, it ought not to go on record here as outlawing such a tax.

FRANKLIN S. EDMONDS (Pennsylvania): Mr. President, there is scarcely a state in the Union which would have its fiscal system made more topsy-turvy than would Pennsylvania, by the adoption of a platform that contains these propositions. The state, up to the present, does not seem to have any sentiment in favor of a personal income tax. We do levy a property tax on tangible property and on intangibles as well, but practically every principle that is found in those first three is not found in our state; yet personally I am willing to vote for this resolution. It presents a coherent plan for a complete program.

In voting, however, for it, it would be definitely understood that I am not representing the sentiment in my state or pledging anybody to support any particular proposition, except this, we all feel the need of some sort of a standardized state program. We all feel that some program ought to be suggested. It may be corrected and eventually made a workable program. We believe that this method which the committee has adopted is the sensible method of getting to that result and therefore, like my friend from Utah, while I feel certain that my own state would not go along these lines next year or the year after that, yet I feel sure that in our state we should be glad to see a coherent program worked out that might be made the basis of a standardized state and municipal program.

THOMAS W. PAGE (District of Columbia) : Just one moment, Mr. Chairman; it seems to me that we are in a little danger here—that has been illustrated by the gentleman from Utah — of misunderstanding just what the object of this motion is that Dr. Gerstenberg has made, and I think that a clear statement of that would simplify the voting on the subject. He has an expression here, it is true, that the conference recommends to the states such a system of taxation. It is not his idea that the delegations that have come here from separate states have come empowered by the governors who appointed them, or the institutions that they represent, to promise that their states are going to follow the recommendations that are made at this conference. We are not committing any state at all in the adoption of this motion, we are simply expressing the approval of this conference of the model system and these model taxes that have been prepared, and these other suggestions that have been incorporated by Dr. Gerstenberg; we are approving those principles and we are, as Senator Edmonds has just said, setting up as a model, as a goal, as an aim, something definite, which those working along the line of tax reform in their several states, may use as a model towards which they may work. It will be years before the states adopt it as a whole. Many states probably never will adopt it as a whole. Nevertheless, it still has its value as an ideal, as a goal towards which those who really want tax reform in their respective states may aim, and it will be of great assistance to them in systematizing and clarifying the proposals for reform which they make.

We are voting, then, as I understand it—and if I am mistaken

Dr. Gerstenberg will correct me—we are voting not with the idea of committing any delegation here to the duty of trying to persuade their respective governors or legislatures at the next meeting to adopt this thing as a whole, but we are simply expressing an approval of what has been worked out by this conference, and the hope that it may be helpful to real tax-reformers in every state in the Union.

ROYAL B. CUSHING (Illinois) : I rise to ask a question. I am not a delegate. I am a member of the organization, the National Tax Association.

CHAIRMAN GRAVES: This is an open forum. You are entitled to speak, even though you are not a delegate.

MR. CUSHING: Am I entitled to vote on the question?

CHARLES W. GERSTENBERG: I think the idea is, we should like to get the sentiment of the people, and not of the conference, it would be a whole lot more helpful to us if we had the sentiment of the individuals. That certainly would not bind the conference in any way, because we are not taking any kind of a formal vote. I think what the committee would like would be a vote of everybody present.

CHAIRMAN GRAVES: The Chair will rule that anyone in the room desiring to vote on this motion has a right to do so. The conference itself acts through resolutions which must first be submitted without debate to the resolutions committee. All this purports to do is to express the sentiment of this session of this tax conference.

ROY G. BLAKEY (Minnesota) : I have merely an incidental suggestion to make. This is one of the most important suggestions that has been presented, especially if it is adopted or approved. I want to mention with respect to the second part of it that at the next annual conference an entire day be set apart for discussion of this. I don't think we have ever had a session that would be more important than that. If the general sense of that is adopted and we do have a day of such discussion, the incidental suggestion I want to make is I hope that the executive committee, or whoever decides, will set the next meeting—not in criticism of any place we have been in the past—at a very central place in the United States, so that the fullest possible attendance of everybody interested in this subject, local, state and other tax officials, may be present.

ZENAS W. BLISS (Rhode Island) : I move the following amendment under Section 3: A business tax on the net income of business carried on within the state, and so forth; I move to strike out the word " net " before " income ". The purpose of this is to prevent the exclusion of consideration of a tax on gross income, or a com-

22

bination tax on gross and net income. It seems to me that it would be a great mistake to confine that to simply the net income.

As you probably know, there are a number of states that are seriously considering business taxes on gross income, and I do not think in the consideration of this subject those states should be left out in that manner; so I move under Section 3 to strike out the word "net".

(Motion duly seconded)

CHAIRMAN GRAVES: Governor Bliss has moved, and his motion has been seconded, that we strike out the word "net" before the word "income" in the item marked 3, so that it will read a business tax on the income, not the net income. That amendment is open to discussion. Does anyone wish to speak on that proposition to amend? If not, are you ready for the question?

(Call for the question)

(Ayes and Noes)

(Motion carried)

CHAIRMAN GRAVES: The motion is carried.

JOHN E. BRINDLEY (Iowa): I just want to ask a question here. If we vote on this, I think it is clear, is it not, that we are going on record in favor of a personal income tax, of course, in each of the states, in addition to the present federal income tax. Is that not true, Doctor?

CHAIRMAN GRAVES: We are expressing it as the sense of this meeting.

MR. BRINDLEY: I understand that a state tax system should embrace among other things a personal income tax?

CHAIRMAN GRAVES: Precisely.

CHARLES W. GERSTENBERG: May I answer this last question? My own notion is that we come to these meetings and people at home know we go to them; they want to know what we are talking about and what we are doing; and some day some person would like to have a change in the taxes of the state, would like to know how the taxes might be changed, and they come and say, "Now, you have been attending all these meetings; what does the National Tax Association suggest to us that we ought to do?" The National Tax Association is not going out to the states tonight, or even if we adopted a resolution in the resolutions committee, and say, "You ought to scrap all that you have done and adopt this thing." We stand right here and say, "If you come to the National Tax Association and would like to know what sort of a thing you can do, if you want to give up your present tax system and start fresh and get something new; after a period of sixteen or seventeen years' talking we have put this out as a standard." "If you have problems that impel you to remain exactly where you are, we do not urge you to change."

Certainly we ought not to go on forever without something that we can definitely recommend.

It has been known that I was chairman of this committee, and I have received requests the last two years from a number of gentlemen in several states on the question of what they ought to do. They want to revise. Now, would it not be very nice if this association could get down to brass tacks and say, "Here is the result of twenty years of deliberation; it is not final." Even this model bill is a human document; each year we will probably come here and move amendments, but let us get some place.

So, I hope I have given you the answer. We are not asking your state to change to this law, but if you are dissatisfied with your system and would like to know what this association considers as a system, to which you may aim, here is something that we propose. We don't say your system is the worst for your state. If you want to get some place, we will all work finally towards the same end if this National Tax Association has something definite.

H. M. PEYSER (New York): I venture the thought that the result of the committee's deliberation, followed by the recording of the sense of this meeting, as expressed in the resolution or the motion just unanimously approved, with the result of the committee's labors during the year, be set forth in pamphlet form and mailed to the members of the conference, and in addition to the heads of the various state governments, a reasonable time before the next conference, so that an apportunity would then be afforded to various delegates to offer suggestions of value or criticisms, if they prefer, or such other action as they would deem necessary, so that the brass-tacks scheme would be endorsed by men knowing what they are doing.

CHARLES W. GERSTENBERG: I think Mr. Peysér's suggestion is absolutely indispensable; and it was probably for the lack of following out that program that the model committee did not get any further. In my report I pointed out that Mr. Bond had drawn the model bill and apparently not even the members of the committee had seen it at the time of the conference. Certainly if we adopt these resolutions tonight the committee should be instructed that within six months the model bill should be in shape, should be printed and be sent out, and there ought to be at least four or five months intervening between that time and the time when we come to discuss it.

CHAIRMAN GRAVES: Any further discussion of the question before the house?

E. M. TROWERN (Ontario): May I ask, as a member from Canada, although a member of your association, to be excused from voting, for reasons which you all know?

CHAIRMAN GRAVES: The Chairman will be very happy to excuse you from voting.
Any further discussion? Are you ready for the question?

(Call for the question)

JOHN E. BRINDLEY (Iowa): I do not care to vote on the proposition.

CHAIRMAN GRAVES: If any of you feel reluctant to vote either for or against, remain silent.

R. A. VANDEGRIFT (California): I should like to express publicly my inability to vote intelligently on this resolution. The committee has had some time to study it and present us a resolution, and by putting in the amendments they have already changed it. I have my doubts if a very large percentage here can vote intelligently on it. I cannot, and I ask to be excused in casting my vote.

JOHN E. BRINDLEY (Iowa): I feel exactly the same way about it. I want to be perfectly frank about the thing. I am trying to do the best I can to prepare a report for our state, and we have been working on it now for more than a year. I do not want to be prejudging as to what the report would contain at this time, and I am in doubt personally, as the gentleman who has just spoken, as to the wisdom of hasty action on as comprehensive a set of resolutions as this. I am in harmony with the general spirit; but that is the reason I do not care to vote on the proposition.

REINHOLD HEKELER (New York): As a member of this committee I was working on these suggestions. I think that there are many men here who are confused as to the purpose of the vote. As I see it, this committee merely feels that it would like to know if there are enough men here who think we are on the right track. If we are not on the right track we want to know it; and we want to go ahead with this work if we are on the right track. Let us know and then we will proceed. That is the purpose of the vote.

JOHN A. ZANGERLE (Ohio): I may be mistaken, but from my knowledge of the proceedings of this association, both in the past and now, all resolutions must be sent to the resolutions committee. Now, I readily understand that this is not in the usual stereotype form of a resolution; does not resolve, but nevertheless it is a resolution and it has been so referred to by the distinguished gentleman of the committee.

CHARLES W. GERSTENBERG: May I make this suggestion, if satisfactory to everybody; that the vote be not recorded. I can see your point, and I think it is a good point to propose that the vote be not recorded. I sympathize very much with Mr. Brindley and Mr. Vandegrift. We would rather have their votes five months from now than the vote now, because we should like to know your well-considered opinion on the subject. We had hoped that the fact that this proposition had been before you for eleven years was not taking you by surprise; also, it was rather definitely called to your attention last year; but in spite of that we very much prefer to have your vote at this time the way you are pretty sure to vote next time.

May I make that definite suggestion, then, if it is suitable to the movers? I will ask that the motion be made, so that the result of the vote be not recorded.

JOHN A. ZANGERLE (Ohio): Will that change the effect?

GEORGE VAUGHAN (Arkansas): As I understand this, Dr. Gerstenberg has made it very plain, but I want to use an old Arkansas word. I think we simply want a straw vote here, in the caucus, and that this is not to go on the record as having the force of a resolution, but it will be an expression which will enable this committee to know whether to go on any further with its duties. I am going to vote for it if it is put to a vote, simply on that ground.

CHAIRMAN GRAVES: The Chair feels that perhaps too much emphasis is laid on the importance of it. The conference acts officially through its resolutions committee, through resolutions formally presented and referred to the resolutions committee.

When this was presented to me the thought occurred to me first that perhaps it should take the usual course, and then I noticed it was a motion that it was the sense of this particular session, of this particular tax conference that we are holding here this week, that these things be so and so. The Chair will rule that it is a proper motion to put if the motion is not withdrawn.

CHARLES D. ROSA (Wisconsin): I just want to say that inasmuch as this conforms fairly closely to the Wisconsin system, I can vote for it very heartily. I can vote for it tonight very heartily, and still be open to vote against the report of the model committee when it is presented later, if it does not conform to my ideas of how a model law ought to operate under these general principles.

(Call for the question)

CHAIRMAN GRAVES: Are you ready for the question?

(Call for the question)

(Ayes and Noes)

CHARLES W. GERSTENBERG: May we have a rising vote, please?

CHAIRMAN GRAVES: Those in favor of this motion please stand.

(Standing vote)

CHAIRMAN GRAVES: Those opposed please stand.

(Standing vote)

(Motion carried)

A. G. MACKENZIE (Utah): As the only member of the minority who spoke rather frankly on this subject, I just wish you to understand, as I tried to have you understand when I was talking before, that my negative vote was to those two points only that I mentioned. I do not wish you to think that I am in any sense an obstructionist, or that I do not desire a further discussion on this, or to say that I do not approve of the program; but I simply took the position I did, and still take, in deference to a sentiment in the state I represent, that has been expressed again and again and thoroughly defeated when it has been before every legislature.

CHAIRMAN GRAVES: May we have quiet? That concludes the evening program.

The chairman of the resolutions committee desires to have all members of the resolutions committee meet around the table here immediately following the adjournment.

(Adjournment)

SEVENTH SESSION

Thursday Morning, October 13, 1927

Joint Session with the Canadian Tax Conference
Mr. F. Berry Hayes, President of the Citizens'
Research Institute of Canada, Presiding.

Chairman Hayes: At this time we will go on with the program. We will call on Mr. G. R. Mickle, Mine Assessor of the Province of Ontario.

MINE TAXATION IN ONTARIO

G. R. MICKLE
Mine Assessor, Province of Ontario

The taxation of mines and mineral products in Ontario is dealt with under the Mining Tax Act, which was passed by the legislature in 1907. The original act has not undergone many changes. Of the fifty sections which it contains only eight have been amended substantially, or are new. The copy dated 1927, giving the law complete as it now stands, was passed at the last session of the legislature by repealing the whole act as it then existed and passing a new one with a few amendments of minor importance. There are no regulations or rulings or anything affecting the act which are not contained in the printed copy. It is the writer's purpose to deal with principles only as shown in the act. Three kinds of taxes are dealt with, viz., (1) natural gas tax, (2) acreage tax, (3) profit tax. Of these, the first is very simple, being merely a fixed rate on the amount of gas produced and used in Canada each year. The rate amounts to two dollars per million cubic feet. On gas wasted the rate is ten times as much, as it is not entitled to the rebate mentioned in Section 47 of the act. This proved to be a valuable feature and was the means of saving our most productive field, viz., the one in the County of Kent. As there were a number of very small producers who might be considered private and who would have added to the expense of administration, without bringing in any substantial revenue, there is an exemption on amounts where the tax would not exceed five dollars. Unfortunately the production of natural gas in Ontario is diminishing and the future does not appear to be hopeful.

(343)

ACREAGE TAX

Coming to the second tax mentioned, the acreage tax, all lands patented as mining land in Ontario are subject to this tax, unless they are situated in an organized municipality, in which case they would be liable for a tax to the municipality but not to the province.

In order to consider the acreage tax intelligently it is necessary to understand the conditions under which lands have been granted in Ontario for mining purposes. In the first regulations formed to deal with mining lands the size of the unit or "mining location," as it was called, was fixed at 10 square miles or 6400 acres. The first grant of one of these monsters was made almost exactly 75 years ago, on the 5th of October, 1852. The following year the regulations were modified, so that by securing a license which cost $100, an area not exceeding 400 acres might be bought. In 1869 an act was passed fixing the area of a mining location at 320, 160 or 80 acres. In 1892 the size was changed to 320, 160, 80 or 40 acres, and in 1906 the area was limited to 40 acres. The result of all this is that at the present time, although for over twenty years, covering the period of greatest mining activity in the province, the size of the mining claim has been limited to 40 acres, the average area of all the mining locations or claims subject to the acreage tax is over 80 acres. The fact is that the policy followed in the early days forced those who wished to secure land for mining purposes into purchasing areas which all experience since has shown are unnecessarily large.

The rate levied as acreage tax—five cents per acre—is less than it is in many places and it seems worth while to consider this and determine if possible whether that rate is a reasonable one or not. It appears to the writer that the only way we can arrive at an estimate of this is to imagine that one person who has practically infinite means at his disposal purchases all the land subject to the acreage tax at the same price as is charged by the Government at the present time, viz., $2.50 or $3 per acre, according to position. As there are over 700,000 acres contained in the taxable lands, this would make an expenditure of approximately $2,000,000. There are about 8700 claims among the patented lands, containing on the average, as stated, over 80 acres each. We will imagine that the purchaser cannot pick out the plums, such as the Creighton Mine and a few more, and abandon the rest, but is bound to thoroughly examine and where indications appear favorable enough, to explore and develop each claim. It is clear that many of these claims would have a minus or negative value, under the conditions mentioned above. To examine, explore and develop all these lands would entail an enormous expenditure and would require probably forty years to carry out the program. We will try to estimate the probable cost of the whole undertaking. The preliminary examination of the 8700 claims at, say, $500 each or $6 per acre, would cost $4,000,000, approximately. This would result probably in discarding over 80 per cent of the claims, leaving, we will say, 1600 to be further examined. We will imagine $20,000, on the average, is spent on each claim selected for further trial, making an expenditure of $32,000,000, for this stage of the operation. If we assume that 90 per cent are rejected, as a result of this work, as seems reasonable, this would leave 160 to be more intensively explored. This would involve expensive underground work which should not be undertaken unless the chance of success appears to be favorable. If the writer might be permitted to refer to a paper of his own dealing with this phase of the matter ("Value of Undeveloped Mining Claims," *Trans. Can. Inst. Mining and Metallurgy*, Vol. 8) it will be seen that the thing we have to determine is the value of the chance of the event turning out favorably, or what is called the "expectation" by the mathematicians. The "expectation" is a product of two things, viz., the chance of success multiplied by the sum to be realized in the event of success, less the cost of making the trial. In the paper referred to, the amount to be realized was put at 100 for convenience, making the unit any given value. As pointed out there, the cost of development, including interest, as it might take several years, would probably be 15 per cent of the sum to be realized. Thus, if the unit is given a value of $10,000, the sum to be realized would be 100 x $10,000, or $1,000,000, and the cost of development 15 per cent of this, or $150,000. Now if the chance of success was a certainty or unity the "expectation" would be the chance of success multiplied by the sum to be realized, less the cost of making the determination or $(1/1 \times 100)-15 = 85$. If now the chance of success is 1 in 2 or $\frac{1}{2}$, the expectation is $(\frac{1}{2} \times 100) - 15$ or 35. If it were 1 in 3 or $\frac{1}{3}$, the expectation is $(\frac{1}{3} \times 100) - 15$ or 18. Now it is evident that when the amount that must be hazarded approaches in magnitude the "expectation" as it does in this case, viz., 15 and 18, it would not be prudent to venture on the undertaking, and in the writer's opinion, where the chance of success is estimated to be less than 1 in 2, using the best knowledge and means available at the time, the serious expensive work should not be undertaken. For this reason the writer has assumed that any claim which is not considered to have at least a chance of 1 in 2 is already rejected. We will assume the average value of the proven mines at an outside figure of, say, $3,000,000. The probable average expenditure on the successful ones would then be $450,000, and that work would be abandoned on the others, after spending $100,000, or an average of $275,000 on the 160 claims, or $44,000,000. This would give a total of $82,000,000 and we might have eighty good mines. Now we have to consider, not the ultimate profit that these mines might produce, in the course of a long life, but what value could reasonably be set upon them as soon as it is demonstrated that they are workable mines. About $3,000,000 would seem a high average, or a total valuation for the 80 mines of $240,000,000. It is obvious, moreover, that the expenditure starts immediately and it is some considerable time before any returns come in.

If the probable expenditures and receipts are represented graphically to scale, the effect of time is more clearly seen.

GRAPHIC REPRESENTATION OF EFFECT OF TIME ON VALUE
OF UNDEVELOPED LANDS

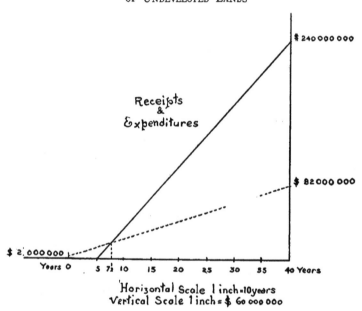

Thus the expenditures start immediately with $2,000,000 for the purchase of lands and are shown at the rate of $2,000,000 per year throughout the forty-year period, making $82,000,000 in all expended. With regard to the receipts, it is assumed that there will be no returns from the development work for the first five years and that thereafter returns from sales would come in uniformly for the rest of the period. Undoubtedly if such a venture were carried out it would be found that neither expenditures or receipts would be represented by a straight line, but in the absence of any information to indicate the position and amount of irregularities it can only be shown by a straight line. If the expenditures and receipts are plotted on the same diagram, it will be noticed that at about 7½ years after the starting point the receipts are greater than the expenditures and it is only the **difference** between the two which need be considered, that is, $240,000,000 less $82,000,000 or $158,000,000, which is the amount to be ultimately received and the period within which it is received is 32½ years, or an annual receipt of $4,861,500, commencing after 7½ years. It is what this prospect is worth at the present time that we have to determine. The problem then is simply to calculate the present value of a payment of $4,861,500 over a forty-year period, with a deference of 7½ years. This results, according to whatever percentage of interest is considered proper, approximately as follows:

At four per cent $65,000,000.
At five per cent $54,000,000.
At six per cent $44,000,000.

As indicated before, many of these lands have been held for many years and have been paying taxes. If we go back ten years, the present value of all the lands would be $44,000,000, $33,000,000 or $26,000,000, at 4.5 and 6 per cent respectively. Going back twenty years, to the time the act came in force, the present value would be $30,000,000, $20,000,000 and $14,500,000, at the same percentages. And it appears that this is the way the matter ought to be considered. The imaginary purchaser has not appeared to energetically develop all the lands, hence whatever value they may have is something that will not be realized on within forty years. Now it is obvious that no well-advised person would be willing to pay the amounts indicated above for the mining lands under consideration, that is, assuming 5 per cent as the proper rate of interest, $54,000,000, $33,000,000 or $20,000,000, according to the time we have in mind. If our calculation should prove to be correct, he would merely in the end get back the money that had been hazarded in the enterprise. Probably not over a quarter, or a fifth of the amounts mentioned could prudently be given for the lands. This would bring the value per acre down to a small amount, probably less than $10, and would appear to indicate that the present rate of taxation is reasonable. The small average value arrived at in the calculation is, of course, due to the inclusion of a large amount of land with a negative or minus value. It is not correct to say that a claim, the possession of which causes a loss of $100,000, has a zero value. It has a value of minus $100,000, and it seems certain that at some time or other all the lands subject to the tax will be tested, as it is inconceivable that the owners will continue paying taxes indefinitely. If after many years any lands should be abandoned, then, as far as the owner is concerned, the purchase price and all taxes paid with interest would constitute the minus value. Approximately 250,000 acres of mining lands have been abandoned for taxes. These certainly, as far as the late owners were concerned, had a minus value, which is the sum of the purchase price and all expenditures on the lands.

We have shown that a purchase of the lands in question on the conditions mentioned is not attractive. If we imagine that there was no obligation to examine and explore, that is, if *all* the lands having a minus value might be ignored, then our imaginary purchaser, instead of debating whether he might give $5,000,000 for the lands, would scarcely hesitate about paying $50,000,000.

While no proof can be given that our assumptions are correct, it can be seen that if they are not within reasonable limits, the result arrived at must be either seriously in excess of the actual facts, or much too low. To anyone who takes the former view it could be pointed out that we do not start with nothing. There are certain well-known and valuable mines which would form a nest-egg, as it were. On the other hand, if it is considered that the results given are too low, it can be shown that in the early days of Cobalt and the surrounding district, something over 2000 claims were staked and about 1 per cent of these developed into valuable mines. The average area of these would not exceed 40 acres. As this was an extraordinarily productive area, somewhat less than one per cent of the 80-acre claims were assumed to be valuable in the above calculation.

If we assume the mines are valued at $2,000,000 each, which seems more probable, then carrying out the calculation in a similar manner, the expenditure on the final stage would be $32,000,000 instead of $44,000,000, and the total expenditure $70,000,000. The difference would be $90,000,000, and plotting this as before, it gives an amount of $2,903,000 over a 40-year period, with a 9 years' deference. The present value of this is $36,000,000, $29,000,000 and $24,000,000, at 4, 5 and 6 per cent respectively.

In the acreage tax, as with the natural gas, we notice that very small areas which would add to the expense of collection and bring no adequate return are eliminated. Accordingly, parcels of land less than ten acres in extent are exempt. These are mostly islands, taken up as mining land but actually intended for summer resorts. One feature worth noticing in the acreage tax is the one whereby a co-owner who pays the whole tax for four years may make an application to the Mining Court to compel the delinquent co-owners to pay their share or lose their interest. The term co-owner includes shareholder in a company. As this fact is becoming more widely known, the number availing themselves of this privilege is increasing and at present thirty to forty applications are being made yearly for this purpose.

THE PROFIT TAX

The way profits are to be determined is set forth in section 5 of the act. According to this section profits in excess of $10,000 are taxable at the rate of three per cent, up to $1,000,000, and at five per cent on profits over $1,000,000 up to $5,000,000, and thereafter on an ascending scale which does not interest us much at present. In effect it is a tax on the value of the ore in the ground, leviable only when it is brought to the surface and either sold or treated. In order to determine the taxable amount, the pit's mouth value is taken and from this is deducted all the expenses of bringing it to the surface, which are mentioned in the act. Certain expenses are excluded—taxes for instance with the exception of the Dominion income tax—and moreover no allowance for exhaustion of the mineral or depletion is made. Depreciation on plant and buildings is limited to a fixed arbitrary amount of fifteen per cent. Each calendar year is taken by itself and returns are made on that, to determine whether there is a profit or not. Thus it will sometimes happen that a mine may operate and produce for some years at a loss and then come into the profit-making stage, when it immediately becomes liable for a tax.

In general it will be seen that the act is framed in such a way as to avoid disputes rather than to attain theoretic justice. Thus things that are incapable of exact determination are excluded altogether. To make the proper allowance for depletion, for instance, would require a complete knowledge of not only all the ore which may exist in the mine but also the market prices of its products in the future. It is safe to say that no one has knowledge of this kind. The attempt to attain theoretic justice would entail very considerable expense and would in the writer's opinion be a delusion. In any mine with extensive workings there will be several members of the staff almost constantly employed in estimating ore reserves. It would obviously be expensive to the Government and intolerable to the mines to attempt to duplicate this, and without such knowledge it would be futile to attempt to estimate the amount that should be allotted to depletion.

The general effect of the profit tax is to throw the burden of taxation on the mines making a very large profit. Thus the statutory exemption of $10,000 which of course chiefly influences those making a small profit, works to this end. For instance, if the profit should happen to be exactly $10,000, the exemption is 100 per cent; if it should be $20,000, the exemption is 50 per cent; if $100,000, 10 per cent, and when the profit is $1,000,000, the exemption is only 1 per cent, or almost vanishes and the higher rate of taxation at 5 per cent, instead of 3 per cent, comes in force. This appears to be reasonable and good policy. The mining lands in the first place, as we have seen, are sold at a fixed moderate price. The acreage tax also is not excessive. The substantial revenue comes in the end, from those who have been fortunate to secure extremely valuable mining lands.

It would seem advisable to examine into the total amount of

taxes which mines in Ontario are required to pay. From the discussion on the acreage tax we have seen that the venture of acquiring undeveloped mining lands and seeking to establish profitable mines on them is essentially hazardous. We are dependent for the main source of revenue on the successful outcome of the efforts of the bold spirits to whom this enterprise appeals and in the end anything which discouraged them or caused them to slacken their effort would affect the revenue adversely. It seems to the writer that we have a better view of this if we consider the gold mines by themselves. They are the most important, from the revenue standpoint, both at present and, as far as one can see in the future. First of all it might be well to review briefly the history of gold mining in Ontario. As far back as the sixties there was a gold excitement in Eastern Ontario. No profitable mines resulted from this. Later on, in various localities, chiefly in the extreme western part of the province, there was another period of activity. The records do not appear to show that a single mine made a profit over any considerable period. In fact, the total production was so small at that time that it was impossible that any substantial profit could have been made. The first year in which any mine showed a profit was in 1912, due to the operation of mines in the Porcupine district. The net result of operations on all gold mines at that time was still a loss and it was not till 1919 that the amount of profit made by the profit-making mines was sufficient to overbalance the expenditures on mines working at a loss and the non-producing mines and mining claims. The figures for that year showed that a little more than $3,000,000 profit was made by the few profit-making mines and approximately $2,000,000 was spent on all the other mines and mining claims. It has often been stated that for every dollar's worth of gold produced in the world, more than a dollar is spent in the effort. It does not seem possible that anyone has sufficient information to make any intelligent estimate of this matter. It does not appear reasonable, as serious expensive work will cease if it brings no results. It is certainly not true of Ontario for the last eight years and will not be true in the future, for a considerable number of years at least. The cost of producing a dollar's worth of gold, including expenditure on non-profit-making and non-producing mines and claims, is between 80 and 90 cents.

If we examine the operations of the profit-making gold mines for the years 1924-5-6 on the mining tax act basis, the following results will be seen:

Total production $84,411,516
Total taxes paid .... $2,996,028 or 3.5 per cent of returns
Total profits before deducting all taxes $27,010,625
Taxes not deductible 1,342,032

Amount retained by owners $25,668,593

That is, the amount accruing to the various tax-levying bodies is 11.6 per cent of that retained by the owners of the mines. Putting it in another way, of the amount available, before payment of any taxes, 89.6 per cent goes to the owners and 10.4 per cent to the public. During this same period, if we include the non-profit-making gold mines, the total production was $87,228,171. There was thus about $2,800,000 yielded by mines operating at a loss. The above figures include the value of the silver contained in bullion. This is about one-half of one per cent of the total.

Long experience appears to show that the maximum amount which may be taken from anyone engaged in an enterprise involving hazard, without discouraging him, is about ten per cent. Thus in the Laws and Orders of the Mendip Mines, set forth about 400 years ago, we find the following, the quaint language and mode of writing being worth reproducing exactly: " That if any Lord or Officer hath once given license to any Man to build or set up an hearth or Washing house, to wash, cleanse or blow the Oare, He that once hath leave shall keep it for ever, or give it to whom he will, so that he doth justly pay his Lotlead, which is the tenth pound which shall be blown at the Hearth or hearths and also that he doth keep it Tenantable, as the Custom doth require." (R. G. Rowe, *Canadian Mining Journal,* May 20th, 1927.) Coming down to our own times, most of the drilling for oil is done on land privately owned, the owner of the land also possessing any oil that may be there. It is the almost universal custom for the one drilling for oil to agree to give the owner of the land and the oil a royalty of one-eighth or 12.5 per cent of the oil found and this is all the payment the owner of the oil receives. The one who takes the hazard gets seven-eighths of what is found. In the case of the gold mines under discussion, whatever mineral may be there is already owned by the company operating the mine, the province having sold both land and minerals.

Undoubtedly our own experience is the most valuable guide to our course of action, and in the matter of determining the maximum percentage which may be exacted from those who take a hazard, we have the course adopted with regard to betting on horse races. Betting is illegal in Canada and penalties are provided for it in the Criminal Code, an exception is made of betting on an authorized race-course. The owners of the race-track are allowed under the Criminal Code to retain a percentage of the amount wagered on each race, which is limited and varies with the amount wagered. In addition to that the province takes 5 per cent of all the amount bet on races and receives a daily license fee from the owners of the track. The combined percentage retained by the track owners and the province out of the amount wagered on each race comes, in the case of races where the amount is not great, say,

$20,000 or $30,000, to over 12 per cent and with larger amounts—
$80,000 for instance—to between 10 and 11 per cent. This amount
is deliberately set as high as the business or diversion of betting on
horse races will stand. At the last session of the legislature the
amount of daily license fee which the province levies on the track
owners was substantially reduced. In the case of horse-racing the
percentage retained by the track owners and the province comes
of course out of the winner of the bet, he takes the hazard and
surrenders from 10 to over 12 per cent of his winnings.

CHAIRMAN HAYES: Mr. Holcomb has some announcements.

(Announcements by Secretary Holcomb of meetings of committees and with respect to entertainment activities)

SECRETARY HOLCOMB: There is one other item. There is a group
of members who are interested particularly in bank taxation. This
group met this morning, and it turned out to be so important that
they intend to continue the discussion tomorrow, under the heading
of unfinished miscellaneous business at the tenth session, the last
item. You will therefore understand—those states that are interested, or anyone interested particularly in bank taxation—that the
subject will be open at that time for discussion.

CHAIRMAN HAYES: We will now call on Mr. Charles R. Howe,
chairman of the Arizona Tax Commission.

CHARLES R. HOWE (Arizona): Mr. Chairman, Members of the
Conference: It is a pleasure for me to be with you at this time.
I have been coming to these conferences since 1912, and each time
that I come I always find something that I can learn from the other
members present.

I am particularly pleased to be called upon to discuss the question
of mine taxation, and consider it an honor to my state, that it is put
on the program at this time, because Arizona is the greatest producing metalliferous mining state in the Union, or, I might say, in
the world. We produce greater metalliferous mineral value than
any other subdivision, so far as I have been able to ascertain.

I was particularly surprised to find that the Province of Ontario
has such a voluminous law for the taxation of mineral property.
In the State of Arizona the only law we have on the statute books
for the assessing of mines or mineral properties is contained in
these few words: " The Tax Commission shall assess all producing
mines in the State." It is left to the tax commission, of which I
have been a member ever since its creation, to value and assess by
the best method they may find, all of the mines in the state.

The mining industry of Arizona is its chief industry. I might
say the taxable wealth of the industry as indicated by the tax rolls

of the state is nearly 43 per cent of the total tax value of the state. You will thus see that it is of great importance to the state that the tax commission uses some method that is equitable, not only between the mines themselves but as between the mines and all other classes of property, and it is on this subject that I have prepared what I am going to say today.

THE TAXATION OF MINES AND MINERAL PROPERTIES

CHARLES R. HOWE
Chairman, Arizona Tax Commission

The title of this discussion is perhaps somewhat too general in character to permit as satisfactory an analysis as might be made, were the discussion confined to producing metalliferous mines. I have, therefore, taken the liberty of changing the subject to "Taxation of Producing Metalliferous Mines," and the paper I have prepared deals with that portion of the general subject only. This has been found necessary, for the reason of my unfamiliarity with non-metalliferous properties.

The subject of mine taxation in any form, though it is admittedly of great importance to many of the states, has received less attention from this association than any other subject of major proportions. Perhaps this has been true in the past because of the animosities provoked by an attempted discussion of the same subject some years ago in the conference at Buffalo. However, time often has a soothing effect on humanity in general and it is only with this idea uppermost that I venture to discuss a subject heretofore taboo for many years, in a frankly plain manner at this time.

While it is true that mines have been taxed in the past and are now taxed in every state wherein they exist, it is also true that no uniform method has ever been adopted, suitable to the needs of all of the states. The laws of most states require that all property shall be assessed and taxed at its "full cash value," or some definition similar thereto. It is comparatively easy to ascertain what may appear to be the true value of most classes of property, under this definition. However, in the case of producing mines, where everything that goes to make the value of the property as a whole is nearly always hundreds and in some cases thousands of feet underground, and the tonnage, assay value, extent of ore body and price to be received for product unknown, it will readily be conceded that if the true or full cash value is *ever actually found* it would be purely a coincidence. This, of course, refers solely to taxation on an ad-valorem basis.

The total or final value of any metalliferous mine must be predicated on not only the ore actually developed, but that which is undeveloped as well. Frequently a mine develops much greater bodies

23

of ore during the period in which the first known ore body is being worked, than it had in the beginning. It is for this reason that a study of the geological formation of the district in which the mine is situated is essential, or at least advisable, particularly when valuing and appraising a property in any new mining district. In a proven district, of course, this is not so much needed.

The problems of mine taxation, while not necessarily calling for an appraisal or valuation of the property to be taxed, nearly always take into consideration the tangible value to a greater or lesser extent. Nearly every state in the Union has from time to time made an effort to tax property under some other method than the ad-valorem or general property tax. While some have succeeded in part, it is still undoubtedly true that by far the greater portion of our revenues come from this source. Bearing this in mind, I believe it is reasonable to conclude that in the states using the ad-valorem system of taxation for practically all other property, some element of physical value should enter into whatever method is adopted for taxing metalliferous productive mines.

The evolution of mine taxation in Arizona during the past twenty years has demonstrated two things very clearly. One of these is that it is absolutely necessary that the taxation of this class of property be placed under the jurisdiction of a centralized body, with ample inquisitorial and quasi-judicial powers. The other is that no specific unyielding formula or method is either necessary or desirable, in order to arrive at an equitable taxation thereof. This would not necessarily be true in other states, where mining is not the chief industry and where annual earnings do not equal the total for all other industries combined, as is the case in Arizona.

For many years the State of Arizona predicated its taxation of producing mines almost entirely on the average net earnings over a period of years. The average thus found was capitalized at various rates, depending on the class of mine to be taxed and other physical information. The sum finally arrived at was the valuation used for that particular year, upon which the various rates of state, county and special district taxes were levied. After a thorough trial of this method it was found too narrow in its scope and not sufficiently elastic to permit equalization of the burdens of taxation as between the mines themselves. Neither did it take into consideration the needs of government or the wasting asset, with reference to the future of the state, to the extent the tax commission believed they should be considered. Still another reason for the method being discontinued, and perhaps the deciding one at the time was the continued and embarrassing litigation brought about by its use. Prior to this time valuation and taxation was fixed by statute, based on both the gross and net yield during the previous year.

For the past three years the method used has been a combination of the capitalized net earnings averaged over a period of years and net earnings for the current year only; average stock sale valuation over a period of years and for the current year only; stock sale valuation as of the date of assessment; ore reserves; physical valuation of property, where it has been made by reputable mining engineers; total costs of production per unit of product as well as costs per unit for taxes only (the latter, of course, being used only for the purpose of ascertaining the extent of the tax burden as between the different mining properties themselves); and any and all other information obtainable from reliable sources while inspecting each individual property annually and at times more often, as conditions seem to warrant.

This method, or rather combination of methods, as heretofore stated, has now been in use for taxation purposes in Arizona for the past three years. As yet the validity of a tax levied thereunder has never been tested. However, the unanimous conclusions of the tax commission are:

1st: It has shown a better equalization of tax burdens, as between the mines as a class, as well as between the mines and other classes of property.

2nd: It has provided for the needs of government in communities created solely by reason of the existence of the mines themselves.

3rd: It has entirely stopped litigation, thereby providing necessary governmental revenues for schools, highways, and bond interest and redemption requirements.

4th: It has created a better feeling between the taxpayers of other classes of property and the mine owners in general.

While I am not prepared to defend the Arizona system as one hundred per cent perfect—it has its faults as does every system yet devised—however, under a conservative administration it has undoubtedly proved the best yet found after years of research and the trial of various other systems.

In this connection perhaps some of the language used in a recent decision of the Ninth Circuit Court of Appeals at San Francisco will be found illuminating.

United Verde Extension Mining Company vs. State Tax Commission and State Board of Equalization of Arizona.

". . . . What form of decree could a court of equity enter in such a case? It seems manifest that it should not attempt to prescribe the mode or manner in which the average annual net income shall be ascertained, nor should it attempt to prescribe or fix the rate or factor to be employed in capitalizing that income, and if it should attempt neither of these things, nothing remains but to condemn the method in its entirety. But why should this be done? The court is concerned with results, not with methods, and why should it condemn a method which can work no injury, unless wrongly or improperly employed. The character of mining property is constantly undergoing change, with exhaustion in some mines and new discoveries in others, and these changes must be met and dealt with as they arise. The problems confronting the state officers are difficult at best. They cannot be solved through the application of some simple unyielding formula, much less can they be solved in advance by the decree of a court of equity."

The relative importance of the mining industry in Arizona from a taxation standpoint can be better appreciated by the quotation of a few statistics, which I trust the conference will pardon me for mentioning at this time:

TAXABLE VALUE OF ALL MINING PROPERTY IN ARIZONA TOGETHER WITH
PER CENT OF TOTAL TAXES PAID BY THE INDUSTRY—1911-1927

Year	Valuation	Per cent of Total Taxes
1911	$ 19,242,331	19.3
1912	45,145,084	31.7
1913	140,488,648	37.2
1914	146,672,395	35.7
1915	159,109,288	37.4
1916	216,879,796	44.2
1917	393,421,536	56.0
1918	491,719,960	58.63
1919	496,262,860	57.66
1920	469,651,131	52.79
1921	424,365,559	50.75
1922	358,536,358	48.97
1923	323,891,322	46.46
1924	275,125,273	42.33
1925	267,582,204	41.75
1926	277,805,484	42.54
1927	288,326,081	42.82

It will be noted that the tabulation commences with the year 1911. This is for the reason that the State Tax Commission was created in 1912 and from that date began a systematized method of assessing all classes of property. For the year 1911 the industry paid only a fraction more than 19 per cent of the total tax burden of the state, while in 1927 it will pay approximately 43 per cent. During the war period, when prices received for the product went to unheard-of figures, mining property paid as high as 58 per cent of all taxes.

My only reason for quoting statistics at this time is to impress upon the members the great importance of the industry to the taxpayers of Arizona, as well as the necessity of some just and workable method by which to arrive at the amount of the tax to be paid.

In no other state is the mining industry of such great importance from a taxation standpoint. Experience has taught us that when an industry is very prosperous, taxes, even though excessive, are seldom questioned and almost never litigated. However, if the industry be only enjoying a moderate degree of prosperity, taxes become more burdensome and litigation invariably ensues. This is especially true where an equalization of the burdens is impossible because of the use of an unyielding method.

Some contend that an elastic method is not advisable and that a hard-and-fast fixed method should be used. In some cases such will doubtless be found true. However, in Arizona so many mines have been penalized while others have escaped their just share of tax burdens under a fixed method of valuation, that it is extremely doubtful if anything resembling a specific method will ever be enacted into law. Of course, the time may come under a less conservative administration than the present, when a supplementary tax of some nature, possibly similar to the Minnesota occupation tax, may seem advisable. However, such a contingency may be considered remote at the present time.

Most taxing officials will agree that it is practically impossible to obtain an exact valuation on any class of property, especially is this true of personal property. A valuable cow assessed at $150 may die three months after assessment; a stock of merchandise or a residence taxed for $10,000 may be consumed by fire shortly after the taxes are paid thereon; a tract of land worth $100 per acre this year may, through a change in soil or marketing conditions, be rendered apparently valueless next year; a valuable city lot or addition may become nearly worthless through migration to the vicinity of an undesirable class of citizens. Thus the conclusion drawn is that only an approximate value, or what may appear to be the true value at time of assessment, is possible. As a matter of fact this is all that is contemplated. If this be true of visible property, how much more should it be true of property to a large extent invisible, such as metalliferous mines? Why should there be complaint if a mine valued for the current year at $1,000,000 becomes worth $10,000,000 next year, through a new ore strike, or only half as much, through unfavorable marketing conditions. The same conditions apply to nearly all other classes of property, yet we hear no loud acclaim for an unyielding method of valuation from them.

Any paper on mine taxation would be incomplete without a short resume of the methods used by the principal mining states for the basis of arriving at the tax:

Arizona: Uses ad-valorem valuation. Taxable value found through a combination of methods consisting of capitalization of net earnings, stock valuation as shown by actual sales over stated periods, ore reserves, physical valuation, where it has been made, together with all other information obtainable during frequent inspection of the properties.

Utah: Uniform ad-valorem valuation of $5 per acre on all mines to which is added a value found by multiplying the net proceeds of the previous year by three. In addition, all improvements and machinery are taxed on an ad-valorem basis, as other similar property.

Idaho: Ad-valorem value consisting of price paid U. S. Government for acreage. In addition to this a valuation of once the annual net proceeds plus the tax on machinery, improvements and structures as levied on other similar property.

Nevada: Specific valuation of once the net annual proceeds plus valuation of machinery and improvements. Ad-valorem value of minimum of $500 per claim for patented mining claims.

Montana: Specific valuation of 100 per cent of net proceeds preceding year. Royalty tax on full cash value of product yielded during preceding year. Also a Metals Mines License Tax based on a sliding scale on the gross production. The same rate of taxation applies on the valuations arrived at by these methods as to other property.

Colorado: Ad-valorem valuation of one-fourth the gross proceeds for preceding year, provided that if the value of the net proceeds for the same year shall be found to be greater, then that shall be used as the taxable valuation of the claims. All machinery and improvements are separately valued.

New Mexico: Ad-valorem value based on a physical appraisal made by J. R. Finlay in 1921, with slight modifications. Once the net proceeds of the preceding year may be used if found to be more than the Finlay valuation. Thus far, only the appraisal method has been used.

Michigan: Ad-valorem valuation based on appraised value of remaining ore in mine plus a reasonable consideration of capitalized value. Annual appraisal made by Geological Survey Mine Appraisal Engineers. Tax commission later equalizes values found between different mines in each district.

California: Ad-valorem valuation by county assessors. No method or formula for finding value is used.

CONCLUSIONS

1st: My experience during a period of something more than twenty years as a tax official in Arizona justifies the conclusion that any systematized method for taxation of all classes of property is better than no system at all. The use of a system or method tends to uniformity, and uniformity promotes equalization of burdens. More especially does this apply to producing mines.

2nd: Metalliferous-producing mines should be assessed and taxed by a centralized state body having large powers and inquisitorial authority, not hampered by undue statutory restrictions.

3rd: A flexible method wisely administered is preferable to an unyielding law or method that administers itself for the reasons:

(a) Equalization between mines in the same class.
(b) Equalization between mines in different classes some of whose ore bodies show signs of exhaustion.
(c) Equalization between mines and other classes of property.
(d) Support of governmental functions in communities created solely because of the existence of the mine itself.

4th: A uniform method or formula of taxation suitable to the needs of all of the mining states is impracticable.

5th: Mines should not be taxed solely with the view of obtaining all the revenue the industry will bear, but rather from the standpoint of an equalization of the burdens of government with other classes of property and of a proper conservation of the ore bodies, always bearing in mind that whether or not a mine may produce at a profit during any particular year, it still enjoys the protection and facilities accorded it by organized government, which in the last analysis is the necessity for economic life and all taxation.

GEORGE G. TUNELL: I wonder if I may ask the speaker a question.

CHAIRMAN HAYES: We are going to have a discussion generally after the next paper.

We will now call on Mr. Mackenzie, Secretary of the Utah Chapter of the American Mining Congress.

Before Mr. Mackenzie starts his paper, I am requested by the secretary to ask the gentlemen who are going to discuss the papers to step forward here instead of just speaking from their seats, so that every one can hear.

A. G. MACKENZIE (Utah):

TAXATION OF MINES AND MINERAL PROPERTIES

A. G. MACKENZIE
Utah Chapter, American Mining Congress

It is significant that no generally acceptable plan for the taxation of minerals has yet been evolved, although mining is an ancient human activity and its physical operations are essentially the same as when desired minerals were first separated from their natural environment centuries ago.

This paper deals with taxation of mineral property and minerals as property. It does not review the history of mineral taxation nor discuss in detail the many methods that have been proposed or applied. The observations and conclusions presented are general in nature and intended to suggest principles only. The financing of mineral enterprises; the business hazards of the industry; the stimulation of it and other phases of the subject, although pertinent in a complete discussion, are therefore ignored.

It is not assumed that a plan of universal and satisfactory application can be evolved. In fact, it is probable that no such desirable solution is imminent, as conditions in the industry and revenue requirements in mineral regions are greatly at variance. But the situation is a challenge to those interested and substantial progress is possible, through accumulation of facts and ideas.

There is no objection by the industry to the proposal that minerals and mineral property should be taxed in proportion to their value, as compared with other property. The difficulty lies chiefly in the determination of the value of mineral deposits so as to arrive at a comparable basis.

In so far as the mineral deposit itself is concerned, it.is obvious that substantial differences exist between the utilization of it and the utilization of other physical property, and that these differences must be recognized in a fair consideration of tax methods. They are known to students of taxation and are indicated here in part by simple comparison, to bring them readily to mind.

The owner of a mineral deposit can have only partial enjoyment of·his property in any given time; that is, he can utilize only as much of his mineral as he can extract and sell within that period · and cannot utilize all of it simultaneously. This difference between mineral and other property may be shown by various comparisons, one of the simplest of which is to compare a mineral deposit with an assumed life of twenty years and a farm of twenty acres.

In this instance, the mineral deposit, converted to terms of the farm, would permit the farmer to cultivate only one of his twenty acres annually, while the other nineteen acres remained idle and unproductive.

The same comparison can be used to illustrate the capital consumption, or "wasting asset" feature of the mineral industry. Thus, the farmer, after one year's operation, would have only nineteen acres, of which he could farm one acre. The following year he would have only eighteen acres and farm one, and so on, until his farm had entirely disappeared. Depletion of mineral deposits, or return of capital, allowance for which is made in some tax systems, is a recognition of this peculiarity of the mineral industry.

These points can be illustrated by comparison of mineral property with property other than farms, such as factories or buildings, that can be fully utilized at all times and kept in service indefinitely.

Cost, a common basis for the determination of non-mineral valuations, presents another difficulty in the adjustment of mineral and non-mineral valuations. Mineral properties are not often sold in their entirety, although the operation of a mineral deposit is a process of continuous, piecemeal sale, prolonged until the deposit has been exhausted, without change of titular ownership. The chief value of much mineral property is the result of development and is frequently attained through skill or good fortune, with capital investment disproportionate to the advantages obtained.

The three methods most generally proposed and employed for the valuation of mineral deposits are the ad-valorem or " physical valuation " plan, the gross output or tonnage basis and the net profits basis.

The ad-valorem plan involves estimation of the extent of mineral reserves, the annual rate and cost of production, the sale price of the mineral, the average profit and the rate of interest on the investment, all of which are uncertain, if not indeterminable factors, except the last, which can be fixed arbitrarily. It is a curious fact that this plan is advocated by a large and respectable school of tax students, who thus insist that mineral shall be valued in accordance with its problematical future, rather than with reference to its known present or past, as in the case of other property. They urge that science and economics afford sufficient knowledge. An industry so dependent upon and so greatly indebted to the scientist and the economist does not deprecate their substantial achievements. Yet the scientist and the economist will not maintain that their estimates, however well grounded, are so conclusively definite as known facts.

The gross output or tonnage basis is incapable of equitable application, even to similar properties in the same locality. It ignores costs and the fact that volume of output is not a measure of value or of ability to pay.

The net-profits plan affords a definite measure of the extent to which possession is enjoyed. It eliminates the uncertainties of the physical-valuation plan and the inequities of the gross-output or tonnage plan. It can be administered efficiently and economically and will probably produce, throughout the life of the mineral deposit, more revenue than either of the other plans and with less hardship to the taxpayer. It is further desirable, in that it does not tend to encourage uneconomic extraction of the mineral.

Net profits should, therefore, be employed in mineral valuations. The manner in which they should be employed can be adequately determined only with knowledge of attendant conditions. Application of the principle in various jurisdictions where it has been accepted shows variations, due to differences in physical conditions and revenue requirements, to expediency and other considerations, but the principle commends itself and when properly applied is superior to other methods, with their many uncertainties and inequalities.

The statements thus far made herein relate to the valuation of the mineral deposit itself. This distinction is mentioned preparatory to subsequent observations with reference to mineral property other than the mineral deposit, but appurtenant to it.

It is apparent that a plan dependent entirely upon earnings or profits as a basis of valuation might subject a jurisdiction in which the mineral industry is the paramount tax source to sudden and perhaps greatly injurious fluctuations in revenue, with changes in business conditions of the industry. The menace of such a situation has frequently been pointed out and constitutes a substantial argument against reliance on net profits as the sole basis for valuation. Protection can be obtained through adaptations of the net-profits plan and through valuation of the mineral property, other than the mineral itself, on an equitable basis. Such other property is considerable in amount and can readily be valued, as it consists of land, buildings, machinery and supplies, and, therefore, subject to the same methods employed in the valuation of non-mineral property.

Since mineral production accords closely with business conditions, revenue therefrom, under the plan proposed herein, would be as constant as revenue from other property, the valuation of which also fluctuates with general business conditions. Cessation or curtailment of operations in an exclusively mineral community is no greater hardship on the inhabitants there than like cessation or curtailment in an exclusively agricultural or manufacturing community. And suspension of mineral activities is probably not more frequent than crop failures or suspension of manufacturing.

Such a plan would also insure against idleness of mineral property for other than justifiable economic reasons. This is, however, largely an imaginary situation, as selfish considerations require the extraction of mineral as rapidly as consistent.

The authentication of the views herein expressed on behalf of the industry is that they have the approval of several mineral organizations and of many individuals that have long been associated with mineral production and with the study of taxation, as it relates especially to the industry. Suggestions for the improvement of the situation are invited, as the industry would benefit greatly through freedom from the adverse effects of the numerous changes and proposed changes in mineral tax laws upon its stability.

CHAIRMAN HAYES: General discussion is now open on the papers read by Mr. Mickle, Mr. Howe and Mr. Mackenzie.

I call upon Mr. Tunell, who desired to ask a question.

GEORGE G. TUNELL (Illinois): I will now ask the question that I intended to ask Mr. Howe a moment ago.

He spoke of a strained method of assessment. I wonder if you meant to imply that it was also an assessed value method. It struck me at the time that the alternative was one that was favorable to the owner of the property rather than unfavorable. Most industries, I imagine, would be very happy to be assessed on the basis of the net return of the single year, if their current aggregate assessment did not exceed the net return of a single year, they would feel the assessment was a very favorable one to them. I am sure the corporation I represent would feel that such was the case.

MR. HOWE: Your question, Mr. Tunell, I presume, refers to my suggestion with reference to the New Mexico—

MR. TUNELL (interrupting): Colorado.

MR. HOWE (continuing): And Colorado situation. The suggestion on my part that it was a strained method was that they could use either of two methods, not that I had any knowledge of which they did use or which was the most preferable, but the fact that they could use either one of the two methods and still be correct, according to their law. Neither do I know or have any knowledge as to the percentage of assessment on other classes of property in those states. It merely goes to the fact that they had the option of using one of two methods, something that no other states I know of have.

MR. LINK (Colorado): This system that you may take one-quarter of the gross or the net is not optional, Mr. Howe. It is mandatory. You must take the higher amount. It is not optional.

MR. HOWE: I did not mean to say yours was optional — New Mexico.

MR. LINK (Colorado): I was just trying to illustrate the proposition that the law is mandatory; you must take the higher amount. I fully concur in Mr. Tunell's deduction that the one alternative results in a very favorable assessment for the producing mine, in a state where we attempt to assess other classes of property at full value.

As Mr. Howe well stated, this is a subject of very vital importance to the mining states. I am sorry to say, and some of you will be rather surprised to know that metal mining in Colorado has come to be a very minor occupation instead, as it was for many years in the early days, a major occupation.

Fifty years have gone by since Colorado was a territory. For quite a number of years after the state was admitted, we received a fair tax from producing metal mines, as compared with other classes of property. There was a complete exemption of metal mines for ten years. Since that time we have had assessment at one-quarter of the gross, or the net, with the exception of 1913, the year when Colorado attempted to go from one-third value to full value.

As a matter of fact Colorado has always been in law a full value state, but all of the county assessors, with no centralization in the state, had agreed to assess on a one-third value.

When the tax commission was created, we went to work immediately and proceeded to reach a full-value basis. The legislature in 1913 increased the metal mining assessment from 25 per cent of gross to 50 per cent of the gross, plus the net, which made a material increase in the value of the assessment of the net producers, and did considerable towards equalization.

I wish to say that I am in full concurrence with Mr. Mackenzie on the proposition of gross being a very unfair method. You may have an enormous gross taken out at a terrific loss. On the other hand, you may have a comparatively small gross with a very large profit. So it is unfair to base any valuation upon a gross. That is the reason that I have never favored a gross income tax. I think that a net income is very much better.

It is of vital importance in Colorado in a state way, as to what may be done. We always have to apologize for our law there. It is not only that the net must be used when it is higher, but unfortunately, there are other provisions of the law which for the purpose of taxation limit the valuation to a group of claims, no matter how large, and we have some very large groups, which must be considered one claim, for the purposes of taxation.

To show you the result of that at the present time, the assessors in mining counties are assessing non-producing claims in the main at from $30 to $60 per acre. The average, I should say, is about $40 to $50 per acre for non-producers at the present time. There are a few producing groups, considered fairly valuable as gold and silver mines, which under this present statute are being assessed at $10 to $25 per acre, or very much less than the non-producers, which now or never had any known value at all. So, we probably have the most favorable law to metal mines that has ever been enacted in any state.

This association, in so far as its committees are concerned, has practically unanimously favored the assessment of metal mines upon the same basis as other real estate in the same locality. I was very glad, indeed, to hear Mr. Mackenzie concede this. Mr. Mackenzie, on the part of the mining men, is very fair. The big problem is to get a law which permits an intelligent administration and the finding of a fair value.

Those of us in the mining states, who have been in tax work for a good while, have for many years realized that states like Minnesota, Wisconsin and Michigan first accomplished a very fair adjustment of this difficult problem.

I think, Mr. Howe, that Arizona got its law for ad-valorem assessment in about 1913.

With due deference to the states just mentioned, which had splendid assessments, and with great satisfaction to the mining interests, Arizona has set the banner in recent years for fair metal mining taxation and administration. Anxious as we are to see the mining industry pay its part, we must not be unmindful of the difficulties and hazards of the metal mining industry, especially in states like Colorado, where it is mostly gold, silver and lead mining. The assessment should be carefully considered and the industry given the advantage of all reasonable doubts.

The metal-mining counties in Colorado, on account of the unfair law, are in very serious financial condition, because the producing mines are the only real wealth. Perhaps Colorado will some time secure a fair law for the assessment of metal mines, but it will be too late to be of great assistance to many of our mining counties.

G. C. BATEMAN (Toronto) : Mr. Chairman, I was quite struck in listening to Mr. Howe and Mr. Mickle at the difference between the Province of Ontario and the State of Arizona. Mr. Howe claims we have a voluminous act, consisting of some fifty sections, while in Arizona the law is confined to a single sentence, vesting all powers in the Arizona State Tax Commission.

In Ontario the Government recognizes that the preliminary exploration of mines is an extremely hazardous and speculative enterprise. The Government considers, or takes the stand, that it is better to encourage mining and have a large number of properties having a moderate tax, rather than have a few paying a high tax.

I used to be an operator in this province, and welcomed Mr. Mickle's visits, when he came to the mine for the purpose of assessing the tax, which is a condition which does not arise with the visit of most tax officers. We would sit down around the table, and probably in an hour our whole taxation problems for the year would be settled.

In this province the administration of the act is extraordinarily simple, while it seems to me that in Arizona it is quite complicated. The simplicity of the operation of the act proves its worth. I think the administration of the Ontario act costs no more than two per cent of the total amount collected, which is extraordinarily reasonable, and I should like to ask Mr. Howe how much it costs them to collect the tax in Arizona.

C. R. HOWE (Arizona) : The gentleman would be surprised if I could give the exact figures of the cost of the total assessment collection and everything else of the mining tax. The Tax Commission of Arizona not only assesses mining properties, but it assesses all railroads, telephone, telegraph, private car line and express companies and supervises the work of all the assessors of the state; visits every county in the state at least once annually, and, after its work of assessing is through, it sits as a board of equalization on all of the property of the state. The total expense of the Arizona Tax Commission per annum runs less than $25,000, and we have a state with a valuation of $700,000,000, of which the mining industry, as I said, constitutes 43 per cent. So you see that the expense of this entire proposition would be almost nominal. We hire no experts, and the only expense we have, possibly other than through the attorney general's department, when we have a case of litigation, which is very infrequent. I do not presume it would be more than one-half as much as your Canadian tax expense, considering the total amount of the assessment.

C. P. LINK (Colorado) : If I am not mistaken, the total expense of your entire department would amount to less than one per cent.

MR. BATEMAN (Toronto) : Does that include the total cost?

MR. HOWE: That includes everything but the county treasurer. The county treasurer, of course, collects the taxes, not only on mines but on other property; and the county treasurer in each county, of course, has a certain budget for his unit. There are five or six mining counties in the state, so I presume there would be a small amount chargeable to mining from the county treasurer's office; but the entire amount, I am very sure, would not run anything like two per cent of the amount collected.

CHAIRMAN HAYES: Is there any other gentleman who wishes to make any comments on the papers read?

(No response)

(Adjournment)

EIGHTH SESSION

Thursday Afternoon, October 13, 1927

(Joint Session with the Canadian Tax Conference)

Chairman Matthews: The first is a paper on the subject of Forest Preservation and its Relation to Public Revenue and Taxation, by Professor Fred R. Fairchild of Yale University.

Fred R. Fairchild (Connecticut): Mr. President and Gentlemen of the Conference: My paper might, perhaps, be more correctly stated as a sub-title under the general title of the meeting which the President has read, as Forest Taxation in a Cutover Region. It is that limited part of that general subject that I shall present to you.

FOREST TAXATION IN A CUTOVER REGION

FRED ROGERS FAIRCHILD

Professor of Political Economy in Yale University,
Director of the United States Forest Taxation Inquiry

HERMANN H. CHAPMAN [1]

Professor of Forest Management in Yale University

The materials of this paper have been snatched, so to speak, out of the works of the Forest Taxation Inquiry. In making my first public presentation of the results of the Inquiry's study of the problem of forest taxation in America I should have preferred to wait until something in the nature of a finished report of at least a part of our investigation could be offered. Actually I am about to set before you that which is far from a finished product, as though a manufacturer should offer his customers what the industrial jargon knows as "goods in process." The Forest Taxation Inquiry, authorized by Congress in the Clarke-McNary law, was organized in April, 1926, and during most of the intervening time has been engaged in field study in the Lake States region, particularly in the State of Minnesota. Only last month was the field work in Minnesota completed, and the necessary office work is still in process.

---

[1] This paper is presented by Professor Fairchild, with acknowledgment of the aid of Professor Chapman, the member of the Forest Taxation Inquiry staff directly in charge of the Minnesota field study.

Although the Minnesota study is thus incomplete, I propose never-theless to lay before you today some of the results of that project. Our facts are far from complete; our statistics have not had the checking which they will eventually require; above all, I have not yet been able to give the facts that deliberate examination, upon which alone sound conclusions must rest. My only excuse for ap-pearing thus before you is my faith that there may be something of value in the facts already brought to light and that certain more obvious conclusions therefrom may not be wholly devoid of interest at the present time.

The region chosen for this study comprises the following sixteen counties of northeastern Minnesota: Cook, Lake, St. Louis, Itasca, Koochiching, Beltrami, Lake of the Woods, Aitkin, Carlton, Cass, Clearwater, Crow Wing, Hubbard, Kanabec, Mille Lacs and Pine. This region was chosen obviously as being the chief seat of the forest problem of Minnesota and typical of the great cutover areas of the Lake States. In addition to these sixteen counties, we made corresponding investigations in Winona County, an agricultural dis-trict with some forests, in the extreme southeastern corner of the state. This county served as a control, so to speak.

These sixteen northern counties were, not so long since, in the heart of one of America's great virgin forest regions. Today the original forests are mostly gone. In their place are some farms, some second-growth forests, and vast areas of cutover lands, in-cluding swamps and barren wastes. Under parts of this region are some of the most valuable iron deposits of the United States; par-ticularly in the three counties of St. Louis, Itasca and Crow Wing, though in certain other counties undeveloped mineral deposits of value are known or suspected.

In area these counties comprise a little more than one-third (37 per cent) of the State of Minnesota, containing 19,301,120 acres out of a total state area of 51,749,120.

The population of the region in 1926 was 486,000, the population of the state being 2,596,000. While thus comprising more than one-third of the area of the state, this region is the home of less than one-fifth (19 per cent) of the people. The density of population is only a little more than one-third that of the rest of the state.

St. Louis County occupies a peculiar and predominant position in this region. In the first place, it contains more than twice the area of the next largest county, and more than one-fifth of the area of the entire region. Including the large city of Duluth, its resi-dents comprise nearly half of the population of the region. If St. Louis County is excluded, the density of population of the rest of the region is only one-fourth that of the balance of the state. Finally, in St. Louis County is located the great bulk of the valuable iron deposits, which, together with the great wealth, real and personal, concentrated in Duluth, makes the tax situation in St. Louis quite distinct from that of the other counties.

Beginning with the last quarter of the nineteenth century, this region has been the scene of a vigorous industrial life, reaching its climax in the first decade of the twentieth century and since declining. The economic structure of the community was based upon the lumbering industry; other industries that developed on the farms and in the towns were ancillary. Everything depended on the exploitation of the forest wealth. As the demand for lumber increased with the country's growing population and as more capital and superior technique came to the lumber industry, large profits were made, not only in lumbering, but in the associated industries as well, and prosperity prevailed.

Misgivings for the future had no part in this picture. Why should they? The big lumber operators were concerned only with the profits of their industry. They had no permanent link with the region. As their holdings were cleared of merchantable timber they intended to pass on to other fields. What became of the cutover lands was of little concern to them; they expected to sell them for what they could get, and at the worst, were prepared to abandon them, an operation which in most cases would involve very little write-off of invested capital.

To other elements of the community the future appeared rosy, on account of prevailing optimism as to the agricultural future of the cutover lands. In other parts of the United States a flourishing agriculture had followed in the wake of the virgin forests. Indeed, in some places the real problem had been to clear away the forests, in order that agriculture might prevail. That the cutover lands of northern Minnesota should furnish the foundation for an agricultural development supporting an even larger population and a more flourishing industry than had the original forests was the natural assumption.

This spirit of optimism was naturally fostered and taken advantage of by those who had land to sell. By 1910 the climax of the lumbering industry was passed, and the big operators had long since begun unloading their lands. Today the lumbering industry is only the shadow of its former bulk: The large operators have disposed of their holdings to such an extent that only a small part of this region is now held by owners of more than 400 acres each. This includes all the larger blocks of uncut private timber (about 510,000 acres), some cutover lands belonging to operators who are still cutting on other parts of their properties, and lands held on account of their mineral values.

But now note that, although sold on the expectation of future agricultural development, these lands have not been sold to farmers. By 1925 only 18.34% of the area of these sixteen counties had been

24

acquired by farmers, whereas the great bulk was in the hands of those who had no intention of developing the lands but hoped to sell at a profit to future farmers. The past generation has witnessed in Minnesota a vast land speculation, based on the general expectation of an agricultural future. And it should be further noted that even the area which is in farms is not being generally farmed as in a real agricultural community; this is shown by the fact that less than one-third (30 per cent) of the land in farms is plow land or plowable pasture.

The lack of agricultural development places this region in marked contrast with other parts of the state, as is shown by the following figures:

LAND CLASSIFICATION—MINNESOTA—1925

	TOTAL AREA	LAND IN FARMS		PLOW LAND	
	Acres	Acres	Per cent	Acres	Per cent
The state	51,749,120	30,059,137	58.09	20,814,531	40.22
The 16 counties	19,301,120	3,540,159	18.34	1,050,496	5.44
Rest of the State...	32,448,000	26,518,978	81.73	19,764,035	60.91
Winona County	407,680	363,212	89.09	217,035	53.24

The ratio of area in farms to total area in the region we are studying is less than one-fourth of that which prevails in the rest of the state, while the ratio of plow land here is only one-eleventh that of the rest of the state. Winona County, chosen as typical of the good farming regions of the state, shows a similar contrast with the 16 northern counties. For corresponding figures for the separate counties, see Table I in the Appendix.

At the rate at which farm development has proceeded since 1900 (1900 to 1925) it would take 169 years to bring the entire area of this region into the hands of farmers and 560 years to bring the region wholly into plow land and plowable pasture.

It is evident that the expectation of a flourishing agriculture following in the wake of the forest exploitation in northern Minnesota has not been realized. For this result there are doubtless many causes, the complete disclosure of which has not yet been undertaken. But we do not have to go far to find one fundamental condition, which of itself is quite sufficient to explain the situation.

The Inquiry has gone to considerable pains to discover the character of the topography and soil of this region, in order to determine what part of the land has agricultural possibilities and what part is valuable for nothing but forest-growing. A detailed soil survey of this whole region has never been made and was not undertaken by us. Useful studies have been made, however, by various experts. The results of all such studies were brought together and supplemented by extensive questionnaires and field observation

by our staff.[2]   From all the evidence thus available the Inquiry has
been able to make a tentative classification of the area of this region
into potential agricultural and non-agricultural lands, dividing the
second group further into that which is barren peat swamp and that
which is suitable for forest-growing.   This classification does not
claim to be more than a careful estimate, with a considerable margin
of error.   Our effort was always to give the benefit of the doubt to
the agricultural land, so that the results, if in error, tend to show
too much, rather than too little potential agricultural land.   The
result for the whole region is shown in the table below, in which
is included also the classification of land in farms and plow land
already given:

LAND CLASSIFICATION, 16 COUNTIES OF MINNESOTA—1925

Potential agricultural:
In farms:
    Plow land .... 1,050,496 acres   5.44%
    Other land 2,489,663   "   12.90

    Total 3,540,159   "   18.34
Not in farms 4,813,778   "   24.94

    Total ....   8,353,937 acres 43.28%
Non-agricultural:
    Barren peat swamp 2,162,670   "   11.21
    Potential forest land.... 8,784,513   "   45.51

    Total   10,947,183   "   56.72

Total area   19,301,120   "   100.00

It appears that on the basis of purely physical cause more than
half of the land in this region is unsuited for agriculture and will
probably never be successfully employed in farming.   Of course the
region is not uniform.   Certain counties are largely composed of
land suitable ultimately for agricultural use, such as Kanabec and
Mille Lacs, with nearly 90 per cent.   Two other counties, Pine and
Aitkin, have over 60 per cent potential agricultural land.   But 9 of
the 16 counties have less than 50 per cent agricultural land, and
these include generally the largest counties; for example, Cook

[2] A map of the surface formations of the state published in 1914 shows
the work of Frank Leverett and Frederick W. Sardeson.   This map was used
by T. Schantz Hansen as the basis of a classification of agricultural and
forest lands in St. Louis County in 1923 and in Lake County in 1927, in
conjunction with an extensive survey of forest cover types, stocking, and
age classes.   The Inquiry has received also valuable assistance from Professor
Hansen and Professor E. G. Cheyney and from certain of the county agents.
The Department of Soils of the University of Minnesota was shown the
classification as compiled by the Inquiry and given opportunity to criticize it.

County, only 14 per cent, Lake County, 24 per cent, and St. Louis County, the largest of all, 34 per cent. The details for the separate counties are given in Table II in the Appendix.

The financial history of this region is consistent with its industrial history. During the prosperous years, when the lumbering industry was cutting its way through the virgin forest, the population was small; the needs of local government were modest, and there were ample taxable values in the standing timber and the properties of the lumber companies and other related interests. The burden of taxation was light.

Removal of the timber was expected to usher in a period of even greater prosperity, based on agricultural development. Land values were kept relatively high by the prevailing spirit of speculation, favorable to and therefore encouraged by those who were unloading their cutover lands. Expectation of increased population gave plausible justification for ambitious programs of road building and school development. There was inaugurated also in certain counties an ambitious drainage policy, by which the peat bogs or muskeg swamps were ditched and drained, in order to make them suitable for farming. This was done at public expense, the money obtained through the issue of bonds guaranteed by the counties, and the lands assessed for the annual interest and sinking-fund charges. Thus did these counties mortgage their future with heavy public expenses and debt obligations.

The success of this program depended upon the fulfillment of the expectations on which it was based. If in fact the cutover lands and the drained swamps had proved to be good agricultural land; if other economic conditions had proved favorable and farmers had come in and made profitable use of the land, the communities might easily enough have borne the taxes and assessments required to maintain their roads, their schools, their drainage systems, and their other government services. In the opposite event, disaster threatens in some of these counties.

Let us glance at the present financial situation of these sixteen counties, propounding first the question: What services do the people require of their local governments? The following table exhibits the percentage distribution, among the three leading functions, of the government cost payments (i. e. excluding payments of principal of public debt) of the counties, cities, townships, and school districts, so far as these were to be determined from the county accounts, with the aid of certain deductions from the statistics of tax levies. Practically all of the expenditures of the local governments are thus accounted for.

TABLE I
PERCENTAGE DISTRIBUTION OF GOVERNMENT COST PAYMENTS
Minnesota, 1925

County	Education	Roads	Cities, Villages and Townships	Other	To State (Net)
Cook	26.82	36.14	8.09	28.95	0.00
Lake	50.43	20.76	7.18	21.63	0.00
Group 1	43.41	25.33	7.45	23.38	0.00
St. Louis	41.04	11.97	33.81	10.03	3.15
Itasca	45.98	17.53	21.57	14.92	0.00
Group 2	41.94	13.65	32.78	10.65	1.95
Koochiching	49.88	10.91	14.04	25.17	0.00
Beltrami	48.92	8.35	10.98	31.75	0.00
Lake of the Woods	39.28	19.78	5.27	35.67	0.00
Group 3	47.56	11.09	11.36	29.69	0.00
Aitkin	41.30	21.77	9.35	29.58	0.00
Carlton	54.46	19.32	13.46	12.76	0.00
Cass	54.17	13.20	11.21	21.42	0.00
Clearwater	46.55	24.47	7.17	21.81	0.00
Crow Wing	51.12	12.38	21.16	15.34	0.00
Hubbard	60.89	13.06	5.90	20.15	0.00
Group 4	51.90	16.32	13.22	18.56	0.00
Kanabec	38.54	31.86	7.37	22.23	0.00
Mille Lacs	48.61	19.37	11.69	20.33	0.00
Pine	46.53	29.37	7.91	16.19	0.00
Group 5	45.56	26.93	8.91	18.60	0.00
Total—16 counties	44.43	14.29	27.53	13.75	0.00
Winona	48.16	12.19	24.83	12.24	2.58

As with local government generally throughout the United States, education and roads stand out as the two predominant functions, accounting for 44.43 per cent and 14.29 per cent respectively of the total government cost payments. General governmental expenses of cities, townships, etc. (not including schools and roads) are an important group, which we are not able to split up into their details. This group, 27.53 per cent, is made to appear disproportionately large by the inclusion of St. Louis County, with its very heavy expenditures and the large expenditures of the City of Duluth. Only two other counties have as much as 20 per cent in this group, while half of the counties are below 10 per cent.

The relative expenditure for education in the several counties is remarkably uniform. The lowest percentage is 26.82 in Cook County, the highest 60.89 in Hubbard County. All the other fourteen counties fall between 38 and 55 per cent. There is somewhat more variety in the proportionate expenditure for roads; from 8.35 per cent in Beltrami County to 36.14 per cent in Cook.

The percentage distribution of payments shows nothing peculiar in this region; the distribution in the southern agricultural county of Winona is almost identical with the average for the sixteen northeastern counties.

On the reverse side of the account the one important fact is that taxation is virtually the sole resource of the local governments, for money to meet their public expenditures. Ninety-four per cent of all revenue receipts of the region come from taxes. The figures for the several counties are presented in Table II below.

TABLE II

PERCENTAGE DISTRIBUTION OF REVENUE RECEIPTS

Minnesota, 1925

County	Taxes	Other County Receipts	Federal and State (Net)
Cook	84.99	7.75	7.26
Lake ....:...............	71.50	3.41	25.09
Group 1	75.69	4.76	19.55
St. Louis	97.71	2.18	.11
Itasca	80.16	2.40	8.44
Group 2	97.62	2.23	.15
Koochiching	82.30	6.04	11.66
Beltrami	68.00	17.66	14.34
Lake of the Woods	74.61	4.85	20.54
Group 3	74.54	11.45	14.91
Aitkin	86.48	7.18	6.34
Carlton	83.25	5.24	11.51
Cass	73.90	5.75	20.35
Clearwater	74.37	7.67	17.96
Crow Wing	89.01	5.55	5.44
Hubbard	71.00	6.11	22.89
Group 4	81.63	5.98	12.39
Kanabec	80.58	10.20	9.22
Mille Lacs ....·....	74.55	7.69	17.76
Pine	80.92	7.56	11.52
Group 5	78.92	8.16	12.92
Total—16 counties	93.89	3.76	2.37
Winona	96.53	3.47	0.00

There is some variation among the counties. The one that draws the largest percentage (97.71) from taxes is the large, populous, and prosperous county of St. Louis, containing the city of Duluth. St. Louis County occupies a predominant position in any weighted average for the whole region, which often gives a false appearance to the average. In this case, while the percentage of tax receipts for the whole region is 93.89, no other county has as much as 90 per cent. Eleven of the counties run between 70 and 85 per cent. Winona, a prosperous agricultural county, is like St. Louis, deriving 96.53 per cent of her revenue receipts from taxes. These northern counties in general thus show a distinctly smaller reliance upon taxation than is to be found in the ordinary prosperous community. The difference is made up generally by net contributions from the state, which, while entirely lacking in St. Louis and Winona counties, account for more than 10 per cent of the receipts in ten of the counties and more than 20 per cent in four of these. Here is distinct evidence of financial weakness.

Table III presents a picture of the tax base upon which the people of this region must depend for their tax revenue.[3]

Of the total assessed valuation of the sixteen counties of 465 million dollars, St. Louis County alone has 356 millions. The other counties have assessed valuations ranging from less than 2 million dollars in Cook County to over 13 millions in Crow Wing and 25 millions in Itasca. These fifteen counties (outside of St. Louis), having 30 per cent of the area of the state, have less than 6 per cent (5.6%) of the taxable property of the state. Further evidence of poverty may be derived from the figures of assessed valuation per capita. Here also St. Louis stands high—double the average for the whole state, $748.90. Two other counties, Cook and Itasca, have per-capita assessments slightly higher than the state as a whole. Of the rest, none is as high as $500; they range from $264 in Beltrami to $476 in Hubbard. In Winona County the average is $618.

Those counties which have valuable iron deposits are especially fortunate. Three are in such situation, St. Louis, Itasca, and Crow Wing. More than two-thirds of the total assessed valuation of St. Louis County and of Itasca County consists of iron ore; in Crow Wing, iron ore accounts for about one-fourth of the assessed value. In most of the counties, the great bulk of the taxable property consists of rural (unplatted) real estate. In only a few counties are platted real estate and personal property important. St. Louis County is one of these. Her enormous values in iron ore and the large value of platted real estate and personal property in the City of

---

[3] In connection with all figures of assessed values in Minnesota it must be remembered that these are not the true values. The law requires the assessor to determine the full and true value and then to assess the following classes of property at the following ratios of true value:

Iron ore 50%
Rural lands and buildings 33⅓%
Urban lands and buildings 40%
Personal property (generally) 33⅓%
Other personal property .... 25% and 10%

TABLE III

TOTAL ASSESSED VALUATION

Minnesota, Levy of 1926

County	Total	ASSESSED VALUATION Unplatted Real Estate	Platted Real Estate	Unmined Iron Ore	Personal Property	Assess Value p Capit
ok ....$	1,834,930	$ 1,619,397	$ 146,244	....	$ 69,289	$ 842.
ke	3,928,212	2,967,407	778,548	....	182,257	467.
Group 1	5,763,142	4,586,804	924,792	....	251,546	544.
Louis	355,799,572	13,577,771	70,366,215	$239,358,688	32,496,898	1,512.
sca	25,234,771	5,115,057	1,647,131	16,980,655	1,491,928	826.
Group 2	381,034,343	18,692,828	72,013,346	256,339,343	33,988,826	1,433.
ochiching	5,480,915	3,635,530	1,172,642	....	672,743	300.
ltrami	6,673,641	4,238,163	1,786,927	....	648,551	264.
ke of the Woods.	2,285,952	1,908,175	202,538	....	175,239	326.
Group 3	14,440,508	9,781,868	3,162,107	....	1,496,533	285.
kin	7,680,449	6,387,061	864,877	....	428,511	422.
rlton	9,552,146	5,647,177	1,687,779	....	2,217,190	463.
ss	6,077,684	4,898,233	730,631	....	448,820	323.
arwater	3,644,259	3,108,278	281,664	....	254,317	375.
ɔw Wing	13,182,146	4,724,264	3,426,343	3,475,022	1,556,517	443.
bbard	4,917,634	3,850,779	665,395	....	401,460	475.
Group 4	45,054,318	28,615,792	7,656,689	3,475,022	5,306,815	419.
nabec	3,746,736	3,031,795	336,395	....	378,546	345.
lle Lacs	5,278,557	3,736,378	923,954	....	618,225	319.
e	9,447,804	7,735,149	863,790	....	848,865	383.
Group 5	18,473,097	14,503,322	2,124,139	....	1,845,636	355.
tal—16 counties..	464,765,408	76,180,614	85,881,073	259,814,365	42,889,356	955.
nona	20,903,300	9,272,937	8,367,920	....	3,262,443	618.
tal—state	1,943,879,780	780,675,381	673,658,376	259,814,365	229,731,658	748.0

Duluth account for all but 14 millions of her total assessment of 356 million dollars. We have here the explanation also of the high figure for per-capita assessment and the general state of prosperity of this large county.

Tax rates in this region are, as would be expected of a poor community, high. Whereas the average rate for the state is 58.4 mills and for the prosperous agricultural county of Winona, 60.4 mills, the average for this region is 71.61 mills.[4] Moreover this average is made low by the predominance in the average of St. Louis County, whose relatively easy circumstances are indicated by a tax rate of 63.83 mills. Outside St. Louis County the lowest rate

[4] These tax rates are to be considered in the light of the legal ratios of assessed to true values, as noted above.

is 68.32 mills; only two other counties are below 78 mills; while six are above 100 mills. The highest is Koochiching, with 157.31 mills. The details are presented in Table IV below.

TABLE IV

AVERAGE TAX RATE IN MILLS

County	Average Tax Rate in Mills	
Cook	124.29	
Lake	110.64	
Group 1		114.99
St. Louis	63.83	
Itasca	100.96	
Group 2		66.29
Koochiching	157.31	
Beltrami	132.68	
Lake of the Woods	97.66	
Group 3		136.48
Aitkin	89.18	
Carlton	91.10	
Cass	108.68	
Clearwater	68.32	
Crow Wing	87.90	
Hubbard	69.80	
Group 4		88.04
Kanabec	70.90	
Mille Lacs	79.71	
Pine	78.08	
Group 5		77.09
Total—16 counties		71.61
Winona	60.36	
Total for state		58.40

·Although, as has been shown, assessed valuations per capita are in most of the northern counties comparatively meagre, the per-capita cost of local government is not correspondingly low. In most counties the cost is higher than in Winona County, where it is $37.40; twelve are higher, up to $104.57 in Cook, while four are lower, down to $32.73 in Clearwater. The region as a whole is about on a par with the entire state, eight counties having a per-capita cost higher than the state average of $47.72, while eight are lower. The average for the whole region, $75.20, is made disproportionately high by the predominant influence of St. Louis County, with $103.66, together with two other counties that run above $100.

Evidence of financial strain is shown by the high cost of local government per dollar of assessed value. (See Table V.) With an average of 62.70 mills for the whole state and 60.35 mills for Winona County, the average for this region is 75.44 mills. But this does not disclose the true situation, since this figure is greatly depressed by the predominant influence of St. Louis County, where the government cost payments (65.60 mills) are only slightly above the state average. Only three other counties have payments under 100 mills per dollar of assessed value, the remaining twelve ranging from 101.18 in Hubbard to 166.69 in Koochiching.

TABLE V

GOVERNMENT COST

SPECIFIED CLASSIFICATION OF PAYMENTS

Minnesota, 1925

COUNTY	PER CAPITA			PER DOLLAR ASSESSED VALUE (MILLS)		
	Total Payments	Educa-tion	Roads	Total Payments	Educa-tion	Roads
Cook $104.57	$28.05	$37.78	$120.67	$32.37	$43.61
Lake 61.80	31.16	12.83	132.97	67.06	27.61
Group 1 .... 70.35	30.54	17.82	129.07	56.03	32.69
St. Louis 103.66	42.55	12.41	65.60	26.93	7.85
Itasca 104.48	48.04	18.31	107.82	49.57	18.90
Group 2 .... 102.84	43.13	13.04	67.89	28.48	8.61
Koochiching 53.15	26.51	5.80	166.69	83.14	18.19
Beltrami 41.87	20.48	3.49	152.37	74.55	12.72
Lake of the Woods ... 51.18	20.10	10.12	153.45	60.27	30.36
Group 3 .... 47.19	22.59	5.24	158.00	75.63	17.53
Aitkin 34.37	14.19	7.48	77.12	31.85	16.79
Carlton 50.76	27.64	9.81	108.02	58.83	20.88
Cass 48.14	26.08	6.36	140.80	76.28	18.59
Clearwater 32.73	15.24	8.01	84.01	39.11	20.55
Crow Wing 40.72	20.82	5.04	86.70	44.33	10.73
Hubbard 47.34	28.83	6.18	101.18	61.61	13.21
Group 4 .... 42.81	22.22	6.99	109.74	56.97	17.90
Kanabec 37.35	14.40	11.90	101.91	39.28	32.47
Mille Lacs 36.56	17.78	7.09	107.47	52.24	20.82
Pine 42.49	19.77	12.48	103.44	48.13	30.38
Group 5 .... 39.54	18.02	10.65	104.28	47.51	28.08
Total—16 counties ... 75.20	33.41	10.74	75.44	33.51	10.78
Winona 37.40	18.01	4.56	60.35	29.07	7.36
Total—State (Levy).. 47.72	17.26	7.27	62.70	22.67	9.55

Interesting side-lights on this situation are furnished by the figures for cost of particular functions of government. Note, for example, that some of these counties are paying as much as $20 and

$30 per capita for education, while the corresponding levy is $18.01 in Winona County and averages $17.26 for the whole state, and are paying $10 and $12 for roads, which cost the people of Winona County only $4.56 per capita and the whole state but $7.27. Consider the payment in certain poor counties of 60, 70 and 80 mills per dollar of assessed value for education and half as much for roads, while in Winona County the expenditure is 29.07 mills for education and 7.36 mills for roads, and in the state as a whole 22.67 mills and 9.55 mills respectively.

TABLE VI

RECEIPTS FROM TAXES

Minnesota, 1925

County	Per Capita	Per Dollar Assessed Value (mills)
Cook	$93.75	$108.19
Lake	43.71	94.06
Group 1	53.72	98.55
St. Louis	103.32	65.39
Itasca	94.69	97.72
Group 2	102.40	67.60
Koochiching	49.49	155.23
Beltrami	34.40	125.17
Lake of the Woods	34.80	104.35
Group 3	39.85	133.43
Aitkin	37.16	83.38
Carlton	41.55	88.43
Cass	36.74	107.48
Clearwater	24.82	63.70
Crow Wing	39.03	83.12
Hubbard	34.82	74.43
Group 4	37.11	95.12
Kanabec	30.47	83.13
Mille Lacs	26.42	77.63
Pine	30.63	74.56
Group 5	29.26	77.16
Total—16 counties	72.56	72.79
Winona	37.34	60.25
Total—State (Levy)	47.72	62.70

The final evidence of the burden of government costs on the people of these counties is furnished by the amount of taxes paid in relation to population and to assessed valuation. In Winona County the tax burden per capita is $37.34. In the state as a whole it is $47.72. Four of the sixteen counties pay less per capita than

Winona; the lowest is $24.82, in Clearwater; twelve pay more, ranging up to $103.32 in St. Louis County. St. Louis and one or two others are well able to pay, on account of their mineral wealth, but most of these are distinctly poor counties, as compared with Winona. The average for the sixteen counties is made disproportionately high by the presence of St. Louis County.

The most telling evidence of all is from the burden of taxes per dollar of assessed value. For the whole state this is 62.70 mills; for Winona County it is 60.25 mills. For the region under consideration it is 72.79 mills, but this average, great as it is, is misleading, on account of the disproportionate influence of St. Louis County, with its tax burden of only 65.39 mills per dollar. Every one of the sixteen counties stands higher than Winona, most of them much higher. Clearwater, with 63.70 mills, is the lowest; Koochiching, with 155.23 mills, is highest. Five of the sixteen counties have rates over 100 mills; six have rates between 80 and 100 mills.

With heavy assessed valuations and high tax rates, based either on the expectation of agricultural values or simply upon the financial necessities of the counties and townships, many owners of rural lands have found themselves unable to bear the burden and have permitted their lands to go delinquent. The Forest Taxation Inquiry has made a careful study of the delinquency in certain of these counties, with results which are shown in the table below.

TABLE VII

TAX-PAYING, TAX-DELINQUENT, AND TAX-EXEMPT ACREAGE

PERCENTAGE OF TOTAL LAND AREA

Minnesota, 1926

County	Federal Lands All Classes	State Lands All Classes	Absolute Un-redeemed Land	Delinquent 3rd Year
Beltrami	21.01	1.30	20.28	6.51
Cass	14.18	5.61	10.53	3.79
Hubbard	.14	2.27	5.58	7.70
Itasca	10.91	11.21	6.70	4.06
Koochiching	8.78	38.78	10.26	3.56
Lake	25.64	11.37	5.85	3.14
St. Louis	7.09	10.33	4.02	1.30

County	Delinquent 2nd Year	Delinquent 1st Year	Tax-Paying Land	Platted Property and Railroad Rights of Way
Beltrami	7.35	4.53	36.70	.47
Cass	4.14	3.98	57.35	.42
Hubbard	11.19	5.42	67.22	.49
Itasca	6.80	4.53	55.29	.50
Koochiching	4.12	3.97	30.34	.19
Lake	3.05	4.80	46.02	.13
St. Louis	2.34	2.67	71.20	1.15

Absolute unredeemed land has little prospect of going back to the owner or to any other private holder. Land delinquent for only one, two, or three years has a better chance, diminishing with the lapse of time it has remained delinquent. Our figures for seven counties show that absolute unredeemed land makes up one-fifth (20.28 per cent) of the area of Beltrami County, over 10 per cent in two others (Cass, 10.53 per cent, and Koochiching, 10.26 per cent) and from 4 per cent to 6.7 per cent of the other four. These are percentages of the entire land area of the respective counties. Taking account of the fact that each of these counties contains considerable tax-exempt land, belonging to the Federal Government or to the state, it appears that of the taxable land, the percentages that are absolutely delinquent are as follows:

Beltrami County	26.10%
Cass County	13.13
Hubbard County	5.72
Itasca County	8.60
Koochiching County	19.57
Lake County	9.29
St. Louis County	4.87

If we add together all the land on which taxes are delinquent, whether for one year or more, we get the following percentages, (1) of the total area and (2) of the taxable land:

	Percentage of	
	Total Area	*Taxable Land*
Beltrami County	40.52%	52.16%
Cass County	22.44	27.98
Hubbard County	29.89	30.63
Itasca County	22.09	28.36
Koochiching County	21.91	41.78
Lake County	16.84	26.73
St. Louis County	10.33	12.51

Of the taxable land in Beltrami County, more than half is in some stage of delinquency, more than one quarter being absolute unredeemed. Nearly half the taxable land in Koochiching is delinquent, and more than a quarter is delinquent in four of the other five counties, St. Louis being the exception.

No account of public finance is complete without reference to the public debt. The table below gives for each of eight selected counties in the northern region the total of all public indebtedness, including obligations of the school districts and the townships, as well as those of the counties, expressed as a percentage of the assessed valuation of taxable property.[5] St. Louis County, as usual, appears to advantage. Three other counties (Hubbard, Lake and Itasca) are in fairly good shape. Of the other four, two have public indebtedness in the neighborhood of one-fourth their assessed valuation (Cass, 26.91 per cent, and Aitkin, 22.57 per cent), while Koochiching has just under one-half (47.57 per cent) and Lake of the Woods has slightly more than half (52.21 per cent).

TABLE VIII

PUBLIC AND PRIVATE INDEBTEDNESS

PERCENTAGE IN RELATION TO ASSESSED VALUATION

Minnesota, 1926

County	Public Debt, Including County, School Districts and Townships	Federal Land Bank Mortgages	State Rural, Credit Loans
Lake	10.30	1.98	.21
St. Louis	5.40	7.36	1.27
Itasca	10.72	5.29	5.00
Koochiching	47.57	7.78	2.86
Lake of the Woods	52.21	7.95	12.29
Hubbard	8.04	7.66	9.75
Cass	26.91	3.92	15.24
Aitkin	22.57	4.79	11.87

County	Other Private Mortgages	Total	Residual Assessed Value
Lake	20.73	33.22	66.78
St. Louis	23.68	37.71	62.29
Itasca	34.99	56.00	44.00
Koochiching	15.34	73.55	26.45
Lake of the Woods	21.34	93.79	6.21
Hubbard	13.86	39.31	60.69
Cass	57.02	103.09	—3.09
Aitkin	40.19	79.42	20.58

Local public debts are in effect a mortgage upon the taxable property of the community. The ability of the property to bear this load is in some degree at least dependent upon the amount of other obligations for which such property has been pledged. To bring out this part of the picture we have compiled for these eight counties the amount of federal land bank mortgages, state rural credit loans, and other private mortgages resting upon the local unplatted real estate. The results are shown in Table VIII. The totals of public and private obligations show that in one county, Cass, the taxable

[5] It is to be recalled, as previously pointed out, that assessed valuations in Minnesota are at certain fractions of true values. If translated into the percentage of true values, as determined by the assessors, the figures in this table would be reduced to approximately one-third.

property is thus pledged to the extent of 103 per cent of its assessed valuation. In another county, Lake of the Woods, the total is 94 per cent, while in two others, Koochiching and Aitkin, the mortgage is about three-fourths of the assessed valuation.

Certain aspects of the public finances of this region which have been set forth as present-day cross-sections, gain added significance if their recent development is shown. For this purpose we have studied certain tendencies, by taking the facts for selected years since 1880. The years selected were 1880, 1890, 1900, 1910, 1915, 1920, 1925, and in some cases also 1926.

For example, Table IX shows that the total assessed valuations of these sixteen counties have been universally increasing since 1880, generally reaching a climax in the year 1920 (though in two

TABLE IX

TOTAL ASSESSED VALUATION *

Minnesota, 1880–1926

County	1880	1890	1900	1910	1915	1920	1925	1926
)k	$ 27	$ 461	$ 1,255	$ 2,228	$ 1,993	$ 1,908	$ 1,820	$ 1,8
ke	119	1,666	2,882	4,384	3,863	4,013	3,903	3,9
Group 1	146	2,127	4,137	6,612	5,856	5,921	5,723	5,7
Louis	1,563	42,890	44,390	272,450	324,256	372,658	365,469	355,7
sca	253	885	5,674	23,650	25,179	28,831	26,843	25,2
Group 2	1,816	43,775	50,064	296,100	349,435	401,489	392,312	381,0
)chiching	.....	......	......	6,178	6,591	6,702	5,580	5,4
trami	90	451	3,298	5,889	7,836	10,775	6,788	6,6
:e of the Woods.	.....	......	......	......	......	......	2,255	2,2
Group 3	90	451	3,298	12,067	14,427	17,477	14,623	14,
:in	195	572	1,481	4,001	5,956	8,166	7,888	7,6
lton	295	2,151	2,582	5,342	6,191	9,455	9,586	9,5
s	669	1,649	2,160	4,413	5,494	7,613	6,257	6,0
irwater	.....	......	......	2,071	2,832	4,260	3,701	3,6
w Wing	308	2,171	2,899	6,024	13,502	14,073	13,572	13,1
)bard	.....	575	2,028	3,187	3,476	5,245	4,819	4,9
Group 4	1,467	7,118	11,150	25,038	37,451	48,812	45,823	45,0
abec	586	551	658	1,999	3,134	5,164	3,885	3,7
le Lacs	592	1,110	1,309	2,563	4,239	6,922	5,478	5,2
)	635	1,504	2,380	4,685	6,588	10,760	9,900	9,4
Group 5	1,813	3,165	4,347	9,247	13,961	22,846	19,263	18,4
il—16 counties .	5,332	56,636	72,996	349,064	421,130	496,545	477,744	464,7
ona	8,990	11,692	11,920	13,567	16,692	22,373	20,944	20,9
il for state	258,056	588,820	588,017	1,194,962	1,491,965	2,084,286	1,951,031	1,943,8

* In thousands of dollars.

Minnesota, 1880–1926

County	1880	1890	1900	1910	1915	1920	1925	1926
Cook	$ 413.17 *	$4,708.08 *	$1,549.20	$1,667.73	$1,240.00	$1,022.59	$ 855.58	$ 842.10
Lake	1,123.37	1,282.39	619.33	547.19	474.56	485.64	465.42	467.03
Group 1	853.41	1,522.70	757.18	707.35	60.76	584.55	544.35	544.21
St. Louis	347.14	956.04	535.26	1,668.67	7852	1,786.36	1,583.36	1,512.37
Itasca	2,037.06	1,190.88	1,240.71	1,3 74.35	1,211.38	1,190.39	970.68	826.18
Group 2	392.42	959.87	572.13	1,640.61	1,729.16	1,724.37	1,517.81	1,433.52
Koochiching	......	......	......	960.63	644.07	482.61	318.19	300.06
Beltrami	9,047.60 *	1,444.19	299.02	304.54	333.58	392.14	274.78	264.17
Lake of the Woods	......	......	......	......	......	......	333.51	326.61
Group 3	9,047.60 *	1,444.19	299.02	468.28	427.80	422.51	298.42	285.79
Aitkin	531.43	232.44	219.56	385.75	462.49	534.34	445.91	422.68
Carlton	239.67	407.98	257.80	304.25	333.92	485.27	469.24	463.31
Cass	1,378.45	1,322.52	277.77	379.83	394.82	472.37	341.52	323.97
Clearwater	......	......	......	301.45	363.96	492.17	388.28	375.46
Crow Wing	132.64	245.24	203.38	357.27	643.12	563.75	469.13	443.48
Hubbard	......	407.57	308.34	324.15	347.78	516.62	467.44	475.59
Group 4	333.29	369.90	245.77	342.46	445.29	515.69	435.54	419.82
Kanabec	1,161.13	348.59	142.55	309.45	398.22	559.96	367.47	345.54
Mille Lacs	394.59	390.22	162.25	239.36	337.32	482.06	339.19	319.80
Pine	464.92	371.22	206.17	295.07	352.51	503.11	411.05	383.68
Group 5	537.90	373.38	179.43	279.84	356.83	508.05	379.14	355.44
Total—16 counties	423.86	754.80	420.51	1,084.88	1,126.34	1,171.24	1,007.89	955.89
15 counties (excluding St. Louis)	466.64	455.58	315.53	483.43	516.69	575.32	461.68	4821
Rest of State (excluding 16 counties)	328.98	430.83	326.42	482.28	572.98	802.21	705.07	701.20
State	330.51	449.38	335.74	575.69	665.23	867.31	761.07	748.90
Winona	330.56	345.94	334.02	406.21	497.74	64.53	619.70	618.00

* Based on population of less than 100.

cases the climax came in 1910 and in one case in 1925).[6] Since the climax there has been for the whole region a gradual falling-off to 1925 and 1926, though a few counties show slight gains in the last year. For the remainder of the state there has been the same general tendency since 1880, except that there has been on the average a slight gain in 1926.

TABLE XI

AVERAGE TAX RATES IN MILLS

Minnesota, 1880–1926

County	1880	1890	1900	1910	1915	1920	1925	1926
Cook	7.5	19.0	24.5	46.42	61.37	94.44	132.06	124.29
Lake	14.2	17.8	22.1	42.37	53.74	91.79	104.06	110.64
Group 1	13.0	18.1	22.8	43.73	56.33	92.64	112.96	114.99
St. Louis	27.6	21.9	25.1	21.90	28.77	65.62	65.78	63.83
Itasca	8.0	9.3	25.5	35.72	44.90	104.68	101.88	100.96
Group 2	24.9	21.6	25.1	23.00	29.93	68.42	68.25	66.29
Koochiching	...	...	...	36.00	75.10	101.94	146.82	157.31
Beltrami	3.5	6.4	28.6	51.70	80.57	96.09	134.23	132.68
Lake of the Woods..	...	...	...	....	....	....	108.30	97.66
Group 3	3.5	6.4	28.6	43.66	78.07	98.33	135.04	136.48
Aitkin	30.6	33.8	32.4	44.30	68.17	84.41	87.20	89.18
Carlton	27.7	24.1	38.1	42.67	57.00	73.60	94.20	91.10
Cass	11.5	8.0	26.8	39.20	66.73	88.63	105.87	108.68
Clearwater	...	...	...	35.20	41.89	62.87	70.65	68.32
Crow Wing	25.0	30.3	29.7	40.40	45.08	80.93	86.09	87.90
Hubbard	...	20.5	31.7	43.87	62.40	61.64	73.87	69.80
Group 4	20.1	22.7	31.8	41.31	55.26	77.64	88.15	88.04
Kanabec	14.6	35.0	47.2	40.20	44.34	67.40	69.81	70.90
Mille Lacs	16.3	27.3	39.9	45.15	49.47	70.59	75.91	79.71
Pine	30.5	23.8	36.8	42.15	51.63	73.06	76.15	78.08
Group 5	20.7	27.0	39.3	42.56	49.34	71.03	74.80	77.09
Total—16 counties	21.5	21.8	27.0	25.94	34.84	70.79	73.00	71.61
Winona	13.5	21.9	25.0	28.28	34.55	48.04	61.65	60.36
Total for state	16.2	21.6	25.4	27.92	34.89	52.43	59.78	58.40

The assessed valuation per capita in this region has been generally falling since 1880 or 1890. In most of the counties there was a rapid drop to 1900. Since then there was a moderate decline, or a level tendency, or even a slight rise, with a secondary peak in 1920, followed universally by a distinct drop to 1925.

St. Louis County is a conspicuous exception, showing a general

[6] Lake of the Woods having been carved out of Beltrami County in 1922, these counties are treated as a unit in this comparison.

25

marked rise of assessed value per capita throughout the period, though with a sharp drop from 1890 to 1900 and again from 1920 to 1925, but with very pronounced rises from 1880 to 1890, and from 1900 to 1920.

This region (outside St. Louis County) is in marked contrast to the rest of the state. In Winona County assessed valuation per capita has been rising rapidly since 1900, although a decline from 1920 to 1925 is observed. The same tendency is shown for the state as a whole, outside these sixteen counties.

The tax rates of the sixteen counties show universal increases from 1880 to 1925, increases which are very great, are continuous through the whole period (with one exception, i. e. Kanabec County from 1900 to 1910), and have generally been accelerating, especially since 1910. St. Louis County is a partial exception, showing a fairly level curve from 1880 to 1910 and from 1920 to 1925. This great increase in tax rates is one of the most significant developments of the past forty-five years. Up to 1915 the progress of tax rates in this region was fairly representative of the state as a whole. Since then the increase in these sixteen counties has been much more rapid and the point reached in 1926 substantially higher than in the rest of the state.

The tax burden per capita is of course the resultant of the assessed valuation per capita and the tax rate. In it the decreasing tendency of the former and the increasing tendency of the latter have in some measure neutralized each other, with the result that there has gradually been (1) a virtually level curve or a slow increase from 1880 to 1910, (2) a quite sharp increase from 1910 to 1920, and (3) from 1920 to 1925 a slight rise in twelve counties and a slight drop in four, with the average about level. See Table XII. Here, while the general tendency in this region is in harmony with what has taken place in Winona County and in the state as a whole, the comparison is nevertheless very significant. Note that the tax burden per capita in this region, despite deficient tax-paying capacity, is continuously higher than in the well-to-do county of Winona and in the state as a whole. Note also that this discrepancy shows a marked increase, beginning in 1900.

We have already noted the amount of land at present delinquent in seven selected counties. Of great significance from the point of view of public finance is the effect of delinquency upon the current revenues of the counties. This may be shown by comparing with the current tax levy for each year, the amount collected, which latter amount we have separated into two parts: that collected on the current year's levy and that which represents collection of back taxes. The difference is the current deficit in county tax revenue. The figures are best expressed as percentages of the current year's tax levy. We have the results of such a comparison for each of the sixteen counties covering the past decade, 1917-1926. They are presented in the accompanying diagram.

TABLE XII

TAXES AND SPECIAL ASSESSMENTS PER CAPITA

Minnesota, 1880–1926

County	1880	1890	1900	1910	1915	1920	1925	1926
Cook	$ 2.91 *	$89.64 *	$38.04	$77.42	$76.10	$96.58	$113.00	$104.66
Lake	16.01	22.79	13.69	23.06	25.60	44.58	48.88	52.55
Group 1	11.03	27.48	17.30	30.83	33.93	54.15	61.85	63.28
St. Louis	9.61	20.91	13.44	36.47	50.76	118.34	105.89	98.20
Itasca	16.30	20.13	31.60	49.08	54.39	125.75	100.61	84.83
Group 2	9.79	20.90	14.39	37.67	51.12	119.11	105.33	96.67
Koochiching	....	....	....	34.61	48.74	60.42	54.43	53.49
Beltrami	31.67 *	9.24	8.56	15.74	26.88	50.74	45.09	42.62
Lake of the Woods.	....	....	....	....	....	....	54.59	48.15
Group 3	31.67 *	9.24	8.56	20.45	33.51	53.99	49.74	47.31
Aitkin	16.29	7.87	7.12	17.10	31.53	50.87	43.82	42.68
Carlton	6.64	9.32	9.83	12.98	19.03	36.82	45.95	44.40
Cass	15.64	10.58	7.44	14.88	26.39	46.12	38.06	36.84
Clearwater	....	....	....	10.61	15.25	30.95	28.96	27.09
Crow Wing	3.36	7.43	6.03	14.44	28.84	46.59	41.33	39.82
Hubbard	....	8.37	9.78	14.22	22.38	32.10	35.40	34.15
Group 4	6.71	8.28	7.82	14.15	24.66	42.20	40.37	38.96
Kanabec	16.88	12.15	6.73	12.43	17.71	38.76	26.48	25.30
Mille Lacs	6.43	10.59	6.47	10.81	16.69	34.68	27.45	26.14
Pine	15.04	9.09	7.59	12.44	18.20	37.12	32.30	30.77
Group 5	11.48	10.17	7.05	11.91	17.62	36.68	29.55	28.16
Total—16 counties ..	9.20	16.53	11.37	28.10	39.63	85.29	76.08	70.75
Rest of state	5.31	9.28	8.23	13.87	19.93	40.70	43.02	41.98
State	5.37	9.70	8.54	16.08	23.21	48.57	49.13	47.37
Winona	4.45	7.58	8.34	11.49	17.20	32.25	38.90	37.97

* Based on population of less than 100.

AND SPECIAL ASSESSMENTS PAID AND DELINQUENT
SSED IN PERCENTS OF THE AMOUNTS LEVIED BY YEARS.

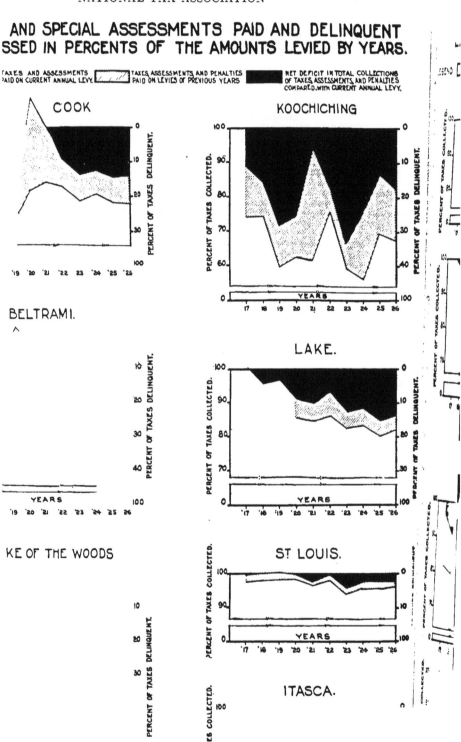

S AND SPECIAL ASSESSMENTS PAID AND DELINQUENT
ESSED IN PERCENTS OF THE AMOUNTS LEVIED BY YEARS

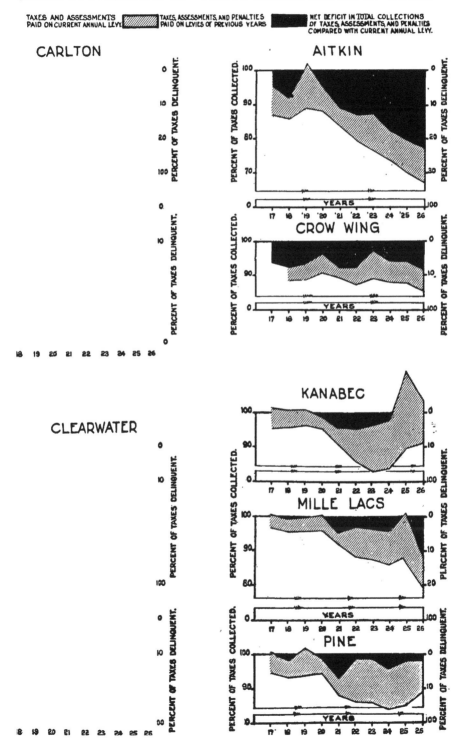

TAXES AND ASSESSMENTS PAID ON CURRENT ANNUAL LEVY.

TAXES, ASSESSMENTS, AND PENALTIES PAID ON LEVIES OF PREVIOUS YEARS

NET DEFICIT IN TOTAL COLLECTIONS OF TAXES, ASSESSMENTS, AND PENALTIES COMPARED WITH CURRENT ANNUAL LEVY.

CARLTON

AITKIN

CROW WING

CLEARWATER

KANABEC

MILLE LACS

PINE

D SPECIAL ASSESSMENTS PAID AND DELINQUENT
ED IN PERCENTS OF THE AMOUNTS LEVIED BY YEARS.

AND ASSESSMENTS / TAXES ASSESSMENTS AND PENALTIES / NET DEFICIT IN TOTAL COLLECTIONS
CURRENT ANNUAL LEVY. / PAID ON LEVIES OF PREVIOUS YEARS / OF TAXES, ASSESSMENTS, AND PENALTIES
COMPARED WITH CURRENT ANNUAL LEVY.

COOK

KOOCHICHING

LTRAMI.

LAKE.

OF THE WOODS

ST LOUIS.

ITASCA.

XES AND SPECIAL ASSESSMENTS PAID AND DELINQUENT
PRESSED IN PERCENTS OF THE AMOUNTS LEVIED BY YEARS

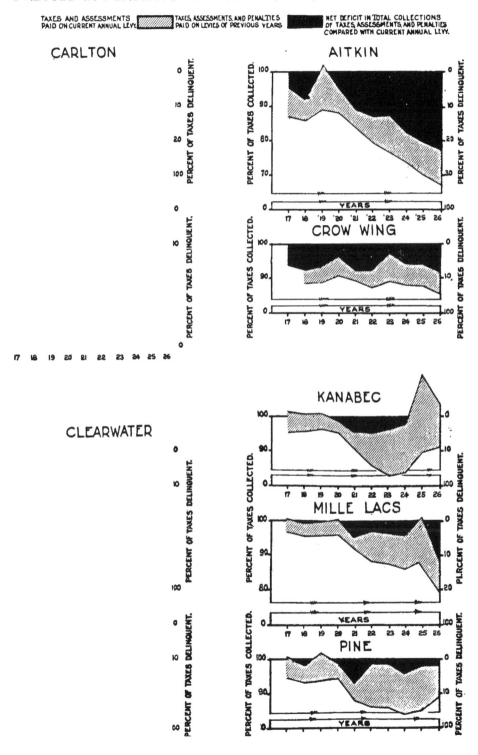

TAXES AND SPECIAL ASSESSMENTS PAID AND DELINQUENT EXPRESSED IN PERCENTS OF THE AMOUNTS LEVIED BY YEARS.

LEGEND

TAXES AND ASSESSMENTS
PAID ON CURRENT ANNUAL LEVY

TAXES, ASSESSMENTS AND PENALTIES
PAID ON LEVIES OF PREVIOUS YEARS.

NET DEFICIT IN TOTAL COLLECTIONS
OF TAXES, ASSESSMENTS AND PENALTIES
COMPARED WITH CURRENT ANNUAL LEVY.

REMAINDER OF STATE.

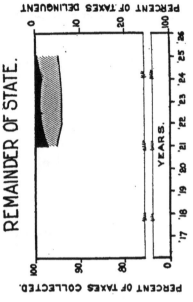

TOTAL 16 COUNTIES.

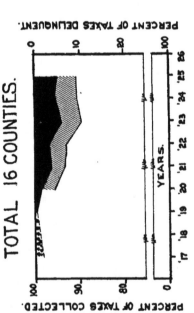

Perhaps nothing shows more clearly the discouraging financial outlook which most of these northern counties face. A few of these counties are prosperous and need feel no serious concern over delinquency; such are St. Louis, Itasca (both helped by their iron ore and St. Louis by its valuable city property in Duluth), Kanabec, which has recently been collecting more than 100 per cent because of its success in bringing in back taxes, and Pine, where the deficit is small and not increasing of late. All the other counties show a serious condition, due to heavy deficits for several years past, or to a tendency of the deficits to increase, or to both. Deficits from 15 per cent to 45 per cent appear for the year 1926, and the most discouraging feature is that in most cases the percentages not collected have been increasing during the decade and especially during the last year or two.

This picture of the critical financial situation of the cutover region of northeastern Minnesota should not be taken as evidence that something is wrong with this particular state. Far from it. Minnesota is made the example in this essay simply because it was the state chosen for our first field study and because it is the one state whose study is now approaching completion. This region of Minnesota represents a certain phase in economic development which I am confident will be found to be representative of many other parts of the United States. In certain parts of the East and North, this phase has been passed. In other places, particularly in the other Lake states but by no means only there, this is the present situation. In other regions, as in the great virgin forest areas of the Pacific coast states, this phase has not yet been reached. Every region which was once covered by virgin timber has passed through this stage, or is now in it, or is destined to reach it, unless the problem of transition is in the meantime solved. The destiny of the virgin forest is to be cut. When cut, something else takes its place; it may be a flourishing agriculture; it may be a healthy second growth of forest; it may be a new forest industry on a sustained yield basis, or it may be a barren waste. The cutover region which we have studied represents the critical stage in which the future is hanging in the balance.

The discussion of the tax situation of these northern counties of Minnesota may appear thus far to have little relation to the problem of forest taxation. As a matter of fact there is no aspect of the public finances of a forest region which is not intimately related to forest taxation. It is a mistake, altogether too frequently made, to think of forest taxation as a problem apart, dissociated from the general problem of the public revenues and expenditures of the community in question. Only upon the foundation of full knowledge of the whole financial system can we hope ever to erect the structure of a sound policy of forest taxation.

It is not my intention at this time to lay down any rules for the taxation of forests in Minnesota or elsewhere. But certain relations between the financial and industrial situation in the cutover region of Minnesota and the question of forest taxation should by now be so clear that he who runs may read.

First of all it should be obvious that no one will long continue to pay taxes upon land from which he sees no prospect of a reward, at least somewhat greater than the taxes. If lands which, on account of their soil or topography or location, are permanently unsuited for agriculture, are nevertheless assessed on the basis of agricultural values, the owner will sooner or later refuse to pay the taxes and let the lands go to the county or the state. No one who understands the situation will be found to buy the land, and, if perchance some ignorant purchaser appear, he will soon learn his lesson, and the land will again be back on the delinquent roll. We shall have to learn that the only thing that gives value to land is the future income which it is expected to yield, when put to its most profitable use. Any attempt to tax land upon any higher valuation than this, defeats its own end, through the process of delinquency.

Now it has been demonstrated that the most profitable use of a very great part of the land in these sixteen counties of northern Minnesota, probably more than half of it, is for forest-growing. It is idle to try to increase the public revenues by assessing such land as though it had agricultural value. Delinquent lands pay no taxes. If the revenues are to be maintained, this can be done only by increasing the burden upon the tax-paying lands. Sooner or later some of these lands, which are hanging on the margin, will give up the struggle and go delinquent. Once more, assessments or tax rates are raised to make up the loss, and so the vicious circle revolves. This is the way to public bankruptcy and ruin for the whole community.

Reasonable taxation, on the other hand, would make it possible for the owners to devote to forest-growing, lands which were, except for taxation, capable of yielding a profit from such use. Moderate taxes are better than no taxes at all. The immediate burden on other property is in some small degree at least relieved, and, as the forests grow and begin to yield income, the tax base is correspondingly increased and the prosperity of the community enhanced.

The economic and social future of large parts of northern Minnesota, as well as many other portions of the United States, depends upon a healthy, profitable forest industry in the hands of private owners. There is no magic in tax reform to make profits where profits are not possible. But taxation may be so arranged that it will cease to be a bar holding back the owner of natural forest land from such economic use of his land as will redound both to his own profit and to the well-being of the community. It may take some years of research and experiment to find out how this end is to be accomplished, but in the meantime, general recognition of the baleful effects of our present unsound taxation methods will be a long step toward the desired goal.

APPENDIX

TABLE I

LAND CLASSIFICATION

Minnesota, 1925

COUNTY	TOTAL AREA	LAND IN FARMS		PLOW LAND	
	Acres	Acres	Per cent	Acres	Per cent
Cook	958,720	23,371	2.44	3,603	.38
Lake	1,343,360	32,394	2.41	6,257	.47
Group 1	2,302,080	55,765	2.42	9,860	.43
St. Louis	4,161,920	545,162	13.10	127,408	3.06
Itasca	1,747,200	229,513	13.14	41,312	2.36
Group 2	5,909,120	774,675	13.11	168,720	2.81
Koochiching	2,010,240	184,512	9.18	32,457	1.61
Beltrami	1,619,863	297,806	18.38	77,930	4.81
Lake of the Woods ..	826,217	139,146	16.84	28,957	3.50
Group 3	4,456,320	621,464	13.95	139,344	3.13
Aitkin	1,171,200	300,564	25.66	92,682	7.91
Carlton	554,880	194,270	35.01	58,695	10.58
Cass	1,346,560	276,645	20.54	89,299	6.63
Clearwater	652,160	223,439	34.26	81,901	12.56
Crow Wing	676,480	207,004	30.60	71,368	10.55
Hubbard	613,120	202,488	33.03	79,490	12.96
Group 4	5,014,400	1,404,410	28.01	473,435	9.44
Kanabec	341,760	177,114	51.82	63,427	18.56
Mille Lacs	373,120	170,926	45.81	71,041	19.04
Pine	904,320	335,805	37.13	124,669	13.79
Group 5	1,619,200	683,845	42.23	259,137	16.00
Total—16 counties ..	19,301,120	3,540,159	18.34	1,050,496	5.44
Winona	407,680	363,212	89.09	217,035	53.24
State	51,749,120	30,059,137	58.09	20,814,531	40.22

TABLE II
LAND CLASSIFICATION
Minnesota, 1925

COUNTY	TOTAL AREA	POTENTIAL AGRICULTURAL		NON-AGRICULTURAL Barren Swamp		Potential Forest	
	Acres	Acres	Per cent	Acres	Per cent	Acres	Per cent
Cook	958,720	138,056	14.40	4,546	.47	816,118	85.13
Lake	1,343,360	321,735	23.95	20,205	1.50	1,001,420	74.55
Group 1	2,302,080	459,791	19.97	24,751	1.08	1,817,538	78.95
St. Louis	4,161,920	1,416,718	34.04	227,587	5.47	2,517,615	60.49
It sca	1,747,200	908,020	51.97	93,206	5.33	745,974	42.70
Group 2	5,909,120	2,324,738	39.34	320,793	5.43	3,263,589	55.23
Koochiching	2,010,240	903,603	44.95	449,232	22.35	657,405	32.70
Beltrami	1,619,863	565,170	34.89	485,798	29.99	568,895	35.12
Lake of the Woods	826,217	225,392	27.28	348,887	42.23	251,938	30.49
Group 3	4,456,320	1,694,165	38.02	1,283,917	28.81	1,478,238	33.17
Aitkin	1,171,200	735,162	62.77	167,939	14.34	268,099	22.89
Carlton	554,880	259,462	46.76	52,561	9.47	242,857	43.77
Cass	1,346,560	658,872	48.93	88,170	6.55	599,518	44.52
Cler	90	379,166	58.14	103,532	15.88	169,462	25.98
Crow Wing	676,480	290,616	42.96	16,502	2.44	369,362	54.60
Hubbard	613,120	334,212	54.51	22,068	3.60	256,840	41.89
Group 4	5,014,400	2,657,490	53.00	450,772	8.99	1,906,138	38.01
Kanabec	341,760	301,398	88.19	2,667	.78	37,695	1 n3
Me Lacs	3?0	330,808	88.66	3,152	.84	39,160	10.50
Pine	90	585,547	64.75	76,618	8.47	242,155	26.78
Group 5	1,619,200	1,217,753	75.21	82,437	5.09	319,010	19.70
Total—16 counties	19,301,120	8,353,937	43.28	2,162,670	11.21	8,784,513	45.51

CHAIRMAN MATTHEWS: Before we proceed with the next paper I have one or two announcements to make.

(Announcements)

CHAIRMAN MATTHEWS: It may be interesting to the members of the National Tax Conference to have me give you this report from the registration desk; there are six provinces represented by 30 people, the District of Columbia and thirty-nine states represented by 365 people; ladies 88, making a total of 483.

The next speaker is Mr. C. D. Howe, Dean of Forestry of the University of Toronto.

DR. C. D. HOWE (Toronto): Mr. Chairman and Gentlemen: I have no set paper; just a few notes. I want to say in the first place that we have no serious tax problems in connection with forest lands in eastern Canada or in Canada as a whole. We think we have managed things a little better than they have in Mr. Fairchild's country.

Forest lands have not been alienated. Over 80 per cent of our forest lands belong to the Crown. As we say, they are Crown lands; that is, the ownership is a public ownership. Indirectly, however, there are tax problems in connection with the administration of our forests; and in order to make that clear to you, I should like to sketch the method of administration or the method of utilizing the timber from the Crown lands. I will take Ontario for an illustration, because I know more about that.

When the Government desires to sell any area, that area is usually cruised; surveyed by foresters in the government employ. These surveyors, these foresters, make maps of the area, classifying the forest types, different kinds of forests, the density of the stand, the yield of the stand, in terms of board feet or cords of pulp wood or ties, as the case may be. They also make rough topographic maps, showing the water courses and the presence of lakes, of which there are a great many, as you know, in the north country; and when the Government is ready to sell this area it is advertised, and tenders are asked, and these tenders are sealed tenders. The man who makes the tender must submit a substantial deposit to indicate his financial responsibilities and to indicate good intentions, and at the present time they tender by thousand feet of logs or by cords of pulp wood.

I was looking over records and the price of pine, our principal saw-log product, last year ranged from $6 to $16 per 1000 board feet; board rule pine has brought in Ontario within recent years as high as $20 per 1000 feet, on the stump. For pulp wood—soft wood, spruce and balsam—actual sales have not been much more than 50 cents a cord for what we call stumpage or bonus.

Now, the licenses to cut saw logs are renewable every year. They are good for only twelve months. The licenses, or concessions, as we usually speak of them, for pulp-wood operations, usually extend over twenty years, because, you know, a pulp-wood company makes a very large initial investment. The cut in the woods is measured usually by a company and is checked up by Government scaler, and they usually work together. The company pays each year for the amount of wood or lumber that is cut. If, at the end of the fiscal year the operator has not paid, he is charged six per cent interest on his delinquency.

Certain conditions always go with the sale. It is always stated in the sales that the Department of Crown Lands reserves the privilege of changing the regulations at any time. As a matter of fact, these regulations are not changed at any time; they usually give the operator due notice. As it works out, regulations are modified only about once in five years. The saw-log operator may be required to purchase his supplies locally, or, at any rate, he may be required to buy all of his supplies in Canada. The pulp-wood operator may be required to operate to a certain capacity, employ a certain number of men, and in some cases he must produce a certain quality of paper for a definite purpose. He must develop usually a certain amount of hydro-electric energy, and he may be required to sell that energy and the surplus energy to neighboring towns. The pulp-wood operator may even be required to purchase a certain amount of his pulp wood from the settlers. The object of this is to stimulate settlement. You know, this province is endeavoring to settle the north country—our great clay-belt region—and the farmer usually has to clear pulp wood off of this land before he can cultivate it. To encourage this settlement, I say, the Government may require the company to buy in some cases as high as 40 per cent of their pulp wood from settlers.

In addition to the purchase price, which is usually spoken of as bonus, in this province, the saw-log operator pays a certain specific tax which we call dues. This is $2.50 per 1000 feet for white pine, and $2.00 for spruce saw timber. This tax is considered separately and is regarded separately in the records of the lands department. There is a historical reason for that. In the early days the dues were all that were paid. They did not pay any stumpage. Then, not so many years ago, the areas were sold for a lump sum; the timber was not sold by 1000 feet or by cords. The man paid a lump sum for his whole area, and in addition to that he paid the dues. The dues on spruce pulp wood this year are about $1.40 a cord. The operator pays that in addition to his stumpage.

Some of the older pulp and paper companies pay 20 cents, 30 cents and 40 cents stumpage dues.

In addition to this direct tax which the operator pays each year on measurement, made before it goes into the streams, the operator has to pay a ground rent, and at the present time this ground rent is five dollars per square mile, for the saw-log operator, at any rate. The pulp and paper companies pay ground rent.

This ground rent has an interesting history. When it was first introduced, way back in 1851, the object of the ground rent was to prevent speculation in timber, and this ground rent at that time was to be doubled every year that the mills were not operative. That provision, however, was dropped within a few years. I think I am safe in saying that this ground rent has been retained by the Government, as an expression of its ownership in the land. Only the timber is sold. The forest soil belongs to the people.

The saw-log operator pays this ground rent of five dollars a square mile for the use of the land, for going over it in connection with his logging operations.

At the present time the saw-log operators are charged one cent per acre fire tax each year, and it is usually less than that with the pulp-wood operators, usually about one-half of that. This fire tax has had an interesting history. In the old days, in the early 80's, when fire protection began in Ontario, the Government paid half the cost and the operator paid half. That was carried on for a good many years. Then about twenty years ago the Government made the operator pay all that fire protection, and in 1916, about ten years ago, the Government imposed this direct tax on the operator for fire protection. This tax pays really only about one-half, and some years only about one-third of the actual amount expended in fire protection of our forests.

In Ontario we have 32,000,000 acres, roughly, in pulp-wood concessions, and about 12,000,000 acres in timber license. Now, that is not an exact expression of spacial relations, because some of these pulp-wood concessions overlap the old timber licenses.

We have in Ontario roughly about 14½ million acres in forest reserves or parks. Ontario derives a revenue from its forests each year of between four and five million dollars, of which about two million dollars is in the form of dues, direct tax, and about one million dollars stumpage. The rest of it is in minor revenues.

Quite a number of years ago, I think it was in the 90's, this Government passed an act by which farm woodlots or forest lands that were being cared for from the standpoint of growing timber, might be exempt from taxation. The exemption of this tax rested with the municipalities. I don't know just how well that exemption worked out. I can say as a whole it was disappointing. The municipalities did not take advantage of it.

At the last session of the legislature an amendment to the ordinary assessment act was passed, in which farm woodlots that were being cared for for the protection of timber, were placed in the class of non-assessable property. They were placed in the class with churches and schools and school property. As I say, this was just passed, at the last session of the legislature, and we don't know yet how this is going to work out. Under the definition of the act not over 10 per cent of a man's farm acreage in woodlot can be exempt; that is, if he has a 200-acre farm, only 20 acres can be exempt, and the woodlot must have at least 400 trees per acre of all sizes on it; 300 trees over two inches in diameter; 200 trees over five inches in diameter, and 100 trees over eight inches in diameter. The act specifically states that the land must be set apart by the owner for the sole purpose of fostering the growth of trees, and is not used for grazing or any other agricultural purpose.

This act, although not specifically stated, evidently will apply to forest plantation, and we have in Ontario at the present time about 15,000 acres of forest plantations, and they are increasing at the rate of about 5,000 acres a year; so it is evident that the forest plantation, if this act works out, will be exempt from taxation.

I am not a student of taxation; do not pretend to be, but as a matter of principle I am not in favor of tax exemption. That is, I think our woodlots, as some of the states are trying to do, should be taxed only once, and that is when the crop is removed. Woodlots should not be taxed every year as they are taxed in a great many states and as they are taxed in Ontario. There should be a just and equitable tax at the time the crop is harvested.

The pulp-wood paper industry and the saw-log industry in Ontario, the two industries together, have invested capital of 223 million dollars, and they produce materials each year to the value of 126 million dollars, and they employ about 20,000 men, and distribute about 25 million dollars in wages each year. So, it is evident that our revenues, direct and indirect, from the forest, are very important; and this is evidence that we should keep our forests, if possible, continuously productive.

We have in Ontario very nearly the same conditions which Mr. Fairchild has described in the State of Minnesota. In the central Ontario region, which has yielded enormous quantities of pine, I want to say, our pineries were originally second even to those of the lake states. This pine has been practically all cut out in central Ontario. The settlers followed the lumbermen, and while the lumbermen were there they had a market for their products. When the lumbermen moved out, these settlers were stranded, and a great many of them are existing there now, almost on the verge of starvation, eking out a poor existence by fishing, hunting and trapping.

Some of you know the present Minister of Lands and Forests is trying to correct this evil, trying to move the men out of these places and give them good farm land in the clay-belt region, and these areas that were never intended by nature to be used for agriculture will be restored in timber. At this time, in its actual operation, a few settlers have been removed from this district into the clay belt.

In general we have, and as you have done in the states, abused very greatly our forests and their products. It is probable that over 60 per cent of the forest area in the Province of Ontario does not bear merchantable material at the present time, because of the prevalence of forest fires.

The Province of Ontario a few years ago made a survey of this pine country in central Ontario, and of 6,000,000 acres, former pineries, they found that 4,000,000 acres had not burned, while 2,000,000 had been burned over and over again, until there was nothing on it except scrub. Approximately 1,000,000 acres in that area contains young white pine, regenerated on these old burned areas, in potential commercial quantities. And the Government is making every effort to protect that young pine, which is a very valuable asset to us. We still have considerable virgin pine left in this province. I don't know if anyone knows exactly how much; it has been variously estimated from six billion to ten billion feet, which means twenty to thirty years' supply, at the present rate of cutting.

The original timber regulations were based on the assumption that the lumberman was to prepare the way for the farm, and he did it in certain instances, and he is doing it in northern Ontario in this clay belt and in larger portions of the clay belt, but the great majority of soils, soils particularly from which pine is being cut today, never will be agricultural, until we have a very much denser population than we have at the present time.

Although it is very evident, and has been evident for years, that these pine lands cannot be used for agriculture, the regulations of cutting have not been changed. We are cutting virgin pine today, just as we did fifty or sixty years ago, and there are no cutting regulations to insure regrowth or regeneration of pine on those areas. It seems evident that if we are to have white pine supplies in the future we must concentrate our fire protection on these young growth areas, and there are millions of acres of them in the central Ontario region. That does not refer to the region north of the Georgian Bay District; and the Government is making a very vigorous attempt to protect its forests from destruction by fire.

The efficiency of fire prevention has been increased enormously in this province in the last few years. The country is being greatly covered with lookout towers, connected up with telephone lines. These lookout towers have considerable range of vision. They are arranged so that when the man in one tower spots a fire, he gets the range and direction on it, and telephones to another man over there and asks him what the barrier is of that smoke, and they project those lines until they intersect, and they locate fires now ten or fifteen or twenty or thirty miles away, on a 100-acre lot, and within a few minutes men with fire-fighting apparatus, pumps and hose, are on their way to that fire. And airplane control has been greatly developed in the past few years, especially in the far-removed regions; so that at the present time I believe conditions are improving. Rain has helped us out considerably in the past few seasons. We have had some wet seasons in the north country.

Fire losses in the past few years have been only about one-fifth the average of fire losses for the past ten years.

The Province of Ontario, as I have already indicated, is doing a great deal to restock waste and barren areas. Our waste areas of the central Ontario region are being planted with pine.

The Government has under consideration now a very large re-forestation scheme for pulp wood in the north country. While our forests have been abused very greatly in the past, I believe that a period of correction is at hand, and that we are doing now really constructive work for the preservation of these millions of dollars which we derive from our forests. I thank you.

CHAIRMAN MATTHEWS: The next speaker on the program is Mr. Avila Bédard of the Department of Lands and Forests of the Province of Quebec.

MR. AVILA BÉDARD (Quebec): Mr. Chairman, Ladies and Gentlemen: I am afraid that the previous speaker has imposed upon me a rather heavy tax, by leaving to me only a very few things to say, and by having dealt with this problem of forest preservation, under consideration, in such an able manner.

The problem of the relationship between forest preservation and the collecting of the revenues or taxes for public utilities' purposes is a complex problem, the solution of which varies, so to say, with every country. First because forest ownership is not the same kind everywhere. In several countries, forests are in the hands of private individuals. In some countries, however, forests still belong to the state. It is specially the case with forests in the Province of Quebec. Statistics reveal that out of a total area of 203,490 square miles of timber-producing territory, private individuals own only about 12,000 square miles. And even on these 12,000 square miles, 2,000 consist of woodlots under location tickets, that is, where the owners' rights are limited by certain government restrictions. Let us first bear in mind that state forests are not taxable and we shall then understand that they cannot share in the same degree, in the same proportions and in the same way, as private property in yielding public revenues.

In the Province of Quebec all private property is taxed under a special article of the municipal code. This is not a heavy tax, as a rule, because private property is generally undervalued for municipal purposes. Statistics establish that landed property, including farms, pastures and woods, is estimated in most cases at one-half of its commercial value. One cannot, therefore, complain that timbered property is unfairly taxed. The taxes on private woodlots are accordingly not so heavy as to compel owners to denude their property rapidly.

We must, however, admit that the valuation of timbered property, dependent as it is on assessors too often ignorant of the fundamental principles of such valuation and having neither time nor interest in ranging forests, to ascertain their nature and wealth, is necessarily uncertain. Are not such assessors liable to give the same value to forest stands equal in area, but unequal in wealth and age? Thus, wood lots scientifically cut will be taxed at the same rate as abusively-cut lots, and lots in process of regeneration or reforestation will, in the assessors' mind, have practically the same value as matured timber. Hence timbered land can only be assessed by really competent assessors.

Furthermore, such valuation must be governed by certain sylvicultural considerations and by a general principle, that is: forests in all countries must be deemed an asset, whose preservation and judicious exploitation is conducive to public welfare. Have not forests much to do for the common welfare? Is it not generally admitted that they safeguard other cultures; that they have a rather beneficial influence on climatic conditions; that they prevent soil erosion in mountainous countries; that they maintain the regularity of water courses, thereby enabling them to supply all the energy demanded by industry, and that they are a sanctuary for game?

All these services, to which may be added that of supplying the raw material necessary for maintaining a large number of industries and for trade expansion, make the forest an asset which must be preserved at all costs in every country. It may even be said that if certain districts, unfit for agriculture, are habitable and draw tourists, it is only on account of their forests.

Let us bear in mind that timber culture cannot be confused with any other production and specially with agricultural production.

While agricultural exploitation is apt to give an annual yield which to a certain extent compensates the invested capital, the timber culture, being unfit to yield commercial products before many years, leaves the owner without any immediate compensation for his capital outlay. One must not forget that the forest wealth, which can be assimilated to a working capital, is liable to be impoverished or diminished by certain accidental factors, such as insets, epidemics, diseases and fire, the occurrence of which cannot be foretold or remedied at short notice. The private owner has not the same facilities for protecting timber property against fire as the

26

farmer has for his implements and buildings. He cannot depend upon the services of an insurance company.

This shows clearly that between agricultural exploitation and timber culture there are essential differences, to the advantage of the former. Those differences are such that one cannot attribute to the forest a value proportionate to its annual returns, as is the case with an agricultural exploitation. To be equitable, taxes should in the case of timber culture, be based on the annuity representative of the productive power of the soil, irrespective of the growing timber.

But there is another consideration which overrules equity; that is the part which the forest plays in the public interest. It can easily be understood that a too high valuation of timber property would induce the owner to cut his forest without cultivating it; in a word, to derive therefrom the maximum timber crop, as soon as possible, without caring at all for its regeneration and improvement.

This is particularly true in countries like the Province of Quebec, where the Government does not believe in restricting individual liberty by burdening the right of ownership with restrictions analogous to those imposed in some European countries.

In the Province of Quebec, the lessees of Crown or state forests have to pay an annual rent of $8.00 per square mile. Such a rental, together with the interest on the purchase price, would be high enough, in certain cases, we must admit, to induce the lessee to cut abusively. Cuttings of this kind cannot, however, be done because the Crown imposes certain restrictions on the forest operations. Thus a special regulation forbids the licensee from cutting trees of less than a certain specified diameter. If, on the other hand, the licensee wishes to cut contrary to this regulation, he has to prove by a proper working plan, that such cutting will not be disastrous for the forest, but will be conducive to the regeneration of the forest stand.

Must we add that the Government, being thoroughly aware of the importance of forest cover and of the necessity of encouraging reforestation of denuded land, has deemed it expedient to pass legislation under which private replanted lands with 300 trees per acre for thirty years, "shall retain for this period the valuation which they had previous to the planting."

On the other hand, according to the same law, the municipal valuation of such plantations, at the end of the thirty years' period, can be modified only every ten years, provided such plantations remain timbered land.

By adopting such legislation, the Quebec Government showed the importance of establishing a difference between the valuation of agricultural and forest property. It was established that timber in the process of growth could not have a value based solely on its future wealth, but on the wealth considered in the present. The Government understood that the time required for the growth of mature wood demanded prolonged sacrifices for the proprietor, for which he had no immediate compensation. It was only fair that such a proprietor should receive, under the form of a reduction of taxation, an adequate compensation for such sacrifices.

Without contending that this legislation is an ideal one, the principles governing it might inspire all legislation respecting taxation of private forest property.

CHAIRMAN MATTHEWS: The last speaker on the program is Mr. E. T. Allen. Mr. Allen represents the private forest owners' organization of the Pacific Coast; also the National Lumber Manufacturers Association, and he was asked to speak for the forest industries of the United States. Mr. Allen.

HARRY SNEED (Louisiana): If Mr. Allen will permit me, I want to ask, as chairman of the resolutions committee, if there are any resolutions to be presented, that they be handed in to the presiding officer now, so that they will be considered by the committee in time for subsequent submission to the conference.

E. T. ALLEN (Forester, Western Forestry and Conservation Association, Oregon): Mr. Chairman and Gentlemen: I have come a long way, from Portland, Oregon, and I want to say how much it means to me in a rather peculiar way. It appears that a great many years ago there was some difference of political opinion in Ontario as to the efficiency of the government relations with the lumber industry, and the astute suggestion was made by the Premier, that perhaps a Yankee could be imported, preferably from a great distance, to reconcile the situation a little bit, and if he succeed, obviously it was a creditable thing for the Government to have thought of it, and if he should not succeed, he might be dropped, without hurting any local feelings. I was offered the job, but on thinking it over it occurred to me that if the job was thoroughly attractive, my political shrewdness would not permit me to hold it, against home talent; that it was a long way to walk, and if the job was not much good I could get one like it at home, and consequently, being a long way from home, and having no return ticket, I am here for the first time.

FOREST PRESERVATION AND ITS RELATION TO PUBLIC REVENUE AND TAXATION

E. T. ALLEN

It takes a citizen of the United States some time to get the significance of the topic " forest preservation and its relation to public revenue and taxation." A Canadian may get it at once, being familiar with the way the provinces lay various taxes on private holders of public forest, and see as quickly that perpetuated production is essential to perpetuated revenue. But an American is likely to think somebody got his syntax twisted (That wouldn't sound so much like a pun to a lumberman) and meant to say "the relation of public revenue and taxation to forest preservation." We rarely hear it discussed from any angle except the prohibition of forest preservation by short-sighted taxing methods.

I think your title has vast possibilities for us. It is hard to wean our states away from the archaic, confiscatory, general property tax that forces uneconomical cutting of our old timber and penalizes the growing of new. Too many people are indifferent to these evils. But few are indifferent to taxation. If we can establish in the public mind a better knowledge of the vast public revenue that our forest lands can be made to yield perpetually, if taxing methods are wise and fair, but not otherwise, it is possible that in a few years the whole subject will receive entirely different consideration.

About a quarter of the United States surface is forest land. About 82 per cent of this, or nearly 370,000,000 acres, is privately owned and taxable. It represents every condition of virgin timber and reforestation, with comparatively little mistreated, so as to be without productive value. Here is a tremendous revenue source demanding such taxation as can be kept continuous. It also supplies the lumber, wood-working and pulp industries, the former alone said to represent a ten-billion dollar investment, with a yearly product worth three billion, and a large share of our railroad tonnage. All these and other related activities are taxed. So, in many ways, are the millions of individuals they directly or indirectly support. It is obvious that immediate annihilation of this resource, representing nearly a quarter of our land surface, mostly usable only to produce forest, would absolutely derange public revenue, as well as public welfare generally. Every gradual insidious attack on its preservation approaches the same result, like the Chinese method of execution, by cutting slices from the victim till he dies. He grows less and less valuable, even for slicing purposes.

Forest fire caused by human indifference is the most spectacular form of slicing forest revenues to death, but not really the most discouraging. It gives forest owner and community some sporting chance of protective effort and good luck. There is no chance against a spirit of forest taxation that disregards the future, that gives no thought of sustainable earnings, that actually makes preservation financially impossible, that inexorably compels owner and community alike to unite in a program of exploitation, liquidation and abandonment, because both believe the victim's death inevitable and that resurrection, if ever, is so far off as to be beyond their interest.

That such a spirit governs in the United States cannot be denied. There are exceptions. Mature timber exists that has not as yet demonstrably been over-taxed, so as to force over-cutting. Many states have adopted legislation to encourage reforestation. On the other hand, in regions where virgin timber supply is greatest, and consequently has to incur longest carrying charges, the tendency to increase the tax cost is greatest and is certainly beginning to influence over-cutting, price demoralization and general undermining of community prosperity. It is just such regions also, because they depend heavily on forest taxation for public revenue, that are loth to relieve cutover land, in order to encourage reforestation. They need the money. I know counties in more than one Pacific Coast state that raise 80 per cent or more of their revenue by taxing forest land. They want roads and improvements built before the forest is cut, so they initiate ambitious projects and increase taxes accordingly. The forest owner consequently cuts as fast as he can, often at an actual loss on his investment, because he thinks the loss will be greater if he waits. As cutting proceeds, the county increases either the forest tax or the cutover land tax, or both, to compensate. The cutover land tax goes to a point which destroys profit in another crop. The owner wavers between abandoning it, to become untaxable immediately, and hanging on, because abandonment now would merely shift the charge to his uncut timber, until he is able to appraise more exactly all the factors involved—one of which, that would take too long to go into fully, being the cost of fire prevention.

This process goes on until timber may be taxed anywhere up to $10 an acre annually and cutover land up to 50 cents an acre. In the Douglas fir region of Washington, for example, merchantable timber taxes on the average have advanced 324 per cent in twelve years and seem to be advancing 12½ per cent a year at present. Fire prevention on both uncut and cutover land of the same character runs from three to twenty-five cents an acre, not including losses.

Let me give you a few examples that I think will astonish you: A 640-acre section of timber in Washington has had its annual tax advanced 10,500 per cent in 28 years—from 10 cents to $10.50 an acre. It has cost over $69,000 or $108 an acre for taxes, not counting any interest. Another in the same region has advanced 9,290 per cent in the same period, now paying $7.17 an acre. It has $73 an acre taxes charged against it, without reckoning interest. In another county the same company is paying $10.52 an acre on timber taxed 12 cents at the time of purchase. Another Washington company had a 50 per cent increase last year, not in valuation but in rate imposed.

An Oregon company paid $415 for a small tract in 1907. In 20 years the annual tax has risen from $3.30 to $84.64, total paid being $632. Cost and taxes at 6 per cent, amount now to $2,286. The best gross return from cutting being estimated at only $600, the owners are letting it revert to the county, timber and all. The same company has just logged 320 acres, bought in 1909, for $16,000. Taxes had advanced from $141 a year to $935, $6,413 having been actually paid. To get 6 per cent interest back on these costs, with no profit, would require $54,566. The gross return was $52,406. The same company has 640 acres, on which in 21 years the tax charge has risen from $50 to $1394. Cost was $7000 and taxes paid $11,000. It would have to bring $37,000 to meet 6 per cent interest on this, but is about to be logged at an estimated return of $31,000 in order to raise money to pay taxes.

Cutover land in this same Douglas fir region, usually restocks swiftly and certainly, if held and protected. But what would you say is the inducement to wait for the crop when in one county it is taxed 35 cents an acre, in another 47 cents, and in another the average on one tract for 12 years has been 82½ cents?

None of the above figures for timber or cutover land include administration and fire-protection costs, or loss, or risk.

Nor do I want to be too sectional. The state forestry board of Minnesota recently reported to a senate committee a 698 per cent increase in 13 years of annual tax on the timber of one company. A Wisconsin company had 300 per cent increase in 12 years. A Maine company testified to taxation of 9 per cent on an assessed valuation double the market value, and to being obliged to strip the land. In another case, after 300 per cent increase, after operations were already losing, it stripped the land, moved out and let the community go down hill.

A Mississippi company found the state revenue agent not only counting reforestation in order to increase assessment, but also including non-commercial species. Seeing no way to break even on another timber crop, it contracted for the cutting of every living thing longer than a man's thumb. There are said to be over 7,000,000 acres of cutover land in Michigan, and perhaps 3,000,000 in Wisconsin, left delinquent and a public burden.

What will become of such communities and regions no one knows. The result will by no means be uniform throughout the United

States. Much experimenting in taxation to encourage reforestation is being tried or talked about. It mostly aims at reforestation, with too little consideration of the importance of sound permanent taxation as a basis. Rich states that want forests may incline to regard sacrifice of present revenue as a reasonable subsidy to get them, so are willing to wait for a yield tax. States that feel unable to forego forest revenue now have small patience with anything that defers it, although occasionally persuadable to give some assurance against taxing the crop at all in future, if they may continue to receive about the present annual land tax. There is so much confusion between these ideas and as to what is now acceptable, and in future will be, that neither state nor land owner feels safe without an anchor to windward; often on the public side consisting of time limits, supervision of forest management to compel production, or absurdly high combinations of annual and yield taxes, or on the private side consisting of contract protection against confiscatory amendments; all of which makes the whole effort extremely uncertain of result.

Meanwhile, to the tendency toward higher taxation of mature timber under the general property tax, is being added frequent attempts to levy a severance tax, in no way to relieve or substitute for the former, but to be superimposed for revenue only. Here the owner, already driven to liquidation because all his accumulated investment in land, taxes and protection seems becoming unrecoverable, is not influenced to hold in order to avoid the severance tax, because he must pay it some day, but speeds up still more. And he has no help in competing with the cheaper product of other states unless he can cut wages or make his nearest customer pay more for the product up to the point determined by cost of transportation from such other states. Neither of these courses is likely to be effective nor in the long run good for him and the community.

A fact of profound significance is that the price of lumber cannot be advanced indefinitely to make the consumer pay accumulated charges. When he thinks he can get along without it awhile, or if it reaches a price met by substitutes, he stops buying. There are few regions where timber values may be expected to advance much more, except in so far as inaccessible tracts are opened up by expensive railroad building, which itself must be absorbed. Consequently, let us consider what two factors cause the increase of stumpage values up to the breaking point where they stop advancing. One is a true rise of intrinsic value, due to diminishing supply and increasing demand. This alone affords a profit. The other is the accumulation and compounding of carrying costs; including fire prevention, taxation and interest on investment; which, without possibility of profit, must be reimbursed to avoid loss. To tax that portion of this increase due to other carrying costs is bad enough, but to tax an increase created by nothing but past tax payments is worse. Taxation has not created value.

At a certain point, if continued long enough, the process inevitably results in all profit from true value increase being swallowed by carrying costs, because the product will not pay both. When this is reached, or foreshadowed sufficiently, values go down again, being nothing but the best salvage possible through enforced liquidation. Much timber has reached this point but is still subjected to rapidly increasing taxation, based on confusion as to what its selling price means, upon a desire for immediate public revenue, and sometimes upon a shrewd realization of the situation and an attempt to bleed the victim before his death makes this impossible and to build up public improvements without cost to his survivors. Rarely is there much thought of prolonging his life; less even than of accomplishing some sort of resurrection through reforestation.

It should not be difficult to outline the general aim of a policy which would correctly relate forest production and forest tax revenue. The difficulty lies in detail to meet varying conditions and in getting the subject understood. Forest industry, in the main, is only temporarily migratory. With us, beginning in New England, it has taken a 300-year course westward to the Pacific, always leaving for a time a wake of depleted resources and temporary economic loss, except where agriculture has occupied a part of the land. But in time, with few exceptions, the land eventually recovers in large degree its community-sustaining value. Maine, our first typically lumbering state, has still 78 per cent of its area in forest use. Forty-four per cent of its industrial capital is invested in wood-using industries. Forest products constitute 44 per cent of its transportation tonnage. More than a third of its industrial population is directly employed in forest industry. Where would Maine be, for tax revenue or public welfare in general, with its forests annihilated?

As we approach the middle of the long westward march — the Lake states — we find the old timber well depleted, with recovery less advanced. On the Pacific Coast, virgin forest and fresh-cut land lie side by side, showing sharp contrast, yet even there much of the earliest-logged land is nearly ready to cut again, where it has escaped fire, because it is a region of ready natural reforestation and fast growth. But every region has a lean and dangerous period between old and new forest, when the economic fabric, built largely on forests, suffers in every way while at the same time obliged to carry its tax burden without substantial forest aid. The aim should be to bridge this gap; to tax existing forests and industry consistently with their continuance as long as possible and the cutover land and reforestation, so as to permit their being held and managed to carry on without a break in either productiveness or taxation. In no other way can the maximum revenue come from forest land, or can it most successfully continue to sustain community prosperity and therefore community ability to stand other taxation.

Without such an aim, we can hardly hope to meet another inherent problem. None knows today what permanent forest land in the United States will eventually be held by government, state and private enterprise, or what lumbermen will represent the latter. Only a part are so situated by the character and amount of their lands, and by mature timber supply to keep up operations and earnings, that they can do so under any circumstances. There will be much shifting of ownership until eventually private enterprise controls a portion best suited therefor while states and government are obliged to assume the rest, in order to protect the country's forest needs. This will not be taxable, but will entail cost of protection and management for long periods, even if eventually profitable. Much will never prove profitable in a revenue sense.

It is evident enough that the public of today is not sufficiently worried by forest shortage to assume voluntarily any great burden of purchasing promising land and caring for it; consequently any burden destroying private interest means leaving the land in bad condition, to be badly cared for. The amount and condition of that which private enterprise will hold, grow trees on and pay taxes on, and of that which reverts to public responsibility, both depend greatly on how encouraging conditions are made for private enterprise during an experimental period of several years. The single greatest object of public forest policy should be to keep all the land productive during these years of ownership adjustment.

Forest land owners as a class appreciate very keenly that we are entering just such an experimental period; they are greatly interested; they are alive to the evil of enforced over-production; they no longer regard their land as mere storage ground for trees, to be abandoned when the trees are cut; they want to perpetuate their industry and either utilize their property or put it in good condition for sale to someone who will. Some are already being forced to liquidation, abandonment and neglect—quite enough to be a warning that without wiser taxation soon, the tax-revenue curve will stop rising and fall rapidly. A few, in the best position, are taking a chance and planning on sustained yield, but in the main they are hanging on and watching. Their views of forestry are changing. Quicker crops and shorter carrying-cost calculations are being promised by new wood uses; pulp wood is an example. They no longer say forest preservation is not a feasible private enterprise. They say it is feasible, with reasonable public reciprocity, with the service recognized as necessary and justly compensated, with public carelessness with fire reduced, with the public sincerely seeking to find methods of taxing the enterprise only what it can justly bear and what will permit its preservation on a sound profitable business basis. Naturally they would prefer this, rather than to be forced in self-defense to liquidate and invest in unfamiliar enterprises, merely because the latter are not penalized for preservation.

An extremely intelligent lumberman, in discussing this subject with me, summed up much as follows: The general property tax has broken down as applied to forest, without further actual value increase with which to pay it. Therefore the system defeats itself and is exhausting this source of tax revenue. The Government which thus despoils the owner is at least under obligation to make it economically possible for him to find some remaining value in his lands, through putting them to the only profitable use of which they are capable—that is, growing trees. If taxation of forest goes beyond taking a portion of the profit to taking all of the profit, or beyond this, to taking a portion of the principal, then more has been taken than is fair and a return is owed. If it can be argued that Government has the moral right to impose such taxation for public benefit, there certainly exists the moral right to give sufficient assurance of relief hereafter, to make productive forest management inviting and enduring. This assurance is possible only through contract or thoroughly established and secure principle. Such guaranteed assurance for the future may not be justified as to the taxation of wealth realized from producing forest, but is absolutely due property devoted to producing forest; and this from both public and private viewpoints.

So, to a very great degree the future of our forests and forest industries, the supply of wood products for our people, and the continuance of so great a land and industrial resource to contribute to public revenue, all depend upon the rapidity with which the inexorable economics of the situation and a reciprocal co-operative spirit can be established in the public mind. This has been left too much to purely forestry effort: to professional foresters and forestry-interested laymen, not sufficiently equipped technically or with influence to deal with the whole legal, administrative and legislative problem of land utility and revenue collection.

It is usually a problem of intricate relations. Every commonwealth should develop a correlated, understood land policy, seeking to bring agricultural, forest, and other lands into a clear perspective which assures their soundest use and future for the general good. Land taxation must be consistent to this end, with fairness as between interests affected. Agriculture and forestry are closely allied, requiring much the same underlying consideration, as productive necessities, although annual and long-separated crops involve very different carrying burdens for the grower. Alike they must be fairly balanced against speculative land ownership and against other industrial enterprises of the community.

Probably no agency is as able to do all this disinterestedly and influentially, while at the same time conversant with public revenue needs which bear on the entire citizenship industrially and individually, as tax officials and taxation experts. They sit on the heights, like the gods of mythology and verse, and watch each group of us in our mortal struggle for existence. Asked to come here representative of one group, the American forest owner, I have presented to you no specific taxation plan to endorse. I know enough of the subject to know blanket rules are impossible; that the situation and exigencies of both the commonwealth and industry vary regionally and greatly. But I do ask you, with all the earnestness I can command, to use your power, not only as tax-gatherers but as economists and publicists, with your reputation at stake and your country's welfare at heart, to study the problem of this great industry and do your best to enable it to survive and keep its lands, its capital, its inventiveness, its traditional courage in fighting the obstacles of fire and flood and all the troubles and hardships that would have broken any but stout-hearted men, still working, with public encouragement, to keep our forest heritage a perpetual contribution to commonwealth prosperity; financially, industrially and inspirationally; without cause or excuse for faltering in this public service.

CHAIRMAN MATTHEWS: The address of Mr. Allen completes the list of speakers who are named upon the program.

I suppose the subject of the afternoon is now open for general discussion. Before proceeding with that, however, I will say that if you have a copy of the program, it appears that from 4:00 to 4:15 the item of the appointment of resolutions committee of the Citizens Research Institute of Canada will be taken up, but I am informed that this has been shifted about, so that the forum is now open for discussion of the subject of this afternoon.

Does anybody wish to speak?

(No response)

CHAIRMAN MATTHEWS: If no one cares to speak, I suppose adjournment is in order.

R. A. VANDEGRIFT (California): I think this is a proper time to bring in a resolution for the resolutions committee, so that they may have it.

CHAIRMAN MATTHEWS: It should be read in the convention, and then passed on to the resolutions committee. (Reading)

The resolution having been read is referred, under the rules, to the resolutions committee.

HARRY P. SNEED (Louisiana): I am going to again take the liberty of directing the attention of the audience to the necessity of intro-during such resolutions as they may desire to introduce now, so the resolutions committee may have opportunity to consider them.

CHAIRMAN MATTHEWS: Are there any delegates present who have resolutions that they wish to present to the resolutions committee?

(No response)

CHAIRMAN MATTHEWS: It is obvious, as Mr. Sneed states, that they should be in soon, if they are to have consideration.

HARRY P. SNEED: We will regard this as the zero hour, Mr. Chairman.

CHAIRMAN MATTHEWS: You will now have to speak, or forever hold your peace.

If there is nothing further to be said, the meeting may be adjourned until this evening.

(Adjournment)

NINTH SESSION

Henry F. Long (Massachusetts) presiding.

Chairman Long: Will the delegates please be seated? Before we start this evening to partake of all the good things that have been laid out for us, I am requested to announce that only 150 certificates have been turned in to the registration desk. This means that it will be impossible for the delegates to secure half full-fare return tickets.

Also, for the purposes of the record, I wish to report for the committee on credentials as follows:

The committee on record has examined all of the evidences and credentials offered by the delegates, and beg to report that the attached list is a correct record of persons entitled to sit as delegates at this particular conference from the various states, the District of Columbia, the Provinces of the Dominion of Canada and the Territories of the United States. Signed, Charles A. Tobin, Edward P. Tobie, Simeon E. Leland.

I will also have to announce that there will not be sufficient time this evening for the business meeting of the National Tax Association, which will be held tomorrow morning. The rest of the program will probably proceed as planned.

This evening, as you all know who have consulted the program, which has been very nicely arranged by the Canadian Tax Conference, is a joint conference between the National Tax Association and the Canadian Conference. Perhaps all of you haven't the Canadian program, but all of you, I think, have the National Tax Association program.

I may be permitted to read what the Canadian Tax program says. It is headed "Reciprocity in Inheritance Taxation." It speaks of Mr. Edmonds, and then says afterwards, "Discussion led by Mr. J. P. White, Hon. Mark Graves, and Mr. R. M. Fisher," and I might as well now announce, so that you will all be prepared for the pleasure of it, that after Mr. Edmonds is through our President is to have the floor for a short talk, or long talk, whichever he chooses, on the flat-rate plan.

Some few years ago the Commonwealth of Pennsylvania found

(413)

itself for the first time probably in its history, either in need of funds or in need of some new method of distributing the tax burden. If there is one thing that the National Tax Association expects of all its people, it is that they shall be courteous and shall not cast any reflections upon the tax system of any of the states of the Union. Therefore, I shall make very little or no reference to Pennsylvania, before the advent of the special taxation commission.

There was a special taxation commission provided for by the legislature of Pennsylvania, and, strangely enough, and quite apart from the usual practice in many states, they selected a very excellent group of people, and I have yet to find how they found the time to give to this very important work.

One Benjamin Franklin left Massachusetts a great many years ago and went to Pennsylvania, and since that time we have looked to Pennsylvania for a great deal of wisdom. I have a suspicion that the wisdom of Franklin was handed down to Franklin Spencer Edmonds, who was the chairman of this special taxation commission of the Commonwealth of Pennsylvania. All of us who have attended these tax associations have come to have a very high respect and almost love for Mr. Edmonds, who was the chairman of the Penn-Pennsylvania committee. None of us who were at Philadelphia last year can forget the very delightful entertainment that we had there through the kindness of Mr. Edmonds and Mrs. Edmonds, as it was largely through their efforts that things worked out so well in Philadelphia.

I have an unusual respect for a person engaged in active practice, as was Senator Edmonds and his associates on the special taxation committee, who will devote so much of their time and energy to working out something for which they will be not thanked at all; for which they probably will get a great many black and blue marks, but out of which they will take a great deal of comfort, as years go on, and the system they established in Pennsylvania shows that it was a worth-while job.

We think so much of Senator Edmonds and the work that his commission did in Pennsylvania that all of us were glad to follow any suggestions that Pennsylvania had, and one of the suggestions that early grew out of this work of the Pennsylvania commission, so ably managed by Senator Edmonds, was along the line of reciprocity in inheritance taxation.

A great many people had fretted under the trouble growing out of inheritance taxation, particularly as it applied to non-resident decedents. To show the unusual influence that this commission had; just at about the right time they staged a suit in the United States Supreme Court in the case of one Frick, and the court clarified the law in relation to non-resident taxation. I think there is no question but what Senator Edmonds and his committee were largely instrumental in seeing that the United States Supreme Court decided that in the way that would be useful to us.

But, Senator Edmonds in addition to doing all this work in Pennsylvania has done a tremendous amount of work in spreading the gospel of reciprocal inheritance taxation, and those who have served on the committee with him know the tremendous amount of work he has done.

Tonight we are to have the pleasure of welcoming Senator Edmonds here and hearing his report, and I for one hope that when Senator Edmonds gets up you will give him a real National Tax Association ovation, so that it will at least in a measure indicate to him the respect in which we hold him.

I have, therefore, great honor and privilege in introducing to you tonight Franklin Spencer Edmonds of Philadelphia, in the United States of America.

FRANKLIN S. EDMONDS (Pennsylvania) : Mr. Chairman and Members and Guests of the Canadian Tax Conference, Canadian Research Conference, and National Tax Association: It is good to have so kindly a welcome. I am afraid you won't feel like so much cordiality when I get through, but I would rather have it at the beginning than not at all.

RECIPROCITY IN INHERITANCE TAXATION

REPORT OF COMMITTEE OF THE NATIONAL TAX ASSOCIATION

FRANKLIN S. EDMONDS, CHAIRMAN

At the convention of the National Tax Association, held in Philadelphia in November, 1926, the following resolution was adopted:

> " WHEREAS, The operation of and the procedure under the recently enacted statutes of several states, with respect to the taxation of the intangible property of non-residents, known as ' reciprocal ' statutes, have resulted in a substantial amount of satisfaction to taxpayers generally and have greatly simplified the procedure involved in the settlement of decedents' estates and have operated as a wholesome influence upon interstate taxation relations; therefore, be it
>
> RESOLVED, That the National Tax Association be requested to appoint a committee to conduct a country-wide investigation of the possibilities of extension of these reciprocal inheritance tax laws, to states other than those at present administering such laws; such committee to consist of such number of members and of such persons, whether within or without the membership, as the association may determine."

Pursuant to the terms of this resolution, the president of the National Tax Association appointed a committee of nine, including representatives from both the Dominion of Canada and the United States of America. It is the report of that committee which I am about to present, and with your permission a portion of it will be presented orally and the balance will be read, for the purposes of the record.

Let me preface what I have to say by stating that reciprocity in this discussion has nothing whatever to do with the Canadian tariff or the tariff of the United States. We understand by "Reciprocity in Inheritance Taxation" the movement of co-operation or comity between the states, tending to eliminate multiple taxation upon the stocks and bonds of non-resident decedents. As we understand the term, there has been no greater evil in the taxation system of the states than the development of methods, whereby when a man dies, his estate may find that his assets are taxable not only by one jurisdiction but by two, three, four or even five jurisdictions, on different bases and at different rates. The result has been to add to the expense of administration, and the uncertainty of inheritance, and frankly, to stimulate a feeling of injustice in connection with the administration of inheritance tax laws.

I read at the New Orleans conference two years ago a summary of the legislation in the United States, showing the number of states that had attempted to reach assets over which they had taxable jurisdiction but which belonged to the estates of non-residents. We now report upon the changes that have been made in two years by the legislatures of the states of the Union.

These changes have come about largely because of a series of conferences initiated in 1924, in which the tax commissions of several states, New York, Pennsylvania, Connecticut, Rhode Island and Massachusetts, took part. We raised the question as to the injustice of attempting to tax stocks and bonds, not only by the jurisdiction at the domicile of the decedent, but by a multiple number of jurisdictions which might, under some fiction of our American law, obtain taxable jurisdiction over these assets. We were at the time prepared to suggest that the states should abandon the taxation of the estates of non-resident decedents, but we recognized that the state which started the movement prevented itself from getting revenue from non-residents, and yet its own residents would be taxed by other states; and that seemed unfair. Out of those conferences grew the idea of reciprocity, and at the 1925 convention of the National Tax Association in New Orleans, in the report upon inheritance taxation, there was included a clause which, if added to the inheritance tax law, would provide that the enacting state would not collect taxes on the stocks and bonds of non-resident decedents of those states which reciprocally would not collect from the estates of decedents of the enacting states.

So the reciprocity movement was born. Running over the progress very briefly: in 1925, New York, Massachusetts, Connecticut and Pennsylvania enacted such reciprocity laws, and that brought them into reciprocity, not only with each other but also with Florida, Nevada, Alabama, and the District of Columbia, which had no inheritance taxes, and also with Georgia, Tennessee, Rhode Island and Vermont, which did not tax the estates of non-resident decedents. Then these twelve states endeavored to agree upon a certain degree of uniformity, in regard to forms and affidavits, in order to make easy and uniform the method for the transfer of securities in each of these states.

In 1926, we reported to the Philadelphia convention of the National Tax Association that New Jersey had been added to the number of reciprocal states, by the repeal of its tax on the stocks and bonds of non-resident decedents. We now have great pleasure in reporting that during the past year eleven states in the American Union have enacted legislation upon this subject: Massachusetts, Colorado and Delaware have repealed all taxes on the stocks and bonds of non-resident decedents; and Maine, New Hampshire, Maryland, Oregon, Ohio, California, Illinois and Georgia have enacted reciprocity statutes. At the present time there are twenty-one states and the District of Columbia, comprising sixty per cent of the population of the American Union, and more than sixty per cent of the wealth, which as among themselves, will not tax the stocks and bonds of non-resident decedents of each other. We will append to our report a list of these reciprocity statutes. (See Exhibit B.) You will notice that some are not as broad as others, but in the main the whole procedure has been worked out harmoniously along the same general idea of attempting to eliminate multiple taxation.

What has brought about this interesting result? The arguments for reciprocity may be briefly summed up as follows: First, to all thinkers upon taxation, the principle of reciprocity in inheritance taxation is recognized as just. It is not fair that several different jurisdictions should tax the same assets, at different rates, under varying methods, under varying conditions. It has been the general recognition of the injustice of the muddle that existed before 1925 which has given great impetus to the reciprocity plan.

In the second place, it frankly has not cost the states very much revenue. So far as we have been able to work out, all that the states of the Union collected from the stocks and bonds of non-resident decedents, prior to 1925, was probably less than ten millions a year, and I think it would be safe to say that almost half of that amount was collected by New York, Pennsylvania and New Jersey. It is not a serious element, as far as the fiscal program of the states is concerned, except under certain special circumstances.

And now, by simplifying the transfer of securities, we not only

27

save the tax to the estate but we also save the tremendous burden of preparing to pay the tax by ascertaining the tax liability. Those who administer decedents' estates have welcomed the reciprocity movement with hearty good-will, because they have recognized that the long delays in obtaining waivers, costly reports, careful analyses, and many other things, which often developed, to complicate the settlement of an estate, disappear when there is only one state to which a report should be made, viz. the state of domicile. Reciprocity has, therefore, materially aided our taxing situation, because it eliminates material items of cost in the settlement of estates.

There is, however, a third reason, a broader reason, which I frankly think has been even more potent with the American people than the other two; and that is that gradually the development of multiple taxes on securities was warping the free course of investment in our country. Men of means were asking themselves: "Is it worth while to leave securities of certain states in my assets? In the event of my death, will my family have trouble in realizing upon such securities? Will my estate be subject to one set of taxes, or two sets of taxes, or three sets of taxes?" In a great many parts of the country, particularly in those parts where there is capital for investment, capital was commencing to shrink from going into jurisdictions where, in the event of death, it might be subjected to unusual hardships, before it could be made liquid. From the point of view of the development of the country, it is tremendously important that the flow of capital should be free. We are inclined to think that the elimination of these multiple taxes has done more to help the flow of capital along economic lines than anything else we could do.

Is there any argument against it? During the past year our committee has conferred with many state tax commissions, and has suggested that they join us in this reciprocity movement. In some cases, we have heard from states whose Tax Commissioner says, " I would be glad to recommend reciprocity, but it happens that our state is the home state of a large corporation, most of whose stock is held by non-residents, and we get a very large income from these non-residents and it is very hard for us to give up that income. We do not know what we would do if we were obliged to give up that income." And then there is quoted to us the stock example of the State of Utah, which is the home state of the Union Pacific Railroad, and which received $780,000 by the death of Mr. E. H. Harriman, the great railroad builder, which sum was used to build the State Capitol. Visitors to this state are told, " We built this Capitol from a non-resident's estate."

As an encouragement towards reciprocity for the states, where this argument is used, we have pursued the following method of inquiry: We prepared a list of thirty-six corporations in the United

States having one million or more shares of stock, all of which are incorporated in the states offering reciprocity, and consequently the stock, if held by non-residents of non-reciprocal states, would be taxable when the transfers came. We asked the Stock Transfer Association to assist us in ascertaining the number of stockholders and the number of shares of stock held in the various states in which this argument against reciprocity has been presented. In eighteen of these corporations, the association was able to secure exact figures, a summary of which is given in " Exhibit A ". It is interesting to find that in some of the states which have not yet accepted reciprocity, the holdings are very much greater than anticipated. If these states will accept reciprocity, each will give up a small income for itself, but they are aiding their own citizens in simplifying for them the problem of obtaining quick transfers, when this stock passes into the executors' hands.

Our committee would be very glad to secure figures for any state in which there is a desire to carry on a campaign of reciprocity, and we believe it will be possible to convince the authorities of these states that reciprocity is an economy to their citizens, even if it may result in a slight decrease in revenue.

I believe that, as time goes on, the general investor will be interested in knowing whether his securities are in a state that permits, without tax, the transfers of stocks and bonds of non-residents. or whether they are in a state which requires that a difficult and elaborate procedure be gone through, before such transfers can be made.

There are four matters which I am instructed to present in this report, which I will read, as follows:

I. Comity between Canada and the United States in Inheritance Taxation

The business interests of the United States of America and the Dominion of Canada are closely interwoven. With the remarkable growth and development of these two countries, it is not at all strange that the boundary line between them, which for more than a hundred years has required no defenses and the integrity of which has been maintained on the basis of mutual confidence and respect, has formed no barrier to the flow of investment capital from one side to the other. Detailed statistics are not available but it is safe to say that residents of Canada have enormous sums of money invested in stocks and securities within the United States and that residents of the United States have like investments within the Dominion.

The same considerations which led to the development of death tax reciprocity among so many of the states of the United States furnish potent reasons for the inauguration of a reciprocal move-

ment between the states of the Union and the provinces of the Dominion. It is felt that the occasion of the holding of the conference
of the National Tax Association in one of the provinces is a particularly happy time for a careful examination of the existing laws
of the several jurisdictions and the discussion of methods whereby
such changes may be made in these laws as may be necessary to
extend the benefits of death tax reciprocity to residents of the
United States having investments in Canada and residents of Canada having investments in the United States.

The theory underlying the reciprocity movement in the United
States has been that multiple taxation of intangible personalty included in estates of decedents should be abolished and such property
should be taxed only by the jurisdiction of which the decedent died
a resident. The extent to which, as between the United States and
Canada, intangible personal property of deceased residents of one
jurisdiction is subject to death taxation in the other becomes of
importance.

We find that intangible personalty of residents of Canada may be
subjected to death taxes (a) by the United States, under the estate
tax law, and (b) by the following states, territories and possessions
of the United States, viz. the states of Arizona, Arkansas, California, Connecticut, Georgia, Idaho, Illinois, Indiana, Iowa, Kansas,
Kentucky, Louisiana, Maine, Maryland, Michigan, Minnesota, Mississippi, Missouri, Montana, Nebraska, New Hampshire, New Mexico, New York, North Carolina, North Dakota, Ohio, Oklahoma,
Oregon, Pennsylvania, South Carolina, South Dakota, Texas, Utah,
Virginia, Washington, West Virginia, Wisconsin, Wyoming; the
territories of Alaska and Hawaii and the possessions of Porto Rico
and the Philippine Islands. Intangible personalty of deceased residents of the United States is not subjected to a death tax by the
Dominion of Canada, as the Dominion has no death tax law, but
death taxes (or succession duties) are imposed thereon by each of
the provinces of the Dominion.

No attempt will be made to discuss the kinds of intangible personalty which are subjected to taxation by the several jurisdictions,
nor the theories upon which the taxes are based. Suffice it to say,
that some jurisdictions exercise the power of taxation over the non-
resident to the fullest possible extent, whereas others tax only certain specified kinds of property, and that the legal bases for the
imposition of the taxes vary.

At the present time the revenue act of the United States, which
contains the estate tax law, does not incorporate any provision for
reciprocal exemptions, but the inclusion of such a provision will be
advocated. This subject is discussed elsewhere in this report. Of
the states listed above, ten (California, Connecticut, Georgia, Illinois, Maine, Maryland, New Hampshire, Ohio, Oregon and Penn-

sylvania) make provision for death-tax reciprocity. Three of the states (Alabama, Florida and Nevada) and the District of Columbia have no death-tax laws. Seven of the states (Colorado, Delaware, Massachusetts, New Jersey, Rhode Island, Tennessee and Vermont) have death-tax laws but do not impose the tax upon intangible personalty of non-residents.

The laws of the provinces of New Brunswick, Newfoundland, Nova Scotia and Ontario contain provisions whereby death taxes payable outside of the province may be credited against the tax imposed upon the same property by the province. In New Brunswick, the credit is only allowed with respect to foreign jurisdictions to which the provision for credit has been extended by the lieutenant-governor-in-council. In Newfoundland no conditions are attached to the allowance of the credit. In Nova Scotia the credit is allowed only with respect to property brought or sent into the province after the death of the owner. In Ontario credit is only allowed in the case of a foreign jurisdiction to which the provision has been made applicable by the lieutenant-governor-in-council, but in all other cases the amount of the duty payable outside the province may be allowed as a deduction from the value of the succession in Ontario. The provinces of Prince Edward Island and the Yukon Territory allow no credit for death taxes payable elsewhere, nor do their laws contain any provision for reciprocity. The succession duty acts of the provinces of Alberta, British Columbia, Manitoba, Quebec and Saskatchewan contain provisions for reciprocity, with respect to credit for taxes payable outside the province. These provisions are of a somewhat peculiar nature. They state that the province will allow a credit to its residents for death taxes payable elsewhere, if the jurisdiction in which such taxes are levied allows a similar credit to its residents for taxes payable in the province. In British Columbia, the credit may be allowed with respect to the other provinces even if such provinces do not allow a similar credit to their residents, for taxes payable to British Columbia. It is significant to observe that in each instance reciprocity is only effective as to those jurisdictions to which it has been extended by order of the lieutenant-governor-in-council and to date no such order has been made in any province except British Columbia, which is now on a reciprocal basis with Great Britain, and the province of Ontario.

The exact theory underlying the provincial reciprocal provisions referred to is somewhat difficult to trace. It does not seem that a province seeking to do justice to its residents by allowing a credit against its taxes for taxes payable elsewhere should be greatly concerned with the question of whether the jurisdiction levying the taxes so to be credited allows a credit to its citizens for taxes payable to the province. In fact these provisions seem to exactly reverse the theory of reciprocity in the United States. The usual form of reciprocity statute in the United States exempts the non-resident from death taxation if the jurisdiction of residence of such non-resident allows a similar exemption to residents of the enacting jurisdiction. The provisions last described furnish an incentive which encourages the enactment of reciprocal laws.

Under existing laws there is and can be no reciprocity between the United States and the provinces of Canada, for the reason that where the reciprocal provisions exist they are of an entirely different nature and do not operate in harmony. In a few of the provinces it is possible that a credit against the provincial taxes for taxes payable to the states may be allowed. Under the decision of the United States Supreme Court in Frick v. Pennsylvania, certain taxes payable to provinces may be deductible from the value of the property transferred, before the state taxes are levied, but there is no provision in any state whereby a provincial tax may be credited against a state tax.

Several of the states have adopted the model succession tax reciprocal exemption provision appearing on page 77 of the report of the National Committee on Inheritance Taxation to the National Conference on Estate and Inheritance Taxation held at New Orleans, Louisiana, November 10, 1925.

" The tax imposed by this act in respect of personal property (except tangible personal property having an actual situs in this state) shall not be payable (a) if the transferor at the time of his death was a resident of a state or territory of the United States, or of any foreign country, which at the time of his death did not impose a transfer tax or death tax of any character in respect of property of residents of this state (except tangible personal property having an actual situs in such state or territory or foreign country), or, (b) if the laws of the state, territory or country of residence of the transferor at the time of his death contained a reciprocal exemption provision under which nonresidents were exempted from transfer taxes or death taxes of every character in respect of personal property (except tangible personal property having an actual situs therein), provided the state, territory or country of residence of such nonresidents allowed a similar exemption to residents of the state, territory or country of residence of such transferor. For the purposes of this section the District of Columbia and possessions of the United States shall be considered territories of the United States."

Elsewhere in this report is contained a suggestion for the amendment of this provision. If the provinces were to adopt this model provision (with necessary changes of phraseology) they would at once establish reciprocal relations with the states whose laws now contain such provisions and with those states which either do not impose death taxes at all or do not impose such taxes upon intangible personalty of non-residents. However, until the United States Revenue Act is amended an exception should be made of the federal estate tax, as otherwise, reciprocity with the states could not be effective.

It is probable that the states of the Union whose laws contain reciprocal provisions not in accord with the model provision will at the first opportunity adopt the model provision. It is also probable that many of the states which now impose death taxes upon intangible personalty of non-residents will in the near future enact the model provision.

Your committee concludes that the greatest promise for early and satisfactory death-tax reciprocal relations between the states and the provinces will be found in the enactment by both, of this model succession-tax reciprocal exemption provision, and it urges that this course shall receive the early and earnest consideration of the proper authorities.

This is the conclusion of this section of the Report, and I desire to express our sincere acknowledgments to Seth T. Cole, Esq., Counsel to the New York State Department of Taxation and Finance, who has prepared this portion of our report, and also to our friends in the taxing departments of the Canadian provinces, who have assisted with suggestions and helpful criticism.

II. THE FEDERAL ESTATE TAX

After careful consideration your committee has reached the conclusion that the principle of reciprocal death-tax exemption ought to be adopted by the Congress of the United States and incorporated in the federal estate tax law, if this tax is continued. It so recommends. Every reason that has been advanced for the elimination of multiple taxation of intangibles of non-residents among the states themselves and between the states and foreign jurisdictions applies with equal force in favor of its elimination as between the United States and foreign jurisdictions. By virtue of the clause of the United States Revenue Act of 1926 which allows credit against the estate tax for taxes payable to the states, to an amount not exceeding eighty per cent of the federal tax, multiple taxation has been substantially reduced as between the states and the Federal Government.

Reciprocity should be of world-wide application. The embracement by the nations of the world of this opportunity to benefit their respective peoples, through the granting of reciprocal death-tax exemptions, should add another link to the chain of good will which is fast being forged and which it is hoped will bind the nations together as one great family, among the members of which suspicion and ill-will shall have no place, but whose guiding principles shall be fair dealing and mutual respect and consideration. It is the thought of your committee that the National Tax Association, by appropriate action, should bring the matter of death-tax reciprocity to the attention of the proper committee of the League of Nations, to the end that it may be presented to the several nations of the world.

III. The Decision in Smith vs. Loughman

The decision of the Court of Appeals of New York in Smith vs. Loughman (245 N. Y. 486, 157 N. E. 753), which held unconstitutional the provisions of the New York tax law imposing a flat-rate transfer tax upon property of non-resident decedents, has aroused a great deal of interest in death tax circles. The New York Tax Commission has already applied for certiorari to bring the case before the United States Supreme Court for review and has issued a statement indicating that it is hopeful that a reversal of the Court of Appeals will result. So far as your committee is concerned, its interest in this decision is confined to its effect upon the reciprocity movement.

The framework of the New York act was such that the provisions for reciprocal exemptions were included in the article imposing the flat-rate tax and the New York attorney general has held that the decision has caused the entire article to fall, carrying with it the reciprocity provision. This has led to some more or less loose talk and possibly loose thinking, so that some have gained the impression that the reciprocity provision was declared to be unconstitutional. Nothing could be farther from the fact. The case did not in any way involve the validity of reciprocity; not only is this true but more important still is what may be regarded as an implied endorsement of the movement for reciprocity by Chief Judge Cardozo, when he said:

> "Much has been said in argument about the desire of the tax commission and the Legislature to avoid multiple taxation. There is a section of the statute to the effect that the tax shall not be payable 'if the transferor is a resident of a state or territory of the United States which at the time of the transfer did not impose a transfer tax or death tax of any character in respect of personal property within said state or territory of residents of this state,' or if the laws of such state or territory contain other provisions insuring reciprocity of treatment. Section 248-p. *The power of the state to forego a tax upon a transfer by a nonresident in order to give effect thereby to a plan of reciprocity does not mean that a tax may* be imposed at excessive or unequal rates when reciprocity is lacking."

Your committee is pleased to report that there is nothing in the decision in Smith vs. Loughman which need cause the slightest apprehension on the part of those who are anxious to see the principle of reciprocity preserved unimpaired. The only regrettable feature connected with the decision, so far as it relates to reciprocity, is that for the time being the State of New York must withdraw from the reciprocal group. It is cheering, however, to know that as soon as the New York legislature convenes, in 1928, the Tax Commission will recommend the enactment of legislation which will reinstate reciprocity and probably will include in its recommendation a suggestion that the proposed legislation be made retroactive to July 1, 1925, the date of the enactment of the provision which has fallen, thereby stilling the troubled waters and eliminating the complicated questions which otherwise seem unavoidable.

In view of this prompt action by the New York Tax Commission, it may be worth while for those who are administering estates containing assets taxable in New York under present conditions, to delay applying for waivers until February or March, 1928, when the course of this anticipated legislation will become clearer. New York is still with us at heart, and we believe that it will not be long before the Empire State is with us again in law.

IV. THE MODEL SUCCESSION TAX RECIPROCAL EXEMPTION PROVISION

Your committee has given careful consideration to the model succession-tax reciprocal exemption provision, set forth at page 77 of the report of the National Committee on Inheritance Taxation to the National Conference on Estate and Inheritance Taxation, held at New Orleans, Louisiana, November 10, 1925, set forth above. Due no doubt to a typographical error the word " personal " appears to have been omitted before the word " property " in the eighth line of such provision. It is also suggested that this provision may be clarified and improved by the addition of two new sentences, as follows:

> " The terms ' foreign country ' and ' country ' as used herein shall mean both any foreign country and any political subdivision thereof, and either of them of which the transferor was domiciled therein at the time of his death."
> " For the purposes of this section, intangible personal property means incorporeal property, including money, deposits in banks, mortgages, debts, receivables, shares of stock, bonds, notes, credits, evidences of an interest in property and evidences of debt."

The first sentence clears up any possible ambiguity, because of the power of subdivisions of countries to make laws, as well as the country itself, and makes it clear that exemption is only allowed in the case of a non-resident decedent if the intangible personal property of a resident of the jurisdiction granting the exemption be subject to no death tax in the jurisdiction of which such non-resident was a resident, either by the sovereign Government of such jurisdiction or any subdivision thereof, whether because of reciprocity or otherwise.

The second sentence is intended to clearly define intangible personal property, so that no question may arise as to what is meant by the term.

Such has been the progress of the reciprocity movement during the past year. We ask those of you who believe that it is just and right to eliminate multiple taxation to join with us in the sincere hope that this idea may eventually become of universal application throughout the United States. And in speaking of it as of universal application, we include not only the territorial possessions of the United States, but our neighbors in Canada. Anything that we can do to strike down artificial economic barriers is unquestionably a great gain for our people.

I regard this as a sound movement towards rational taxation, and if you agree with us, we ask your backing.

Exhibit A

An effort has been made to ascertain the number of shareholders and stockholdings in corporations of the reciprocity states in six states of the Union which have not yet accepted reciprocity, namely, Kansas, Kentucky, Michigan, Utah, West Virginia and Wisconsin.

Through the co-operation of the New York Stock Transfer Association, an inquiry was addressed to thirty-six corporations, each having a million or more shares of stock, and each incorporated in a reciprocity state, inquiring as to the number of shareholders and number of shares held by residents of the above six states. Answers were received from eighteen corporations, or one-half of those to whom the inquiry was addressed. It is to be noted that one large railroad corporation was only able to give the required statistics for the State of Kentucky, and that a second gave the number of stockholders but not the number of shares.

The totals are as follows:

	Stockholders	Number of Shares
Kansas	3403	66,405
Kentucky	5759	260,268
Michigan	11082	348,160
Utah	1381	33,502
West Virginia	5398	300,389
Wisconsin	10006	227,079

If these states do not accept reciprocity and there is no change in the existing state law relating to the taxation of non-residents, then upon the death of any of the above stockholders, his estate will be obliged to pay duplicate taxes upon the assets included in the above summary.

This inquiry justifies the conclusion that there are more stockholders of large corporations throughout the United States than has generally been conceded; and furthermore justifies the conclusion that the states accepting reciprocity will save their residents from inordinate taxation, high administrative costs, and much delay in the settlement of estates.

F. S. EDMONDS, *Chairman*
C. C. BOLTON
R. H. BERRY
MARK GRAVES
H. F. LONG
W. G. ROWE
R. L. RILEY
J. L. SAYLER
J. T. WHITE

EXHIBIT B

RECIPROCITY STATUTES

(Prepared by the Prentice-Hall Service)

California

Sec. 6½. *Reciprocal exemption.*—The tax imposed by this act in respect of intangible personal property shall not be payable if the decedent is a resident of a state or territory of the United States which at the time of his death did not impose a legacy or succession tax or a death tax of any character in respect of intangible personal property within said state or territory of residents of this state, or if the laws of the state or territory of residence of the decedent at the time of his death contained a reciprocal provision under which non-residents were exempted from legacy or succession taxes or death taxes of every character in respect of intangible personal property providing the state or territory of residence of such non-residents allowed a similar exemption to residents of the state or territory of residence of such decedent. For the purposes of this section the District of Columbia shall be considered a territory of the United States. (Added by L. 1927, c. 646, effective July 29, 1927.)

Connecticut

Sec. 20. *Taxability of non-resident's property.* — The following property owned by a non-resident of this state at the time of his decease which shall pass by will or inheritance under the laws of any state shall be subject to a transfer tax of two per centum of its fair market value upon the death of such owner. Moneys on deposit within this state; all stocks or registered obligations of any national bank located in this state, or of any corporation organized or existing under the laws of this state. The provisions of this act shall not apply if the state of domicile of such decedent imposes no succession, inheritance, transfer or similar tax upon moneys on deposit therein or upon the stock or registered obligations of any national bank or corporation located in such state or organized or existing under the laws of such state held at their decease by residents of this state. For the purposes of this section, the word " state " shall be construed to include any territory of the United States, the District of Columbia and any foreign country. (As amended by L. 1925, c. 239; L. 1927, c. 57, approved April 13, 1927, effective July 1, 1927.)

Georgia

Reciprocity. — Be it further enacted by the authority aforesaid that the tax imposed by this Act on personal property (except tangible personal property having an actual situs in this state) shall not be payable if the laws of the state of residence of the decedent at the time of his death exempted residents of this state from transfer taxes or death taxes on such property.

Illinois

Reciprocity.—The tax imposed by this Act in respect of personal property of non-residents (other than tangible personal property having an actual situs in this state) shall not be payable (1) if the transferor at the time of his death was a resident of a state or territory of the United States which at the time of his death did not impose a transfer tax or death tax of any character in respect of personal property of residents of this state (other than tangible personal property having an actual situs in such state or territory), or (2) if the laws of the state or territory of residence of the transferor at the time of his death contained a reciprocal provision under which non-residents were exempted from transfer taxes or death taxes of every character in respect of personal property (other than tangible personal property having an actual situs therein) provided the state or territory of residence of such non-residents allowed a similar exemption to residents of the state or territory of residence of such transferor. For the purposes of this section the District of Columbia and possessions of the United States shall be considered territories of the United States.

Maine

Sec. 24. *Reciprocity.*—The tax imposed by section one shall not be payable in respect of intangible personal property if the decedent

is a resident of a state or territory of the United States which at the time of his death did not impose a legacy or succession tax or a death tax of any character in respect of intangible personal property within said state or territory on residents of this state, or if the laws of the state or territory of residence of the decedent at the time of his death contained a reciprocal provision under which non-residents were exempted from legacy or succession taxes or death taxes of every character in respect of intangible personal property providing the state or territory of residence of such non-residents allowed a similar exemption to residents of the state or territory of residence of such decedent. For the purposes of this section the District of Columbia shall be considered a territory of the United States. The provisions of this section shall apply only to the estates of non-residents who die after July first, nineteen hundred twenty-eight. (Added by L. 1927, ch. 231, approved April 16, 1927. Public Laws 1927 become effective at 12: 01 A. M., July 16, 1927. This chapter applicable only to estates of non-residents dying after July 1, 1928.)

Maryland

Reciprocity.—Except as to tangible personal property having an actual situs in the State of Maryland, no tax on commissions of executors or administrators of non-resident decedents, and no inheritance, estate, or death or transfer tax of any character, in respect of personal property (including also therein mortgages upon real or personal property located within the State of Maryland) of non-resident decedents, shall be payable (a) if the decedent at the time of his death was a resident of a state or territory of the United States, or of any foreign country, which at the time of the distribution, transfer, or other disposition of such personal property of such decedent in Maryland did not impose a transfer tax or death tax of any character in respect of personal property of residents of this state (except tangible personal property having an actual situs in such state or territory or foreign country), or (b) if the laws of the state, territory or country of residence of the decedent at the time of such distribution, transfer or other disposition contained a reciprocal exemption provision under which residents of Maryland are exempted from transfer taxes or death taxes of every character in respect of personal property (except tangible personal property having an actual situs in such state or territory or foreign country) provided the State of Maryland allows a similar exemption to residents of the state, territory or country of residence of such decedent. For the purposes of this section the District of Columbia and possessions of the United States shall be considered territories of the United States. Nothing herein shall be construed to subject to taxation anything heretofore exempt therefrom; and any and all laws or parts of laws of Maryland in conflict or inconsistent with the provisions of this Section 148-A are hereby repealed to the extent of such conflict or inconsistency. (Added by L. 1927, c. 350, approved April 5, 1927, effective June 1, 1927.)

New Hampshire

29. *Reciprocal exemption.*—The tax imposed by this chapter, except upon the transfer of tangible personal property having an actual situs in this state, shall not be payable, in the case of estates of persons deceased subsequent to the passage of this act, (a) if the non-resident owner at the time of his death was a resident of a state or territory of the United States, or of any foreign country which at the time of his death did not impose a transfer tax or death tax of any character in respect to personal property of residents of this state, except tangible personal property having an actual situs in such state or territory or foreign country, or (b) if the laws of the state, territory, or country of residence of such non-resident owner at the time of his death contained a reciprocal exemption provision under which non-residents were exempted from transfer taxes or death taxes of every character in respect to personal property, except tangible personal property having an actual situs therein, provided the state, territory or country of residence of such nonresidents allowed a similar exemption to residents of the state, territory or country of residence of such non-resident owner. For the purpose of this section the District of Columbia and possessions of the United States shall be considered territories of the United States. (Added by L. 1927, c. 37, approved and effective March 9, 1927, 4:47 P. M., as amended by L. 1927, c. 104, approved and effective April 7, 1927.)

Ohio

Method of assessing tax; apportionment exemption.—When assessing tax upon a succession passing from a non-resident decedent the court shall determine the value of the aggregate succession, which shall be the fair market value of all the property, real or personal, whether within or without the state, passing to the successor from the estate of the decedent after making the deductions computed as though the decedent had been a resident of this state and all of his property were located in this state. It shall further determine the value of the Ohio succession, which shall be the fair market value of that part of the aggregate succession which passes to the successor in property subject to inheritance tax under this chapter, after allowing the deductions aforesaid. Out of the Ohio succession so determined the successor shall be allowed such proportion of the exemption to which he would be entitled under the section 5334 as is represented by the ratio borne by the value of his Ohio succession to the value of his aggregate succession. Tax shall then be assessed on the balance of the Ohio succession remaining at the rates and in the method provided for by section 5335 of the General Code. Except that the inheritance tax imposed by this chapter in respect of personal property, except tangible personal property having an actual situs in this state, shall not be payable if the laws of the state, territory or country of residence of the transferor at the time of his death contained a reciprocal exemption provision under which non-residents were exempted from transfer or death taxes of every character in respect of personal property, except tangible personal property having an actual situs therein, provided the state, territory or country of residence of such non-residents allowed a similar exemption to residents of the state, territory or country of residence of such transferor. For the purposes of this section the District of Columbia and possessions of the United States shall be considered territories of the United States. (Added by 111 v. 97—1925, amended by Laws 1927 (H. B. No. 136,), approved March 31, 1927, effective June 30, 1927.)

Oregon

Reciprocal exemption of intangible personal property of non-resident decedent.—Intangible personal property of a non-resident decedent upon which an inheritance tax is imposed by sections 1191 (par. 1), 1192 (pars. 2-4) and 1228 (par. 41), Oregon Laws, shall not be subject to the tax so imposed if a like exemption is made by the laws of the state or country of decedent's residence in favor of residents of the state of Oregon. (L. 1927, c. 118, effective May 27, 1927.)

Pennsylvania

Personal property of a non-resident decedent made taxable under this section shall not be subject to the tax so imposed if a like exemption is made by the laws of the state or country of the decedent's residence in favor of residence of this Commonwealth. (As amended by C. 391, L. 1925, effective May 14, 1925.)

CHAIRMAN LONG: I am not certain that we should now ask for any action on the part of this conference on the report just rendered, but I suspect that it would have been well for me to have, as a matter of record, accepted the report of the committee on credentials, and in order to speed up that matter I will recognize that Mr. Conner of South Dakota moves that this report be accepted, on the credentials, and that it has been seconded, and that those in favor say aye. It is carried.

There are several things that we of New England are proud of. One of them at the present time is that we have a sterling son of New England as the President of the National Tax Association;

one of the others is that we all feel in this great land of the United States of America, perhaps some in the Dominion of Canada, that by each fireside there exists some thought of New England. I know in my contact with delegates of various states of the United States of America I find that they trace back, not without pride, to some ancestor in New England. Being from Massachusetts, and joining with the President of this Association in the pride of New England, I am greatly pleased to come in contact with so many who feel that way.

We are sometimes prone to wait until a person dies before we show any affection for him. We have a President of this association who has had many times laid before him the wreaths of affection and esteem in which we hold him, but one who probably has done more than any one else in relation to inheritance taxes, and particularly in relation to non-resident inheritance taxes. He has erected a monument which he himself cannot now erase. Who is there who claims to know anything about inheritance tax who does not know of the Matthews flat-rate plan?

We frequently find from the reading of history and learning from the lips of those who have lived a long while, of the deeds of some who have passed from us, and we feel sometimes that we should like to call them back to us that we might get from them in life the wisdom that we have to get from the books; but we are greatly to be honored tonight, and we are greatly to be congratulated that we do not have to call from the past, with a triumph of guns, but by the ordinary speaking voice we can call to us one whose monument is already erected, and one that he conceived before he even passed into the presidency of the National Tax Association. It is, therefore, with a degree of pride, and I think rather an unusual situation, when we can point to a man who has already placed his own name on the pages of history. I have very great pleasure in introducing to you the man who made the Matthews Flat Rate Plan known throughout the world.

JOSEPH S. MATTHEWS: Mr. Chairman, Ladies and Gentlemen: The plan to which the speaker, or the chairman, has referred is the one which was brought out before Senator Edmonds conceived the idea of reciprocity. It was brought out at that time because such a plan as Senator Edmonds has discussed with you was not then in sight, and it did not appear that there was any immediate prospect that the states could be induced by any means to forego the tax upon the intangible personal property of non-residents.

In that situation, at the meeting at Bretton Woods, in 1921, I suggested this plan, which did not reach to the elimination of the duplicate taxation, but was intended to alleviate the situation while such taxes were bound to be enforced and remained upon the statute books.

If and when the reciprocity idea is adopted generally throughout the states, this plan will no longer be useful, but in the meantime several states have adopted it, and until reciprocity is brought about, its usefulness should continue.

The idea was to simplify the administration of the tax by a flat-rate plan, which would enable an easy computation of the tax, enable executors to quickly obtain their transfers; eliminate expense, and do everything that was then apparently in sight to be accomplished, except to rid the country of the tax itself.

The plan is not involved in this opinion of the New York Court, to which Senator Edmonds has referred, and it is for that reason that I want to discuss it.

It has gone abroad throughout the country that the flat-rate plan was held to be unconstitutional in that New York decision. I am going to try to present an argument to sustain my own view, which is that the flat-rate plan was not involved and is not affected by the New York decision, and that those states which have adopted the plan as originally proposed have no reason to be anxious in regard to the constitutionality of their law, for the reasons upon which the New York opinion was based.

THE CONSTITUTIONALITY OF THE FLAT-RATE INHERITANCE TAX PLAN

HON. J. S. MATTHEWS
Associate Justice New Hampshire Superior Court,
President, National Tax Association

An opinion recently handed down by the New York Court of Appeals in the case of Smith vs. Loughman and others has given rise to much discussion as to the constitutionality of the flat-rate plan which has heretofore been endorsed and approved by this association and adopted in several states.

The headnote is as follows:

> " The statute imposing a tax on taxable transfers of the property of non-resident decedents, which is a modification of the method known as the ' Matthews flat-rate plan,' is unconstitutional as being discriminatory between residents and non-residents, denying to the latter the privileges and immunities extended to citizens of this state."

Upon an examination of the New York statute, however, I am convinced that the principle of the flat-rate plan, as we have understood it, was not involved, and I can find nothing in the opinion of the court to account for the reference to the flat-rate plan in the headnote. The flat rate imposed by the New York statute applied to both real and personal property, and was evidently based upon the theory that in imposing inheritance taxes a state could discrimi-

28

nate between estates of residents and those of non-residents. The flat rate which we have discussed at our conferences was intended to apply to personal property only and was based upon the theory that an inheritance tax, as such, could not be imposed at all upon personal property, by any state except the state of domicile; that the tax imposed upon personal property in other states, although termed an inheritance tax, was not such in fact, and did not operate as such.

Real estate passes at death, under the laws of the state where it is located, regardless of the domicile of the deceased. Inheritance taxes upon real estate have been levied by the state of location, and not elsewhere. There has been no duplication in the case of real estate. The expense and annoyance which the flat-rate plan was intended to avoid did not apply to that class of property. In other words, there was no occasion for the flat rate, so far as real estate was concerned. In the case of personal property the law of inheritance is just the other way around. Such property passes at death, under the laws of the state of the decedent's domicile, regardless of the location of the property.

The whole difficulty which the flat rate was calculated to alleviate had to do with personal property and grew out of the attempt to tax the inheritance of personal property, not only in the state of domicile, under whose laws the property passed, but also in other states, whose laws did not pretend to control the right of inheritance. I discussed the theory of the flat rate as a remedy for these evils in a paper which was read at the conference held at Bretton Woods in 1921, from which I will quote:

"The idea of the flat rate as a remedy for these evils was evolved from a consideration of the character of the inheritance tax as interpreted by the courts, and its relation to the laws regulating intestate succession. The courts say that it is a tax imposed upon the right or privilege of the heirs or legatees to take at death the property of a deceased person and not a tax upon the property itself; that the right which is taxed is one which emanates from the law of the state of domicile and is subject to tax by the state which grants the right and is not in fact taxed or subject to tax in other states; that the tax assessed by other states refers only to the transfer of the property within their several jurisdictions to the executor or administrator; and that the payment thereof merely reduces the net assets, like the payment of a debt of the testator, or the payment of money for funeral expenses or expenses of administrator, and does not otherwise affect the interest of the heirs or legatees.

"Speaking of the non-resident tax, the New Jersey Court says in Carr v. Edwards, 84 N. J. L. 667: 'We had in Neilson v. Russell, 76 N. J. L. 655, just prior to the passage of the Act of 1909, held that a legacy under a non-resident's will was not taxable here because, among other reasons, it depended for its validity and amount upon the law of the testator's domicile. We said that the justification of special taxes of this character, imposed without regard to the limitation contained in our constitution upon property taxes, was found in the fact that the rights of testamentary disposition and of succession were creatures of law, upon the exercise and operation of which the law-maker might impose terms, and that it followed logically that the only law that could impose the terms was the law that created the right. The only special right given by the New Jersey law, in case of a non-resident decedent, is the right of an executor or administrator to succeed to the property having its situs in New Jersey. Unless, therefore, the legislature meant by the Act of 1909 to tax this right—the transfer, by grace of our law of the property having its situs here, from the decedent to his representative—its enactment was futile as far as the estates of non-residents are concerned.'

"Now, assuming that the executor of a New Hampshire estate has paid a tax to New Jersey in order to secure the transfer of shares in a New Jersey corporation, let us consider how the New Hampshire court says he must account for it in the settlement of his account. The subject is covered by the opinion in Kingsbury v. Bazeley, 75 N. H. 13, which is, in part, as follows: ' In the absence of statutory provisions on the subject, the question seems to be: What force, if any, can be given the foreign law in the distribution under New Hampshire law? This must be the sole question, unless there can be drawn from the terms of the will, expressly or by implication, evidence sufficient to justify a conclusion as to the testator's intention. In a gift of a pecuniary legacy of a certain amount, the apparent intention is to benefit the legatee to the full amount named. . . . . To hold that the effect of the foreign law is to reduce the legacy given by the will, construed in accordance with the law of the testator's domicile, is to permit the foreign law to regulate the testamentary capacity of a citizen of this state. But the foreign law cannot extend beyond the jurisdiction which created it. . . . .

" ' As the foreign tax depends upon the jurisdiction over the property, and is not sustainable as a regulation of the exercise of testamentary power by the citizen of another state, it follows that the tax is merely a charge upon the particular property, and not upon pecuniary legacies given by the will. That the foreign state may regulate the amount of the imposition made by it, or determine whether it will make any at all, by the character of the legacies given by the will, is immaterial. Having jurisdiction over the property, it is for such state alone to determine upon what basis it will exact payment. While in giving effect to a foreign will courts are governed by the law of the testator's domicile, it has never been held that in the administration of an estate the courts of the testator's domicile would be governed by the law of the situs of personal property. The estate within the control of the court is to be administered according to the law of the state. The property to be administered embraces all that was originally within the state, or that the executor has been able to find elsewhere and bring here. Whatever sums the executor may be obliged to pay to bring the property within the state merely reduce the amount within the control of the court. . . . .

" ' The executors have in hand, if they are ready to settle, so much property. The will, construed by the laws of this state, directs how the distribution shall be made. The fact that the executors have less than they would have had, except for the demands of jurisdictions to which they were obliged to go to get the property and bring it here for distribution, cannot alter the law of the state or the terms of the will.

" ' In the absence of evidence from which a contrary direction can be implied from the will, the amounts deducted by other states, before permitting the transfer of property within their limits to the executor for distribution here (Greves v. Shaw, 173 Meads 205, 209) are not properly within this state for distribution. The executors are chargeable only for what has come to their hands—the property less the duties paid. If they charge themselves with the full value of the property, a practical method of accounting would permit them to discharge themselves by accounting for the foreign duties paid as expenses of administration.' "

From this I drew the conclusion that this tax, although called an inheritance tax and ordinarily made a part of the inheritance tax law, is in fact nothing more or less than the price which the executor appointed in the state of domicile must pay for the privilege of taking possession of the property and not an inheritance tax at all.

The New Jersey law to which I have referred, as later amended, was before the United States Supreme Court in Maxwell vs. Bugbee, 250 U. S. 525, and the view of the nature of the tax which I have expressed seems to be supported by the opinion in that case. The Court there says, " Before taking up these objections, it is necessary to briefly consider the nature of the tax." The Court then cites the case of Carr vs. Edwards and says: " It was held by the New Jersey Court of Errors and Appeals to be a tax upon the special right, the creation of the statute, of an executor or administrator of a non-resident decedent to succeed to property having its situs in New Jersey."

The Court then goes on to say that " The language correctly characterizes the nature and effect of the tax as imposed under the amendment of 1914," which was the Act there under consideration; and again, " The tax is, then, one upon the transfer of property in New Jersey, to be paid upon turning it over to the administrator or executor at the domicile of the decedent."

Unlike the statute which the New York Court has declared to be unconstitutional, the flat-rate plan does not propose to tax inheritances from estates of non-residents at a different rate from that imposed upon inheritances from estates of residents. On the contrary, it proposes the abandonment of the inheritance tax as affecting personal property of non-residents, and the replacement of the revenue derived from such taxes, by a tax upon the privilege extended to a foreign executor to take possession of the property for administration under the laws of another state. And since the tax deals only with the transfer of personal property within the state to the foreign executor, and has no reference to any other property or to the individual interests, relationship or residence of the beneficiaries, it is urged that it is not necessary to adjust the rate to conform to the rates imposed upon inheritances and in fact that there is no point in doing so.

In New Hampshire the flat-rate tax is not included in the statute imposing a tax upon inheritances, but is made the subject of an entirely separate act.

In the case which was the subject of the recent opinion of the New York Court of Appeals the only property involved was real estate located in the State of New York, but belonging to the estate of a non-resident. The transfer of this property to the beneficiaries under the decedent's will had been taxed at a different rate from that which would have been imposed if the decedent had been a resident of the State of New York, and the Court said that " a state is not at liberty to establish varying codes of law, one for its citizens and another, *governing the same conduct,* for citizens of sister states."

What the New York Court might have said, if the property involved had been limited to personal property and if the New York statute had also been limited to a tax upon the transfer of personal property to the foreign executor does not appear.

I wish to make it clear that I am not undertaking in this address to comment upon the merits of the opinion of the New York Court. The point I am endeavoring to make is that the principle of the flat-rate plan, as endorsed by this association, was not involved in the case in which that opinion was rendered.

CHAIRMAN LONG: We all listened with a great deal of interest to the report of the President of the Association, and in it we find a breath of the freshness of the hills of New England. Just for a moment we will get a breath of the freshness of the mouth of the Mississippi in asking Mr. Sneed from New Orleans to say something that he wishes to announce to you in relation to the committee on resolutions. Mr. Sneed.

HARRY P. SNEED (Louisiana) : I have forgotten all about water since I have been in Canada, but I want to ask the resolutions committee to meet me just a moment at the registration desk in the outer hall, so that we can formulate our report. It will only take a moment or two.

CHAIRMAN LONG: Any of the resolutions committee who are here can be absented for just that two minutes.

On the Canadian program there was written something which is not written on the United States program, and that was in relation to the reciprocal inheritance taxation; that some people would lead the discussion; and the first person to lead this discussion is Mr. J. T. White. Before introducing Mr. White I think it is well for us to recall that there has not been a meeting of the National Tax Association in Canada for many of us for a great many years, and I think that most of us who have been connected with the association for a few years looked with favor upon coming to Canada, largely through our very pleasant associations with the representatives who had been sent to the National Tax Association from Canada, and one of those whom we have used very freely on our committees is Mr. White. We have dipped deeply into the talent that he has very freely offered to us, and I think we all owe a very deep debt of gratitude to the person who will lead this discussion of the very interesting subject that we have had here.

On the Canadian program it is said that this discussion is to be led by Mr. J. T. White, K. C. I won't undertake to say what " K. C." means, but he is Controller of Revenue of the Province of Ontario. If Mr. White is here I wish that he may come forward so that we can look upon him again.

J. T. WHITE (Ontario) : Mr. Chairman, I thank you for your very kind reference to myself, little as it may be deserved, and I thank the delegates present. In fact, I feel rather embarrassed at the very warm welcome with which my name was received. I cannot say how pleased I am to. see so many delegates here at this convention. I was a little bit nervous in inviting you here, because I thought it might be of some inconvenience to yourselves to leave the United States, of which you are all so dearly fond; to get away even for such a short time from your pleasant associations; but I do trust that you will feel the time has not been wasted.

As to the report which Senator Edmonds has put before you in such eloquent language, I am a member of the committee of which he was the able chairman, and I only wish to say that I very heartily concur in everything contained in the report, and I can only emphasize one of the reasons contained in that report which I think should strongly induce the Canadian provinces to bring themselves within the scope of your legislation along the lines of reciprocity in the succession duties or inheritance taxes. That is, that it will break down the barriers and leave the line open to the free flow of capital into this country. That, I think, is a great advantage to Canada as, in the development of this great country of ours, we shall, for a great many years, need capital for development purposes, and, I think, it will in no less degree be a benefit to the people of the states who have money to invest, to have this market open for investment, and I doubt if you will find—in fact, I am sure you will not find—any safer place for the investment of whatever capital you may see fit to employ outside of your own country.

I thank you all for your very kind attention, and I again thank you, Mr. Chairman, for your very kind remarks.

CHAIRMAN LONG: Following further the Canadian program, and keeping more or less in line with those who are supposed to speak upon this subject, I am going to ask next as a speaker one of our own members from the United States of America, and a man who has been connected with tax work and with government work for a good many years, in the empire state of New York. He needs no introduction, but in order to introduce him I want to say that I think that probably there is no one of us but what has always profited by whatever the next speaker has said upon any subject that he chose to speak upon, and I am sure that we shall listen with a great deal of interest to what he may have to say tonight.

I rather suspect that he has not had any great warning that he was upon this program, because being busy with other activities he may not even have had the opportunity to read the program that the Canadian Conference had printed, or even to know that the Canadian Conference had printed a program.

With these brief remarks, which are more or less meant as an excuse and a help for him, in anything he may want to slide out from under, I have again the very great pleasure of introducing to you the Honorable Mark Graves of New York.

MARK GRAVES (New York): Mr. Chairman, Ladies and Gentlemen: We of New York have learned very much from New England. It has pleased me tonight to have a New England gentleman in the chair, and the President of the National Tax Association from New England as a speaker.

In my brief career in tax work I have learned very many of the few things that I know from New England. The very first contact that I had was back several years ago. They invited me to come over to a New England tax conference to make a speech. My recollection is we had this conference in Vermont, and every speaker traced his origin back to Vermont, somehow. I got up in a somewhat flippant mood, and explained that my ancestors were an old New England family; that I had traced them back to Thomas

Hadfield Graves, who settled from somewhere in Massachusetts or Connecticut, and I was sorry I had no real connection with Vermont except this fact. My wife was not present at that time. I really had never been in Burlington before, but to make the story good I said the only real relation I had to Vermont was that I came over to Burlington once in my boyhood days and kissed a girl there. The joke was on me when, after the conference was over that evening, one of the Burlington men came around and said, "Would you mind telling me the name of that girl?"

We have almost been adopted into this New England tax conference. I have paid quite a heavy tribute to New England. I have accumulated several sore throats by saying " That is good " when I have attended New England tax conferences.

I have been very much interested in President Matthews' speech. I am going to trespass on your good nature to let me tell a story which many of you have heard before from our good friend Professor Belknap of Kentucky.

I really don't know whether we adopted the Matthews Flat Rate Plan in New York or whether we did not. I will take it for granted that we did not. I will illustrate it this way.

Belknap tells this story about some New England family down in the Back Bay district. This lady came of a very distinguished family, and was very high-toned; had a couple of children, and one night she found the little girl scratching the boy's face and having a terrible fight with him; finally the girl spit in the boy's face. The mother said, "Why, now, Helen, you must have been inspired by the devil to do that." " Well," Helen said, " the devil may have inspired me to scratch his face, but the spit was my own idea."

When we started out with what we thought was the Matthews' Flat Rate Plan in New York, and coupled it up with reciprocity, I admit we worked some of our own ideas into the plan. I hope none of you will charge that to President Matthews. Apparently we muffed the ball somewhere along the line, but I do wish to say to all of you from the United States, as well as to you distinguished men from Canada, that if New York has made a mistake—and we are not prepared to admit it, because we shall carry our case to the United States Supreme Court — when they have told us we are wrong, we will believe that Cardozo was right; but be that as it may, we shall undertake to correct by legislation, without waiting for the Supreme Court's decision. You may all look forward to see New York four-square in the reciprocity column by the first of March of next year.

This reciprocity program that we have in the United States originated down in Harrisburg. Senator Edmonds, who has presented the report here, invited Commissioner Long and myself and some others to come to Harrisburg in 1924, I believe. We talked over various matters; we talked about multiple taxation, and we conceived the idea that we could do something to do away with multiple taxation in the states. To be perfectly frank about it, while I participated in the conference, I did not anticipate that within three years it would gain so much headway. I think Senator Edmonds, if he told you how he really felt in December, 1924, would say he did not expect so many results as we have had. We believe it is the right principle.

In the few remaining minutes I have I should like to talk to our neighbors of Canada. We are not here to sell you something from the states. We have come here on this particular program to try and convince you that reciprocity is the sound principle of death-taxation. To a very great extent you can borrow money from the states. Financiers from the United States tell me that we have loads of money over there; the trouble is to keep it working.

You have natural resources to develop here. We believe that it is sound economics to do away with multiple taxation between the provinces of Canada and the states of the United States. We believe, as the Senator from Pennsylvania has said, that we should not, by artificial man-made laws, set up barriers which interfere with the economic laws of the nations and of the world. We believe that capital should be permitted to flow for the most unrestricted development of the resources of the world, and that is all we are asking for in this reciprocal plan. We believe it is to your benefit; we believe it is to our benefit; we believe it is to the benefit of the rich states and the poor states, and we appeal to you on that simple proposition only. I thank you.

CHAIRMAN LONG: It was my good fortune last evening, together with some others from the National Tax Association, to sit in for the first time with some of our Canadian friends in relation to inheritance taxation, more as a round-table talk, and it proved a very enjoyable gathering. We came there in contact with the next speaker, who will speak for the provinces of Canada and in particular the province of Manitoba. I know that you will like the next speaker, because I liked him, and I feel that our first impressions are generally pretty good. It has been one of the very great pleasures to me to meet these Canadian tax officials, and find them so much like ourselves in many respects, and it really is more than an unusual pleasure to introduce to you as the next speaker on the program Mr. R. M. Fisher, barrister-at-law and administrator of the succession duty office, department of the provincial treasurer of Winnipeg.

R. M. FISHER (Manitoba): Mr. Chairman, Ladies and Gentlemen: I want to preface the few remarks that I make tonight with

a profession of faith. I am whole-heartedly in favor of the abolition of multiple inheritance taxation. I do not want anything that
I may say in the course of my remarks to in any way detract from
that simple sincere statement.

I thought it might be interesting for the American delegates to
have a very brief review of the Canadian situation as regards this
province.

In Canada, unfortunately, we have not yet settled our domestic
problem, and in considering an international program, its bearing
upon our local situation must be considered. Now, I want to simply,
in headings, point out a few differences between the Canadian and
the American legislation, and in so far as I make reference to the
American legislation, anything that I say is with the utmost deference, because I do not profess an intimate knowledge of your law.

In the first place, as regards the incidence of the tax, as I understand it, the theory in the United States is that the tax is on the
right. In Canada, in the common-law provinces, the tax is on the
property, and in the province of Quebec, which is under the civil
law, the tax is on the transmission.

Now, as to constitutionality. I am not going to discuss your constitutional problems in the United States, but let me point out that in
Canada we have, as has already been pointed out, no federal inheritance tax, and our provincial succession-duty legislation is subject
to two constitutional limitations.

First, the tax must be direct, and, second, it must be within the
province.

The third difference, or at least, the third point I want to make,
is that we have found in the consideration of the problem in Canada, of abolishing multiple taxation, three main obstacles. First,
our constitutional problem, as I have already indicated. The tax
must be direct and it must be within the province. Secondly, we
have an economic situation. Capital in Canada is largely centralized in the provinces of Ontario and Quebec. On the other hand,
we have in the province of British Columbia something which is
somewhat similar to the situation as regards Florida in the United
States. They have advantages which make them prone to favor a
system of taxation based on domicile. Then, thirdly, we have an
economic development which I think is probably true both in your
country and in ours; that the trend of investment is gradually from
investment in realty to investment in personalty; and, finally, the
legal problem.

As I have already intimated, there is the question of the civil
code in Quebec; and there is another thing which is purely local
but which is very important to us at the present time, and that is
the uncertainty as to the ultimate control of the corporations,
whether it is to rest with the Federal Government, or whether it is
to rest with the Provincial Government.

I want to make four very brief observations on the report as presented by the committee of the National Tax Association, and at the outset I should like it distinctly understood that these observations are not offered in any spirit of criticism, but in the hope that by testing any plan from any or every angle we can finally solve our problem, fundamentally, equitably and absolutely and forever.

The first observation I want to make is, that unfortunately in Canada at the present time there is no consensus of opinion as to how multiple taxation is to be abolished interprovincially; secondly, in Canada we are not familiar legally with the division of personal property into tangibles and intangibles. We have had no decision in our courts which in any way resembles or in any way discusses the questions that were settled by the Frick decision. Thirdly, I would suggest that it is possible that the plan as advocated by the National Tax Association does not provide as fundamental a solution as uniform legislation abolishing the possibility of multiple taxation?

Just on this point I want to throw out two questions: First, how is the question of international dispute to be settled? You may or may not, the first time you come to this reciprocal provision, find that you have a conflict of opinion, as between one state and another, as to what it means, how it operates. That, I take, could be settled by your Supreme Court, Mr. Chairman, but when you come into the international field there is at the present time no court to settle those difficulties.

The second question I want to throw out is: What are you going to do about the doctrine of equitable conversion, as applied to real estate? I believe that doctrine has had some support in the United States and some support in England. It has not yet been discussed by the Canadian court; but I prophesy that we are not yet at the final solution as regards that particular phase of the question.

The fourth suggestion I want to make is that in certain stages of economic development the taxation of intangible personalty on the bases of domicile alone is possibly unfair to the jurisdiction of situs.

I am not going to amplify that. What I have in mind, I think, is evident to all of you. The only thing I would draw your attention to is the fact that the financial committee of the League of Nations, a committee composed of Josiah Stamp of England, Professor Seligman of the United States, and Professor Durms of Europe, in struggling with this problem, decided that to be absolutely fair there must be some division of the tax between the jurisdiction of domicile and the jurisdiction of situs.

I want to repeat again, I throw out these suggestions, not in the spirit of criticism but simply to indicate that before we apply this principle internationally we should be absolutely satisfied that it is fundamental and equitable and that it cannot in any way be improved upon.

Mr. Chairman, I do not want to exceed my allotted time.

CHAIRMAN LONG: Say whatever you want to say.

MR. FISHER: Then, with the Chairman's permission, may I take just a few minutes to sketch in the very briefest way a suggestion by which you may test the proposal of the National Tax Association and satisfy yourself that the plan as advocated is the international solution of the problem. I have put this suggestion down in abbreviated form, and I think if I read it slowly you will get what is involved.

The premises: A uniform act embodying as a basic principle the imposition of a duty with the following incidences and times of payment.

(a) A primary payment to be made by the estate, as a condition of obtaining probate or administration, according to a rate based on the aggregate value of the estate wherever situate, applicable to all property real and personal actually situate within the jurisdiction, irrespective of its destination under the will or intestacy and irrespective of the domicile of the deceased.

That is what your national committee, I believe, has called an estate tax. Its basis is situs, and it would require, necessarily, a codification of the rules regarding the situs of personal property.

(b) A deferred payment, to be made by beneficiaries at the time of actual distribution of the estate, according to a rate based on the relationship of the beneficiary and what he receives; applicable to all real estate within the jurisdiction, irrespective of the domicile of the deceased, and to all personal estate wherever situate, of a deceased person domiciled within the jurisdiction.

In conformity with the Frick decision, I take it you would have to add real estate and tangible personalty.

The deferred payment is a true succession duty, and the two payments would aggregate what was considered to be a reasonable rate, under the present imposition of one tax.

I have just summarized very briefly certain advantages of this principle:

(1) A uniform act would simplify administration and lessen expenses for estates.

(2) Would abolish possibility of multiple taxation.

(3) Would interfere as little as possible with the free circulation of capital.

(4) I think this is important: Would lighten initial payment and make the balance payable when the estate is administered.

(5) Would avoid many of the difficulties inherent in the application of one principle to the exclusion of the other. And finally:

(6) Would materially lessen litigation on constitutional points, because based on principles of private international law.

So far as I can see the only point that could be questioned would be in connection with the deferred payment, where the deceased leaves intangible personalty with a legal situs in a jurisdiction outside the jurisdiction of the domicile devised to beneficiaries who are also non-residents.

I think there is no question under our Canadian law, and I submit the Frick decision casts no doubt on the right of jurisdiction of domicile to tax all intangible personalty.

However, if you still have doubts I submit that it is good law and within the competence of the jurisdiction of domicile to make it a condition precedent to any one inheriting under that law, whether as a resident or non-resident, that he shall discharge the tax imposed by the jurisdiction of the domicile as a condition of inheriting.

In conclusion, let me make this quite frank statement: I am not advocating this plan in lieu of the plan suggested by the National Tax Association, but simply tendering it as a suggestion, so that you may satisfy yourselves that your solution is as fundamental and as equitable a solution as may be found.   Thank you.

CHAIRMAN LONG: I wish to recognize one of our former presidents and dearly beloved members, Dr. Page.

THOMAS W. PAGE (District of Columbia): Mr. Chairman, we have heard on this interesting subject the men who are better qualified than any others in the world to talk to us about reciprocity in inheritance taxation, because they are the men who have been chiefly active in framing the idea and getting genuine reciprocity in the states of the Union; and yet, in spite of their experience and competence, they leave me a little puzzled.

Senator Edmonds has told us that reciprocity is not going to suffer at all from that New York decision.   President Matthews has told us that the Matthews Flat Rate Plan is thoroughly constitutional and could not have been repealed by that New York decision. Mr. Graves says that he does not know whether they ever did have the Matthews Plan in New York or not, but, at any rate, whatever it was they once had, they are going to make it good again by the 4th of next March.   So that my state of puzzlement is much the same as that of a Pullman porter who runs between Washington and Atlanta.   A man got on at Washington about 10 o'clock at night and told the porter he wanted to get off at Greensboro, North Carolina.   The train was to get there about 4 o'clock in the morning. He said, "Now, Porter, I am a heavy sleeper, and I never like to get up in the morning, and it is very important that I should get off; I am going to give you five dollars now and tell you no matter how I resist, I want you to put me off the train at Greensboro." The porter promised faithfully he would do it, and of course the man went to sleep, and he slept peacefully and did not wake up until about 9:30 the next morning. By that time he was far past Greensboro, and he lost his temper somewhat, rang for the porter, and said, " I thought I told you to put me off at Greensboro, and I paid you to do it." The porter looked a little dilapidated; one eye was swollen, and his face was scratched, and he was in pretty bad physical condition; and he looked at this man and said, " You certainly has got me puzzled, boss. I jest wonder who in de name o' Gawd dat was I did put off at Greensboro!"

I am just wondering what it was that this New York decision did put off.

CHAIRMAN LONG: I am not certain, but I suppose that it is a proper thing for the Conference to accept or reject this report.

FRANKLIN S. EDMONDS: I should like to move the acceptance of the report, and with your permission I should like to spend a few minutes to discuss some of the questions that have been raised.

It is true that we all recognize the great difficulty in this multiple taxation of the intangibles of non-residents. It is true that six or seven years ago Judge Matthews developed from the New Hampshire experience the plan of the flat-rate tax, which was an infinite improvement upon the chaos which existed previous to that time. It is true that certain states have adopted the flat-rate plan. Then, shortly after that, came the suggesion of reciprocity, which has been all too kindly attributed to myself but was really the result of a joint conference of a number of states, in which New York was one of the pioneers.

We like reciprocity better than the flat-rate plan, because while the flat-rate plan limits its tax to two per cent, it still means that those assets are being subjected to two kinds of taxation, and we felt that upon principle, it was better that they should be only subject to one kind of taxation, and with the taxation at domicile; and that these states which had adopted the flat-rate plan could add reciprocity on as an additional feature.

As a matter of fact Georgia, within the last two months has adopted the flat-rate plan, with reciprocity, which means that it will charge nothing at all to the decedents of the reciprocal states, but will charge two per cent to the decedents of the non-reciprocal states. That was an improvement over the original chaos, but at the same time it leaves the way open for the abolition completely of the tax on intangibles of non-residents, as soon as all states enter into the reciprocal condition.

Then came this New York decision, which was erroneously reported as a decision against the flat-rate plan. Judge Matthews felt that that legally was not a correct statement of the decision.

As a matter of fact, I am reminded of the statement about the relationship between Erasmus and Martin Luther, with reference to the Reformation, which used to appear in our history books, which said that "Erasmus laid the egg which Luther hatched, but afterwards disowned the chicken."

The New York decision against the flat-rate plan as applied to realty carried down reciprocity with it because, unfortunately, in the section of the New York law the two were joined together. One sentence imposed the two per cent flat rate, when no deductions were taken, or three per cent if deductions were taken, upon the property of non-residents; and then came the second sentence, that started out like this: That from the tax imposed by this section there be an exemption to the decedents of the reciprocal states. The language was, "from the tax imposed by this section."

When the Supreme Court wiped out that first sentence, what was left was the provision for reciprocity in exemptions from the tax imposed by the section. The attorney general of New York was obliged to conclude that reciprocity had fallen also, because the two were joined together.

Mr. Graves and his colleagues have told us that the sentiment in New York is strongly in favor of reciprocity. We believe that is true, because no state could have given the movement more cordial assistance than the State of New York. It will doubtless come before the next session of the legislature in the form of a separate bill. If, in the meantime, the Supreme Court of the United States has reversed the Court of Appeals of New York, then we are where we were originally. If the Supreme Court does not reverse the Court of Appeals of New York, there will doubtless be in New York a new reciprocity statute.

Now, I want to say just a few words of appreciation of the excellent discussion which Mr. Fisher has given and of the aid which he gave us prior to this session.

Speaking generally, according to our American law we divide all property into real property, tangible personalty—that is, articles of furniture, statuary and things of that kind, and automobiles—and intangible personalty, or stocks and bonds of one sort or another.

Our Supreme Court has said that realty and tangible personal property are to be taxed only by the state where they are permanently located. That is all right. That is one form of taxation. There is no violation of the rule of simplicity of taxation in that; but, our Supreme Court has also said that intangible personal property may be taxed by any jurisdiction that acquires jurisdiction of the same. There is where the difficulty comes.

There is, first of all, the jurisdiction of the domicile of the testator, and then there are one, two, three, four or five jurisdictions which may have, in some way or other, jurisdiction over the asset. It is that double taxation which we are trying to get rid of.

Mr. Fisher has called attention to the fact that there may be a jurisdiction which in its economic development needs capital. There may be an investor who has capital in that jurisdiction, although he is not a resident there. Shouldn't that jurisdiction tax his estate upon the transfer of his intangible assets?

I think it is a matter of opinion, but investors are getting better educated as the years go on, and it is a question to my mind as to whether you are going to be able to attract investors if, by coming in from the outside and investing, they are going to make themselves subject to two or three kinds of taxation. Won't they be more likely to select for their investments the jurisdiction where they will only be subject to one form of taxation?

To my mind the great economic question before the jurisdiction confronted with this situation is self-denial, and sound policy would prescribe that it should say: "We won't tax these intangibles of non-residents, even if we have a right to do so." The great advantage of this policy is that it will make it possible for investors to come in freely and invest, and it is from that point of view that we support this reciprocity movement, not only as in line with simple taxation but in line also with sound economics.

JOSEPH S. MATTHEWS: I should like to say just another word. I agree entirely with Senator Edmonds when he says he thinks more of reciprocity than he does of the flat-rate plan. The idea of the flat-rate plan was something like the idea of the physician who is called to attend a patient who is in great pain. The first thing a physician does is to administer an opiate to quiet the patient until he can find some way to cure him.

The flat-rate plan was intended to operate as the opiate. Senator Edmonds apparently has still his way to find a cure in the reciprocity proposition. If it goes through and is adopted generally, it will operate as a cure, and when the patient is well, then of course the opiate will no longer be necessary.

CHAIRMAN LONG: I recognize Mr. Atterbury of New York.

J. FRANCIS ATTERBURY (New York): There are two ideas I should like the members of the conference to carry away with them tonight, and they are both facts. One is this, I will cite the argument that has to do with the State of New Jersey. When a resident of New York state died, the total tax on his estate was $3600, and it was thought that that was all the estate would have to pay, but they were reminded by the corporate securities department of the State of New Jersey that the estate had to pay a tax of $6000. In other words, they penalized the estate for investing in New Jersey.

A year ago I had the privilege and pleasure of making an address before the State Bankers Convention, and on my way, realizing that I had to give them something new and instructive, I stopped in

Albany and spent the evening with my good friend Hon. Mark Graves and Deputy Commissioner Cole, and discussed the question of extending the reciprocal idea into the Dominion, with respect to the free flow of capital.

After delivering that address and being invited to dine with Mr. Frederick Taylor of Montreal, he asked me to reiterate my idea of reciprocity. I gave it to him, and the best evidence in the world in favor of it lies in the fact that the New York state bankers gave me Hell, because of my endeavor to have capital flow into Canada.

I am aware of the fact that the states of the United States never would have prospered to the extent they have if it had not been for outside capital. Canada and the United States have similar national resources. We have developed, largely through the fact that we had capital; we had it from Canada, we had it from Europe—and why? Because we could show them an investment that would give greater returns.

One other fact I should like to indelibly impress upon the gentlemen here is the fact that this question of multiple taxation does not affect the wealthy man as much as it does the person of moderate means. A man may think he is leaving $100,000 to his family, but before he gets through with the multiple taxation it is very much reduced. The wealthy man can afford competent lawyers to advise him as to methods of protecting his estate or whatever it may be. In conclusion I should like to call your attention to one thing: In 1924 when the New York Stock Transfer Association, of whom I happen to be secretary, took up this question, due to our contract with the dear public, it was brought to my mind in discussing the subject with a young chap in a broker's office. He was wise enough to see the opportunity presented with the law as it existed in 1924. He went into the investment business and studied capital, and found out that he could change investments for a number of wealthy people, whereby they could get away from this multiple taxation, with the result that that young man today, with all our modifications of the laws, has an income of from anywhere between $50,000 and $100,000 a year in brokerage fees.

Furthermore, I have in mind one estate with some $300,000 worth of securities, and because of this inheritance taxation it was multiplied three times, by virtue of the man's domicile.

PHILIP ZOERCHER (Indiana) : I should like to second the motion of the gentleman from Pennsylvania in adopting this report.

CHAIRMAN LONG: Senator Edmonds moves the adoption of the report, and Mr. Zoercher of Indiana seconds the motion. Is there anything to be said on the acceptance of the report?

I may be permitted to ask Senator Edmonds if there is any suggestion in this report that the committee continue its investigations,

29

or if, so far as he knows, the lemon has been completely squeezed or whether there is still something left.

SENATOR EDMONDS: I understand that Mr. Cole has prepared two resolutions for the committee on resolutions, to be reported to-morrow; one of which will continue the committee and the other of which will carry with it the authority to present to Congress the suggestion with reference to the federal estate tax. I think those resolutions will come up tomorrow morning.

RUSSELL BRADFORD (New York): Referring to the income tax report of last Tuesday, I want to say that I just understand that there is no resolution before the resolutions committee on that subject. So that they may have something before them, I beg to present this resolution; that this association express its great appreciation and thanks to the committee that rendered the report on income taxes, which was presented last Tuesday, and that the committee be kept alive, and that this report be brought to the attention of the committee on ways and means of the House of Representatives and the finance committee of the United States Senate, for its consideration upon the merits of the report itself and not upon any adoption by the association of that report.

CHAIRMAN LONG: In accordance with the rules, that will be accepted and referred to the committee on resolutions.

Is there anything further to be said on this motion that is now before the house? We have one other thing this evening that will take some time, but I do not wish to stop any one from saying anything they wish to say in regard to this most important subject of inheritance taxes. Those of us engaged in tax work do not have to worry about inheritance taxes, but some of the rest of you may have to. This is a good time to say anything you want to say about it. If there is nothing further to be said, all those in favor of the acceptance of this report manifest it by saying aye.

(Ayes and Noes)

CHAIRMAN LONG: There is no opposition. It is unanimous.

The next matter we have on the program, and which was put down for 9: 30, is: The Efficacy of Individual and Associated Work Toward Reform in State and Local Taxation, by Professor Charles J. Bullock of Harvard University.

If Professor Bullock is about, I should like to have him come forward. If he is not, I shall have to appoint a committee to go out and get him.

CHARLES J. BULLOCK: Mr. Chairman, Ladies and Gentlemen: We have had three long sessions today; we have been here over two hours, in this bad air, and it is twenty minutes past ten. I do not believe that at such an hour, and under such conditions, anyone ever heard of anything that was worth while about taxation, and I do not believe even that anybody ever said anything about that subject that was worth learning.

I shall not attempt to try. I shall say just a word about the matter of the incorporation of the National Tax Association.

The fact that this association has lasted twenty years; that interest in its work has grown; that increasing results are every year seen from the deliberations of these conferences, from the investigations of our committees and the contacts established between tax officials and tax payers, the students of taxation and the public generally, are all sufficient evidence of the value of associated work, and have brought us to a time when it is impossible, I take it, for any of us to visualize such a thing as the dissolution of this tax association.

We are so constituted that we never appreciate any good thing until we lose it; and if we just stop a minute and reflect what we should lose in those contacts between taxpayers and tax officials, students of taxation matters, and what we should lose in the way of investigations and such splendid reports as we have had here today, I am sure that if we try to visualize that loss and estimate it, we shall all agree that it is unthinkable that this associated effort towards progress and reform in taxation matters should ever come to an end.

Last year the executive committee of the National Tax Association met and voted to appoint a committee on incorporation, and later I was informed that I was chairman of that committee and that my associates would be two ex-presidents, Professor Page and Professor Thomas S. Adams.

A date was set in May for a meeting in New York, in plenty of time to have some papers to read for presentation here at Toronto, but when the time came, Tommy Adams was on the high seas on the way to Geneva to attend a ten-day conference on taxation as the representative of the United States, and he did not get back until June. In June things came up at home that made it impossible for me to leave Cambridge, and the matter had to go over until July. Something happened then again, so that we have done nothing, except look over the ground and hold some informal conferences.

Fortunately, our work is pretty simple. We have in the first place the original constitution of the National Tax Association. It ought not to be scrapped; it is an admirable document in many respects. It provides for this dual organization of the tax association; a continuing body, which calls meetings, appoints committees, publishes the bulletin, reports of the conferences; and in general performs administrative services, and provides for this conference delegates, which is a deliberative body. The two things are frequently confused in people's minds, but the method of organization is really simple, natural and appropriate. If we had had nothing but these annual conferences — no continuing organization — we might have had one or two, or perhaps three of them, and they would presently have come to an end.

The committee bound to call the next meeting, might not have functioned. It has been the existence of the tax association that has insured a continuance of the conferences and of the various lines of administrative work that have contributed so greatly to the general result.

Now, that wants to be preserved. The original constitution can be simplified in some respects. The document can be shortened; but it is not going to be scrapped. We are going to build on what we have and shall retain everything substantial in the original constitution, with one or two exceptions that I am going to mention.

In the matter of these new provisions that we are thinking of making, we are fortunate in having to fall back upon the very excellent report submitted by Professor Fairchild at the last meeting of this conference, and we have had the advantage of reading the discussion following the submission of that report.

We find that Professor Fairchild in his report, and the participants in the discussion which followed, agreed that the original constitution of the N. T. A. was very wise in making liberal provision for representation in the conference; welcoming not only public officials but associated certified public accountants, professors of economics conducting courses in public finance, and others, and it is agreed that liberal provision for representation in the conference should be made in our new articles.

Professor Fairchild also found, and nearly everybody who subsequently spoke seemed to agree, that in the conferences it was desirable to limit the voting power on many matters of tax policy and other things to the delegates appointed by the governors of states and territories and provinces and the executive of the District of Columbia. That seems to us to be absolutely wise.

Other people, representatives of certified public accountants' associations, taxpayers' associations, college professors if they have standing in their own states, can get themselves appointed as delegates and can participate as a rule, in proportion to their standing in their several communities.

In the next place, we are agreed that the Fairchild report, with respect to the great desirability of continuing the law that has been unwritten to date, as to substantial unanimity on matters on which it resolves, has been well taken. However, the majority of the committee think it might be well to put something into the constitution of the N. T. A. just to serve as a reminder about the principle of proceeding only by substantial unanimity.

One other question remains, as to how the delegates appointed by governors of states and territories and provinces shall vote. The Fairchild report was very clear and very satisfactory to the committee on the point that each state, territory, province and the District of Columbia should have one vote. That was simply to prevent local representation from the community where the meeting is being held, swamping those who may have come from one to three thousand miles.

One thing that came up in the discussions subsequent to the Fairchild report, and which was not covered by that report, is, whether, when the states vote, they should vote by unit rule, or whether, if the delegates appointed by the governor of the state have divided opinion, say two and two, the states should have a one-half vote for and one-half vote against. In our view that is not particularly important, one way or the other. We don't care. We may be wrong in thinking that it is not important. I think that since what we want is an expression of opinion, the provision for fractional voting gives you probably a better expression of opinion; but to my mind it is not important. The thing can be done either way.

That is the way in which the thing heads up at the present moment. Probably incorporation will be sought under the general act of the District of Columbia, since we are a national organization, and there is a perfectly suitable act there, under which we can incorporate, without seeking a special charter, which the American Bar Association found it impossible to get.

I think, Mr. Chairman, our committee would welcome any expressions on these points, particularly on this matter of how the states should vote, 'whether by unit rule or by fractional vote. We want to do this thing in such a manner as will be approved by the members of the association and the representatives at this conference, with a view to making our incorporated association just as effective and useful as possible.

I take this occasion to raise these questions, and the committee will be glad to have any expression of opinion on it.

MILBANK JOHNSON (California) : As I seem to be the only official representative of the taxpayers' associations, I want to say first that I have always secured the appointment of the governor of our state. I have it at this time. I have no quarrel with our own governor, and I hope to be able to secure appointment by our governor as often as I want to come to this conference.

I do, however, want to bring to the attention of this conference, and particularly to the committee on new constitution, the fact that there is growing in the United States a very definite movement of organization among taxpayers, known as the taxpayers' movement. There is, as you know, in the West a federation of taxpayers' associations, covering twelve states. There are isolated taxpayers' associations throughout the United States. There is a southern group forming. There is one forming in the northwest; and at Santa Fe this year we had several suggestions from taxpayers' groups of a federation of those sections or groups into a national organization.

Personally I believe it would be a mistake to have a national tax-payers' association. I believe that the potentialities of this National Tax Association are so great, and the advantages of the contact between taxpayer and the tax collector so important, that we should do all we can to preserve—what shall I say—the single purpose of this one organization; and I have opposed for two years among those taxpayers' organizations the organization of a national tax-payers' association. I have opposed it in the hope that recognition of the taxpayer, that is, equal recognition, would be given to the taxpayer as is now given to the tax official.

You must understand—and I have harped on this often—that it is inevitable that any taxpayers' association that begins to object to a governor's plan or program is going to make that governor just a little bit ticklish about sending any of those taxpayers to a place where his voice may be heard. I can say that in some of the states it has happened, and it has happened here at this particular confer-ence, that certain state taxpayers' associations were unable to secure the recognition of the governors.

I want to give a warning to the National Tax Association—much as I hate to do it—and I hope none of you will consider it a threat, it is purely a warning—that I believe that the taxpayers' movement is of sufficient importance and of sufficient size to be recognized by this association, and I would urge upon this body that if they do not want to see a national taxpayers' movement in the United States, they will have to give equal recognition to the recognized, *bona fide* taxpayers' associations with the officials, or they will certainly see a dual tax association in the United States.

I thank you for this opportunity of saying this, and what I have said it due to my great desire that we preserve such a unanimity of feeling between the taxpayer and the tax collector in this organiza-tion that such a move will be unnecessary.

CHARLES J. BULLOCK: The committee, of course, in its informal conferences has given very careful consideration to that problem. It was covered by Professor Fairchild's paper and taken up in the subsequent discussion.

Of course, it is true that sometimes taxpayers' associations will not secure representation by appointment of their governor, and it may very well be that they will fail to secure such recognition when they deserve it. On the other hand, the great difficulty of bringing into our provisions for voting power the taxpayers' associations seems to the committee to be decisive.

In the first place, the mortality among them has been pretty great. I hope that the best of these taxpayers' associations are going to live and attack the big problem of public expenditures, which is at the root of most of our taxation troubles of the present day. I am getting to be a crank on that matter of public expenditures, and I welcome the growth of these associations; but there is very great difficulty in discriminating between them, if we should have to discriminate.

I have known a good deal about them, first and last. Some have been very excellent organizations, and others have been fly-by-night concerns, with no bottom and no prospective permanency. They can have representation in personnel; they can participate in committee work, and their representatives have done so. They can probably, for the most part, most of the time, secure recognition as voting delegates by appointment of their governors. Therefore, though we realize that instances may arise where recognition cannot be secured, we feel that, on the whole, the difficulties of giving these associations voting power are greater than the advantages.

As to the rise of another such organization, I do not know how the committee feels, but personally I do not dread it at all. I should welcome a first-rate national taxpayers' association, if the thing can be done on a national scale and kept straight.

To get right down to brass tacks, some of them are straight and some are not. Mr. Johnson represents one of the very excellent associations. I know that as long as he stays on the job, with his present colleagues, they will be all right; but it is not easy to keep these associations straight. I know, because I got one up and helped run it for some years, and finally we dissolved it because it was getting to be a public menace. It took three years to dissolve it, because the secretary was getting a salary out of it and the president was interested in it. He did not realize the difficulties that lay ahead of it. It is a very difficult proposition.

There is every possibility for cooperation with them within the association as it now stands, without going to this length of giving them voting power. Therefore, our committee is decided in regard to its views in the case. However, that is a matter for the association to decide and not for the committee. We heard the discussion last year and concluded that on the whole there was no strong sentiment in favor of giving official recognition to these associations; and we thought that probably our decision would be in line with the general sentiment of the conference.

If such a national taxpayers' association arises, and if it prospers and does good work and keeps straight, and doubtless it will, it is not going to hurt the N. T. A. We are twenty years old. We have had considerable experience with such suggestions, as that other organizations would arise and supplant us. If they can supplant us, the answer is, they ought to, because it will be that they are better. We do not want to preserve the N. T. A. if there is some better way of doing the job. But, three, four or five times, according to my certain recollection, we have seen this prospect before us, and we have decided to keep on the even tenor of our way, welcoming everybody to our open forums, giving representation to everybody in our committee work, and giving recognition also, as far as certified public accountants' or economists' or taxpayers' associations or officials are concerned, to those who can secure appointment by the governor. Personally I am not alarmed on other accounts, at the prospect of the growth of the national taxpayers' association. I can see that it might be a mighty good thing, and would be disposed, within the limits of my time, to go for it. If it comes, it probably will not do this association any harm.

On the other hand, if it does us any harm it will be because it turns out to be a better organization than we are. In that case we haven't any priority of organization, that should lead us to change our ways.

CHARLES W. GERSTENBERG: I have a short observation to make that may seem to some facetious. I am wondering if the committee was intending to incorporate immediately. It is possible that it is not the best thing to do. I take it that the organization will consist of a very short charter, and then that all these questions will come up in the by-laws.

We have been talking about the avoidance of inheritance taxes. One of the best ways to avoid the inheritance tax is to make a gift to a charitable institution. It may seem that nobody would be interested in leaving some money to the National Tax Association, but the Clark estate left $60,000 to an institution that was not nearly as important as this one. As a matter of fact it was a glee club, and they are trying still to get that $60,000. If some person thought it were a wise thing and should leave $10,000 or $15,000 to us, as a legal proposition we could not take it.

I should like to see this committee incorporate immediately and leave all these questions for the by-laws, which would go on for an indefinite time.

J. F. ZOLLER (New York): Mr. Chairman, I did not expect to say anything at this time, and I don't know that this is a matter that should be discussed by me. However, I think here is a vital thing, which is coming up before this association.

I speak as a representative of a taxpayer or taxpayers; and I want to say, as the representative of taxpayers that I hope the time will never come when the taxpayers themselves have any deciding vote or voice in this organization, because I think that would be a very bad thing for the taxpayers themselves.

There are plenty of organizations representing the taxpayer. Nearly every state in the Union has an association of manufacturers, or of merchants, or of public utilities, and all that sort of thing, and we have national organizations of taxpayers. They may not be called taxpayers' associations, but nevertheless their purpose is to represent the selfish interests of the taxpayer, and they admit it, and everybody knows it, and they do not have the voice and force that an impartial organization like this has.

I have attended these meetings since 1914, and there never has been a time that I know of that the taxpayers have not had every right to express their opinions before these conferences, but I have always felt that this association should not be an association that was representing the wishes of the taxpaying public; that it was a place where taxpayers themselves could go to get an impartial opinion; that when that opinion came from this organization it was looked upon by Congress and by state legislatures and by everybody as a truly impartial opinion, in respect of the principles of taxation.

It seems to me that just as soon as you give the taxpaying public a voice in the running of this organization you are going to convert it into a different organization from what it is at the present time. I think that would be a very unfortunate thing, and I am speaking from the standpoint of a taxpayer and not from the standpoint of the professors of colleges or from the tax commissioners of the different states.

I think the important thing is to keep what I might call a highbrow institution; one which is impartial; one which does not represent anybody who really pays the money, because I do not believe it possible to bring in a taxpaying public and give them a voice in the running of an institution of this kind, without those taxpayers trying to use it for their own selfish purposes. That is the natural thing.

We have plenty of our own organizations to protect our interests and all that sort of thing, and I believe that this is the only institution of its kind that can be pointed to, as expressing impartial opinions in respect to taxation.

We need, and the taxpayers themselves need, an institution of this kind; one which will announce impartial, fair, honest, equitable and sound principles of taxation.

All that the taxpayers need in this country, I take it, is a square deal, and I believe that through an institution of this kind, as it now exists, they can get a square deal. I believe that there has been great improvement in taxation measures throughout the country, as the result of the work that this association has done for a number of years in an impartial way, and I think that it would be the worst thing that could happen to the taxpaying public to convert in any way this institution into one where the taxpaying public—the fellow who pays the taxes and cannot be impartial—would have a controlling voice. Therefore, I think it would be unwise to bring in these taxpayers' associations and give them, as such, a voice in the running of an institution of this kind. I will go further than that: I think it would be unwise to put taxpayers on the governing board of this institution, because if it goes out that this is operated by people who are interested in making certain taxes impossible, then it is not going to have the standing in the future that it has had in the past. We need in this country an institution that has that standing, and we cannot get it, if it is composed of the fellows who really have to pay the bill. I thank you.

C. P. Link (Colorado) : It has been the policy of the governors of our State of Colorado, during the twenty years' existence of this organization to appoint a very representative list of delegates, starting in with all of the commercial organizations, the manufacturers and merchants, and just a few assessors, because the counties were not able to pay their expenses. I know of not a single case in my state—and I think our state is just like other states—where any individual, or company, or organization of taxpayers has made a request to be appointed delegates, but what the governor has granted that request. I don't think there is an exception. There might be. As Dr. Bullock has well said, this is a very difficult problem, of course. Dr. Johnson has, as we all recognize, the best taxpayers' organization that we have known of in the United States, and it is doing very excellent work in California. Well and good for that; but all of us know, in all of our states, that there are many of these local organizations which Dr. Bullock called fly-by-night organizations. They are not so well founded; they are frequently very radical and even dangerous, and they have been very selfish in their inclinations.

The voting proposition is the main thing, and I know that the California organization is thinking chiefly of the expenses. That is their preliminary work. I have talked with Dr. Johnson for some years, and other members of his organization. When their duties along that line are accomplished, I know that they are going to join along lines to distribute the burden. Isn't that true, Doctor? That would be just fine if we knew that all organizations would be of that nature, but, unfortunately, that cannot be true.

The only objection that I can see to your present plan, which is excellent and well-safeguarded, is that some governor of a state with a splendid organization, such as exists in California, might be disgruntled and might decline to recognize it.

I am asking the chairman, and Dr. Bullock especially, and the past presidents, if this might not be perfectly proper. Suppose a contingency should arise; suppose the California organization should come here next year without credentials; without recognition on the part of the governor; might it not be possible, Mr. Chairman, in such an emergency, to suspend our rules and give that organization recognition? Might not that be permissible?

I thought that possibly, by unanimous consent, we might do that. That seems the only contingency. There are certainly many poor risks on these organizations. This organization has gone on record to tackle the great problem of expenditures; it is enormous; it will take a lot of work and an enormous amount of money, but we are on record for it, if it becomes possible; and if these organizations must be separate, we shall welcome their support. I certainly concur in the splendid suggestion made by Dr. Bullock.

CHAIRMAN LONG: Anything further to be said on this question? I am not quite certain in my own mind whether there is anything really before the conference either to accept or reject.

MR. LINK: If it is permissible—Dr. Bullock asked for suggestions on the vote—just as an informal matter, I move you that the sense of this conference is that we vote by the fractional plan, to give minority as well as majority representation.

CHAIRMAN LONG: Don't you think, Mr. Link, that it ought to be defined? For example, suppose the State of New York has perhaps 100 delegates here, do you mean that they should have one vote for the State of New York, and then if 50 vote one way and 49 the other way, and they have a split vote, the majority should control, or do you want to define how this is going to be split?

MR. LINK: As I understand Dr. Bullock's suggestion, each state will have one vote, but that vote will be divided into fractions. Is that right?

CHARLES J. BULLOCK: That is the only thing that seemed to us, after going through the record in the case, especially the Fairchild report, to be not fairly well covered by previous expressions of sentiment, previous discussions, and which was left open last year. I should like to have an expression one way or the other on that point.

RAY RILEY (California): Is it moved and seconded?

CHAIRMAN LONG: It has not been seconded yet.

RAY RILEY: If it has not been seconded, then I move to amend.

C. L. TURNER (Pennsylvania): I second the motion of Mr. Link of Colorado.

RAY RILEY: I move an amendment to vote on unit rule, majority to control.

CHAIRMAN LONG: Anything to be said on the amendment offered by Mr. Riley of California?

MARK GRAVES (New York): Mr. President, I am wondering if it is necessary to write into the rigid constitution of the organization a rule on the voting? I am wondering if it could not be left with the delegations to decide whether to vote on the fractional plan or on the unit rule. When we have a conference in the east, in the State of New York, it may happen to have a very considerable delegation. On a fractional plan the fractions would be very small. I think it would be more acceptable, under most circumstances, for the New York delegation to meet and decide for itself, at that particular conference, whether it would vote fractional or on the unit rule. I am just wondering if it is essential we write into the fundamental law the provision on that particular point.

C. L. TURNER (Pennsylvania): I think it is not absolutely essential but that it is desirable to have something, because the question will continually come up, as it did last year. You make still a third suggestion; that each state shall have one vote and that the delegates from each state shall decide whether to follow the unit rule or do it the other way. That is the third proposition for consideration. We may have no preference, but we know perfectly well that if we do not get some expression the thing will come up every year.

CHAIRMAN LONG: Professor Fairchild; are you seeking to speak?

FRED R. FAIRCHILD: No, I was not, Mr. Chairman.

CHAIRMAN LONG: Is there anything to be said on this question?

CHARLES W. GERSTENBERG: If this motion is lost then there is an alternative suggested, is that the idea?

CHAIRMAN LONG: I take it that we do not need to be particular what the motion is. I think the committee merely wishes to get the sense of this session as to what is the best way to handle this voting proposition. I do not believe that Dr. Bullock intended to start a row here tonight, as to how we should vote. It may have had the counterpart down in New Orleans, but I do think what the Doctor wants to know is really what is the sense of this meeting as a whole, on this question of voting. I think it ought to be made perfectly clear to the committee. Governor Bliss of Rhode Island.

ZENAS W. BLISS: Mr. Chairman, it seems to me that if you want the unit rule, all that is necessary to do is not to do anything, because the majority will naturally control, if there is no special limitation. The majority naturally would carry the state. The delegation would take care of the matter themselves. But it seems very important to me that the minority in each state should be represented, particularly in an organization of this kind. It might very well be that we might have, as is usually the case, three delegates, with two one way and one the other, and it would be very well for the organization to have the minority delegate from that state voice his opinion and vote, and we should know very much better when the vote was counted what the actual situation was. I think it would be very advisable to have fractional voting.

CHAIRMAN LONG: I take it, Governor Bliss, that what you have back in your mind, in addition to what you said, is that we should not place ourselves in a position where a minority would have no voice. A division would absolutely lose some voice in the proceedings.

ZENAS W. BLISS: That is what you will have if you have the unit rule, and you will have the unit rule, unless you specifically provide for the fractional vote.

CHARLES J. BULLOCK: We have three proposals. Our committee hasn't any opinion, but would like an expression on one of them, either the unit rule or the fractional vote or Mr. Graves' suggestion of referring it to each delegation, for home rule.

C. L. TURNER: I understand there are two motions.

CHAIRMAN LONG: No. One is an amendment.

C. L. TURNER: One was made for the fractional vote and seconded, and one for the unit rule and seconded.

DELEGATE: That is an amendment.

CHARLES J. BULLOCK: You might have the question on the amendment. As I understand, Mr. Riley, your amendment is to vote on the unit rule?

RAY RILEY (California): My purpose in making this amendment was to get the question fairly before the delegates; to have the delegates vote on one part of it or the other.

CHAIRMAN LONG: I am not entirely clear on this question myself, but that is a reasonably fair expression of it. Under the unit rule the State of California and the Commonwealth of Massachusetts would have one vote, but if the delegations should split 50-50 they would have no vote.

RAY RILEY: That is true.

CHAIRMAN LONG: Does that make it clear to all of you in voting on this amendment on the unit rule, that that situation might very well develop?

RAY RILEY: Or a vote which in substance is the same thing. I want to correct myself.

CHAIRMAN LONG: Would that be unit rule?

RAY RILEY: Yes.

GEORGE VAUGHAN: I want some one to explain to me, then, what would be the difference between the unit rule as so interpreted and the fractional rule, so far as each state is concerned?

PHILIP ZOERCHER (Indiana): Mr. Chairman; the unit rule would mean that if the majority of the delegation voted one way, one vote would be counted for it. That is what is meant by the unit rule; at least that is what we Democrats call it in our Democratic convention, but it is really left to the states, as to whether the unit rule should apply.

Suppose seven vote one way and three the other. As Governor Bliss has said, it would indicate that there were at least three on that delegation that stood out for one thing, and seven the other. I think it ought to be the fractional rule; each state would still be entitled to one vote if it would be fractional. It would be seven-tenths for and three-tenths against, but it would show that there were three individual fellows that had the courage to stand out. That is the way it should be.

CHAIRMAN LONG: I suspect that it might be the other way, that the seven have the courage to stand out.

Before we really put the question, I think every one ought to understand what might develop under this situation, and we ought to have it clear in our minds just what is going to happen. If you have it all perfectly clear in your minds, there is no reason why I should not put the motion.

DELEGATE: I don't know what we are voting on.

C. L. TURNER: Let the Secretary read the motion as it now stands.

CHAIRMAN LONG: I am going to save the Secretary that trouble, Mr. Turner, because I do not think that is going to clarify it. Early in the evening I suggested where Pennsylvania gets some of its intelligence, and inasmuch as the senator, or former senator, from that territory inherited some of it from Benjamin Franklin, I am going to ask Senator Edmonds of Pennsylvania if he will state what he thinks this situation is.

FRANKLIN S. EDMONDS: As I understand it, Mr. Chairman, Mr. Link is in favor of the fractional vote, as Mr. Zoercher stated it; that the vote of each delegate will be a fraction, but it will be divided between the two sides, seven-tenths one way and three-tenths the other way. Mr. Riley has moved to amend by inserting the unit vote. That means that if there was a majority of the delegation for the proposition, it would go all one way; if the vote was equally divided, it would be one-half one way and one-half the other, but there could be no other fraction.

As I take it, the vote is first on Mr. Riley's amendment. Those who vote aye on Mr. Riley's amendment vote in favor of unit rule as he explained it; namely, one vote for each state, except in the case of equal division; and then those who are opposed to that, who are in favor of Mr. Link's plan, will vote no on that.

CHAIRMAN LONG: Without injecting any politics into it, both the Democrats and the Republicans understand this.

(Call for the question)

GEORGE VAUGHAN: In view of the explanation, I think it is really best for this organization to have the fractional rule, because the questions to be voted upon for the most part will be economic questions that affect matters of taxation throughout the whole country, regardless of state lines. I think it would rather have that complexion. That being true, it will be interesting to know how at least a majority have voted and how they stood on these questions, and not on the basis of state lines. It is not like electing presidents of the United States, so I think there is a little more in favor of the fractional vote than there would be in favor of the unit rule. If there were forty-five states represented, we should have forty-five votes, and twenty-three would carry the result, and we should know nothing more about it; whereas, if the entire 450 delegates should vote, you would know then about how strong the sentiment was. I think the fractional vote would be the thing.

(Calls for the question)

CHAIRMAN LONG: All those in favor of the amendment offered by Mr. Riley of California signify by saying aye.

(No response)

CHAIRMAN LONG: All those opposed, signify by saying no.

(Noes)

CHAIRMAN LONG: It seems to have been lost.
Now, all of those in favor of— Dr. Page.

THOMAS W. PAGE: I rise to a point of order.

CHAIRMAN LONG: Not unless it is a good one.

THOMAS W. PAGE: During the discussion in regard to the incorporation of the tax association, Professor Bullock said that the committee, which has been appointed to draw up the document, would be glad to have some general suggestions from the members of this conference in regard to various things. I think he did not contemplate that there would be formal votes taken in regard to what was going to be done, in respect to a document that was not yet drafted. It seems to me that we are a little bit hasty. I happen to be a member of that committee, and I didn't know it until Professor Bullock told me so yesterday. I think that we are talking here about a thing without any special purpose to it. I think you would save time and do better work if you waited until we could get the draft that this committee is going to prepare. I don't see much use in taking votes on what this committee is going to do. We are in conférence now, and in the National Tax Association, and I am a member of that committee; but I do not believe I should be bound by any vote of this kind.

CHARLES J. BULLOCK: If we have a vote I feel in my bones that we shall save a lot of time.

FRANKLIN S. EDMONDS: That is the best argument for fractional vote you can get. Dr. Bullock wants it and Dr. Page does not want it. There would be fractions on each side.

CHAIRMAN LONG: Dr. Page warns us whichever way we vote he won't pay a damned bit of attention to it.
All in favor of Mr. Link's motion signify by saying aye.

(Ayes)

CHAIRMAN LONG: All opposed signify by saying no.

(No response)

(Motion carried)

CHAIRMAN LONG: That is the sense of the meeting.

(Adjournment)

TENTH SESSION

FRIDAY FORENOON, OCTOBER 14, 1927

CHAIRMAN MATTHEWS: If the conference will come to order we will have the next business.

HARRY P. SNEED (Louisiana): Mr. Chairman; on behalf of the resolutions committee I offer and move the adoption of the following resolutions:

> BE IT RESOLVED, that from the viewpoints both of public revenue and perpetuating forest resources and industries, we urge research and legislation to effect more just forest taxation, to encourage the preservation and production of forests, commercially and on farm wood-lots.

CHAIRMAN MATTHEWS: You have heard the resolution as proposed by the committee. What is your pleasure?

W. H. BLODGETT (Connecticut): Move its adoption.

(Motion duly seconded)

(Ayes and Noes)

(Motion carried)

CHAIRMAN MATTHEWS: It is a vote.

HARRY P. SNEED: The committee offers and moves the adoption of the following resolution:

> WHEREAS, it appears from the report of the committee appointed under the resolution of the 1925 conference to study uniformity in state taxation of business organizations, that a suggested model system for the taxation of such organizations should be prepared sufficiently in advance of the time of its consideration to enable intelligent discussion thereof; therefore be it
>
> RESOLVED, That the National Tax Association be requested to continue the committee, subject to such changes in personnel as may appear to the National Tax Association desirable and that its recommendations be distributed at least ninety days before the conference of 1928.

I may say in explanation, that this is a resolution copied from last year's meeting, the change of date being the only change made.

30 (465)

CHAIRMAN MATTHEWS: This resolution having been read, Mr. Sneed moves its adoption.

(Motion duly seconded)

CHAIRMAN MATTHEWS: The motion is seconded. Is there any discussion?

(Ayes and Noes)

(Motion carried)

HARRY P. SNEED: The committee presents and moves the adoption of the following resolution:

> RESOLVED, That the National Tax Association be requested to appoint a committee to make further study into the problem of taxation of all classes of motor vehicles, with special attention to the taxation of those vehicles engaged in commercial transportation.

CHAIRMAN MATTHEWS: You have heard this resolution read. Is the motion that it be adopted seconded?

(Motion duly seconded)

(Ayes and Noes)

(Motion carried)

HARRY P. SNEED: The committee presents and moves the adoption of the following resolution:

> RESOLVED, That the thanks of this conference be extended to the chairman and members of the committee on the simplification of the income tax and that the committee be continued, with authority to present its findings and suggestions to the appropriate congressional committees.

(Ayes and Noes)

(Motion carried)

HARRY P. SNEED: Mr. Chairman, the committee is going to depart slightly from its regular routine and defer the vote of thanks until a few moments later, believing that the vote of thanks is of sufficient dignity and importance to be made a special order of business. With the consent of the Chair, that part of the committee's report will be deferred for a short time.

On behalf of the resolutions committee I present and move the adoption of the following resolution:

> WHEREAS, The report of the committee on reciprocity in inheritance taxation not only shows remarkable progress toward the goal of complete reciprocity among the states, but also

shows the necessity for the continuance of its efforts, therefore
RESOLVED, That the National Tax Association be requested
to continue said committee, for the purpose for which it was
created, and that it be authorized, in accordance with the
recommendations contained in its report, to further the principles of reciprocity in inheritance taxation between the states
and nations.

GEORGE VAUGHAN (Arkansas): Motion seconded.

CHAIRMAN MATTHEWS: Is there any discussion?

(No response)

(Ayes and Noes)

(Motion carried)

SECRETARY HOLCOMB: Mr. White is anxious to have it brought
to your attention, that tickets for the banquet tonight may be obtained by those who have not received any, at the Oak Room on the
ground floor, at 7 o'clock P. M. They desire very much that there
will be a large attendance, and it would be a nice thing to show our
appreciation of this courtesy.

I have a request to make. I have here a letter from the assessment commissioner of Toronto, Mr. Forman, explaining Toronto's
assessing system. He says that in answer to many requests of delegates regarding the present system, this summary was prepared.
My suggestion is that I be authorized to include that in the record
of the conference.

R. A. VANDEGRIFT (California): I move it be placed in the record
and properly recorded in the proceedings.

ZENAS W. BLISS: Motion seconded.

CHAIRMAN MATTHEWS: Those in favor of the passage of this
motion manifest it in the usual manner.

(Ayes and Noes)

(Motion carried)

TORONTO'S ASSESSING SYSTEM

J. C. FORMAN
Assessment Commissioner of Toronto

Answering the many requests of delegates to the National Tax
Conference regarding the present system of taxation in Toronto,
this summary was prepared.

Our taxable assessment amounts to $926,000,000 and our exemp-
tions to $127,000,000, or a total assessment of $1,053,000,000, all of
which is shown in the assessment rolls as required by statute.

Our Assessment Act provides that land is to be assessed at its actual value and buildings at the amount which they add to the value of the land. Our land assessment is $359,000,000, buildings $409,000,000, a total realty assessment of $768,000,000 or 83% of the $926,000,000 taxable total.

Our business assessment of $96,000,000 and income assessment of $61,000,000 take the place of the personal property assessment, which was abandoned in Ontario in 1905 as the result of a Government committee appointed in 1901.

It was generally conceded that the carrying-out of the personal property assessment was impracticable, because it was levied, subject to certain exemptions, on all goods, chattels, interest on mortgages, dividends from bank stocks, dividends on stocks of other incorporated companies, money, notes, accounts and debts, income, and all other property except land and real estate.

In the assessment of personal property, the honest man suffered; the widow suffered, because of the information obtained from the Surrogate Court and, furthermore, it was necessary for the assessor to delve into the private affairs of the merchant, manufacturer and others.

There is no doubt in my mind but that, were the right to assess personal property still in vogue, instead of an assessment of $157,000,000, business and income combined, we should have at least three times that amount, and while it is not claimed that the business assessment is perfect, it appears to work out reasonably.

The Statute Revision Commission, composed chiefly of our Judges, which was appointed in 1925 by the Ontario Government to revise the Assessment Act and other Acts, made no suggested changes in the business assessment.

The business assessment is based on the assessed value of premises occupied for business purposes, whether it be a small portion of a building or a building used entirely by one company or individual, different ratings being applicable to the various classes of business.

One of the main arguments in its favor is that it is easy of application. The assessor has before him in his field book the assessment of land and building and has but to use his common sense in applying the proper percentage.

For example, a retailer is assessable personally, in respect of business assessment for 25% of the assessed value of the lands and building used for business purposes. A manufacturer's rating is 60%, department stores 50%, wholesalers 75%, banks, loan and trust companies and other financial companies 75%, and so forth. Lastly is the distiller, who has the highest of all ratings, namely 150% of the assessed value of the real property he occupies.

Income is assessable against the beneficiary, in the municipality in which he resides, subject to the exemptions following:

On income from investments, an exemption of $1,000 is allowed, where the total income does not exceed $2,000, but in the case of a· widow or of any person over sixty years of age, the sum of $2,000 is exempt, where the total does not exceed $3,000. If this class of income exceeds the totals mentioned, the whole amount is taxable.

On personal earnings, a householder receives an exemption of $3,000, no matter what the total income, with an additional $400 for each dependent child or parent, while the non-householder receives $1,500 exemption.

The farmer is exempt on the income from his farm but is liable to assessment on the above-mentioned income. However, as there are no farms within the limits of our city, this exemption does not affect us, but the other exemptions, particularly those applicable to personal earnings, materially affect our assessments. These generous exemptions were increased to the present figures at the last session of the Ontario legislature and resulted in a loss to this municipality of over $17,000,000 in income assessment or, in taxes, over $510,000.

As an example of the generous treatment given, a married man with three dependent children who receives $4,200 per annum is totally exempt from income assessment. One would think he would be able and perhaps willing to pay some reasonable taxes on his income, for the many privileges enjoyed by him and his family in our parks, bowling greens, tennis courts, free libraries, etc., all without cost to him, apart from the general taxes on his real property.

In the case of an individual or partnership engaged in business, the amount of the business assessment is allowed as an exemption in addition to the other exemptions mentioned, so that there is in no sense double taxation.

Incorporated companies are exempt on their capital, except that invested in real estate. Their dividends, however, are assessable (subject to the exemptions above) in the hands of the beneficial shareholders. Some have claimed that this is double taxation, but as all taxes, allowance for depreciation, reserve fund, etc., are deducted from the profits of a business before a dividend is declared, it will readily be seen that there is no double taxation.

The exemptions on real property are often mentioned as an assessment problem, but while our exemptions total $127,000,000, or over 12% of our total assessment, the result when analyzed is not quite so serious.

Properties owned by the City of Toronto account for $30,000,000, to which must be added $18,000,000 for public schools, $2,000,000 for Roman Catholic separate schools, another million for free libraries, as well as five and a half million for the buildings of our municipally-owned transportation and hydro-electric systems (the land being taxable) and over six and a half millions for the land reclaimed by our Harbor Commission, a total municipal exemption of over $63,000,000, or one-half of the grand total.

The Dominion Government, Ontario Government and Provincial University, and the County of York are responsible for about $27,000,000 more, leaving $37,000,000, or approximately 3½% of the total assessment for what might be termed private exemptions. This amount is divided, approximately, as follows:

Churches	$19,000,000
Hospitals	9,000,000
Cemeteries	3,000,000
Private schools	2,000,000
Charitable institutions, etc.	4,000,000

Of the whole, the only class that might be termed a private business and, as such, not entitled to exemption from taxation is the private schools, which are conducted on commercial business principles and which should be taxed in the same manner as other real property.

This information, in brief, regarding the working of the Assessment Act as at present constituted, is presented for your consideration. Generally speaking, it is a most reasonable act and I am confirmed in my belief by the assistance given to this department by so many of our taxpayers.

For current expenses, in addition to its ordinary revenue, Toronto finds it necessary to raise $27,000,000 annually by direct taxation. Our other revenue is derived from rentals of city-owned land, from licenses, etc.

The main expenditures are for education, which, with free libraries, takes well over one-third of the total; for public health which, including our park system, hospitals, street cleaning, mothers' allowances, etc., requires five and a quarter millions; fire and police protection which cost four and three-quarter millions; and our good roads, both within and outside our limits, which cost a million and three-quarters annually.

These services are of the best and, while we are not content with our present tax rate of 31.8 mills on the dollar or $31.80 per $1,000 of assessment, there is a strong feeling with the taxpayers that they are receiving value for the taxes paid.

CHAIRMAN MATTHEWS: The next item in order here is the consideration of the time and place for the next conference.

SECRETARY HOLCOMB: Mr. Chairman, I want simply to say that I have received a large number of invitations from one city or another throughout the country. I have in my hand, for instance, a letter from the Mayor of the City of Detroit, but there are some, I should say, twenty or thirty places as well — Memphis, Columbus,

Seattle, San Francisco, Los Angeles and Milwaukee. I won't undertake to run them all over, but I simply wanted to have you know that there is a large number. Montreal is included in that list.

THOMAS W. PAGE: Mr. President, I believe it is customary for the conference to leave the determination of the time and place of the meeting of the association to the executive committee.

CHAIRMAN MATTHEWS: That is true.

THOMAS W. PAGE: I have no desire to have that practice upset. I should like, however, to say just one or two things about the next place of meeting. It has been a number of years since we have met in the far west. We have met in Virginia, New Orleans, St. Louis, Philadelphia, and now in Toronto, and there are, I admit, some very excellent reasons why the conference should go to the far west, even as far as the Pacific Coast, next year. Nevertheless, there are some very excellent reasons why the National Tax Association should meet next year in the City of Washington. I have in my hand here invitations addressed to the president and executive committee of the National Tax Association, from the commissioners of the District of Columbia, from the chamber of commerce of the District of Columbia, from the merchants and manufacturers association, bankers association, and from other business organizations, which will indicate that there is a universal desire in Washington to have the National Tax Association meet there. It happens that this association has never met in the national capital. There are some very excellent reasons why it should meet next year at that place. One, of course, is that the whole matter of federal taxation is now in an unsettled condition, and the subject is one that for several years has taken up a great deal of time in our discussions. It is of most vital interest to all of us, and the proper place to make a study of that subject, and to make your opinions carry weight in shaping federal tax legislation is, of course, Washington. Moreover, the tax situation in the District of Columbia is unique in the United States. It is the only part of the United States where the residents have no voice whatsoever in the appropriations that are made, or in the taxes that are imposed to meet those appropriations. Tax legislation is effected by Congress. The situation at present is partly colored by chaos. It is inevitable that there must be a revision of the tax system of the District of Columbia, and it is the one place in the Union where there are no obstacles presented by constitutional limitations and other things standing in the way of putting into practical operation what we have agreed to call amongst ourselves a model tax system.

Your presence in Washington, your advice and your aid would go a long way toward bringing to definite and actual fulfilment the application of the model tax system to one of our states, for to all intents and purposes, except in the matter of voting, the District of Columbia functions as a state.

I am not going to debate this question at the present time. I merely want to bring it to your attention, and if the president does call for any expression of preference on the part of this association as to where the next meeting shall be, I trust that you will bear that in mind. Personally I do not want to oppose the sentiment of the conference if they feel there is a duty to go to the far west, but I should like, before that decision is made, to have you consider the matter very carefully and to give full weight to these various considerations, which would indicate that for effective accomplishment and achievement of this association at its next meeting, Washington would be the very best place you could possibly meet.

GEORGE VAUGHAN (Arkansas): Just one word. I don't know that it is in order for any of us to make any extended speech in behalf of our respective cities, but I want to seriously extend an invitation to this body to meet if possible in the City of Hot Springs, Arkansas. While it is a small city, it has ample hotel accommodations, and without more ado, knowing that this will be left to the executive committee, I want to call attention to one advantage that you would have over the city that has just been recommended by Dr. Page.

My idea is that the prevailing problem right now with this association—one of the main problems—is that of the conflict between federal and state taxes, particularly the estate tax, and I am wondering, if we should be in Washington, if so many of the members of Congress would not militate against the fulfilment of the long-cherished sentiment for substantial unanimity which our body is trying to achieve, and without question, substantial unanimity will not be interfered with in Arkansas for we have politically almost 100 per cent unanimity in the Democratic rule.

J. F. ZOLLER (New York): I should like to ask Mr. Holcomb if he received any communication from Memphis, Tennessee. The chamber of commerce at Memphis, Tennessee, the public utility organization there, and the merchants and manufacturers organization there, thinking I might be in position to present the matter, asked me to mention the fact that Memphis, Tennessee, would like to have this convention in Memphis next year.

RAY RILEY (California): California has no desire to embarrass the executive committee. In conformity with the custom of the past two years I again invite you to California, to Los Angeles or San Francisco, at your option, whenever and wherever you please. If next year isn't the time, it is all right.

J. VAUGHAN GARY: Mr. Chairman; having respect for Dr. Page's opinions, as I have, I want to suggest to the conference that they follow his suggestion, but like some other famous characters in history, follow it from afar off, and come 116 miles from Washington to Richmond, Virginia, where the latch-string is always on the door. I have been authorized by the chamber of commerce, from year to year, to extend this invitation, and while I don't want to embarrass the executive committee, I want you to know that the invitation is always open.

JOHN H. LEENHOUTS (Wisconsin)): Mr. Chairman; on behalf of the City of Milwaukee and the officials of the association of commerce, I am pleased to ask this conference to decide to hold their next meeting, in 1928, in our city. This city is no longer famous for its beverages, but it really is famous for its many manufacturing industries, whose products are distributed throughout the entire world. I am sure it is so centrally located that every one can come to Milwaukee from either the east, west, north or south; and since we are going to discuss some of those very important matters that were mentioned on the floor, which might affect all of our states, I believe a central location next year would be most happy for our purposes.

CHAIRMAN MATTHEWS: Any others who wish to offer any assistance to the executive committee?

G. B. BJORNSON (Minnesota): I am authorized by the Mayor of St. Paul and the chamber of cemmerce of St. Paul to invite the association to come to our beautiful city next year. We have there the Twin Cities, as you know. We have in Minnesota a standing invitation, not only on behalf of the City of St. Paul but the whole state of Minnesota, the state of 10,000 lakes, the state of the iron mines and the state of the best roads in the Union. We should like to have you come to Minnesota.

CHESTER M. PULFORD: I would like to extend an invitation to the association to come to Detroit.

WALTER W. BURNHAM (Rhode Island): Mr. President and Gentlemen: I appreciate the desirability of these places mentioned, but it occurs to me that the proposition to go to Washington is opportune. Here is the District of Columbia which is in need of a modern system of taxation. It is the head and center of all the tax operations. Why wouldn't the strength and aid that this association could give in Washington be reflected upon the operations of the District of Columbia. It looks to me as though it is a ready-made situation and the opportune time.

CHAIRMAN MATTHEWS: Mr. Sneed has another resolution which he wishes to present.

HARRY P. SNEED (Louisiana): I ask the adoption, by rising vote, of the following resolution:

RESOLVED, That the sincere and grateful thanks of the twentieth national conference on taxation be extended to the Prime Minister of Ontario and the members of the Cabinet; the Honorable J. D. Monteith, Treasurer of the Province of Ontario, and Mr. F. Martin Turnbull and Misses Georgiana Mac- Nachtan and Margaret Magill of his staff; Hon. J. T. White, K. C., Comptroller of Revenue for the Ontario Government; Capt. W. A. Orr, Assistant Comptroller of Revenue and his assistants; The Citizens Research Institute of Canada; Mr. E. R. Wood, President, Dominion Securities Company; the Honorable Thomas Foster, Mayor of Toronto; Hon. T. G. McConkey, General Manager, Canada Life Insurance Co., and the management of the King Edward Hotel; Mr. Walter G. Query, Chairman of the South Carolina Tax Commission and his assistants, Miss Julia Ethel Hodge, secretary to the chairman, and F. Dawson Beattie, Assistant Inheritance Tax Examiner; Mr. Chas. J. Tobin, President, New York State Tax Association; The Robert Simpson Company, Ltd., Mrs. J. D. Monteith, Mrs. T. G. McConkey, Mrs. Mary Monteith and their associates on the women's local committee; the officers and members of the executive committee of the National Tax Association; the presiding officers at the various sessions; the speakers upon the program; the chairmen and members of its several committees reporting to the conference; the Press of Toronto, and all others whose cordial and untiring assistance, cooperation and participation in the proceedings and in the entertainment of the members and guests, have contributed so signally to the success of the conference and to the pleasure and comfort of all concerned.

The ladies in attendance upon the twentieth annual tax conference heartily concur in and endorse the above resolution, and in addition desire to express appreciation of the exceptional arrangements provided for their special pleasure, comfort and convenience.

I move the adoption of that resolution by a rising vote.

(Rising vote, adopting the resolution)

CHAIRMAN MATTHEWS: It appears to be unanimous.

Is there any further business to be brought before the conference?

I will say that following the adjournment of the conference a meeting of the National Tax Association will be called. The members of the association are requested to remain and all others.

If there is no further business a motion to adjourn the conference is in order.

MR. RIGBY: I move that the conference adjourn.

(Motion duly seconded)

(Ayes and Noes)

(Motion carried)

(Adjournment of National Tax Conference)

BUSINESS MEETING OF THE NATIONAL TAX ASSOCIATION

FRIDAY, OCTOBER 14, 1927

PRESIDENT MATTHEWS: We are now in session as the National Tax Association. Gentlemen, listen to the report of the secretary.

SECRETARY HOLCOMB: The secretary hasn't much to report, because it is too late in the day to do much reporting, but there are two or three outstanding events that I do feel like mentioning, even at this late time.

During the year one of the most important steps ever taken by the association has been accomplished, through the kindness of Professor and Mrs. Roy G. Blakey of the University of Minnesota. This book which you have seen—most of you probably have seen it—is the index and digest prepared by Professor and Mrs. Blakey, containing a brief digest of all the papers in the various proceedings, and the index to them, and the index as well to the articles in the *Bulletin,* from the start of the association to 1925. It is an invaluable book, and the thanks of all of us are due to Professor and Mrs. Blakey. Copies may be had by addressing me, an announcement having gone out in the *Bulletin.*

Another outstanding event is the taking over of the editing of the *Bulletin* by Professor M. H. Hunter of the University of Illinois. I do not suppose that you can appreciate the load that is removed from the secretary's shoulders by these two outstanding events. Our thanks are due to Mr. Hunter for his kindness.

The other outstanding event is of a financial nature, and it is a marvel, and I want to make particular reference to it, because it is an exception.

The Philadelphia conference was a great success, as you know, probably attended by more delegates than any other conference we ever held. It was a splendid occasion, and the success was due almost entirely to Senator Edmonds. As a result of that conference something happened that will astonish you. There was a balance left over, after attending to our wants, amounting to some $517, which was turned over to the association through the kindness of Senator Edmonds.

I want to make just a very hasty report of operations of the treasury, and I will merely mention the receipts, amounting to some $10,500, and expenses of some $6,900, but the slack will be taken up, because the publication bill was not paid until after June 30th, which was the end of our fiscal year, so that we have probably used up our entire receipts for this year.

I won't take up any more of your time with these things, except as I shall have to appear again shortly, I expect, with some other suggestions. I should like, perhaps, to have my report accepted.

HENRY F. LONG (Massachusetts): I move this able, intelligent and clarifying report of the treasurer be accepted, and anything else he says.

(Motion duly seconded)

PRESIDENT MATTHEWS: Moved and seconded that the report be accepted.

(Ayes and Noes)

PRESIDENT MATTHEWS: It is a unanimous vote.

SECRETARY HOLCOMB: There are certain routine votes that ought to be taken, drawn from last year. For instance, the routine vote for the expenses carrying the appropriation of some $3000 for clerical services, rent, supplies and other contingencies incident to the conduct of the routine work of the office of the secretary and treasurer, in addition to the cost of printing.

DELEGATE: So move.

(Motion duly seconded)

PRESIDENT MATTHEWS: You have heard the motion. Those who favor it manifest by saying aye.

(Ayes and Noes)

(Motion carried)

SECRETARY HOLCOMB: Votes should be taken to carry out the votes taken in the conference, first, for the continuation of the committee on business taxation, which is Dr. Gerstenberg's committee. Perhaps if you will authorize me in general terms, if that would be sufficient, I will put it into language, that the committee be continued. That also applies to the committee on federal income tax simplification and the committee on motor vehicle taxation.

PRESIDENT MATTHEWS: Is it your pleasure that that be done?

(No response)

PRESIDENT MATTHEWS: Hearing no dissent,—

Mr. Rigby: I move the committees all be continued.

Secretary Holcomb: Appropriate wording to be furnished by the secretary.

Mr. Rigby: By the secretary.

President Matthews: It is moved that the suggestions of Mr. Holcomb be adopted. Those who favor that manifest by saying aye.

(Ayes and Noes)

(Motion carried)

Secretary Holcomb: That includes the inheritance tax, as I understand it.

It is highly desirable that the work of selection of the time and place and details of the next conference be turned over to a sub-committee. The secretary has usually attended to that, until last year we adopted the idea of having a committee, and Mr. Graves, Mr. White and myself attended to the details for this year. I should like a resolution that the president be authorized to appoint a sub-committee of the executive committee, consisting of three members,. to canvass the situation with respect to the time and place, and then to report back to the executive committee their suggestions and the possibilities.

Voice: So moved.

(Motion duly seconded)

(Ayes and Noes)

(Motion carried)

Secretary Holcomb: The committee on motor vehicle taxation is not an extension, it is a new committee. I take it that would require a little change in that vote, because the motor vehicle taxation committee is not an extension of an existing committee.

President Matthews: What is your motion?

Secretary Holcomb: I thought somebody would move that a committee be appointed on motor vehicle taxation.

R. A. Vandegrift (California): As there seems to be some confusion in that blanket resolution, I move that the chair be authorized to appoint a committee to undertake to study the motor vehicle tax situation.

President Matthews: You mean the president of the association?

Mr. Rigby: Seconded.

PRESIDENT MATTHEWS: Moved that the president of the association be authorized to appoint a committee on motor vehicle taxation.

MR. RIGBY: Seconded.

PRESIDENT MATTHEWS: Those in favor manifest by saying aye.

(Ayes and Noes)

(Motion carried)

PRESIDENT MATTHEWS: If there is no further business, the report of the nominating committee is next in order.

R. A. VANDEGRIFT (California): Might it be in order to present one matter as to the time and place for the next meeting? I would suggest that information be gotten out as soon as possible, for the reason that there are a number of research organizations and a number of national statistical associations holding their meetings annually. A number of us happen to be holding membership in these various organizations. If we travel some 3000 miles from the Pacific Coast, it sometimes is possible for us to attend two or three of these meetings, if they come within some reasonable period, but if they are widely separated as to time, but still close as to location, it is impossible, and some of these meetings can be set before the National Tax Association if we know early enough.

SECRETARY HOLCOMB: How early would you suggest?

MR. VANDEGRIFT: If we had notice of about three or four months.

SECRETARY HOLCOMB: We had the notice out in May this year.

CHARLES J. BULLOCK: Mr. President, the committee on nominations begs to submit the following list of names:

For President of the association, Professor H. L. Lutz of California; Vice-President, the Hon. Mark Graves of New York; for Secretary, the Hon. W. G. Query of South Carolina; for Treasurer, Mr. Alfred E. Holcomb of New York.

We have the usual three vacancies on the executive committee, and for the terms expiring in 1930 we recommend the Hon. Henry F. Long, Tax Commissioner of Massachusetts, the Hon. Philip Zoercher, Tax Commissioner of Indiana, and the Hon. S. M. Chase, chairman of the Tax Commission of the State of Washington; for vacancies on the executive committee, for terms expiring in 1928, we recommend Mr. John J. Merrill of the Tax Commission of the State of New York, Judge T. M. Milling of the State of Louisiana, and finally, as honorary member of the executive committee, we recommend Mr. E. Brassard, of the Province of Quebec.

PRESIDENT MATTHEWS: Gentlemen, you have before you the report of the nominating committee. What is your pleasure?

FRANCIS N. WHITNEY (New York): I move that the report be received and that the secretary be authorized to cast one ballot.

PRESIDENT MATTHEWS: For all the officers?

FRANCIS N. WHITNEY: For all the officers.

(Motion duly seconded)

PRESIDENT MATTHEWS: It is moved and seconded that the report be received and that the secretary be authorized to cast one ballot for all the officers named.

Those who favor that motion manifest it in the usual manner.

(Ayes and Noes)

PRESIDENT MATTHEWS: It is a unanimous vote.

SECRETARY HOLCOMB: The secretary announces that he casts the ballot as requested.

PRESIDENT MATTHEWS: Gentlemen, the secretary has cast one ballot for president, H. L. Lutz, for vice-president, Hon. Mark Graves, for secretary, Hon. W. G. Query, for treasurer, Mr. A. E. Holcomb, for members of the executive committee for the term expiring in 1930, Mr. Henry F. Long of Massachusetts, Mr. Philip Zoercher of Indiana, Mr. S. M. Chase of Washington; for members of the executive committee to fill the unexpired vacancies for the term expiring in 1928, Mr. John J. Merrill of New York and Judge T. M. Milling of Louisiana, and for honorary member, Mr. E. Brassard of the Province of Quebec.

I will request Mr. Long and Mr. Vaughan to escort the newly elected president to the Chair.

MR. RIGBY: Mr. President, do I understand that the President now has declared its officers elected?

PRESIDENT MATTHEWS: I have declared them elected. That is what I thought I was doing.

MR. RIGBY: I did not catch the declaration.

PRESIDENT MATTHEWS: If I did not do so, then I do so now. I will ask Dr. Page and Senator Edmonds to discover the vice-president.

(President-elect and vice-president-elect escorted to Chair)

PRESIDENT-ELECT LUTZ: As the young lady so often said, " This is so sudden," that I find myself without an inaugural speech.

It was my privilege to serve the association the past year in the very humble capacity of vice-president. I once heard a gentleman say, who filled the position of vice-president of a large bank and trust company, that the vice-president is the lowest form of animal life.

Now that you have elevated me to the very responsible position of president of the National Tax Association, I can only assure you at this time that I shall not choose to run in 1928.

Seriously, I thank you very profoundly and sincerely for the honor. I beseech your cooperation and assistance, and I assure you that, so far as within my power, I shall serve the association as president to the very best of my ability. I thank you.

Mr. GEORGE VAUGHAN (Arkansas): Mr. President, in introducing the next victim of the occasion, I am reminded of the status of a convict who was sitting in the penitentiary on a bench, when his colored friend came up, who was also incarcerated in the penitentiary. He said, "Sam, how come you here?" "Oh," said he, "I have been here a good while." "What do they charge?" "Oh, no charge; it's all free." "I mean, what is you did?" He said, "I kill my wife." He said, "How long you in here for?" "Two weeks." "Just two weeks for killing your wife?" "That's all; then I gets hung."

I want to introduce to you this morning Mr. Mark Graves, who is in here for a short vacation.

VICE-PRESIDENT-ELECT GRAVES: I am at a loss to know just what to say to you on an occasion of this kind. I have always proceeded on the theory that a vice-president should be seen and not heard. I was not aware until this morning, when my illustrious predecessor acquainted me with the fact, that the vice-president was the lowest form of animal life.

I am mindful of the honor which this association has conferred on me. My hope will be that I shall be able to contribute something to the success of the association. I have the earnest desire and shall hope to be of service in the future as I have tried to be in the past. I thank you.

CHAIRMAN MATTHEWS: Since the newly elected President does not assume the chair, I suppose it devolves upon me to inquire if there is any further business, and, if not, to entertain a motion to adjourn. Do I hear the motion to adjourn?

MARK GRAVES (New York): I move we adjourn.

(Motion duly seconded)

(Ayes and Noes)

(Motion carried)

ADJOURNMENT SINE DIE.

ARKANSAS

Hammond, W. T.	Chairman, State Tax Com'n	Little Rock
Vaughan, George		Little Rock

ARIZONA

Howe, C. R.	Chairman, State Tax Com'n	Phoenix

CALIFORNIA

Cattell, H. G.		Pasadena
Hardison, A. C.		Santa Paula
Johnson, Milbank	600 Burleigh Drive	Pasadena
Lutz, H. L.	1400 Webster St.	Palo Alto
Lutz, Mrs. H. L.	1400 Webster St.	Palo Alto
Martin, Irving		Stockton
Martin, Mrs. Irving		Stockton
Johnson, Miss Adeline		Stockton
Patten, Miss Josephine A.		Stockton
Plehn, C. C.		Berkeley
Riley, Ray	State Controller	Sacramento
Riley, Mrs. Ray		Sacramento
Vandegrift, R. A.	Subway Terminal Bldg.	Los Angeles

COLORADO

Collins, C. W.	Manager of Revenue, 1801 Dahlia Ave.	Denver
Guerrero, A. M.	County Assessor	Walsenburg
Lee, C. S.	County Assessor	Ft. Morgan
Link, C. P.	Member State Tax Com'n	Denver
Seaman, J. R.	Member State Tax Com'n	Denver
Seaman, Mrs. J. R.		Denver
Walpole, N. S.	325 W. 15th St.	Pueblo

CONNECTICUT

Blodgett, Wm. H.	State Tax Commissioner	Winsted
Connelly, Wm. F.	Tax Com'r, 71 Bancroft Ave.	Bridgeport
Fairchild, F. R.	Yale University	New Haven
Knapp, Farwell	45 Outlook Ave.	West Hartford

DELAWARE

Neilsen, A. C.		Wilmington
Wootten, B. L.		Wilmington

DISTRICT OF COLUMBIA (Washington)

Beale, W. L.	728 15th St., N.W.
Brewster, Kingman	815 15th St.
Coleman, F. J.	620 A. St., N.E.
Collady, E. F.	3734 Northampton St.
Coombs, Whitney	2013 New Hampshire Ave.
Eby, R. J.	725 13th St.
Fleming, R. V.	2200 Wyoming Ave.
Moore, B. F.	1615 H. St.
Page, T. W.	26 Jackson Place
Richards, Wm. P.	Assr of Dist., 1457 Harvard St.
Williams, N. B.	Union Trust Bldg.

GEORGIA

Jarnagin, M. P.		Athens
Lyle, Edward	Hurt Bldg.	Atlanta
Lyle, J. N.	13 Brookhaven	Atlanta
McPherson, J. H. T.	623 Milledge Ave.	Athens
Norman, R. C.	State Tax Commissioner	Atlanta

ILLINOIS

Bogg, H. B., Jr.	Armour & Co.	Chicago
Bogg, Mrs. H. B., Jr.		Chicago
Bristol, A. E.	10 So. LaSalle St.	Chicago
Cushing, R. B.	208 So. LaSalle St.	Chicago
Cushing, Mrs. R. B.		Chicago
Feldman, M. J.		Chicago
Griggs, E. 'M.	Nat'l Bd. Fire Underwriters	Chicago
Griggs, Mrs. E. M.		Chicago
Huntington, F. B.	Grand Central Station	Chicago
Morrison, K. E.	547 W. Jackson Blvd.	Chicago
Morrison, Mrs. K. E.		Chicago
Paddock, H. W.	Ill. Bell Tel. Co.	Chicago
Patten, A. E.	547 W. Jackson Blvd.	Chicago
Patten, Mrs. A. E.		Chicago
Sayler, J. L.	6529 Woodlawn Ave.	Chicago
Sayler, Mrs. J. L.		Chicago
Sutherland, Douglas	105 W. Monroe St.	Chicago
Sutherland, Mrs. Douglas		Chicago
Tunell, G. G.	A. T. & S. Fe. R. R.	Chicago
Tunell, Mrs. G. G.		Chicago
Watson, J. C.	608 So. Dearborn St.	Chicago

INDIANA

Haldtead, B. G.	Ind. Bell Tel. Co.	Indianapolis
Harrison, Wm. C.	716 Continental Bank Bldg.	Indianapolis
Hough, W. A.	State Tax Commissioner, 231 State House	Indianapolis
Hough, Mrs. W. A.		Indianapolis
Zoercher, Philip	State Tax Commissioner, 231 State House	Indianapolis
Zoercher, Mrs. Philip		Indianapolis

IOWA

Brindley, J. E.	Iowa State College	Ames
Hammill, John	Governor of Iowa	Des Moines
Johnson, R. E.	Treasurer of State	Des Moines
Long, J. W.	State Auditor	Des Moines
Merckins, W. C.	Sec'y of Executive Council	Des Moines
Ramsay, W. C.	Secretary of State	Des Moines
Thornberg, Mark	Secretary of Agriculture	Des Moines

KANSAS

Carroll, J. A.		Independence
Carroll, Mrs. J. A.		Independence
Guy, R. A.	Sedgwick Bldg.	Wichita
Jensen, J. P.		Lawrence
Mulholland, A. R.	316 West 8th Ave.	Topeka
Smith, Clarence	Member, Pub. Service Com'n	Topeka

KENTUCKY

Leland, S. E.	1336 Fontaine Road	Lexington

LOUISIANA

Ferry, E. R.	I. C. R. R.	New Orleans
Jeter, J. W. A.	Assessor	Shreveport
McGraw, John		New Orleans
Milling, T. M.		Shreveport
Sneed, H. P.	Whitney Bldg.	New Orleans
Sneed, Mrs. H. P.		New Orleans

MARYLAND

Griffith, F. J.	B. & O. R. R. Co.	Baltimore
Leser, Oscar	Member, State Tax Com'n	Baltimore
Lindsay, M. J.	Union Tr. Bldg.	Baltimore
MacLeod, D. R.	13 Leland St.	Chevy Chase
MacLeod, Mrs. D. R.		Chevy Chase
Murray, T. A., Jr.,	Secretary, State Tax Com'n, Union Tr. Bldg.	Baltimore
Murray, Mrs. T. A., Jr.		Baltimore
Price, J. D.	State Tax Commissioner	Salisbury
Ray, J. E.	Chairman, State Tax Com'n	Hyattsville
Ray, Mrs. J. E.		Hyattsville

MASSACHUSETTS

Alexander, Thornton	B. & M. R. R.	Boston
Brown, C. C.	209 Dodge St.	Beverly
Bullock, C. J.	Harvard University	Cambridge
Comstock, Miss Alzada	Mount Holyoke College	South Hadley
Currier, A. P.	c/o Hood Rubber Co.	Watertown
Doherty, J. F.	1013 Barristers Hall	Boston
Fischer, F. L.	N. E. Tel. & Tel. Co.	Boston
Fish, E. F.	84 State St.	Boston
Holmes, Alexander	Deputy Com'r of Corp's and Taxation	Boston
Huse, J. W.	Director, Mass. Inher. Tax	Boston
Kent, L. B.	N. E. Tel. & Tel. Co.	Boston
Locke, J. W.	15 State St.	Boston
Long, H. F.	Com'r of Corp's and Tax'n	Boston
Lyon, H. S.	State Official, 221 N. Main St.,	West Bridgewater
Rich, G. A.		Boston
Silbert, Coleman	73 Tremont St.	Boston
Wakefield, E. E.	Chamber of Commerce Bldg.	Boston

MICHIGAN

Benfield, G. G.	1818 Buhl Bldg.	Detroit
Berry, R. H.	331 Marlborough Ave.	Detroit
Boice, J. A.	Prudden Bldg.	Lansing
Boice, Mrs. J. A.		Lansing
Bond, A. W.	Union Tr. Co.	Detroit
Corcoran, T. M.	Assistant Assessor	Detroit
Finn, G. J.	City Assessor	Detroit
Hutchinson, W.	M. C. R. R. Co.	Detroit
Hutchinson, Mrs. W.		Detroit
Lillie, J. S.	Canadian Nat'l Rys.	Detroit
Lucking, Dean	Ford Bldg.	Detroit
Newton, R. W.	Michigan State College	Lansing
Richards, A. E.	State Tax Commissioner	Lansing
Righter, Chester	Bureau of Gov. Res.	Detroit
Scott, J. J.	City Assessor	Detroit
Peelford, C. M.		Detroit

MINNESOTA

Armson, J. G.	State Tax Commissioner	St. Paul
Bjornson, G. B.	State Tax Commissioner	St. Paul
Blakey, R. G.	University of Minnesota	Minneapolis
Butler, F. D.	Merchants Nat'l Bank Bldg.	St. Paul
Dooley, F. E.		Minneapolis
Erdall, J. L.	Soo Line Ry.	Minneapolis
Hilton, C. L.	Attorney General	St. Paul
McNiven, J. H.	Member, State Tax Com'n	St. Paul
Mueller, Wm.	C. St. P. M. & O. Ry.	St. Paul
Scott, J. A.	City Assessor	Duluth
Sullivan, G. H.		Stillwater
Thomson, H. A.	Soo Line Ry.	Minneapolis
Walquist, John	Court House	Minneapolis
Youngquist, G. A.	Ass't Atty. Gen'l, State Capitol, St. Paul	

MISSISSIPPI

May, G. W.		Jackson
Inman, C. E.	Chairman, State Tax Com'n	Jackson

MISSOURI

Barker, Carl		St. Louis
Barrett, R. H.	414 Joplin St.	Joplin
Cast, W. B.	Union Station	Kansas City
Cast, Mrs. W. B.		Kansas City
Cast, Miss Dorothy		Kansas City
Friganza, W. T.	S. W. Bell Tel. Co.	St. Louis
Friganza, Mrs. W. T.		St. Louis
Friganza, Miss Marjorie		St. Louis
Hagee, G. M.	1810 Boatmens Bank Bldg.	St. Louis
Laun, A. C.	3119 Osceola Ave.	St. Louis
Matthews, D. B.	5801 Enright Ave.	St. Louis
Naylor, J. C.	Pet Milk Co.	St. Louis
Phelps, E.	Kansas City Southern Ry.	Kansas City
Phelps, Mrs. E.		Kansas City
Rowe, W. G.	St. Louis Union Tr. Co.	St. Louis
Rowe, Mrs. W. G.		St. Louis
Smith, Forrest	Member, State Tax Com'n	Jefferson City
White, J. W.	Mercantile Tr. Co.	St. Louis
White, Mrs. J. W.		St. Louis

NEBRASKA

Buckingham, Wm. H.	Attorney, N. W. Bell Tel. Co.,	Omaha
Buckingham, Mrs. Wm. H.		Omaha
Williams, T. E.	State Tax Commissioner	Lincoln

NEW HAMPSHIRE

Hirst, E. C.	State Tax Commissioner	Concord
Matthews, J. S.	Superior Court Judge	Concord
Morse, M. H.	Assistant Attorney General	Berlin
Tremblay, J. O.	City Assessor	Manchester
Whittemore, L. F.	State Tax Commissioner	Concord

NEW JERSEY

Bates, A. E.		Montclair
Berry, J. J.	City Tax Commissioner, 770 DeGraw Ave.	Newark
Brewster, S. L.	Tax Assessor	Montclair
Davenport, G. I.	51 Ardilly Rd.	Montclair
Fast, L. A.	President, Board of Ass't	Newark
Fitzsimmons, J. J.	Sec'y, Newark Tax Board	Newark
Fitzsimmons, Mrs. J. J.		Newark
Humphreys, H. R.		Atlantic City
Hyland, J. F.	County Tax Board	Newark
Hyland, Mrs. J. F.		Newark
Leighton, W. M.		Maplewood
Mungle, J. A.	345 Plane St.	Newark
Park, H. M.	28 Central Ave.	Cranford

NEW MEXICO

Jaffa, Nathan	Chief State Tax Com'r	Santa Fe
Joerns, John	Secretary, State Tax Com'n	Santa Fe
Seaberg, Hugo		Raton

NEW YORK

Andrews, Kent	The Solvay Process Co.	Syracuse
Andrews, Mrs. Kent		Syracuse
Arthur, Donald	56 Pine St.	New York City
Atterbury, J. F.	23 Wall St.	New York City
Bowers, T. W.	150 East 73rd St.	New York City
Bailey, Miss Beulah	State Tax Commission	Albany
Burke, W. J.	City Assessor, 403 Porter Ave.,	Buffalo
Bonbright, J. C.	Columbia University	New York City
Butterweck, H. S.	22 William St.	New York City
Broderick, J. P.	143 West Eagle St.	Buffalo
Bradford, R. L.	22 Exchange Place	New York City
Brownell, G. G.	60 Wall St.	New York City
Callahan, T. J.	c/o State Tax Commission	Albany
Chipman, C. J.	Mutual Life Bldg.	Buffalo
Cole, S. T.	Deputy State Tax Com'r	Catskill
Cole, Mrs. S. T.		Catskill
Condon, D. P.	416 East 136th St.	New York City
Dalton, C.	60 Wall St.	New York City
Doyle, E. P.	12 East 41st St.	New York City
Doyle, E. S.	1777 East 21st St.	Brooklyn

Duncan, H. A.		Bellerose, L. I.
Frazer, C. R.	41 Park Row	New York City
Freeman, H. H.	507 White Bldg.	Buffalo
Garrett, Thomas, Sr.	44 Wall St.	New York City
Garrett, Mrs. Thomas, Sr.		New York City
Gerstenberg, C. W.	70 Fifth Ave.	New York City
Goldfogle, H. M.	President, Dep't of Taxes, Municipal Bldg.	New York City
Graves, Mark	State Tax Commission	Albany
Graves, Mrs. Mark		Albany
Hall, A. G.		Highland Mills
Hamlin, Will		Canandaigua
Hamlin, Mrs. Will		Canandaigua
Hanaran, F. V.	Dep. Com'r, 515 Plymouth Ave.,	Buffalo
Harding, Miss Ruth J.	254 Seaman Ave.	New York City
Harpfinger, Fred	Board of Supervisors, 1035 Ridge Road	Lackawanna
Hekeler, Reinhold	17 Battery Place	New York City
Hickman, W. G.	6 Granger Place	Buffalo
Holcomb, A. E. .	195 Broadway	New York City
Holcomb, Mrs. A. E.		New York City
Holmes, G. E.	15 William St.	New York City
Holmes, W. W.		Olean
Howard, M. S.	Deputy Commissioner	Albany
Hubbard, F. M.	49 Wall St.	New York City
Jonsson, G. W.	25 West 43rd St.	New York City
Jonsson, Mrs. G. W.		New York City
Kendrick, M. S.		Ithaca
Knox, G. W.		Niagara Falls
Kuhn, J. L.	16 Wall St.	New York City
Long, E. M.		Buffalo
Loughman, M. F.	President, State Tax Com'n, 220 W. 40th St.	New York City
Mastick, S. C.		Pleasantville
Major, C. A.	143 Liberty St.	New York City
Merrill, J. J.	State Tax Commission	Alfred
Merrill, Mrs. J. J.		Alfred
Merwin, E. M.	351 Crescent Ave.	Buffalo
Moriarty, E. J.	195 Broadway	New York City
Murphy, Miss E. F.	45 Prospect Place	New York City
Murphy, J. M.	140 Broadway	New York City
Murray, Timothy	City Tax Commissioner	Yonkers
O'Brien, Wm. A.	424 Cumberland Ave.	Buffalo
Orcutt, B. S.	Wall Street Journal	New York City
Payne, Wm. K.		Auburn
Perons, R. S.		East Aurora
Peyser, H. M.	1089a Prospect Place	Brooklyn
Reeves, C. E.	2202 Liberty Bank Bldg.	Buffalo
Renling, C. J.	1541 Abbott Road	Buffalo
Riely, L. M.	38 Chauncey Road	Astoria, L. I.
Rice, Miss Florence M.	524 West 124th St.	New York City
Rothschild, Julius	292 Madison Ave.	New York City
Rothschild, M. D.	6 West 48th St.	New York City
Rothschild, Mrs. M. D.		New York City
Ryan, J. B.	68 St. Pauls Place	Brooklyn
Ryan, P. L.	60 Wall St.	New York City
Sack, Isidor	285 Madison Ave.	New York City

Salt, F. H.	128 Fourth St.	Niagara Falls
Saxe, Martin	27 Pine St.	New York City
Seilheimer, Henry	65 Niagara St.	Buffalo
Schultz, W. J.	120 West 12th St.	New York City
Smith, Everett	1839 Union St.	Schenectady
Smith, H. B.	44 Wall St.	New York City
Sonderling, S. J.	16 William St.	New York City
Sowers, J. T.	Income Tax Bureau	Albany
Spalding, J. W.		New Rochelle
Spalding, Mrs. J. W.		New Rochelle
Spratt, D. R.	Deputy State Tax Com'r	Albany
Staeber, J. L.	County Board of Supervisors	Lancaster
Stephens, W. E.	84 So. Pine Ave.	Albany
Stephens, Mrs. W. E.		Albany
Stephenson, M. A.	Dep. Com'r, 220 West 40th St.,	New York City
Sutton, G. W.	City Com'r, 60 Sutton Manor	New Rochelle
Tobin, C. J.		Albany
Tyng, Arthur	206 Richmond Ave.	Buffalo
Turchin, A. I.	Imperial Hotel	New York City
Tyler, F. H.	1183 Fulton St.	Brooklyn
Vickers, Leslie	292 Madison Ave.	New York City
Watt, H. B.	78 Prospect Park, West	Brooklyn
Whitney, F. N.	195 Broadway	New York City
Wilber, W. J.	11 Park St.	Gowanda
Zoller, J. F.	General Electric Co.	Schenectady
Zoller, Mrs. J. F.		Schenectady

NORTH CAROLINA

Lee, W. T.		Raleigh
Maxwell, A. J.	Chairman, Tax Commission	Raleigh

NORTH DAKOTA

Thoresen, T. H.	State Tax Commissioner	Bismarck

OHIO

Chandler, G. B.	1188 E. Broad St.	Columbus
Cherrington, Homer	Ohio University	Athens
Dickey, M. R.	Cleveland Trust Co.	Cleveland
Dickey, Mrs. M. R.		Cleveland
Doty, C. E.	Hippodrome Bldg.	Cleveland
Doty, Mrs. C. E.		Cleveland
Dunn, James, Jr.	1537 Lewis Drive	Lakewood
Dunn, Mrs. James, Jr.		Lakewood
Dyer, C. A.	Southern Hotel	Columbus
Forney, S. E.		Columbus
Gibbs, V. H.	Assistant Attorney General	Columbus
Hunt, J. G.		Fremont
Koars, Anthony	Huntington Bank Bldg.	Columbus
Marshall, E. J.	Spitzan Bldg.	Toledo
Minor, R. H.	Goodyear T. & Rubber Co.	Akron
Morgan, Gilbert		North Olmsted
Newman, F. A.	Deputy Auditor	Akron
Pomeroy, G. E.		Toledo
Schuler, H. L.	1423 Arthur Ave.	Cleveland
Schuler, Mrs. H. L.		Cleveland

Schulke, L. A.		Cleveland
Stone, H. A.	Electric Bldg.	Cleveland
Swetland, F. L.	Swetland Bldg.	Cleveland
Swetland, Mrs. F. L.		Cleveland
Walsh, J. F.	Williamson Bldg.	Cleveland
Watson, J. P.	201 Marshall Ave.	Columbus
Zangerle, J. A.	County Auditor	Cleveland

OKLAHOMA

Deardorff, C. C.	Skelly Oil Co.	Tulsa
Harley, D. D.	211 East Independence	Tulsa
King, J. B.	Assistant Attorney General	Oklahoma City
King, Mrs. J. B.		Oklahoma City
Meyer, Leo		Tulsa
Parkinson, Fred	Oklahoma Gas & Electric Co.	Oklahoma City
Parkinson, Mrs. Fred		Oklahoma City
Patrick, F. L.	County Ass'r, 1302 E. Univ. St.	Sapulpa
Patrick, Mrs. F. L.		Sapulpa
Plank, F. B.	c/o Empire Gas & Fuel Co.	Bartlesville
Pyle, T. M.	Oklahoma Gas-Electric Co.	Oklahoma City
Rowe, D. A.	County Ass'r, 415 So. Olympia,	Tulsa
Thompson, G. E.	Tidal Oil Co. Bldg.	Tulsa
Thompson, Mrs. G. E. and daughter		Tulsa
Wells, A. J.	Carter Oil Co.	Tulsa
Williamson, J. M.		Oklahoma City

OREGON

Allen, E. T.	Spalding Bldg.	Portland

PENNSYLVANIA

Berryman, Wm. I.	Union Tr. Co.	Pittsburgh
Biegeman, H., Jr.	Finance Bldg.	Philadelphia
Edmonds, F. S.	111 So. 15th St.	Philadelphia
Edmonds, Mrs. F. S.		Philadelphia
Elkin, E. M.	Westinghouse Elec. & Mfg. Co.	Pittsburgh
Heim, G. H.	Broad Street Station	Philadelphia
Herde, G. F.	Farmers Bank Bldg.	Pittsburgh
Hunt, F. R.	Lafayette College, 522 Parsons St.	Easton
Johnston, Samuel	Gulf Refining Co.	Pittsburgh
Johnston, Mrs. Samuel		Pittsburgh
Kalisher, S. S.	260 So. Broad St.	Philadelphia
Lamb, C. S.	Pittsburgh Plate Glass Co.	Pittsburgh
Lamb, Mrs. C. S.		Pittsburgh
Littleton, W. G.	327 Chestnut St.	Philadelphia
Littleton, Miss Anne K.		Philadelphia
Makiver, H. J.		Media
Makiver, Mrs. H. J.		Media
Martin, Edward	Auditor General	Washington
Mayer, R. A.	Provident Tr. Co.	Philadelphia
Mayer, Mrs. R. A.		Philadelphia
McKay, M. K.	University of Pittsburgh	Pittsburgh
McKay, Mrs. M. K.		Pittsburgh
McKay, Miss Marian		Pittsburgh

Murray, J. V.	Mechanics Tr. Bldg.	Harrisburg
Pollock, W. W.	4021 Walnut St.	Philadelphia
Ramey, J. M.	Broad Street Station	Philadelphia
Ramey, Mrs. J. M.		Philadelphia
Reese, D. R.		Scranton
Rial, W. S.	Huff Bldg. .	Greensburg
Rigby, J. L.	Deputy Auditor General	Media
Rigby, Mrs. J. L.		Media
Ruslander, S. L.	Farmers Bank Bldg.	Pittsburgh
Sheaffer, M. C.	Auditor General's Dept.	Shiremanstown
Shumberger, J. C.	Lehigh Portland Cement Co.	Allentown
Sisson, S. A.	Marine Bank Bldg.	Erie
Spahr, M. C.	Pittsburgh Plate Glass Co.	Pittsburgh
Spahr, Mrs. M. C.		Pittsburgh
Steere, J. M.	Girard Tr. Co.	Philadelphia
Steere, Mrs. J. M.		Philadelphia
Turner, C. L.	468 Lyceum Ave., Roxborough,	Philadelphia
Wheeler, A. R.		Endeavor

RHODE ISLAND

Adelman, D. C.	15 Westminster St.	Providence
Bliss, Z. W.	State Tax Commissioner	Providence
Bliss, Mrs. Z. W.		Providence
Massey, Mrs. Alice I. B.		Providence
Burnham, W. W.	Ch'man, City B'd of Assessors	Providence
James, H. W.	State Inheritance Tax Atty.,	
	33 Windsor Road	Providence
Makepeace, C. MacR.	Hospital Tr. Bldg.	Providence
Sheldon, C. D.	66 Shirley Blvd.	Cranston
Sheldon, Mrs. C. D.		Cranston
Sherman, A. A.		Portsmouth
Spring, H. W.	R. I. Hospital Tr. Co.	Providence
Tobie, E. P.	Chief Clerk, State Board of	
	Tax Commissioners	Providence

SOUTH CAROLINA

Beattie, A. J.	Comptroller General	Columbia
Beattie, F. D.	Inheritance Tax Dept.	Columbia
Crouch, Thomas	So. Bell Tel. Co.	Columbia
Derham, J. P.	State Tax Commission	Columbia
Gross, H. H.		Harleyville
Hodge, Miss Julia Ethel	Secretary, Chairman S. C. Tax	
	Commission	Columbia
Lyon, J. F.	State Tax Commission	Columbia
McCaslan, R. E.		Greenwood
Query, W. G.	Chairman, State Tax Com'n	Columbia
Scarborough, J. H.	State Treasurer	Columbia

SOUTH DAKOTA

Baer, B. W.	State Tax Department	Pierre
Bell, W. W.	Northwestern Pub. Ser. Co.	Huron
Conner, E. E.	City Assessor	Aberdeen
Sandstedt, C. L.	Northwestern Pub. Ser. Co.	Huron

TENNESSEE

Booton, W. S.	Director, State Excise Tax Div.,	Nashville
Booton, Mrs. W. S.		Nashville
Hall, F. S.	Com'r State Finance & Taxat'n,	Nashville
Hall, Mrs. F. S.		Nashville
Logsdon, R. E.	1397 Peabody Ave.	Memphis

UTAH

Beatty, Wm. N.	Utah Power & Light Co.	Salt Lake City
Beatty, Mrs. Wm. N.		Salt Lake City
Brown, C. M.	1459 So. 13 East	Salt Lake City
Brown, Mrs. C. M.		Salt Lake City
Mackenzie, A. G.		Salt Lake City
Preece, J. H.	108 City & County Blvd.	Salt Lake City
Preece, Mrs. J. H.		Salt Lake City
Winder, M. S.	Am. Farm Bureau Federation	Salt Lake City

VERMONT

Harvey, E. M.	Commissioner of Taxes	Montpelier
Harvey, Mrs. E. M.		Montpelier

VIRGINIA

Ballinger, R. A.	Va. Agr. Ext. Sta.	Blacksburg
Benton, Miss Grace Browning	138 Hume Ave., Potomac	Alexandria
Benton, W. C.	Commissioner of Revenue	Middleburg
Chamblin, Mrs. H. B.		White Post
Gary, J. V.	State Planters Bank Bldg.	Richmond
Lewis, M. C.		Farnham
Snavely, T. L.	University of Virginia	University

WISCONSIN

Arnold, L. A.	City Tax Commissioner	Milwaukee
Brabant, E. J.		Madison
Dudley, A. S.	1108-221 Wisconsin Ave.	Milwaukee
Koester, E. J.	852 Grant Blvd.	Milwaukee
Leenhouts, J. H.	Assessor of Incomes	Milwaukee
Leenhouts, Mrs. J. H.		Milwaukee
Reynolds, P. N.	Burgess Laboratories	Madison
Rosa, C. D.	Member, State Tax Com'n	Madison
Wendt, Mrs. Anne M.	621 Grant St.	Wausau

HAWAIIAN ISLANDS

Hapai, H. C.	Treas., Territory of Hawaii	Honolulu

CANADA

MANITOBA

Watts, E. W.	Manitoba Tax Commission	Winnipeg
Watts, Mrs. E. W.		Winnipeg
Nichols, R. R.	Canadian Nat'l Railways	Winnipeg
Fisher, R. M.		Winnipeg

ONTARIO

Brittain, H. L.	Citizens Research Inst. of Can.,	Toronto
Clarke, H. A.		Toronto
Cronyn, Hume	Mutual Life Ins. of Canada	London
Currie, D. H.		Toronto
Davidson, W. G.	National Trust Co.	Toronto
Forman, J. C.	Assessment Commissioner	Toronto
Freek, J. P.	Assessment Commissioner	St. Thomas
Henry, W. J.	Assessment Commissioner	Peterborough
Kemp, H. R.	Professor of Economics, 152 Howland Ave.	Toronto
MacNachtan, Miss	682 Huron St.	Toronto
Magill, Miss Margaret	387 Albany Ave.	Toronto
McConkey, T. G.	Canada Life	Toronto
McConkey, Mrs. T. G.		Toronto
Innes, Capt. Wm. C. C.		Port Credit
McLean, E. M.		Walkerville
Orr, Wm. A.	Ass't Comp. of Rev.	Toronto
McPhillips, F.		Toronto
Monteith, Mrs. J. D.		Toronto
Paterson, H. D.	Dominion Income Tax	Toronto
Saunders, Mrs. E. M.		Toronto
Sloan, C. J.	Royal Bank of Canada	Toronto
Ramsay. Mrs. A. G.		Toronto
Roberts, Mrs.		Toronto
Taylor, Mrs. W. B.		Toronto
Turnbull, F. M.	Ass't Treas., Parliament Bldgs.,	Toronto
White, J. T.	Controller of Revenue	Toronto

QUEBEC

Brassard, Evariste	Succession Duty Dep't	Quebec
McMahon, L. I.	Bell Tel. Co. of Canada	Montreal
McMahon, Mrs. L. I.		Montreal
Trowern, E. M.	18 Rideau St.	Ottawa
Veale, P. H.	Ass't Com'r, City Hall	Ottawa
Watson, T. G.	Canadian National Railways	Montreal

SASKATCHEWAN

Smith, J. J.	Minister of Municipal Affairs	Regina
Westgate, R. J.	City Ass'r & Tax Collector	Regina
Ward, P. G.	Civil Service Commission	Regina

FOREIGN

Braeuer, Karl	University of Breslau	Germany

INDEX

INDEX 495

Lightning Source UK Ltd.
Milton Keynes UK
UKHW020804271218
334504UK00008B/528/P